MCSE Guide to
Managing a Microsoft® Windows® Server 2003 Environment, Enhanced

Dan DiNicolo
Brian McCann

THOMSON

COURSE TECHNOLOGY

Australia • Canada • Mexico • Singapore • Spain • United Kingdom • United States

THOMSON
™
COURSE TECHNOLOGY

MCSE Guide to Managing a Microsoft® Windows® Server 2003 Environment, Enhanced

is published by Course Technology

Managing Editor:
Will Pitkin III

Product Manager:
Nick Lombardi

Production Editor:
Brooke Booth
Kristen Guevara

Technical Edit/Quality Assurance:
Marianne Snow
Chris Scriver
Sean Day
Christian Kunciw

Associate Product Manager:
Mirella Misiazek
David Rivera
Sarah Santoro

Editorial Assistant:
Jenny Smith

Senior Manufacturing Coordinator:
Melissa Hulse

Senior Marketing Manager:
Guy Baskaran

Text Designer:
GEX Publishing Services

Compositor:
GEX Publishing Services

Cover Design:
Steve Deschene

Disclaimer
Course Technology reserves the right to revise this publication and make changes from time to time in its content without notice.

ISBN 0-619-21752-9

BRIEF
Contents

TABLE OF
Contents

Introduction

Welcome to *MCSE Guide to Managing a Microsoft Windows Server 2003 Environment, Enhanced*. This book provides in-depth coverage of the knowledge and skills required to pass Microsoft certification exam 70-290: *Managing and Maintaining a Microsoft Windows Server 2003 Environment*. This course of study prepares a network professional to have the ability to manage a network running Windows Server 2003. These solutions include configuring, administering, and troubleshooting elements ranging from user accounts to server security. You will also learn how to create, configure, and manage network resources such as file, print, and Web resources as well as various Active Directory objects such as users and groups.

The goal of *MCSE Guide to Managing a Microsoft Windows Server 2003 Environment, Enhanced* is to teach strategies for network management to individuals who desire to learn about that topic for practical purposes, as well as those who wish to pass Microsoft exam #70-290. This book provides the content for all the skills measured on that exam, but also provides related information that is not directly tested

The Intended Audience

This book was written with the network professional in mind. It provides an excellent preparation for the Microsoft exam 70-290, and also for the real-life tasks involved in managing today's networks, which must support an ever-increasing variety of applications. To fully benefit from the content and the projects presented here, you will need access to a classroom lab containing computers configured as listed here.

- Windows Server 2003 installed with the default settings. Name the first computer Instructor, and then subsequent servers Server01, Server02, etc.

- DNS should be installed and configured on the Instructor server prior to the installation of Active Directory. Use Dovercorp.net as the domain name, creating the zone as type Standard Primary. A reverse lookup zone based on your IP subnet should also be created. Run dcpromo.exe to upgrade the Instructor server to a domain controller in a domain called Dovercorp.net. Run dcpromo.exe on subsequent servers, making them domain controllers in their own child domain, using the naming convention Domain01, Domain02, etc.

- For the Domain Users group in each domain, add the right to allow log on locally to the default domain controllers security policy.

- In each child domain, create a user account named Admin01, Admin02, etc. This name should correspond to the associated domain name, and the account should be added to the Domain Admins group. These accounts should also be added to the Enterprise Admins group in the forest root domain.

For more detailed setup instructions, see the "Set-up Instructions" section.

New to This Edition

- A new, full-color interior design brings the material to life and full-color screenshots provide a more detailed look at the Microsoft Server 2003 interface.

- Appendix B provides detailed lab setup instructions to assist instructors in preparing labs for class.

- Appendix C features expanded and more comprehensive chapter summaries to assist students in reviewing the material covered in each chapter.

- Two new Practice Exams are provided. One is located in the back of the textbook and is perforated so that it can be handed in as a homework assignment or test. The second is posted on *www.course.com* in the password protected Instructor's Resource section, along with the Solutions to both exams. The questions on these Practice Exams are modeled after the type of questions students will see on the actual MCSE 70-290 certification exam. In addition to helping students review what they have learned, they have the added benefit of preparing them for the certification exam.

- Our CoursePrep ExamGuide content is now included in PDF format on the CD that accompanies this textbook. This content features key information, bulleted memorization points, and review questions for every exam objective in an easy-to-follow two-page-spread layout. This is an excellent resource for self-study before taking the 70-290 certification exam.

Chapter Descriptions

Chapter 1, "Introduction to Windows Server 2003," provides an overview of network administration and procedures, introduces Windows Server 2003 Active Directory, and compares the different editions of Windows Server 2003.

Chapter 2, "Managing Hardware Devices," emphasizes the importance of planning an installation and assessing hardware and software needs in advance. It shows how to install and configure hardware devices, as well as how to install and manage Windows Server 2003 updates.

Chapter 3, "Creating and Managing User Accounts," outlines how to create and administer Windows Server 2003 user accounts and related settings.

Chapter 4, "Implementing and Managing Group and Computer Accounts," outlines the different types and scopes of group accounts available in Windows Server 2003, as well as providing an introduction to computer accounts and related management activities.

Chapter 5, "Managing File Access," focuses on creating and managing shared folders and monitoring access to them. This chapter also teaches how to configure shared folder and NTFS permissions, both critical file management concepts.

Chapter 6, "Managing Disks and Data Storage," provides an overview of disk management concepts, explains how to manage disk partition and volumes, and introduces a variety of different disk management utilities included with Windows Server 2003.

Chapter 7, "Advanced File System Management," takes a closer look at Windows Server 2003 file management concepts with a look at file and folder attributes, disk quotas, and implementing and managing the Distributed File System (DFS).

Chapter 8, "Implementing and Managing Printers," provides an overview of printing concepts and terminology in Windows Server 2003 environments, explains how to install and configure local and network printers, and outlines steps towards troubleshooting printer-related issues.

Chapter 9, "Implementing and Using Group Policy," introduces Group Policy and explains how to manage Group Policy inheritance and how to deploy software using Group Policy.

Chapter 10, "Server Administration," provides an overview of the different tools and techniques that can be used to locally and remotely manage a Windows Server 2003 system. Examples of tools and services outlined in this chapter include the Microsoft Management Console (MMC), Terminal Services, Remote Desktop, and Microsoft Software Update Services (SUS).

Chapter 11, "Monitoring Server Performance," outlines issues involved in monitoring Windows Server 2003 health and performance. It also discusses troubleshooting Windows Server 2003 startup procedures, advanced startup options, and troubleshooting methods.

Chapter 12, "Managing and Implementing Backups and Disaster Recovery," provides an overview of different backup and recovery procedures in Windows Server 2003 environments, including a look at the tools and utilities available to deal with disaster recovery events, such as a server failure.

Chapter 13, "Administering Web Resources," outlines the new features of Internet Information Services (IIS) 6.0, and explains how to configure Windows Server 2003 as a Web or FTP server. This chapter also outlines the various authentication and security settings that can be configured to make an IIS server or site more secure.

Chapter 14, "Windows Server 2003 Security Features," provides a broad overview of different security-related issues and tools that a Windows Server 2003 administrator should be familiar with.

Features and Approach

To ensure a successful learning experience, *MCSE Guide to Managing a Microsoft Windows Server 2003 Environment, Enhanced* includes the following pedagogical features:

- **Chapter Objectives**—Each chapter begins with a detailed list of the concepts to be mastered. This list gives you a quick reference to the chapter's contents and is a useful study aid.

- **Activities**—Hands-on Activities are incorporated throughout the text, giving you practice in setting up, managing, and troubleshooting a network system. The activities give you a strong foundation for carrying out network administration tasks in the real world. Because of this book's progressive nature, completing the hands-on activities is essential before moving on to the end-of-chapter projects and subsequent chapters.

- **Chapter Summary**—Each chapter's text is followed by a summary of the concepts introduced in that chapter. These summaries provide a helpful way to recap and revisit the ideas covered in each chapter.

- **Key Terms**—All of the terms within the chapter that were introduced with boldfaced text are gathered together in the Key Terms list at the end of the chapter. This provides you with a method of checking your understanding of all the terms introduced.

- **Review Questions**—The end-of-chapter assessment begins with a set of review questions that reinforce the ideas introduced in each chapter. Answering these questions will ensure that you have mastered the important concepts.

- **Case Projects**—Each chapter closes with a section that proposes certain situations. You are asked to evaluate the situations and decide upon the course of action to be taken to remedy the problems described. This valuable tool will help you sharpen your decision-making and troubleshooting skills, which are important aspects of network administration.

- **Tear-Out Practice Exam**—A 50-question tear-out practice exam is included in the back of the text. The questions are modeled after the actual MCSE certification exam and are on perforated pages so students can hand them in as an assignment or an exam. The answers to the Practice Exam are included as part of the Instructor Resources.

- **On the CD ROM**—The CD-ROM includes CoursePrep® test preparation software, which provides sample MCSE exam questions mirroring the look and feel of the MCSE exams. The CD also contains a complete CoursePrep ExamGuide workbook in PDF format. It devotes an entire two-page spread for every exam objective, featuring bulleted memorization points and review questions for self-study before exam day.

Text and Graphic Conventions

Additional information and exercises have been added to this book to help you better understand what is being discussed in the chapter. Icons throughout the text alert you to additional materials. The icons used in this textbook are as follows:

Tips offer extra information on resources, how to attack problems, and time-saving shortcuts.

Notes present additional helpful material related to the subject being discussed.

The Caution icon identifies important information about potential mistakes or hazards.

Each Activity in this book is preceded by the Activity icon.

Case project icons mark the end-of-chapter case projects, which are scenario-based assignments that ask you to independently apply what you have learned in the chapter.

Instructor's Resources

The following supplemental materials are available when this book is used in a classroom setting. All of the supplements available with this book are provided to the instructor on a single CD-ROM.

Electronic Instructor's Manual. The Instructor's Manual that accompanies this textbook includes additional instructional material to assist in class preparation, including suggestions for classroom activities, discussion topics, and additional activities.

Solutions. Solutions are provided for the end-of-chapter material, including Review Questions, and, where applicable, Hands-On Activities and Case Projects. Solutions to the Practice Exams are also included.

ExamView®. This textbook is accompanied by ExamView, a powerful testing software package that allows instructors to create and administer printed, computer (LAN-based), and Internet exams. ExamView includes hundreds of questions that correspond to the topics covered in this text, enabling students to generate detailed study guides that include page references for further review. The computer-based and Internet testing components allow students to take exams at their computers and also save the instructor time by grading each exam automatically.

Practice Exam. A second 50-question Practice Exam is included as part of the Instructor Resources. Like the Tear-Out Practice Exam in the text, the questions are modeled after the actual MCSE certification exam. The answers to this exam are also included as part of the Instructor Resources.

PowerPoint presentations. This book comes with Microsoft PowerPoint slides for each chapter. These are included as a teaching aid for classroom presentation, to make available to students on the network for chapter review, or to be printed for classroom distribution. Instructors, please feel at liberty to add your own slides for additional topics you introduce to the class.

Figure files. All of the figures and tables in the book are reproduced on the Instructor's Resource CD, in bitmap format. Similar to the PowerPoint presentations, these are included as a teaching aid for classroom presentation, to make available to students for review, or to be printed for classroom distribution

Minimum Lab Requirements

Hardware:

All hardware should be listed on Microsoft's Hardware Compatibility List for Windows Server and the hand-on projects should meet the following hardware requirements.

Hardware Component	Windows 2000 Advanced Server
CPU	Pentium III 533 or higher
Memory	128 MB RAM (256 MB RAM recommended)
Disk Space	Minimum of two 4-GB partitions (C and D), with at least 500 MB of free space left on the drive
Drives	CD-ROM (or DVD-ROM) Floppy Disk
Networking	All lab computers should be networked. Students will work in pairs for some lab exercises. A connection to the Internet via some sort of NAT or Proxy server is assumed.

Software:

The following software is needed for proper setup of the labs:

- Windows Server 2003

- The following tool from the Microsoft Software Update Services Web site:
  - Microsoft Software Update Services, client and server components.

Set Up Instructions:

To successfully complete the lab exercises, set up classroom computers as listed here:

(1) Install Windows 2000 Server onto drive C: of the instructor and student servers. The following specific parameters should be configured on individual servers during the installation process:

Parameter	Setting
Disk Partitioning	Create two 4 GB primary NTFS partitions during the installation process, C and D. Ensure that at least1 GB of free space is left on the hard disk for student exercises.
Computer Names	Instructor (first server), ServerXX (subsequent student servers)
Administrator Password	Password01
Components	Default Settings
Network Adapter	IP Address: 192.168.1.X. The instructor computer should be l allocated a unique IP address on the same subnet as client computers. The suggested IP address for the Instructor machine is 192.168.1.100. Subnet Mask: 255.255.255.0 DNS: The IP address of the Instructor computer Default Gateway: The IP address for the classroom default gateway. If the Instructor computer will be used to provide Internet access via ICS or NAT, it will require a second network adapter card or modem.
Workgroup Name	Workgroup

In the table above, "*X*" or "*XX*" should represent a unique number to be assigned to each student. For example, student "1" would be assigned a computer name of Server01 and an IP address of 192.168.1.1.

(2) Once the installation process is complete, use Device Manager to ensure that all devices are functioning correctly. In some cases, it may be necessary to download and install additional drivers for devices listed with a yellow question mark icon.

(3) Create a new folder named Source on drive D of all classroom servers. Copy the entire contents of the Windows Server 2003 CD to this folder on all servers.

(4) Create a new folder named Shared on drive D of the Instructor computer only. Share this folder using the shared folder name Shared, and ensure that the

Everyone group is granted the Full Control shared folder permission. This folder will be used to store any supplemental files that may need to be made available to students during the course.

(5)   Download both the client and server components of Microsoft Software Update Services (SUS) to the Shared folder on the Instructor computer. Links to both downloads can be found at *www.microsoft.com*/windowsserversystem/sus/default.mspx.

(6)   Run dcpromo.exe on the Instructor computer to install Active Directory and DNS. Name the new domain (the first in a new forest) Dovercorp.net, ensure that both nonsecure and secure dynamic updates are allowed, and accept all other default options.

(7)   On the Instructor server, open Active Directory Users and Computers. Right-click the Dovercorp.net domain and click Raise Domain Functional Level. Change the domain functional level of the Instructor server only to Windows Server 2003.

(8)   After the previous steps are completed and the Dovercorp.net domain is completely installed on the Instructor server, run dcpromo.exe on each student server to install Active Directory, making each a child domain of Dovercorp.net. Name the student domains Domain*XX*.Dovercorp.net, where *XX* is the student number assigned to each student. Once the process is completed on all classroom servers, all DNS zones should be configured to allow nonsecure and secure dynamic updates. The Active Directory structure in the classroom once this is complete is illustrated in the following figure.

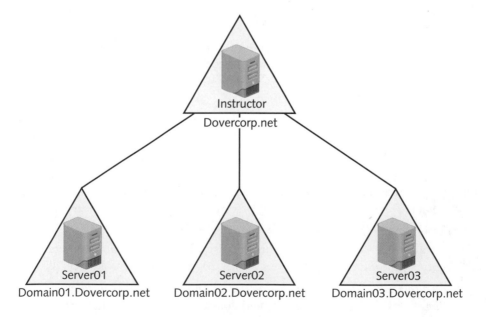

(9)   In each child domain, use Active Directory Users and Computers to create a user account named AdminXX in the Users container, where XX corresponds to the student number assigned to each student. The password associated with this account should be Password01. This account should be added to the Domain Admins group in the same domain.

(10)   On each server, edit the Default Domain Controllers Group Policy object to grant the Domain Users group the right to log on locally. This is accomplished by opening Active Directory Users and Computers, right-clicking the Domain Controllers OU, and clicking Properties. Click the Group Policy tab, click the Default Domain Controllers Policy, and then click Edit. In the Group Policy Object Editor window, browse to the Computer Configuration\Windows Settings\Security Settings\Local Policies\User Rights Assignment node. Double-click the Allow log on locally right, and then add the Domain Users group to the list.

ACKNOWLEDGMENTS

I would like to thank the folks at Course Technology for giving me the opportunity to write this book. The end result wouldn't have been possible without the involvement of Nick Lombardi, Brooke Booth, the QA department, and reviewers Patty Gillilan and Robert Sherman of Sinclair Community College, C.J. Gray of Pittsburgh Technical Institute, and Ronald Mashburn of West Texas A & M University. My eternal gratitude to Moirag Haddad, without whose involvement I certainly would have packed up and moved to a cabin in the woods a long time ago. A special thanks to Mike Aubert for all his help. I'm always thankful to have a server-side prodigy working with me; dealing with my rants, making suggestions, and always willing to help. Last but not least, a special thank you to all the people who serve to inspire me, especially my brother Dave, his better half Lynn, Mark the wise, my incredible girlfriend Jessica, Jack the master gardener, and the person without whom none of this would have ever come to be, my mom. Thanks to each of you for making me one of the luckiest people ever to have walked this planet.

INTRODUCTION TO WINDOWS SERVER 2003

After reading this chapter and completing the exercises, you will be able to:

- ◆ Differentiate between the different editions of Windows Server 2003
- ◆ Explain Windows Server 2003 network models and server roles
- ◆ Identify concepts relating to Windows Server 2003 network management and maintenance
- ◆ Explain Windows Server 2003 Active Directory concepts

Windows Server 2003 network administration consists of two major goals. The first is to ensure that network resources such as files, folders, and printers are available to users whenever they need access. The second goal is to secure the network so that available resources are only accessible to users who have been granted the proper permissions.

To acquire the skills needed to meet your network administration goals, you need to understand a number of concepts, from the account creation process to server and resource management. A Windows Server 2003 network administrator also requires an understanding of **Active Directory (AD)** concepts and management, as well as general troubleshooting tools and techniques.

The first section of this chapter explains the main elements of the four Windows Server 2003 editions, including hardware specifications and supported features. Ultimately, the Windows Server 2003 edition best suited to a particular environment or server implementation will depend upon the performance, scalability, and reliability needs of an organization, along with the intended purpose of a particular system. In order to provide you with a better perspective on Windows networking concepts, the second section of this chapter introduces the different logical models used to group network resources, namely workgroups and domains. A look at member servers and domain controllers explains the roles of each type of server in a domain, and why an administrator might choose to configure a server in one role over another.

The third section of this chapter outlines the tasks network administrators are expected to understand and implement as part of managing and maintaining a Windows Server 2003 network. This section provides a basic outline of the concepts and procedures covered in the subsequent chapters of this book.

It is also essential to understand the basic concepts of Windows Server 2003 Active Directory and how it influences network management procedures because most network management tasks take place within domain environments. The final section of this chapter discusses Active Directory concepts and provides a solid foundation on which to build your network administration skills. To become a successful Microsoft Certified Systems Administrator (MCSA) or Microsoft Certified Systems Engineer (MCSE), you need practical, hands-on experience with products like Microsoft Windows Server 2003. This book includes numerous hands-on activities and case studies to help ensure that you not only understand the theory behind the concepts covered but also that you feel comfortable carrying out common system administration tasks. To help simulate a real-world network environment, all of the activities in the book relate to a fictitious multinational organization calif led Dover Leasing Corporation, a property management company with a head office based in Boston. For the purpose of the activities and case projects, you have been hired by Dover Leasing Corporation as a junior network administrator responsible for looking after the day-to-day administration of an Active Directory domain within their Windows Server 2003 network. The scenarios presented are designed to help you relate the concepts that you learn to tasks typically performed by a system administrator in a corporate Windows Server 2003 environment.

WINDOWS SERVER 2003 EDITIONS

Businesses today have a wide variety of needs, making it difficult for a single operating system to include all required features. The Windows Server 2003 product line is divided into four distinct operating system editions. Each edition has similar core capabilities but is differentiated from the others by features (and limitations) that make it suitable for different server environments. This allows businesses to choose the platform that best meets their needs in terms of features, performance, and price.

The Windows Server 2003 operating system comes in the following editions, each of which are discussed in the following sections:

- Windows Server 2003, Standard Edition
- Windows Server 2003, Enterprise Edition
- Windows Server 2003, Datacenter Edition
- Windows Server 2003, Web Edition

Windows Server 2003, Standard Edition

Windows Server 2003, Standard Edition, is designed to meet the everyday needs of small to large businesses. It provides file and print services, secure Internet connectivity, and centralized management of network resources. Windows Server 2003, Standard Edition, provides the logical upgrade path for companies currently running its predecessor, Windows 2000 Server.

This edition of Windows Server 2003 provides basic operating system elements that enable file and printer sharing over a network, along with secure management of resources using NTFS permissions. It supports up to four processors in a symmetric multiprocessor (SMP) system, and up to 4 GB of RAM. Table 1-1 provides an overview of the system requirements and basic feature support for Windows Server 2003, Standard Edition.

Table 1-1   Windows Server 2003, Standard Edition, system requirements and feature support

Specification/Feature	Value
Minimum CPU speed	133 MHz
Recommended minimum CPU speed	550 MHz
Minimum RAM	128 MB
Recommended minimum RAM	256 MB
Maximum RAM supported	4 GB
Multiprocessor support	Up to 4 CPUs
Operating system disk space requirements	1.5 GB Free space
Clustering support	None
Itanium support	None
Active Directory support	Domain controller, Member server
Supported upgrades	Windows NT 4.0 Server (SP5), Windows NT 4.0 Terminal Server Edition (SP5), Windows 2000 Server

NOTE   Itanium is the name of Intel's line of 64-bit processors aimed at higher-end application, security, and transaction processing servers. Only the Enterprise and Datacenter editions of Windows Server 2003 support these CPUs. For more information on the Itanium processor lines see *http://www.intel.com/itanium*.

Windows Server 2003, Standard Edition is designed to support the everyday business needs of small to medium organizations, or to function as a departmental server in larger environments. Key considerations for companies choosing this edition are the fact that it does not support the Itanium platform or clustering, and that it can only scale to a maximum of four processors and 4 GB of RAM.

Windows Server 2003, Enterprise Edition

Windows Server 2003, Enterprise Edition, is designed to meet the needs of organizations that support higher-end applications that demand better performance, reliability, and availability. Windows Server 2003, Enterprise Edition, supports up to eight processors in an SMP system and is available for both 32-bit x86 and 64-bit Itanium processors. In addition to these features, this platform has the following advantages:

- Supports up to 32 GB of RAM for x86 systems and up to 64 GB for Itanium systems.

- Provides **clustering** capabilities for up to eight nodes. Clustering is the ability to increase access to server resources and provide fail-safe services by linking two or more computer systems so they appear to function as though they are one.

- Supports hot-add memory in which RAM can be added to a system without shutting down the server.

- Provides Non-Uniform Memory Access (NUMA) support for SMP computers, allowing a processor to access memory designated for other processors. Applications can be written so that they take advantage of NUMA capabilities, including faster memory access.

- Supports Microsoft Metadirectory Services to facilitate networks that use multiple directory services to track and manage access to such resources as user accounts, shared folders, and shared printers.

- Provides Windows System Resource Manager (WSRM) to allow administrators to allocate and dedicate CPU and memory resources on a per-application basis.

Table 1-2 provides an overview of the system requirements and basic feature support for Windows Server 2003, Enterprise Edition.

Table 1-2   Windows Server 2003, Enterprise Edition, system requirements and feature support

Specification/Feature	Value
Minimum CPU speed	133 MHz (x86), 733 MHz (Itanium)
Recommended minimum CPU speed	733 MHz
Minimum RAM	128 MB
Recommended minimum RAM	256 MB
Maximum RAM supported	32 GB (x86), 64 GB (Itanium)
Multiprocessor support	Up to 8 CPUs
Operating system disk space requirements	1.5 GB (x86), 2.0 GB (Itanium)
Clustering support	Up to 8 nodes
Itanium support	Yes
Active Directory support	Domain controller, Member server

Table 1-2   Windows Server 2003, Enterprise Edition, system requirements and feature support (continued)

Specification/Feature	Value
Supported upgrades (x86 only)	Windows NT 4.0 Server (SP5), Windows NT 4.0 Terminal Server Edition (SP5), Windows NT 4.0 Enterprise Edition (SP5), Windows 2000 Server, Windows 2000 Advanced Server, Windows Server 2003 Standard Edition

Windows Server 2003, Enterprise Edition, is designed to support the higher-end business needs of medium to large organizations that require support for mission-critical applications. Key considerations for companies choosing this edition are the fact that it does support the Itanium platform and 8-way clustering, can scale to a maximum of eight processors, and supports more RAM than Standard Edition.

Windows Server 2003, Datacenter Edition

Windows Server 2003, Datacenter Edition, is designed for environments with mission-critical applications, very large databases, and information access requiring the highest possible degree of availability. This platform offers support for between eight and 32 processors in an x86 SMP system (64 processors maximum on Itanium systems), along with 8-way clustering. The maximum RAM capabilities for Datacenter Edition are the most robust at 64 GB for x86 systems and 512 GB for Itanium models. Table 1-3 provides an overview of the system requirements and basic feature support for Windows Server 2003, Datacenter Edition.

Table 1-3   Windows Server 2003, Datacenter Edition, system requirements and feature support

Specification/Feature	Value
Minimum CPU speed	400 MHz (x86), 733 MHz (Itanium)
Recommended minimum CPU speed	733 MHz
Minimum RAM	512 MB
Recommended minimum RAM	1 GB
Maximum RAM supported	64 GB (x86), 512 GB (Itanium)
Multiprocessor support	Minimum 8 CPUs required, Maximum 32 CPUs supported (x86), Maximum 64 CPUs supported (Itanium)
Operating system disk space requirements	1.5 GB (x86), 2.0 GB (Itanium)
Clustering support	Up to 8 nodes
Itanium support	Yes
Active Directory support	Domain controller, Member server
Supported upgrades (x86 only)	Windows 2000 Datacenter Server

Windows Server 2003, Datacenter Edition, is the most industrial-strength platform designed for large mission-critical database and transaction processing systems. Unlike the other Windows Server 2003 editions, the Datacenter edition can only be obtained from original equipment manufacturers (OEMs).

Windows Server 2003, Web Edition

Windows Server 2003, Web Edition, is designed for hosting and deploying Web services and related applications. This platform supports up to two processors (x86 only) and a maximum of 2 GB of RAM. It is specifically optimized to run Microsoft Internet Information Services (IIS) 6.0, and provides companies that only need to deploy Web-related services with a more cost-effective solution than the other Windows Server 2003 editions. Table 1-4 provides an overview of the system requirements and basic feature support for Windows Server 2003, Web Edition.

Table 1-1   Windows Server 2003, Web Edition, system requirements and feature support

Specification/Feature	Value
Minimum CPU speed	133 MHz
Recommended minimum CPU speed	550 MHz
Minimum RAM	128 MB
Recommended minimum RAM	256 MB
Maximum RAM supported	2 GB
Multiprocessor support	Up to 2 CPUs
Operating system disk space requirements	1.5 GB
Clustering support	None
Itanium support	None
Active Directory support	Member server only
Supported upgrades	None

Small to large companies, or departments within an organization that develop and deploy Web sites are examples of the intended audience for this platform. One limitation of Windows Server 2003, Web Edition, is that it cannot be configured as a domain controller, a function that is available on all other Windows Server 2003 platforms. You'll learn more about Active Directory later in this chapter.

NOTE   For a complete high-level overview of the features included in the different editions of Windows Server 2003 visit *www.microsoft.com/windows server2003/ evaluation/features/compareeditions.mspx*.

ACTIVITY

Activity 1-1: Determining the Windows Server 2003 Edition Installed on a Server

1

Time Required: 5 minutes

Objective: Determine the edition of Windows Server 2003 installed on your server.

Description: The edition of Windows Server 2003 that is installed on a server can be determined in a number of different ways ranging from the operating system selection screen during the boot process to the graphic displayed as part of the logon dialog box. In this exercise you will use the System Properties windows to determine the edition of Windows Server 2003 installed on your server.

1. At the Welcome to Windows dialog box, press **Ctrl+Alt+Delete**.

2. At the Log On to Windows dialog box, type **AdminXX** in the User name text box, where *XX* is your assigned student number. In the Password text box, type **Password01**.

3. Click the **Options** button. Ensure that Domain*XX* is selected in the Log on to drop down box, where *XX* is your assigned student number. Click **OK**.

4. At the Manage Your Server window, check the **Don't display this page at logon** check box, and then close the window.

5. Click **Start**, right-click **My Computer**, and click **Properties**. Notice that the Windows Server 2003 edition installed on your server appears in the System section of the General tab, as shown in Figure 1-1.

6. Click **Cancel** to close the System Properties window.

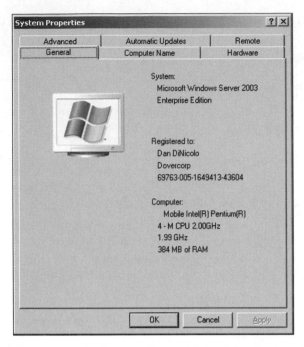

Figure 1-1   Using the General tab of the System Properties window to determine the Windows Server 2003 edition

WINDOWS NETWORKING CONCEPTS OVERVIEW

As part of managing a Windows Server 2003 network environment, a network administrator needs to be familiar with both of the different security models that can be implemented as well as the roles that a server can hold. The two different security models used in Windows network environments are the workgroup model and the domain model. While almost all larger organizations use the domain model (and by extension, Active Directory), the workgroup model is often implemented in smaller environments. As part of understanding a Windows network, you should be familiar with both models, including the benefits and limitations of each.

When a Windows Server 2003 system is deployed, it can participate on the network in one of three major roles. These roles include being configured as a standalone server, member server, and domain controller. The decision as to which role a server should be configured in is a function of the network model in use (workgroup or domain), as well as the types of tasks that the server will be handling. In the following sections you'll learn more about both of the Windows networking models, as well as each Windows Server 2003 server role.

Workgroups

A Windows **workgroup** is a logical group of computers characterized by a decentralized security and administration model. Instead of implementing a server to facilitate functions like centralized authentication, systems in a workgroup rely upon a local account database known as the **Security Accounts Manager (SAM) database**. When a user logs on to their workstation in the workgroup, they are authenticated by the local SAM database on that system. One of the benefits of the workgroup model is that it is simple and does not explicitly require a server at all—users can share resources directly from their desktop systems as necessary.

While this model may initially sound appealing, it does present many limitations. First, a user needs a unique user account to be configured on each and every workstation that they will log on to, rather than a single, centralized account. This may not be difficult in a small environment with only three workstations, but would be very difficult to manage on a larger network. Second, individual users effectively manage their own systems in the workgroup model, which can lead to potential security issues. Finally, the workgroup model is not scalable to very large sizes—as such, it is only recommended for smaller networks. As a general rule, workgroups should only be used in networks with 10 or less client systems, although workgroups up to 20 systems are not uncommon.

Although the workgroup model does not explicitly require a server, a Windows Server 2003 system can still be made part of a workgroup. In the workgroup model, a server would be used for traditional purposes such as providing a centralized location for the storage of user data files or acting as an e-mail server. A Windows Server 2003 system configured as part of a workgroup does not, however, authenticate users in a centralized manner, and configuring security settings (such as file and folder permissions) is more difficult due to the lack of a single user database. When a Windows Server 2003 system is configured as a member of a workgroup, it is properly referred to as a standalone server.

Figure 1-2 illustrates the Computer Name tab of the System Properties window for a server configured as part of a workgroup. Most organizations use the default workgroup name "Workgroup," but any valid NetBIOS name can be chosen to identify the logical group.

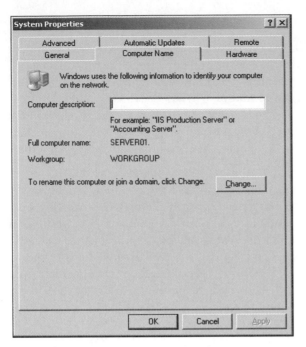

Figure 1-2   A Windows Server 2003 system configured as part of a workgroup named Workgroup

Domains

In contrast to a workgroup, a **domain** is a logical group of computers characterized by centralized authentication and administration. In the domain model, user, group, and computer accounts are stored in a centralized directory database—Active Directory, in the case of Windows Server 2003. While the directory conceptually centralizes both authentication and administration, the database itself is stored on one or more computers configured in a role known as a domain controller. In a Windows Server 2003 environment, a domain controller can be a server running Windows Server 2003, Windows 2000, or even Windows NT 4.0. In order to function as a domain controller, a server must explicitly be configured to hold this role.

The versions of Windows supported as domain controllers in a Windows Server 2003 Active Directory environment depends upon the configured functional level of both the domain and the forest. For more information on domain and forest functional levels see the Windows Server 2003 Help and Support Center.

When a user attempts to log on in a domain environment, they are authenticated by a domain controller rather than by the local SAM database of the workstation under normal circumstances. The authentication request is passed from their workstation to a domain controller where the supplied user name and password are compared to information stored in the directory database. The obvious benefit of this model is that a user requires only a single account to be created to gain access to the network, rather than an account in the SAM database of many different workstations. By extension, this model also facilitates easier administration of the network since users and their properties can be managed centrally.

The domain model is highly recommended in any environment that consists of more than 10 users or workstations. One drawback of this model is that it requires at least one server to be configured as a domain controller, which means additional expense. Optimally, a domain environment will consist of a minimum of two domain controllers for the purpose of fault tolerance and load balancing. In this case, the second domain controller provides fault tolerance by ensuring that a domain controller is available to service requests should the other fail. Load balancing is achieved by having both domain controllers (rather than just one) handle requests, which results in better performance. Later in this chapter you'll learn more about Windows Server 2003 domains, and specifically Active Directory.

Member Servers

A **member server** is a Windows Server 2003 system that has a computer account in a domain, but is not configured as a domain controller. Member servers are typically used for a wide variety of functions including file, print, and application services. Member servers also commonly host network services such as the Domain Name Service (DNS), Routing and Remote Access Service (RRAS), and others. Each of the four Windows Server 2003 editions can be configured in the role of a member server in a domain environment.

Figure 1-3 illustrates the Computer Name tab of the System Properties window for a member server configured as part of a domain named Domain01.Dovercorp.net.

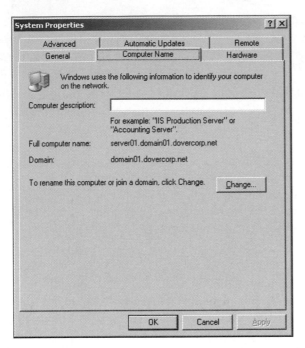

Figure 1-3   A Windows Server 2003 system configured as a member of a domain named Domain01.Dovercorp.net

Domain Controllers

While still a member of a domain, a **domain controller** is a Windows Server 2003 system explicitly configured to store a copy of the Active Directory database, and service user authentication requests or queries about domain objects. While many companies choose to dedicate servers to the role of a domain controller exclusively, other companies will use their domain controllers to also provide file, print, application, and networking services on the network. The main considerations when deciding which additional roles a domain controller should take on are the current utilization of the server, as well as whether sufficient resources (such as memory) are available to handle those roles. Of the four Windows Server 2003 editions, only Windows Server 2003, Web Edition, cannot be configured as a domain controller.

Servers are promoted to the role of a domain controller using either the Active Directory Installation Wizard (DCPROMO.EXE) or the Configure Your Server wizard. The Configure Your Server wizard is illustrated in Figure 1-4.

1

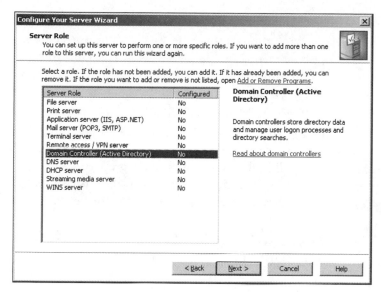

Figure 1-4   The Server Role screen of the Configure Your Server wizard

Activity 1-2: Determining the Domain or Workgroup Membership of a Windows Server 2003 System

Time Required: 5 minutes

Objective: Determine the domain or workgroup membership of a Windows Server 2003 system.

Description: Windows Server 2003 systems can be configured in different roles depending upon the Windows network environment in use and the intended purpose of the server. In this exercise you will use the System Properties window in order to determine the current role of your server as well as domain or workgroup membership settings.

1. Click **Start**, right-click on **My Computer**, and then click **Properties**.

2. Click the **Computer Name** tab. This tab displays both the full computer name of your server along with the domain that it is currently a member of.

3. Click the **Change** button. When the Computer Name Changes dialog box appears, read the message you are presented with and click **OK**. This message appears because your server is currently configured as a domain controller.

4. Notice in the lower portion of the Computer Name Changes window that the Member of section is grayed out and cannot be changed. If your system were not a domain controller, this screen would be used to add the server to a domain or workgroup. Your server is currently configured as a domain controller in domain*XX*.dovercorp.net, where *XX* is your assigned student number.

5. Click **Cancel** to close the Computer Name Changes window.

6. Click **OK** to close the System Properties window.

Computer Accounts

Computers running Windows NT, Windows 2000, Windows XP, or Windows Server 2003 are assigned computer accounts as part of joining a domain. A computer account provides a method to authenticate computers that are members of a domain, as well as audit access to network resources. While systems running Windows 95/98/ME can participate in a domain, these operating systems are not assigned computer accounts.

In an Active Directory environment, computer accounts are represented as computer objects, and can be viewed using administrative tools like Active Directory Users and Computers. In Activity 1-3, you will explore some of the basic properties associated with the computer account for your server. Later in this book you will learn more about the process of creating and managing computer accounts in an Active Directory environment.

ACTIVITY

Activity 1-3: Viewing and Configuring Computer Account Settings in Active Directory Users and Computers

Time Required: 5 minutes

Objective: Use Active Directory Users and Computers to view and configure computer account settings and properties.

Description: When a Windows Server 2003 system is configured as a member of an Active Directory domain, a computer account is created for the system in the Active Directory database. In this exercise you will use the Active Directory Users and Computers administrative tool to view the location and settings of the computer account associated with your server.

1. Click **Start**, point to **Administrative Tools**, and click **Active Directory Users and Computers**.

2. Click on the **plus sign (+)** next to the domain*XX*.dovercorp.net (where *XX* is your assigned student number) icon to expand it.

3. Click on the **Domain Controllers** folder to view its contents. This object is an organizational unit in the domain*XX*.dovercorp.net domain.

4. Right-click the **ServerXX** computer object shown in Figure 1-5, and click **Properties**.

5. Review the information provided on the General tab. Notice that this system currently holds the role of Domain controller. In the Description text box, type **Domain Controller for domainXX.dovercorp.net**, where *XX* is your assigned student number.

6. Click the **Operating System** tab. This tab displays information about the operating system installed, along with version number and service pack information. Notice, however, that Windows Server 2003 edition information is not provided. Click **OK**. You will review the remaining tabs found in the properties of a computer account in a later chapter.

7. Close Active Directory Users and Computers.

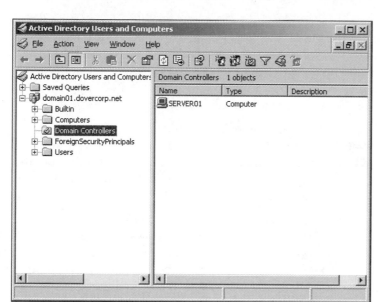

Figure 1-5   Using Active Directory Users and Computers to view a computer object

NETWORK MANAGEMENT AND MAINTENANCE OVERVIEW

Although managing and maintaining a Windows Server 2003 network environment requires an administrator to be familiar with a variety of different tools, concepts, and troubleshooting procedures, most of these tasks can be broadly categorized into one of the following five major focus areas:

- Managing and maintaining physical and logical devices
- Managing users, computers, and groups
- Managing and maintaining access to resources
- Managing and maintaining a server environment
- Managing and implementing disaster recovery

The following sections outline the key tasks associated with each of these five focus areas, which make up the core concepts that a network administrator needs to be familiar with for Microsoft exam 70-290, Managing and Maintaining a Microsoft Windows Server 2003 Environment. Outside of providing a broad overview of each focus area and related tasks, each section also provides details of where these topics are covered within this book.

Managing and Maintaining Physical and Logical Devices

A large part of managing and maintaining any network environment involves ensuring that network hardware is configured and functioning correctly. In a typical environment, a network administrator will be responsible for installing and configuring server hardware devices, managing server disks, and generally ensuring that devices are performing optimally. Key tools that are used to manage server hardware and related settings include various Control Panel applets, Device Manager, and the Computer Management MMC.

A network administrator would typically be responsible for installing new server hardware, such as an additional network adapter card or perhaps a modem. Apart from the physical act of inserting the card in an expansion slot, the administrator needs to be sure that resource settings are configured correctly, the correct driver is installed, and that the installed driver is certified for Windows Server 2003.

As part of managing server disks, an administrator will need to be familiar with the different types of disks available in Windows Server 2003, and how to configure these disks with different logical volumes or partitions. Once partitions or volumes have been created, an administrator will need to manage them to ensure optimal performance using utilities like Disk Defragmenter. In cases where disk redundancy is required, an administrator will need to be familiar with the various fault tolerance techniques available in Windows Server 2003, such as **Redundant Array of Independent Disks (RAID)**.

Although a proactive approach to network management and maintenance will help to ensure that server hardware problems are minimized, there will still be times when problems occur without warning. In these situations, it is imperative that a network administrator be able to identify the problem using the various tools provided in Windows Server 2003 in order to minimize the potential impact to network users.

Managing and maintaining hardware devices and related settings is detailed in Chapter 2. Managing disks and data storage is covered in Chapter 6.

Managing Users, Computers, and Groups

One of the most common day-to-day tasks encountered by a Windows Server 2003 network administrator is the administration of user accounts. New user accounts need to be created, existing settings may need to be changed, and users will invariably forget their passwords from time to time. In large environments, the management and maintenance of user accounts can consume a great deal of time and energy for any administrator.

To help alleviate some of this burden, Windows Server 2003 Active Directory includes a variety of new tools and features that allow an administrator to automate and simplify many account-related tasks. For example, the primary user administration tool, Active Directory Users and Computers, now supports drag-and-drop functionality to make moving objects easier. Similarly, a number of new command-line utilities are available to help automate the process of adding, changing, and deleting user accounts. These powerful utilities give an administrator more flexibility in effectively managing their user environment. In a similar manner, these same tools can be used to manage the computer accounts required for Windows NT, Windows 2000, Windows XP, and Windows Server 2003 systems that will be part of a domain.

Windows Server 2003 supports a number of different group types and scopes. Groups can be created for the purpose of assigning network rights and permissions to multiple users, as well as to create distribution lists for e-mail. An administrator needs to be familiar with the different group types and scopes available in Windows Server 2003, and, subsequently, how and when each should be used. Group accounts, like user accounts, can also be managed using a variety of new command-line utilities included with Windows Server 2003.

Outside of the creation and management of users, computers, and groups, a network administrator also needs to manage the user desktop environment. In Windows Server 2003, the desktop environment is managed using user profiles. Depending upon the environment and needs of an organization, user profiles may be configured to save settings locally, enforce a standard profile for all users, or follow users to any system that they happen to log on to.

Once network objects are created and settings are configured, an administrator is still responsible for troubleshooting related problems as they arise. In some cases solving these problems may be simple, such as resetting a user's forgotten password. In others, a variety of issues may impact the user's ability to authenticate and access network resources. An administrator must be familiar with the authentication process and the different policy settings that can impact user access to the network.

Managing and maintaining user accounts, computer accounts, profile settings, and troubleshooting authentication issues are looked at in more detail in Chapter 3. The creation and management of group accounts is covered in Chapter 4.

One of the most common tasks for a network administrator involves resetting forgotten user passwords. In Activity 1-4 you will use Active Directory Users and Computers to reset the password associated with your AdminXX user account.

Activity 1-4: Resetting a Domain User Account Password Using Active Directory Users and Computers

Time Required: 10 minutes

Objective: Use Active Directory Users and Computers to reset a user password and force the user to change their password the next time they log on.

Description: One of the common tasks of a network administrator is to reset forgotten user passwords. While an administrator can explicitly control the passwords that users will need to provide during the logon process, this is not a common configuration. Instead, when a user forgets their password, an administrator will typically reset the account password to a temporary value, supply this password to the user, and then force them to change it to a new value during the logon process. In this exercise you will use Active Directory Users and Computers to reset the password associated with your AdminXX account, and then create a new personal password during the logon process.

1. Click **Start**, point to **Administrative Tools**, and then click **Active Directory Users and Computers**.

2. Click the **Users** folder to view its contents. The Users folder is a built-in container in Windows Server 2003 Active Directory environments.

3. Right-click the **AdminXX** user object, where XX is your assigned student number. From the shortcut menu, click **Reset Password**.

4. In the Reset Password dialog box displayed in Figure 1-6, type **Password02** in the New password text box and **Password02** in the Confirm password text box.

5. Check the **User must change password at next logon** check box. This will force you to change your password immediately the next time you log on. Click **OK**.

6. When the Active Directory dialog box appears, click **OK**.

7. Close Active Directory Users and Computers.

8. Click **Start**, and then click **Log Off**. In the Log Off Windows dialog box, click the **Log Off** button.

9. Log on using your **AdminXX** account and the password **Password02**. At the Logon Message dialog box, click **OK**.

10. In the Change Password dialog box, type a new password in the New Password text-box and then re-type the new password in the Confirm New Password check box. Click **OK**. If the password you chose does not meet the complexity requirements read the dialog box that appears, click **OK**, and then enter a sufficiently complex password.

11. At the Change Password dialog box, click **OK**.

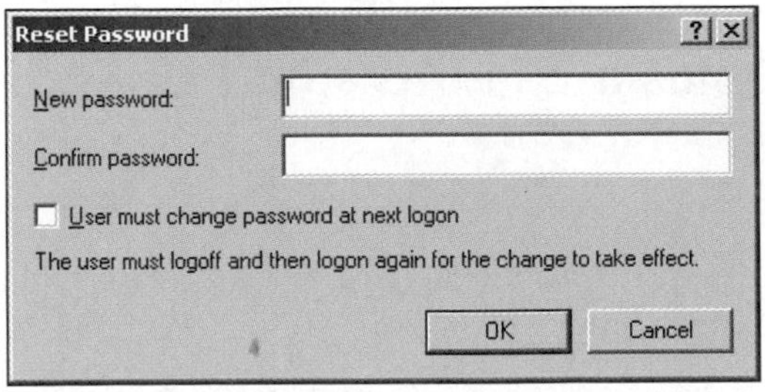

Figure 1-6 The Reset Password dialog box in Active Directory Users and Computers

1

Managing and Maintaining Access to Resources

The primary reason for implementing a network is to allow users to share resources. Examples of common network resources that users need access to include files saved on network servers and shared network printers. An administrator not only needs to ensure that resources are accessible to users, but also that they are properly secured.

In Windows Server 2003, resources are made available to network users via a technique known as sharing. When a folder or printer is shared over the network it becomes possible for users to connect to and remotely access the resource. The two most common methods of sharing resources are using the Windows Explorer interface and the Computer Management administrative tool. Other methods are also possible including using the command line.

Although sharing resources is the primary reason for implementing a network, it is imperative that resources are properly secured. While it might be fine for all users to access certain network folders or printers, others will need to be restricted to certain users or groups. Windows Server 2003 provides two main methods of securing resources, shared folder permissions and NTFS permissions. Shared folder permissions are only applicable when a user tries to access a resource over a network, while NTFS permissions apply both locally and remotely.

An administrator needs to understand the difference between each type of permission and the effects of combining them in order to properly plan permissions. If these concepts are not correctly understood and accounted for, the security of the network is put at risk, and unauthorized users may be able to access resources they shouldn't be able to.

Windows Server 2003 also includes a service known as **Terminal Services**. Terminal Services allows a user to connect to a central server and access applications as though working from the user desktop. This is a popular method of granting users access to certain applications without the need to deploy those applications to all desktops. Along the same lines, Terminal Services can also be used to give users running different operating systems (such as Windows 98 or Windows NT) the ability to use applications that were designed for Windows Server 2003. Once the decision to use Terminal Services has been made, a network administrator not only needs to ensure that a client can access the environment, but also that the environment is properly secured.

 Managing the access to files and configuring security permissions is looked at in more detail in Chapter 5. Terminal Services and related settings are covered in Chapter 10.

Managing and Maintaining a Server Environment

A wide variety of tasks are involved in the general management and maintenance of a Windows Server 2003 server environment. Tasks included in this focus area range from managing server licensing to deploying software updates to managing Web servers. As part of the day-to-day operations of a network, a network administrator needs to be familiar with a wide variety of software tools and concepts aimed not only at management, but also the monitoring of resources.

Two of the most popular tools used to monitor and troubleshoot a server environment are Event Viewer and System Monitor. Event Viewer handles the primary event logging functions on a Windows Server 2003 system, creating entries when any event of significance occurs. When an error occurs, Event Viewer should be the main tool accessed by a network administrator to gather more information. In cases where the overall performance of a server is in question, the System Monitor tool allows an administrator to gather current performance information that can be compared against the baseline of normal performance. Both tools are key utilities in helping an administrator to identify problem areas or performance issues.

Timely application of software patches and security updates is another key maintenance task for the network administrator. Microsoft typically releases patches for known exploits or issues shortly after they are identified, and then later includes these updates in a Service Pack release. Because managing individual updates for hundreds of computers is time-consuming and difficult, Microsoft has released a tool known as **Software Update Services (SUS)** for managing updates in a centralized manner. Administrators of Windows Server 2003 networks should be familiar with this tool and the capabilities that it provides.

Managing printing is yet another key component of a Windows Server 2003 network. Outside of physically connecting and then sharing printers, an administrator needs to ensure that printers are properly secured, and troubleshoot print queue issues as they arise.

While users should be encouraged to save their data files to a network server, an administrator also needs to prevent misuse of this space. For example, users may begin using their server storage space for non-critical files, such as MP3s. Ultimately such misuse of corporate resources leads to higher costs since additional disk space must consequently be acquired. In order to help control these types of issues, an administrator should be familiar with the disk quota feature of Windows Server 2003, which allows an administrator to control the amount of disk space allocated and available to each user.

Windows Server 2003 also includes Web server software in the form of Internet Information Services (IIS) 6.0. Although not installed by default, a Windows Server 2003 network administrator should be familiar with installing the service, and then subsequently ensuring that it is properly secured.

In order to simplify the administration of Windows Server 2003 servers, a variety of remote administration tools are included. One of these tools, the **Microsoft Management Console (MMC)**, provides an administration framework that allows different tools (known as snap-ins) to be added in custom configurations for different management and maintenance tasks. Almost all MMC snap-ins can be focused locally or remotely, allowing an administrator to manage settings on both local and remote servers from a central location. Another very useful remote management tool included with Windows Server 2003 is Remote Desktop, which allows an administrator to remotely connect to a server and manage it as though sitting in front of it. Both tools are key components of any Windows Server 2003 remote administration strategy.

Advanced file system management concepts, including the configuration of disk quotas, are looked at in Chapter 7. Implementing and managing printing are detailed in Chapter 8. Software Update Services (SUS) and the remote administration of servers are covered in Chapter 10. Monitoring and managing server performance using tools like Event Viewer and System Monitor is looked at in more detail in Chapter 11. The administration and configuration of Web resources is covered in Chapter 13.

In Activity 1-5 you will create a custom Microsoft Management Console.

Activity 1-5: Creating a Custom Microsoft Management Console

Time Required: 10 minutes

Objective: Create a custom MMC.

Description: The MMC is the common environment in which all of the Windows Server 2003 administrative tools run. Although these tools are individually available from the Administrative Tools section of the Start menu, administrative tasks can be simplified by grouping commonly used tools into a single customized MMC. The IT manager at Dover Leasing has asked you to create and save a custom MMC to access both Event Viewer and Device Manager. In this activity, you will create a custom MMC and save it to your desktop for more convenient access.

1. Click **Start**, click **Run**, and then type **mmc** in the Open text box. Click **OK**. Figure 1-7 shows an empty MMC window.

2. Click the **File** menu, and click **Add/Remove Snap-in**. Figure 1-8 shows an open Add/Remove Snap-in dialog box.

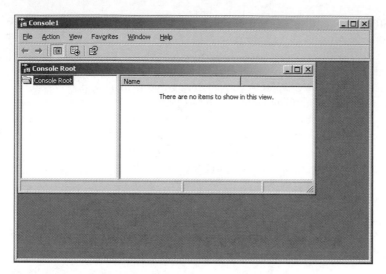

Figure 1-7   An empty MMC

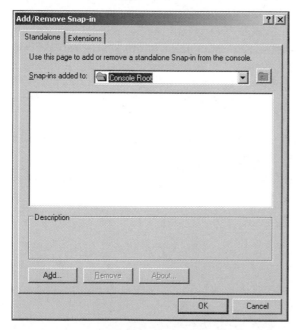

Figure 1-8   The Add/Remove Snap-in dialog box

3. Click the **Add** button to open the Add Standalone Snap-in dialog box listing the available snap-ins, as shown in Figure 1-9.

4. From the list of available snap-ins, click **Event Viewer** and click **Add**. When the Select Computer dialog box opens, make sure that the **Local computer** radio button is selected, as shown in Figure 1-10, and click **Finish**.

Figure 1-9   The Add Standalone Snap-in dialog box

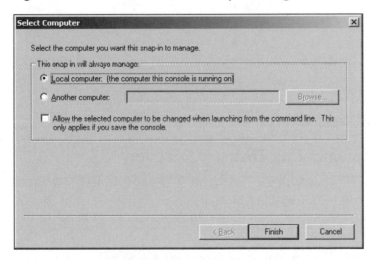

Figure 1-10   Selecting the snap-in focus

5. Click **Device Manager** on the list of available snap-ins and click **Add**. In the Device Manager dialog box, ensure that the **Local computer** radio button is selected and click **Finish**.

6. Click **Close** in the Add Standalone Snap-in dialog box.

7. Click **OK** in the Add/Remove Snap-in dialog box.

8. To save the console, click the **File** menu, and click **Save As**. In the Save in drop-down box, select your desktop, type the file name **My Console** in the File name text box, and click **Save**. Figure 1-11 shows a finished console.

9. Close the My Console window. If prompted to save changes, click **Yes**.

10. Double-click the **My Console** file on your desktop to open the custom console. Notice that it includes both the Event Viewer and Device Manager snap-ins. Close the **MMC**.

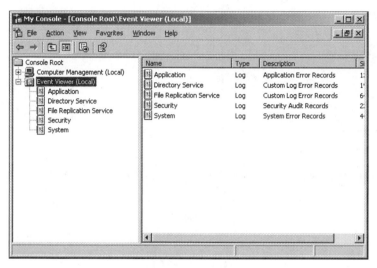

Figure 1-11   A customized MMC

Managing and Implementing Disaster Recovery

The final major focus area for a Windows Server 2003 network administrator is implementing and managing disaster recovery. This focus area concentrates on tasks that ensure both data and system settings are properly backed up and then available in cases like the failure of a server or the accidental deletion of files.

The backup tool provided with Windows Server 2003 is Windows Backup. This tool includes not only a graphical interface where the files to be backed up or restored can be selected, but also a wizard that can be used to simplify the same tasks. A network administrator should be familiar with the different types of backups available using this tool, along with how to schedule backup operations to occur automatically.

The Windows Backup tool can also be used to back up critical system information by selecting the System State option. System State information includes a variety of operating system components, including the Registry and critical system files. An administrator should be familiar with both backing up and restoring System State information using the Windows Backup tool.

Windows Server 2003 also includes a new feature known as Automated System Recovery. This feature, which is accessible from the Windows Backup utility, allows an administrator to create a floppy disk to which critical configuration information will be copied, allowing a server operating system to be restored using a combination of the disk and the Windows Server 2003 installation media. This provides a fast and effective way for an administrator to restore the operating system to a more current configuration rather than reinstalling from scratch.

Finally, another new and important feature in Windows Server 2003 is Shadow Copies of Shared Folders. Shadow Copies of Shared Folders is a feature that maintains previous versions of files on a server in a manner accessible to individual users. In the event that the current copy of a file has been deleted or overwritten, Shadow Copies of Shared Folders allows a user to restore a previous version of the file without having to contact an administrator. Ultimately, this feature can save an administrator a great deal of time and effort traditionally expended restoring individual user files from backup.

 Concepts relating to implementing and managing disaster recovery are looked at in more detail in Chapter 12.

INTRODUCTION TO WINDOWS SERVER 2003 ACTIVE DIRECTORY

Active Directory is the native directory service included with Windows Server 2003 operating systems. Active Directory provides the following services and features to the network environment:

- A central point for storing, organizing, managing, and controlling network objects, such as users, computers, and groups
- A single point of administration of objects, such as users, groups, computers, and Active Directory-published resources, such as printers or shared folders
- Logon and authentication services for users
- Delegation of administration to allow for decentralized administration of Active Directory objects, such as users and groups

The Active Directory database is stored on any Windows Server 2003 server that has been promoted to the role of domain controller. Each domain controller on the network has a writeable copy of the directory database. This means that you can make Active Directory changes to any domain controller within your network, and those changes are replicated to all of the other domain controllers. This process is called **multimaster replication**, and provides a form of fault-tolerance. If a single server fails, Active Directory does not fail because replicated copies of the database are available from other servers within the network.

Active Directory uses the **Domain Name Service (DNS)** to maintain domain-naming structures and locate network resources. What this means to a network designer is that all Active Directory names must follow standard DNS naming conventions. An example of a standard DNS naming convention would be *Dovercorp.net*. A child domain of *Dovercorp.net* would add its name as a prefix, such as *Europe.Dovercorp.net*.

Active Directory Objects

Active Directory stores a variety of objects within the directory database. An **object** represents network resources such as users, groups, computers, and printers. When an object is created in Active Directory, various attributes are assigned to it to provide information about the object. For example, Figure 1-12 illustrates creating a new user object and the ability to add various attributes, such as First name, Last name, and User logon name.

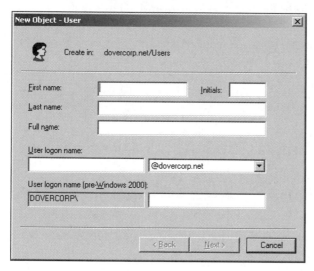

Figure 1-12   Creating a new user object

If you need to locate information about an object from Active Directory, you can perform a search of specific attributes relating to the object. For example, Figure 1-13 shows how you can find the e-mail address of a user object by searching for the specific user name in Active Directory and then viewing the attributes for the object.

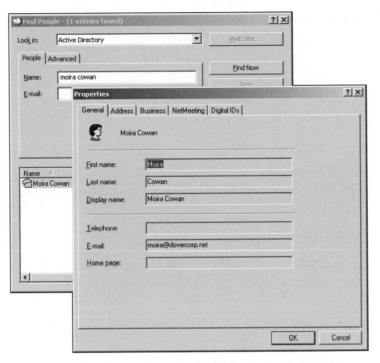

Figure 1-13   Viewing the e-mail address for a user object

Active Directory Schema

All of the objects and attributes that are available in Active Directory are defined in the **Active Directory schema**. In Windows Server 2003, the schema defines the objects for the entire Active Directory structure. This means that there is only one schema for a given Active Directory implementation, and it is replicated among all domain controllers within the network.

The Active Directory schema consists of two main definitions: **object classes** and **attributes**. Object classes define the types of objects that can be created within Active Directory, such as user objects and printer objects. All object classes consist of various attributes that describe the object itself. For example, the user and printer object classes may both have an attribute called description, which is used to describe the use of the object. Attributes are created and stored separately in the schema and can be used with multiple object classes to maintain consistency.

The Active Directory database stores and replicates the schema partition to all domain controllers in an Active Directory environment. Storing the schema within the Active Directory database provides the ability to dynamically update and extend the schema, as well as instant access to information for user applications that need to read the schema properties.

Active Directory Logical Structure and Components

Active Directory is made of several components that provide a way to design and administer the hierarchical, logical structure of the network. The logical components that make up an Active Directory structure include:

- Domains and organizational units
- Trees and forests
- A global catalog

To ensure efficient maintenance and troubleshooting within Active Directory, it is essential that you understand these logical components. The next sections discuss each component in greater detail.

Domains and Organizational Units

A Windows Server 2003 domain is a logically structured organization of objects, such as users, computers, groups, and printers that are part of a network and share a common directory database. Each domain has a unique name and is organized in levels and administered as a unit with common rules and procedures. Windows Server 2003 domains provide a number of administrative benefits including the ability to configure unique security settings, decentralize administration (if necessary), and control replication traffic. By default, members of the Administrators group are only allowed to manage the objects within their own domain. All domain controllers within a single domain store a copy of the Active Directory database, and domain-specific information is only replicated between the domain controllers of the same domain.

An **organizational unit (OU)** is a logical container used to organize objects within a single domain. Objects such as users, groups, computers, and other OUs can be stored in an OU container. For example, you may want to organize your users based upon the department in which they work. You might create a Sales OU to store all of your sales department users and objects and a Marketing OU to store all of your marketing department users and objects. Not only does this make it easier to locate and manage Active Directory objects, but it also allows you to apply **Group Policy** settings to define more advanced features such as software deployment or desktop restrictions based upon department, job function, or perhaps geographic location. Figure 1-14 illustrates an example of a domain with several OUs.

Another main advantage of using an OU structure is the ability to delegate administrative control over OUs. For example, you may want to give a set of users the right to add or remove new users within the Sales OU. You do not have to provide the group with full administrative rights to accomplish this task because Active Directory allows you to delegate very specific tasks, if necessary.

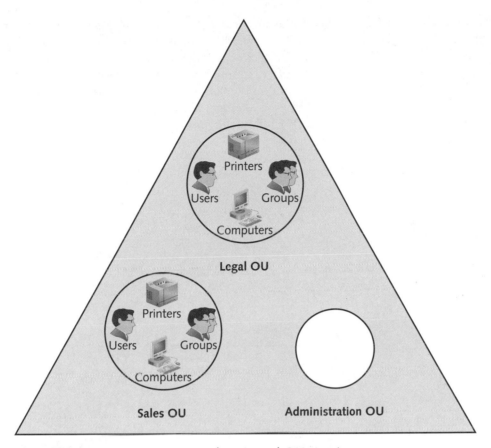

Figure 1-14   An Active Directory domain and OU structure

Trees and Forests

When designing a Windows Server 2003 network infrastructure, there may be times when you are required to create multiple domains within an organization. Reasons for doing this include the following:

- Divisions within the company may be administered on a geographic basis. To make administration easier, a separate domain is created for each division.
- Different password policies are needed between divisions within an organization.
- An extraordinarily large number of objects need to be defined.
- Replication performance needs to be improved.

The first Active Directory domain created in an organization is called the **forest root domain**. When multiple domains are needed, they are connected to the forest root to form either a single **tree** or multiple trees, depending upon the design of the domain name structure. A tree is a hierarchical collection of domains that share a contiguous DNS namespace. For example, Dover Leasing has its head office in Boston with a forest root domain called *Dovercorp.net*. Dover has two divisions, one located in London and the other located in Hong Kong. Because of geographic and administrative differences, you might decide to create a distinct domain for each division. Two child domains can be created off of the forest root domain. The London domain can be named *Europe.Dovercorp.net*, which follows the contiguous DNS namespace design. Similarly, the Hong Kong domain can be called *Asia.Dovercorp.net*. Figure 1-15 illustrates an example of this structure.

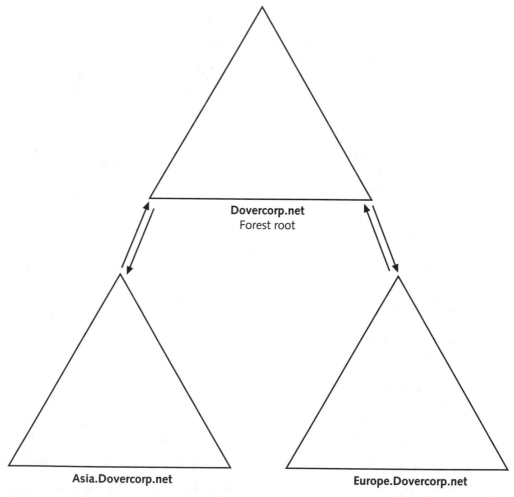

Dovercorp.net
Forest root

Asia.Dovercorp.net

Europe.Dovercorp.net

Figure 1-15   The Dovercorp.net domain tree

Whenever a child domain is created, a two-way, transitive trust relationship is automatically created between the child and parent domains. A **transitive trust** means that all other trusted domains implicitly trust one another. For example, because *Europe.Dovercorp.net* trusts the *Dovercorp.net* forest root domain, Europe also implicitly trusts the *Asia.Dovercorp.net* domain via the *Dovercorp.net* domain. These two-way, transitive trusts allow for resource access anywhere throughout the Active Directory structure. Windows Server 2003 also allows explicit trusts to be created between domains in the same forest, as well as between forests if necessary.

A **forest** is a collection of trees that do not share a contiguous DNS naming structure. For example, Dover Leasing purchases a large international company called Seven Acres Property Management. It may not make sense to make the Seven Acres domain a child of *Dovercorp.net* because of the renaming required to maintain a contiguous naming convention based on *Dovercorp.net*. Instead, you could create a new tree and allow Seven Acres to start its own contiguous naming hierarchy. Both trees make up an Active Directory forest. See Figure 1-16 for an illustration. Although the term "forest" implies a number of trees, an Active Directory forest might consist of only a single domain.

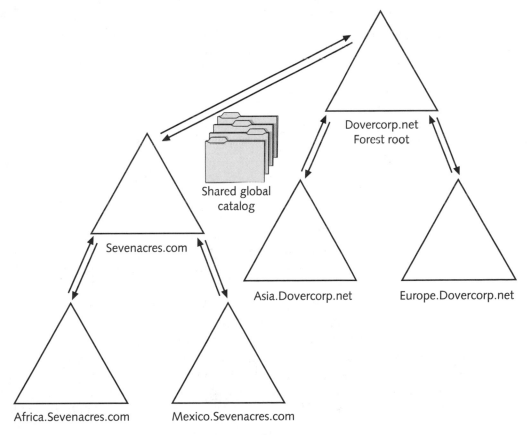

Figure 1-16 Creating an Active Directory forest

Even though the trees within a forest do not share a common namespace, they do share a single Active Directory schema, which ensures that all object classes and attributes are consistent throughout the entire structure. A special group called Enterprise Admins is also created, which allows members to manage objects throughout the entire forest. The Enterprise Admins group is created within the initial forest root domain and has a scope throughout the entire forest. Another component that is shared throughout the forest is a **global catalog**.

Global Catalog

A global catalog is an index and partial replica of the objects and attributes most frequently used throughout the entire Active Directory structure. Some of the common attributes that are stored in a global catalog include a user's first and last names, logon name, and e-mail address. A global catalog is replicated to any server within the forest that is configured to be a global catalog server.

A global catalog is used primarily for four main functions:

- To enable users to find Active Directory information from anywhere in the forest.

- To provide universal group membership information to facilitate logging on to the network. During the logon process in a multiple-domain environment, a global catalog server is contacted to provide universal group membership information.

- To supply authentication services when a user from another domain logs on using a **User Principal Name (UPN)**. (A UPN is a representation of a user's logon credentials in the form user@domain.com. When a UPN is used, a domain name does not need to be explicitly specified in the Log on to drop-down box.)

- To respond to directory lookup requests from Exchange 2000 and other applications. Global catalog servers also host the Exchange 2000 Global Address List (GAL).

The first domain controller in the forest root domain automatically becomes a global catalog server. To provide redundancy, additional domain controllers can easily be configured to also be global catalog servers. Multiple global catalogs can improve user query and logon authentication performance, especially in Active Directory environments that include geographically distant sites connected by wide area network (WAN) links. Microsoft recommends that each Active Directory site be configured with at least one domain controller acting as a global catalog server.

In cases where placing a global catalog in a specific site is not practical (possibly due to slow WAN links between locations], Windows Server 2003 Active Directory provides a new feature known as universal group caching. Universal group caching allows the domain controllers within a particular site to query a global catalog server in another location for a user's universal group membership information, and then cache that information locally for use in subsequent logons.

Active Directory Communications Standards

As mentioned previously, Active Directory uses the DNS naming standard for hostname resolution and for providing information on the location of network services and resources.

1

For example, if you need to locate a server called *database.Dovercorp.net*, your workstation first queries a DNS server to resolve the IP address of the database server. Once the IP address is known, a direct communication session can take place.

The same process occurs when you need to log on to the domain. Your workstation queries DNS to find a domain controller to perform authentication. Once the location of a domain controller is known, then the authentication process can take place, thus allowing a user access to network resources.

When users need to access Active Directory, the **Lightweight Directory Access Protocol (LDAP)** is used to query or update the Active Directory database directly. Just as a DNS name contains a specific naming convention (e.g., *Dovercorp.net*), LDAP also follows a specific naming convention. LDAP naming paths are used when referring to objects stored within the Active Directory. Two main components of the naming paths include:

- *Distinguished name*—Every object in Active Directory has a unique **distinguished name (DN)**. For example, the *Dovercorp.net* domain component (DC) has a user object with a common name (CN) of Moira Cowan that is stored within the Marketing OU. The distinguished name for the object would be CN=Moira Cowan, OU=Marketing, DC=Dovercorp, DC=Net.

- *Relative distinguished name*—A portion of the distinguished name that uniquely identifies the object within the container is referred to as the **relative distinguished name (RDN)**. For example, the distinguished name OU=Marketing, DC=Dovercorp, DC=Net would have a relative distinguished name of OU=Marketing. For the distinguished name CN=Moira Cowan, OU=Marketing, DC=Dovercorp, DC=Net, the relative distinguished name would be CN=Moira Cowan.

Active Directory Physical Structure

The Active Directory physical structure relates to the actual connectivity of the physical network itself. Because the Active Directory database is stored on multiple servers, you need to make sure that any modification to the database is replicated as quickly as possible between domain controllers. You must also design your topology so that replication does not saturate the available network bandwidth. One replication problem that you may encounter is when domain controllers are separated over a slow WAN connection. In this scenario, you likely want to control the frequency and the time that replication takes place.

In addition to replication, you may also want to control logon traffic. Referring back to the previous scenario, you generally would not want any user authentication requests to have to cross over slow WAN links during the logon process. Optimally, users should authenticate to a domain controller on their side of the WAN connection.

NOTE

Keep in mind that the physical structure of Active Directory is totally separate from the logical structure. The logical structure is used to organize your network resources, whereas the physical structure is used to control network traffic.

You can control Active Directory replication and authentication traffic by configuring sites and site links. An Active Directory **site** is a combination of one or more Internet Protocol (IP) subnets connected by a high-speed connection. It is assumed that domain controllers that belong to the same site all have a common network connection. It is also assumed that any connection between sites that are not reliable at all times must have replication controlled through replication schedules and frequency intervals.

A **site link** is a configurable object that represents a connection between sites. Site links created using the Active Directory Sites and Services snap-in are the core of Active Directory replication. The site links can be adjusted for replication availability, bandwidth costs, and replication frequency. Windows Server 2003 uses this information to generate the replication topology for the sites, including the schedule for replication. Figure 1-17 shows an example of a site structure within a domain. Each site contains domain controllers that share a high-speed connection. Because of a slower WAN connection between Boston, Hong Kong, and London, sites and site links have been defined to better control replication and logon traffic.

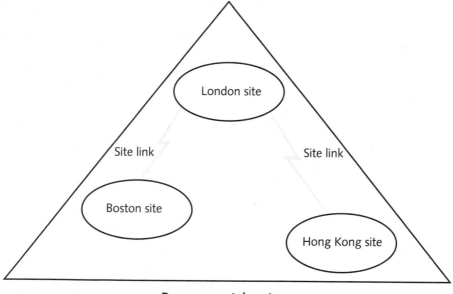

Figure 1-17   The site structure of Dovercorp.net

Replication within a site takes place based on a change notification process. If any change is made within Active Directory, the server waits 15 seconds and then announces the changes to another domain controller. In cases where a domain controller has multiple replication partners within a site, changes are sent out to additional domain controllers at three-second intervals. Replication between sites is initially set at every three hours by default, but can easily be changed by editing the properties of the site link object.

1

CHAPTER SUMMARY

- ❑ Windows Server 2003 is available in four different editions—Standard Edition, Enterprise Edition, Datacenter Edition, and Web Edition. The edition chosen for a particular environment or server implementation depends upon the individual performance, scalability, and reliability needs of the business or organization.

- ❑ Windows networks use one of two models to logically group computers. A workgroup is a model characterized by decentralized authentication and administration, and is typically used on smaller networks. A domain provides centralized authentication and administration, and is more common in larger environments.

- ❑ Managing and maintaining a Windows Server 2003 environment consists of five major focus areas: managing physical and logical devices; managing users, computers, and groups; managing and maintaining access to resources; managing and maintaining a server environment; and managing and implementing disaster recovery.

- ❑ Active Directory is the native directory service for Windows Server 2003 operating systems. Active Directory provides a variety of services to a network environment including centralized management and administration, authentication services, and more.

- ❑ The logical components of Active Directory include domains, organizational units, trees, forests, and the global catalog. The physical components of Active Directory include domain controllers and sites.

KEY TERMS

Active Directory (AD) — The directory service included with Windows Server 2003 that provides a single point of administration, authentication, and storage for user, group, and computer objects.

Active Directory schema — Contains the definition of all object classes and attributes used in the Active Directory database.

attributes — Used to define the characteristics of an object class within Active Directory.

clustering — The ability to increase access to server resources and provide fail-safe services by linking two or more computer systems so they appear to function as though they are one. Clustering is only supported in Windows Server 2003 Enterprise and Datacenter editions.

distinguished name (DN) — An LDAP component used to uniquely identify an object throughout the entire LDAP hierarchy by referring to the relative distinguished name, domain name, and the container holding the object.

domain — A logically structured organization of objects, such as users, computers, groups, and printers, that are part of a network and share a common directory database. Domains are defined by an administrator and administered as a unit with common rules and procedures.

domain controller — A Windows Server 2003 system explicitly configured to store a copy of the Active Directory database, and service user authentication requests or queries about domain objects.

forest — A collection of Active Directory trees that do not necessarily share a contiguous DNS naming convention but do share a common global catalog and schema.

forest root domain — The first domain created within the Active Directory structure.

global catalog — An index of the objects and attributes used throughout the Active Directory structure. It contains a partial replica of every Windows Server 2003 domain within Active Directory, enabling users to find any object in the directory.

Group Policy — The Windows Server 2003 feature that allows for policy creation that affects domain users and computers. Policies can be anything from desktop settings to application assignments to security settings and more.

Lightweight Directory Access Protocol (LDAP) — An access protocol that defines how users can access or update directory service objects.

member server — A Windows Server 2003 system that has a computer account in a domain, but is not configured as a domain controller.

Microsoft Management Console (MMC) — A customizable management interface that can contain a number of management tools to provide a single, unified application for network administration.

multimaster replication — A replication model in which any domain controller accepts and replicates directory changes to any other domain controller. This differs from other replication models in which one computer stores the single modifiable copy of the directory and other computers store back-up copies.

object — A collection of attributes that represent items within Active Directory, such as users, groups, computers, and printers.

object classes — Define which types of objects can be created within Active Directory, such as users, groups, and printers.

Organizational unit (OU) — An Active Directory logical container used to organize objects within a single domain. Objects such as users, groups, computers, and other OUs can be stored in an OU container.

Redundant Array of Independent Disks (RAID) — A collection of hard disks that act as a single unit for the purpose of providing fault tolerance or increasing performance.

relative distinguished name (RDN) — An LDAP component used to identify an object within the object's container.

Security Accounts Manager (SAM) database — The local security and account database on a Windows Server 2003 standalone or member server.

site — A combination of one or more Internet Protocol (IP) subnets connected by a high-speed connection.

site link — A low-bandwidth or unreliable/occasional connection between sites. Site links can be adjusted for replication availability, bandwidth costs, and replication frequency. They enable control over replication and logon traffic.

Software Update Services (SUS) — Microsoft software that allows security patches and updates to be deployed from a centralized server.

Terminal Services — A Windows Server 2003 service that allows a user to connect to and run applications on a server as if sitting at the server console.

transitive trust — The ability for domains or forests to trust one another, even though they do not have a direct explicit trust between them.

User Principal Name (UPN) — A user-account naming convention that includes both the user name and domain name in the format user@domain.com.

workgroup — A logical group of computers characterized by a decentralized security and administration model.

REVIEW QUESTIONS

1. What is the name of the first domain installed within the Active Directory database?
   a. Master root domain
   b. Forest root domain
   c. Main root domain
   d. Tree root domain

2. Assuming a user name of John Doe with a user account located in the Sales OU of the domain *Dovercorp.net*, what would be the object's distinguished name?
   a. OU=Sales, CN=John Doe
   b. CN=John Doe
   c. CN=John Doe, OU–Sales, DC=Dovercorp, DC=Net
   d. DC=Net, DC=Dovercorp, OU=Sales, CN=John Doe

3. In Windows Server 2003, a two-way, transitive trust relationship is maintained between which of the following?
   a. Child and parent forests
   b. Child and parent groups
   c. Child and parent domains
   d. None of the above

4. What is the absolute minimum RAM requirement for Windows Server 2003, Standard Edition?
   a. 64 MB
   b. 128 MB
   c. 256 MB
   d. 512 MB

5. Which of the following are not supported features or configurations for a Windows Server 2003, Web Edition system? (Choose all that apply.)
   a. Standalone server
   b. Domain controller
   c. Member server

6. Which edition of Windows Server 2003 cannot be configured as an Active Directory domain controller?

    a. Windows Server 2003, Web Edition

    b. Windows Server 2003, Standard Edition

    c. Windows Server 2003, Enterprise Edition

    d. Windows Server 2003, Datacenter Edition

7. How often does Active Directory replication between sites take place by default?

    a. Every hour

    b. Every 2 hours

    c. Every 3 hours

    d. Never

8. What is the recommended minimum CPU speed for Windows Server 2003, Enterprise Edition?

    a. 550 MHz

    b. 1 GHz

    c. 733 MHz

    d. 133 MHz

9. How many seconds after a change notification process is triggered does replication between domain controllers occur?

    a. 10

    b. 20

    c. 15

    d. 5

10. The global address list (GAL) for Exchange 2000 e-mail systems is stored on which of the following systems?

    a. All domain controllers

    b. All member servers

    c. All desktop systems

    d. Global catalog server

11. Which group has administrative privileges in all forest domains by default but exists within the forest root domain only?

    a. Administrators

    b. Enterprise Admins

    c. Domain Admins

    d. Forest Admins

1

12. Which of the following domain controllers will become global catalog servers by default?

    a. First domain controller in all domains

    b. All domain controllers in the forest root domain

    c. First domain controller in the forest root domain

    d. None

13. If a customer network needs to support Windows Server 2003 systems configured in a 4-node cluster, which edition(s) of Windows Server 2003 could be used?

    a. Windows Server 2003, Web Edition

    b. Windows Server 2003, Standard Edition

    c. Windows Server 2003, Enterprise Edition

    d. Windows Server 2003, Datacenter Edition

14. Which of the following operating systems can be upgraded to Windows Server 2003, Standard Edition?

    a. Windows 2000 Server

    b. Windows 2000 Advanced Server

    c. Windows NT Server 4.0 (SP5)

    d. Windows 2000 Datacenter Server

15. Which of the following operating systems can be upgraded to Windows Server 2003, Web Edition?

    a. Windows 2000 Server

    b. Windows NT Server 4.0 (SP5)

    c. Windows 2000 Advanced Server

    d. None of the above

16. Which of the following Windows Server 2003 editions are capable of running on Itanium-based systems?

    a. Windows Server 2003, Web Edition

    b. Windows Server 2003, Standard Edition

    c. Windows Server 2003, Enterprise Edition

    d. Windows Server 2003, Datacenter Edition

17. What is the maximum number of CPUs supported in an SMP configuration on a Windows Server 2003, Datacenter Edition, system running on the x86 platform?

    a. 64

    b. 32

    c. 8

    d. 16

18. Which of the following operating systems can be upgraded to Windows Server 2003, Enterprise Edition?

    a. Windows 2000 Server

    b. Windows Server 2003, Standard Edition

    c. Windows NT Server 4.0 (SP5)

    d. Windows 2000 Advanced Server

19. Which of the following logical Active Directory components is created mainly for the delegation of administrative authority and the implementation of group policy settings?

    a. Tree

    b. Domain

    c. Forest

    d. Organizational unit

20. Which of the following statements best describes an Active Directory forest?

    a. A collection of domains that share a common schema

    b. A collection of organizational units

    c. A collection of trees with different schemas

    d. A collection of users with common settings

CASE PROJECTS

CASE PROJECTS

Case Project 1-1

Dover Leasing Corporation has recently implemented Windows Server 2003 and Active Directory. Dover's network consists of three main locations with offices in Boston, Hong Kong, and London. The Boston location is the head office and connects to London via a dedicated T1 WAN link, whereas the Hong Kong location connects to London via a 256-Kbps Frame Relay link. Dover had recently considered opening a new office in San Francisco, which would connect via WAN links to both the Boston and Hong Kong offices. Different password policies need to be implemented in the Boston, Hong Kong, and London locations. Ultimately, the San Francisco office will become the administrative responsibility of IT staff in Boston. Based on what you know of Windows Server 2003 thus far and the information provided above, the IT manager has asked you to assess Dover Leasing's Active Directory design by answering the following questions:

1. Which of the factors listed in the scenario would influence the logical design of Dover Leasing's Active Directory implementation?

2. What type of domain structure would you suggest for Dover Leasing?

3. Based on Dover Leasing's current and future locations, what would be the best naming strategy for their Active Directory domain structure?

4. How many sites would likely be configured as part of Dover Leasing's Active Directory implementation once the San Francisco office opens, and how many site links would be required?

5. Once the San Francisco office is opened, how many global catalog servers should be implemented on the network to ensure adequate performance?

Case Project 1-2

Dover Leasing is currently planning the deployment of three new Windows Server 2003 systems in its head office location. The company plans to deploy one server as a dedicated Web server running IIS 6.0. The second server will be used for file and print services, and will be deployed on an SMP system with 4 CPUs and 8 GB of RAM. The last system will be used as a database server, and will be deployed in conjunction with an existing server as part of a 2-way cluster. Based on these configurations, the IT manager at Dover Leasing has asked you to identify the most appropriate Windows Server 2003 edition for each system.

1. Which Windows Server 2003 edition would be most appropriate for the server that will run IIS? Why?

2. Which Windows Server 2003 edition would be most appropriate for the file and print server? Why?

3. Which Windows Server 2003 edition would be most appropriate for the database server? Why?

2

MANAGING HARDWARE DEVICES

After reading this chapter and completing the exercises, you will be able to:

♦ Understand the importance of managing hardware

♦ Understand the purpose of device drivers

♦ Configure hardware resource settings and resolve resource setting conflicts

♦ Configure driver signing options

♦ Optimize server processor and memory usage

♦ Create and configure hardware profiles

♦ Configure server power options

One key responsibility of any network administrator is managing and maintaining server hardware. After installing Windows Server 2003, there may be a number of additional hardware-related tasks you need to perform before the server is ready for the production environment. Examples include reviewing hardware settings, updating device drivers, and ensuring that no resource conflicts exist. Once a server is deployed, hardware also needs to be maintained, and changes to individual devices or other updates may be necessary. If not managed correctly, server hardware problems may lead to a variety of errors, and potentially server failure.

Managing and maintaining server hardware involves a variety of different tasks. For example, there may be hardware components that were not automatically detected and configured during the Windows Server 2003 installation process. Similarly, you may need to obtain and update device drivers to ensure the functionality expected under the new operating system.

When new hardware is added to a server, you need to be sure that no resource conflicts exist. Although specifications like Plug and Play will allocate resources to devices automatically, the manual configuration of legacy hardware may lead to conflicts, and by extension, the inability of hardware to function correctly. As a network administrator, it is your job to not only identify but also resolve these conflicts.

Windows Server 2003 supports a variety of new and familiar tools and features to aid in the management and maintenance of server hardware. Tools like Device Manager and the Add Hardware Wizard make it easy for an administrator to add, manage, and monitor server hardware settings. Features like driver signing help to ensure the quality of installed drivers, while at the same time promoting server stability. The new Roll Back Driver feature allows an administrator to quickly return to a previous driver version if an update causes unexpected problems. Similar to Windows 2000, Windows Server 2003 continues to support the configuration of power management settings and the use of hardware profiles. Each of these features, along with processor and memory optimization techniques, is looked at in detail throughout this chapter.

INTRODUCTION TO MANAGING HARDWARE

Managing and maintaining server hardware is a key responsibility of any network administrator. Windows Server 2003 supports a wide variety of both internal and external hardware components that you should be familiar with. Examples of internal hardware components include network adapter cards and disk drives, while external components are typically peripheral devices like a Universal Serial Bus (USB) mouse or printer. The following list outlines the more common internal and external hardware devices that need to be managed and maintained on a Windows Server 2003 system:

- Disk drives
- CD-ROM/DVD-ROM drives
- Modem
- Network adapter cards
- Video adapter cards
- Printers and scanners
- Keyboard
- Mouse
- USB devices
- IEEE 1394 (FireWire) devices

The following sections provide more detail about Windows Server 2003 hardware compatibility, the functions of device drivers, and an introduction to Device Manager, the primary tool used to manage hardware on a Windows Server 2003 system.

Hardware Compatibility

Your Windows Server 2003 infrastructure is only as reliable as the hardware upon which it is based. For this reason, it is vital that you understand the system requirements of Windows

Server 2003. Before you install Windows Server 2003, make sure that your hardware meets or exceeds the minimum requirements set forth by Microsoft, as outlined in Chapter 1.

In previous versions of Windows, Microsoft provided an index of compatible hardware known as the Hardware Compatibility List (HCL). The HCL served as a reference guide to determine which hardware (and associated drivers) had been tested to function correctly on operating systems like Windows 2000 Server. Beginning with Windows Server 2003, Microsoft has moved towards a new model of providing this information known as the **Windows Server Catalog**. The Windows Server Catalog contains listings of hardware devices that have been certified to function with Windows Server 2003, and officially carry the "Designed for Windows Server 2003" logo. The Windows Server Catalog Web site shown in Figure 2-1 can be accessed from the Help and Support Center by clicking on the Compatible Hardware and Software link in the Support Tasks section of the Help Contents page.

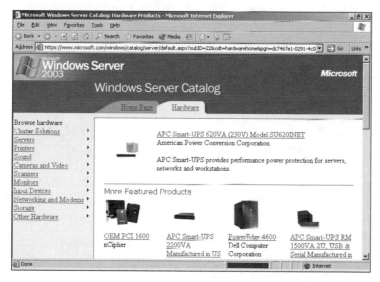

Figure 2-1   The Windows Server Catalog Web site

Although you may find that many non-certified hardware devices perform well on your server, Microsoft may not provide troubleshooting support if the hardware has not been specifically tested and certified for Windows Server 2003.

The Windows Server Catalog can also be accessed online at *http://www. microsoft.com/windows/catalog/server/default.aspx.*

UNDERSTANDING DEVICE DRIVERS

Hardware devices like modems, network adapter cards, and graphics adapters are manufactured by a wide variety of vendors. Because different vendors use different processes, components, and standards when manufacturing their equipment, specialized software is required in order for an operating system to interact and communicate with a specific hardware device. This software is generically referred to as a **device driver**.

Device drivers act as intermediaries between specific hardware devices and an operating system such as Windows Server 2003. They contain the instructions necessary for the operating system to use the full capabilities of the hardware correctly. Once installed, device drivers load automatically for all enabled hardware as part of the Windows boot process.

In some cases, a driver not specifically designed for a particular hardware device will allow that device to function. This is because many of the basic capabilities of a particular type of device (such as video adapter cards) are similar, and follow common standards. However, installing or using the wrong device driver for a particular hardware component usually results in less than optimal performance, and generally does not allow you to take advantage of many of the advanced features of a specific device. Installing the correct device driver for a given hardware component and operating system is important in terms of both system stability and performance.

Vendors, as well, often update device drivers after they have initially released them. In some cases this is to fix a known flaw, while in others it is to take advantage of additional features or capabilities. Subsequently, the driver software that was originally provided with a hardware device (usually on an accompanying disk) is often not the best driver to install, since it may be outdated. Vendors typically post updated drivers to their Web or FTP sites in order to allow the most recent version to be downloaded and installed. When hardware is not performing optimally or is generating errors, downloading and installing an updated driver is often the most appropriate solution.

Device drivers have a significant impact on system stability and performance. Because of this, Microsoft uses a technique known as **driver signing** to verify that the drivers for a particular hardware device have undergone rigorous testing and will function correctly with Windows Server 2003. Microsoft recommends that only digitally signed device driver files be installed on a Windows Server 2003 system. You learn more about device driver signing later in this chapter.

Device Manager

The primary tool used to manage device drivers on a Windows Server 2003 system is known as Device Manager. The main purpose of Device Manager is to allow you to view and modify different hardware device properties. Some of the tasks that can be accomplished with Device Manager include:

- Determining whether installed hardware is functioning correctly
- Viewing and changing hardware resources settings

- Determining and changing the drivers used by a device

- Enabling, disabling, and uninstalling devices

- Configuring advanced settings for devices

- Viewing and printing summary information about devices installed on a server

Device Manager is accessible from the Hardware tab of the System program in Control Panel as shown in Figure 2-2, and can also be accessed from the Computer Management administrative tool.

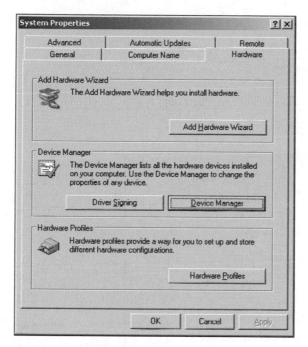

Figure 2-2   The Hardware tab of the System program

After installing Windows Server 2003 on a new or existing server, one of your first tasks should be to verify that all hardware devices have been detected and that no conflicts or problems exist. The same is true any time you install a new hardware device. To accomplish this task, open Device Manager to view all of the installed devices. Devices are organized by type in the Device Manager interface by default. Expanding a particular type of device, such as Display adapters, will show any display adapters installed on the server. This is shown in Figure 2-3.

As illustrated in Figure 2-4, any device that is not functioning correctly is indicated with a yellow exclamation point, while manually disabled hardware is indicated with a small red "x" over the device icon.

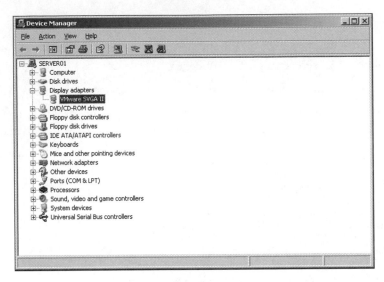

Figure 2-3   The Device Manager interface

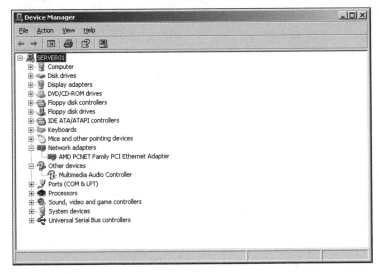

Figure 2-4   Using Device Manager to identify hardware problems

If a specific device is missing or is not functioning, Windows Server 2003 provides two ways to troubleshoot or repair the problem. The first method is to obtain a new driver from the manufacturer's Web site and then install the new driver through Device Manager. The Driver tab in the properties of a device is used to view current driver details and access the Update Driver button, as shown in Figure 2-5.

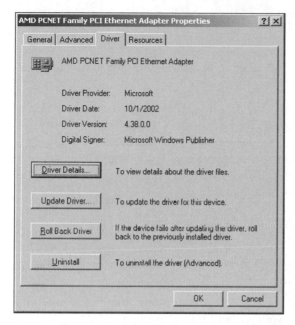

Figure 2-5   The Driver tab in the properties of a hardware device

Windows Server 2003 also allows you to update drivers from Device Manager by using the Hardware Update Wizard, as shown in Figure 2-6. This wizard guides you through the task of selecting and installing the updated device driver. In Activity 2-1, you explore both hardware and configuration settings for your server using Device Manager.

Figure 2-6   The Hardware Update Wizard

Activity 2-1: Exploring Device Manager

Time Required: 10 minutes

Objective: Use Device Manager to gather information about existing hardware and ways of viewing information.

Description: The IT manager at Dover Leasing plans to give all network help desk staff access to the Device Manager utility to enable them to gather information about the hardware status of existing servers. In this activity, you use Device Manager to view the properties of the existing hardware devices, including driver options and settings, resource usage, hardware status icons, and the different ways in which information can be displayed with this tool.

1. Click **Start**, right-click **My Computer**, and click **Properties**.

2. On the System Properties screen, click the **Hardware** tab.

3. In the Device Manager section, click the **Device Manager** button. Maximize Device Manager once it opens.

4. Click the **plus sign (+)** next to Network adapters to expand it, if necessary. A list of network adapters installed on your system will appear.

5. Right-click the first network adapter listed and review the shortcut menu options.

6. On the shortcut menu, click **Properties**.

7. On the General tab, notice that the device type, manufacturer, and location are listed. Review all messages in the Device status box to ensure that the network adapter is functioning correctly.

8. In the Device usage list box (see Figure 2-7), click **Do not use this device (disable)**. Click **OK**.

9. Notice that the icon associated with this specific network adapter has changed to signify that it has been disabled. Double-click the network adapter again to access its properties. On the General tab, click **Use this device (enable)** in the Device usage list box. Click **OK** to enable the device.

10. Double-click the network adapter icon again to access its properties. Click the **Advanced** tab, and notice both the Property and Value settings. Note that different network adapter cards and drivers will support different advanced features. Make no changes on this screen, and click the **Driver** tab.

11. Note the driver provider, date, version, and digital signer information. Click the **Driver Details** button to view more information about the driver, including its filename and location.

12. Click **OK** to close the Driver File Details window.

13. Click the **Resources** tab, and note both the IRQ and I/O Range associated with the network adapter card. Click **OK** to close the network adapter's properties and return to Device Manager.

14. Click **View** on the menu bar. Notice that Devices by type is selected as the Device Manager view in use. Click **Devices by connection** to switch the view of Device Manager.

15. In the PCI bus section, expand the various items (if necessary) until you find your network adapter listed.

16. Click **View** on the menu bar and click **Resources by type**. Click the **plus sign (+)** next to Interrupt request (IRQ) to expand it. Note that all IRQs assigned by the system and their associated devices are listed.

17. Click **View** on the menu bar. Click **Devices by type** to switch the Device Manager view back and close Device Manager. Close all open windows.

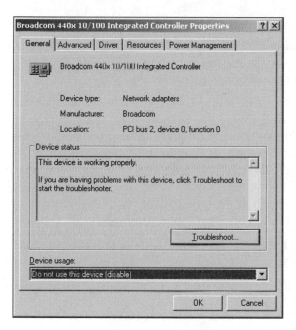

Figure 2-7   Disabling a hardware device in Device Manager

ADDING NEW DEVICES

Windows Server 2003 makes it easy to install and configure new hardware devices. The two main types of hardware typically installed in a server can be broadly categorized as Plug and Play and legacy devices. In most cases, Windows Server 2003 will automatically install and configure the correct driver and resources settings for a Plug and Play device, although certain system requirements must be met. Legacy devices are older hardware components that typically need to be configured manually. In the following sections you learn more about both Plug and Play and legacy devices.

Plug and Play Devices

One important capability in computer hardware and operating system software is the ability to automatically detect and configure newly installed hardware devices, using a specification referred to as **Plug and Play**. Windows Server 2003 is a Plug and Play-compliant operating system. However, in order for this feature to function correctly, Plug and Play support must be:

- Built into the device
- Enabled in the computer's **Basic Input/Output System (BIOS)**
- Built into the computer operating system kernel

Almost all computer hardware today, including peripheral devices, support Plug and Play. Plug and Play eliminates the hours of time that server administrators and computer users once spent installing and configuring hardware devices. When you purchase a computer or a new hardware device, ensuring that it is Plug and Play compatible goes a long way towards minimizing potential configuration issues on Windows Server 2003.

Installing a Plug and Play device is a relatively simple process. After installing or attaching the hardware device, Windows Server 2003 should detect it automatically, install the appropriate drivers, and configure resource settings. In some cases, the driver that Windows Server 2003 assigns to the resource may not be the most current version, and may need to be updated using a tool like Device Manager. In others, Windows Server 2003 may not have the required driver for the device, and will prompt you for the driver disk that was supplied with the hardware. Keep in mind that you should review the manufacturer's installation instructions before installing or connecting the device to your computer.

In Activity 2-2, you first use Device Manager to uninstall a device, and then use the Add Hardware Wizard to allow the Plug and Play feature of Windows Server 2003 to re-detect and configure the device.

Activity 2-2: Installing a Plug and Play Hardware Device

Time Required: 5 minutes

Objective: Use Device Manager and the Add Hardware Wizard to uninstall and then reinstall a device.

Description: While exploring Device Manager in Activity 2-1, you noticed that one of the options available was the ability to uninstall a device. In this activity, you test what happens when a device is uninstalled using Device Manager, and then attempt to reinstall the device using the Add Hardware Wizard from Control Panel.

1. Click **Start**, and then click **Run**.
2. In the Open text box, type **devmgmt.msc** and click **OK**. This is simply another method of accessing Device Manager.

3. Click the **plus sign (+)** next to DVD/CD-ROM drives to expand it. Right-click the DVD or CD-ROM device associated with your computer and click **Uninstall**.

4. Click **OK** on the Confirm Device Removal screen.

5. Close Device Manager.

6. Click **Start**, and then click **My Computer**. Confirm that your DVD or CD-ROM drive is unavailable. Close My Computer.

7. Click **Start**, select **Control Panel**, and then click **Add Hardware**. On the Add Hardware Wizard welcome screen, click **Next**.

8. The wizard should search for, find, and configure your DVD or CD-ROM drive automatically.

9. Click **Finish** to close the Add Hardware Wizard.

10. In the System Settings Change dialog box, click **No** if prompted to restart your computer. Click **Start**, and then click **My Computer** and verify that your DVD or CD-ROM drive is present.

11. Close My Computer.

Legacy Devices

While most new hardware devices sold today adhere to the Plug and Play hardware specification, many older devices do not. Generically referred to as **legacy devices**, these devices may be detected as hardware components by Windows Server 2003, but typically require that drivers and resource settings be installed and configured manually. Devices that use the old **Industry Standard Architecture (ISA)** bus are typically categorized as legacy devices.

When a legacy device, such as an ISA modem, is physically installed on a server, Windows Server 2003 may recognize the fact that hardware has been added to the system, but usually cannot configure the hardware automatically. In such cases, the Add Hardware Wizard can be used to manually install the driver required by the device. The Add Hardware Wizard can also be used to add hardware that has not been detected by Windows Server 2003. When the option to Add a new hardware device is chosen, you are given the ability to configure the device using a variety of methods, including choosing the type of hardware to be installed and then ultimately supplying the correct driver. The Add Hardware Wizard is shown in Figure 2-8.

Besides the installation of the appropriate device driver, it may be necessary to manually configure resource settings for the installed hardware in Device Manager, especially in cases where conflicts have occurred. You learn more about modifying resource settings for hardware devices in the next section.

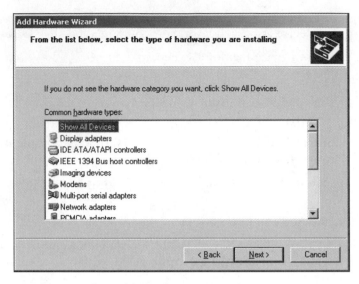

Figure 2-8   The Add Hardware Wizard

HARDWARE RESOURCE SETTINGS

When hardware devices are installed on a server, they are assigned resource settings that allow them to access the system processor and memory in different ways, depending upon the type of device. The four main types of resources that a hardware device can use are:

- Direct Memory Access (DMA) channels
- Input/Output (I/O) ranges
- Memory address ranges
- Interrupt request (IRQ) lines

When a Plug and Play hardware device is detected and installed by Windows Server 2003, the necessary resource settings are allocated to the device automatically. In almost all cases, you will not need to manually configure these settings. However, when older legacy hardware is installed (such as an ISA modem), resource settings may need to be configured manually.

Resource settings are configured from the Resources tab of the properties of a hardware device in Device Manager. In some cases, you may notice that the resources associated with a device cannot be manually configured. In this scenario, resource settings have been allocated by Plug and Play automatically, and cannot be changed.

When resource settings are configured manually, it is important to ensure that no conflicts exist. Devices typically require their own unique resource settings, and when conflicts occur, the associated devices may cease to function. In some cases, resources can be shared amongst multiple devices, such as IRQ settings for PCI devices.

Because resource conflicts can result in hardware devices not functioning correctly, a method of determining conflicts is required. Device Manager allows you to view resource conflicts in the lower portion of the Resources tab for a device, as shown in Figure 2-9.

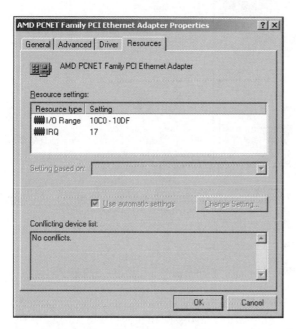

Figure 2-9 The Resources tab for a network adapter card

In the following sections you learn more about the purpose of each of the four hardware resource types.

Direct Memory Access Channels

As the name suggests, **Direct Memory Access (DMA) channels** allow a hardware device to access system memory (RAM) directly. When DMA is implemented, a device, such as a CD-ROM drive, can transfer information directly to RAM, without requiring the intervention of the system CPU. This ultimately makes data transfer much faster, while reducing the processing burden of the CPU.

Not all hardware devices use or require DMA channels. The most common devices for which DMA channels are allocated include hard disk controllers, floppy disk controllers, and sometimes sound cards. Because DMA can significantly speed up data transfer between a hardware device like a CD-ROM drive and memory, enabling DMA for disk controllers is highly recommended. Figure 2-10 illustrates the Advanced Settings tab for the Primary IDE Channel in Device Manager, configured to use the "DMA if available" transfer mode.

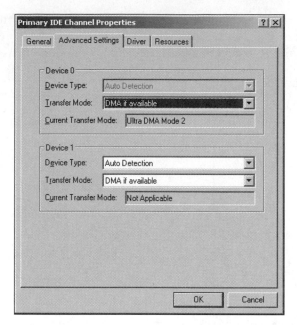

Figure 2-10   Configuring the Primary IDE Channel to use DMA if available

The DMA channel used by a particular hardware device can be determined from the Resources tab of the properties of a device in Device Manager. To view all DMA channels in a more simplified fashion, choose the Resources by type option from the Device Manager View menu, and then expand the DMA node.

Input/Output Ranges

Input/Output ranges are small, dedicated memory areas that are allocated for the purpose of transferring information between a computer and a hardware device. Because a device always uses the same I/O memory range, the hardware knows where to place data to be transferred to the computer, and where to find data transferred from the computer. Some devices, such as network adapter cards, typically have higher data transfer requirements, and thus use a larger range of I/O addresses. In contrast, an LPT port uses a smaller I/O address range.

The I/O ports used by a particular hardware device can be determined from the Resources tab of the properties of a device in Device Manager. To view all I/O ports in a more simplified fashion, choose the Resources by type option from the Device Manager View menu, and then expand the Input/Output (IO) node.

Interrupt Request Lines

Hardware devices use **interrupt request (IRQ) lines** to gain the attention of the system processor. For example, the floppy disk controller typically uses IRQ 6 on a Windows Server 2003 system. When the floppy disk controller has finished sending data to the processor, it sends an interrupt message to it on IRQ 6. Traditionally, individual hardware devices used a dedicated IRQ number, and sharing of IRQ resources was limited. However, as a Plug and Play-compliant operating system, Windows Server 2003 supports IRQ sharing amongst Plug and Play devices connecting to the PCI bus on systems that support the Advanced Configuration and Power Interface (ACPI) motherboard specification. On a Windows Server 2003 system, the PCI bus uses IRQ 9 for IRQ steering, allowing multiple devices to share a single IRQ without generating conflicts.

In the case of legacy hardware devices, IRQ settings usually need to be configured manually to use an IRQ line not currently in use. In most cases, the optimal IRQ will be specified in the documentation that accompanied the legacy hardware device. If that IRQ is already in use, it can often be reserved (and thus not allocated by Windows) in the system's BIOS configuration settings.

The IRQ line used by a particular hardware device can be determined from the Resources tab of the properties of a device in Device Manager. To view all IRQ lines in a more simplified fashion, choose the Resources by type option from the Device Manager View menu, and then expand the Interrupt request node. Figure 2-11 displays the IRQ lines in use by different hardware devices on a Windows Server 2003 system.

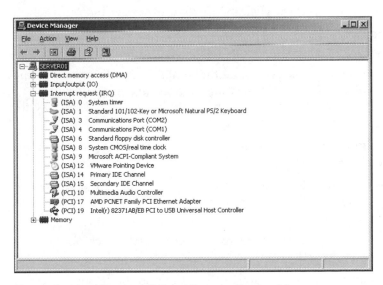

Figure 2-11   Viewing IRQ settings in Device Manager

Memory Addresses

Memory addresses are used for communication between a hardware device and the operating system. Devices on a Windows Server 2003 should be configured with dedicated and unique memory address ranges. By default, Windows Server 2003 will allocate these memory ranges automatically for Plug and Play–compliant devices. However, in the case of legacy devices, it may be necessary to configure resources manually. In such cases, the memory ranges to be configured are usually specified in the vendor documentation.

In Activity 2-3 you use Device Manager to view information about memory address and other system resource settings for hardware installed on your server.

ACTIVITY

Activity 2-3: Viewing Resource Settings Using Device Manager

Time Required: 5 minutes

Objective: Use Device Manager to view hardware resource settings.

Description: In order to get a better sense of the types of resources used by the hardware on the Dover Leasing servers, you have been asked to explore resource settings using Device Manager. In this activity you explore the settings of various hardware devices and take a closer look at how settings like IRQ assignments can be changed.

1. Click **Start**, right-click **My Computer**, and click **Properties**.

2. On the System Properties screen, click the **Hardware** tab.

3. In the Device Manager section, click the **Device Manager** button.

4. Click the **plus sign (+)** next to Display adapters to expand it. Right-click on your server's display adapter and click **Properties**.

5. Click the **Resources** tab. Scroll through the settings in the Resource settings section, noting the different I/O and Memory Ranges used by the device. Notice also that the Use automatic settings check box cannot be unchecked to allow the device to be configured manually. Click **Cancel**.

6. Click the **plus sign (+)** next to Keyboards to expand it. Right-click on your server's keyboard and click **Properties**.

7. Click the **Resources** tab. Scroll through the settings in the Resource settings section, noting the different I/O Ranges and the IRQ used by the device. Click **Cancel**.

8. Click the **plus sign (+)** next to Ports to expand it. Right-click on **Communications Port (COM1)** and click **Properties**.

9. Click the **Resources** tab. Scroll through the settings in the Resource settings section, noting the I/O Range and IRQ used by the device.

10. Uncheck the **Use automatic settings** check box.

2

11. Click the **arrow** next to Setting based on, and choose the last entry in the list (Basic configuration 0001, for example).

12. In the Resource settings section, click **IRQ**, and then click **Change Setting**.

13. In the Edit Interrupt Request window, click the **arrows** next to Value to scroll through the available IRQ values, as shown in Figure 2-12. Pay particular attention to any data that appears in the Conflict information section for a particular IRQ.

14. Click **Cancel** to close the Edit Interrupt Request window.

15. Click **Cancel** to close the Communications Port (COM1) Properties window.

16. Close Device Manager.

Figure 2-12   Manually configuring IRQ settings

Troubleshooting Resource Setting Conflicts

Because Windows Server 2003 automatically allocates resources to Plug and Play devices, the manual configuration of resource settings is usually unnecessary. However, when legacy devices need to be configured manually, resource settings may overlap or be duplicated between devices, which may result in those devices not functioning correctly or at all.

Earlier in this section you learned that the Resources tab in the properties of a hardware device will display any known conflict between one device and another. While this is an effective way to determine conflicts, it is not the only available method. Windows Server 2003 includes another utility that can be used to determine hardware settings and conflicts, known as the System Information tool. To open the System Information tool, type msinfo32.exe at the Run command and click OK.

The System Information tool is a reporting utility rather than a configuration tool. It allows you to view quickly and easily a wide variety of system settings, including the configuration of hardware devices. The Hardware Resources section displays summary information about resource settings, as well as any conflicts that may exist. The Forced Hardware node in this section is particularly useful, because it allows you to easily identify any hardware devices whose resource settings have been configured manually. The I/O node of the System Information tool is shown in Figure 2-13.

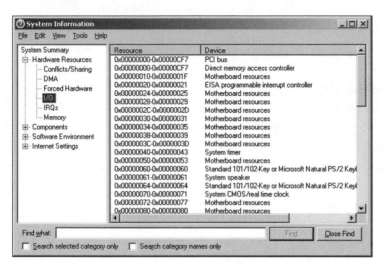

Figure 2-13   The I/O node in the Hardware Resources section of the System Information tool

The Components node of System Information is another useful troubleshooting tool, because it allows you to obtain all critical pieces of information about a device from one location. For example, clicking on the Adapter node under Network allows you to view not only resource settings such as the IRQ and I/O settings of the device, but also information about the device driver and configuration settings. In cases where you suspect that a hardware device is not functioning correctly, use the Problem Devices node in this section to obtain more information. In Figure 2-14, the Problem Devices node specifies that the Multimedia Audio Controller on the system is not functioning correctly because the drivers for the device are not installed.

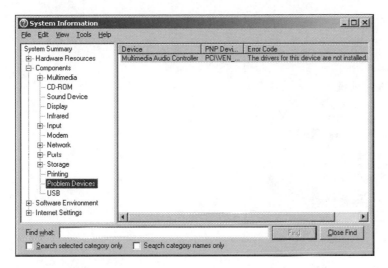

Figure 2-14   Viewing Problem Devices using the System Information tool

CONFIGURING DEVICE DRIVER SIGNING

Every Windows Server 2003 operating system file and built-in driver has been digitally signed by Microsoft to ensure compatibility, quality, and authenticity. Driver signing ensures that a driver for a specific device has been verified by Microsoft to work with Windows Server 2003, and that Microsoft's digital signature has been associated with the driver. This digital signature assures you that the driver has met quality testing standards, and that the file has not been altered or overwritten by another program or driver installation process.

Windows Server 2003 supports three different driver signing options, as outlined in Figure 2-15:

- Ignore—This option effectively turns off driver and file verification. If this option is selected, driver signing is ignored.

- Warn—If this option is selected, a message appears when you attempt to install an unsigned driver. This alerts you that a digital signature was not found on the driver and there is no guarantee that the driver is going to work with Windows.

- Block—This option prevents the installation of any driver that is not signed.

In Activity 2-4, you configure driver signing options on your server to block the installation of unsigned drivers.

After a Windows Server 2003 installation, the Warn driver signing option is selected by default.

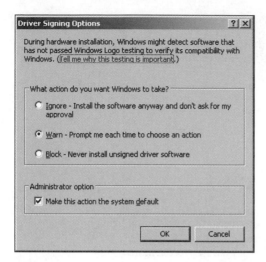

Figure 2-15   Configuring driver signing options

Activity 2-4: Configuring Driver Signing Options

Time Required: 10 minutes

Objective: Configure Windows Server 2003 to block the installation of all driver files that are not digitally signed.

Description: For Dover Leasing's original Windows Server 2003 deployment, the IT manager made a decision that only driver files digitally signed by Microsoft should be installed on corporate servers. In this activity, you have been asked to configure the driver signing options on your server so that it will block the installation of any unsigned driver files.

1. Click **Start**, and then right-click **My Computer**. Click **Properties** to access the System Properties tool.

2. Click the **Hardware** tab. In the Device Manager section, click the **Driver Signing** button. This will open the Driver Signing Options dialog box, as shown in Figure 2-15.

3. Click the **Tell me why this testing is important** hyperlink. The Help and Support Center opens automatically.

4. In the Hardware section to the left of the Help and Support Center window, click the **Driver signing for Windows** hyperlink. Read the Driver signing for Windows help topic displayed on the right. Close the Help and Support Center window.

5. Note each of the three options listed in the What action do you want Windows to take? section. Click the **Block** radio button.

6. In the Administrator option section, ensure that the **Make this action the system default** check box is selected, and click **OK**.

7. To ensure maximum compatibility in future activities, change the configured driver signing option to **Ignore** before continuing.

8. Click **OK** to close the System Properties dialog box.

If you decide to leave the driver signing option set to Warn, it is possible that unsigned or incompatible device drivers can inadvertently be installed. If you are having problems with operating system instability, you can run a verification check to see which existing drivers on your computer are not digitally signed. Windows Server 2003 includes a utility called the **File Signature Verification**. This utility can identify unsigned files and give you information such as the filename, location, modification date, and version number, as shown in Figure 2-16.

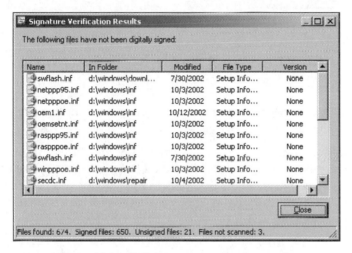

Figure 2-16   The File Signature Verification utility

By default, the File Signature Verification utility only checks device drivers and Windows Server 2003 system files. If you want to check other files to see if they are digitally signed, you must configure this in the program's advanced settings, as shown in Figure 2-17. In Activity 2-5, you use the File Signature Verification utility to scan your server for unsigned system files and drivers.

Figure 2-17   Advanced File Signature Verification settings

Activity 2-5: Using the File Signature Verification Utility

Time Required: 10 minutes

Objective: Use the File Signature Verification utility to verify that Microsoft has digitally signed all installed system files and device drivers.

Description: Dover Leasing uses a variety of hardware on the servers from different vendors. Because of his concern about system stability, the IT manager would like to ensure that all system and device driver files are digitally signed. In this activity, you have been asked to use the File Signature Verification utility to scan your server for any system or device driver files that may not be digitally signed.

1. Click **Start**, and then click **Run**.

2. In the Open text box, type **sigverif.exe**, and then click **OK**.

3. Click the **Advanced** button.

4. In the Advanced File Signature Verification Settings window, click the **Logging** tab. Ensure that the **Save the file signature verification results to a log file** check box is selected, and click **OK**.

5. Click the **Start** button to begin the file signature verification scanning process. Note that this process may take several minutes to complete.

6. Once scanning is complete, click the **Close** button.

7. Click the **Advanced** button and then click the **Logging** tab.

8. Click the **View Log** button to open the SIGVERIF.TXT file in Notepad.

9. Scroll through the contents of the log file being sure to note the number of files scanned and signed, as well as the Status column for individual files. Close the SIGVERIF.TXT file.

10. Click **Cancel** to close the Advanced File Signature Verification Settings window.

11. Click **Close** to close the File Signature Verification utility.

Roll Back Driver Feature

Earlier in this chapter you learned that vendors commonly release new or updated drivers for hardware devices to fix known issues or take advantage of updated features. While these drivers are typically tested in advance by the vendor on a variety of different hardware configurations, updating a driver can sometimes also result in system stability problems and errors.

Windows Server 2003 includes a feature that allows you to "roll back" to a previous version of a driver in cases where an updated driver is causing problems. Accessible from the Driver tab in the properties of a device in Device Manager, the Roll Back Driver button provides a simple and effective method to reinstall a previously used driver version. In Activity 2-6 you test this feature by first installing a new driver for your system's video adapter, and then rolling back to the version you are currently using.

Activity 2-6: Using the Roll Back Driver Feature

Time Required: 15 minutes

Objective: Use the Roll Back Driver feature to return to a previous version of a device driver.

Description: The IT manager at Dover Leasing wants to ensure that servers can be quickly recovered in the event that installing an updated or incorrect device driver leads to server problems. In this activity you update an existing device driver and then use the roll back driver feature to return to the original driver.

1. Click **Start**, right-click **My Computer**, and click **Properties**.

2. On the System Properties screen, click the **Hardware** tab.

3. In the Device Manager section, click the **Device Manager** button.

4. Click the **plus sign (+)** next to Display adapters to expand it. Right-click on your server's display adapter and click **Update Driver**.

5. At the Hardware Update Wizard welcome screen, click the **Install from a list or specific location (Advanced)** radio button, and click **Next**.

6. Click the **Don't search, I will choose the driver to install** radio button, and click **Next**.

7. Click **Standard VGA Graphics Adapter** in the Model list and click **Next**.

8. Click **Finish** to complete the wizard.

9. At the System Settings Change dialog box, click **Yes** to restart your server.

10. Once your server has rebooted, log on using your Admin*XX* account.

11. Click **Start**, right-click **My Computer**, and click **Properties**.

12. On the System Properties screen, click the **Hardware** tab.

13. In the Device Manager section, click the **Device Manager** button.

14. Click the **plus sign (+)** next to Display adapters to expand it. Right-click on your server's display adapter and click **Properties**.

15. Click on the **Driver** tab.

16. Click the **Driver Details** button. Notice that the current driver is the Standard VGA Graphics Adapter. Click **OK**.

17. Click the **Roll Back Driver** button, as shown in Figure 2-18.

18. At the Standard VGA Graphics Adapter dialog box, click **Yes**.

19. Click the **Driver Details** button. Notice that the previous driver is again being used. Click **OK**.

20. Click **Close** to exit the properties of your graphics adapter.

21. At the System Settings Change dialog box, click **Yes** to restart your server. Once your server has rebooted, log on using your Admin*XX* account.

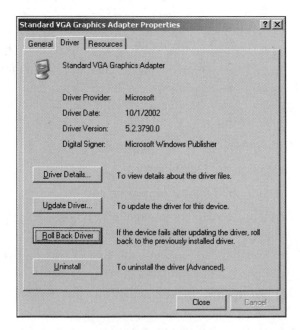

Figure 2-18   The Driver tab in the properties of a display adapter

CONFIGURING PROCESSOR AND MEMORY SETTINGS

Windows Server 2003 enables you to configure and optimize your server's memory and processor settings for optimal performance. There are three basic areas that you can configure:

- Processor scheduling and memory usage
- Virtual memory
- Memory for network performance

Processor Scheduling

Processor scheduling allows you to configure how processor resources are allocated to programs. The default setting on Windows Server 2003 is Background services, which means that all running applications receive equal amounts of processor time. Normally you should leave the default setting as it is for a server system. However, there may also be times when it might be better to select the Programs option to give most of the processor's resources to a particular foreground application. For example, if you determine that a disk drive is likely to fail and you want to back up its contents as fast as possible using the Windows Backup utility, selecting this option would give the Backup tool more processor time, and thus allow it to work faster.

Memory usage options are used to configure how much system memory is used to run programs versus how much is allocated to traditional server functions. Select the Programs option if your computer is temporarily acting as a workstation, mainly running programs at the console. Select the System cache option shown in Figure 2-19 (this is the default setting) if your computer is acting as a network server or running programs that require a large amount of memory.

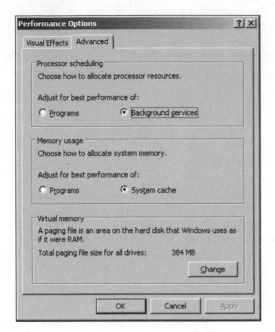

Figure 2-19   The Performance Options Advanced tab

Virtual Memory

Virtual memory is disk storage used to expand the capacity of the physical RAM installed in the computer. When the currently running programs and processes exceed the RAM, they treat disk space allocated for virtual memory as if it were real memory. The disadvantage of this is that memory activities performed through virtual memory are not as fast as those performed in RAM. Virtual memory works through a technique called paging, whereby blocks of information, called pages, are moved from RAM into virtual memory on disk. On a Pentium computer, data is paged in blocks of 4 KB. For example, if the system is not presently using a 7 KB block of code, it divides the code block between two pages, each 4 KB in size (part of one page will not be completely full). Next, both pages are moved to virtual memory on disk until needed. When the processor calls for that code block, the pages are moved back into RAM.

Before virtual memory can be used, it must first be allocated for this purpose by tuning the operating system. The area of the disk that is allocated for this purpose is called the **paging file**. A default amount of virtual memory is always established when Windows Server 2003 is installed, but the amount should be checked by the server administrator to ensure that it is not too large or too small. The name of the paging file on a Windows Server 2003 system is pagefile.sys.

In addition to size, the location of the paging file is important. Some tips for placement of the paging file are:

- Server performance is better if the paging file is not placed on the boot partition (the one with the \Windows folder) of basic disks or the boot volume of dynamic disks (you'll learn more about the types of disks later in this book).

- If there are multiple disks, performance can be improved by placing a paging file on each disk (but avoid placing the paging file on the boot partition or volume that contains the system files in the \Windows folder).

- In a mirrored set or volume, place the paging file on the main disk, and not on the mirrored (backup) disk.

- Do not place the paging file on a stripe set, striped volume, stripe set with parity, or RAID-5 volume, which are all disks specially set up to increase performance and fault tolerance.

When you tune the size of the paging file there are two parameters to set: initial size and maximum size. A general rule for configuring the initial size is to start with the size recommended when you view the default virtual memory setting, which is the amount of installed RAM times 1.5. For a server with 256 MB of RAM, the initial paging file size should be at least 384 MB (256 x 1.5). Set the maximum size so it affords plenty of room for growth—such as twice the size of your initial paging file setting (the default value). When it is operating, Windows Server 2003 always starts using the initial size and only expands the size of the paging file as additional space is needed. In Activity 2-7 you view and configure virtual memory settings on your Windows Server 2003 system.

Activity 2-7: Viewing and Configuring Virtual Memory Settings

Time Required: 10 minutes

Objective: Configure virtual memory settings on a Windows Server 2003 system.

Description: In order to increase the performance of virtual memory on the servers at Dover Leasing, you have been asked to move the paging file to a different volume. In this activity you remove the paging file from drive C and create a new paging file on drive D.

1. Click **Start**, right-click **My Computer**, and click **Properties**.
2. Click the **Advanced** tab.
3. In the Performance section, click the **Settings** button.
4. Click the **Advanced** tab.
5. In the Virtual memory section note the total paging file size listed, and click the **Change** button.
6. In the Virtual Memory window, ensure that C: is selected in the Drive section, and then note the initial and maximum size values for the current paging file as shown in Figure 2-20.

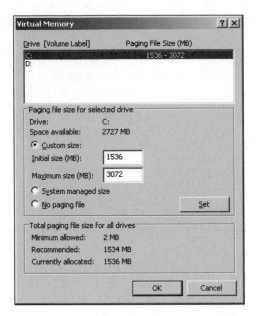

Figure 2-20   Configuring virtual memory settings

7. Click the **No paging file** radio button, and click the **Set** button.

8. When the System Control Panel Applet dialog box appears, click **Yes**.

9. Click on **D:** in the Drive section, and then click the **Custom size** radio button.

10. In the Initial size (MB) text box, type **384**.

11. In the Maximum size (MB) text box, type **512**.

12. Click the **Set** button, and then click **OK**.

13. When the System Control Panel Applet dialog box appears, click **OK**.

14. Click **OK** to close the Performance Options window.

15. Click **OK** to close the System Properties window.

16. At the System Settings Change dialog box, click **Yes** to restart your server.

17. Once your server has rebooted, log on using your Admin*XX* account.

18. Click **Start**, and click **My Computer**.

19. Double-click on drive **D** to view its contents.

20. Click the **Tools** menu, and then click **Folder Options**.

21. Click the **View** tab.

22. In the Advanced setting section, uncheck the **Hide protected operating system files (Recommended)** check box.

23. When the Warning dialog box appears click **Yes**, and then click **OK**.

24. Notice that protected system files now appear in the contents of drive D. In the list of files, notice the size of pagefile.sys. The file size should be consistent with the initial size configured in Step 10.

25. Close all open windows.

Memory for Network Performance

Memory can be divided between server functions and network connectivity functions. The server functions include software applications, printing, and currently running services. Network connectivity is related to the number of user connections at a given time. Server functions use RAM and paging. The network connectivity only uses RAM. If the server performance is slow because memory is busy, the network memory parameters should be checked and tuned.

Network memory is adjusted from the Network Connections option in Control Panel, by configuring the properties of File and Printer Sharing for Microsoft Networks. These settings are shown in Figure 2-21.

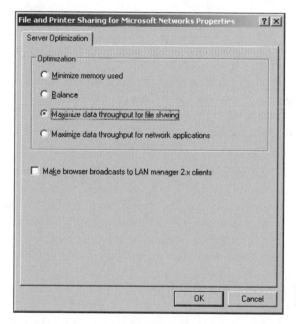

Figure 2-21 File and Printer Sharing for Microsoft Networks, Server Optimization tab

The memory optimization settings are described in Table 2-1. For example, if a server has 120 users who regularly access word processing and spreadsheet files on the server or who regularly install software from the server, the Maximize data throughput for file sharing option should be checked; or if there are only 32 users on a small network, check the Balance option button.

Table 2-1   Configuring server memory for network optimization

Option	Description
Minimize memory used	Optimizes the memory used on servers with 10 or fewer simultaneous network users
Balance	Optimizes memory use for a small LAN with about 64 or fewer users
Maximize data throughput for file sharing	Used for a large network with over 64 users where file and print serving resources need more memory allocation to make the server efficient
Maximize data throughput for network applications	Used in servers that primarily handle network connections and to reduce paging activity when this affects server performance, such as on a server that mainly authenticates users to the network or that handles databases that distribute functions to the client (in client/server systems)
Make browser broadcasts to LAN manager 2.x clients	Used for networks that have both Windows Server 2003 and the Microsoft (and IBM) early server operating system, LAN Manager

HARDWARE PROFILES

A **hardware profile** is a set of instructions telling the operating system which devices to start and drivers to load when your computer starts. By default, there is one hardware profile (named Profile 1) created when you install Windows Server 2003. Every device installed on your computer is enabled in the default profile.

One of the most common uses for hardware profiles is with portable computers. Most portable computers are, at different times, used in the office, at home, and on the road when traveling. You can create multiple profiles and use Device Manager to enable or disable specific devices for each one. For example, you may have a hardware profile for home that disables your network card if you only use a modem. You can create a second hardware profile for the office that enables your network card and disables your modem. In Activity 2-8 you configure and test a new hardware profile for your Windows Server 2003 system.

Activity 2-8: Creating a Hardware Profile

Time Required: 15 minutes

Objective: Create a new hardware profile with certain hardware devices disabled.

Description: Because all of the IT staff at Dover Leasing have access to the server room, the IT manager is concerned that a user might accidentally or maliciously use the floppy or

2

DVD/CD-ROM drive to install non-standard software or updates. In this activity you create a new hardware profile for your server that disables both the floppy and DVD/CD-ROM drive.

1. Click **Start**, right-click **My Computer**, and click **Properties**.

2. Click the **Hardware** tab, and then click the **Hardware Profiles** button.

3. In the Hardware Profiles window, review the available settings, and then click the **Properties** button.

4. In the Profile 1 Properties window, check the **Always include this profile as an option when Windows starts** check box, as shown in Figure 2-22. Click **OK**.

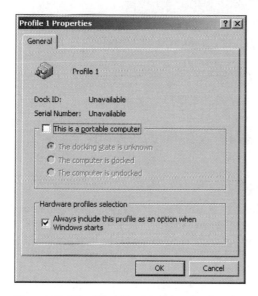

Figure 2-22   The Properties of a hardware profile

5. In the Hardware Profiles window, click the **Copy** button.

6. In the To text box, type **No CD/Floppy Drive**, and click **OK**.

7. Click **OK** to exit the Hardware Profiles screen, and then click **OK** to close the System Properties window. Restart your server.

8. At the Hardware Profile/Configuration Recovery Menu, select **No CD/Floppy Drive** as shown in Figure 2-23, and press **Enter**.

9. Log on to your server using your Admin*XX* account.

10. Click **Start**, right-click **My Computer**, and click **Properties**.

11. On the System Properties screen, click the **Hardware** tab.

12. In the Device Manager section, click the **Device Manager** button.

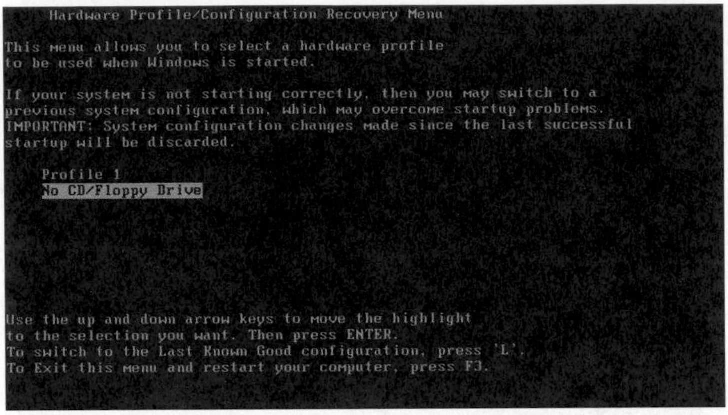

Figure 2-23   The Hardware Profile/Configuration Recovery Menu

13. Click the **plus sign (+)** next to DVD/CD-ROM drives to expand it.

14. Right-click on your CD or DVD drive and click **Properties**.

15. On the General tab, click the Device usage list box and select **Do not use this device in the current hardware profile (disable)**. Click **OK**.

16. Click the **plus sign (+)** next to Floppy disk drives to expand it.

17. Right-click on your floppy drive and click **Properties**.

18. On the General tab, click the Device usage list box and select **Do not use this device in the current hardware profile (disable)**. Click **OK**. Notice that both your DVD/CD-ROM drive and floppy drive now appear as disabled devices in the Device Manager interface.

19. Close Device Manager and restart your server.

20. At the Hardware Profile/Configuration Recovery Menu, select **No CD/Floppy Drive** and press **Enter**.

21. Log on to your server using your Admin*XX* account.

22. Click **Start**, and double-click **My Computer**. Verify that both your DVD/CD-ROM drive and floppy drive are not currently available.

23. Restart your server, select **Profile 1**, and then log on using your Admin*XX* account.

CONFIGURING POWER OPTIONS

After you have installed Windows Server 2003, check the power management options to make sure that they are set appropriately for the server and the way you are using the server on the network. The default power scheme is set at Always On, which means that it turns the monitor off after 20 minutes of no activity, and never turns off the hard disks. Also, the

2

default configuration runs the shutdown procedure when you press the power off button, instead of placing the computer in standby mode. Standby is a mode in which the computer components are shut down and information in memory is not written to hard disk—which means if the power goes out in standby mode, information in memory is lost. The power supply and CPU remain active, waiting to start up all components when you press a key or move the mouse.

Configure power options by clicking Start, pointing to Control Panel, and clicking Power Options. Access the Power Schemes tab first to establish the power settings, which include settings for desktop and portable computers. The settings change on the basis of the power scheme that you select, Portable/Laptop or Minimal Power Management, for example. In most situations, you will likely select Always On or Minimal Power Management, which are options that primarily involve display monitor power management. Another option is to create your own settings by specifying how soon to turn off the monitor, whether to turn off the hard disks, and whether to use standby mode. In Activity 2-9 you create a new custom power scheme for your server.

ACTIVITY

Activity 2-9: Defining a Power Scheme

Time Required: 5 minutes

Objective: Configure a new power scheme for use on a Windows Server 2003 system.

Description: The IT manager at Dover Leasing is very concerned that all servers are configured to use appropriate power management settings to reduce energy costs while at the same time ensuring resource availability. In this activity you create a new power scheme according to the supplied specifications.

1. Click **Start**, select **Control Panel**, and click **Power Options**.
2. Ensure that the Power Schemes tab is displayed.
3. Click the Turn off monitor box, and click **After 1 hour**, as shown in Figure 2-24.
4. Ensure that the Turn off hard disks list box displays Never.
5. Ensure that the System standby list box displays Never.
6. Click **Save As**, type **ServerXX** in the Save Scheme dialog box, and click **OK**. Click **Apply**.
7. Click each of the other three tabs to view the additional parameters that can be set.
8. Click **OK**, and then close Control Panel.

When you configure the power options, also check the Advanced tab to determine whether the computer powers off or goes into standby mode, which is determined by what you enter in the When I press the power button on my computer box. Because you will likely be working on the computer hardware or want to perform a cold boot when you power the computer off, the default is set to Shut down, as shown in Figure 2-25. If you select Stand by, consider checking the box Prompt for password when computer resumes from standby, so that only an authorized server administrator can access the server.

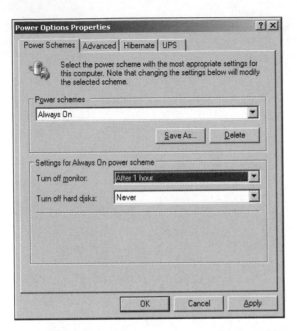

Figure 2-24   Configuring power scheme settings

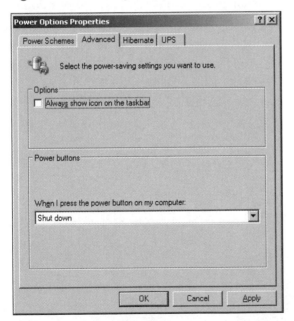

Figure 2-25   Configuring Power Options advanced settings

The third tab, Hibernate, enables you to set up the computer to hibernate when it is not in use. Hibernate mode is similar to standby, but with an important difference: the memory

2

contents are saved before shutting down the disks, allowing you to restart your system in a manner identical to when hibernation occurred. For example, if an application was running prior to hibernation, it will be returned to that state when the system is restarted.

The fourth tab, UPS, enables you to configure an **uninterruptible power supply (UPS)**, which is a battery backup device that temporarily supplies power to the server when the main power goes out. You can set up communications between the UPS and Windows Server 2003 usually through a serial connection so that the UPS notifies the server when there is a power outage and the server sends you an alert.

NOTE   Disk drives, memory, and other key server components can sustain damage from power outages and fluctuations, such as brownouts. Also, the server may lose valuable data when a sudden power problem causes it to shut down without the opportunity to save data. A UPS is the best fault-tolerance method to prevent power problems from causing data loss and component damage.

All UPS systems are designed to provide power for a limited time period, such as 10 to 20 minutes, so that a decision can be made (based on how long the power failure will last) as to whether to shut down computers immediately. Of course, the amount of time the batteries can provide power depends on how much and what equipment is attached to the UPS. This is why most people attach only critical equipment to a UPS, such as computers and monitors, external disk arrays, and tape drives. Most UPS systems also include circuitry to guard against power surges and power brownouts.

CAUTION   Some manufacturers recommend against plugging laser printers into a UPS, because those printers draw excessive power when turned on, risking damage to the UPS.

The general steps for configuring a UPS connection to Windows Server 2003 are:

1. Click **Start**, point to **Control Panel**, click **Power Options**, and click the **UPS** tab, as shown in Figure 2-26.

2. Click the **Select** button and in the Select manufacturer list box, select the UPS manufacturer, such as **American Power Conversion**.

3. Select the specific UPS model in the Select model box, such as **PowerStack**.

4. In the On port box, specify the COM port to which the UPS is attached, such as **COM2**. Click **Finish**.

5. Click the **Configure** button in the Power Options Properties dialog box.

6. Configure the options that are appropriate to the UPS, including how to send out notifications of a power failure, when to sound a critical alarm that the UPS is almost out of power, the option to run a program just before the UPS is out of power, and if you want the computer and UPS to shut down just before the UPS is out of power. Click **OK**.

7. Click **Apply**.

8. Check the message at the bottom of the dialog box to make sure that the UPS is connected and communicating with the server. A large "X" in a red circle appears if it is not properly connected and communicating. If it is not, make sure that the serial cable is attached, ensure that you configured the same server port in Step 4 as is used for the cable, and make sure that the UPS is turned on.

9. Click **OK**.

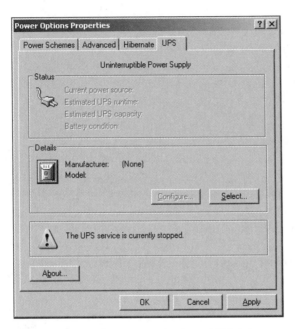

Figure 2-26   The Power Options UPS tab

CHAPTER SUMMARY

❏ Windows Server 2003 supports a variety of different internal and external hardware devices. The Windows Server Catalog contains listings of hardware devices that have been certified to function with Windows Server 2003.

❏ Device Manager is the primary tool used to manage and modify hardware on a Windows Server 2003 system. Features of this tool include the ability to configure resource settings, device drivers, enable and disable hardware, and more.

❏ Device driver files allow Windows Server 2003 to communicate with a hardware device. Digitally signed drivers are always preferred, but unsigned driver files can be used if necessary. An administrator can configure driving signing options to control which drivers can be installed.

2

❏ Windows Server 2003 provides the ability to control the allocation of processor and memory resources, as well as the use of virtual memory.

❏ Hardware profiles allow an administrator to control which drivers are loaded during the boot process, and by extension, which hardware devices will be available. This feature is primarily used with portable computers, but can also be used to control access to hardware devices on server systems if necessary.

KEY TERMS

Basic Input/Output System (BIOS) — A program stored on a flash memory chip attached to the motherboard that establishes the initial communication between the components of the computer, such as the hard drive, CD-ROM, floppy disk, video, and memory.

device driver — Software that includes the instructions necessary in order for an operating system to communicate with a hardware device.

Direct Memory Access (DMA) channels — A resource that allows hardware to access RAM directly without the intervention of the system CPU.

driver signing — A digital signature that Microsoft incorporates into driver and system files as a way to verify the files and to ensure that they are not inappropriately overwritten.

File Signature Verification — A utility used to identify unsigned system and driver files, that provides information such as the filename, location, modification date, and version number.

hardware profile — A set of instructions telling the operating system which devices to start and drivers to load when a computer starts.

Industry Standard Architecture (ISA) — A legacy 16-bit bus architecture that does not support the Plug and Play standard.

Input/Output (I/O) ranges — Dedicated memory areas that are allocated for the purpose of transferring information between a computer and a hardware device.

interrupt request (IRQ) lines — Resource used by hardware devices to gain the attention of the system processor.

legacy devices — Devices that do not follow the Plug and Play standard, such as older Industry Standard Architecture (ISA) expansion cards.

Memory Address range — Memory ranges allocated for the purpose of communication between a hardware device and the operating system.

paging file — Disk space, in the form of a file (pagefile.sys), for use when memory requirements exceed the available RAM.

Plug and Play — A set of specifications originally developed by Intel that enables a system to automatically detect hardware and configure driver and resource settings.

uninterruptible power supply (UPS) — A device built into electrical equipment or a separate device that provides immediate battery power to equipment during a power failure or brownout.

virtual memory — Disk storage used to extend the capacity of the physical RAM installed in the computer.

Windows Server Catalog — The main listing of hardware devices that have been certified to function with Windows Server 2003, and officially carry the "Designed for Windows Server 2003" logo.

REVIEW QUESTIONS

1. Which of the following is the list of hardware devices certified for Windows Server 2003?
   a. Windows Hardware Qualifier
   b. Windows Server Catalog
   c. Hardware Compatibility List
   d. Windows Hardware List

2. What is the default driver signing option in Windows Server 2003?
   a. Block
   b. Allow
   c. Deny
   d. Warn

3. Which of the following are driver signing options on a Windows Server 2003 system? (Choose all that apply.)
   a. Block
   b. Warn
   c. Deny
   d. Ignore

4. Which of the following resources is used for communication between a hardware device and the operating system?
   a. IRQ
   b. I/O range
   c. Memory address
   d. DMA channel

5. Which of the following resources allows a hardware device to directly access RAM?
   a. IRQ
   b. I/O range
   c. Memory address
   d. DMA channel

6. Which of the following resources does a hardware device use to send a notification to the CPU?

    a. IRQ

    b. I/O range

    c. Memory address

    d. DMA channel

7. Which of the following tools can be used to diagnose a resource conflict in Windows Server 2003? (Choose all that apply.)

    a. Device Manager

    b. System Information

    c. MSCONFIG

    d. AUTOEXEC.BAT

8. Which IRQ does Windows Server 2003 use for PCI steering?

    a. 5

    b. 4

    c. 9

    d. 6

9. Which of the following tools is used to verify digital signatures for system files and device drivers?

    a. SIGVERIF

    b. VERIFYSIG

    c. SIGNAT

    d. SIGVERIFY

10. Which File and Printer Sharing setting optimizes memory use for a small LAN with 64 or fewer users?

    a. Minimize memory used

    b. Balance

    c. Maximize data throughput for network applications

    d. Maximize data throughput for file sharing

11. Which File and Printer Sharing setting optimizes the memory used on servers with 10 or fewer simultaneous network users?

    a. Minimize memory used

    b. Balance

    c. Maximize data throughput for network applications

    d. Maximize data throughput for file sharing

12. How many hardware profiles are configured on a Windows Server 2003 system by default?

    a. 2

    b. 0

    c. 1

    d. 3

13. Which Windows Server 2003 feature allows you to return to a previous driver version with a push of a button?

    a. Roll Back Driver

    b. Driver Steering

    c. Driver Updates

    d. Driver Fallback

14. What is the name of the file used by virtual memory on a Windows Server 2003 system?

    a. Swap.sys

    b. Swap.pag

    c. Pagefile.sys

    d. Page.sys

15. Which tab in the properties of a hardware device would be used to determine the IRQ assigned to the device?

    a. Advanced

    b. Resources

    c. Hardware

    d. Drivers

16. Which of the following would most likely be referred to as a legacy device?

    a. PCI display adapter

    b. USB hub

    c. DVD-ROM drive

    d. ISA modem

17. Which of the following is not required in order for Plug and Play to function correctly?

    a. Plug and Play built into the device

    b. Plug and Play enabled in the computer's BIOS

    c. Plug and Play built into the computer operating system kernel

    d. Driver signing

18. What would the initial page file size be by default for a Windows Server 2003 system with 1 GB of RAM?

a. 1 GB

b. 2 GB

c. 4 GB

d. 1.5 GB

19. The Windows paging file must reside on drive C.

a. True

b. False

20. Which IRQ does a floppy disk controller typically use by default?

a. 4

b. 5

c. 6

d. 7

CASE PROJECTS

Case Project 2-1

Dover Leasing is planning to implement a new Windows Server 2003, Standard Edition, server in one of its branch office locations. The server will have 2 GB of RAM, and will be used to host databases running Microsoft SQL Server 2000. At the present time, this branch office has 100 users who will be accessing the server regularly. The server will be configured with multiple disks—one for the operating system, one for the SQL Server database, and a third which is currently not associated with any particular task. Based on the intended usage of this system, which processor scheduling, memory usage, virtual memory, and network memory settings would best meet the needs of Dover Leasing?

Case Project 2-2

The IT Manager at Dover Leasing has asked you to confirm that the main hardware components installed in your server are listed in the Windows Server Catalog. Use Device Manager to find manufacturer and model information for the display adapter, network adapter, and DVD/CD-ROM installed on our server. Use this information to search the online Windows Server Catalog found at *http://www.microsoft.com/windows/catalog/server/default.aspx,* and to verify that each of these devices is compatible with Windows Server 2003.

3

CREATING AND MANAGING USER ACCOUNTS

After reading this chapter and completing the exercises, you will be able to:

♦ Understand the purpose of user accounts

♦ Understand the user authentication process

♦ Understand and configure local, roaming, and mandatory user profiles

♦ Configure and modify user accounts using different methods

♦ Troubleshoot user account and authentication problems

Good management is essential for all modern networks. Active Directory enables you to effectively manage a potentially chaotic group of resources, such as user accounts, shared folders, and shared printers. Active Directory accomplishes this by providing a hierarchy of management elements that allow you to organize resources, control access to them, and advertise their existence—making the lives of users easier.

The most basic unit of any Active Directory environment is a user account. Without a user account object defined in Active Directory, a user cannot log on and gain access to network resources. Aside from being used for authentication purposes, a user account also describes the user associated with that account, including information about that individual and various configuration settings for their working environment.

As part of authenticating a user on a network, Windows Server 2003 uses different authentication types and protocols. This chapter explores the differences between interactive and network authentication, as well as the two primary authentication protocols used in Windows Server 2003 domain environments: Kerberos v5 and the NT LAN Manager (NTLM) protocol.

A user's desktop environment and related settings is known as their user profile. Windows Server 2003 supports three different types of profiles known as local, roaming, and mandatory profiles. The profile type implemented impacts how a user interacts with their desktop environment, whether their settings follow them to different workstations, and whether they have the ability to customize these settings. Later in this chapter you learn more about each profile type, including how to configure them in a Windows Server 2003 environment.

Although Active Directory Users and Computers is the primary tool used to create and manage domain user accounts, Windows Server 2003 includes a variety of new tools to allow user accounts to be configured and modified from the command line. For administrators looking to import or export user account settings from existing databases or directory services, familiar bulk import and export tools originally introduced in Windows 2000 continue to be supported. This chapter familiarizes you with a variety of tools that can be used to create and manage user accounts.

Finally, there are an array of issues that can impact the user authentication process in a network environment. At the end of this chapter you learn some of the specific settings that impact user authentication, as well as ways to troubleshoot and resolve common user authentication problems.

INTRODUCTION TO USER ACCOUNTS

A **user account** is an object that is stored in Active Directory that represents all of the information that defines a user with access to the network. The information that defines a user may include attributes such as a first and last name, a password, group membership information, as well as a number of other data.

Any person who needs access to resources on the network requires a user account. User accounts can assist in the administration and security of the network by making it possible to:

- require authentication for users connecting to the network
- control access to network resources such as shared folders or printers
- monitor access to resources by auditing actions performed by a user logged on with a specific account

When creating a new user account, it is important that an organization set standards on the various elements of a user object. Some of these standards might include:

- Establishing a naming convention—The user account names within the domain follow a consistent naming convention. Common examples include:
  - First name and last initial—The account name for Kirk Jefferies would be KirkJ
  - First initial and last name—The account name for Karen Armstrong would be Karmstrong
  - Last name and first initial—The account name for Mike Smith would be Smithm; adding additional initials, such as the first letter of a user's middle name, accommodates multiple users with the same name

■ Controlling password policy and ownership—The best password policy requires that a password consist of at least eight characters, contain a variety of alphanumeric characters, and have an expiration setting; either the network administrator or the user can control and maintain the password.

■ Including additional required attributes— For example, requiring that all phone numbers and e-mail addresses are part of the account information.Keep in mind that every additional attribute requires additional replication bandwidth and storage space within Active Directory.

NOTE A user logon name is referred to as a User Principal Name (UPN) when combined with the domain suffix (for example, @dovercorp.net). The UPN allows users to log on from any trusted domain within a forest by providing only a UPN name and password at the Windows logon screen.

User Account Properties

The primary tool used to create and manage user accounts in an Active Directory environment is **Active Directory Users and Computers**. Through this interface, a variety of different properties can be configured for a user account. While the configurable settings available represent the most commonly used settings, there remain dozens of other attributes that can be configured for a user account. To open the property page for a user object, simply right-click the object in Active Directory Users and Computers and choose Properties. The window shown in Figure 3-1 appears. You can open the same window by double-clicking a user object, or choosing Properties from the Action menu with the user object selected.

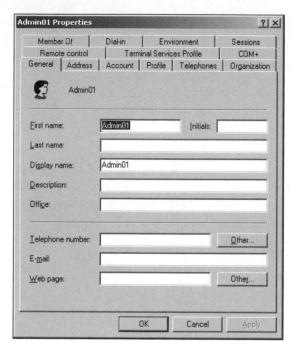

Figure 3-1   Properties of a user account

NOTE   Although the properties page of a user account displays the most common attributes for a user object, additional attributes can be managed programmatically with code, script, or tools like ADSI Edit.

The number of tabs and the tab headings that appear in this chapter may differ from what you see on your system. Because Active Directory is extensible (that is, the schema can be extended with new attributes and new classes), Active Directory-aware applications may add tabs to the property pages of Active Directory objects such as user accounts. A good example of this is when Microsoft Exchange Server 2000 is installed it adds three new tabs to the user property page.

The following is a brief summary of the account properties that can be set for a user:

- General—Contains personal information about the account holder including the first name, last name, and name as it is displayed in the console, description of the user or account, office location, telephone number, e-mail address, and home page; also provides optional buttons for additional telephone numbers and Web page addresses for the account holder

- Address—Stores information pertaining to the account holder's street address, post office box, city, state or province, postal code, and country or region

3

- Account—Holds information regarding the logon name, domain name, and account options, such as requiring the user to change a password at next logon, and account expiration date, if one applies; includes a Logon Hours button to set up the account so that the user only logs onto the domain at designated times, such as during backups and designated system work times on the server; also provides a Log On To button to limit from which computer the user can log on to the server or domain

- Profile—Enables the particular profile (discussed later in this chapter) to be associated with the user or a set of users, such as a common desktop; also used to associate the logon script (a file of commands that are executed at logon) and the home folder (a folder that is the users main folder, such as a folder on a particular system)

- Telephones—Stores specific telephone contact numbers for the account holder, which include one or more numbers for home, pager, mobile, fax, and IP

- Organization—Provides a place to enter the account holder's title, department, company name, and the name of the person who manages the account holder

- Member Of—Adds the account to an existing group of users that have the same security and access requirements; also used to remove the account from a group

- Dial-in—Controls remote access from dial-in modems or from virtual private networks (VPNs)

- Environment—Configures the startup environment for accessing one or more servers using terminal services (for running programs on the server)

- Sessions—Configures session parameters for the user utilizing terminal services, such as session time limits, limits on how long a session can be idle, what to do when a connection is broken, and how to reconnect

- Remote control—Sets up remote control parameters for the client using terminal services; enabling the administrator to view and manipulate the client session while it is active in order to troubleshoot problems

- Terminal Services Profile—Sets up the user profile for using terminal services

- COM+—Specifies which COM+ partition set the user is a member of

NOTE   Some additional tabs available in the properties of a user account are hidden by default. These tabs include Object, Published Certificates, and Security. To view these tabs, click on the View menu item in Active Directory Users and Computers and click Advanced Features. For more information on the purpose of each tab, see the Windows Server 2003 Help and Support Center.

In Activity 3-1 you review the property pages associated with a user account in Active Directory Users and Computers.

ACTIVITY

Activity 3-1: Reviewing User Account Properties

Time required: 10 minutes

Objective: Review the properties of a user account.

Description: The IT manager at Dover Leasing has recently decided that one of your primary responsibilities will be the configuration of user accounts and related settings for all corporate users. As such, you have decided to familiarize yourself with the configurable elements of a user account in Active Directory Users and Computers. In this activity you review the main tabs associated with configuring the properties of a user account.

1. Click **Start**, select **Administrative Tools**, and click **Active Directory Users and Computers**.

2. Click on the **Users** container located in the left pane to view its contents.

3. Right-click on the **AdminXX account**, where *XX* is your assigned student number, and click **Properties**.

4. Review the configurable settings on the General tab, noting that information such as a telephone number, description, and office can be configured on this screen. Click the **Address** tab.

5. Review the configurable settings on the Address tab. Note the types of information that can be configured on this screen, and click the **Account** tab.

6. Review the settings available on the Account tab, as shown in Figure 3-2. Notice both the user logon name, and the domain name that follows it. Together, these two elements form a UPN, which a user can use to log on to the network. Click the **Logon Hours** button.

7. The Logon Hours for AdminXX appears. This window allows you to configure the days and hours when this user is allowed to log on to the network. By default, a user can log on at any time, as illustrated in Figure 3-3. Click the **Cancel** button to close the Logon Hours for AdminXX window.

8. Click the **Log On To** button. When the Logon Workstations window appears, note that a user can log on to all computers by default. If a user needs to be limited to logging on to specific computers only, this window allows you to configure appropriate settings by computer name. Click the **Cancel** button to close the Logon Workstations window.

9. In the Account options section of the Account tab, review the various configurable properties available, and then click the **Profile** tab.

10. Review the settings available on the Profile tab, noting that it allows you to configure the network path for a user profile, the location of a logon script, and the location of the user's home folder. User profile settings are covered in more detail later in this chapter. Click the **Telephones** tab.

3

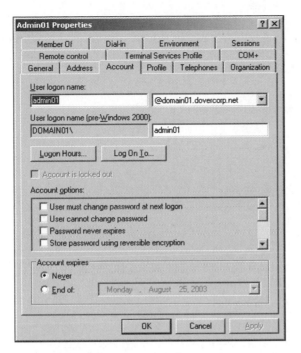

Figure 3-2   The Account tab

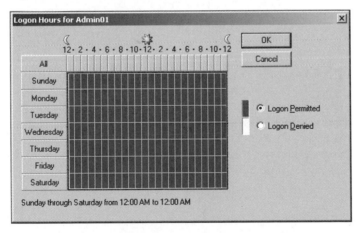

Figure 3-3   The Logon Hours window

11. Review the settings that can be configured on the Telephones tab. The Notes section on the bottom of this page could be used to configure additional information, such as which phone number is preferred for the user. Click the **Organization** tab.

12. Review the settings that can be configured on the Organization tab. Note that information about the user's manager and reporting status within the organization can also be configured on this page. Click the **Member Of** tab.

13. Notice that the Member Of tab displays information about the groups this user is a member of, as shown in Figure 3-4. Users can be added or removed from groups by using the Add and Remove buttons respectively. Group accounts are looked at in more detail in Chapter 4. Click the **Dial-in** tab.

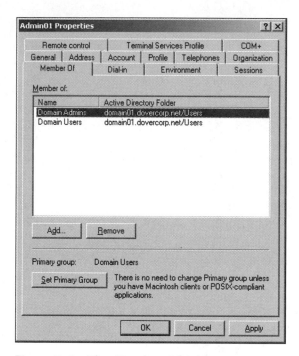

Figure 3-4   The Member Of tab

14. Review the settings that can be configured on the Dial-in tab, as shown in Figure 3-5. Notice that this tab allows you to configure Dial-in and VPN settings for the user, and that remote access permissions are set to the Deny access setting by default. Click on the **Environment**, **Sessions**, **Remote control**, **Terminal Services Profile**, and **COM+** tabs to review their settings as time permits.

15. Click **Cancel** to close the Admin*XX* Properties window.

16. Close Active Directory Users and Computers.

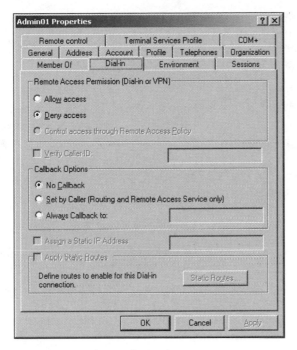

Figure 3-5   The Dial-in tab

USER AUTHENTICATION

In order for a user to gain access to network resources in an Active Directory environment, they must first be authenticated. **Authentication** is the process by which a user's identity is validated and subsequently granted or denied access to network resources. When logging on to the network from a client operating system such as Windows XP or Windows 2000 Professional, a user inputs their user name and password, and then specifies the resource that they wish to log on to (such as a particular domain or the local computer). In an Active Directory environment, a user generally logs on to a domain, where a server configured as a domain controller authenticates the user in a centralized manner. In a workgroup, authentication is handled by the local computer's SAM database. The authentication method used ultimately impacts the manner in which a user interacts with the network and available resources.

Authentication Methods

Authentication in a Windows Server 2003 environment consists of two main processes. The first process is known as interactive authentication, and relates to the act of supplying user account information at the Log On to Windows dialog box. The second process is known as network authentication, and relates to the process by which a user's credentials are confirmed when they attempt to access a network resource. The following sections define both interactive and network authentication in greater detail.

Interactive Authentication

Interactive authentication is the process by which a user provides their user name and password to be authenticated from the Log On to Windows dialog box. In a Windows Server 2003 Active Directory environment, a user can choose to log on to either a domain or the local workstation as part of this process.

The option to log on to the local computer is not available on a Windows server configured as a domain controller.

If a user chooses to log on to a domain, the supplied user name and password credentials are compared to information stored on a domain controller in its Active Directory database. If the supplied credentials are correct, the user is validated, and the logon process completes successfully. If the credentials are not correct, the user is not validated, and must supply correct credentials to complete the process. Figure 3-6 illustrates the dialog box encountered when an incorrect user name or password combination is supplied in the Log On to Windows dialog box.

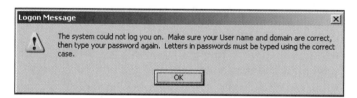

Figure 3-6   The Logon Message dialog box

Windows Server 2003 also supports interactive authentication using smart cards. When smart cards are configured for users, a user inserts their smart card into a card reader as part of the authentication process. After doing so, the user is prompted to supply a PIN number rather than a password. The need to supply both the physical smart card and associated PIN number as part of the authentication process makes smart card authentication a more secure option than the traditional user name/password combination.

When a user chooses to log on to the local workstation, the supplied user name and password is validated by the local SAM database of the computer rather than by an Active Directory domain controller. In order for this interactive authentication method to successfully validate a user, they must have a configured user account on the computer they are logging on to. If the credentials supplied are correct, the user is validated and the logon

3

process completes successfully. If the credentials are not correct, the user is not validated, and must supply correct credentials to complete the process.

In a domain environment, users normally do not have local user accounts configured on their workstations, so the domain method of interactive authentication is typically used. This method ultimately makes the process of accessing network resources transparent, as you learn in the next section.

Network Authentication

Network authentication is the process by which a network resource or service confirms the identity of a user. For example, when a user attempts to access the contents of a shared folder on the network, their credentials must be validated. The manner in which network authentication occurs is different for a user who chooses to log on to a domain versus a user who logs on to their local computer.

If a user logs on to a domain during the interactive authentication process, the network authentication process is completely transparent. This is because the same credentials that were supplied as part of the interactive authentication process are used to validate their identity when they attempt to access a network resource. For example, if a user logged on interactively using the user name jsmith in the domain*XX*.dovercorp.net domain, these are the credentials that would be supplied to a network server in the event that this user attempts to access a network resource or service. Since the user is already authenticated in the domain, they are not prompted to provide their user name and password again. This makes the process of accessing resources seamless and transparent to an authenticated domain user.

If a user logs on to their local computer during the interactive authentication process, however, that particular computer is the only one to have authenticated them. When a user in this scenario attempts to access network resources such as a shared folder on another computer, they are prompted to supply an appropriate user name and password for that resource. An example of a network authentication dialog box is illustrated in Figure 3-7.

Figure 3-7   A network authentication dialog box

Authentication Protocols

Windows Server 2003 supports two main authentication protocols; **Kerberos version 5 (Kerberos v5)** and **NT LAN Manager (NTLM)**. While Kerberos v5 is the primary authentication protocol used in Active Directory domain environments, it is not supported on all client operating systems. For this reason, Windows Server 2003 also includes support for NTLM authentication, which is the primary authentication protocol of older Microsoft operating systems like Windows NT 4.0 and Windows 98. The following sections reveal more about the Kerberos v5 and NTLM authentication protocols.

Kerberos v5

Kerberos v5 is the primary authentication protocol used in Active Directory domain environments. Microsoft operating system versions that support Kerberos v5 authentication include:

- Windows 2000
- Windows XP
- Windows Server 2003

Although the process used by Kerberos to authenticate users and network services is seamless and transparent in the eyes of the user, it helps to understand the manner in which Kerberos authentication occurs. The following example illustrates the steps involved in the Kerberos authentication process in an Active Directory domain environment.

1. A user logs on interactively from a computer that is a member of a domain by providing a user name/password/domain combination or smart card. The authentication request is passed to a **Key Distribution Center (KDC)**. The KDC in this case is a Windows Server 2003 domain controller.

2. The KDC authenticates the user, assuming they have provided the correct user name and password combination. As part of this process, the KDC creates and issues what is known as a **ticket-granting ticket (TGT)** to the client system. The TGT proves that the client has been successfully authenticated.

3. When a client attempts to access a network resource in the domain, such as a shared folder on another server, the client presents its TGT to the KDC requesting a **service ticket** for the server on which the resource resides.

4. The client then contacts the server hosting the requested network service, and presents the service ticket obtained in Step 3 to this server. This ticket proves the identity of the client to the network service, and proves the identity of the network service to the client. At this point the user can access the requested service on the server, assuming they have appropriate permissions or rights to do so.

The Kerberos v5 process for accessing resources across domains is similar to those listed in the previous steps, but slightly more involved. For more information on the specific Kerberos process for accessing resources in other domains, see the topic "Accessing resources across domains" in the Windows Server 2003 Help and Support Center.

From this example, it should be clear that a KDC is a trusted intermediary (or third party) in the Kerberos authentication process. Every domain controller in a Windows Server 2003 (or Windows 2000) Active Directory environment holds the role of KDC. It is also important to recognize, however, that not all operating systems are capable of functioning as Kerberos clients. Clients not capable of using Kerberos for authentication rely upon NTLM authentication, as looked at in the next section.

NTLM

For clients that do not support Kerberos v5, Windows Server 2003 continues to support authentication using the NTLM protocol. NTLM is a challenge-response protocol that is used for authentication purposes with operating systems running Windows NT 4.0 or earlier (often referred to as "down-level" systems). In cases where Kerberos-based authentication is not possible, Windows 2000 and Windows Server 2003 systems are also capable of using NTLM authentication. NTLM authentication would most commonly be used in conjunction with a Windows Server 2003 system when:

- A Windows Server 2003 system attempts to authenticate to a Windows NT 4.0 domain controller

- A Windows NT 4.0 Workstation system attempts to authenticate to a Windows 2000 or Windows Server 2003 domain controller

 The original version of NTLM is sometimes referred to as NTLMv1. A newer version, known as NTLMv2, was introduced in Windows NT 4.0 with Service Pack 4 installed, and offered a variety of security improvements. Operating systems like Windows 95 and Windows 98 can be configured to support NTLMv2 if they have Active Directory Client Extensions software installed.

The following example illustrates the steps involved in the NTLM authentication process between a **down-level operating system** such as Windows NT 4.0 and a domain controller:

1. A user logs on interactively from a computer that is a member of a domain by providing user name, password, and domain information. The client system calculates a cryptographic hash of the supplied password, and then discards the original password information.

2. The client system sends the supplied user name to the domain controller.

3. The domain controller generates a 16-bit random number, and sends it back to the client. This number is known as the "challenge".

4. The client encrypts the challenge with the hash of the user password and sends this value back to the domain controller.

5. The domain controller computes the value that it expects the client to return using the password information stored in the user account database. If the two values match, authentication is successful.

After successful NTLM authentication takes place, a token is generated for the client and attached to their user process. Each time the user attempts to access a resource on the network, their token is checked as part of the authentication process.

 Windows Server 2003 supports a variety of different configuration settings for NTLM security. For more information about configurable NTLM security settings, see the Windows Server 2003 Help and Support Center.

USER PROFILES

Microsoft operating systems since Windows NT 4.0 have automatically stored the unique settings for a user's desktop environment in what is known as a **user profile**. A user profile is simply a collection of settings specific to a particular user. For example, if two users share a PC running Windows XP, each user is provided with their own customizable desktop environment and related settings when they log on using their personal user name and password. In this way, a single system can support the unique desktop settings of many different users.

When a new user logs on to a Windows NT 4.0, Windows 2000, Windows XP, or Windows Server 2003 system for the first time, a new and dedicated user profile is created for that user locally. The default location for all local user profiles is a folder bearing the same name as the user located in the %systemdrive%\Documents and Settings folder, as illustrated in Figure 3-8. User profiles are local by default, and as such do not follow users when they log on to different computers.

Although user profiles are stored locally by default, Windows Server 2003 also supports the ability to have a profile follow a user to different computers with a technique known as a roaming profile. Furthermore, administrators can configure a user profile with a mandatory profile so that a user cannot modify it. Both roaming and mandatory user profiles are covered later in this chapter.

User profiles are often only associated with a user's desktop environment, such as the placement of icons, creation of shortcuts, and the desktop wallpaper that they have chosen. However, a user profile actually consists of a wide variety of items, including a user's My Documents folder, Internet Explorer Favorites menu, and more. Table 3-1 outlines the key folders that make up a user profile, along with the types of information that they store.

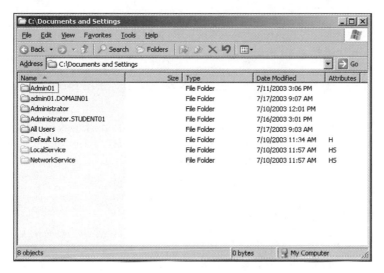

Figure 3-8   The Documents and Settings folder

Table 3-1   User profile folders and contents

Folder Name	Folder Contents
Application Data	Program-specific data such as the data files associated with a particular application
Cookies	Cookie files from visited Web sites
Desktop	User desktop items such as shortcuts, files, and folders
Favorites	Shortcuts to Internet locations
Local Settings	Program data, history information, and temporary files
My Documents	User files and folders
My Recent Documents	Shortcuts to recently used files and folders
NetHood	Shortcuts to items found in My Network Places
PrintHood	Shortcuts to items found in the Printers folder
SendTo	Shortcuts to file-handling utilities, such as the ability to create a desktop shortcut
Start Menu	Shortcuts to programs that appear on the Start Menu
Templates	User templates

Local Profiles

When a user logs on to a Windows Server 2003 system for the first time, a new local user profile is created for them by default. The settings contained in this new profile are copied from a pre-configured profile folder in the Documents and Settings folder named Default User. As its name suggests, the Default User folder contains all of the settings that will be applied to new profiles as they are created. One benefit of this method is that it allows an administrator to edit the contents of the Default User profile such that the default desktop environment applied to users contains specific settings, if these are required.

After a new **local profile** is created for a user, any changes made by the user are saved in their associated profile folder when they log off. For example, if a user logs on, changes their desktop wallpaper, and then logs off, their customized desktop wallpaper settings would be presented the next time they log on to that system. However, if a different user were to log on to that system for the first time, their new profile would consist of the settings found in the Default User folder to begin with.

Although local user profiles are created automatically when a new user logs on to a Windows Server 2003 system for the first time, an administrator can manage various elements of a local user profile. For example, the System program in Control Panel provides access to user profile settings from the Advanced tab, as shown in Figure 3-9.

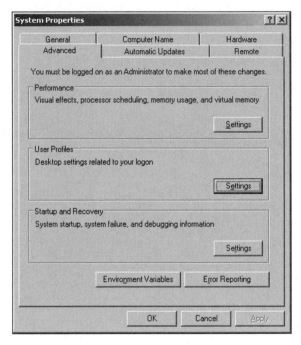

Figure 3-9 The Advanced tab of the System program

Clicking on the Settings button in the User Profiles section opens the User Profiles window, as shown in Figure 3-10. As its name suggests, the Profiles stored on this computer section provides a list of all profiles stored on this computer, including their size, type, status, and last modification date.

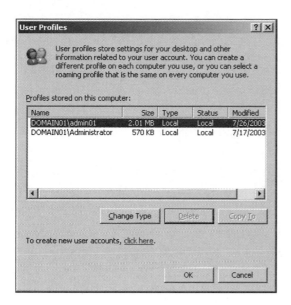

Figure 3-10   The User Profiles window

When an individual profile is selected from the list, one or more of the following three buttons become available:

- Change Type—Allows you to change the type of user profile from local to roaming or vice versa.

- Delete—Allows you to delete a profile if necessary. In some cases, such as when many unnecessary user profiles exist on a system, an administrator may delete old or unused profiles to save disk space.

- Copy To—Allows you to copy a user profile to a different location, such as a central server location. This is useful for maintaining a user's existing desktop settings while switching their profile from local to roaming.

If you select the profile of the currently logged on user in the User Profiles window, both the Delete and Copy To buttons appear unavailable. You can neither delete nor copy the profile of the currently logged on user. To accomplish either of these tasks, you need to log on to the system using a different user account with administrative privileges.

In Activity 3-2 you explore and test local user profile settings on your Windows Server 2003 system.

Activity 3-2: Testing Local Profile Settings

Time required: 10 minutes

Objective: Configure and test a local user profile.

Description: The IT manager at Dover Leasing is currently debating whether Dover would be better served by using local or roaming user profiles for domain users. As part of determining the capabilities of each, he has asked you to explore and test local user profile settings to get a better sense for how they function. In this exercise you create two new user accounts and then test the impact of changing various local user profile settings on your server.

1. Click **Start**, select **Administrative Tools**, and then click **Active Directory Users and Computers**.

2. Right-click on the **Users** container, select **New**, and then click **User**.

3. In the New Object – User window, type **Testuser1** in the First name text box, and type **Testuser1** in the User logon name text box. Click **Next**.

4. In the Password text box type **Password01**, and then type **Password01** in the Confirm password text box. Uncheck the **User must change password at next logon** check box, click **Next**, and then click **Finish**.

5. Right-click on the **Users** container, select **New**, and then click **User**.

6. In the New Object – User window, type **Testuser2** in the First name text box, and type **Testuser2** in the User logon name text box. Click **Next**.

7. In the Password text box type **Password01**, and then type **Password01** in the Confirm password text box. Uncheck the **User must change password at next logon** check box, click **Next**, and then click **Finish**.

8. Close Active Directory Users and Computers, and log off.

9. Log on using the Testuser1 account, using the password Password01. Once the logon process completes, notice that you are presented with the default user desktop environment.

10. Right-click on a blank area of the desktop, and click **Properties**.

11. Click on the **Desktop** tab. In the Background list, click on **Ascent**, and then click **OK**. The Ascent desktop wallpaper will appear on your desktop.

12. Log off, and then log back on using the Testuser1 account with a password of **Password01**. Notice that the Ascent wallpaper appears because it was saved as part of the Testuser1 profile.

13. Log off, and then log back on using the Testuser2 account with a password of **Password01**. Notice that the default user profile appears, because Testuser2 has not logged on to this system before.

14. Log off, and then log on using your Admin*XX* account.

15. Click **Start**, select **Control Panel**, and then click **System**.

16. Click the **Advanced** tab, and then click the **Settings** button in the User Profiles section. Notice that both the Testuser1 and Testuser2 profiles appear on the list as local profiles.

17. In the Profiles stored on this computer section, click **Domain*XX*\Admin*XX*** (where *XX* is your assigned student number) to select it if necessary. Notice that both the Delete and Copy To buttons are grayed out because you cannot delete or copy the profiles of the currently logged on user.

18. Click the **Domain*XX*\Testuser1** profile. Notice that all three buttons are now available.

19. Click the **Change Type** button. Notice that only the Local profile option is available, as shown in Figure 3-11. This is because a roaming profile does not exist for Testuser1. Click **Cancel**.

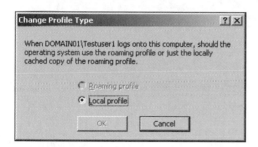

Figure 3-11   The Change Profile Type window

20. Click the **Delete** button. When the Confirm Delete dialog box appears, click **Yes**. Notice that the Testuser1 profile no longer appears on the list.

21. Click **OK** to close the User Profiles window, and then click **OK** to close the System Properties window.

22. Log off, and then log on using the Testuser1 account with the password **Password01**. Notice that the Ascent wallpaper no longer appears because the previously stored profile for Testuser1 was deleted in Step 20. Because a local profile did not exist, Testuser1 has had a new profile created based on the Default User profile.

23. Click **Start**, and then click **My Computer**.

24. Double-click on drive **C:**, and then double-click on the **Documents and Settings** folder. Double-click on the **Testuser1** folder. A list of some of the folders originally mentioned in Table 3-1 appears.

25. Click the **Tools** menu, and then click **Folder Options**. Click the **View** tab. In the Advanced settings section click the **Show hidden files and folders** radio button, and then click **OK**. Notice that all of the profile folders originally mentioned in Table 3-1 now appear, some of which were previously hidden from view. This is illustrated in Figure 3-12. Close the Testuser1 window.

26. Remain logged on to your server with the Testuser1 account.

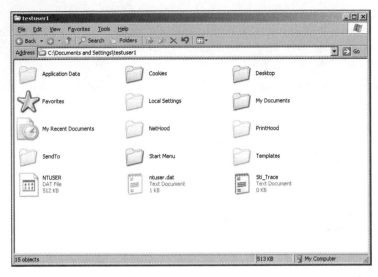

Figure 3-12   Folders in the Testuser1 local user profile

Roaming Profiles

In small and large organizations alike, users sometimes need to log on to different workstations. Although a user in a large organization may use the same workstation every day, a user working in a call center or bank may regularly log on to different computers. Regardless of frequency, the ability of a user's profile to be stored centrally on a server and follow them to different workstations is definitely useful.

In organizations where users always use the same workstation, **roaming profiles** provide the advantage of storing user desktop settings in a single, centralized location rather than locally on many different systems. This provides the advantage of being able to back up user profile settings in a central manner. In cases where users change workstations, the obvious benefit is that their user profile settings will follow them and remain consistent on different computers.

Roaming profiles are configured from the Profiles page of a user account's properties in Active Directory Users and Computers. The location in which the profile is stored is a shared folder on a network server, specified by a Universal Naming Convention (UNC) path such as \\serverXX\profiles\user name, where *profiles* is a shared folder, and *user name* is the specific folder in which a user's profile will be stored. Typically, roaming profiles are stored in a shared folder that resides on an NTFS partition, so that permissions can be configured such that only a specific user has access to their own profile. You learn more about NTFS permissions later in this book.

The network storage location for roaming profiles can be any Windows server system. There is no requirement to store roaming profiles on a domain controller.

3

Because user profiles are local by default, an administrator needs to give serious consideration to the implementation of roaming user profiles. For example, if a user has been using a local profile for some time, and that profile contains a large number of settings, the user would likely want (or need) to continue using those settings. Because of this, it is generally recommended that an administrator copy a user's existing local profile to a central server location first, and then configure the properties of the user's account to access this profile. This technique helps to ensure that the user's existing profile settings are not lost when a roaming profile is configured.

When a user logs on using a roaming profile for the first time, a copy of this profile is downloaded to the computer they have logged on to. If the user makes any changes to this profile, these changes are saved to the server location when the user logs off. Then, the updated profile settings are available to the user the next time they log on to the same computer or a different computer on the network.

In Activity 3-3 you configure and test roaming profile settings.

Activity 3-3: Configuring and Testing a Roaming Profile

Time required: 15 minutes

Objective: Configure and test a roaming user profile.

Description: The IT manager at Dover Leasing is concerned that local profiles will quickly become unmanageable since so many users at Dover need access to different desktops regularly. In particular, he is concerned about the decentralized nature of local profiles, and backing up user settings. As such, he has asked you to configure and test roaming profile settings on your Windows Server 2003 system. In this activity you create a shared folder in which to store roaming profiles, copy an existing local profile to this shared folder, and then configure the properties of a user account to use this network-based roaming profile.

1. Right-click on a blank area of the desktop, and click **Properties**.

2. Click on the **Desktop** tab. In the Background list, click on **Azul**, and then click **OK**. The Azul desktop wallpaper will appear on your desktop.

3. Log off, and then log back on using the Testuser1 account with a password of Password01. Notice that the Azul wallpaper appears because it was saved as part of the Testuser1 profile.

4. Click **Start**, click **Control Panel**, and then double-click **System**.

5. Click the **Advanced** tab, and then click the **Settings** button in the User Profiles section. Notice that the Testuser1 profile appears on the list as a local profile.

6. Click **Cancel** to exit the User Profiles window, and then click **Cancel** to exit the System Properties window. Close the Control Panel window.

7. Log off, and then log on using your Admin*XX* account.

8. Click **Start**, and then click **My Computer**.

9. Double-click on drive **D** to view its contents. Right-click on a blank area, select **New**, and click **Folder**.

10. Name the new folder **Profiles**. Right-click on the **Profiles** folder and click **Sharing and Security**.

11. On the Sharing tab, click the **Share this folder** radio button. This folder will be used to store roaming user profiles.

12. Click the **Permissions** button. In the Permissions for Profiles window, check the check box next to **Full Control** in the **Allow** column. Click **OK**. Click **OK** again to close the Profiles Properties window.

13. Close the **My Computer** window.

14. Click **Start**, select **Control Panel**, and then click **System**.

15. Click the **Advanced** tab, and then click the **Settings** button in the User Profiles section. Click on the **Domain*XX*\Testuser1** account, and then click the **Copy To** button.

16. In the Copy To window, type **\\Server*XX*\profiles\testuser1** in the Copy profile to text box, where *XX* is your assigned student number, as shown in Figure 3-13.

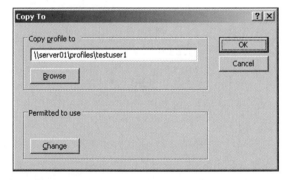

Figure 3-13   Copying a local profile to a network location

17. Click the **Change** button in the Permitted to use section. In the Enter the object name to select text box, type **Domain*XX*\Testuser1**, where *XX* is your assigned student number, and then click **OK**. Click **OK** to close the Copy To window.

18. Click **OK**. Click **OK** again to close the System Properties window. The local profile for Testuser1 has now been copied to the shared location specified.

19. Click **Start**, select **Administrative Tools**, and then click **Active Directory Users and Computers**.

3

20. Click on the **Users** container to view its contents if necessary.

21. Right-click on the **Testuser1** user account, and click **Properties**.

22. Click the **Profile** tab. In the Profile path text box, type
\\serverXX\profiles\testuser1, as shown in Figure 3-14. This is the path from
which Testuser1 will obtain their roaming profile the next time they log on.
Click **OK**.

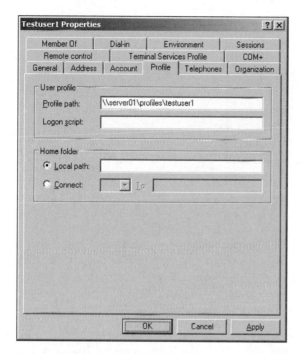

Figure 3-14   Configuring profile path settings in the properties of a user account

23. Close Active Directory Users and Computers, and then log off.

24. Log on using the Testuser1 account with the password Password01. Notice that the
Azul wallpaper configured for Testuser1 continues to appear as part of their profile.

25. Click **Start**, click **Control Panel**, and then double-click **System**.

26. Click the **Advanced** tab, and then click the **Settings** button in the User Profiles
section. Notice that the Testuser1 user profile now appears as a roaming profile, as
shown in Figure 3-15. Click **Cancel** to exit the User Profiles window, and then
click **Cancel** again to close the System Properties window. Close the Control Panel
window.

27. Log off and then log back on to your server using your AdminXX account.

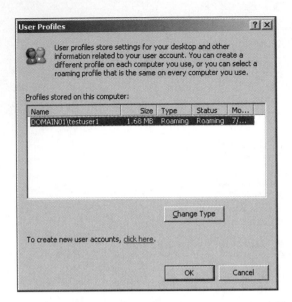

Figure 3-15   Confirming a roaming user profile

Mandatory Profiles

Both local and roaming user profiles allow a user to make changes to their profile settings according to their own preferences by default. For example, a user can change their desktop wallpaper, add additional shortcuts to their desktop, change the placement of desktop icons, add Internet Explorer favorites shortcuts, and more. While this customization provides the user with a flexible desktop environment, it is not suitable in all environments.

Consider the example of a large organization that needs to support many users. Some users may choose to change their wallpaper, delete desktop icons, remove shortcuts, and more. In cases where an organization is trying to standardize a desktop environment for training and support purposes, all users having different desktop environments can lead to increased support costs. Similarly, tellers at a bank probably expect to find applications and related shortcuts in the same desktop location, regardless of which workstation they log on to. If users change their desktop settings, it can ultimately lead to an inconsistent user environment, less efficiency, and increased support costs.

For this reason, Windows Server 2003 supports an alternate type of profile known as a **mandatory profile**. Mandatory profiles allow a user to change their profile while logged on, but the changes are not ultimately saved. For example, if a user is assigned a mandatory profile, they always receive the same profile when logging on. Although they can change or add desktop icons while logged on, any changes made are never saved to their profile when they log off. Because of this, the user always receives a consistent desktop environment at logon.

Both roaming and local user profiles can be configured as mandatory profiles. Changing a profile to be mandatory is not difficult, and simply involves renaming a single file stored in the profile, namely ntuser.dat. When the ntuser.dat file is renamed to ntuser.man, the settings in the profile become mandatory, and cannot be permanently changed by the user.

In Activity 3-4 you change the roaming user profile assigned to Testuser1 from a normal roaming profile to a mandatory roaming profile.

Activity 3-4: Configuring a Mandatory Profile

Time required: 10 minutes

Objective: Configure and test a mandatory user profile.

Description: The IT manager at Dover Leasing is interested in the possibility of implementing mandatory roaming profiles in order to ensure a consistent desktop environment for support and training purposes. In this activity you configure the roaming user profile for Testuser1 as a mandatory roaming profile.

1. Click **Start**, and then click **My Computer**.
2. Double-click on drive **D:**, double-click on the **Profiles** folder, and then double-click on the **Testuser1** folder.
3. In the Testuser1 folder, locate the file named ntuser.dat. Right-click on the **ntuser.dat** file, and click **Rename**.
4. Rename the ntuser.dat file to **ntuser.man**. The ntuser.man file is illustrated in Figure 3-16.

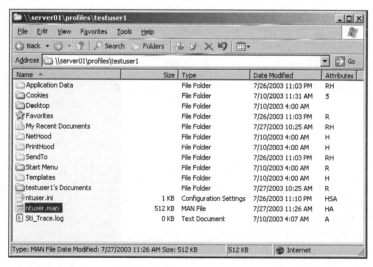

Figure 3-16 Creating a mandatory profile by renaming ntuser.dat to ntuser.man

5. Close the My Computer window.
6. Log off and then log on as Testuser1 with a password of Password01.

7. Right-click on a blank area of the desktop, and click **Properties**.

8. Click on the **Desktop** tab. In the Background list, click on **Autumn**, and then click **OK**. The Autumn desktop wallpaper will now appear on your desktop.

9. Log off and then log back on as Testuser1 with a password of **Password01**. Notice that the Autumn desktop wallpaper does not appear, and that the Azul wallpaper that is part of the mandatory profile is again used. Because the profile for Testuser1 is now mandatory, changes made to the profile are no longer saved when the user logs off.

10. Log off, and then log on using your AdminXX account.

CREATING AND MANAGING USER ACCOUNTS

Earlier in this chapter you learned that every user who needs access to a Windows Server 2003 network requires a unique user account. In an Active Directory environment, user accounts are created and stored on domain controllers, in the Active Directory database. Windows Server 2003 supports a number of different methods and tools for creating user account objects. Although the standard tool used for this purpose is Active Directory Users and Computers, Windows Server 2003 also provides a number of command line tools and utilities for adding, deleting, modifying, importing, and exporting user accounts.

This variety of tools allows an administrator to work from whichever environment they feel most comfortable with, or the environment most appropriate to a situation. For example, if an administrator is creating or editing the properties of a single user account, Active Directory Users and Computers would probably be the most logical tool to use. However, in cases where an administrator is creating or managing the properties of multiple users simultaneously, the process might be better undertaken or automated by using some of the command-line tools and utilities available in Windows Server 2003.

In the following sections you learn how to create and manage user accounts using both Active Directory Users and Computers as well as various command line utilities.

Active Directory Users and Computers

The primary tool used to create and manage user accounts in an Active Directory environment is Active Directory Users and Computers. Available from the Administrative Tools menu, it can also be added to a custom Microsoft Management Console (MMC) or opened directly from the Run command by its filename, dsa.msc. This graphical tool makes it easy for administrators to add, modify, move, and delete user accounts as necessary based on the needs of a specific organization. Because Active Directory implementations may ultimately scale to very large sizes with thousands of user objects, this tool also includes the ability to search for user objects based on different settings or criteria.

The version of Active Directory Users and Computers supplied with Windows Server 2003 is functionally very similar to the Windows 2000 version. It has been enhanced, however, to include some additional features, such as the ability to move objects between containers, such as the Users container and an organizational unit (OU), for example, using common Windows techniques like drag and drop. Another new feature is the inclusion of a node called Saved Queries, which allows an administrator to search for user accounts quickly based on specific settings, such as all users with a particular manager or all accounts that have been disabled. The Active Directory Users and Computers interface is illustrated in Figure 3-17.

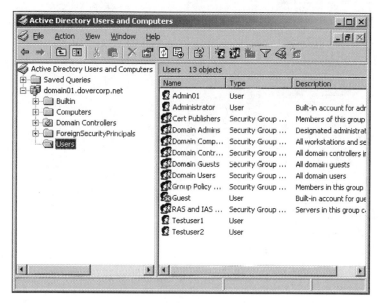

Figure 3-17   Active Directory Users and Computers

As you learned in Activity 3-2, creating user accounts in Active Directory Users and Computers is as simple as right clicking on a particular container (such as Users), selecting New, and then clicking User. This opens the New Object – User window, as shown in Figure 3-18.

Although the built-in Users container may seem like the most logical place to create new user objects, it is not the only place they can be created or located. In larger Active Directory implementations, administrators will typically create additional OU objects to organize users for administration and **Group Policy** application. For example, an OU named Marketing might contain all of the user, computer, and group accounts associated with users in the Marketing department. After a user object is created in one container, it can easily be moved to another, either by selecting the object and then dragging it onto the new destination container, or by right-clicking on the object and selecting Move. The Move window is shown in Figure 3-19.

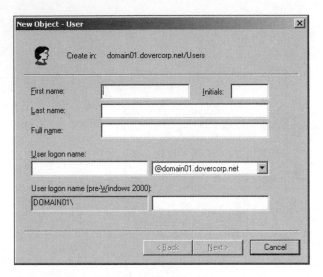

Figure 3-18   The New Object – User window

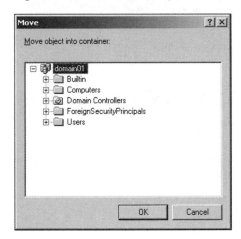

Figure 3-19   The Move window

In Activity 3–5 you create a number of new user objects using Active Directory Users and Computers.

Activity 3-5: Creating User Accounts Using Active Directory Users and Computers

Time required: 20 minutes

Objective: Use Active Directory Users and Computers to create user accounts.

Description: In the past, Dover Leasing hasn't had a set naming convention for user accounts. Some accounts were created using first names only, while other variations were used as the company grew larger. Hoping to address some of the scalability issues previously encountered, Dover's IT manager has decided that all corporate user names should follow a convention of first initial and last name. For cases where two users have the same name, the solution will be to use the first initial of subsequent users' middle names to ensure uniqueness. In this activity, you create a number of new user accounts within your dedicated child domain.

1. Click **Start**, select **Administrative Tools**, and click **Active Directory Users and Computers**.

2. Right-click the **Users** container, select **New**, and click **User**.

3. In the New Object – User dialog box, type **John** in the First name text box.

4. Press the **Tab** key twice to reach the Last name text box and type **Smith**. Notice that the Full name text box is populated automatically.

5. Press the **Tab** key twice to reach the User logon name field. Type **jsmith** and press the **Tab** key.

6. In the list box, ensure that your domain name in the form @Domain*XX*.Dovercorp. net is selected rather than the @Dovercorp.net domain. Click the **Next** button.

7. In the Password text box, shown in Figure 3-20, type **Password01** and press the Tab key. In the Confirm password text box, type **Password01** again.

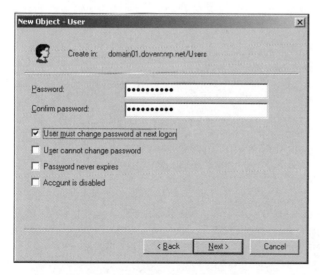

Figure 3-20   Configuring an initial password for a new user object

8. Uncheck the **User must change password at next logon** check box and click **Next**. Click **Finish**.

9. Repeat Steps 2 through 8 to create user accounts for **Mark Manore**, **Frank Adili**, **Christy Jackson**, **John Harold Smith**, **Chris Medved**, **Moira Cowan**, **Mike Aubert**, and **Alan Finn**. Remember to use the user account naming convention originally specified in the description for this activity.

10. When finished, close Active Directory Users and Computers.

The settings configured as part of creating a new user object in Active Directory Users and Computers are fairly limited. Once a new user object has been created, additional attribute settings are configured from the properties of the account, as originally explored in Activity 3-1. From the properties of a user object an administrator can easily add a user to different groups, configure profile settings, and so forth.

Although configuring the properties of each user account individually is possible, it can also be very time consuming, especially when hundreds or even thousands of user accounts need to be created. In many cases, multiple user accounts require the same property settings, and configuring these settings simultaneously can greatly reduce the amount of time and administrative effort required. For this reason, Active Directory Users and Computers includes another new feature in Windows Server 2003, namely the ability to configure the properties of multiple user objects simultaneously. When multiple user objects are selected (by pressing the CTRL key and clicking on different user accounts), accessing the properties of those objects allows you to configure settings on the following tabs once, for all selected accounts:

- General
- Account
- Address
- Profile
- Organization

For example, an administrator could select multiple user accounts and then configure all of them with the same Office setting on the General tab, as illustrated in Figure 3-21.

TIP

One of the benefits of being able to configure settings on multiple user objects simultaneously is that you can take advantage of variables. For example, when configuring the UNC path for a user's profile, you can use the %username% variable in the place of a folder bearing the user's name. This ultimately creates a folder bearing their user name automatically.

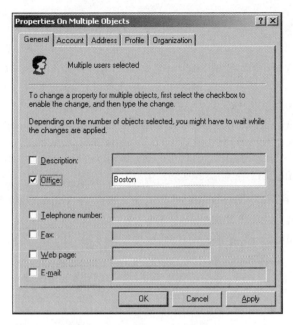

Figure 3-21   Configuring properties for multiple user objects simultaneously

User Account Templates

In order to reduce the time and administrative burden associated with creating new user accounts, many administrators create new user objects by copying a pre-defined template. A **user account template** is simply a user account that is pre-configured with the common settings associated with a particular type of user. For example, when creating new user accounts for users in the Marketing department, a large number of settings are likely to be similar. Because of this, an administrator could create a new user account called Marketing Template, and then populate this account with the common settings required by all marketing users, such as group membership, user profile, and organizational information. Then, when a new user account in the marketing department needs to be created, an administrator can simply copy this account, providing new user name and password information specific to the user.

Only the most common configuration settings are copied to a new user account by default. The settings that are copied when a new user account is created from a template can be controlled by modifying the "Attribute is copied when duplicating user" check box in the Active Directory schema. For more information on the Active Directory schema, see the Windows Server 2003 Help and Support Center.

In Activity 3-6 you configure a new user account template in Active Directory Users and Computers, and then copy that template in order to create a new user account.

ACTIVITY

Activity 3-6: Creating a User Account Template

Time required: 10 minutes

Objective: Create a user account template and then use that template to create a new user account.

Description: The IT manager at Dover Leasing has asked you to standardize on a method of creating new user accounts. Ultimately, the goal is to reduce the administrative effort and risk of misconfiguration associated with creating new user accounts, especially by junior administrators. In this activity you first create a new user account template, and then copy that template in order to create another new user account.

1. Click **Start**, select **Administrative Tools**, and then click **Active Directory Users and Computers**.

2. Right-click the **Users** container, select **New**, and click **User**.

3. In the New Object – User dialog box, type **_Contractor Template** in the First name text box. Be sure to add the underscore "_" character at the beginning of the name. This will ensure that the template account appears at the top of the user listing when sorted alphabetically by name, making it easier to find when required.

4. Press the **Tab** key four times to reach the User logon name field. Type **contractortemplate** and click **Next**.

5. In the Password text box, type **Password01** and press the **Tab** key. In the Confirm password text box, type **Password01** again. (Passwords are not copied as part of creating a new user account from a template.)

6. Uncheck the **User must change password at next logon** check box and click **Next**. Click **Finish**.

7. Right-click on the **_Contractor Template** user account, and click **Properties**.

8. In the Description text box on the General tab, type **Contractor User**.

9. Click the **Profile** tab. In the Profile path text box, type **\\serverXX\profiles\%username%**. The use of the %username% variable will automatically populate this field with the name of the user account when copied to new accounts.

10. Click the **Member Of** tab. Notice that this account is a member of the Domain Users group by default.

11. Click the **Add** button. In the Enter the object names to select text box on the Select Groups window, type **Domain Guests** and click **OK**. This adds the template account to the Domain Guests group, as shown in Figure 3-22. Click **OK**.

12. Right-click on the **_Contractor Template** user account and click **Disable Account**. User account templates should always be disabled for security purposes. When the Active Directory dialog box appears, click **OK**.

13. Right-click on the **_Contractor Template** user account and click **Copy**.

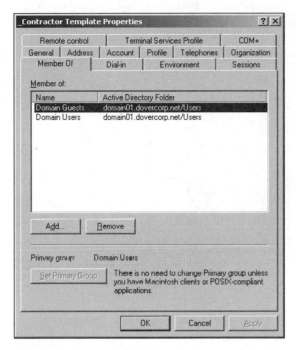

Figure 3-22   The Member Of tab for a user account template

14. The Copy Object – User dialog box appears. Type **Jim** in the First name text box.

15. Press the **Tab** key twice to reach the Last name text box and type **Johnson**.

16. Press the **Tab** key twice to reach the User logon name field. Type **jjohnson** and click **Next**.

17. In the Password text box, type **Password01** and press the **Tab** key. In the Confirm password text box, type **Password01** again. Notice that the Account is disabled check box is checked by default.

18. Uncheck the **Account is disabled** check box, and click **Next**.

19. Review the settings shown in Figure 3-23. Notice that this screen explicitly states that this user is being copied from _Contractor Template. Click **Finish**.

20. Right-click on the **Jim Johnson** user account and click **Properties**. Click on the **General**, **Member Of**, and **Profile** tabs to confirm that settings configured in the _Contractor Template account have been copied to the Jim Johnson user account. Click **Cancel** once you have confirmed these settings.

21. Close Active Directory Users and Computers.

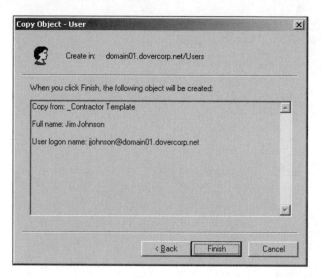

Figure 3-23   Creating a new user by copying a user account template

Command Line Utilities

While Active Directory Users and Computers is the primary tool used to create and manage domain user accounts, Windows Server 2003 includes a variety of new utilities that allow you to create and manage user accounts from the command line. These utilities are aimed at administrators with a preference for working from the command line, or those looking to automate the creation or management of user accounts in a more flexible manner. The command line utilities to be looked at in the following sections include:

- DSADD—Adds objects such as users.
- DSMOD—Modifies object attributes and settings.
- DSQUERY—Queries for objects.
- DSMOVE—Moves objects to different locations within a domain.
- DSRM—Deletes objects from the directory.

DSADD

DSADD allows various object types to be added to the directory. Examples of objects that can be added to the directory with DSADD include computer accounts, contacts, quotas, groups, OUs, and users.

The basic syntax for creating a user account with DSADD is DSADD USER, followed by a variety of different switches that allow you to configure everything from profile paths to group membership information for a single account. The basic syntax for adding a user with the DSADD USER tool consists of only a single piece of information, namely the distinguished name of the account to be created. In Chapter 1 you were introduced to the concept of a distinguished name, which identifies an object in LDAP format.

For example, to create a user account name Mark Jones in the Users container of the domain01.dovercorp.net domain, the correct command syntax would be:

```
dsadd user "cn=Mark Jones,cn=users,dc=domain01,dc=dovercorp,dc=net"
```

In cases where any spaces exist in the distinguished name, the entire name must be enclosed in quotes in a manner similar to this example. If the DSADD USER command completes successfully, a message stating "dsadd succeeded" will be displayed, similar to Figure 3-24.

```
Command Prompt                                                      _ □ ×
C:\>dsadd user "cn=Mark Jones,cn=users,dc=domain01,dc=dovercorp,dc=net"
dsadd succeeded:cn=Mark Jones,cn=users,dc=domain01,dc=dovercorp,dc=net

C:\>
```

Figure 3-24   The DSADD USER command

The DSADD account supports a wide variety of switches used to configure different account attributes. The list below provides examples of the more common attributes that might be configured with the DSADD USER command.

- -pwd—Specifies a password for the user account being added.
- -memberof—Specifies groups that the user should be made a member of.
- -email—Specifies the e-mail address of the user.
- -profile—Specifies the profile path for the user.
- -disabled—Specifies whether the account will be initially enabled or disabled.

The following command is an example of creating a new user account named Paul Kohut in the Users container of the domain01.dovercorp.net domain, including values for the switches just explored. Note that the entire command is a single line:

```
dsadd user "cn=Paul Kohut,cn=Users,dc=domain01,dc=dovercorp,dc=net" -pwd
Password01 -memberof "cn=domain
guests,cn=users,dc=domain01,dc=dovercorp,dc=net" -email
paul@dovercorp.net -profile "\\server01\profiles\paul kohut" -disabled no
```

For a complete list of the various switches and options available with the DSADD USER command, see the DSADD topic in Windows Server 2003 Help and Support or type DSADD USER /? at the command line.

In Activity 3-7 you create two new user accounts using the DSADD utility.

Activity 3-7: Creating User Accounts Using DSADD

Time required: 10 minutes

Objective: Create new user accounts using the DSADD USER command.

Description: The IT manager at Dover Leasing has asked you to explore different processes for creating user accounts from the command line. Ultimately, the goal is to be able to create user accounts via a telnet session with remote servers when necessary. In this activity you will use the DSADD USER command to create two new user accounts from the command line.

1. Click **Start**, and then click **Run**.

2. In the Open text box, type **cmd.exe**, and click **OK**.

3. At the command prompt window, type **cd ..** and press **Enter**. Type **cd ..** again and press **Enter**. This will help to reduce the on-screen clutter associated with the command prompt path.

4. Type **cls** and press **Enter** to clear the screen.

5. At the command line, type the following, all in one line: **dsadd user "cn=Mark Jones,cn=users,dc=domainXX,dc=dovercorp,dc=net"**, where *XX* is your student number. Press **Enter**. If the dsadd succeeded message appears, the new user account has been created successfully. If you receive an error message, type the command again being careful to avoid errors.

6. Minimize the Command Prompt window.

7. Click **Start**, select **Administrative Tools**, and then click **Active Directory Users and Computers**.

8. Click on the **Users** container to view its contents. Notice that the Mark Jones user account now appears in the container, but that it is disabled by default.

9. Minimize Active Directory Users and Computers, and maximize the Command Prompt window.

10. At the command line, type the following, all in one line: **dsadd user "cn=Paul Kohut,cn=Users,dc=domainXX,dc=dovercorp,dc=net" –pwd Password01 –memberof "cn=domain guests, cn=users,dc=domainXX,dc=dovercorp, dc=net" –email paul@dovercorp.net -profile "\\serverXX\profiles\paul kohut" –disabled no**, where *XX* is your student number. Press **Enter**. If the dsadd succeeded message appears, the new user account has been created successfully. If you receive an error message, type the command again being careful to avoid errors.

11. Close the Command Prompt window, and then maximize the Active Directory Users and Computers window.

12. Right-click on the **Users** container, and then click **Refresh**. Notice that the Paul Kohut user account now appears in the Users container.

13. Right-click on the **Paul Kohut** user account and click **Properties**.

14. On the General tab, confirm that the configured e-mail address is paul@dovercorp.net.

15. Click the **Profile** tab. Confirm the profile path specified in \\server*XX*\profiles\paul kohut, where *XX* is your assigned student number.

16. Click on the **Member Of** tab. Confirm that this account is a member of the Domain Guests group.

17. Click **Cancel**, and then close Active Directory Users and Computers.

DSMOD

DSMOD allows various objects types to be modified from the command line. Examples of directory objects that can be modified with DSMOD include computer accounts, contacts, quotas, groups, OUs, servers, partitions, and users.

The basic syntax for modifying a user account with DSMOD is DSMOD USER, followed by a variety of different switches that allow you to modify everything from profile paths to group membership information for a single account. Since DSMOD USER is used to modify an existing user account, the command requires that you specify the distinguished name of the object to be modified, along with at least one switch (which would specify a particular modification).

For example, to add the description "Marketing Manager" to an existing user account named Mark Jones in the Users container of the domain01.dovercorp.net domain, the correct command syntax would be:

```
dsmod user "cn=Mark Jones,cn=users,dc=domain01,dc=dovercorp,dc=net"
-desc "Marketing Manager"
```

If the DSMOD USER command completes successfully, a message stating "dsmod succeeded" will be displayed, similar to Figure 3-25.

Figure 3-25 The DSMOD USER command

Similarly, the DSMOD USER command can be used to change settings associated with multiple user accounts simultaneously. For example, to change the fax number associated with both the Mark Jones and Paul Kohut user accounts in the Users container of the domain01.dovercorp.net domain, the correct command syntax would be:

```
dsmod user "cn=Mark Jones,cn=users,dc=domain01,dc=dovercorp,dc=net"
"cn=Paul Kohut,cn=users,dc=domain01,dc=dovercorp,dc=net" -fax "800-
555-5555"
```

For a complete list of the various switches and options available with the DSMOD USER command, see the DSMOD topic in Windows Server 2003 Help and Support or type DSMOD USER /? at the command line.

In Activity 3-8 you modify the settings of two user accounts using the DSMOD USER command.

Activity 3-8: Modifying User Accounts Using DSMOD

Time required: 10 minutes

Objective: Modify existing user account properties using the DSMOD USER command.

Description: The IT manager at Dover Leasing has asked you to explore different processes for modifying user accounts from the command line. Ultimately, the goal is to be able to modify user accounts via a telnet session with remote servers when necessary. In this activity you use the DSMOD USER command to modify two existing user accounts from the command line.

1. Click **Start**, and then click **Run**.

2. In the Open text box, type **cmd.exe**, and click **OK**.

3. At the command prompt window, type **cd ..** and press **Enter**. Type **cd ..** again and press **Enter**.

4. Type **cls** and press **Enter** to clear the screen.

5. At the command line, type the following, all in one line: **dsmod user "cn=Mark Jones,cn=users,dc=domainXX,dc=dovercorp,dc=net" –desc "Marketing Manager"**, where *XX* is your assigned student number. Press **Enter**. If the dsmod succeeded message appears, the modification has completed successfully. If you receive an error message, type the command again being careful to avoid errors.

6. Minimize the Command Prompt window.

7. Click **Start**, select **Administrative Tools**, and then click **Active Directory Users and Computers**.

8. Click the **Users** container if necessary to view its contents. Right-click on the **Mark Jones** user account and click **Properties**.

9. On the General tab, confirm that the words Marketing Manager now appear in the Description text box. Click **Cancel**.

10. Minimize Active Directory Users and Computers, and maximize the Command Prompt.

11. At the command line, type the following, all in one line: **dsmod user "cn=Mark Jones,cn=users,dc=domainXX,dc=dovercorp,dc=net" "cn=Paul Kohut,cn=users,dc=domainXX,dc=dovercorp,dc=net" –fax "800-555-5555"**, where *XX* is your assigned student number. Press **Enter**. If the dsmod succeeded message appears, the modification has completed successfully. If you receive an error message, type the command again being careful to avoid errors.

12. Close the Command Prompt window, and then maximize the Active Directory Users and Computers window.

13. Right-click on the **Paul Kohut** user account in the Users container and click **Properties**.

14. Click on the **Telephones** tab to confirm that the fax number configured using the DSMOD command is displayed in the Fax text box. Click **Cancel**.

15. Repeat Steps 13 and 14 to confirm that the fax number has also been configured for the Mark Jones user account.

16. Close Active Directory Users and Computers.

DSQUERY

DSQUERY allows various objects types to be queried from the command line. Examples of directory objects that can be queried for with DSQUERY include computer accounts, contacts, quotas, groups, OUs, servers, partitions, and users. The DSQUERY command also supports the wildcard character (*), effectively allowing it to query for any type of directory object.

At the most basic level, DSQUERY allows you to query the directory for a particular type of object, and return a value. For example, to view all of the user objects in the Users container of the domain01.dovercorp.net domain that are currently disabled, the correct command syntax would be:

```
dsquery user "cn=users,dc=domain01,dc=dovercorp,dc=net" -disabled
```

This command returns a list of the distinguished names of all disabled user accounts in the Users container, as illustrated in Figure 3-26.

Figure 3-26 The DSQUERY USER command

Along the same lines, the DSQUERY USER command can be used to view all of the accounts in a particular domain that have not changed their password in the past 14 days. The correct syntax for this command would be:

```
dsquery user domainroot -name * -stalepwd 14
```

One of the most powerful uses of the DSQUERY command is that its output can be redirected to another command. For example, an administrator might want to automatically disable all of the user accounts that have not changed their password in the last 30 days. Rather than searching for this information using DSQUERY USER and then using DSMOD USER or Active Directory Users and Computers to modify the accounts, the output of the DSQUERY USER command could be piped as input to the DSMOD USER command. In this example, the correct command syntax would be:

```
dsquery user domainroot -name * -stalepwd 30 | dsmod user -disabled
yes
```

The results of piping the output of the DSQUERY USER command to the DSMOD USER command are illustrated in Figure 3-27.

Figure 3-27   Piping the output of the DSQUERY USER command to the DSMOD USER command

 For a complete list of the various switches and options available with the DSQUERY USER command, see the DSQUERY topic in Windows Server 2003 Help and Support or type DSQUERY USER /? at the command line.

DSMOVE

DSMOVE allows various object types to be moved from the object's current location to a new location in the directory, or to rename an object without moving it to a new location.

For example, an administrator might want to move a user account from the Users container into an OU named Marketing. Assuming that the user to be moved is named Paul Kohut and the domain is domain01.dovercorp.net, the correct command syntax to move the user to the new OU would be:

```
dsmove "cn=Paul Kohut,cn=users,dc=domain01,dc=dovercorp,dc=net"
-newparent "ou=marketing,dc=domain01,dc=dovercorp,dc=net"
```

Along the same lines, if Paul Kohut had left the company and was to be replaced by a new user named Johnny Wong, the administrator might chose to simply rename the Paul Kohut user account. Assuming that this account will still exist in the Marketing OU, the correct syntax for this command would be:

```
dsmove "cn=Paul Kohut,ou=marketing,dc=domain01,dc=dovercorp,dc=net"
-newname "Johnny Wong"
```

It is important to understand that the DSMOVE command can only be used to move objects within the same domain. It cannot be used to move an object from one domain to another. If you need to move an object from one domain to another, use the MOVETREE command available when the Windows Server 2003 Support Tools are installed.

For a complete list of the various switches and options available with the DSMOVE USER command, see the DSMOVE topic in Windows Server 2003 Help and Support or type DSMOVE USER /? at the command line.

NOTE

DSRM

The **DSRM** command allows objects to be deleted from the directory. This tool is powerful because it supports the ability to delete not only a single object, but also an entire subtree of objects.

For example, an administrator can specify that only a single object should be deleted by specifying the object's distinguished name. To delete the Mark Jones user account in the Users container of the domain01.dovercorp.net domain, the correct command syntax is:

```
dsrm "cn=Mark Jones,cn=users,dc=domain01,dc=dovercorp,dc=net"
```

After issuing this command, the administrator is prompted to confirm deletion of this object by default, as shown in Figure 3-28.

Figure 3-28 Confirming the deletion of an object with the DSRM command

If the administrator wants to delete the Mark Jones user object without the need to confirm the deletion, the correct command syntax would be:

```
dsrm "cn=Mark Jones,cn=users,dc=domain01,dc=dovercorp,dc=net"
-noprompt
```

The DSRM command can also be used to delete an existing object and its contents if necessary. For example, to delete the Marketing OU (along with all of the objects that it contains) without being prompted to confirm the action, the correct command syntax would be:

```
dsrm -subtree -noprompt -c "ou=marketing,dc=domain01,
dc=dovercorp,dc=net"
```

Conversely, if the administrator wants to delete all of the objects in the Marketing OU, but leave the Marketing OU itself intact, the correct command syntax would be:

```
dsrm -subtree -exclude -noprompt -c "ou=marketing,
dc=domain01,dc=dovercorp,dc=net"
```

Be very careful when using the -noprompt switch with the DSRM command, as you might inadvertently delete required objects.

For a complete list of the various switches and options available with the DSRM USER command, see the DSRM topic in Windows Server 2003 Help and Support or type DSREM USER /? at the command line.

Bulk Import and Export

In large environments, companies may be in the process of transitioning from one directory service to another, or have reams of user data stored in various databases. Rather then manually create hundreds or thousands of user accounts and related objects from scratch, many companies look towards utilities that allow them to import existing stores of data.

Along the same lines, the information stored in a directory service like Active Directory contains a wealth of useful information if properly maintained and kept up-to-date. Companies might be interested in exporting this information for the purpose of populating secondary databases, such as an application used by human resources staff.

To provide administrators with the flexibility to import and export data to or from Active Directory, Windows Server 2003 includes two main utilities, known as **CSVDE** and **LDIFDE**. You learn more about each of these utilities in the following sections.

CSVDE

CSVDE is a command-line tool that supports the bulk export and import of Active Directory data to and from comma-separated value (CSV) files. One of the benefits of the CSV file format is that its structure allows these files to be easily created or opened in a traditional text editor, database program, or spreadsheet application like Microsoft Excel. When data is exported from Active Directory using CSVDE, the first line of the file contains the name of each attribute being exported, separated by commas. Each subsequent line represents a specific object stored in the directory, with attribute values ordered according to that first line.

For example, CSVDE can be used to export information about all current objects stored in Active Directory to a text file. In the following example, information about objects stored in Active Directory would be exported to a text file named output.csv:

```
csvde -f output.csv
```

Opening the resulting file in a text editor like Notepad would display the exported information in CSV format, as illustrated in Figure 3-29.

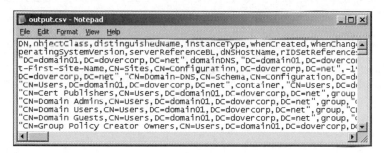

Figure 3-29   Data exported using the CSVDE command

Ultimately, an administrator might choose to import the information stored in the CSVDE file to a different directory or application. In a similar manner, data stored in an existing CSV file, perhaps exported from another LDAP directory, can also be imported into Active Directory to create new objects (such as user accounts) using a bulk process. When importing a file for the purpose of creating new user objects, the key consideration is that the format of the CSV file is correct. For best results, use the first line of an exported CSV file to determine the correct syntax required for such a file to be imported.

For more information about the CSVDE command, see the CSVDE topic in Windows Server 2003 Help and Support Center, or type CSVDE /? at the command line.

LDIFDE

In a manner similar to CSVDE, the LDIFDE utility is a command line tool that can be used to import and export data from Active Directory. Unlike CSVDE, which works with CSV files, LDIFDE uses a file format known as LDAP Interchange Format (LDIF). LDIF is an industry standard method for formatting information imported to or exported from LDAP directories.

Some common uses of LDIFDE and the LDIF file format include extending the Active Directory schema; adding, modifying, and deleting user and group objects; and importing bulk data from an existing directory to populate the Active Directory database.

Unlike a CSV file, where a comma separates every attribute, LDIF files place each attribute and its associated value on a separate line, with a blank line separating individual objects.

The file format associated with LDIFDE is LDF, but these files can be read in any text editor in a manner similar to those created with CSVDE. In Activity 3-9 you export data from Active Directory using the LDIFDE utility.

ACTIVITY

Activity 3-9: Exporting Active Directory Users Using LDIFDE

Time required: 5 minutes

Objective: Export Active Directory data using LDIFDE.

Description: The IT Manager at Dover Leasing has asked you to determine a way to export Active Directory user account settings to ultimately be imported into another LDAP-compliant application. In this activity you use LDIFDE to export user accounts and selected attributes to an LDF file.

1. Click **Start**, and then click **Run**.

2. In the Open text box, type **cmd.exe**, and then press **Enter**.

3. Type **d:** at the command prompt and press **Enter**.

4. Type the following command, all on one line: **ldifde –f exportusers.ldf –s Server*XX* –d "dc=Domain*XX*,dc=Dovercorp,dc=net" –p subtree –r "(&(objectCategory=person)(objectClass=User)(givenname=*))" –l "cn,givenName,objectclass,samAccountName"**, where *XX* is your assigned student number, and press **Enter**. This will export all user accounts from your domain to the LDIF file named exportusers.ldf. If you receive an error message, type the command again being careful to avoid errors.

5. Close the **Command Prompt**.

6. Click **Start**, and then click **My Computer**.

7. Double-click on drive **D:** to view its contents.

8. Double-click on the **exportusers.ldf** file.

9. At the Windows dialog box, click the **Select the program from a list** radio button, and then click **OK**.

10. At the Open With window, click **Notepad**, and then click **OK**.

11. When the exportusers.ldf file opens in Notepad, scroll through the entries in the file, noticing that each entry corresponds to an Active Directory user account, as shown in Figure 3-30.

12. Close all open windows.

```
exportusers.ldf - Notepad                                      _ □ X
File  Edit  Format  View  Help
dn: CN=Admin01,CN=Users,DC=domain01,DC=dovercorp,DC=net          ▲
changetype: add
objectClass: top
objectClass: person
objectClass: organizationalPerson
objectClass: user
cn: Admin01
givenName: Admin01
sAMAccountName: admin01

dn: CN=Testuser1,CN=Users,DC=domain01,DC=dovercorp,DC=net
changetype: add
objectClass: top
objectClass: person
objectClass: organizationalPerson
objectClass: user
cn: Testuser1
givenName: Testuser1
sAMAccountName: Testuser1

dn: CN=Testuser2,CN=Users,DC=domain01,DC=dovercorp,DC=net
changetype: add
objectClass: top
objectClass: person
objectClass: organizationalPerson
objectClass: user                                                ▼
◄                                                              ► ⸢
```

Figure 3-30   User data exported using the LDIFDE command

For more information about the LDIFDE command, see the LDIFDE topic in Windows Server 2003 Help and Support Center, or type LDIFDE /? at the command line.

NOTE

TROUBLESHOOTING USER ACCOUNT AND AUTHENTICATION ISSUES

Although creating and configuring user accounts is a relatively straightforward process, a number of issues can impact a user's ability to log on to a Windows Server 2003 Active Directory network. Some of these issues are directly related to the configuration of a user account, such as account lockout. In other cases, various policy settings may prohibit a user from being successfully authenticated either interactively or over the network. In the following sections learn some of the key policy settings that can impact the user authentication process, methods of gathering more information about authentication issues, and solutions to common authentication problems.

Account Policies

A variety of configuration settings can and do impact the user authentication process in an Active Directory domain environment. Some of the most important settings to consider are those configured in the Account Policies node of Group Policy objects applied at the domain level. While Group Policy objects and related settings is looked at in more detail in Chapter 11, this section focuses on authentication-related settings, namely those dealing with account lockout, passwords, and Kerberos.

Windows Server 2003 creates a default Group Policy object at the domain level called the Default Domain Policy. Although this object can be configured with a wide variety of different settings, the domain level is the only level at which account lockout, password, and Kerberos settings can be configured for all domain users. The Default Domain Policy can be accessed from Active Directory Users and Computers by right-clicking the domain object, clicking Properties, and then clicking on the Group Policy tab, as shown in Figure 3-31.

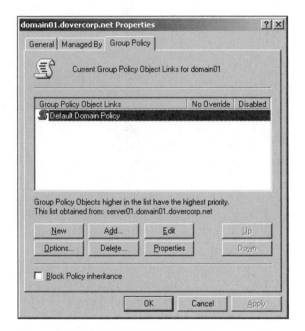

Figure 3-31   The Group Policy tab

Clicking the Edit button opens the Group Policy Object Editor window. The Account Policies node is found in the Computer Configuration section, under Windows Settings – Security Settings – Account Policies, as shown in Figure 3-32.

In the following sections you learn more about each of the three main Account Policies nodes:

- Password Policy
- Account Lockout Policy
- Kerberos Policy

In learning about each node and its configurable settings, pay particular attention to the impact it can have on authentication-related issues.

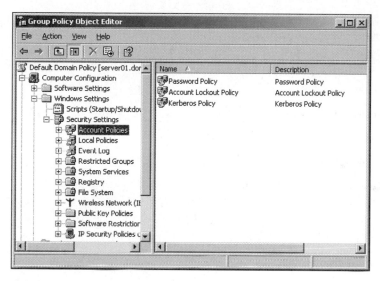

Figure 3-32   The Account Policies node

Password Policy

The Password Policy node contains configuration settings that refer to the required history, age, length, and complexity of user passwords. Settings found in this section don't usually impact a user's ability to authenticate (if they know and submit their current and correct password), but they do impact how often a user must change their password, when their password expires, and so forth. The following list outlines each individual policy item, its default setting, and its intended purpose:

- Enforce password history—Defines the number of passwords that have to be unique before a user can reuse an old password. The default configuration setting is 24 passwords remembered.

- Maximum password age—Defines the number of days that a password can be used before the user is required to change it. The default configuration setting is 42 days.

- Minimum password age—Defines the number of days that a password must be used before a user is allowed to change it. The default configuration setting is one day.

- Minimum password length—Defines the least number of characters required in a password (values can be from 1 to 14 characters); if no password is required, set the value to zero. The default configuration setting is seven characters.

- Passwords must meet complexity requirements—Increases password complexity by enforcing rules that passwords must meet. This setting is enabled by default. A complex password cannot include any portion of the user's account name, must be at least six characters in length, and must include three of the four elements below:
  - English uppercase letters
  - English lowercase letters
  - Numbers
  - Non-alphanumeric (for example, !, $, #)
- Store passwords using reversible encryption—This setting is the same as storing passwords in clear text; this policy provides support for applications using protocols that need the passwords in clear text for authentication purposes. This setting is disabled by default.

Account Lockout Settings

The Account Lockout Policy node contains configuration settings that refer to the password lockout threshold and duration, as well as reset options. Settings configured in this section may impact the user authentication process by locking out user accounts after a specified number of incorrect logon attempts, such as when a user enters an incorrect user name and password combination. The following list outlines each individual policy item, its default setting, and its intended purpose:

- Account lockout duration—Defines the number of failed logon attempts that results in the user account being locked. This setting is not defined by default.
- Account lockout threshold—Defines the number of incorrect logon attempts that must occur before an account is locked out. The default value is zero, meaning that accounts will never be locked out.
- Reset account lockout counter after—Determines the number of minutes that must elapse after a single failed logon attempt before the bad logon counter is reset to zero. This setting is not configured by default.

Kerberos Policy

The Kerberos Policy node contains configuration settings that refer to the Kerberos ticket-granting ticket (TGT) and session ticket lifetimes and time stamp settings. Settings configured in this section may impact both a user's ability to log on to the network, as well as their ability to access network resources. For example, Kerberos relies upon time-stamped tickets in order to ensure that old tickets cannot be reused. If the clock on a user desktop is greatly out of sync with the KDC (a domain controller), the user will not be allowed to log on to the network. The following list outlines each individual policy item, its default setting, and its intended purpose:

- Enforce user logon restrictions—Requires the Key Distribution Center (KDC), a service of Kerberos V5, to validate every request for a session ticket against the user rights policy of the target computer; if enforced, there may be performance degradation on network access. This setting is enabled by default.

- Maximum lifetime for service ticket—Determines the maximum amount of time, in minutes, that a service ticket is valid to access a resource; the default is 600 minutes (10 hours).

- Maximum lifetime for user ticket—Determines the maximum amount of time, in hours, that a TGT may be used; the default is 10 hours.

- Maximum lifetime for user ticket renewal—Determines the amount of time, in days, that a user's TGT may be renewed; the default is seven days.

- Maximum tolerance for computer clock synchronization—Determines the amount of time difference, in minutes, that Kerberos tolerates between the client machine's clock and the time on the server's clock; the default is five minutes.

Auditing Authentication

Although the auditing feature of Windows Server 2003 is looked at in more detail in Chapter 14, the ability to audit account logon events can provide administrators with useful troubleshooting information relating to authentication.

Windows Server 2003 is capable of auditing one type of event related to users logging on to an Active Directory domain. This setting, known as Audit account logon events, is configured in a Group Policy object linked to the Domain Controllers OU. The name of this policy is the Default Domain Controllers Policy.

By default, a Windows Server 2003 domain controller is configured to audit "success" account logon events only. A success account logon event is related to a user being able to log on to the domain successfully. In cases where user logon is successful, a Windows Server 2003 domain controller will add an event to its Security log, which is accessible in Event Viewer. Administrators should also consider auditing "failure" account logon events for both a higher degree of security and troubleshooting purposes. A failure account logon event would be generated when a user fails to log on successfully, such as if they provided an incorrect user name or password. In cases where you are trying to determine why a user cannot logon, failure events can be a very useful source of information.

While success account logon events are configured by default, failure logon events must be configured manually. To access the Default Domain Controllers Policy, open Active Directory Users and Computers, right-click on the Domain Controllers OU, and click Properties. Click the Group Policy tab to view the Default Domain Controllers Policy, and then click Edit.

To enable the auditing of failure account logon events, access the Audit Policy node, which is available under Computer Configuration – Windows Settings – Security Settings – Local Policies, as shown in Figure 3-33. In the Audit Policy node, double-click on the Audit account logon events policy, check the Failure check box, and then click OK. Domain controllers will now audit both success and failure events related to account logon.

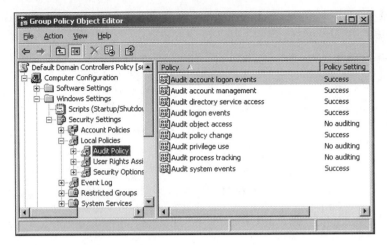

Figure 3-33   The Audit Policy node

Both success and failure account logon events can be viewed using the Security log in the Event Viewer administrative tool. A "key" icon designates success events, while a "lock" icon designates failure events. To open a particular entry in the Security log, simply double-click on it to view more information. Figure 3-34 illustrates a log entry for a failure account logon event. In this case, reading through the information provided makes it clear that the event is a failure event, and that it is related to the user name Admin01. In this case the Event ID listed is 675, which is typically associated with a user providing an incorrect password.

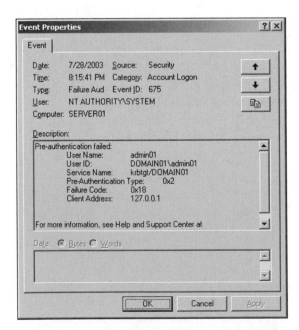

Figure 3-34   A failure event in the Security log

When users are unable to log on to an Active Directory domain, failure auditing for account logon events is one of the best sources of information available to an administrator. Although most account logon failure events will fall into Event IDs 675 and 676, the particular Failure Code associated with these errors can vary widely, and provides much more detailed information about the cause of the failure. For more information about Event ID and specific failure codes, your best source of information is the Microsoft Knowledge Base available at *http://support.microsoft.com*.

Resolving Logon Issues

In an Active Directory environment, users may not be able to log on to the domain for a variety of different issues. In some cases, the problem may be as simple as the user forgetting or mistyping their user name or password, while in others network settings may potentially be to blame. The following list outlines some of the more common logon issues that may occur in an Active Directory environment, and how they can be resolved.

- Incorrect user name or password — Most commonly caused by a user forgetting or mistyping their user name or password. The obvious solution to this problem is to reset the user's password using an administrative tool like Active Directory Users and Computers.

- Account lockout — After multiple incorrect logon attempts, a user's account may be locked out, depending on the Account lockout policy settings configured in the domain. User accounts can be unlocked manually from the Account tab in the properties of a user account.

- Account disabled — A user is unable to logon unless their account has been enabled. In some cases, such as when a new user is created based on a template account, their account may not have been enabled. Use Active Directory Users and Computers or the DSMOD USER command line utility to explicitly enable the user's account.

- Logon hour restrictions — A user is having trouble logging on at certain times during the day. Check to ensure that no logon hour restrictions are configured for their account. If a user needs access after normal business hours, ensure that the logon hour restrictions for their account are configured appropriately.

- Workstation restrictions — A user is not able to log on from certain workstations. Check to ensure that workstation restrictions have not been configured in the properties of their user account. Permit their account to log on to additional workstations or all workstations if necessary.

- Domain controllers — Workstations running Windows XP/2000/2003 seem unable to contact a domain controller. Check to ensure that their configured DNS settings are correct. Their operating systems query DNS to find the IP address of a domain controller, and incorrect settings may prohibit them from doing so.

- Client time settings — A user cannot log on to Windows XP, 2000, or 2003 workstations or member servers. Check to ensure that the user's clock is less than five minutes out of sync with the domain controller. Synchronization settings more than five minutes apart will prohibit users from logging on due to Kerberos policy settings.

- Down-level client issues — Down-level clients like workstations running Windows 95/98 and Windows NT are experiencing logon issues. Consider installing the Active Directory Client Extensions software on their systems.

- UPN logon issues — A user cannot log on using their UPN in a multiple-domain environment. Ensure that a Global Catalog server is configured and accessible. Global Catalog servers must be available when a user attempts logon using a UPN.

- Users unable to log on locally — A user needs to log on locally to specific servers or domain controllers. Grant them the right to log on locally in the policy settings on that server.

- Remote access logon issues — A user cannot log on via a dial-up or VPN connection. Be sure that their account is configured to allow access on the Dial-up tab in the properties of their user account.

- Terminal Services logon issues — A user cannot log on to a Terminal Server in the domain. Ensure that the Allow logon to terminal server check box is checked on the Terminal Services Profile tab in the properties of their user account.

CHAPTER SUMMARY

- The two primary authentication protocols used in Windows Server 2003 Active Directory environments are Kerberos v5 and NTLM.

- Windows Server 2003 supports three different types of user profiles; local profiles, roaming profiles, and mandatory profiles.

- The primary tool used to create and manage user accounts in a Windows Server 2003 Active Directory environment is Active Directory Users and Computers. This tool can also be used to configure user templates that can then be copied as a means of simplifying the user account creation process.

- Windows Server 2003 introduces a number of tools to allow user accounts to be created and managed from the command line including DSADD, DSMOD, DSQUERY, DSMOVE, and DSRM.

- The LDIFDE and CSVDE command-line utilities can be used to import and export settings to and from LDIF and CSV text files respectively.

KEY TERMS

Active Directory Users and Computers — An Active Directory MMC tool that allows you to create various objects such as OUs, user accounts, groups, computers, and contacts.

authentication — The process by which a user's identity is validated, which is subsequently used to grant or deny access to network resources.

CSVDE — A command-line utility that can be used to import and export data to and from Active Directory in a comma-separated file format.

down-level operating system — An operating system running Windows NT 4.0 or earlier.

DSADD — A command-line utility used to add objects to Active Directory.

DSMOD — A command-line utility used to modify Active Directory objects.

DSMOVE — A command-line utility used to move or rename Active Directory objects.

DSQUERY — A command-line utility used to query for Active Directory objects.

DSRM — A command-line utility used to delete Active Directory objects.

Group Policy — Enables the centralized management of user desktop settings, desktop and domain security, and the deployment and management of software throughout your network.

interactive authentication — The process by which a user provides their user name and password to be authenticated from the Log On to Windows dialog box.

Kerberos version 5 (Kerberos v5) — The primary authentication protocol used in Active Directory domain environments.

Key Distribution Center (KDC) — An Active Directory domain controller that stores the directory database containing all users and passwords.

LDIFDE — A command-line utility that can be used to import and export data to and from Active Directory using the LDAP Interchange Format file format.

local profile — A user profile stored on a particular computer that doesn't follow a user across the network.

mandatory profile — A user profile with settings that are not changed when a user logs off.

network authentication — The process by which a network resource or service confirms the identity of a user.

NT LAN Manager (NTLM) — The challenge-response protocol that is used for authentication purposes with operating systems running Windows NT 4.0 or earlier.

roaming profile — A user profile stored on a centralized server that follows a user across a network.

service ticket — A Kerberos ticket granted by a KDC allowing a client to gain access to a network resource or service.

ticket-granting ticket (TGT) — A ticket passed to a client system by the KDC once successful authentication occurs.

user account — An object that is stored in Active Directory that represents all of the information that defines a physical user who has access permissions to the network.

user account template — A special user account configured with settings that can be copied in order to simplify the creation of user accounts with common settings.

user profile — The desktop and environment settings associated with a particular user account.

REVIEW QUESTIONS

1. Which of the following tools can be used to modify the properties of existing user accounts from the command line?

   a. DSADD

   b. DSMOD

   c. DSQUERY

   d. DSRM

2. Which of the following tools can be used to create new user accounts?

   a. DSADD

   b. DSMOD

   c. DSQUERY

   d. DSMOVE

3. Which of the following tools can export user objects to a comma-separated text file?

   a. LDIFDE

   b. Active Directory Users and Computers

   c. DSADD

   d. CSVDE

4. Which of the following tools can import settings in LDAP Interchange Format?

   a. LDIFDE

   b. CSVDE

   c. DSRM

   d. DSQUERY

5. Which of the following is not a tool to create user accounts?

   a. DSADD

   b. Active Directory Users and Computers

   c. LDIFDE

   d. DSMOD

6. The Default Domain Policy specifies that a user password must be how long by default?

   a. five characters

   b. six characters

   c. seven characters

   d. eight characters

7. Which of the following is not a required element in a complex password?

   a. Minimum of six characters

   b. Minimum of eight characters

   c. Cannot include the user name

   d. Must include three of four defined character types

8. After how many days must a domain user change their password by default?

   a. 30

   b. 10

   c. 42

   d. 34

9. Active Directory user accounts are configured to lockout after three incorrect logon attempts.

   a. True

   b. False

10. When a user account template is copied, group membership information is also copied.

    a. True

    b. False

11. How many user passwords are remembered by a domain controller as part of password history setting by default?

    a. 6

    b. 8

    c. 16

    d. 24

12. On which tab of a user account's properties is the user's home directory configured by default?

    a. Home Directory

    b. Profile

    c. Account

    d. General

13. When a new user account is created in Active Directory Users and Computers, which group is it a member of by default?

    a. Domain Admins

    b. Domain Users

    c. Domain Guests

    d. Users

14. Which type of user profile does not save user settings when the user logs off?

    a. Local

    b. Roaming

    c. Null

    d. Mandatory

15. What type of user profile is used by default when a user logs on to a Windows XP system in an Active Directory domain?

    a. Local

    b. Roaming

    c. Null

    d. Mandatory

16. Which authentication protocol do Windows 2000 clients logging on to a Windows Server 2003 domain use?

    a. NTLM

    b. NTLMv2

    c. Kerberos

    d. RADIUS

17. Which authentication protocol is not configured with the Active Directory Client Extensions software used by Windows NT 4.0 clients when logging on to a Windows Server 2003 domain?

    a. NTLM

    b. NTLMv2

    c. Kerberos

    d. RADIUS

18. Logging on to an Active Directory domain from the console of a Windows XP system is referred to as which type of authentication?

    a. Interactive

    b. Network

    c. Domain

    d. Local

19. Which of the following folders in not part of a user profile?

   a. NetHood

   b. PrintHood

   c. My Documents

   d. Networks

20. Creating a mandatory user profile involves renaming which file?

   a. NTUSER.DAT

   b. NTUSER.MAN

   c. NTUSER.PRO

   d. NTUSER.SET

CASE PROJECTS

Case Project 3-1

Dover Leasing currently has information about all users stored in a human resources database application. The IT manager has asked you to explore some of the possible ways that this information could be used to create user accounts and populate the Active Directory database. Which tools could be used to accomplish this, and what are some of the issues involved with using these utilities?

Case Project 3-2

The DSADD command provides an effective method for administrators to create new user accounts from the command line. Use the DSADD utility to create the four new user accounts listed in the table below. All the user accounts should be created in the Users container in your Domain*XX*.Dovercorp.Net domain. Use the DSADD topic in the Help and Support Center to determine the appropriate switches required to configure these accounts from the command line.

User Name	Group Membership	Title	Pager number	Account Disabled?
Elliot Maxwell	VP Operations		555-1111	Yes
Nick Peers	Domain Guests	Contractor		No
Bob Mackenzie	Domain Admins	Administrator	555-1112	Yes
Doug Mackenzie	Backup Operators	Contractor		Yes

Case Project 3-3

In many companies, user account templates are created to help ease the administrative burden of creating many similar accounts. Create an account template called "TempUsers" in the Users container that is made a member of the Guest Users global group and has logon denied on Sundays. After completing the template, use it to create a new user account named "Mary Walsh" and ensure that the properties configured on the template apply to the new user account.

IMPLEMENTING AND MANAGING GROUP AND COMPUTER ACCOUNTS

After reading this chapter and completing the exercises, you will be able to:

♦ Understand the purpose of using group accounts to simplify administration

♦ Create group objects using both graphical and command-line tools

♦ Manage security groups and distribution groups

♦ Explain the purpose of the built-in groups created when Active Directory is installed

♦ Create and manage computer accounts

Although user accounts represent the primary method utilized to identify users on a network, trying to configure permissions or rights for multiple users according to their individual account can quickly become unmanageable, especially in large environments. For this reason, most network operating systems, including Windows Server 2003, include the ability to aggregate user accounts into entities known simply as groups.

Groups help to reduce the administrative effort associated with assigning rights and permissions to users by grouping users with common needs. For example, an administrator might choose to create a group to represent all users in the marketing department, or all users who work in a particular location. Ultimately, groups make administration easier by allowing an administrator to configure rights or permissions for several users at once rather than individually for each user. When a user requires certain rights or permissions, they are simply added to the group to which an appropriate level of access is granted.

In a manner similar to user accounts, Active Directory Users and Computers is the primary tool used to create and manage group accounts in an Active Directory environment. The various directory service command-line tools introduced in Chapter 3 for creating and managing user accounts can also be used to create and manage groups. You learn more about these methods of group management later in this chapter.

In much the same way that a user object represents an individual user in a domain environment, computer objects represent workstations and servers. In this chapter you also learn how to create and manage computer accounts using both Active Directory Users and Computers, and the DSADD command-line utility.

INTRODUCTION TO GROUP ACCOUNTS

A Windows Server 2003 **group** is a container object that is used to organize a collection of users, computers, contacts, or other groups into a single security principal. You would use a group object to simplify administration by assigning rights and resource permissions to a group rather than to individual users. Groups sound similar to OUs in that both organize other objects into logical containers. The main differences between an OU and a group are as follows:

- OUs are not security principals and as such cannot be used to define permissions on resources or be assigned rights. Active Directory Security Groups are security principals that can be assigned both permissions and rights.

- OUs can only contain objects from their parent domain. Some groups can contain objects from any domain within the forest.

In the following sections you learn more about the different group types and scopes available in a Windows Server 2003 Active Directory environment, as well as the various membership rules that apply to those groups.

Group Types

A group's type is used to define how that group can be used within an Active Directory domain or forest. Windows Server 2003 supports two different group types, known as Distribution Groups and Security Groups. The distinction between each type of group is important, because each is created for a different purpose and has different characteristics. The following sections look at both security and distribution groups in more detail.

Security Groups

Security groups are typically the most popular group type in an Active Directory environment. In a manner similar to a user account, security groups are defined by a Security Identifier (SID) that allows them to be assigned both permissions for resources in **discretionary access control lists (DACLs)**, as well as rights to perform different tasks. When trying to determine whether to create a **security group** or a distribution group, an administrator first needs to consider how that group will be used. Any group that will ultimately be assigned permissions or rights must be a security group, because distribution groups cannot be assigned permissions and rights.

Although the assignment of permissions and rights is the primary function of security groups, these groups can also be used as e-mail entities. Sending an e-mail message to an Active Directory Security Group (such as when Microsoft Exchange 2000 is installed) sends the message to all of the members of that group.

Distribution Groups

Distribution groups are the other type of group in an Active Directory environment. Unlike security groups, distribution groups do not have an associated SID and therefore cannot be used to assign permissions or rights to members. The primary purpose of a **distribution group** is for use with e-mail applications like Microsoft Exchange 2000, where sending an e-mail message to the distribution group sends the message to all members of that group.

While distribution groups may not seem useful in light of the fact that e-mail messages can also be sent to security groups, they differentiate themselves in an important way. Distribution groups do not have an SID associated with them, therefore they do not impact the user authentication process unnecessarily with excess information not required for security purposes. For this reason, if a group will never be used for security purposes, it should be configured as a distribution group rather than a security group.

Group Scopes

A group's scope refers to the logical boundary within which a group can be assigned permissions to a specific resource within an Active Directory domain or forest. Security and Distribution Groups in Active Directory can be assigned one of three possible scopes:

- global
- domain local
- universal

The following sections explore each group scope in more detail.

Global Groups

Global groups are created for the purpose of logically organizing users, computers, and potentially other groups that exist within the same domain in an Active Directory forest. For example, a **global group** created in Domain A can include objects (such as users) from Domain A, but not from Domain B.

When an administrator creates global groups, it is usually to organize objects associated with a geographic location or job function into logical groups. An administrator might create a global group called Marketing Users that includes all users in the marketing department, for example. Then, when permissions need to be assigned to all users in the Marketing Department for a specific folder or printer, the administrator can assign the permissions once for the Marketing Users global group, rather than for each user account individually. This obviously helps to reduce the administrative effort associated with configuring security settings like rights or permissions.

The type of objects that can be added to a global group is directly related to the configured functional level of a domain. Windows Server 2003 supports three main domain functional levels in environments that include various combinations of Windows 2000 Server and Windows Server 2003 domain controllers. These include:

- Windows 2000 mixed—This **domain functional level** is the default configured when Windows Server 2003 Active Directory is installed. This level supports a combination of Windows NT Server 4.0, Windows 2000 Server, and Windows Server 2003 domain controllers. Because each type of domain controller is supported, this domain functional level still follows many of the group member-ship rules associated with Windows NT 4.0 domain environments (to be explored shortly).

- Windows 2000 native—This domain functional level supports a combination of Windows 2000 Server and Windows Server 2003 domain controllers only. When configured to this functional level, a domain can support a variety of advanced group membership features, including the ability to nest global groups from the same domain. Supported group membership features at the Windows 2000 native domain functional level is covered shortly.

- Windows Server 2003—This domain functional level supports Windows Server 2003 domain controllers only. When configured to this domain functional level, a domain supports the same group membership features as the Windows 2000 native function level.

As outlined in the previous list, the configured functional level of a domain is directly related to the types of domain controllers present in an environment. For example, a company upgrading an existing Windows NT 4.0 domain needs to exist at the Windows 2000 mixed domain functional level for at least some period of time. Once all of the domain controllers have been upgraded to at least Windows 2000 Server, the domain functional level can be raised to Windows 2000 native. If all domain controllers are ultimately upgraded to Windows Server 2003, the functional level can then be upgraded again. Ultimately, the functional level of a domain impacts much more than group membership rules, but that is beyond the scope of this section.

For more information on the different capabilities of different Windows Server 2003 domain functional levels, see the Domain and forest functionality: Active Directory topic in Help and Support Center.

When a domain is configured to the **Windows 2000 mixed** domain functional level, global groups within an Active Directory forest can:

- Contain user accounts from the same domain
- Be added to local groups or domain local groups in any domain

When a domain is configured to the Windows 2000 mixed domain functional level, global groups within an Active Directory forest cannot:

- Be added to universal groups in the forest, since universal groups do not exist at the Windows 2000 mixed domain functional level

When a domain is configured to the **Windows 2000 native** or **Windows Server 2003** domain functional levels, global groups within an Active Directory forest can:

- Contain user accounts or other global groups from the same domain
- Be added to universal groups
- Be added to local groups or domain local groups in any domain

The process of creating different groups and changing the functional level of a domain is looked at in more detail later in this chapter.

Domain Local Groups

Domain local groups are typically created for the purpose of assigning rights and permissions to groups of users in an Active Directory environment. Created on domain controllers, a **domain local group** can be assigned rights and permissions to any resource within the same domain only. However, domain local groups can also contain groups from other domains in addition to users.

For example, a domain local group named Marketing is configured on a domain controller in Domain A. This domain local group is then assigned permissions to a folder on a server in Domain A. Then, instead of assigning permissions on this folder for multiple groups, global groups from Domain A (as well as other trusted domains) can be added to the Marketing domain local group. This ultimately grants users in those global groups the permissions associated with the Marketing domain local group.

In much the same way that the functional level of a domain impacts the membership rules for global groups, the same is true of domain local groups. When a domain is configured to the Windows 2000 mixed domain functional level, domain local groups within an Active Directory forest can:

- Contain user accounts from any domain
- Contain global groups from any domain

When a domain is configured to the Windows 2000 native or Windows Server 2003 domain functional levels, domain local groups within an Active Directory forest can:

- Contain user accounts from any domain

- Contain global groups from any domain

- Contain universal groups

- Contain other domain local groups from the same domain

 Groups created on Windows Server 2003 member servers or Windows XP Professional clients are called local groups. Local groups can only be assigned permissions to a resource available on the local machine on which it is created.

Universal Groups

Universal groups are typically created for the purpose of aggregating users or groups in different domains throughout an Active Directory forest. Stored on domain controllers configured as global catalog servers, a **universal group** can be assigned rights and permissions to any resource within a forest. Universal groups can contain not only users and global groups from any domain, but also other universal groups.

For example, a universal group named Enterprise Marketing is configured in a large organization with multiple domains. Then, the Marketing Users global groups from various domains (which contain individual marketing user accounts) is added to the Enterprise Marketing universal group, forming a single group that encompasses all of the marketing users within an organization across domain boundaries. Then, when rights or permissions need to be assigned to all marketing users in the forest, they can be assigned once to the Enterprise Marketing universal group, rather than individual Marketing Users groups from each domain.

Unlike global and domain local groups, which can exist at the Windows 2000 mixed domain functional level, universal groups can only be created once a domain is configured to the Windows 2000 native or Windows Server 2003 domain functional level. When a domain in configured to the Windows 2000 native or Windows 2003 domain functional level, universal groups in an Active Directory forest can:

- Contain user accounts from any trusted domain

- Contain global group accounts from any trusted domain

- Contain other universal groups

TIP Use universal groups with caution. All universal groups along with their memberships are listed in the global catalog. When there is any change to any member of a universal group, this change must be replicated to every global catalog in the forest. Global and domain local groups are also listed in the global catalog but do not have their memberships listed. A best practice is to place individual members within the global groups and then place the global groups within universal groups.

Table 4-1 provides a summary of each group type, its use, and its membership options within an Active Directory forest.

Table 4-1   Windows Server 2003 Group Summary

Group Scope	Usage	Windows 2000 Mixed Domain Functional Level Membership Options	Windows 2000 Native/ Windows Server 2003 Domain Functional Level Membership Options
Local	Assigns permissions to resources on the local computer only	User accounts from any domain; global groups from any domain	User accounts from any domain; global groups from any domain
Domain local	Assigned to resources within local domain	User accounts from any domain; global groups from any domain	User accounts, global groups, and universal groups from any domain; domain local groups from the same domain only
Global	Aggregates individual objects such as user accounts within a domain	User accounts from the same domain only	User accounts and global groups from the same domain only
Universal	Aggregates individual objects such as users or global groups from any domain in a forest	Not available	User accounts, global groups, and universal groups from any domain

CREATING GROUP OBJECTS

Global, domain local, and universal groups are created and stored in the Active Directory database like domain user accounts. Windows Server 2003 supports a number of different methods and tools for creating and managing group account objects. Although the standard tool used for this purpose is Active Directory Users and Computers, Windows Server 2003 also provides a number of command-line tools and utilities for the purpose of managing group accounts from the command line.

This variety of tools allows an administrator to work from whichever environment they feel most comfortable with, or the environment most appropriate to a situation. For example, if an administrator needs to create or edit the properties of a single group, Active Directory Users and Computers is probably the most logical tool to use. In cases where an administrator needs to create or manage the properties of multiple groups simultaneously, however, using some of the command-line tools and utilities available in Windows Server 2003 is a better, more automated process. Examples include DSADD, DSMOD, DSQUERY, and so forth.

In the following sections you learn how to create and manage group accounts using both Active Directory Users and Computers as well as various command line utilities.

Active Directory Users and Computers

The primary tool used to create group accounts in an Active Directory environment is Active Directory Users and Computers. Fundamentally, creating groups of different types and scopes with this tool is very similar to the process used to create new user accounts.

New group accounts can be created in any of the built-in containers found in Active Directory Users and Computers, as well as in the root of the domain object. For organizational purposes, however, group accounts are often created with custom OU objects. For example, if an administrator creates all user accounts for users in the Marketing Department in an OU named Marketing, it makes sense to also create all marketing-related group accounts in this same OU. However, this method of locating group accounts is not strictly required, and the placement of group objects is at the discretion of the administrator.

Like new user objects, new groups are created in Active Directory Users and Computers by right-clicking on a particular container or OU (such as Users), selecting New, and then clicking Group. Doing so opens the New Object - Group window, shown in Figure 4-1.

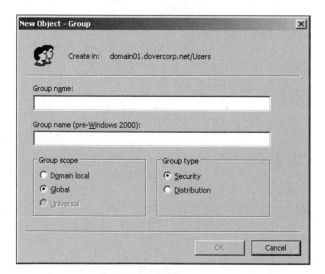

Figure 4-1   The New Object - Group window

Notice in Figure 4-1 that while both group types are available for selection, the Universal group scope option is not. In this case, the universal group option is not available because the functional level of the domain is not yet configured to Windows 2000 native or Windows Server 2003.

Active Directory Users and Computers, like user accounts, can also be used to configure the properties associated with a group account. The properties dialog box for a group account consists of four main tabs:

- General—Allows a description and e-mail address to be configured for the group, and allows the type and scope of a group to be changed.

- Members—Allows members to be added or removed from the group.

- Member Of—Displays any groups that this group is a member of, and allows this group to be added to or removed from other groups.

- Managed By—Displays information about the user or contact responsible for the management of the group object.

NOTE

When the Advanced Features view is enabled within Active Directory Users and Computers, two additional tabs become visible in the properties of a group account. The Object tab displays information about the properties of the group object, while the Security tab shows the configured permissions for the group object.

In Activity 4-1 you create and add members to global groups using Active Directory Users and Computers.

ACTIVITY

Activity 4-1: Creating and Adding Members to Global Groups

Time Required: 15 minutes

Objective: Use Active Directory Users and Computers to create global groups.

Description: Having read about the different group types and scopes in Windows Server 2003, you have decided to try and take advantage of some of the reduced administrative effort associated with using groups to manage resource access in an Active Directory environment. In this activity, you create a series of global groups that will be associated with different job functions at Dover Leasing, and then populate these global groups with user accounts.

1. Log on with your Admin*XX* account if you haven't already done so. Click **Start**, select **Administrative Tools**, and click **Active Directory Users and Computers**.

2. Right-click the **Users** container, select **New**, and then click **Group**.

3. In the New Object – Group dialog box, type **Marketing Users** in the Group name text box.

4. Under Group scope, ensure that the **Global** radio button is selected.

5. Under Group type, ensure that the **Security** radio button is selected. Click **OK** to create the group.

6. Repeat Steps 2 through 5 to create global groups named **Help Desk Users**, **Finance Users**, **IT Users**, **Network Support Users**, and **Sales Users** within the Users container.

7. Double-click the **IT Users** global group to view its properties, as shown in Figure 4-2.

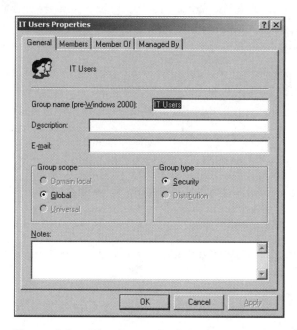

Figure 4-2   The General tab in the properties of a global group

8. Click the **Members** tab.

9. Click the **Add** button. In the Select Users, Contacts, Computers, or Groups dialog box, type **Mark Manore** in the Enter the object names to select text box and click **OK**. The Mark Manore user account should be listed as a member of the group, as shown in Figure 4-3.

10. Click **OK** to close the properties of the IT Users global group.

11. Click the **Moira Cowan** user account to select it. Hold down the **Ctrl** key and click the **John H. Smith** user account. Both accounts should now be selected. Release the **Ctrl** key.

12. Right-click the **John H. Smith** account and click **Add to a group**.

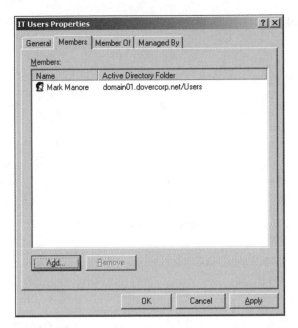

Figure 4-3   The Members tab in the properties of a global group

13. In the Select Group dialog box, type **marketing users** in the Enter the object name to select text box as shown in Figure 4-4, and click **OK**. At the Active Directory dialog box, click **OK**.

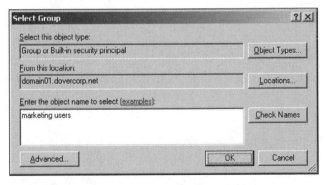

Figure 4-4   The Select Group dialog box

14. Using any combination of the steps outlined here, add the **Chris Medved** account to the Finance Users group, the **Mike Aubert** and **Alan Finn** accounts to the Network Support Users group, the **Frank Adili** and **Christy Jackson** accounts to the Sales Users group, and the **John Smith** account to the Help Desk Users group.

15. Leave Active Directory Users and Computers open.

In Activity 4-2 you create and add members to domain local groups using Active Directory Users and Computers.

Activity 4-2: Creating and Adding Members to Domain Local Groups

Time Required: 10 minutes

Objective: Use Active Directory Users and Computers to create domain local groups.

Description: In this activity, you create a series of domain local groups associated with resource access at Dover Leasing, and then populate these domain local groups with global group accounts.

1. In Active Directory Users and Computers, right-click the **Users** container, select **New**, and then click **Group**.

2. In the New Object – Group dialog box, type **Marketing Resources** in the Group name text box.

3. Under Group scope, click the **Domain local** radio button.

4. Under Group type, ensure that the **Security** radio button is selected. Click **OK** to create the group. Notice that a group's scope and type can be distinguished via the Type header when viewing the contents of a container.

5. Repeat Steps 1 through 4 to create domain local groups named **Help Desk Resources**, **Finance Resources**, **IT Resources**, **Network Support Resources**, and **Sales Resources** within the Users container.

6. Right-click on the **Marketing Resources** domain local group, and then click **Properties**.

7. Click the **Members** tab, and then click the **Add** button.

8. In the Select Users, Contacts, Computers, or Groups window, type **Marketing Users** in the Enter the object names to select text box. Click **OK**.

9. Click **OK** to close the Marketing Resources Properties window.

10. Repeat Steps 6 through 9 to add the **Help Desk Users** global group to the Help Desk Resources domain local group, the **Finance Users** global group to the Finance Resources domain local group, the **IT Users** global group to the IT Resources domain local group, the **Network Support Users** global group to the Network Support Resources domain local group, and the **Sales Users** global group to the Sales Resources domain local group.

11. Leave Active Directory Users and Computers open.

As you learned earlier in this chapter, universal groups cannot be created until the functional level of a domain is set to Windows 2000 native or Windows Server 2003. The functional level of a domain is configured using the Active Directory Users and Computers tool. In

Activity 4-3 you first configure the functional level of your domain to Windows Server 2003, and then create and add members to universal groups.

Activity 4-3: Changing the Functional Level of a Domain and Creating and Adding Members to Universal Groups

4

Time Required: 10 minutes

Objective: Change the functional level of a domain to Windows Server 2003, and use Active Directory Users and Computers to create universal groups.

Description: Because the Dover Leasing Active Directory forest will eventually consist of multiple domains, the IT manager has asked you to determine the process for raising the functional level of a domain and then create and populate universal groups. In this activity you first raise the functional level of your domain to Windows Server 2003, and then create and add a member to a universal group.

1. In Active Directory Users and Computers, right-click the **DomainXX.Dovercorp.net** domain (where *XX* is your assigned student number) and click **Raise Domain Functional Level**.

2. In the Raise Domain Functional Level dialog box, click **Windows Server 2003** in the Select an available domain functional level list box. Note the warning message that appears below the list box, as shown in Figure 4-5.

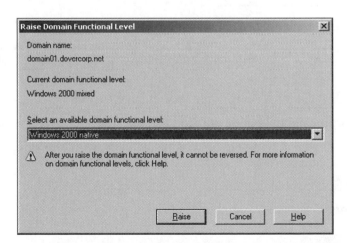

Figure 4-5   The Raise Domain Functional Level dialog box

3. Click the **Raise** button.

4. Click **OK** to confirm that this action will affect the entire domain.

5. Click **OK** when prompted that the functional level was raised successfully, being sure to read the associated message that appears.

6. Right-click on the **Users** container, select **New**, and then click **Group**.

7. In the New Object – Group dialog box, type **Universal Marketing** in the Group name text box.

8. Under Group scope, click the **Universal** radio button, which is now available, as shown in Figure 4-6.

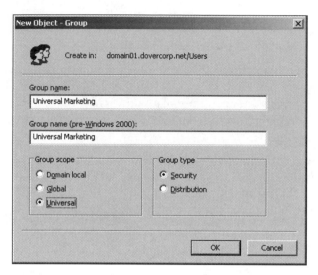

Figure 4-6   Creating a Universal group

9. Under Group type, ensure that the **Security** radio button is selected. Click **OK** to create the group.

10. Right-click on the **Universal Marketing** group, and click **Properties**.

11. Click the **Members tab**, and then click the **Add** button.

12. In the Select Users, Contacts, Computers, or Groups window, type **Marketing Users** in the Enter the object names to select text box. Click **OK**.

13. Click **OK** to close the Universal Marketing Properties window.

14. Leave Active Directory Users and Computers open.

CONVERTING GROUP TYPES

When creating new Active Directory groups, it is important to select the appropriate group type based on how the group will be used. When a group needs to be assigned permissions or rights, you have already learned that security groups are required. It is also conceivable, however, that an administrator might accidentally create a distribution group when a security group is required, or vice versa. For this reason, Active Directory Users and

Computers allows an administrator to change the type of an existing group if required. In order to take advantage of this capability, the domain in which the group account exists must be configured to at least the Windows 2000 native domain functional level. The type of a group cannot be converted if the domain is configured to the Windows 2000 mixed domain functional level.

In Activity 4-4 you use Active Directory Users and Computers to create a new distribution group, and then convert it to a security group.

Activity 4-4: Converting Group Types

Time Required: 5 minutes

Objective: Use Active Directory Users and Computers to change group types.

Description: The IT manager at Dover Leasing is worried that new administrators may accidentally create distribution groups where security groups are necessary, and vice versa. He has asked you to test the ability to change the type of groups using the Active Directory Users and Computers tool to be sure that changes to a group's type can be made when necessary. In this activity you first create a new distribution global group and then change the type of the group to security.

1. In Active Directory Users and Computers, right-click on the **Users** container, select **New**, and click **Group**.

2. In the New Object – Group dialog box, type **Testing Type** in the Group name text box.

3. Under Group scope, ensure that **Global** is selected.

4. Under Group type, click the **Distribution** radio button, and then click **OK** to create the group.

5. Verify that the Testing Type group appears as a Distribution Group in the Type column of the Users container, as shown in Figure 4-7.

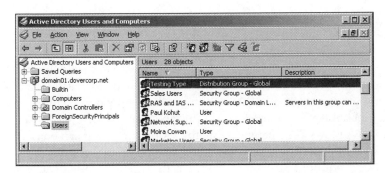

Figure 4-7   Viewing group types in Active Directory Users and Computers

6. Right-click on the **Testing Type** group and click **Properties**. Notice that the group is currently listed as a Distribution group in the Group type section of the General tab.

7. Click the **Security** radio button, as shown in Figure 4-8. Click **OK** to change the type of the Testing Type group from distribution to security, and to exit the properties of the group.

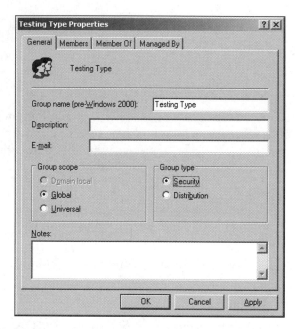

Figure 4-8   Changing a group's type from distribution to security

8. Verify that the Testing Type group now appears as a Security Group in the Type column of the Users container. Leave Active Directory Users and Computers open.

CONVERTING GROUP SCOPES

In much the same way that the type of a group can be changed after it has been created, so can the scope of a group. For example, if an administrator accidentally creates a global group instead of a universal group, the scope of the group can be changed from one to the other, but certain restrictions apply. First and foremost, the functional level of a domain must be configured to at least Windows 2000 native before the scope of a group can be changed. The Windows 2000 mixed domain functional level does not support changing the scope of a group. Additionally, an administrator must consider the membership of a group when attempting to change its scope. The list below outlines the various group scope changes supported in Windows Server 2003 Active Directory, along with restrictions based on group membership:

- Global to universal—This change is supported as long as the global group is not a member of any other global groups. If it were, the result would be a universal group being a member of a global group, which is not supported.

- Domain local to universal—This change is supported as long as the domain local group does not have any other domain local groups as members. If it did, the result would be a domain local group being a member of a universal group, which is not supported.

- Universal to global—This change is supported as long as the universal group does not have any other universal groups as a member. If it did, the result would be a universal group being a member of a global group, which is not supported.

- Universal to domain local—This change is always supported without restrictions.

In Activity 4-5 you attempt to change the scopes of various groups using Active Directory Users and Computers.

Activity 4-5: Converting Group Scopes

Time Required: 5 minutes

Objective: Use Active Directory Users and Computers to change group scopes.

Description: The IT manager at Dover Leasing is worried that new administrators may accidentally create groups of the wrong scope when creating new group accounts. He has asked you to test the ability to change the scope of groups using the Active Directory Users and Computers tool to be sure that changes to a group's scope can be made when necessary. In this activity you attempt to change the scope of different groups based on what you have learned about the ability to change group scope relative to the group's existing membership.

1. In Active Directory Users and Computers, right-click on the **Users** container, select **New**, and click **Group**.

2. In the New Object – Group dialog box, type **Testing Scope** in the Group name text box.

3. Under Group scope, ensure that **Global** is selected.

4. Under Group type, ensure that the **Security** radio button is selected, and then click **OK** to create the group.

5. Right-click on the **Testing Scope** group, and click **Properties**.

6. Click the **Members** tab, and then click the **Add** button.

7. In the Select Users, Contacts, Computers, or Groups window, type **Marketing Users** in the Enter the object names to select text box. Click **OK**. This will add the Marketing Users global group to the Testing Scope global group. Click **OK** to close the properties of the Testing Scope group.

8. Right-click on the **Testing Scope** group and click **Properties**.

9. On the General tab, notice that the Group scope section allows you to change the group to the Universal scope. This is because the Testing Scope global group is not a member of any other global groups. Do not make any changes, and click **OK**.

10. Right-click on the **Marketing Users** group, and click **Properties**.

11. On the General tab, notice that the Group scope section allows you to change the group scope to Universal. However, if you select the Universal radio button and click OK, you will receive an error message stating that a global group cannot have a universal group as a member. Click **OK** to close the properties of the Marketing Users group.

12. Right-click on the **Testing Scope** group and click **Properties**.

13. On the General tab, click the **Universal** radio button, and then click **OK**. This will change the scope of the Testing Scope group from global to universal.

14. Close Active Directory Users and Computers.

Command Line Utilities

While Active Directory Users and Computers is the primary tool used to create and manage domain group accounts, Windows Server 2003 also includes a variety of utilities that allow you to create and manage user accounts from the command line. These utilities are aimed at administrators with a preference for working from the command line, or those looking to automate the creation or management of group accounts in a more flexible manner. The command-line utilities to be looked at in the following sections include:

- DSADD—Adds objects such as groups
- DSMOD—Modifies object attributes and settings
- DSQUERY—Queries for objects
- DSMOVE—Moves objects to different locations within a domain
- DSRM—Deletes objects from the directory

DSADD

As you learned in Chapter 3, DSADD is one of the new command-line utilities introduced in Windows Server 2003 to allow various object types to be added to the directory. In much the same way that this utility can be used to add new user accounts to the directory, it can similarly be used to create new group accounts.

The basic syntax for creating a user account with DSADD is DSADD GROUP, followed by a variety of different switches that allow you to configure everything from the members of a scope to its scope and type. The basic syntax for adding a group with the DSADD GROUP tool consists of only a single piece of information, specifically the distinguished name of the group account to be created.

For example, to create a new security global group account named Database Users in the Users container of the domain01.dovercorp.net domain, the correct command syntax would be:

```
dsadd group "cn=Database Users,cn=users,dc=domain01,dc=dovercorp,
dc=net" -secgrp yes -scope g
```

If the DSADD GROUP command completes successfully, a message stating "dsadd succeeded" is displayed, as shown in Figure 4-9.

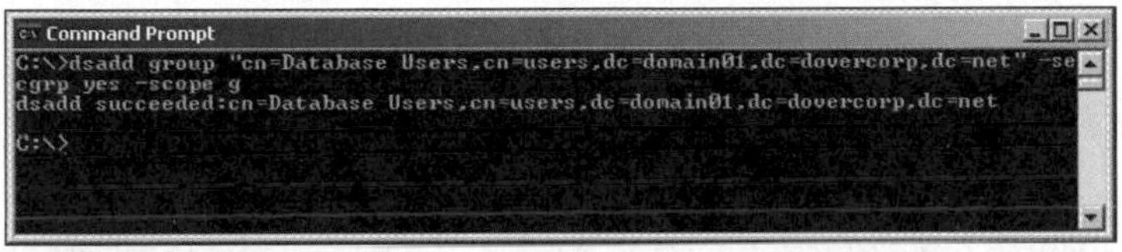

Figure 4-9   The DSADD GROUP command

The DSADD GROUP command supports a wide variety of switches used to configure different group account attributes. The list below provides examples of the more common attributes that might be configured with the DSADD GROUP command.

- –secgrp:
- –scope:
- –memberof:
- –members:

The following command is an example of creating a new domain local security group account named Archive Resources in the Users container of the domain01.dovercorp.net domain, including values for the switches just explored. Note that the entire command is a single line:

```
dsadd group "cn=Archive
Resources,cn=users,dc=domain01,dc=dovercorp,dc=net"
-secgrp yes -scope l -memberof "cn=Marketing
Resources,cn=users,dc=domain01,dc=dovercorp,dc=net"
-members "cn=Marketing Users,cn=users,dc=domain01,
dc=dovercorp,dc=net"
```

In this example, a new domain local security group named Archive Resources is created. This group has been made a member of the Marketing Resources domain local group, and the Marketing Users global group has been added to it as a member.

> **NOTE** For a complete list of the various switches and options available with the DSADD GROUP command, see the DSADD topic in Windows Server 2003 Help and Support or type DSADD GROUP /? at the command line.

In Activity 4-6 you use the DSADD GROUP command to create two new groups from the command line.

Activity 4-6: Creating Groups Using DSADD

Time Required: 10 minutes

Objective: Use the DSADD GROUP command to add groups of different types and scopes.

Description: The IT manager at Dover Leasing has asked you to explore different processes for creating group accounts from the command line. Ultimately, the goal is to be able to create group accounts via a telnet session with remote servers when necessary. In this activity you use the DSADD GROUP command to create two new group accounts from the command line.

1. Click **Start**, and then click **Run**.

2. In the Open text box, type **cmd.exe**, and click **OK**.

3. At the command prompt window, type **cd ..** and press **Enter**. Type **cd ..** again and press **Enter**. This will help to reduce the on-screen clutter associated with the command prompt path.

4. Type **cls** and press **Enter** to clear the screen.

5. At the command line, type the following, all in one line: **dsadd group "cn=Database Users,cn=users,dc=domainXX,dc=dovercorp,dc=net" −secgrp yes −scope g**, where *XX* is your student number. Press **Enter**. If the dsadd succeeded message appears, then the new user account has been created successfully. If you receive an error message, type the command again being careful to avoid errors.

6. Minimize the Command Prompt window.

7. Click **Start**, select **Administrative Tools**, and then click **Active Directory Users and Computers**.

8. Click on the **Users** container to view its contents. Notice that the Database Users group now appears.

9. Minimize Active Directory Users and Computers, and maximize the Command Prompt window.

10. At the command line, type the following, all in one line: **dsadd group "cn=Archive Resources,cn=users,dc=domainXX,dc=dovercorp,dc=net" –secgrp yes –scope l –memberof "cn=Marketing Resources,cn=users, dc=domainXX,dc=dovercorp,dc=net" –members "cn=Marketing Users,cn=users,dc=domainXX,dc=dovercorp,dc=net"**, where *XX* is your student number. Press **Enter**. If the dsadd succeeded message appears, then the new user account has been created successfully. If you receive an error message, type the command again being careful to avoid errors.

11. Close the Command Prompt window, and then maximize the Active Directory Users and Computers window.

12. Right-click on the **Users** container, and then click **Refresh**. Notice that the Archive Resources group now appears in the Users container.

13. Right-click on the **Archive Resources** group and click **Properties**.

14. On the General tab, confirm that the group is of domain local scope and the security type.

15. Click the **Members** tab. Confirm that the Marketing Users group is a member of this group.

16. Click on the **Member Of** tab. Confirm that this group is a member of the Marketing Resources group.

17. Click **Cancel**, and then close Active Directory Users and Computers.

DSMOD

DSMOD is another new utility introduced in Windows Server 2003 that allows various object types to be modified from the command line. In the same way that the DSMOD USER command allows the properties of a user account to be changed, the DSMOD GROUP command allows the properties of a group account to be modified.

The basic syntax for modifying a group account with DSMOD is DSMOD GROUP, followed by a variety of different switches that allow you to modify everything from the type or scope of a group to the group membership. Since DSMOD GROUP is used to modify an existing group account, the command requires that you specify the distinguished name of the object to be modified, along with at least one switch (which would specify a particular modification).

For example, to add the description "Domain01 Marketing Users Global Group" to an existing group account named Marketing Users in the Users container of the domain01. dovercorp.net domain, the correct command syntax would be:

```
dsmod group "cn=Marketing Users,cn=users,dc=domain01,dc=dovercorp,
dc=net" -desc "Domain01 Marketing Users Global Group"
```

If the DSMOD GROUP command completes successfully, a message stating "dsmod succeeded" will be displayed, similar to Figure 4-10.

Figure 4-10   The DSMOD GROUP command

In a similar manner, the DSMOD GROUP command can also be used to add or remove users from a particular group. For example, to remove the Archive Resources group from the Marketing Resources group, and then subsequently add the Universal Marketing group to Marketing Resources in the domain01.dovercorp.net domain, the correct command syntax would be:

```
dsmod group "cn=Marketing Resources,cn=users,dc=domain01,
dc=dovercorp,dc=net" -rmmbr "cn=Archive Resources,cn=users,
dc=domain01,dc=dovercorp,dc=net" -addmbr "cn=Universal
Marketing,cn=users,dc=domain01,dc=dovercorp,dc=net"
```

 For a complete list of the various switches and options available with the DSMOD GROUP command, see the DSMOD topic in Windows Server 2003 Help and Support or type DSMOD GROUP /? at the command line.

In Activity 4-7 you change the properties of two existing group accounts from the command line using the DSMOD GROUP command.

Activity 4-7: Modifying Groups Using DSMOD

Time Required: 10 minutes

Objective: Use the DSMOD GROUP command to modify group accounts.

Description: The IT manager at Dover Leasing has asked you to explore different processes for modifying group accounts from the command line. Ultimately, the goal is to be able to modify group accounts via a telnet session with remote servers when necessary. In this activity you use the DSMOD GROUP command to modify two existing group accounts from the command line.

1. Click **Start**, and then click **Run**.
2. In the Open text box, type **cmd.exe**, and click **OK**.
3. At the command prompt window, type **cd ..** and press **Enter**. Type **cd ..** again and press **Enter**.

4. Type **cls** and press **Enter** to clear the screen.

5. At the command line, type the following, all in one line: **dsmod group "cn=Marketing Users,cn=users,dc=domainXX,dc=dovercorp,dc=net" –desc "DomainXX Marketing Users Global Group"**,where *XX* is your assigned student number. Press **Enter**. If the dsmod succeeded message appears, then the modification has completed successfully. If you receive an error message, type the command again being careful to avoid errors.

6. Minimize the Command Prompt window.

7. Click **Start**, select **Administrative Tools**, and then click **Active Directory Users and Computers**.

8. Click the **Users** container if necessary to view its contents. Right-click on the **Marketing Users** group and click **Properties**.

9. On the General tab, confirm that the words DomainXX Marketing Users Global Group now appear in the Description text box on the General tab. Click **Cancel**.

10. Minimize Active Directory Users and Computers, and maximize the Command Prompt.

11. At the command line, type the following, all in one line: **dsmod group "cn=Marketing Resources,cn=users,dc=domainXX,dc=dovercorp, dc=net" –rmmbr "cn=Archive Resources,cn=users, dc=domainXX,dc=dovercorp, dc=net" –addmbr "cn=Universal Marketing,cn=users,dc=domainXX, dc=dovercorp,dc=net"**, where *XX* is your assigned student number. Press **Enter**. If the dsmod succeeded message appears, then the modification has completed successfully. If you receive an error message, type the command again being careful to avoid errors.

12. Close the Command Prompt window, and then maximize the Active Directory Users and Computers window.

13. Right-click on the **Marketing Resources** group in the Users container and click **Properties**.

14. Click on the **Members** tab to confirm that the Archive Resources group is no longer a member of the group, and that the Universal Marketing group is a member. Click **Cancel**.

15. Close Active Directory Users and Computers.

DSQUERY

As you learned in Chapter 3, DSQUERY is another new utility introduced in Windows Server 2003 that allows various object types to be queried from the command line. In the same way that the DSQUERY USER command is used to query for and return information about user accounts, the DSQUERY GROUP command is used to query for and return information about groups. Recall that the DSQUERY command also supports the wildcard character (*), effectively allowing it to query for any type of directory object.

At the most basic level, DSQUERY allows you to query the directory for a particular type of object, and return a value. For example, to view all of the group objects in the Builtin container of the domain01.dovercorp.net domain, the correct command syntax would be:

```
dsquery group "cn=builtin,dc=domain01,dc=dovercorp,dc=net"
```

This command would return a list of the distinguished names of all group accounts in the Builtin container, as illustrated in Figure 4-11.

```
C:\>dsquery group "cn=builtin,dc=domain01,dc=dovercorp,dc=net"
"CN=Server Operators,CN=Builtin,DC=domain01,DC=dovercorp,DC=net"
"CN=Account Operators,CN=Builtin,DC=domain01,DC=dovercorp,DC=net"
"CN=Pre-Windows 2000 Compatible Access,CN=Builtin,DC=domain01,DC=dovercorp,DC=ne
t"
"CN=Windows Authorization Access Group,CN=Builtin,DC=domain01,DC=dovercorp,DC=ne
t"
"CN=Terminal Server License Servers,CN=Builtin,DC=domain01,DC=dovercorp,DC=net"
"CN=Administrators,CN=Builtin,DC=domain01,DC=dovercorp,DC=net"
"CN=Users,CN=Builtin,DC=domain01,DC=dovercorp,DC=net"
"CN=Guests,CN=Builtin,DC=domain01,DC=dovercorp,DC=net"
"CN=Print Operators,CN=Builtin,DC=domain01,DC=dovercorp,DC=net"
"CN=Backup Operators,CN=Builtin,DC=domain01,DC=dovercorp,DC=net"
"CN=Replicator,CN=Builtin,DC=domain01,DC=dovercorp,DC=net"
"CN=Remote Desktop Users,CN=Builtin,DC=domain01,DC=dovercorp,DC=net"
"CN=Network Configuration Operators,CN=Builtin,DC=domain01,DC=dovercorp,DC=net"
"CN=Performance Monitor Users,CN=Builtin,DC=domain01,DC=dovercorp,DC=net"
"CN=Performance Log Users,CN=Builtin,DC=domain01,DC=dovercorp,DC=net"

C:\>
```

Figure 4-11   The DSQUERY GROUP command

In the same manner as with the DSQUERY USER command, the output of the DSQUERY GROUP command can be piped as input to other directory service command line tools such as DSADD, DSMOD, or DSRM.

NOTE   For a complete list of the various switches and options available with the DSQUERY GROUP command, see the DSQUERY topic in Windows Server 2003 Help and Support or type DSQUERY GROUP /? at the command line.

DSMOVE

The DSMOVE command allows various object types to be moved from the object's current location to a new location in the directory, or an object to be renamed without moving it to a new location. In the same manner that this tool can be used to move or rename user objects, it can also be used to move or rename groups.

For example, an administrator might want to move a group account from the Users container into an OU named Marketing. Assuming that the group to be moved is named Marketing Users and the domain is domain01.dovercorp.net, the correct command syntax to move the user to the new OU would be:

```
Dsmove   "cn=Marketing Users,cn=users,dc=domain01,dc=dovercorp,
dc=net" -newparent "ou=marketing,dc=domain01,dc=dovercorp,dc=net"
```

Along the same lines, if the Marketing Users group was not named according to the correct naming convention and needed to be renamed to Global Marketing Users, the administrator might chose to simply rename the Marketing Users group. Assuming that this account now exists in the Marketing OU, the correct syntax for this command would be:

```
dsmove "cn=Marketing Users,ou=marketing,dc=domain01,dc=dovercorp,
dc=net"-newname "Global Marketing Users"
```

Remember that the DSMOVE command can only be used to move objects within the same domain. To move objects between domains, use the MOVETREE command available when the Windows Server 2003 Support Tools are installed.

For a complete list of the various switches and options available with the DSMOVE command, see the DSMOVE topic in Windows Server 2003 Help and Support or type DSMOVE /? at the command line.

DSRM

In much the same way that you learned to delete user objects with the DSRM command in Chapter 3, this command can also be used to delete group accounts. For example, if your goal were to delete the Marketing Users global group in the Users container of the domain01.dovercorp.net domain, the correct command syntax would be:

```
dsrm "cn=Marketing Users,cn=users,dc=domain01,dc=dovercorp,dc=net"
```

As when deleting a user account, the DSRM command prompts you to confirm deletion of the specified objects. To delete the Marketing Users group without being prompted, the correct command syntax would be:

```
dsrm "cn=Marketing Users,cn=users,dc=domain01,dc=dovercorp,dc=net"
-noprompt
```

Remember to be very careful when issuing the DSRM command with the −noprompt switch, as this might cause you to accidentally delete required objects.

For a complete list of the various switches and options available with the DSRM command, see the DSRM topic in Windows Server 2003 Help and Support or type DSRM /? at the command line.

MANAGING SECURITY GROUPS

As you start to implement the use of security groups, a general strategy is to use the acronym A G U DL P. This refers to the following:

1. Create user Accounts (A), and organize them within Global groups (G). Often users are grouped in global groups based on departments in the organization.

2. Optional: Create Universal groups (U) and place global groups from any domain within the universal groups.

3. Create Domain Local groups (DL) that represent the resources in which you want to control access, and add the global or universal groups to the domain local groups.

4. Assign Permissions (P) to the domain local groups.

For example, Dover Leasing has a shared file called Reports. All users in all domains that work in the Marketing Department must have access to the Reports Share. Following the steps previously discussed, this is how you could organize access:

1. In each domain, create a global group called Marketing Users, and add any appropriate user account to the group.

2. Optional: Create a universal group called Dovercorp Marketing, and add all global groups created in Step 1, from all domains to the universal group.

3. Create a domain local group called Reports Share, and add the Dover Marketing universal group to the local group. (If you skipped Step 2, you can add the Marketing Users global group instead.)

4. Assign the Reports Share domain local group to the access control list of the actual share on the network, and specify the appropriate permissions.

If your domain is running in Windows 2000 native mode or the Windows Server 2003 functional level, you can use the option of nesting groups to simplify administrative tasks. For example, Dover Leasing may have three global groups called Help Desk, IT Managers, and Network Support. Together, these three groups of users may represent the Information Technology department of Dover Leasing. You could create the Information Technology global group and put the Help Desk, IT Managers, and Network Support groups into this one group, thus simplifying the assignment of permissions for resources to which all three groups should have access. You do not need to add individuals to the Information Technology group. When you are assigning permissions to resources, assign the permissions to domain local groups.

If you are working in a single domain, you can use global groups or universal groups interchangeably. Choose one of these options to group your users, and then add these groups to the local domain groups.

Determining Group Membership

One of the most important jobs of any Windows Server 2003 network administrator is to ensure that users are members of the correct groups. If not managed effectively, membership (or a lack thereof) in incorrect groups can lead to problems with user access to required resources, or worse still, the ability to access restricted resources.

The easiest method to determine the groups that a user is a member of is via the Member Of tab in the properties of their user account. As you learned earlier in this chapter, this tab lists all of the global, domain local, and universal groups in which a user's account is a member. Unfortunately, the Member Of tab only displays those groups in which a user has been directly added. For example, if a user account is made a member of a global group named Marketing Users, they appear as a member of this group. However, if the same user account is a member of the Marketing Users global group, and the Marketing Users global group is in turn a member of the Marketing Resources domain local group, the Member Of tab displays membership in the Marketing Users group only. This is not a design flaw—instead, the Member Of tab is designed to strictly list the groups in which the user account is directly a member. To dig deeper, an administrator could use the Member Of tab for the Marketing Users global group to gather additional information.

One additional tool that provides an exceptionally easy method of determining a user's group membership from the command line is DSGET. The DSGET command allows you to display the results of a query on-screen, in a manner similar to DSQUERY, but with different switches supported. For example, the DSGET GROUP command could be used to gather information about all the members of the Marketing Users group in the Users container of the domain01.dovercorp.net domain if the following command were issued:

```
dsget group "cn=Marketing Users,cn=users,dc=domain01,cn=dovercorp,
cn=net"-members
```

Similarly, the DSGET GROUP command could also be used to view all of the groups that the Marketing Users group is a member of:

```
dsget group "cn=Marketing Users,cn=users,dc=domain01,cn=dovercorp,
cn=net"-memberof
```

The DSGET USER command can also be used to determine the groups that a specific user is a member of. For example, to view all of the groups that the user Alan Finn in the Users container of the domain01.dovercorp.net domain is a member of, the following command would be issued:

```
dsget user "cn=Alan Finn,cn=users,dc=domain01,cn=dovercorp,cn=net"
-memberof
```

By default, the output of the DSGET command is displayed onscreen. In some situations, however, it might be better for the output of this command to be saved to a text file, perhaps to ultimately be imported to a spreadsheet or database application. This is easily accomplished by using a standard redirect at the command line. For example, issuing the command below would output a listing of all members of the Marketing Users group to a text file named mktgusers.txt:

```
dsget group "cn=Marketing Users,cn=users,dc=domain01,cn=dovercorp,
cn=net"-members >> mktgusers.txt
```

For a complete list of the various switches and options available with the DSGET command, see the DSGET topic in Windows Server 2003 Help and Support or type DSGET /? at the command line.

BUILT-IN GROUPS

When Windows Server 2003 Active Directory is installed, a number of built-in local security groups with various pre-assigned rights are created, which you may want to use to allow users to perform certain network tasks. Whenever possible, you should use one of the built-in local groups to assign rights because this eases the implementation of delegation and security rights throughout the network. For example, rather than creating a special group with rights to back up and restore servers, you can use the built-in backup operators group.

The built-in groups created automatically when Active Directory is installed are stored in two different locations, namely the Builtin container and the Users container. The following sections outline the built-in groups found in each location.

The Builtin Container

The Builtin container contains a number of domain local group accounts that are allocated different user rights based on common administrative or network-related tasks. Table 4-2 outlines the name of each of the built-in domain local groups found in this container, as well as a description of the purpose or capabilities of members of the group.

Table 4-2   Domain local groups found in the Builtin container

Group Name	Description
Account Operators	Able to create, delete, and modify user accounts and groups within the domain; they cannot place themselves or anyone else in the administrators group
Administrators	Assigned complete unrestricted access to the domain
Backup Operators	Able to override security restrictions for the purpose of backing up or restoring files
Guests	Have no default permissions or rights (The guests group is a member of the special group named Everyone; this means that any access permissions to the Everyone group gives permission to the Guests group)
Incoming Forest Trust Builders	Able to create one-way incoming trusts to the forest; this group is only available in the forest root domain

4

Table 4-2   Domain local groups found in the Builtin container (continued)

Group Name	Description
Network Configuration Operators	Able to change TCP/IP settings on domain controllers within the domain
Performance Log Users	Able to remotely access servers to schedule logging of performance counters
Performance Monitor Users	Able to remotely access servers to monitor performance
Pre-Windows 2000 Compatible Access	This group is created to support applications that work with Windows NT 4.0, but may have problems with Windows Server 2003 security; has read access on all users and groups within the domain; used primarily for Windows NT RAS servers that require access to Active Directory
Print Operators	Have all print administration rights
Remote Desktop Users	Able to log on to domain controllers within the domain remotely
Replicator	Used by the File Replication Service
Server Operators	Able to share disk resources, back-up and restore files, and shut down or restart the server
Terminal Server License Servers	Contains computer accounts for all servers configured as Terminal Server License Servers
Users	Have no default permissions, except for permissions assigned by the administrator
Windows Authorization Access Group	Allows members to query user accounts for the group membership information of a user

Depending upon the services installed and configured on your server, some of the groups listed in Table 4-2 may not appear in the Builtin container.

The Users Container

The Users container contains a number of different domain local and global group accounts. Table 4-3 outlines the name of each of the domain local and global groups found in this container, as well as a description of the purpose or capabilities of members of the group. Note that some of the groups listed are only found in the root domain of an Active Directory forest rather than each individual domain.

Table 4-3   Domain local and global groups found in the Users container

Group Name	Group Scope	Description
Cert Publishers	Domain local	Able to publish certificates in Active Directory
DnsAdmins	Domain local	Able to administer DNS server settings and configuration

Table 4-3   Domain local and global groups found in the Users container (continued)

Group Name	Group Scope	Description
DnsUpdateProxy	Global	Able to perform DNS dynamic updates on behalf of other clients
Domain Admins	Global	Able to perform domain administration tasks
Domain Computers	Global	Contains all workstations and server computer accounts in the domain
Domain Controllers	Global	Contains all domain controller computer accounts in the domain
Domain Guests	Global	Guest accounts in the domain should be added to this group
Domain Users	Global	All domain user accounts are added to this group
Enterprise Admins	Global	Able to perform administrative tasks throughout an Active Directory forest; this group only exists in the forest root domain
Group Policy Creator Owners	Global	Able to modify group policy objects and settings in the domain
RAS and IAS Servers	Global	Servers in this group can access the remote access properties of a user account
Schema Admins	Global	Able to perform administrative tasks related to the Active Directory schema; this group only exists in the forest root domain
WINS Users	Domain local	Allows read-only access to WINS server settings

CREATING AND MANAGING COMPUTER ACCOUNTS

In much the same way that users on a network require user accounts, computers running Windows NT 4.0, Windows 2000, Windows XP, and Windows Server 2003 require computer accounts to be members of an Active Directory domain. While computer accounts can be created in a domain during the operating system installation processes, they can also be added manually after the fact. While the primary tool used to create and manage computer accounts is the familiar Active Directory Users and Computers, computer accounts can also be created from the System applet in Control Panel from the workstation being added to the domain, as long as the user doing so has been granted appropriate privileges in Active Directory.

NOTE   Computers running Windows 95 and Windows 98 do not support advanced security features and, as such, are not assigned computer accounts in a domain.

In the same way that user and group accounts can be created and managed using the various directory service command-line tools looked at earlier in this chapter, so too can computer accounts. For example, the DSADD COMPUTER command can be used to create new computer accounts from the command line, while DSMOD COMPUTER can be used to change the settings of existing computer accounts. For more information on creating and modifying computer accounts from the command line, see the appropriate command in Windows Server 2003 Help and Support.

In Activity 4-8 you use Active Directory Users and Computers to create a new computer account.

Activity 4-8: Creating and Managing Computer Accounts

Time Required: 10 minutes

Objective: Use Active Directory Users and Computers to create and manage computer accounts.

Description: The IT manager at Dover Leasing has asked you to document the process for creating new computer accounts in Active Directory Users and Computers. In this activity you create and configure the properties of a new computer account.

1. Click **Start**, select **Administrative Tools**, and click **Active Directory Users and Computers**.

2. Right-click the **Computers** container, select **New**, and then click **Computer**. The New Object – Computer window appears, as shown in Figure 4-12.

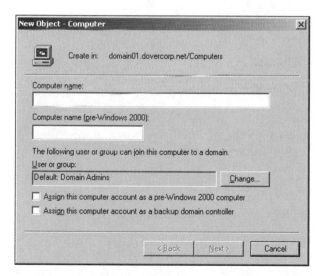

Figure 4-12   The New Object – Computer window

3. In the Computer name text box, type **WorkstationXX**, where *XX* is your assigned student number. Notice that the Computer name (pre-Windows 2000) text box is populated automatically. Click **Next**.

4. At the Managed screen, click **Next**. A managed computer is one associated with the Windows Server 2003 Remote Installation Services (RIS).

5. Click **Finish**. The new computer account will appear in the Computers container.

6. Right-click on **WorkstationXX** and click **Properties**.

7. Review the settings on the General tab, as shown in Figure 4-13. Click the **Operating System** tab.

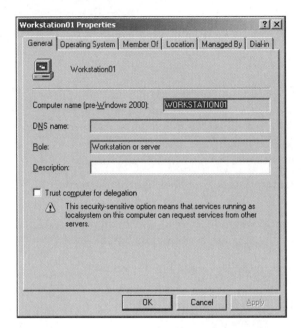

Figure 4-13   The properties of a computer account

8. Notice that no information is available on the Operating System tab. This information would be generated automatically if a computer named WorkstationXX actually existed on the network. Click the **Member Of** tab.

9. Notice that WorkstationXX is a member of the Domain Computers group by default. Click the **Location** tab.

10. In the Location text box, type **Miami**. Click the **Managed By** tab.

11. In a manner similar to a group account, the Managed By tab can be used to configure information about the user responsible for managing the computer. Click the **Dial-in** tab.

12. Review the settings available on the Dial-in tab, and click **OK**.

13. Close Active Directory Users and Computers.

Resetting Computer Accounts

Computers that are members of a domain use a secure communication channel known as a secure channel to communicate with a domain controller. A password is associated with this secure channel that is changed every 30 days, and is synchronized automatically with the domain controller and the workstation. In rare cases, such as if a particular computer has not been connected to the network (or turned off) for longer than 30 days or the channel is somehow disrupted, a user logging on to that workstation may not be able to authenticate due to synchronization issues. The error messages associated with this problem are typically listed in Event Viewer as Event IDs 3210 and 5722.

When synchronization problems of this manner occur, an administrator must reset the computer account associated with the workstation. The two primary ways to accomplish this include:

- Using Active Directory Users and Computers
- Using the Netdom.exe command from the Windows Support Tools

To reset a computer account using Active Directory Users and Computers, simply right-click on the computer account object and choose the Reset Account option.

To reset a computer account using Netdom.exe, the following command should be issued from the command line:

```
Netdom reset computername /domain: domainname
```

In this example, computername is the name of the workstation to be reset, and domainname is the domain in which the computer account resides.

Chapter Summary

- The primary purpose of groups in a network environment is to ease the administrative burden associated with assigning rights and permissions to individual user accounts.

- Windows Server 2003 supports two group types, known as security groups and distribution groups. Security groups have an associated SID and can be assigned rights and permissions. Distribution groups are primarily used as e-mail entities and do not include an SID.

- Windows Server 2003 supports three different group scopes, known as global, domain local, and universal. The scope of a group impacts how it can be used in an Active Directory environment. The configured functional level of a domain also impacts the scopes of groups that can be created and associated membership rules.

- The primary tool used to create and manage group accounts in a Windows Server 2003 Active Directory environment is Active Directory Users and Computers. The directory service command-line tools can also be used to manage group accounts, such as DSADD, DSMOD, DSQUERY, DSMOVE, and DSRM.

❑ The most scalable method of managing security groups to assign rights and permissions is A G U DL P. The method provides an administrator with maximum flexibility and a minimal need to assign rights and permissions more often than necessary.

❑ The primary tools used to gather group membership information are the Member Of and Members tabs in the properties of objects, and the DSGET command-line utility.

❑ Windows Server 2003 Active Directory includes a number of built-in global and domain local groups in both the Users and Builtin containers. Many of these groups are pre-assigned rights and permissions to perform common administration-related functions.

❑ Workstations running Windows NT 4.0, Windows 2000, Windows XP, and Windows Server 2003 require computer accounts in Active Directory. Computer accounts are typically created and managed using Active Directory Users and Computers, but can also be created and managed from the command line using tools like DSADD and DSMOD.

KEY TERMS

distribution group — A group that is only used for an e-mail distribution list.

domain functional level — The level at which a Windows Server 2003 domain is configured, such as Windows 2000 mixed mode, Windows 2000 native mode, or Windows Server 2003.

domain local group — A group that can only be assigned permissions to a resource available in the domain in which it is created. However, group membership can come from any domain within the forest. Created on domain controllers within the domain.

global group — A group that is mainly used for organizing other objects into administrative units. A global group can be assigned permissions to any resource in any domain within the forest. The main limitation of a global group is that it can only contain members of the same domain in which it is created.

group — A container object that is used to organize a collection of users, computers, contacts, or other groups into a single object reference.

security group — A group that can be used to define permissions on a resource object.

universal group — A group that can be assigned permissions to any resource in any domain within the forest. Universal groups can consist of any user or group object except for local groups.

Windows 2000 mixed — The default domain functional level for a Windows Server 2003 Active Directory domain. Supports Windows NT Server 4.0, Windows 2000 Server, and Windows Server 2003 domain controllers.

Windows 2000 native — A domain functional level that supports both Windows 2000 Server and Windows Server 2003 domain controllers.

Windows Server 2003 — A domain functional level that supports Windows Server 2003 domain controllers only.

REVIEW QUESTIONS

1. Which of the following are considered group types? (Choose all that apply.)

    a. Global

    b. Domain local

    c. Security

    d. Distribution

2. Which of the following are considered group scopes? (Choose all that apply.)

    a. Global

    b. Universal

    c. Domain local

    d. Distribution

3. Which of the following objects can be added to a global group when a domain is configured to the Windows Server 2003 domain functional level?

    a. Users

    b. Global groups

    c. Domain local groups

    d. Universal groups

4. Which of the following objects can be added to a domain local group when a domain is configured to the Windows 2000 mixed domain functional level?

    a. Users

    b. Global groups

    c. Domain local groups

    d. Universal groups

5. Which of the following group types cannot be created when a domain is configured to the Windows 2000 mixed domain functional level?

    a. Global groups

    b. Domain local groups

    c. Universal groups

    d. None of the above

6. A Windows Server 2003 Active Directory domain is configured to the Windows 2000 mixed domain functional level by default.

    a. True

    b. False

4

7. When can a domain local group be converted to a universal group?

    a. Always

    b. Never

    c. When the domain local group does not contain any other domain local groups as members

    d. When the domain local group does not contain any global groups as members

8. When can a global group be converted to a universal group?

    a. Always

    b. Never

    c. When the global group does not contain any other global groups

    d. When the global group is not a member of any other global groups

9. When can a universal group be converted to a domain local group?

    a. Always

    b. Never

    c. When the universal group does not contain any other universal groups

    d. When the domain local group does not contain any other universal groups

10. Which of the following command-line utilities is used to convert a group's scope?

    a. DSMOD

    b. DSADD

    c. DSGET

    d. DSRM

11. Which of the following command-line utilities is used to obtain a listing of all group members?

    a. DSMOD

    b. DSGET

    c. DSADD

    d. DSRM

12. Which of the following command-line utilities is used to create new group objects?

    a. DSADD

    b. DSMOD

    c. DSGET

    d. DSMOVE

13. Which of the following built-in global groups are all user accounts added to automatically?

    a. Domain Guests

    b. Domain Users

    c. Domain Admins

    d. Schema Admins

14. Which of the following built-in global groups are all workstations and member servers added to automatically?

    a. Domain Computers

    b. Domain Controllers

    c. Domain Servers

    d. Domain PCs

15. Which of the following tools is used to reset a computer account?

    a. Active Directory Users and Computers

    b. NETSH

    c. NETDOM

    d. NETCONF

16. Which of the following group scopes contains global groups as a member in a domain configured to the Windows 2000 mixed functional level?

    a. Domain local groups

    b. Global groups

    c. Universal groups

17. What is indicated when a domain local group cannot be converted to a universal group?

    a. The functional level of the domain is set to Windows 2000 mixed

    b. The functional level of the domain is set to Windows 2000 native

    c. The functional level of the domain is set to Windows Server 2003

18. Which of the following built-in groups is only found in the forest root domain?

    a. Domain Admins

    b. Enterprise Admins

    c. Schema Admins

    d. Domain Guests

19. Which tab in the properties of a user account is used to view that user's group membership information?

    a. Member Of

    b. Members

    c. Policies

    d. Membership

20. Which tab in the properties of a group account is used to view the other groups that are members of this group?

    a. Member Of

    b. Members

    c. Policies

    d. Membership

CASE PROJECTS

CASE
PROJECTS

Case Project 4-1

Using the information learned in this chapter, create three new security group accounts named Global Test, Domain Local Test, and Universal Test, using the scope designated in their names. For each group scope, attempt to add each of the other two groups to that group as members, and document whether each attempt is successful or not.

CASE
PROJECTS

Case Project 4-2

The DSADD command provides an effective method for administrators to create new group accounts from the command line. Use the DSADD utility to create the four new groups accounts listed in the table below. All the group accounts should be created in the Users container in your DomainXX.Dovercorp.Net domain. Use the DSADD topic in Help and Support Center to determine the appropriate switches required to configure these accounts from the command line.

Group Name	Group Type	Group Scope	Group Description
Project Users	Security	Global	Project management users
Project Resources	Security	Domain Local	Project management resources
Universal IT Staff	Security	Universal	All Dover Leasing ITstaff
Marketing Distribution	Distribution	Universal	All Dover Leasing marketing staff

CASE
PROJECTS

Case Project 4-3

The IT Manager at Dover Leasing has asked you to create documentation for the membership of all existing groups at Dover Leasing. Use the DSGET command to create a series of text files that list the membership of all existing groups in the Builtin and Users containers, naming the files according to the names of these groups.

MANAGING FILE ACCESS

After reading this chapter and completing the exercises, you will be able to:

♦ Identify and understand the differences between the various file systems supported in Windows Server 2003

♦ Create and manage shared folders

♦ Understand and configure the shared folder permissions available in Windows Server 2003

♦ Understand and configure the NTFS permissions available in Windows Server 2003

♦ Determine the impact of combining shared folder and NTFS permissions

♦ Convert partitions and volumes from FAT to NTFS

The main reason for implementing a network is to allow users to access shared resources. Examples of shared resources commonly found on a network include files, folders, and printers. While the ability to share resources is the primary goal of any network, these resources also need to be properly secured to ensure that they are made available to only those users who require access. Furthermore, the level of access that users need for a particular resource also needs to be considered, since it is likely to be different for different users or groups.

Resources such as files, folders, and printers are secured on a Windows Server 2003 network through the use of permissions. By configuring various permissions on a particular resource, an administrator can limit a certain group of users' ability to read files only, while granting another group complete control. The ability to configure resource permissions in a very granular fashion ultimately gives an administrator a high degree of control over resource access. However, these permissions must be managed carefully. An understanding of how permissions apply in a Windows Server 2003 environment is critical for all network administration staff.

Windows Server 2003 supports two types of permissions in order to secure file and folder resources: NTFS and shared folder. NTFS permissions can be applied to resources that are stored on partitions or volumes formatted with the NTFS file system. Shared folder permissions can be applied to any folder that has been shared to allow access from network workstations. The combination of NTFS and shared folder permissions has often been the basis of intensive troubleshooting tasks for administrators. It is important to understand how permissions are applied to ensure that clients obtain appropriate access to resources. To ensure an understanding of this concept, the integration of NTFS and shared folder permissions is discussed in this chapter, as is monitoring access to folders that are shared on the network.

WINDOWS SERVER 2003 FILE SYSTEMS

Like its predecessor Windows 2000, Windows Server 2003 supports three main file systems, namely File Allocation Table (FAT), FAT32, and NTFS. The file system choice for a particular partition or volume on a Windows Server 2003 system is usually a function of how the system will be used, whether multiple operating systems will be installed on the same system, and the security requirements for the system. For example, if Windows Server 2003 is installed on a system in a lab environment, it might be configured in a dual-boot configuration with another operating system such as Windows 98. Because Windows 98 only supports the FAT and FAT32 file systems, an administrator might not format any partitions or volumes using NTFS, because Windows 98 cannot access this file system locally.

On a production server, however, a dual-boot configuration is exceptionally rare. Because of the security features provided by NTFS, this file system is highly recommended for all partitions on volumes on a Windows Server 2003 system, with very few exceptions. The following sections look at the basic characteristics of the FAT, FAT32, and NTFS file systems.

FAT

FAT is a file system used by MS-DOS and supported by all versions of Windows created since. Although traditionally limited to partitions up to 2 GB in size, the version of FAT included with Windows Server 2003 supports partitions up to 4 GB. The two biggest limitations of the FAT file system are the relatively small supported partition sizes, and the fact that FAT provides no file system security features, such as those available with NTFS. Comparatively speaking, disk space usage on a FAT partition is also poor when compared to both FAT32 and NTFS. For these reasons, most administrators shy away from formatting partitions using the FAT file system on Windows Server 2003 systems.

FAT32

A derivative of the FAT file system, **FAT32** was originally introduced in Windows 95 OSR2. The main difference between FAT32 and the FAT file systems is that FAT32 supports much larger partition sizes, up to 2 terabytes (TB). However, much like the FAT file system, FAT32 does not provide any of the advanced security features of NTFS, namely the ability to configure permissions on file and folder resources.

NTFS

Microsoft introduced a new file system known as **NTFS** beginning with the Windows NT operating system. The current version of NTFS is version 5, which is supported by systems running Windows NT 4.0 (SP5 or later), Windows 2000, Windows XP, and Windows Server 2003. The NTFS file system theoretically supports much larger partition sizes than both FAT and FAT32, since it is capable of addressing up to 16 Exabytes (EB) of disk space. In practice, however, the maximum NTFS partition sizes range from 2 TB up to approximately 16 TB, depending on the disk type and cluster size used.

NTFS is the preferred file system for all partitions and volumes on a Windows Server 2003 system. Some of the advantages of NTFS over both FAT and FAT32 include:

- Greater scalability for large disks, and better performance than FAT-based systems on larger partitions
- Support for Active Directory on systems configured as domain controllers; all domain controllers must have at least one NTFS partition or volume available to hold the Sysvol folder
- The ability to configure security permissions on individual files and folders stored on an NTFS partition or volume
- Built-in support for both compression and encryption
- The ability to configure disk space quotas for individual users
- Support for Remote Storage, the ability to extend disk space using removable media
- Recovery logging of disk activities, allowing information relating to NTFS partitions or volumes to be recovered quickly in the event of system problems

For the purpose of this chapter, the most important consideration when choosing a file system is its ability to support security permissions. In the following sections you learn more about the types of security permissions available on Windows Server 2003 systems.

CREATING AND MANAGING SHARED FOLDERS

Shared folders must be configured with the proper access-control permissions to permit general user access to data on a network. A **shared folder** is a data resource that has been made available over the network to authorized network clients. These clients can then view or modify the contents of the folder, depending upon the level of permissions granted to either the user or group of which the user is a member.

Users are required to have appropriate rights to create shared folders. A member of the Administrators or Server Operators groups has the right to create shared folders within a domain. Members of the Power Users group can also configure shared folders on Windows Server 2003 systems not configured as domain controllers. There are several ways to create shared folders; two of the more popular methods include using the Windows Explorer interface and the Computer Management console. Beyond simply allowing you to create new shared folders, the Computer Management console also allows shared folders to be monitored, as explored later in this section.

Using Windows Explorer

Windows Explorer is the standard method used to create and share folders for all versions of Windows since Windows 95. It can be used to create, maintain, and share folders on any drive connected to the computer. There are many ways to open Windows Explorer. For example, you can click the Windows Explorer icon on the Accessories menu, or you can right-click almost any drive-related object and click the Explore command on the shortcut menu. Figure 5-1 illustrates the Windows Explorer window.

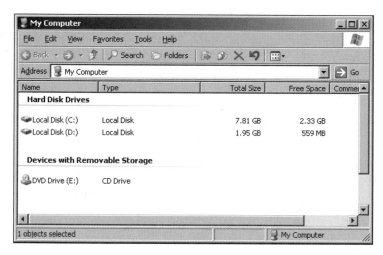

Figure 5-1   The Windows Explorer window

In Activity 5-1 you create a new folder and then share it using Windows Explorer.

Folders are shared in Windows Server 2003 by accessing the Sharing tab of a folder's properties, as illustrated in Figure 5-2.

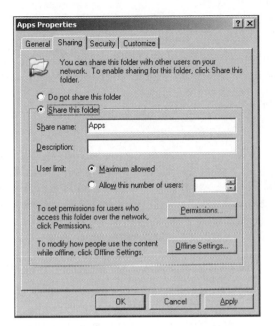

Figure 5-2   The Sharing tab in the properties of a folder

Activity 5-1: Creating a Shared Folder Using Windows Explorer

Time Required: 5 minutes

Objective: Create a shared folder using Windows Explorer.

Description: The IT manager at Dover Leasing has asked you to create a shared folder on a new Windows Server 2003 system that will ultimately be used to store network-accessible applications for users in the Marketing Department. In this activity, you create a new folder called Apps and then share it over the network using Windows Explorer.

1. Log on with your **AdminXX** account, where *XX* is your assigned student number. Click **Start**, select **All Programs**, select **Accessories**, and then click **Windows Explorer**.

2. Click the **plus sign (+)** next to My Computer to expand it, then click drive **D:**. Click **File** on the menu bar, select **New**, and then click **Folder**. Name the new folder **Apps**.

3. Right-click the **Apps** folder and then click **Sharing and Security**.

4. On the Sharing tab, click the **Share this folder** radio button, as shown in Figure 5-2.

5. In the Share name text box, type **Applications**.

6. In the Description text box, type **Applications for Marketing Users**.

7. Click **OK** to share the folder and close the Apps Properties dialog box. Close the Windows Explorer window.

8. To verify that the new shared folder called Applications is available over the network, open a command prompt, and at the command line type **net view \\serverXX**, where *XX* is your assigned student number. Press **Enter**.

9. All of the shared folders available on your server should be visible, including the new Applications folder just created. Close the command prompt window.

10. Click **Start**, and then click **Run**. In the Open text box, type **explorer.exe** and click **OK**. Click the **plus sign (+)** next to My Network Places to expand it. Click the **plus sign (+)** next to Entire Network to expand it. Click the **plus sign (+)** next to Microsoft Windows Network to expand it. Click the **plus sign (+)** next to Domain*XX* (where *XX* is your assigned student number) to expand it. Click on **Server*XX*** to view the shared resources available on your server.

11. Close all open windows.

> By default, the shared name of a folder is the same as the actual folder name, but this is not a requirement. It is important to provide a meaningful share name because this is how your users find the share. Be careful of any share names that are longer than eight characters in cases where you have any legacy clients such as Windows 3.1 or DOS that cannot handle long file names.

Windows Explorer indicates a shared folder by placing a hand icon under the folder, as shown in Figure 5-3.

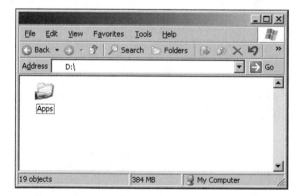

Figure 5-3   Identifying a shared folder by its icon in Windows Explorer

There may be times when you would like to create a shared folder but not have it listed in My Network Places or Network Neighborhood. To hide a shared folder, place a dollar sign ($) after its name. For example, if you create a shared folder called "Salary," you can hide it by giving it the share name "Salary$." To map or connect to a hidden share, a user needs to manually type the share name, including the dollar sign. Windows Server 2003 creates a number of hidden **administrative shares** by default during the installation process. For example, the Admin$ share allows an administrator to easily connect to the Windows folder on a server or workstation across the network, whereas shares like C$ provide an administrator with easy access to the root of the C drive on a computer. Figure 5-4 illustrates the shared folder name associated with the Windows folder on a Windows Server 2003 system.

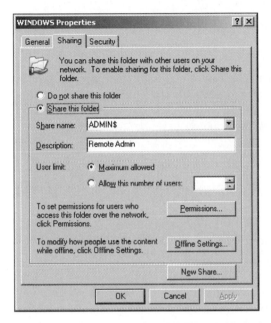

Figure 5-4   The Windows folder is shared as Admin$ by default

Using Computer Management

Another popular method for creating and managing shared folders in Windows Server 2003 is through the use of the **Computer Management console**. Computer Management is a predefined Microsoft Management Console (MMC) application that allows you to perform a variety of administrative tasks, such as sharing and monitoring folders for both local and remote computers.

Shared folders are created in the Shared Folders section of Computer Management using the Share a Folder Wizard. Beyond simply allowing you to create new shared folders, this wizard also allows you to configure shared folder permissions. Three of the choices are preconfigured, whereas the fourth allows custom permissions to be specified. Permission options found in the wizard include:

- All users have read-only access—Grants the Read permission to the Everyone group

- Administrators have full access; other users have read-only access—Grants Full Control permission to the local Administrators group and Read permission to the Everyone group

- Administrators have full access; other users have read and write access—Grants Full Control permission to the local Administrators group and both Read and Change permissions access to the Everyone group

- Use custom share and folder permissions—Allows both share and NTFS permissions to be defined manually

If you want to stop sharing a folder, the easiest way to do this is via the Shares node in the Computer Management console. The list of shares appears in the details pane of the console. To stop sharing a particular folder, you simply right-click the share that is to be discontinued, and click Stop Sharing on the shortcut menu.

Activity 5-2: Creating and Viewing Shared Folders Using Computer Management

Time Required: 10 minutes

Objective: Create and view shared folders using Computer Management.

Description: To streamline the training process for new help desk staff at Dover Leasing, the IT manager has asked you to document the process for using the Computer Management tool to create and view shared folders on network servers. In this activity, you use the Computer Management tool to both view the existing visible and hidden shares, as well as create a new shared folder.

1. Click **Start**, right-click **My Computer**, and click **Manage**. The Computer Management tool opens, as illustrated in Figure 5-5. If necessary, click the **plus sign (+)** next to System Tools to expand it.

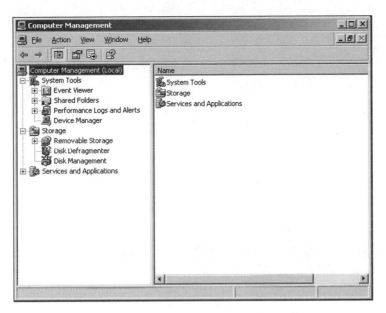

5

Figure 5-5   The Computer Management console

2. Click the **+ (plus symbol)** next to the Shared Folders node to expand it. The Shares, Sessions, and Open Files nodes appear.

3. Click the **Shares** folder to view its contents, as illustrated in Figure 5-6. Notice that the list includes folders that have been manually created (such as Applications), administrative shares (such as C$), and shared folders used by operating system communication processes (such as IPC$). The Shares node also provides the complete file system path to the shared folder.

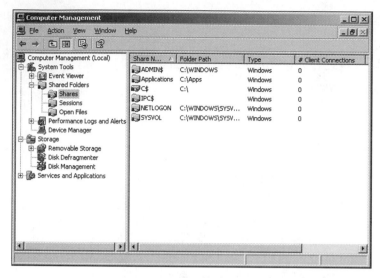

Figure 5-6   Contents of the Shares node

4. Right-click the **Shares** folder and click **New Share**. The Share a Folder Wizard appears. At the welcome screen, click **Next**.

5. At the Folder Path screen, type **D:\mktgdocs** in the Folder path text box, as illustrated in Figure 5-7. Click **Next**.

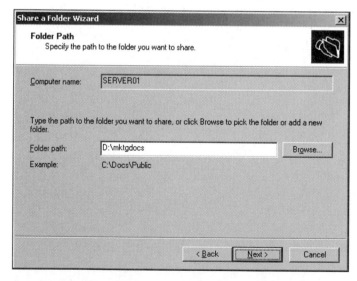

Figure 5-7   Configuring the path for a shared folder

6. When prompted with the dialog box specifying that the folder doesn't exist and asking whether you want to create it, click **Yes**.

7. At the Name, Description, and Settings screen, type **Marketingdocs** in the Share name text box and **All Marketing Documentation** in the Description text box. Click **Next**.

8. At the Permissions screen, select the **Administrators have full access; other users have read–only access** radio button, as shown in Figure 5-8. Click **Finish**.

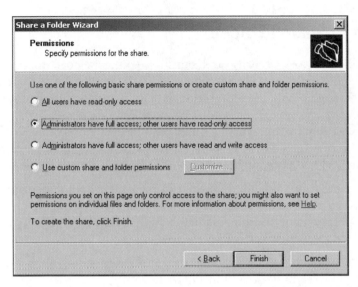

Figure 5-8   Configuring permissions using the Share a Folder Wizard

9. At the Sharing was Successful screen, review the Summary information and then click **Close**.

10. Verify that the new Marketingdocs shared folder is visible in the details pane of the Shares node in Computer Management.

11. To verify that the Marketingdocs folder is accessible over the network, open the Run command and type **\\serverXX\marketingdocs** in the Open text box (where *XX* is your assigned student number) and click **OK**. The Marketingdocs folder should open in a new window.

12. Close all open windows.

A third method sometimes used to share folders on a Windows Server 2003 system is the NET SHARE command. This command can be used to share an existing folder from the command line. For example, to share the folder C:\testfolder with a share name of test, the correct syntax for the command would be net share test="C:\testfolder".

Monitoring Access to Shared Folders

To assist in maintaining network security and statistics, you may need to periodically monitor shared folder and open-file access. Keeping track of the number of users connected to a specific network share helps you plan for future capacity requirements and fine-tuning of performance levels. In Windows Server 2003, you are able to see how many people are connected to a share, who they are, and what files they have open at any given time. You can also disconnect users from a specific share or send network messages alerting users of pending changes to the server's status, such as a planned reboot.

This Computer Management utility is the tool used to perform shared folder monitoring and management tasks on a Windows Server 2003 network. As with most MMC-based tools, the Computer Management console facilitates the management of both local and remote computers on the network.

The Sessions node in Computer Management provides information about the users currently connected to a server, as illustrated in Figure 5-9.

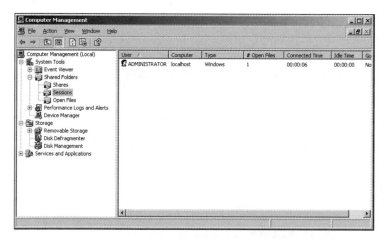

Figure 5-9   The Sessions node under Shared Folders

To manage a different computer, right-click Computer Management (Local), select Connect to another computer, and then provide the name of the server you wish to manage.

The Open Files node in Computer Management provides information about all of the files that users currently have open. This information can be used to troubleshoot file-access problems, such as when two users attempt to access the same file but one of the users is granted read-access only.

If you want to disconnect an open file connection or session, simply right-click the entry in the details pane, and click Close Open File or Close Session on the shortcut menu. This can assist you in situations where you have changed permissions on a folder or file and you want the new permissions to take effect immediatcly.

To help prevent data loss, it is always a best practice to send users a warning message before disconnecting sessions or shutting down a server. The Computer Management tool facilitates this by allowing you to send a console message to all users connected to the server. Illustrated in Figure 5-10, the Send Console Mcssage feature allows you to supply a custom warning message that appears as a dialog box on the user's screen.

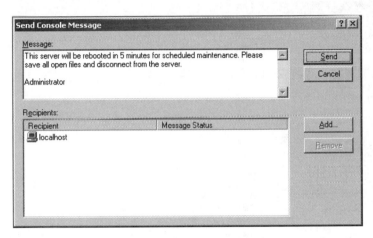

Figure 5-10   The Send Console Message window

Managing Shared Folder Permissions

Each folder that is shared has a **discretionary access control list (DACL)** associated with it. A DACL is part of an object's security descriptor that contains a list of user or group references that have been allowed or denied permissions to the resource. Each user or group name listed in the DACL is referred to as an **access control entry (ACE)**. To access the DACL, click the Permissions button on the Sharing tab of a folder's properties. You can also access it by clicking the Custom button when using the Share a Folder Wizard. Figure 5-8 illustrates the DACL for a shared folder called Apps.

It is important to remember that share permissions only apply to users that connect to a shared folder over the network; they do not apply to a user logged on to the local machine where the shared folder is defined. Windows Server 2003 supports three different share permissions, as explained in Table 5-1.

Table 5-1   Shared folder permissions in Windows Server 2003

Shared Folder Permission	Capabilities
Read	Allows the abilities to browse the file and folder names (including subfolders), read the data in a file, and execute programs
Change	Allows the same abilities as the Read permission, as well as the abilities to add and delete files in the folder, and read and edit the contents of existing files
Full Control	Allows the same abilities as the Read and Change permissions, as well as the ability to change the permissions associated with the folder

Notice that Windows Server 2003 does not include a No Access share permission as found on Windows NT systems. Instead, to deny a user or group access to a shared folder, an administrator must explicitly deny the user that particular permission, as shown in Figure 5-11.

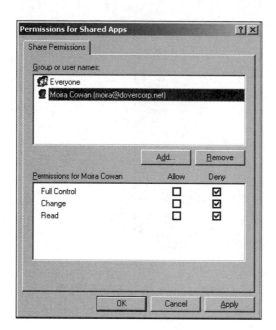

Figure 5-11   Denying permissions for a shared folder

As discussed previously, when a new share is created, the default permission on the shared folder allows the Everyone group read access. One of the first steps an administrator should perform after sharing a folder is to substitute the Everyone group for one that includes authenticated domain users. In many companies, the Users group is given the Full Control shared folder permission, while resources are made more secure through the use of NTFS permissions.

The Everyone group includes all users who have access to the network, regardless of whether they have been authenticated in the domain.

NOTE

When a share is created and a user is assigned permission to that share, the user also has the same level of permissions to all subfolders and files inside that share. In other words, the permissions configured on the shared folder are inherited by all of the objects that it contains. In Activity 5-3, you configure and test the effects of different shared folder permissions.

5

Activity 5-3: Implementing Shared Folder Permissions

ACTIVITY

Time Required: 15 minutes

Objective: Control access to resources using shared folder permissions.

Description: The IT manager at Dover Leasing is very concerned with ensuring that all network resources are properly secured so that only authorized network users can access shared folders and their contents. He has asked you to ensure that only members of the Domain Admins group have Full Control permission for the Marketingdocs shared folder, while members of the Marketing Users group are granted Change permission. All other users should not have access to the folder. In this activity, you configure permissions on the Marketingdocs shared folder to implement the requirements outlined by the IT manager.

1. Open My Computer and access the properties of the D:\mktgdocs folder.

2. Click the **Sharing** tab, and then click the **Permissions** button. The Permissions for Marketingdocs dialog box opens.

3. In the Group or user names list box, ensure that Everyone is selected and click the **Remove** button.

4. Click **Add**. The Select Users, Computers, or Groups dialog box opens.

5. In the Enter the object names to select text box, type **Domain Admins** and click **OK**. Domain Admins should be added to the Group or user names list of the Permissions dialog box, with the configured permission of Allow Read.

6. In the Allow column, check the **Full Control** check box.

7. Click **Add**. In the Enter the object names to select (examples) text box, type **Marketing Users** and click **OK**.

8. Ensure that the Marketing Users group is selected in the Group or user names list box. In the Allow column, check the **Change** box, and then click **OK**. Click **OK** in the mktgdocs Properties dialog box.

9. Close all open windows.

10. Click **Start**, and then click **Run**. In the Open text box, type **\\serverXX\marketingdocs** (where *XX* is your assigned student number) and click **OK**. The Marketingdocs window opens.

11. Right-click an area of white space in the window, select **New**, and then click **Folder**. Name the folder **July Documents** and then close the window.

12. Log off, and log on again using the **mcowan** account with the password **Password01**.

13. At the Run command, type **\\serverXX\marketingdocs** (where *XX* is your assigned student number) and click **OK**. The Marketingdocs window opens.

14. Attempt to create a new folder called **August Documents** in the Marketingdocs folder. This will be possible because all members of the Marketing Users group have the Change permission to the shared folder.

15. Close all open windows and log off.

16. Log on as user **mmanore** with the password **Password01**.

17. At the Run command, type **\\serverXX\marketingdocs** (where *XX* is your assigned student number) and click **OK**. The mmanore account is not able to access the folder because it lacks sufficient permissions.

18. Close all open windows and log off. Log on using your **AdminXX** account.

Shared folder permissions are cumulative. All the permissions assigned to a user, and any group of which the user is a member, are combined and the combination of all the permissions applies. For example, imagine if the user Moira Cowan is a member of both the Marketing and Managers groups. If the Marketing group is assigned the Read permission to a share and the Managers group is assigned Change, Moira's effective permission would be a combination of both, equivalent to Change. A single but important exception to this rule applies: when a user (or a group of which a user is a member) is denied a permission, the denied entry always overrides any permissions that are allowed. So, if the Marketing group were ultimately denied Full Control to the shared folder, Moira would not have access because this permission would override the fact that she is granted the Change permission as a member of the Marketing group.

NTFS PERMISSIONS

Files and folders located on NTFS partitions or volumes can be secured through the use of NTFS permissions. A Windows Server 2003 administrator needs to be familiar with how NTFS permissions are applied, the different standard and special NTFS permissions available, and how the **effective permissions** for a particular user or group can be determined. Each of these concepts is covered in more detail in the following sections.

NTFS Permission Concepts

It is important to understand the different NTFS file and directory permissions that are available, as well as how they are applied. Remember that NTFS permissions can only be applied to files and folders that exist on partitions formatted with the NTFS file system. As such, NTFS permissions cannot be applied to files or folders that reside on partitions formatted using the FAT or FAT32 file systems.

- NTFS permissions are configured via the Security tab, which is accessed by right-clicking any file or folder and clicking Properties.

- NTFS permissions are cumulative. If a user is a member of multiple groups that have different permissions, the final permission is the sum of all permissions.

- Permissions that are explicitly denied always override those that are allowed. For example, if the Mark Manore user account is explicitly denied Full Control on a folder through an individual or group permission assignment, this overrides any permissions that Mark may have been allowed via other group memberships.

- NTFS folder permissions are inherited by child folders and files, unless otherwise specified. Clearing the Allow inheritable permissions from the parent to propagate to this object and all child objects check box in the Advanced section of the Security property sheet can prevent the inheritance of NTFS permissions.

- NTFS permissions can be set at a file level, as well as at a folder level.

- When a new access control entry is added to an NTFS file or folder, the default permissions allow the user or group both the Read and the Read and Execute permissions for files, along with the List Folder Contents permission for folders.

- Windows Server 2003 has a set of standard NTFS permissions, as well as special permissions. Figure 5-12 illustrates the standard NTFS permissions available for a folder.

Figure 5-12   Standard NTFS permissions for a folder

Table 5–2 lists and explains the capabilities of **standard NTFS permissions**.

Table 5-2   Standard NTFS permissions in Windows Server 2003

NTFS Permission	Capabilities
Full Control	Allow the user to make any changes to the file or folder; details of the Full Control permission are listed in Table 5-3
Modify	Gives full permissions except the permission to delete subfolders and files, change permissions, and take ownership
Read & Execute	Gives permissions to traverse folders, list folders, read attributes and extended attributes, read permissions, and synchronize; these permissions are inherited by both files and folders
List Folder Contents	Same as Read and Execute permissions, except that the permissions are inherited only by folders and not by files; visible only on folders
Read	Same as Read and Execute, except without the permission to traverse folder; inherited by files and folders
Write	Gives permissions to create files and folders, write attributes and extended attributes, read permissions, and synchronize
Special Permissions	Used to designate that a user has been allowed or denied one or more of the more granular special permissions configured in the Advanced section of the security settings; Special permissions are detailed in Table 5-3

When assigning shared folder or NTFS permissions to users and groups, never grant them a higher level of access than they actually require. For example, if users only need to be able to read (but not change) files, the Read permission would be sufficient. Granting users too liberal a level of access can result in files being accidentally or purposely deleted, changed, and so forth.

In Activity 5-4 you implement standard NTFS permissions.

Activity 5-4: Implementing Standard NTFS Permissions

5

Time Required: 20 minutes

Objective: Configure and test NTFS permissions on a local folder.

Description: While the IT manager at Dover Leasing is certainly concerned about controlling access to shared folders on network servers, he is equally concerned about controlling access to local files and folders as well. In this activity, you have been asked to implement standard NTFS permission on a folder to review not only the default permissions but also the behavior of permission inheritance.

1. Open My Computer, and double-click on drive **D:**. Right-click an area of white space in the window, select **New**, and then click **Folder**. Name the folder **Test**. Right-click on the **D:\Test** folder and click **Properties**.

2. Click the **Security** tab to view the NTFS permissions assigned to users and groups by default. Click each individual entry in the Group or user names list box to view the properties associated with these accounts. Note that although each group is assigned different permissions to the folder, some assigned permissions appear within a gray box and cannot be changed. This is because these permissions have been inherited from a parent folder, in this case the NTFS permissions assigned to drive D.

3. Access the properties of drive **D:** and click the **Security** tab. Notice that the same NTFS permissions that are applied on the test folder are also applied on the D: drive. The difference is that these permissions were assigned directly to the D: drive by default when the partition was created and can be changed.

4. Click the **Add** button. In the Select Users, Computers, or Groups dialog box, type **moira** in the Enter the object names to select (examples) text box, and click **OK**. Ensure that the Moira Cowan user account is only granted the **Allow Read** permission, and click **OK**. When the Security dialog box appears, click **Yes**.

5. Open the Security tab of the test folder to confirm that the Moira Cowan user account now appears in the list of Group or user names. Click the **Moira Cowan** account to confirm that it has inherited the permissions assigned in the previous step.

6. Click the **Add** button. In the Select Users, Computers, or Groups dialog box, type **Marketing Users** in the Enter the object names to select (examples) text box, and click **OK**. Note that the group is assigned the allow Read & Execute, List Folder Contents, and Read permissions on the folder by default. Click **OK**.

7. Open the D:\Test folder. Right-click an area of white space, select **New**, and then click **Text Document**. Name the file **ntfstest.txt**.

8. Right-click the **ntfstest.txt** file and click **Properties**.

9. Click the **Security** tab to view the NTFS permissions associated with this file. Note that the permissions configured for this file have been inherited from the D:\Test folder.

10. In the Group or user names list box, click **Users** and then click **Remove**. Read the Security dialog box that appears, outlining the fact that the group Users cannot be removed because its settings are inherited from a parent folder. Click **OK**.

11. Click the **Advanced** button. The Advanced Security Settings for test dialog box opens.

12. Uncheck the **Allow inheritable permissions from the parent to propagate to this object and all child objects** check box.

13. When the Security dialog box opens, read its message, click **Copy**, and then click **OK**.

14. Click each user or group in the Group or user names section to view the associated NTFS permissions. Note that permissions are now directly applied to users and groups rather than being inherited. This is a result of clicking the Copy button in the previous step.

15. In the Group or user names list box, click **Users** and then click **Remove**. Notice that this time, the Users group is removed without issue. Close all open windows.

16. Log off and then log on again using the **mcowan** user account.

17. Open My Computer and attempt to create a new text file in the D:\Test folder. Notice that this action is denied because the Moira Cowan user account does not have sufficient permissions for the D:\Test folder as a member of the Marketing Users group.

18. Close all open windows and log off. Log on again using your **AdminXX** account.

Special NTFS Permissions

Windows Server 2003 provides access to 14 individual NTFS permissions that can be used to specify an even more granular level of access to a file or folder. Occasionally, one of the standard permissions may not provide enough control or, conversely, may provide a slightly higher level of access than a user requires. To access the special permissions, click the Advanced button in the Security tab on the Properties dialog box for the folder or file. The resulting Advanced Security dialog box allows you to assign special permissions to user or group accounts. To view the **special NTFS permissions** assigned to a user or group, click the user or group and then click the Edit button. The Permission Entry dialog box opens, as shown in Figure 5-13.

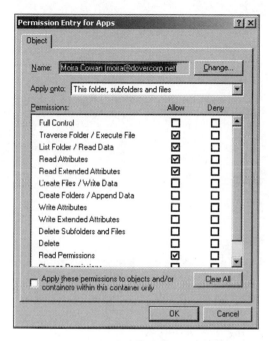

Figure 5-13   Viewing special NTFS permissions

The Permission Entry dialog box enables you to assign special NTFS permissions, while also providing a way to control permission inheritance settings. Special permissions can be applied in the following ways, as illustrated in Figure 5-14:

- This folder only
- This folder, subfolders, and files (default)
- This folder and subfolders
- This folder and files
- Subfolders and files only
- Subfolders only
- Files only

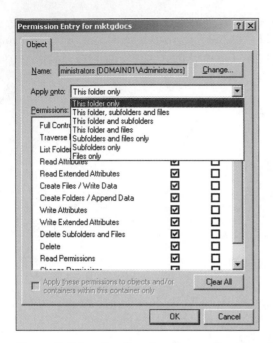

Figure 5-14   Configuring the method in which special permissions will be applied

Table 5-3 shows the special access permissions that you can apply and their functions.

Table 5-3   Special NTFS permissions in Windows Server 2003

Special NTFS Permission	Capabilities
Full Control	Provides the same level of access as the standard Full Control permission, and includes all of the special NTFS permissions listed in this table
Traverse Folder/Execute File	Controls the ability to pass through folders without explicit permission to enter in order to get to an intended folder; for example, a user may not have permission to read the Salesdata folder, but may have Read permission to JuneSales.doc in the Salesdata folder; if the user has traverse folder permissions, the user would be able to open the JuneSales.doc file
List Folder/Read Data	Controls the ability to view the contents of folders and read data files with a folder
Read Attributes	Controls the ability to view the attributes of a file or folder
Read Extended Attributes	Controls the ability to view the extended attributes of a file or folder; extended attributes are additional information attached to a file, as defined by an application
Create Files/Write Data	Controls the ability to create files within a folder (applies to folders only), while also controlling the ability to make changes to files and overwrite any existing content (applies to files only)

Table 5-3   Special NTFS permissions in Windows Server 2003 (continued)

Special NTFS Permission	Capabilities
Create Folders/Append Data	Controls the ability to create additional folders within a folder (applies to folders only), while also controlling the ability to add to the end of the file but not change, delete, or overwrite any existing content (applies to files only)
Write Attributes	Controls the ability to change the attributes of a file or folder, such as read-only or hidden; attributes are defined by NTFS
Write Extended Attributes	Controls the ability to change the extended attributes of a file or folder; extended attributes are defined by programs and can vary
Delete Subfolders and Files	Controls the ability to delete subfolders and files, even if the standard delete permission has not been granted on the sub-folder or file
Delete	Controls the ability to delete a file or folder
Read Permissions	Controls the ability to read the security permissions of a file or folder
Change Permissions	Controls the ability to change the security permissions of a file or folder
Take Ownership	Controls the ability to take ownership of a file or folder

In Activity 5-5 you configure special NTFS permissions.

Activity 5-5: Configuring Special NTFS Permissions

Time Required: 15 minutes

Objective: View, configure, and test special NTFS permissions.

Description: Having now used standard NTFS permissions to configure and test file and folder access, you have been asked by the IT manager to test the ability to control resource access using the special NTFS permissions. In this activity, you attempt to deny Marketing users the ability to read the NTFS permissions associated with a file or folder.

1. Open My Computer and create a new folder on drive D: called **Special Permissions**.

2. Open the properties of the Special Permissions folder and click the **Security** tab.

3. Add the **Marketing Users** group to the Group or user names list, granting it the default permissions only. Close all open windows.

4. Log off and then log on again using the **mcowan** user account.

5. Right-click the **D:\Special Permissions** folder, then click **Properties**. Click the **Security** tab to view the permission settings configured for different accounts. Note that while the permissions can be read by the mcowan user account, they cannot be changed. Close all open windows.

6. Log off and then log on again using your **AdminXX** account.

7. Right-click the **D:\Special Permissions** folder, then click **Properties**. Click the **Security** tab, and then click **Advanced**. The Advanced Security Settings for Special Permissions dialog box opens.

8. In the Permission entries list box, click the entry for the **Marketing Users** group and then click **Edit**.

9. In the Permissions section, click the **Read Permissions** check box in the Deny column to specifically disable the ability to read the NTFS permissions associated with this folder. Click **OK** to close the Permission Entry for Special Permissions dialog box, and then click **OK** to close the Advanced Security Settings for Special Permissions dialog box. Click **Yes** in the Security dialog box.

10. In the Group or user names list box, click the **Marketing Users** group account to view its configured security settings. Notice that the Special Permissions Deny column now includes a check mark. Close all open windows.

11. Log off and then log on again using the **mcowan** user account.

12. Attempt to access the Security tab in the Properties dialog box for the **D:\Special Permissions** folder. This tab is no longer available because, as a member of the Marketing Users group, Moira Cowan has been denied the ability to view permission settings.

13. Close all open windows and log off. Log on again using your **AdminXX** account.

Determining Effective Permissions

In versions of Windows prior to Windows Server 2003, one of the more complex and tedious tasks that administrators were often responsible for was determining a user's effective permissions for network resources. Because the permissions that actually apply to a user can be the result of membership on a variety of different groups, this task could often be very complex and involve a great deal of research. In environments that included thousands of users and shared resources, the amount of time and effort required to do this could quickly become unmanageable.

To easily determine the effective NTFS permissions that apply to a user or group, Windows Server 2003 includes the Effective Permissions tab in the Advanced Security Settings dialog box for a file or folder, shown in Figure 5-15. In Activity 5-6, you use the Effective Permissions tab to determine the effective NTFS permissions that apply to a user and group for a specific folder.

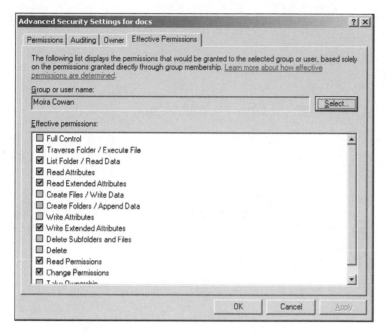

Figure 5-15   The Effective Permissions tab

Activity 5-6: Determining Effective NTFS Permissions

Time Required: 5 minutes

Objective: View effective permissions for a user on an NTFS folder.

Description: Although the IT manager is now convinced of the benefits that NTFS security will provide for Dover Leasing, he is still worried that the application of permissions to many different users and groups may result in mistakes being made with respect to the effective level of permissions assigned to users. In this activity, you use the Effective Permissions tab in the Advanced Security Settings of a folder to view the effective NTFS permissions that apply to both a user and group.

1. Open My Computer and right-click the **D:\Test** folder. Click **Properties** from the shortcut menu, then click the **Security** tab.

2. Click the **Advanced** button to access the Advanced Security Settings for Test dialog box.

3. Click the **Effective Permissions** tab.

4. Click the **Select** button.

5. In the Enter the object name to select (examples) text box, type **Moira** and click **OK**. Review the effective NTFS permissions that apply to the Moira Cowan user account.

6. Click the **Select** button again and, this time, add the **Marketing Users** group. Review the effective NTFS permissions that apply to this group.

7. Close all open windows.

COMBINING SHARED FOLDER AND NTFS PERMISSIONS

NTFS permissions are often combined with share permissions to provide a strong combination of local and remote security for files and directories. When share and NTFS permissions are combined, the following rules apply:

- When a user is accessing a share across a network and both NTFS and share permissions apply, the most restrictive permission of the two becomes the effective combined permission. For example, if the effective shared folder permission is Full Control, but the effective NTFS permission is Read, then the user will be granted the Read permission to the resource.

- When a user accesses a file locally, only NTFS permissions apply.

In Activity 5-7, you test the impact of configuring both NTFS and shared folder permissions.

ACTIVITY

Activity 5-7: Exploring the Impact of Combined Shared Folder and NTFS Permissions

Time Required: 10 minutes

Objective: Determine the impact of combining shared folder and NTFS permissions.

Description: Although you understand how both shared folder and NTFS permissions combine, you are worried that the new junior administrators will have difficulty properly configuring these permissions to allow the correct level of user access. You have decided to test the impact of different permission combinations to develop a set procedure to be used by new junior administrators at Dover Leasing. In this activity, you test the impact of combining both shared folder and NTFS permissions for both local and network resource access.

1. Open My Computer and create a new folder on drive D: named **Combined**. Share this folder using the default name.

2. Access the properties of the **Combined** folder. Click the **Security** tab, and then click the **Advanced** button. Uncheck the **Allow inheritable permissions from the parent to propagate to this object and all child objects** check box. When the Security dialog box opens, click **Remove**, and then click **OK**.

3. Read the message in the Security dialog box that opens, and then click **Yes**.

4. Add the **Domain Users** group to the Group or user names list, granting the group the **Allow Modify** permission.

5. Click the **Sharing** tab, and then click the **Permissions** button. Remove the

Everyone group from the list, and then add the **Domain Users** group with the **Allow Read** permission. Click **OK**, and then click **OK** again to exit the properties of the Combined folder.

6. Attempt to create a new folder called **Documents** in the D:\Combined folder. This operation should complete successfully because the Domain Users group has the NTFS Modify permission on the folder. Close My Computer.

7. Open the Run command, type **\\serverXX\combined** (where *XX* is your assigned student number), and then press **Enter**. The Combined window should open.

8. Right-click an area of white space in the window and then attempt to create a new folder. When the Unable to create folder dialog box opens, read the message and then click **OK**. You are unable to create a new folder because the share permission is Read, and when the folder is accessed over the network, this is the effective permission that applies because it is more restrictive. Close the \\Server*XX* window, and then open **My Computer**.

9. Right-click the **D:\Combined** folder and click **Properties**. Click the **Sharing** tab, click **Permissions** and change the permissions for the Domain Users group to **Allow Full Control**. Click **OK** to exit, and then click **OK** to close the Combined Properties dialog box.

10. Open the Run command again, type **\\serverXX\combined**, then click **OK**. The Combined window should open.

11. Attempt to create a new folder in this window called **Documents2**. The operation should complete successfully because the combination of the Full Control share permission and the Modify NTFS permission make Modify the effective permission on the folder.

12. Close all open windows.

CONVERTING A FAT PARTITION TO NTFS

As you have already learned, the ability to configure files and folders with NTFS permissions requires the volume or partition on which they are stored to be formatted with the NTFS file system. In some environments, it is conceivable that an administrator might have formatted certain partitions with the FAT or FAT32 file system for any number of potential reasons, including accidentally. For the highest degree of security, however, partitions and volumes on a Windows Server 2003 system should always be configured to use the NTFS file system.

Windows Server 2003 provides a command-line utility called CONVERT for the purpose of converting existing FAT or FAT32 partitions and volumes to the NTFS file system. When this utility is used, all existing files and folders on a partition are retained once the conversion process is complete. This is a far more effective method of implementing the NTFS file system than the alternative, which involves formatting the partition.

Although the CONVERT utility can convert existing FAT and FAT32 partitions and volumes to NTFS, the reverse is not true. CONVERT cannot convert an NTFS partition or volume to the FAT or FAT32 file systems; allowing this to occur would potentially represent a serious security risk.

In Activity 5-8 you use the **Disk Management** utility to create a small new FAT32 partition, and ultimately use the CONVERT utility to convert the partition from FAT32 to the NTFS file system.

Activity 5-8: Converting a FAT32 Partition to NTFS

Time Required: 15 minutes

Objective: Convert a FAT32 partition to the NTFS file system.

Description: In the past, one of the administrators at Dover Leasing made the decision to format almost all of the partitions used for storing user data files with the FAT32 file system. The IT manager is interested in converting these partitions to the NTFS file system, but wants to be certain that no existing data files are lost in the process. In this activity you create a small FAT32 partition on your server, create a new folder and file on that partition, and then use the CONVERT utility to convert the partition to the NTFS file system.

1. Click **Start**, right-click **My Computer**, and click **Manage**.

2. Click the **Disk Management** node. Note that you may need to expand the Storage node to access Disk Management.

3. Right-click on an area of free space on Disk 0 and click **New Partition**.

4. At the New Partition Wizard welcome screen, click **Next**.

5. At the Select Partition Type screen, ensure that **Primary partition** is selected, and click **Next**.

6. At the Specify Partition Size Screen, type **50** in the Partition size in MB text box. Click **Next**.

7. At the Assign Drive Letter or Path screen, ensure that drive **F** is selected in the Assign the following drive letter drop down box and click **Next**.

8. At the Format Partition screen, select **FAT32** in the File system drop down box, and check the **Perform a quick format** check box. Click **Next**.

9. Click **Finish** to create the new partition.

10. Close the Computer Management window.

11. Click **Start**, and then click **My Computer**.

12. Double-click on drive **F:** to view its contents.

13. Right-click on a blank area, select **New**, and click **Folder**. Name the folder **permissiontest**.

14. Right-click on the **permissiontest** folder and click **Properties**. Note that the folder does not include a Security tab, since it is stored on a FAT32 partition. Close the permissiontest Properties window.

15. Close the My Computer window.

16. Click **Start**, and then click **Run**. In the Open text box, type **cmd.exe** and click **OK**.

17. Type **convert f: /fs:ntfs** and press **Enter**.

18. At the Enter current volume label for drive F: prompt, type **NEW VOLUME**, and press **Enter**. Note that the conversion process will take a few minutes or more. Once complete, the Conversion complete message appears, as shown in Figure 5-16. When the conversion process is complete, close the command prompt window.

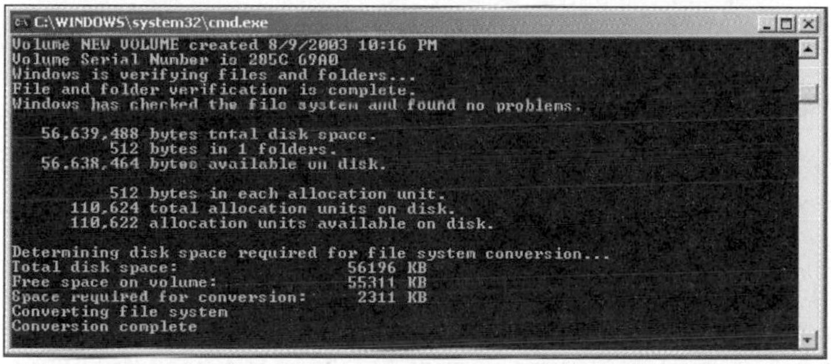

Figure 5-16   Results of the CONVERT command

19. Click **Start**, and then click **My Computer**.

20. Double-click on drive **F:** to view its contents. Notice that the permissiontest folder is still available after the conversion.

21. Right-click on the **permissiontest** folder and click **Properties**. Note that the Security tab is now available.

22. Click on the **Security** tab and review the permissions assigned for the folder. These permissions are inherited from those applied to drive F: by default after the conversion process completed.

23. Click **OK**, and then close all open windows.

CHAPTER SUMMARY

- Windows Server 2003 supports the FAT, FAT32, and NTFS file systems. Only the NTFS file system allows local security permissions to be configured.

- To create a shared folder, you are required to have the appropriate rights. A domain administrator or server operator has the default rights to create shared folders within a domain. The primary tools used to create shared folders are Windows Explorer, Computer Management, and the NET SHARE command-line utility.

❑ Windows Server 2003 supports three share permissions: Read, Change, and Full Control. Share permissions are cumulative. If a user is a member of multiple groups that have different permissions, the final permission is the sum of all permissions.

❑ Windows Server 2003 supports both standard and special NTFS permissions. Special NTFS permissions give an administrator a more granular level of control over how permissions are applied.

❑ NTFS permissions are cumulative. If a user is a member of multiple groups that have different permissions, the final permission is the sum of all permissions.

❑ When a shared folder and NTFS permissions are combined, the most restrictive permission applies.

❑ A denied permission always overrides an allowed permission.

❑ Windows Server 2003 provides the CONVERT utility as a way to convert existing FAT or FAT32 partitions to the NTFS file system without losing existing data.

KEY TERMS

access control entry (ACE) — An entry in an object's discretionary access control list (DACL) that grants permissions to a user or group. An ACE is also an entry in an object's system access control list (SACL) that specifies the security events to be audited for a user or group.

administrative shares — Hidden shared folders created for the purpose of allowing administrators to access the root of partitions and other system folders remotely.

Computer Management console — A predefined Microsoft Management Console (MMC) application that allows administration of a variety of computer-related tasks on the local computer or a remote computer.

discretionary access control list (DACL) — A part of the security descriptor of an object that contains a list of user or group references that have been allowed or denied permissions to the resource.

Disk Management — The Windows Server 2003 utility used to manage disk partitions and volumes.

effective permissions — The permissions that actually apply to a user or group based on the different permissions of the user or groups they are members of on a particular resource.

FAT — A file system supported in Windows Server 2003 but traditionally associated with the MS-DOS operating system. FAT can be used on partitions or volumes up to 4 GB in size.

FAT32 — A derivative of the FAT file system that supports partition sizes up to 2 TB, but provides none of the security features of NTFS.

NTFS — The native file system of Windows Server 2003, provides better scalability and performance than FAT and FAT32, while also providing the ability to configure local security permissions, compression, encryption, and more.

shared folder — A data resource container that has been made available over the network to authorized network clients.

special NTFS permissions — A more granular set of NTFS permissions that allows an administrator a higher degree of control over the abilities assigned to users or groups for a particular resource.

standard NTFS permissions — The permissions available on the Security tab of an NTFS file or folder.

5

REVIEW QUESTIONS

1. What is the default permission assigned to a shared folder?
   a. Allow Full Control to the Everyone group
   b. Allow Read to the Everyone group
   c. Allow Change to the Users group
   d. Deny Read to the Users group

2. Which of the following tools can be used to create shared folders on a Windows Server 2003 system? (Choose all that apply.)
   a. Computer Management
   b. Windows Explorer
   c. Internet Explorer
   d. The NET SHARE command

3. Which of the following are shared folder permissions on a Windows Server 2003 system? (Choose all that apply.)
   a. Read
   b. Modify
   c. Change
   d. Full Control

4. Which of the following shared folders would be hidden in My Network Places?
   a. Documents
   b. Documents$
   c. $Documents
   d. Documents%

5. Assuming that a user is granted the Allow Read shared folder permission as a member of one group and the Deny Full Control permission as a member of another group for the same folder, what is the user's effective permission?

    a. Deny Full Control

    b. Allow Read

    c. Allow Modify

    d. Deny Modify

6. Which of the following are NTFS folder permissions? (Choose all that apply.)

    a. Read & Execute

    b. List Folder Contents

    c. Read

    d. Change

7. Which of the following are NTFS file permissions? (Choose all that apply.)

    a. Read & Execute

    b. List Folder Contents

    c. Read

    d. Modify

8. Which of the following file systems support local security?

    a. NTFS

    b. FAT

    c. FAT32

9. Which of the following commands would be used to convert drive D from FAT32 to NTFS?

    a. Convert fs:ntfs d:

    b. Convert d: ntfs

    c. Convert d: /fs:ntfs

    d. Convert /fs:ntfs d:

10. Which of the following NTFS permissions would allow a user to change the permissions associated with a file?

    a. Full Control

    b. Modify

    c. Read & Execute

    d. Write

11. Which of the following commands would be used to share a folder from the command line?

   a. Net Use

   b. Net Share

   c. Share

   d. Net Config

12. Assuming that a user is granted the Allow Full Control NTFS permission as a member of one group and the Allow Read permission as a member of another group for the same folder, what is the user's effective permission?

   a. Allow Read

   b. Allow Full Control

   c. Allow Modify

   d. Allow Read & Execute

13. Assuming that a user is granted the Allow Modify NTFS permission as a member of one group and the Deny Modify shared folder permission as a member of another group for the same folder, what is the user's effective permission locally?

   a. Allow Modify

   b. Deny Modify

   c. Allow Read

   d. Deny Read

14. Assuming that a user is granted the Allow Full Control NTFS permission as a member of one group and the Allow Read shared folder permission as a member of another group for the same folder, what is the user's effective permission remotely?

   a. Allow Full Control

   b. Allow Read

   c. Allow Modify

   d. Deny Full Control

15. Which of the following file systems allow folders to be shared? (Choose all that apply.)

   a. NTFS

   b. FAT

   c. FAT32

5

16. Which acronym is used to describe an entry in an access control list?

    a. ACL

    b. DACL

    c. SACL

    d. ACE

17. A denied permission always takes precedence over an allowed permission.

    a. True

    b. False

18. Which tool can be used to determine the ultimate set of permissions that impact a user trying to access resources on an NTFS partition?

    a. The Effective Permissions tab

    b. Active Directory Users and Computers

    c. Active Directory Domains and Trusts

    d. DSADD

19. Which of the following are not standard NTFS permissions on a file? (Choose all that apply.)

    a. Read

    b. Read & Execute

    c. Change

    d. List Folder Contents

20. Which of the following are not standard NTFS permissions on a folder?

    a. Read

    b. List Folder Contents

    c. Change

    d. Modify

CASE PROJECTS

Case Project 5-1

This case project involves configuring share and NTFS permissions. Dover Leasing is in the process of reviewing their current structure and practices. There has been talk of minor security breaches occurring in which users are able to gain access to information they should not be permitted to view. Management would like you to make some recommendations as to how permissions can be changed on specific folders.

1. Two network servers maintain confidential information pertaining to financial data and employee data. Users access the folders both locally and on the network. Only members of the Managers group, Human Resources group, and Accountants group should have access to these folders. Explain how permissions can be implemented, including a short description of how share permissions and NTFS permissions work together.

2. Dover Leasing has recently hired a new server administrator to assist you. He has worked with Windows NT 4.0 in the past and is unfamiliar with Windows Server 2003. Prepare a brief explanation for the new administrator about how to configure share and NTFS permissions.

Case Project 5-2

A new junior administrator at Dover Leasing has just configured a variety of NTFS permissions on a shared folder named Marketing on a newly installed server. After completing his configuration, he notices that some of the Marketing users are having trouble accessing the server with the correct level of access, if at all. What are some of the possible permission-related reasons why users might be having trouble connecting?

Case Project 5-3

To understand how NTFS and share permissions work together, consider the following example and answer the accompanying questions:

Users	Group Membership
User1	Sales, Marketing, domain users
User2	Managers, domain users

Directory Structure	Share Permissions	NTFS Permissions
SalesData	Sales—Full Control	Sales—Modify
	Managers—Read	Marketing—Full Control
CompanyData	domain users—Change	default
HRData	Managers—deny Full Control	default

1. What permissions would User1 have to the SalesData folder if the user were accessing the folder across a network connection?

2. What permissions would User1 have to the SalesData folder if the user were logged on to the computer where the folder was located?

3. What permissions would User2 have to the CompanyData folder if the user were accessing the folder across the network?

4. What permissions would User2 have to the HRData folder if the user were accessing the folder across the network?

5. What permissions would User2 have to the HRData folder if the user were accessing the folder on the computer on which it is located?

6

MANAGING DISKS AND DATA STORAGE

After reading this chapter and completing the exercises, you will be able to:

♦ Understand concepts relating to disk management

♦ Manage partitions and volumes on a Windows Server 2003 system

♦ Understand the purpose of mounted drives and how to implement them

♦ Understand the fault tolerant disk strategies natively supported in Windows Server 2003

♦ Determine disk and volume status information and import foreign disks

♦ Maintain disks on a Windows Server 2003 system using a variety of native utilities

When Intel-based servers first appeared on the scene, disk storage options were limited because disk sizes were relatively small at 20 to 40 MB. At 20 GB and well beyond, disk storage has come a long way and is arguably one of the most important server elements that an administrator needs to configure and maintain. Server activities are typically related to making files, databases, and applications available to network clients, and all of these rely upon disk storage.

In this chapter, you learn the fundamentals of Windows Server 2003 disk management. This begins with a look at the two major types of disks supported on Windows Server 2003 systems, as well as the disk space allocation strategies associated and supported by each type.

Windows Server 2003 also supports a variety of disk fault tolerance features in the form of different Redundant Array of Independent Disk (RAID) strategies. The various RAID levels available in Windows Server 2003, as well as the disk configurations necessary to support them, will also be looked at in this chapter.

While the partitions and volumes implemented on Windows-based systems have tradition-ally been designated and associated with drive letters, Windows Server 2003 also supports the ability to mount NTFS partitions and volumes to folders, in a manner similar to UNIX- or Linux-based systems. In this chapter you learn the prerequisites for mounting a drive in this fashion, as well as how it is accomplished using tools such as Disk Management.

Although implementing partitions and volumes on the disks of a Windows Server 2003 system is a relatively straightforward process, these resources still must be maintained in order to ensure that they function at an acceptable level. A variety of different utilities are provided in Windows Server 2003 to manage and maintain disks, volumes, and partitions. This chapter ends with a look at the various graphical and command-line tools that you should be familiar with to ensure that hard disk resources are maintained optimally.

DISK MANAGEMENT CONCEPTS

Windows Server 2003 supports two data storage types: basic disks and dynamic disks. A **basic disk** is one that uses traditional disk management techniques and contains primary partitions, extended partitions, and logical drives. A **dynamic disk** is one that does not use traditional partitioning. Dynamic disk architecture provides new flexibility in that there is virtually no restriction to the number of volumes that can be implemented on one disk. Both types of data storage are discussed in more detail in the following sections.

Basic Disks

A basic disk is a hard disk that is divided into primary and extended partitions, where each partition acts as a separate storage unit. You can configure a basic disk with a maximum of four primary partitions, or three primary partitions and one extended partition, as shown in Figure 6-1.

Figure 6-1   Basic disk configurations

Primary partitions on a basic disk are used by default when Windows Server 2003 is installed on a new server. You can format each primary partition with either the FAT, FAT32, or NTFS file systems, and assign that partition a drive letter. Of the primary partitions that are configured, only one can be marked as the active partition. Also known as the system partition, this is the partition that contains the files required to start the operating system. On Windows operating systems, the system partition is almost always drive C.

The boot partition is where the operating system files are installed. In a Windows Server 2003 installation, this is the partition where the \WINDOWS folder resides. Unlike the system partition, the boot partition can be located on a primary partition, or on a logical drive in an extended partition.

To overcome the limitation of only being able to create four primary partitions on a single basic disk, you also have the option to create up to three primary partitions and one extended partition per disk. An extended partition is created from free hard disk space, but is not formatted or assigned a drive letter. Instead, the space within an extended partition is further divided into logical drives. Each logical drive within the extended partition is formatted and assigned a drive letter.

When you install Windows Server 2003, all disks are automatically initialized as basic disks. You can convert disks from basic to dynamic after the installation, or let them remain as basic if the extended capabilities of dynamic disks are not required. Dynamic disks and their capabilities is explored shortly.

Primary Partitions

A partition can be configured as either primary or extended. A basic disk must contain at least one **primary partition** and can contain a maximum of four primary partitions per disk. A primary partition is one from which you can boot an operating system if required, such as Windows Server 2003. When you boot from a primary partition, it contains the operating system startup files in a location at the beginning of the partition. For example, the startup files for Windows 98 include Io.sys and Msdos.sys. With Windows Server 2003, the startup files include Boot.ini, Ntldr, and Ntdetect.com, for example. At least one primary partition must be marked as active and only one primary partition can be active at a given time. The **active partition** is the partition where your computer looks for the hardware-specific files to start the operating system. Although primary partitions are used to start an operating system when basic disks are used, they can also be used for traditional data storage purposes, such as holding users' home directories.

Extended Partitions and Logical Drives

An **extended partition** is created from space that is not yet partitioned. The purpose of an extended partition is to enable you to exceed the four-partition limit of a basic disk. There can be only one extended partition on a single basic disk. An extended partition is neither formatted nor assigned a drive letter. Once an extended partition is created, the space allocated to it can be further divided into **logical drives**. The logical drives are then formatted and assigned drive letters for the purpose of data storage.

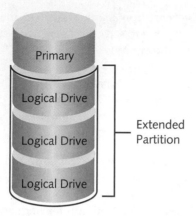

Figure 6-2   An extended partition can be divided into one or more logical drives

Volume Sets and Stripe Sets

On a Windows NT Server 4.0 system you can create multi-disk volumes referred to as volume sets and stripe sets. A volume set consists of two or more partitions combined to look like one volume with a single drive letter. A stripe set consists of two or more disks that combined like a volume set, but that striped for RAID level 0 or RAID level 5 (RAID is discussed later in this chapter). Windows Server 2003 (and Windows 2000 Server) provides backward compatibility with the volume and stripe sets previously created using Windows NT. If you have any of these multi-disk volumes on a computer running Windows NT 4.0, you can still use them after an upgrade to Windows Server 2003, but you cannot create new volume or stripe sets should the disks fail. For this reason, after a Windows NT server is upgraded to Windows Server 2003, you should convert basic disks to dynamic disks in order to implement any new multi-disk volumes.

Dynamic Disks

A dynamic disk is a hard disk that does not use the traditional partitioning strategies of a basic disk. Dynamic disks make it possible to set up a large number of volumes on one disk, while providing the ability to extend volumes onto additional physical disks. Some of the reasons why an administrator might opt to implement dynamic disks include the ability to:

- Extend NTFS volumes
- Configure RAID volumes for fault tolerance or increased performance
- Reactivate missing or offline disks
- Changes disk settings without having to restart the computer

Dynamic disks do not contain primary and extended partitions. Instead, dynamic disks are configured with what are known as volumes. While fundamentally similar in principle to a partition, volumes on dynamic disks provide additional features and capabilities not available to partitions on a basic disk. The different types of volumes that can be configured on a dynamic disk are in the following sections.

Do not convert basic disks to dynamic disks if the system is configured to dual-boot with other operating systems. Once converted, other operating systems may not have access to the disk.

Dynamic disks are not supported on portable computers, removable disks, detachable disks (such as external USB or IEEE 1394 drives) or disks connected to a shared SCSI bus.

6

Simple Volume

A **simple volume** is a dedicated and formatted portion of disk space on a dynamic disk. If you do not allocate all available space on a disk to a simple volume, you have the option to later take all or a portion of the unallocated space and add it to an existing simple volume, which is called extending the volume. Only simple volumes formatted with the NTFS file system can be extended. It is important to note that neither the system nor boot volume on a Windows Server 2003 system can be extended.

Spanned Volume

A **spanned volume** consists of space in between two and 32 dynamic disks that is treated as a single logical volume. For example, you might create a spanned volume if you have four separate small hard disks, as shown in Figure 6-3. Another reason to use a spanned volume is if you have several small areas of free disk space scattered throughout a server's disk drives. You might have 600 MB of free space on one drive, 150 MB on another, and 70 MB on a third. All of these free areas can be combined into a single 820 MB spanned volume with its own drive letter, with the advantage that you reduce the number of drive letters needed to make use of the space.

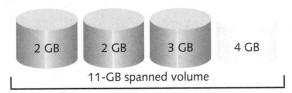

Figure 6-3   Creating a spanned volume using four disks

As you add new disks, the spanned volume can be extended to include each disk. Volumes formatted for NTFS can be extended, but those formatted for FAT16 and FAT32 cannot. The advantage of creating spanned volumes is the ability to maximize the use of scattered pockets of disk space across several disks.

CAUTION The disadvantage of using a spanned volume is that if one disk fails, the entire volume is inaccessible. Also, if a portion of a spanned volume is deleted, the entire disk set is deleted. For these reasons, avoid placing mission-critical data and applications on a spanned volume.

Striped Volume

A **striped volume** is often referred to as RAID level 0. One reason for implementing a striped volume is to extend the life of hard disk drives by spreading data equally over two or more drives. Spreading the data divides the drive load so that one drive is not working more than any other. Another advantage of striping is that it increases disk performance. Contention among disks is equalized and data is accessed faster for both reading and writing than when it is on a single drive, because Windows Server 2003 can write to all drives simultaneously.

In Windows Server 2003, disk striping requires at least two physical hard disks and can use up to 32. The aggregation of space from the various disks is ultimately called a striped volume. Equal portions of data are written in 64 KB blocks in rows or stripes on each disk. For example, imagine that you have set up a striped volume across five hard disks, and are working with a 720 KB data file. The first 64 KB portion of the file is written to disk 1, the next 64 KB portion is written to disk 2, the third portion is written to disk 3, and so on. After 320 KB are spread in the first data row across disks 1 through 5, the next 320 KB are written in 64 KB blocks in the second row across the disks. Finally, there will be 64 KB in the third row on disk 1 and 16 KB in the third row on disk 2, as shown in Figure 6-4.

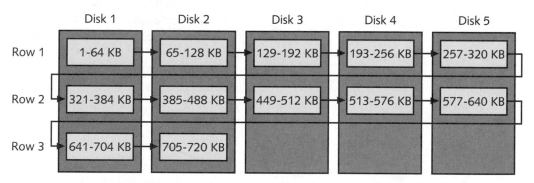

Figure 6-4   Disks in a striped volume

Because of their high performance, striped volumes are useful for storing large databases or for data replication from one volume to another. Striping is not a benefit when most of the data files on a server are very small, such as under 64 KB.

Data can be lost when one or more disks in the striped volume fail, because the system has no automated way to rebuild data. Although often referred to by a RAID-level name, striped volumes do not provide any degree of fault tolerance, and are implemented for performance reasons only.

Windows Server 2003 supports two additional volume types, known as mirrored volumes and RAID-5 volumes. Since both of these volume types provide fault tolerance, they are looked at in more detail in the Fault Tolerant Disk Strategies section later in this chapter.

MANAGING PARTITIONS AND VOLUMES

Disk management tasks are usually performed on a Windows Server 2003 system using the **Disk Management** tool. This tool provides a central facility for viewing disk-related information, and performing tasks such as creating and deleting partitions and volumes. The following sections introduce you to the different tasks you can perform using the Disk Management tool, including viewing disk information, creating and deleting partitions, creating volumes, and converting basic disks to dynamic disks. The Disk Management node of the Computer Management tool is shown in Figure 6-5.

6

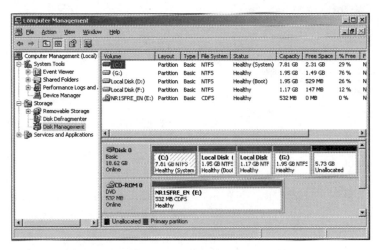

Figure 6-5 The Disk Management node of the Computer Management tool

Managing Disk Properties

Although the Disk Management tool can be added to a custom Microsoft Management Console (MMC), it is most commonly accessed via its node in the Storage section of the Computer Management tool. While primarily used for the creation, deletion, and management of disks, partitions, and volumes the Disk Management tool also provides information about disks, partitions, and volumes that are typically associated with other tools.

For example, right-clicking on a specific partition or volume in Disk Management and clicking Properties provides access to the same property sheets for the disk available from within Windows Explorer, as shown in Figure 6-6.

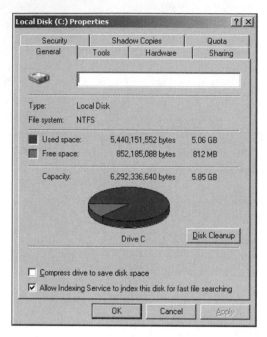

Figure 6-6   The Properties screen for an existing partition

In a similar vein, right-clicking on a disk in the Disk Management tool and clicking Properties opens the same property sheets available from the Device Manager tool for a disk, as shown in Figure 6-7.

In Activity 6-1 you use the Disk Management node of the Computer Management tool to access and view the properties of the hard disk and a partition on your server.

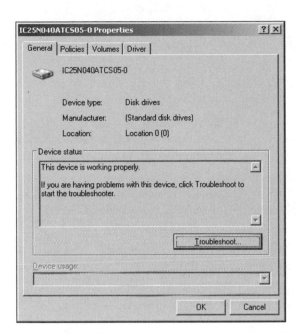

Figure 6-7   The Properties screen for a hard disk

Activity 6-1: Viewing and Managing Disk Properties with Disk Management

Time Required: 10 minutes

Objective: Use the Disk Management node of the Computer Management tool to view the properties of a hard disk and partition.

Description: As part of designing a training seminar for new administrators, the IT manager at Dover Leasing would like to include a section on disk management, and specifically on using the Disk Management tool. He has asked you to explore the different property settings for disks and partitions in order to help identify the elements on which new staff should ultimately be trained. In this activity you use the Disk Management node from within the Computer Management tool to view the properties of both your server's hard disk and an existing partition.

1. Log on using your **AdminXX** account. Click **Start**, right-click **My Computer**, and click **Manage**.

2. Click the **+ (plus symbol)** next to Storage to expand it, if necessary.

3. Click the **Disk Management** node to view its contents.

4. In the upper-right pane of the Disk Management node window, right-click on drive **C:** and click **Properties**. The Properties window for drive C: will open, as shown in Figure 6-6.

5. Review the information and settings available on the General tab. Notice that this tab provides an easy way to determine both the capacity and available free space for the partition. Click the **Tools** tab.

6. Review the descriptions of the tools available on this tab. Some of these tools are looked at in more detail later in this chapter. Click the **Hardware** tab.

7. The Hardware tab provides a list of the drives installed in your server, and provides access to both the properties of the drive and a troubleshooting tool. Click the **Sharing** tab.

8. The Sharing tab allows the root of a partition or volume to be shared over the network. Notice that drive C: is shared over the network using the share name C$ by default. The root of all partitions and volumes on a Windows Server 2003 system are shared for administrative purposes. Click the **Security** tab.

9. The Security tab allows NTFS permissions to be configured for the partition or volume, with settings inherited by subfolders and files. Click the **Shadow Copies** tab.

10. The Shadow Copies tab is used to configure the new Shadow Copies feature of Windows Server 2003. This topic is looked at in more detail later in the text. Click the **Quota** tab.

11. The Quota tab allows an administrator to configure disk space quotas for users on individual volumes or partitions. This feature is looked at in more detail later in the text. Click the **Cancel** button.

12. In the lower-right pane of the Disk Management node window, right-click on **Disk 0** and click **Properties**. This opens the property pages for the disk drive, as shown in Figure 6-7.

13. Review the information available on the General tab, noting that it also provides access to a troubleshooting tool. Click the **Policies** tab.

14. The Policies tab is used to configure write caching and safe removal settings for a disk. Review the default settings and available options, and then click the **Volumes** tab.

15. The Volumes tab lists all available partitions (or volumes) currently configured on this disk. Clicking on a partition or volume and then clicking Properties opens the same property sheets for a partition or volume explored at the beginning of this activity. Click the **Driver** tab.

16. The Driver tab allows an administrator to view details about the currently installed driver for the disk, update the driver, roll back the driver, and uninstall the driver, if necessary. Click the **Cancel** button.

17. Leave the Computer Management window open.

CREATING PARTITIONS AND VOLUMES

The Disk Management tool is the primary tool used to create and manage partitions and volumes on a Windows Server 2003 system. In Activity 6-2 you use the Disk Management node of the Computer Management tool to create, and then delete, a new primary partition on Disk 0.

Activity 6-2: Creating and Deleting a Primary Partition

Time Required: 5 minutes

Objective: Create and delete a new primary partition.

Description: In the past, the IT staff at Dover Leasing has always used the FDISK utility to pre-create partitions for servers. However, you have been asked to walk new staff members through the process of creating and managing different partitions, because the IT manager has dictated that all files must be stored on NTFS partitions only. In this activity, you use Disk Management to create, and then delete, a new primary partition on your server.

1. In the Computer Management window, ensure that the **Disk Management** node is selected. Right-click on an area of free space on Disk 0, and click **New Partition**.

2. Click **Next** at the New Partition Wizard welcome screen.

3. At the Select Partition Type screen, ensure that the **Primary partition** radio button is selected, and click **Next**.

4. At the Specify Partition Size screen, type **50** in the Partition size in MB text box. Click **Next**.

5. At the Assign Drive Letter or Path screen, ensure that drive **G** is selected in the Assign the following drive letter drop down box and click **Next**.

6. At the Format Partition screen, ensure that **NTFS** is selected in the File system drop down box, and check the **Perform a quick format** check box. Click **Next**.

7. Click **Finish** to create the new partition. Leave the Computer Management window open.

8. Click **Start**, and then click **My Computer**. Double-click on drive New Volume **G:** to ensure it is accessible. Close the My Computer window.

9. In the Computer Management window, right-click on drive New Volume **(G:)**, and then select **Delete Partition**. Because Disk 0 already contains four primary partitions, this partition must be deleted to make room for an extended partition in the next activity.

10. When prompted to confirm the deletion of the partition, click **Yes**. Notice that the space previously allocated to drive G: is now listed as free space on the disk once again.

11. Leave the Computer Management window open.

In Activity 6-3 you use some of the existing free space on your hard disk to create an extended partition using the Disk Management tool.

Activity 6-3: Creating an Extended Partition

Time Required: 5 minutes

Objective: Create an extended partition.

Description: Although a basic disk supports up to four primary partitions, the IT manager would prefer to have the additional flexibility that implementing a single extended partition per disk provides. In this activity you use Disk Management to create a new extended partition on your server's hard disk.

1. In the Computer Management window, ensure that the Disk Management node is selected. Right-click on an area of free space on Disk 0, and click **New Partition**.

2. Click **Next** at the New Partition Wizard welcome screen.

3. At the Select Partition Type screen, click the **Extended partition** radio button and read the Description section. Notice that the option to create a logical drive is not currently available because an extended partition doesn't currently exist. Click **Next**.

4. At the Specify Partition Size screen, enter **300** in the Partition size in MB text box and then click **Next**.

5. At the Completing the New Partition Wizard screen, click **Finish**.

6. In the Disk Management window, notice the new extended partition that is visible on Disk 0. Note also that because this is an extended partition, it is not formatted and does not have a drive letter assigned to it.

7. Leave the Computer Management window open.

Since an extended partition was created in Activity 6-3, it is now possible to create logical drives within the extended partition. In Activity 6-4 you use the Disk Management tool to create a new logical drive within an extended partition.

ACTIVITY

Activity 6-4: Creating a Logical Drive

Time Required: 5 minutes

Objective: Create a logical drive from within an extended partition.

Description: In order to use the disk space allocated to an extended partition, logical drives must be defined. In this activity you create a single logical drive that uses all of the space available in the extended partition created in Activity 6-3.

1. In the Computer Management window, ensure that the **Disk Management** node is selected. Right-click within the extended partition on Disk 0, and click **New Logical Drive**.

2. When the New Partition Wizard welcome screen opens, click **Next**.

3. At the Select Partition Type screen, notice that the only available option is to create a logical drive. Click **Next**.

4. At the Specify Partition Size screen, ensure that the Partition size in MB text box matches the value found in the Maximum disk space in megabytes (MB) section and then click **Next**.

5. At the Assign Drive Letter or Path screen, ensure that **G** is selected in the Assign the following drive letter list box and then click **Next**.

6. At the Format Partition screen, ensure that the **Format this partition with the following settings** radio button is selected. In the Volume label text box, type **Logical Drive** and then click **Next**.

7. At the Completing the New Partition Wizard screen, review the summary information provided in the You selected the following settings section and then click **Finish**.

8. After returning to the Disk Management details screen, notice that the Status column of the partition in the upper pane is set to Formatting and provides the percentage information of the format operation currently complete.

9. Once the format operation completes and the new partition's Status is set to Healthy, close Computer Management.

10. Open My Computer and verify that the new logical drive (G:) is now accessible.

11. Close all open windows.

6

Before you can create any volumes on a Windows Server 2003 system, you must first convert disks from basic to dynamic; otherwise, the only option available is to create traditional partitions. You can convert a basic disk to a dynamic one by using the Disk Management snap-in; right-click the disk you want to convert and then click Convert to Dynamic Disk, as illustrated in Figure 6-8.

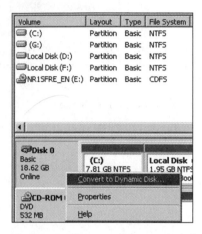

Figure 6-8   Converting a disk from basic to dynamic

Keep the following key points in mind before you upgrade a disk from basic to dynamic:

- You must have administrative privileges to perform the upgrade.

- The disk must contain at least 1 MB of free space for the upgrade to succeed. Windows Server 2003 automatically reserves this space when installed.

- No data is lost when you upgrade from basic to dynamic. To revert back to a basic disk, however, all volumes must first be deleted. You can then restore data from backup once the disk has been reverted to basic.

- Once upgraded, the disk can only be locally accessed by operating systems that support dynamic disks such as Windows 2000, Windows XP, or Windows Server 2003. Converting to a dynamic disk does not affect network access to shared resources on the disk.

- Once upgraded, primary and extended partitions become simple volumes.

To create any new fault-tolerant volumes in Windows Server 2003, such as a mirrored or RAID-5 volume, disks must first be converted to dynamic.

NOTE

In Activity 6-5 you convert your server's hard disk from a basic disk to a dynamic disk.

Activity 6-5: Converting a Basic Disk to a Dynamic Disk

Time Required: 5 minutes

Objective: Convert a basic disk to a dynamic disk.

Description: While all disks on a Windows Server 2003 system are configured as basic disks by default, the IT manager at Dover Leasing would eventually like to take advantage of the ability to extend existing NTFS volumes, as well as implement fault-tolerant techniques such as RAID 1. Because of this, he has asked you to convert your server's disk from a basic disk to a dynamic disk. In this activity you use the Disk Management tool to convert Disk 0 on your server to a dynamic disk.

1. Click **Start**, right-click on **My Computer**, and click **Manage**.

2. Click on the **Disk Management** node to display its contents, if necessary.

3. Right-click on **Disk 0**, and click **Convert to Dynamic Disk**.

4. In the Convert to Dynamic Disk dialog box, click **OK**.

5. Click the **Convert** button.

6. When the Disk Management dialog box appears, click **Yes**.

7. Click **Yes** to confirm that the file systems on the disk will be dismounted.

8. Click **OK** to reboot the computer when prompted. Once the process completes, log on using your **AdminXX** account.

9. Click **Start**, right-click on **My Computer**, and click **Manage**.

10. Click on the **Disk Management** node to display its contents, if necessary. Notice that Disk 0 is now listed as a dynamic disk. Leave the Computer Management tool open.

There are circumstances when you may need to change a dynamic disk back to a basic disk, such as when you want to implement a dual-boot setup, or when you want to remove Windows Server 2003 from the computer so that a different operating system—such as Windows XP—can be installed. Before reverting back to a basic disk, the disk must be empty; therefore, the data on the disk must be backed up or moved to another disk. A dynamic disk can be converted back to a basic disk by using the following general steps:

1. Back up all data on the dynamic disk volume before you start.

2. Delete all dynamic disk volumes using the Disk Management tool by right-clicking on each volume, and then clicking Delete Volume.

3. Once all volumes on the disk have been deleted, right-click the dynamic disk, and choose Convert to Basic Disk.

4. Use the Disk Management tool to partition and format the disk.

6

In Activity 6-5 you used the Disk Management tool to covert Disk 0 on your server from a basic disk to a dynamic disk. Once a dynamic disk is available, an administrator can create different types of volumes, as outlined earlier in this chapter. In Activity 6-6 you use the Disk Management tool to create a new simple volume on Disk 0.

Activity 6-6: Creating a Simple Volume

Time Required: 5 minutes

Objective: Create a simple volume.

Description: After converting your hard disk to a dynamic disk in Activity 6-5, you are now capable of creating volumes on the disk. In this activity you create a small simple volume formatted with the NTFS file system.

1. In the Disk Management tool, right-click on an area of free disk space on Disk 0 and click **New Volume**.

2. At the Welcome to the New Volume Wizard screen, click **Next**.

3. At the Select Volume Type screen, ensure that Simple is selected, and click **Next**.

4. At the Specify Volume Size screen, type **50** in the Partition size in MB text box. Click **Next**.

5. At the Assign Drive Letter or Path screen, ensure that drive **I:** is selected in the Assign the following drive letter list box and then click **Next**.

6. At the Format Volume screen, ensure that the **Format this volume with the following settings** radio button is selected. In the Volume label text box, type **New Simple Volume** and then click **Next**.

7. Click **Finish** to create the new simple volume.

8. Close the Computer Management tool.

EXTENDING VOLUMES

Windows Server 2003 supports the ability to extend NTFS volumes, as long as those volumes are not functioning as the boot or system volume for the system. Although volumes can be extended using the Disk Management tool by right-clicking on a volume and selecting the Extend Volume option, they can also be extended from the command line using the DISKPART utility. In Activity 6-7, you use the DISKPART command-line utility to extend the simple volume created in Activity 6-6. You learn more about the DISKPART command later in this chapter.

Activity 6-7: Extending a Volume Using DISKPART

Time Required: 5 minutes

Objective: Extend an existing volume using the DISKPART command.

Description: In the past, administrators at Dover Leasing have noticed that some servers quickly run out of space in existing partitions. Because NTFS volumes can be extended, you have decided to test this functionality on your server. In this activity, you extend the simple volume created in Activity 6-6 to include additional space by using the DISKPART command-line utility.

1. Click **Start**, and then click **Run**. In the Open text box, type **cmd.exe** and click **OK**.

2. At the command line, type **diskpart** and press **Enter**.

3. At the DISKPART prompt, type **list volume** and press **Enter**.

4. From the list of available volumes, determine the volume number assigned to drive I: in the Volume ### column, and review the volume numbers and letters assigned to other drives.

5. At the DISKPART prompt, type **select volume X**, where X is the number assigned to drive I: on your system. Press **Enter**.

6. At the DISKPART prompt, type **extend size=50** and press **Enter**. This extends the size of drive I: by 50 MB on the same disk.

7. At the DISKPART prompt, type **exit** and press **Enter**. Close the command prompt window.

8. Click **Start**, and then click **My Computer**.

9. Right-click on drive **I:** and click **Properties**. On the General tab, confirm that the size of drive I: is approximately 100 MB, based on the original size of 50 MB, and the extension by another 50 MB.

10. Click **Cancel**, and then close the My Computer window.

MOUNTED DRIVES

Windows Server 2003 enables you to mount a drive as an alternative to giving it a drive letter. A **mounted drive** is one that appears as a folder and that is accessed through a path like any other folder. You can mount a basic or dynamic disk drive, a CD-ROM, or a Zip drive. Only an empty folder on a volume formatted for NTFS can be used for mounting a drive.

There are several reasons for using mounted drives, the most apparent being that Windows operating systems are limited to 26 drive letters and mounting drives enables you to reduce the number of drive letters in use, because they are not associated with letters. As server administrator, you might allocate one drive for all user home directories and mount that drive in a folder called Users. The path to this drive might be C:\Users. In another situation, you might have a database that you want to manage as a mounted drive so that it is easier for users to access. Also, by mounting the drive, you can set up special backups for that database by simply backing up its folder.

In Activity 6-8 you use the Disk Management node of the Computer Management tool to mount an existing NTFS volume to a new empty folder on drive D.

Activity 6-8: Mounting an NTFS Volume

Time Required: 5 minutes

Objective: Mount an NTFS volume.

Description: Some of the servers at Dover Leasing contain many disks, each with many partitions. In the past, administrators have been constrained by a lack of available drive letters on some of these servers. Knowing that Windows Server 2003 allows drives to be mounted to an empty folder on an NTFS partition, you decide to test this functionality. In this activity, you use Disk Management to mount drive I to an empty NTFS folder on drive D.

1. Click **Start**, and then click **My Computer**.

2. Double-click on drive **D:** to view its contents.

3. Right-click on an area of blank space, select **New**, and then click **Folder**. Name the new folder **mounted**, and then close My Computer.

4. Click **Start**, right-click on **My Computer**, and click **Manage**.

5. Click on the **Disk Management** node to display its contents, if necessary.

6. Right-click on volume **I:** and click **Change Drive Letter and Paths**.

7. In the Change Drive Letter and Paths for I: (New Simple Volume) window, ensure that drive **I:** is selected, and then click **Add**.

8. In the Add Drive Letter or Path window, ensure that the **Mount in the following empty NTFS folder** radio button is selected, and type **d:\mounted** in the text box. Click **OK**. Drive I: is now accessible both by using its drive letter (I:) and by accessing the d:\mounted folder.

9. Close the Computer Management window.

10. Click **Start**, and then click **My Computer**. Double-click on drive **I:**, and create a new folder named **Test**. Press the **Backspace** button on the keyboard to return to the list of available drives.

11. Double-click on drive **D:** to view its contents. Double-click on the **mounted** folder, noticing that its icon has changed to what appears to be a disk, rather than a folder. The Test folder created in Step 10 appears, since the mounted folder now acts as another entry point to drive I:.

12. Close all open windows.

Fault Tolerant Disk Strategies

6

Fault tolerance is the ability of a system to gracefully recover from hardware or software failure. Servers often store critical data that must have high availability. Windows Server 2003 provides a level of fault tolerance through software RAID. RAID is not meant as a replacement for performing regular backups of data, but it increases the availability of disk storage. For example, if a hard disk fails and you have not implemented fault tolerance, any data stored on that disk is lost and unavailable until the drive is replaced and data is restored from backup. With fault tolerance, data is written to more than one drive; in the event one drive fails, data can still be accessed from one of the remaining drives using a combination of other parts of the file, and associated parity information.

RAID Levels

Because hard disk drives are prone to failure, one of the best data security measures is to plan for disk redundancy in servers and host computers. This is accomplished in two ways: by performing regular backups and by installing RAID drives.

Redundant Array of Independent Disk (RAID) strategies is a set of standards for lengthening disk life, preventing data loss, and enabling relatively uninterrupted access to data. There are six basic levels of RAID (other RAID levels exist beyond the basic levels), beginning with the use of disk striping.

The six basic RAID levels are as follows:

- RAID level 0—Striping with no other redundancy features is RAID level 0. Striping is used to extend disk life and to improve performance. Data access on striped volumes is fast because of the way the data is divided into blocks that are quickly accessed through multiple disk reads and data paths. A significant disadvantage to using level 0 striping is that if one disk fails, you can expect a large data loss on all volumes. Windows Server 2003 supports RAID level 0, using between two and 32 disks in a set. In Windows Server 2003, this is called striped volumes, previously referred to as striped sets in Windows NT 4.0.

- RAID level 1—This level employs simple disk mirroring and provides a means of duplicating the operating system files in the event of a disk failure. Disk mirroring is a method of fault tolerance that prevents data loss by duplicating data from a main disk to a backup disk, as shown in Figure 6-9. Disk duplexing is the same as disk mirroring, with the exception that it places the backup disk on a different controller or adapter than is used by the main disk, as shown in Figure 6-10. Windows Server 2003 supports level 1, but includes disk duplexing as well as mirroring through the fault-tolerance driver Ftdisk.sys. If there are three or more volumes to be mirrored or duplexed, this solution is more expensive than the other RAID levels. When planning for disk mirroring, remember that write access is slower than read access, because information must be written twice, once on the primary disk and once on the secondary disk. Some server administrators consider disk mirroring and disk duplexing to offer one of the best guarantees of data recovery when there is a disk failure.

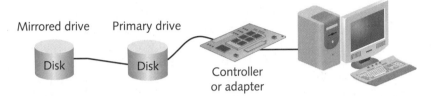

Figure 6-9   Disk mirroring

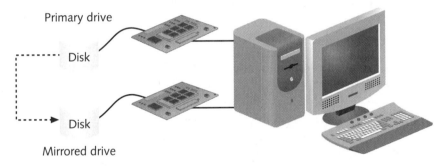

Figure 6-10   Disk duplexing

- RAID level 2—This uses an array of disks whereby the data is striped across all disks in the array. Also, in this method all disks store error-correction information that enables the array to reconstruct data from a failed disk. The advantages of level 2 are that disk wear is reduced and that data can be reconstructed if a disk fails.

- RAID level 3—Like level 2, RAID level 3 uses disk striping and stores error-correcting information, but the information is only written to one disk in the array. If that disk fails, the array cannot rebuild its contents.

- RAID level 4—This level stripes data and stores error-correcting information on all drives, in a manner similar to level 2. An added feature is its ability to perform checksum verification. The checksum is a sum of bits in a file. When a file is recreated after a disk failure, the checksum previously stored for that file is checked against the actual file after it is reconstructed. If the two do not match, the file may be corrupted. Windows Server 2003 does not support RAID levels 2 through 4.

- RAID level 5—Level 5 combines the best features of RAID, including striping, error correction, and checksum verification. Windows Server 2003 supports level 5, referring to it as a "stripe set with parity on basic disks" or a RAID-5 volume (for dynamic disks), depending on the disk architecture. Whereas level 4 stores checksum data on only one disk, level 5 spreads both error-correction and checksum data over all of the disks, so there is no single point of failure. This level uses more memory than the other RAID levels, with at least 16 MB of additional memory recommended for system functions. In addition, level 5 requires at least three disks in the RAID array. Recovery from a failed disk provides roughly the same guarantee as with disk mirroring, but takes longer with level 5. RAID level 5 can recover from a single disk failure; however, if more than one drive in the array fails, all data is lost and must be restored from backup.

Windows Server 2003 supports RAID levels 0, 1, and 5 for disk fault tolerance (each of these levels is discussed further in the sections that follow), with levels 1 and 5 recommended. RAID level 0 is not recommended in many situations because it does not really provide fault tolerance, except to help extend the life of disks while providing relatively fast access. All three RAID levels support disks formatted with FAT or NTFS. When you decide between using RAID level 1 or RAID level 5, consider the following:

- The boot and system files can be placed on RAID level 1, but not on RAID level 5. Thus, if you use RAID level 5, these files must be on a separate disk or a separate RAID level 1 disk set.
- RAID level 1 uses two hard disks, and RAID level 5 uses from three to 32.
- RAID level 1 is more expensive to implement than RAID level 5, when you consider the cost per megabyte of storage. Keep in mind that in RAID level 1, half of your total disk space is used for redundancy, whereas that value is one-third or less for RAID level 5. The amount of RAID level 5 used for parity is $1/n$ where n is the number of disk drives in the array.
- RAID level 5 requires more memory than RAID level 1.
- Read access is faster in RAID levels 1 and 5 than write access, with read access for RAID level 1 identical to that of a disk that does not have RAID. Because RAID level 5 involves more disks and the read/write heads can acquire data simultaneously across striped volumes, however, RAID level 5 has much faster read access than RAID level 1.

Striped Volume (RAID 0)

As you learned earlier in this chapter, the reasons for using a RAID level 0 or a striped volume in Windows Server 2003 are to:

- Reduce the wear on multiple disk drives by equally spreading the load
- Increase disk performance compared to other methods for configuring dynamic disk volumes

Although striped volumes do not provide fault tolerance, other than to extend the life of the disks, there are situations in which they might be used. Consider, for example, an organization that maintains a "data warehouse" in which vital data is stored and updated on a mainframe; and a copy is downloaded at regular intervals to a server housing the data warehouse. The purpose of the data on the server is to create reports and to provide fast lookups of data, without slowing down the mainframe. In this instance, the goal is to provide the fastest possible access to the data and not fault tolerance, because the original data and primary data services are on the mainframe. For this application, you might create a striped volume on the server used for the data warehouse, because it yields the fastest data access.

To create a striped volume, right-click the unallocated space for the volume, click New Volume, after the New Volume Wizard starts click Next, click the option button for Striped, and complete the remaining steps in the New Volume Wizard.

Mirrored Volume (RAID 1)

Disk mirroring, known as RAID level 1, involves creating a copy of data on a backup disk. Only dynamic disks can be set up as a **mirrored volume** in Windows Server 2003. It is one of the most guaranteed forms of disk fault tolerance because the data on a failed drive is still available on the mirrored drive (with a short down time to make the mirrored drive accessible). Also, disk read performance is the same as reading data from any single disk drive. The disadvantage of mirroring is that the time to create or update information is doubled because it is written twice, once on the main disk and once on the shadow disk. However, writing to disk in mirroring is normally faster than writing to disk when you use RAID level 5. A mirrored volume cannot be striped and requires two dynamic disks.

A mirrored volume is particularly well suited for situations in which data is mission-critical and must not be lost under any circumstances, such as with customer files at a bank. A mirrored volume is also valuable for situations in which a computer system must not be down for long, such as for medical applications or in 24-hour manufacturing. The somewhat slower update time is offset by the assurances that when a disk failure occurs, data will not be lost and the system will quickly be functioning again. However, if fast disk updating is the most important criterion for disk storage, such as when copying files or taking orders over a telephone, then a striped volume may be a better choice than a mirrored volume.

A mirrored volume is created through the Disk Management tool. To create the volume, right-click the unallocated space on one disk, click New Volume, click Next, and choose the Mirrored option in the New Volume Wizard.

RAID-5 Volume

Fault tolerance is better for a RAID-5 volume than for a simple striped volume. A **RAID-5 volume** requires a minimum of three disk drives. Parity information is distributed on each disk so that if one disk fails, the information on that disk can be reconstructed. The parity used by Microsoft is Boolean (true/false, one/zero) logic, with information about the data contained in each row of 64 KB data blocks on the striped disks. Using the example of storing a 720 KB file across five disks, one 64 KB parity block is written on each disk. The first parity block is always written in row 1 of disk 1, the second is in row 2 of disk 2, and so on, as illustrated in Figure 6-11. (Compare this figure to the striped volume illustrated earlier in Figure 6-4.)

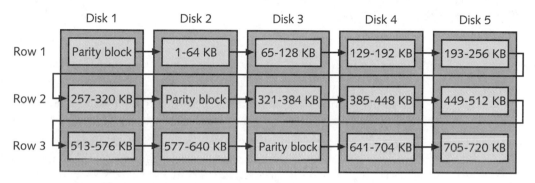

Figure 6-11   Disks in a RAID-5 volume

When you set up a RAID-5 volume, the performance is not as fast as with a striped volume, because it takes longer to write the data and calculate the parity block for each row. However, reading from the disk is as fast as a striped volume. A RAID-5 volume is a viable choice for fault tolerance with mission-critical data and applications where full mirroring is not feasible due to the expense. Also, disk arrays are compatible with RAID level 5. A RAID-5 volume is particularly useful in a client/server system that uses a separate database for queries and report creation, because disk read performance is fast for obtaining data. In applications such as a customer service database that is constantly updated with new orders, disk read performance is slower than with striping without parity.

The amount of storage space used for parity information is based on the formula $1/n$ where n is the number of physical disks in the volume. For example, if there are four disks, the amount of space taken for parity information is $1/4$ of the total space of all disk drives in the volume. This means you get more usable disk storage if there are more disks in the volume. A set of eight 2 MB disks yields more usable storage than a set of four 4 MB disks using RAID level 5.

Use the Disk Management tool to create a RAID-5 volume. To start, right-click the unallocated or free space on a disk that is to be part of the volume, click New Volume, click Next, and select the RAID-5 volume option in the New Volume Wizard.

Software RAID and Hardware RAID

Two approaches to RAID can be implemented on a server: software RAID and hardware RAID. Software RAID implements fault tolerance through the server's operating system, such as using RAID levels 0, 1, or 5 through the Windows Server 2003 Disk Management tool. Hardware RAID is implemented through the server hardware and is independent of the operating system. Many manufacturers implement hardware RAID on the adapter, such as a SCSI adapter, to which the disk drives are connected. The RAID logic is contained in a chip on the adapter. Also, there is often a battery connected to the chip that ensures it never loses power and has fault tolerance to retain the RAID setup even when there is a power outage. Hardware RAID is more expensive than software RAID, but offers many advantages over software RAID, such as:

- Faster read and write response
- The ability to place boot and system files on different RAID levels, such as RAID levels 1 and 5
- The ability to "hot-swap" a failed disk with one that works or is new, thus replacing the disk without shutting down the server (this option can vary by manufacturer)
- More setup options to retrieve damaged data and to combine different RAID levels within one array of disks, such as mirroring two disks using RAID level 1 and setting up five disks for RAID level 5 in a seven disk array (the RAID options depend on what the manufacturer offers)

Monitoring Disk Health and Importing Foreign Disks

The Disk Management tool in Windows Server 2003 provides information on the health of both disks and volumes as a method of allowing administrators to determine the overall health of the disk subsystem. While status messages like Online or Healthy are optimal, it's important to have a basic understanding of the other messages that might appear on disks or volumes.

While monitoring the status of existing disks and volumes is important, Windows Server 2003 also provides the ability to import disks from other servers in the event that another server should fail. Disks that originate from other servers are known as foreign disks, and the process for importing them to another Windows Server 2003 is relatively straightforward.

In the following sections you learn more about both disk and volume status descriptions and the process for importing foreign disks on a Windows Server 2003 system.

Disk and Volume Status Descriptions

Under normal operating conditions, the status associated with a particular hard disk in the Disk Management tool should be "Online", while the status associated with a volume should be "Healthy". These status indicators are listed in the graphical representation of disks or volumes in the Disk Management display, as shown in Figure 6-12.

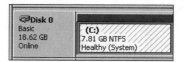

Figure 6-12 Disk and volume status information

Although these status messages are optimal, a variety of additional status messages may appear in their place, and can indicate anything from the failed redundancy of a fault-tolerant volume to different media errors. The most common status messages for a volume are as follows:

- Failed—Indicates that a volume could not be started automatically, or that the disk is damaged. If this status message appears, ensure that the disk is properly connected to the system.

- Failed Redundancy—Indicates that the fault tolerance provided by a RAID-5 or mirrored volume is unavailable because one of the disks in the fault-tolerant volume is not online. Different sub-status messages may appear in parentheses next to the message indicating that the volume at risk is the system or boot volume, holds the paging file, and so forth.

- Formatting—A temporary status message that indicates a format operating is currently being carried out on the volume.

- Healthy—Indicates that a volume is functioning as it should, and no additional actions are required. If this message is followed by a sub-status message in parentheses indicating that the volume is at risk, I/O errors may have been detected, and Check Disk should be run.

- Regenerating—Indicates that a missing disk in a RAID-5 volume has been reactivated and is regenerating its data. Once complete, the status of the volume should return to Healthy.

- Resyncing—Indicates that a mirrored volume is synchronizing information as part of maintaining identical data on both disks. This message may also appear when mirrored disks are imported, or when an offline disk in a mirrored volume is brought back online. Once complete, the status of the volume should return to Healthy.

- Unknown—Indicates that the boot sector for the volume is corrupted, and data on that volume is not accessible.

The most common status messages for a disk are as follows:

- Audio CD—Indicates that an audio CD is located in a CD or DVD drive.

- Foreign—Indicates that the disk is a dynamic disk imported from another computer. To access data on this disk, right-click and select the Import Foreign Disks option.

- Initializing—A temporary status that indicates a basic disk is being converted to a dynamic disk.

- Missing—Indicates that the disk has been removed, is not properly connected, or has been corrupted. If the disk is reconnected, right-click on the disk and choose the Reactivate Disks option to make the disk accessible.

- No Media—Indicates that the CD, DVD, or other removable media drive is empty.

- Not Initialized—Indicates that a new disk has been added to the system without a valid disk signature. To make the disk accessible, right-click on the disk and choose the Initialize Disk option.

- Online—Indicates that the disk is functioning normally, and no additional actions are required.

- Online (Errors)—Indicates that I/O errors have been detected on a dynamic disk. Use the Check Disk utility to scan the disk for errors.

- Offline—Indicates that a disk is no longer accessible. Attempt to fix this problem by right-clicking on the disk and choosing Reactivate Disk. If that doesn't solve the problem, the issue may relate to the connection or a problem with the drive controller.

- Unreadable—Typically indicates I/O errors or corruption on certain portions of the disk. Use the Rescan Disks command to try and bring the disk back online, or try to repair the problem with the Check Disk utility.

TIP

For a complete list of the various disk and volume status and sub-status messages available in Windows Server 2003, see the Volume status descriptions and Disk status descriptions topics in Help and Support Center.

Importing Foreign Disks

In cases where a particular server fails, it is conceivable that the data stored on the server's hard disks could still be intact, and need to be made accessible to network users. Windows Server 2003 supports the ability to import dynamic disks from different operating systems, including Windows 2000, Windows XP, and other Windows Server 2003 systems.

When a dynamic disk from another server is connected to a Windows Server 2003 system, the initial status message associated with that disk is Foreign, and the data is inaccessible. To remedy this situation, right-click on the disk and choose the Import Foreign Disks option. This option allows you to choose the disk group to be imported, and display the type, condition, and size of the volumes available on the disk.

If you need to import multiple foreign disks, you should import each disk individually using the Import Foreign Disk command. If more than one disk is used to form a RAID-5 or mirrored volume, fault-tolerance is restored once all disks have been imported. In the case of a spanned volume, all disks that were part of the spanned volume must be imported in order for the data to be accessible. By default, an imported disk attempts to use the same drive letters assigned to individual volumes from the originating server, but if a conflict exists, the next available drive letters are used instead.

OTHER DISK MAINTENANCE AND MANAGEMENT UTILITIES

Although the Disk Management console is the primary utility used to manage, monitor, and maintain disks on a Windows Server 2003 system, a variety of other disk-related utilities exist. While some of these utilities provide functions or features not available from within the Disk Management interface, others are utilities that allow you to carry out Disk Management-type functions from the command line. The utilities to be explored in this section include:

- Check Disk / CHKDSK
- CONVERT
- Disk Cleanup
- Disk Defragmenter / DEFRAG
- DISKPART
- FORMAT
- FSUTIL
- MOUNTVOL

Check Disk

The Check Disk tool allows you to scan your disk for bad sectors and file system errors. This is a tool that is meant for use when there are no users that need to access the files on the disk you want to check, because the disk is made unavailable during the scan for problems. The Check Disk tool is started from the Properties dialog box for a volume or partition, as shown in Figure 6-13.

There are two options when starting the Check Disk tool, as illustrated in Figure 6-14:

- Automatically fix file system errors—Select this option to have Windows repair any errors in the file system that it finds during the disk-checking process. In order to use this option, all programs must be closed.

- Scan for and attempt recovery of bad sectors—Select this option to have the system find and fix bad sectors and file errors, recovering any information that it can read. Choosing this option also includes the file system fixes that are performed by the Automatically fix file system errors option.

You can also check your disk for errors by running the CHKDSK command (by clicking the CHKDSK command from the command line or Run command). CHKDSK also starts automatically when you boot Windows Server 2003 and the boot process detects a corrupt

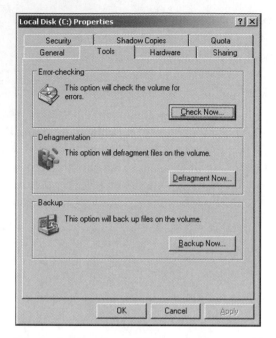

Figure 6-13   Check Disk can be accessed by clicking the Check Now button on the Tools
tab in the properties of a volume

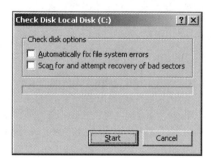

Figure 6-14   The Check Disk tool

file allocation table or corrupted files. In Windows Server 2003, CHKDSK can be used to
check FAT16, FAT32, NTFS, or any combination of these (on a dual-boot computer).
When the file system is FAT16 or FAT32, the utility checks the file allocation table, folders,
files, disk sectors, and disk allocation units. In NTFS, it checks files, folders, indexes, security
descriptors, user files, and disk allocation units. The output of the CHKDSK command is
illustrated in Figure 6-15.

```
Command Prompt                                          _ □ X

G:\>chkdsk
The type of the file system is NTFS.
The volume is in use by another process. Chkdsk
might report errors when no corruption is present.

WARNING! F parameter not specified.
Running CHKDSK in read-only mode.

CHKDSK is verifying files (stage 1 of 3)...
File verification completed.
CHKDSK is verifying indexes (stage 2 of 3)...
Index verification completed.
CHKDSK is verifying security descriptors (stage 3 of 3)...
Security descriptor verification completed.
CHKDSK is verifying Usn Journal...
Usn Journal verification completed.

  4096543 KB total disk space.
  3904616 KB in 12391 files.
     3776 KB in 1117 indexes.
        0 KB in bad sectors.
    63335 KB in use by the system.
    22544 KB occupied by the log file.
   124816 KB available on disk.

     4096 bytes in each allocation unit.
  1024135 total allocation units on disk.
    31204 allocation units available on disk.
```

Figure 6-15   Output from the CHKDSK command

 Allow plenty of time for CHKDSK to run on large disk systems, such as a system having over 10 GB. If you have multiple disks, you may want to stagger running CHKDSK on different disks for each week. Also, the presence of some bad sectors is normal. Many disks have a few bad sectors that are marked by the manufacturer during the low-level format and on which data cannot be written.

When CHKDSK finds lost allocation units or chains, it prompts you with the Yes or No question: Convert lost chains to files? Answer Yes to the question so that you can save the lost information to files. The files that CHKDSK creates for each lost chain are labeled Filexxx.chk and can be edited with a text editor to determine their contents.

CONVERT

The primary purpose of the CONVERT command-line utility is to provide a mechanism for converting existing FAT and FAT32 partitions or volumes to the NTFS file system, while leaving existing data intact. This utility was originally explored in Chapter 5, and cannot be used to convert between FAT and FAT32, or from NTFS to either FAT file system. The syntax of the CONVERT command is fairly basic. The example below reiterates the process for converting an existing FAT or FAT32 partition (drive G in this example) to the NTFS file system:

```
convert g: /fs:ntfs
```

Disk Cleanup

Over time, temporary and unnecessary files (such as those placed in the Recycle Bin) can begin to consume very large areas of disk space that could be used for other purposes. The Disk Cleanup utility allows an administrator to quickly determine how much disk space could potentially be freed up on a particular volume or partition by removing unnecessary files. Examples of elements that the Disk Cleanup tool can be used to remove include:

- Temporary Internet files
- Downloaded program files
- Files stored in the Recycle Bin
- Windows temporary files
- Windows components no longer used
- Installed programs no longer used

Additionally, Disk Cleanup can help to increase the amount of disk space made available by compressing files that are seldom used, or removing old catalog files created by the Indexing service. Figure 6-16 illustrates the Disk Cleanup tab of this utility, while Figure 6-17 shows the contents of the More Options tab.

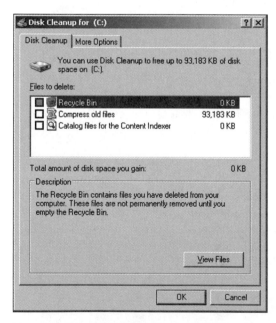

Figure 6-16 The Disk Cleanup utility

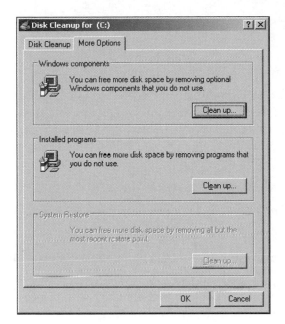

Figure 6-17   The More Options tab in the Disk Cleanup utility

To access the Disk Cleanup tool, right-click the volume or partition and click Properties. On the General tab, click the Disk Cleanup button. The Disk Cleanup utility can also be started from the command line using the CLEANMGR command.

Disk Defragmenter

When you save a file to a disk, Windows Server 2003 saves the file to the first area of available space. The file may not be saved to a contiguous area of free space, and therefore the disk gradually becomes **fragmented**, particularly as more and more files are created and deleted. When your computer attempts to access the file, it may have to be read from different areas on a disk, slowing access time and creating disk wear. The process of **defragmenting** locates fragmented folders and files and moves them to a location on the physical disk so they are in contiguous order.

On a busy server, drives should be defragmented once every week or two. On less busy servers, defragment the drives at least once a month.

TIP

In Activity 6-9 you use the Disk Defragmenter utility to analyze and then defragment drive C on your server.

Activity 6-9: Using the Disk Defragmenter Utility

Time Required: 10 minutes

Objective: Defragment a volume using the Disk Defragmenter utility.

Description: In the past, Dover Leasing has always purchased and installed a third-party disk defragmentation utility for all servers. The IT manager at Dover Leasing is exploring ways to help reduce costs, and as such, has asked you to evaluate the Disk Defragmenter tool included with Windows Server 2003. In this activity you use Disk Defragmenter to first analyze and then defragment drive C on your server.

1. Click **Start**, right-click on **My Computer**, and click **Manage**.

2. Click on the **Disk Defragmenter** node to view its contents.

3. Ensure that Volume **C:** is selected, and then click the **Analyze** button.

4. When the Disk Defragmenter dialog box appears, click the **View Report** button.

5. Review the data in the Volume information section, and then click **Close**. The Estimated disk usage before defragmentation bar will be populated with difficult colors to represent fragmented files, contiguous files, unmovable files and free space, as shown in Figure 6-18.

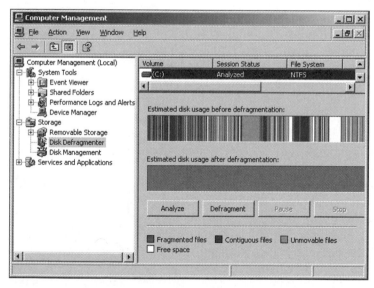

Figure 6-18   Results of analyzing the fragmentation of a volume

6. Click the **Defragment** button to begin the defragmentation process.

7. Once the process completes, click the **View Report** button. After reviewing the report, click the **Close** button.

8. Close the Computer Management window.

Along with the MMC version of the Disk Defragmenter tool, Windows Server 2003 also provides a command-line version of this utility. The DEFRAG command can be used to analyze or defragment an existing volume, partition, or mount point from the command line, and it represents an effective way to schedule disk defragmentation to occur automatically when used in conjunction with a batch file and the Task Scheduler. For example, the following command could be added to a batch file to force a volume (D:) to be defragmented, even if disk space on that volume is low (the disk defragmenter issues a warning when less that 15% of the disk space on a volume is free):

```
defrag d: -f
```

Or, to simply analyze the current fragmentation of drive D from the command line, an administrator could issue the command:

```
defrag d: -a
```

For a list of the complete syntax and switches supported with the DEFRAG command, type DEFRAG /? at the command line and press Enter.

6

DISKPART

The DISKPART command is a powerful utility for managing disks, volumes, and partitions from the command line. Using this tool an administrator can configure the active partition, assign drive letters, control file system mounting, create and extend volumes and partitions, implement fault tolerance schemes, import disks, and more.

One of the most popular uses of the DISKPART utility is to manage disks from within scripts that can be used to automate tasks. For example, the DISKPART tool provides a useful method for creating additional partitions on a system that has been installed using an unattended setup procedure.

For more information on the syntax, commands, and switches available with the DISKPART command, type DISKPART /? at the command line and press Enter.

FORMAT

Users familiar with disk preparation on MS-DOS or Windows 9X systems are likely already familiar with the basic concept of the FORMAT command. Used to implement a file system on an existing partition, the FORMAT command in Windows Server 2003 allows an administrator to not only specify which of the supported file systems should be implemented with the command, but also a variety of advanced settings including the allocation unit (cluster) size. Although the ability to format disks is provided from within the Disk Management console, the command-line version provides administrators with additional flexibility, including formatting partitions from within scripts.

For more information on the syntax, and switches available with the FORMAT command, type FORMAT /? at the command line and press Enter.

FSUTIL

The FSUTIL command is an advanced command-line utility that allows an administrator to gather information and perform tasks relating to FAT, FAT32, and NTFS file systems. Because this utility allows an administrator to control many advanced file system settings and functions, it should only be used by advanced or experienced administrators. Examples of information that can be gathered by the FSUTIL tool include listings of drives, volume information, NTFS-specific data, and so forth. The FSUTIL tool can also be used to manage disk quotas, display the free space available on a volume, and more. For example, to view all of the volumes available on a system, issue the following command:

```
fsutil fsinfo drives
```

To view disk space information about drive C, including the amount of free space and total disk space available, issue the following command:

```
fsutil volume diskfree c:
```

The FSUTIL command supports a variety of sub-commands and switches. For detailed information on the capabilities of the FSUTIL command, see the FSUTIL topic in Help and Support Center.

MOUNTVOL

Although Windows Server 2003 allows NTFS volumes to be mounted to an empty folder from within the Disk Management console, the MOUNTVOL command can also be used to create, delete, or list volume mount points from the command line. Unfortunately, one of the parameters associated with mounting a new volume is VolumeName, and this value is specified using a globally unique identifier (GUID) value that can be exceptionally long. Thankfully, issuing the MOUNTVOL /? command and pressing Enter will not only list the various switches associated with the command, but also the GUIDs of existing volumes and partitions.

For example, the command to mount a volume with the GUID ced284f1-6962-11d7-8400-806d6172696f to an empty NTFS folder named D:\mountpoint would be:

```
mountvol d:\mountpoint \\?\volume{ced284f1-6962-11d7-8400-
806d6172696f}\
```

Although the length of the GUID complicates the task of adding a new mount point, existing mount points can be easily deleted using the command. For example, the mount point created in the previous example would be deleted by issuing the following command:

```
mountvol d:\mountpoint /d
```

For more information on the syntax, and switches available with the MOUNTVOL command, along with the VolumeName values for existing volumes and partitions, type MOUNTVOL /? at the command line and press Enter.

CHAPTER SUMMARY

❑ Windows Server 2003 supports both basic and dynamic disks. Basic disks consist of primary and extended partitions, as well as logical drives. Dynamic disks allow volumes to be created and fault-tolerant disk strategies to be implemented.

❑ Basic disks can support up to four primary partitions, or three primary and one extended partition. Extended partitions can be further divided into logical drives.

❑ Dynamic disks can support simple, spanned, striped, mirrored, and RAID-5 volumes.

❑ Disk Management is the primary tool used to manage disks, partitions, and volumes on a Windows Server 2003 system.

❑ Windows Server 2003 supports two main fault-tolerance techniques for hard disks. Mirrored volumes, also known as RAID 1, mirrors the contents of one volume to another disk. RAID-5 volumes use disk striping with parity to allow continued operation of a volume in the event that a single disk in that volume should fail.

❑ Windows Server 2003 provides a number of tools for managing, maintaining, and monitoring disks and partitions from the command line including CHKDSK, DISKPART, DEFRAG, FORMAT, FSUTIL, and MOUNTVOL.

❑ The Disk Cleanup utility allows Administrators to remove unnecessary files and applications from a partition or volume, as well as save space by compressing seldom-used files.

❑ The Disk Defragmenter tool is used to optimize the performance of a partition or volume by moving fragmented files back into contiguous blocks of disk space.

KEY TERMS

active partition — The partition from which an operating system begins the boot process. Typically drive C: is configured as the active partition on a Windows Server 2003 system.

basic disk — In Windows Server 2003, a partitioned disk that can have up to four partitions and that uses logical drive designations. This type of disk is compatible with MS-DOS, Windows 3.x, Windows 95, Windows 98, Windows NT, Windows 2000, Windows XP, and Windows Server 2003.

defragmenting — A process by which fragmented files are rearranged into contiguous areas of disk space, improving file access performance.

Disk Management — An MMC snap-in used to manage and monitor disks, volumes, and partitions.

dynamic disk — A disk in Windows Server 2003, that does not use traditional partitioning, meaning there are no restrictions on the number of volumes that can be set up on one disk or the ability to extend volumes onto additional physical disks. Dynamic disks are only compatible with Windows Server 2003, Windows 2000, and Windows XP Professional systems.

extended partition — A partition on a basic disk that is created from unpartitioned free disk space, and is not formatted with a file system. Space in an extended partition is allocated to logical drives.

fault tolerance — Techniques that employ hardware and software to provide assurance against equipment failures, computer service interruptions, and data loss.

fragmented — A normal and gradual process in which files become divided into different areas of disk space in a volume, resulting in slower file access.

logical drives — Dedicated and formatted portions of disk space created within an extended partition on a basic disk.

mirrored volume — A fault-tolerant disk strategy in which a volume on one dynamic disk has its contents mirrored to a second dynamic disk.

mounted drive — A partition or volume accessible via an empty folder on an existing NTFS partition. Often implemented to circumvent the need to assign the volume or partition of a drive letter.

primary partition — A dedicated portion of a basic disk that is potentially bootable, and formatted with a file system. A basic disk can support a maximum of four primary partitions.

RAID-5 volume — A fault-tolerant disk strategy that consists of creating a single volume across anywhere between three and 32 dynamic disks. RAID-5 volumes use disk striping with parity to allow the volume to remain accessible in the event that a single disk with the volume should fail.

Redundant Array of Independent Disks (RAID) — Disk performance and fault tolerance strategies that can be implemented on a Windows Server 2003 system with multiple hard disks installed.

simple volume — A dedicated and formatted portion of disk space on a dynamic disk.

spanned volume — Dedicated and formatted space on between two and 32 dynamic disks that is treated as a single logical volume.

striped volume — Dedicated and formatted space on between two and 32 dynamic disks that is treated as a single logical volume, with data striped across the disks in the volume in 64 KB blocks.

Review Questions

1. What is the maximum number of primary partitions that a basic disk can support?

   a. 1

   b. 2

   c. 3

   d. 4

2. What is the maximum number of extended partitions that a basic disk can support?

    a. 1

    b. 2

    c. 3

    d. 4

3. Which of the following can be created on a dynamic disk?

    a. Simple volume

    b. Spanned volume

    c. Primary partition

    d. Extended partition

4. What term is used to describe an installed dynamic disk that originated from another server?

    a. Foreign disk

    b. External disk

    c. Dynamic disk

    d. Basic disk

5. If only one hard disk is installed on a Windows Server 2003 system, what disk number will it be assigned?

    a. 0

    b. 1

    c. 2

    d. 01

6. Which of the following can be created on a basic disk?

    a. RAID-5 volume

    b. Spanned volume

    c. Primary partition

    d. Logical drive

7. RAID-5 volumes can be created on a basic disk.

    a. True

    b. False

8. Which of the following volumes cannot be extended on a Windows Server 2003 system?

    a. System volume

    b. Boot volume

    c. All volumes can be extended on a Windows Server 2003 system, as long as the file system used is NTFS

9. Which of the following file systems supports the ability to extend existing volumes?

   a. FAT

   b. FAT32

   c. NTFS

10. What is the minimum number of hard disks required for implementing a RAID-5 volume?

    a. 2

    b. 3

    c. 4

    d. 5

11. What is the maximum number of hard drives supported for a striped volume on a Windows Server 2003 system?

    a. 3

    b. 6

    c. 16

    d. 32

12. What term is used to describe disk mirroring when each drive is connected to its own hard disk controller?

    a. Disk mirroring

    b. Disk duplexing

    c. Shadowing

    d. Controller mirror

13. What term is used to describe the volume the Windows folder is located on?

    a. Boot volume

    b. System volume

    c. Dynamic disk

    d. Basic disk

14. How many partitions can be marked active on a Windows Server 2003 system at any point in time?

    a. 0

    b. 1

    c. 2

    d. 3

15. Which of the following RAID levels provides no fault tolerance?

    a. RAID level 0

    b. RAID level 1

    c. RAID level 4

    d. RAID level 5

16. All access to a spanned volume is lost if one disk on which the spanned volume resides fails.

    a. True

    b. False

17. Which of the following tools can be used to view and remove unnecessary files on a particular partition or volume?

    a. Disk Cleanup

    b. Check Disk

    c. MOUNTVOL

    d. DISKPART

18. Which of the following command-line utilities can be used to defragment files?

    a. DISKPART

    b. DEFRAG

    c. DEFRAGMENT

    d. DF

19. An extended partition is formatted with a file system.

    a. True

    b. False

20. A volume can be mounted to an empty folder on a drive formatted with the FAT32 file system.

    a. True

    b. False

CASE PROJECTS

Case Project 6-1

The IT manager at Dover Leasing wants all administrative staff to be capable of managing disks from the command line. Using the details provided in Help and Support Center, use the DISKPART command to create a new simple volume using the remaining disk space on DISK 0. Use the FORMAT command to format this new partition with the NTFS file system. Finally, use the MOUNTVOL command to mount the new partition to an empty folder named Newmount on drive D.

Case Project 6-2

Dover Leasing is interested in implementing a disk-management strategy that will allow them to use the fault-tolerance features of Windows Server 2003. Outline each of the fault-tolerant disk methods available on Windows Server 2003, how they work, and the requirements for implementation.

ADVANCED FILE SYSTEM MANAGEMENT

> **After reading this chapter and completing the exercises, you will be able to:**
>
> ♦ Understand and configure file and folder attributes
>
> ♦ Understand and configure advanced file and folder attributes
>
> ♦ Implement and manage disk quotas
>
> ♦ Understand and implement the Distributed File System

Managing resources such as files and folders on a Windows Server 2003 system consists of a variety of tasks. In Chapter 5 you learned about how file resources are shared and then secured using both shared folder and NTFS permissions. While the configuration of file and folder permissions is a critical part of an administrator's overall security strategy, administrators also need to be familiar with other tasks and capabilities relating to managing these resources.

Since the days of MS-DOS, Microsoft operating systems have used file and folder attributes as a method of "describing" and even securing files. Windows Server 2003 supports the four standard file and folder attributes available since MS-DOS, namely the Archive, Hidden, Read-only, and System attributes. An understanding of how these attributes impact files and folders is an important part of any file management strategy. In this chapter you learn how to utilize and configure standard attributes using both the Windows graphical interface as well as command-line utilities.

When a volume or partition is formatted with the NTFS file system, Windows Server 2003 also supports a number of advanced file system attributes. For example, a feature of the NTFS file system known as the Encrypting File System (EFS) allows an administrator to further secure files by encrypting their contents. Another advanced attribute, known as compression, allows an administrator to reduce the amount of disk space occupied by files on an NTFS partition by compressing the contents of selected files and folders. Although other advanced attributes are also discussed, encryption and compression are looked at in detail in this chapter.

In many network environments, the amount of server disk space consumed by user files can quickly fill existing disk space, especially in cases where users are saving non–work-related files to locations such as their home directory. While features like compression can help to reduce the amount of disk space consumed by files, Windows Server 2003 provides administrators with a more granular level of control over how disk space is allocated to users via the disk quotas feature. When implemented, an administrator can control the amount of disk space allocated to users for particular NTFS partitions and volumes. Later in the chapter you learn about how disk quotas are implemented, as well as how they are managed in Windows Server 2003 environments.

As any network environment grows, users may need to access various shared folders on a variety of different servers. Although techniques such as mapping network drives help to make shared folders more easily accessible, shared resources can still be difficult to find. To help account for this, Windows Server 2003 supports a feature known as the Distributed File System (DFS). If correctly designed and implemented, DFS allows an administrator to create a single logical directory structure for shared folders on different servers throughout a network environment, allowing them to appear as though they are simply sub-folders or a single directory tree. Ultimately, the implementation of DFS can make accessing resources spread across multiple servers much simpler for users, and reduce costs associated with time wasted searching for resources.

FILE AND FOLDER ATTRIBUTES

Microsoft Operating systems since MS-DOS have included the ability to apply attributes to files and folders. Broadly speaking, attributes are used to describe files, folders, and their characteristics. On a Windows Server 2003 system, file and folder attributes can be viewed and configured using both graphical tools as well as the ATTRIB command.

The four standard file and folder attributes that have been available since MS-DOS include:

- Read-only
- Archive
- System
- Hidden

Each of these attributes is looked at in more detail in the following sections.

Read-only

As its name suggests, the **read-only attribute** designates that the contents of a file cannot be changed. The read-only attribute provides a degree of security that helps to ensure that files are not accidentally changed or deleted, and is available regardless of the file system in use. For example, attributes can be configured for files located on FAT, FAT32, or NTFS partitions and volumes.

Although the read-only attribute suggests that it provides a degree of security, the level of security associated with the attribute depends upon the file system on which the file resides. For example, setting the read-only attribute on a file stored on a FAT or FAT32 volume will indeed make the contents of that file read-only, but any user could change the attribute, effectively disabling the setting. When attributes are configured on a file stored on an NTFS volume, only users with at least the Allow Modify NTFS permission (or those users who have been explicitly granted the Write Attributes special NTFS permission) have the ability to change attributes. In this way, attributes configured on an NTFS volume can be effectively secured, while attributes configured for files stored on a FAT or FAT32 volume are inherently insecure.

The read-only attribute can be configured for a file or folder from the General tab of its Properties dialog box, as shown in Figure 7-1. When the read-only attribute is configured for a folder, the attribute doesn't apply to the folder itself, but rather the files it contains. For example, checking the read-only attribute for a folder will automatically configure all of the files in that folder as read-only, while unchecking the read-only attribute will remove this attribute for all files within the folder. If the read-only check box on the General tab of a folder appears as solid gray, it means that some, but not all of the files within the folder have their read-only attribute set.

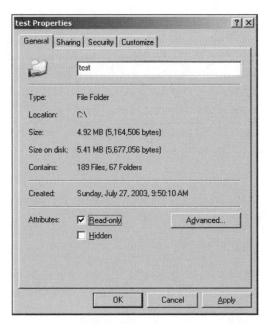

Figure 7-1   Configuring the read-only attribute for a folder

While any user can open a file configured with the read-only attribute, attempts to save changes to this file will result in a warning dialog box similar to the one illustrated in Figure 7-2.

Figure 7-2   The result of trying to save changes to a file configured with the read-only attribute set

Archive

The main purpose of the **archive attribute** is to provide a method for both administrators and applications to determine which files and folders have recently been created or changed. When a new file is created, or an existing file has been changed, the archive attribute for that file is turned on, marking the file as "ready for archiving". The status of the archive attribute is particularly important to backup programs, where different backup methods will manipulate the attribute as part of different backup schemes.

For example, if an administrator uses the Windows Backup utility to perform a full back up on all files on drive C, the archive attribute is cleared on files as part of the process. Then, as new files are created or existing files changed, the archive attribute for these files would be turned out. Ultimately, this allows the backup utility to determine which files are new (or have changed) since the last full backup, and makes it possible to selectively back up only these new files. The various backup techniques used by programs like Windows Backup (and their impacts on the archive attribute) is looked at in more detail in Chapter 12.

When a file or folder is stored on a FAT or FAT32 partition or volume, the archive attribute can be configured from the General tab in the properties of the file or folder, as shown in Figure 7-3.

Configuring the archive attribute using Windows Explorer for files and folders stored on NTFS partitions and volumes is looked at in the Advanced Attributes section later in this chapter.

Determining whether the archive attribute is set or cleared for a particular file is possible by using both Windows Explorer and command-line utilities such as DIR (used to view directory listings) and the ATTRIB command. Both are looked at in more detail later in this chapter.

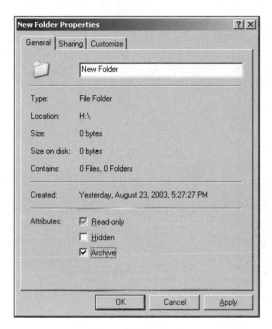

Figure 7-3 The archive attribute can be configured from the General tab of a file or folder residing on a FAT or FAT32 partition or volume

System

Although originally designed to identify operating system files in MS-DOS, the actual application of the **system attribute** has never been entirely consistent or well documented. On a Windows Server 2003 system, a number of files and folders have their system attribute configured, usually in conjunction with the hidden attribute. When both the system and hidden attributes are configured for a file or folder, that file or folder is considered "super hidden", and is not displayed in the Windows Explorer interface, even when the option to show hidden files is configured. Instead, files or folders with both the hidden and system attributes configured are treated as "protected operating system files", which have their own specific display options. You learn more about the display options associated with hidden files in the next section.

NOTE   The system attribute is not configurable from the General tab in the properties of a file or folder in a manner similar to the read-only and hidden attributes. The system attributes can be manipulated using the ATTRIB command, as outlined later in this section.

Hidden

As a method of protecting certain files and folders from being visible to users from Windows Explorer or the command line, another attribute appropriately named hidden is available. In much the same way that a file can be configured as read-only from the General tab of it's properties, the **hidden attribute** can be configured in a similar manner, as shown in Figure 7-4.

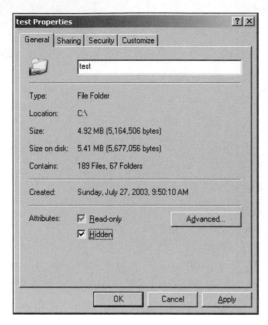

Figure 7-4   Configuring the hidden attribute for a file

Although the name hidden seems to suggest that a file cannot be viewed using a tool like Windows Explorer, the default configuration setting in Windows Server 2003 displays files configured with the hidden attribute using a semi-transparent icon. By default, the only hidden files that do not appear in the Windows Explorer interface by default are those with both their hidden and system attributes configured. The degree to which hidden files and folders are visible from within the Windows Explorer interface is configurable from the View tab of the Folder Options program available from the Tools menu in Windows Explorer, as shown in Figure 7-5.

The two most relevant settings on this tab and their capabilities are as follows:

- Hidden file and folders—When the Show hidden files and folders option is selected (it is not selected by default), hidden files and folders appear in the Windows Explorer interface using transparent icons. When the Do not show hidden files and folders option is selected, any file with its hidden attribute configured is not displayed in the Windows Explorer interface.

- Hide protected operating system files (Recommended)—When this option is selected (the default setting), all files with both their hidden and system attributes set are completely hidden in the Windows Explorer interface. When deselected, all files with the hidden and system attributes configured are visible from Windows Explorer.

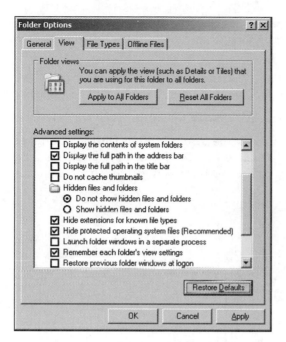

Figure 7-5   Configuring display settings for hidden files and folders

In Activity 7-1 you use Windows Explorer to view and configure attributes, as well as change the display settings for Hidden files and folders.

Activity 7-1: Viewing and Configuring File and Folder Attributes Using Windows Explorer

Time Required: 10 minutes

Objective: Use Windows Explorer to view and configure file and folder attributes.

Description: NTFS permissions are the primary method used to secure files and folders on Dover Leasing's Windows Server 2003 systems. However, the IT manager is also interested in taking advantage of file system attributes for their ability to control which files are included in backup processes, and which files are visible to users, including junior administrators. In this activity you use the Windows Explorer interface to view and configure attribute settings on your server.

1. Log on using your **AdminXX** account (where *XX* is your assigned student number). Click **Start**, and then click **My Computer**.

2. Double-click on drive **C:** to view its contents.

3. Click the **View** menu, and then click **Details**. This view displays the Name, Size, Type, Date Modified, and Attributes associated with files and folders. Review the letters listed in the Attribute column for the files and folders displayed. Each letter

listed represents configured attributes for that folder. For example, the letters RHSA would designate a file or folder that has its read-only (R), hidden (H), system (S), and archive (A) attributes configured.

4. Double-click the **Documents and Settings** folder to view its contents. Make note of the folders that are visible in the Documents and Settings folder by default.

5. Click the **Tools** menu, and then click **Folder Options**. Click the **View** tab.

6. In the Advanced settings section, click the **Show hidden files and folders** radio button, as displayed in Figure 7-6. Click **OK**. Notice that a folder named Default User now appears on the list, and that this folder has its hidden attribute configured.

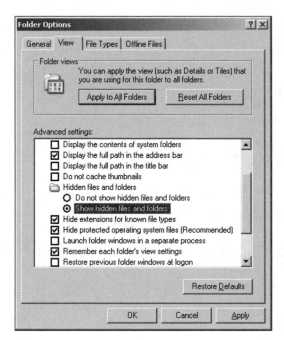

Figure 7-6   Displaying hidden files and folders

7. Press the **Backspace** button on the keyboard to return to the contents of drive C:. Note that no additional files or folders appear in this list as a result of showing hidden files.

8. Click the **Tools** menu, and then click **Folder Options**. Click the **View** tab.

9. In the Advanced settings section, uncheck the **Hide protected operating system files (Recommended)** check box. When the Warning dialog box shown in Figure 7-7 appears, read the message it displays, and click **Yes**. Click **OK**.

10. Review the additional files and folders now displayed in the Windows Explorer interface, noting that each of the new files and folders now visible has its system and hidden attributes configured.

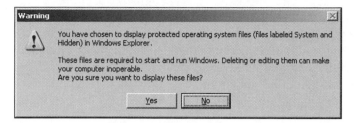

Figure 7-7   Warning message when choosing to view protected operating system files

11. Right-click on the **NTDETECT** file, and click **Properties**. On the General tab, notice that the Read-only check box is checked and can be changed, but that the hidden attribute is checked and cannot be changed. The fact that the Hidden check box is not configurable is a function of the fact that this file also has its System attribute configured. Click **Cancel**.

12. Press the **Backspace** button to view the contents of My Computer. Double-click on drive **D:** to view its contents.

13. Click the **File** menu, select **New**, and then click **Text Document**. Name the new file **attribute-test**.

14. After creating the file, notice that it is automatically assigned the archive attribute by default.

15. Right-click on the **attribute-test** file and click **Properties**.

16. On the General tab, check both the **Read-only** and **Hidden** check boxes, and click **OK**.

17. Notice that the Attribute column now displays RHA, because the read-only, hidden, and archive attributes are configured for the file. Close all open windows.

The ATTRIB Command

ATTRIB is a command-line utility that can be used to add or remove any of the four main attributes to or from files and folders. Although Windows Explorer allows you to configure the read-only and hidden attributes using a graphical interface, the system attribute can only be configured from the command line when necessary. The ATTRIB command can also be used to view the configured attributes for a file or folder. For example, to view the attributes associated with a file named text.txt in the D:\docs directory, the correct syntax would be:

```
D:\>attrib d:\docs\test.txt
```

The basic syntax used to change attributes with the ATTRIB command is outlined below. In the first example, the archive, system, hidden, and read-only attributes are configured for a file named test.txt in the D:\docs directory. In the second command, these same attributes are removed.

```
D:\>attrib +A +S +H +R d:\docs\test.txt
```

```
D:\>attrib -A -S -H -R d:\docs\test.txt
```

One of the major advantages of using the ATTRIB command is that it supports wildcards, allowing the attributes for multiple files and folders to be changed simultaneously. For example, the following command would configure the hidden attribute for all files stored in the D:\docs folder that end in a .TXT extension:

```
D:\>attrib +H d:\docs\*.txt
```

In Activity 7-2 you use the ATTRIB command to view and change file attributes from the command line.

Activity 7-2: Changing File Attributes Using the ATTRIB Command

Time Required: 10 minutes

Objective: View and change file attributes from the command line.

Description: While Windows Explorer provides a simple method to configure attributes for files and folders, this can also be accomplished using the ATTRIB command. In this activity you use the ATTRIB command to view and change the attributes associated with files from the command line, and then view those changes in Windows Explorer.

1. Click **Start**, and then click **Run**. In the Open text box, type **cmd.exe** and click **OK.**

2. At the command line, type **d:** and press **Enter**.

3. Type **mkdir attributes** and press **Enter** to create a new directory called attributes. Leave the command prompt window open.

4. Click **Start**, and then click **My Computer**. Double-click on drive **D:** to view its contents, and then double-click on the **attributes** folder to open it. Create three new text files in the folder named **file1.txt**, **file2.txt**, and **file3.txt**. Once complete, close the My Computer window.

5. In the command prompt window, type **cd attributes** and press **Enter**.

6. Type **attrib file1.txt** and press **Enter**. Notice that the output of the command displays the letter A (meaning the archive attribute is set) and the path to the file, as shown in Figure 7-8.

7. Type **attrib –A file1.txt** and press **Enter**. This removes the archive attribute from file1.txt.

8. Type **attrib file1.txt** and press **Enter**. Notice that the output no longer displays any attributes for file1.txt.

9. Type **attrib +A +H +R +S file1.txt** and press **Enter**. This command adds the archive, hidden, read-only, and system attributes to file1.txt. Close the command prompt window.

Figure 7-8   Viewing file attributes with the ATTRIB command

10. Click **Start**, and then click **My Computer**. Double-click on drive **D:** to view its contents, and then double-click on the **attributes** folder to open it. Notice that all three files are visible in the Windows Explorer interface, along with their associated attributes. Notice also that file1.txt uses a transparent icon, since its hidden attribute is set.

11. Click the **Tools** menu, and then click **Folder Options**. Click the **View** tab.

12. In the Advanced settings section, check the **Hide protected operating system files (Recommended)** check box, and click **OK**.

13. Notice that file1.txt no longer appears in the list of files in Windows Explorer. This is because file1.txt has both the system and hidden attributes set, and as such is hidden from display because it is treated like a protected operating system file as configured in Step 12.

14. Close the My Computer window.

ADVANCED ATTRIBUTES

In addition to the standard file and folder attributes outlined in the previous section, Windows Server 2003 also supports a number of advanced attributes for files or folders stored on NTFS partitions or volumes. Advanced attributes are accessible by clicking the Advanced button on the General tab in the properties of a file or folder that resides on an NTFS partition or volume. This opens the Advanced Attributes window, as shown in Figure 7-9.

The Archive and Index attributes section of the Advanced Attributes windows consists of the following two options for a file:

- File is ready for archiving—Configures the archive attribute for the file.
- For fast searching, allow Indexing Service to index this file—Indexes the contents of the file, allowing searches to be performed within the text and according to properties such as configured attributes, modification dates, and so forth.

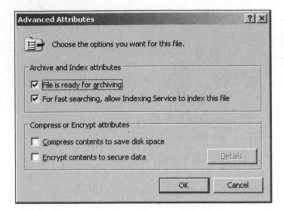

Figure 7-9   The Advanced Attributes configuration window for a file

The Advanced Attributes window for a folder contains similar options, but will set the archiving or indexing attributes for an entire folder (and potentially its contents) rather than just a single file. For example, when the indexing option is changed for a folder it sends a prompt inquiring whether the indexing status should also be changed for subfolders and files, as illustrated in Figure 7-10.

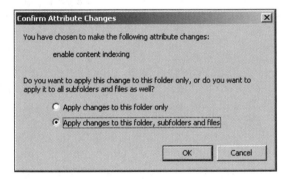

Figure 7-10   The Confirm Attribute Changes window

The Compress or Encrypt attributes section of the Advanced Attributes window consists of the following two options:

- Compress contents to save disk space—Compresses the file or folder to reduce the amount of space that it occupies on the disk.
- Encrypt contents to secure data—Encrypts the contents of a file to secure it. When configured for a folder, new files saved to this folder (and potentially existing files) are encrypted as well.

Compression and encryption settings are only applicable to files and folders residing on NTFS partitions or volumes. Both the compress and encrypt attributes are mutually exclusive. In other words, you cannot encrypt and compress a given file or folder at the same time.

Both the compression and encryption features of Windows Server 2003 are looked at in more detail in the following sections.

File Compression

On volumes that are formatted with NTFS, you can enable **compression** to reduce the amount of disk space that folders and files take up, thus allowing more data to be stored on the volume. Once a volume, folder, or file is compressed, you do not need any additional utilities to uncompress it. When a user accesses the file, it is automatically uncompressed in a manner completely transparent to the user.

Configuring compression is as simple as enabling or disabling the compression attribute of a file or folder within Windows Explorer. Checking the Compress contents to save disk space check box enables compression, as illustrated in Figure 7-11.

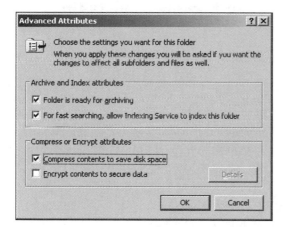

Figure 7-11 Configuring compression settings for a folder

After a folder or file has been compressed, it is displayed in a different color within Windows Explorer (making it easy for an administrator to identify what is and is not compressed). Compressed folders and files are displayed in blue by default, though you can change this option from the View tab in the Folder Options dialog box.

The compression attribute can be affected when copying and moving files. Keep the following points in mind when using the compression attribute:

- If a file is copied to another folder within the same NTFS volume, it automatically inherits the compression attribute of the destination folder.

- If a file or folder is moved within the same NTFS volume, it retains its compression attribute.

- If a file or folder is copied between NTFS volumes, the file or folder inherits the compression attribute of the destination folder.

- If a file or folder is moved between NTFS volumes, the file or folder inherits the compression attribute of the destination folder.

NOTE

Although the previous points specifically list the impact of moving or copying compressed files within or between NTFS volumes or partitions, the same rules apply to moving or copying encrypted files, as well as any NTFS permissions applied to files. For example, if an encrypted file is copied to another folder (with its encryption attribute configured) on the same NTFS volume, it inherits the encryption attribute of the target folder. The configuration of encryption settings is looked at in more detail later in this section.

In Activity 7-3 you will use the compression feature to compress a folder stored on an NTFS volume on your server.

ACTIVITY

Activity 7-3: Configuring Folder Compression Settings

Time Required: 5 minutes

Objective: Configure a folder to compress its contents.

Description: Both the Legal and Marketing Departments at Dover Leasing generate enormous quantities of data over the course of a year. Although much of the old marketing data can be deleted after this time, all files belonging to the Legal Department must be archived indefinitely. Because of the large amount of disk space that this data occupies, the IT manager has asked you to evaluate ways in which the amount of disk space used by these files can be reduced. In this activity, you test the impact of using the NTFS compression attribute to save disk space.

1. Open My Computer, and then browse to drive **D**:. Create a new folder called **Compress** and then copy the setup.bmp file from the C:\WINDOWS\System32 folder into this new folder.

2. Right-click the **Compress** folder and click **Properties**. Note both the Size and Size on disk information provided on the General tab.

3. Click the **Advanced** button to open the Advanced Attributes dialog box.

4. In the Compress or Encrypt attributes section, click the **Compress contents to save disk space** check box and then click **OK**.

5. Click **OK** to exit the properties of the Compress folder.

6. When the Confirm Attribute Changes dialog box opens, ensure that the **Apply changes to this folder, subfolders and files** radio button is selected and then click **OK**.

7. In the My Computer interface, notice that the Compress folder is now listed in blue text, which designates it as having its compression attribute set.

8. Open the **Compress** folder, right-click on the **setup.bmp** file, and click **Properties**. Notice that while the Size value has not changed, the Size on disk value is now significantly reduced from its original value, as shown in Figure 7-12.

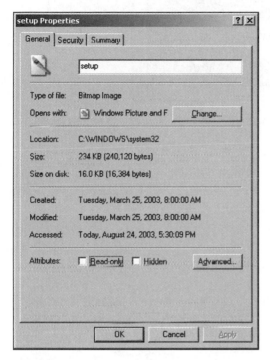

Figure 7-12   Viewing the Size and Size on disk settings for a compressed file

9. Close all open windows.

COMPACT

Windows Server 2003 includes a utility named COMPACT to allow the compression attribute of files and folders to be changed from the command line. When issued without any switches, the COMPACT command will display compression settings for the contents of the current directory, as shown in Figure 7-13.

The most common switches used in conjunction with the COMPACT command are /c (to compress files and folders) and /u (to uncompress files and folders). For example, to compress a single file named setup.bmp in the C:\WINDOWS\system32 directory, the correct syntax would be:

```
C:\WINDOWS\system32>compact /c setup.bmp
```

```
Command Prompt                                              _ □ ×

D:\attributes>compact

 Listing D:\attributes\
 New files added to this directory will not be compressed.

      0 :            0 = 1.0 to 1   file1.txt
      0 :            0 = 1.0 to 1   file2.txt
      0 :            0 = 1.0 to 1   file3.txt
 787512 :       559616 = 1.4 to 1 C test.bmp

Of 4 files within 1 directories
1 are compressed and 3 are not compressed.
787,512 total bytes of data are stored in 559,616 bytes.
The compression ratio is 1.4 to 1.


D:\attributes>_
```

Figure 7-13   Viewing compression information for the current directory using the COM-
PACT command

Similarly, if you wanted to remove the compression attribute from all files and subfolders of
the directory C:\compressed, but not change the compression attribute of the
C:\compressed folder itself, the correct syntax would be:

```
C:\>compact /u c:\compressed
```

Because the COMPACT command requires the NTFS file system to function, it cannot be
used to compress files or folders stored on FAT or FAT32 partitions or volumes.

NOTE   For a complete list of the switches supported with the COMPACT command,
type COMPACT /? at the command prompt, or view the Compact: Command-
line reference topic in Help and Support Center.

File Encryption

Another method to secure files and folders is to use encryption. The ability to encrypt files
adds another level of protection on top of setting share or NTFS permissions. The
Encrypting File System (EFS) uses public key cryptography to transparently encrypt
folders and files.

File and folder encryption is implemented using two main types of encryption keys. When
a file is configured for encryption, EFS encrypts the data using a special session key known
as a **file encryption key (FEK)**. The FEK is added to a header attached to the encrypted
data known as the **data decryption field (DDF)**. The DDF is subsequently encrypted
using the user's public key, so only they can decrypt it using their corresponding private key.

The main challenge associated with using encryption to secure file resources is that if a user
were to leave the company, all data that had been encrypted with their public key would be
inaccessible by other user accounts. One exception to this is when an administrator renames

the user account to which the private key is associated. In this case, the new user would be able to access data encrypted by the private key because only the username associated with the account has changed.

For data recovery purposes, Windows Server 2003 includes a special role known as a **data recovery agent**. In the event that a user encrypts data and then leaves the company or loses their private key, the user designated as the recovery agent can recover the encrypted data. When data is encrypted using EFS, the FEK of the data recovery agent is also stored in a second header called the **data recovery field (DRF)**. This key is encrypted using the data recovery agent's public key, thus making the data recovery agent capable of decrypting or recovering EFS-encrypted files and folders. By default, the local administrator of a standalone workstation or member server is designated as the recovery agent. In a domain environment, the domain administrator account is configured as the only data recovery agent by default, though additional recovery agents can be designated using Certificate Services and Group Policy. Windows Server 2003 also includes a new feature that allows EFS-encrypted files to be shared with other users, which you learn about later in this section.

EFS encryption for a file or folder is configured using advanced attributes in Windows Explorer. The advanced attribute settings for a folder are shown in Figure 7-14.

Figure 7-14   Viewing the encryption settings for a folder

Before using EFS to encrypt data, keep the following in mind:

- If you set the encryption attribute on a folder, the folder itself is not actually encrypted, only the contents of the folder
- Once a folder's encryption attribute is set, any data saved in the folder, or copied or moved into the folder, is encrypted

- If an encrypted file is copied or moved into a folder that is not encrypted, the file retains its encryption attribute as long as the file system is NTFS; encrypted files moved to a FAT partition are automatically decrypted

- Encryption and compression are mutually exclusive; you cannot encrypt and compress data at the same time

In Activity 7-4 you configure a folder to encrypt files using EFS and then attempt to access an encrypted file using different user accounts.

Activity 7-4: Encrypting Files Using Windows Explorer

Time Required: 10 minutes

Objective: Implement and test file encryption security using EFS.

Description: Dover Leasing is interested in having its laptop users utilize EFS to better protect corporate data on these machines should they be lost or stolen. In this activity, you configure a folder to use EFS encryption and then attempt to access files within the folder using different user accounts.

1. Open My Computer and create a new folder on drive D: named **Encrypted**.

2. Right-click the **Encrypted** folder and click **Properties**.

3. On the General tab, click the **Advanced** button to open the folder's advanced attributes settings.

4. Check the **Compress contents to save disk space** check box, and then check the **Encrypt contents to secure data** check box. Notice that only one of these two options can be selected at any time.

5. Click **OK** to exit the Advanced Attributes window, and then click **OK** again to exit the properties of the Encrypted folder. Notice that the text in the name of the Encrypted folder changes to the color green. This is to help easily identify encrypted folders and files.

6. Open the Encrypted folder and create a new text file within it called **encrypted.txt**. In the encrypted.txt file, type **this is an encrypted file**, then save your changes and close the file. Access the Advanced Attributes of this file to ensure that the Encrypt contents to secure data check box is checked. Close the Advanced Attributes dialog box and the encrypted Properties dialog box.

7. Close all open windows and then log off. Log on as the user **mmanore** with the password **Password01**.

8. Open My Computer and attempt to open the D:\Encrypted folder. Remember that although EFS will mark a folder with the encryption attribute, the folder itself is not encrypted. As such, it opens without issue.

9. Attempt to open the **encrypted.txt** file by double-clicking on it. Notice that access is denied, as shown in Figure 7-15, because Mark Manore does not have the private key necessary to decrypt the file. Close all open windows.

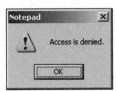

Figure 7-15 Attempting to open a file encrypted by another user

10. Log off and then log on again as **Administrator** with the password **Password01**.

11. Open the D:\Encrypted folder and attempt to open the file **encrypted.txt**. Notice that the file opens because the domain Administrator account is the default recovery agent. Close all open windows.

12. Log off and then log on again using your **AdminXX** account.

Sharing Encrypted Files

On Windows 2000 systems, EFS used only the public keys of both the user encrypting a file and the data recovery agent to encrypt the file encryption key used to secure the file. As such, the contents of an encrypted file were only accessible to these two users by default, and all other users would be denied access if they attempted to access the file.

In order to allow users to share EFS-encrypted files, Windows Server 2003 supports a new feature to provide this functionality. When accessing the Advanced Attributes window for an encrypted file, clicking the Details button opens the Encryption Details window, as shown in Figure 7-16.

From this window, the Add button can be used to allow other users to access the file, effectively using that user's public key to encrypt the FEK that was originally used to encrypt the file. If you plan to use this feature, the following issues must be kept in mind:

- EFS sharing can only be configured for files, not folders.
- You can only share EFS-encrypted files with users, not groups.
- Users who are being granted access to the file must have a certificate located on the computer.
- Users granted access to the file must also have appropriate NTFS permissions to access the file.

Figure 7-16   The Encryption Details window for an EFS-encrypted file

 The management and configuration of user certificates is beyond the scope of this text. For more information on user certificates, see the Certificates overview: Certificates topic in Help and Support Center.

NOTE

The CIPHER Command

In much the same way that the COMPACT command can be used to compress files or folders from the command line, the CIPHER command allows an administrator to encrypt the contents of files stored on NTFS partitions and volumes. When issued without any switches, the CIPHER command will display encryption settings for the contents of the current directory, as shown in Figure 7-17.

The most common switches used in conjunction with the CIPHER command are /e (to encrypt files and folders) and /d (to decrypt files and folders). CIPHER will only set the encryption attribute on folders by default unless the /a switch is also specified. For example, to encrypt a single file named test1.txt in the C:\encrypted directory, the correct syntax would be:

```
C:\encrypted>cipher /e /a test1.txt
```

One of the most popular uses of the CIPHER utility is to perform bulk encryption from the command line. For example, to encrypt all of the files with a .DOC extension in the C:\encrypted folder, the correct command syntax would be:

```
C:\encrypted>cipher /e /a *.doc
```

Because the CIPHER command requires the NTFS file system to function, it cannot be used to encrypt files or folders stored on FAT or FAT32 partitions or volumes.

The CIPHER command cannot encrypt files with their read-only attribute set.

Figure 7-17   Viewing encryption information for the current directory using the CIPHER command

In Activity 7-5 you use the CIPHER command to encrypt files stored in a directory on your server.

Activity 7-5: Encrypting Files Using the CIPHER Utility

Time Required: 5 minutes

Objective: Encrypt and decrypt files using the CIPHER utility.

Description: Although encryption settings can be easily configured from the properties of a file or folder in the Windows Explorer interface, the CIPHER command presents an excellent alternative, especially in cases where large numbers of files need to be encrypted simultaneously. In this activity you use CIPHER to view encryption settings and configured encryption for multiple files simultaneously.

1. Click **Start**, and then click **My Computer**.
2. Double-click on drive **D:** to view its contents.
3. Click the **File** menu, select **New**, and then click **Folder**. Name the new folder **ciphertest**.
4. Double-click the **ciphertest** folder.
5. Click the **File** menu, select **New**, and then click **Text Document**. Name the file **file1.txt**. Repeat this step to create additional files named **file2.txt** and **file3.txt**. Close the My Computer window.

6. Click **Start**, click **Run**, and in the Open text box type **cmd.exe**. Click **OK**.

7. Type **d:** and press **Enter**.

8. Type **cd ciphertest**, and press **Enter**.

9. Type **cipher** and press **Enter**. All files in the ciphertest folder should currently be listed as unencrypted, as designated by the letter U that precedes their file names.

10. Type **cipher /e /a file1.txt** and press **Enter**. This action encrypts file1.txt only.

11. Type **cipher** and press **Enter**. Notice that file1.txt is now preceded with the letter E, meaning the file is encrypted.

12. Type **cipher /e /a *.txt** and press **Enter**. This command encrypts all currently unencrypted text files in the ciphertest folder.

13. Type **cipher** and press **Enter** to confirm that all files in the folder are currently encrypted.

14. Close the command prompt window.

DISK QUOTAS

In all server environments, available disk space eventually becomes an issue. This is often a result of users storing large data files or archiving e-mail messages (which may include attachments) in their home directories. Depending on the number of users on the network and the amount of data they are storing, disk space can easily become scarce and needs to be managed.

Windows Server 2003 uses **disk quotas** as a means of monitoring and controlling the amount of disk space available to users. Administrators can use disk quotas as a capacity-planning tool or as a way of managing data storage.

Using disk quotas has the following advantages:

- Prevents users from consuming all available disk space
- Encourages users to delete old files as they reach their disk quota
- Allows an administrator to track disk usage for future planning
- Allows administrators to track when users are reaching their available limits

You can enable disk quotas on any NTFS volume, but they are disabled by default. By enabling disk quotas on a volume, you can see the amount of disk space that is being consumed by users, allowing you to use them as a capacity-planning tool. To use disk quotas as a management tool, you can set default quotas that specify the maximum amount of space allocated to network users. This is particularly useful for volumes hosting home folders, which tend to consume a lot of disk space. For example, many organizations establish a default quota of 10 to 100 MB per user on home folder volumes. The default quota prevents a few users from occupying disk space that is needed for all users, while also encouraging users to save only essential information and delete files and folders that are no longer needed.

TIP

Disk quotas can be implemented only on NTFS volumes, and they are set on a per-user/per-volume basis.

To configure disk quotas, access the properties of a volume and click the Quota tab, as shown in Figure 7-18.

7

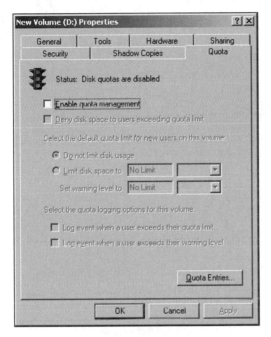

Figure 7-18   The Quota tab in the properties of a volume or partition

Table 7-1 summarizes the options available on the Quota tab of an NTFS volume.

Table 7-1   Disk quota configuration parameters

Parameter	Description
Enable quota management	Tracks disk space on the volume and allows for the configuration of disk quotas
Deny disk space to users exceeding quota limit	Once users reach their quota limit, they are denied access to additional disk space
Do not limit disk usage	Tracks disk usage, but does not limit disk space to users
Limit disk space to	Sets the default amount of disk space that is available to users
Set warning level to	Sets the default amount of disk space that a user can consume before a warning message is sent to the user stating that the quota is being reached
Log event when user exceeds their quota limit	Causes an event to be entered in the System log to notify the administrator that the user has reached their quota

Table 7-1   Disk quota configuration parameters (continued)

Parameter	Description
Log event when a user exceeds their warning level	Causes an event to be entered in the system log to notify the administrator that the user is approaching their quota

Exceptions can be created for users who require more disk space than others. You can set disk quotas for specific user accounts by clicking the Quota Entries button on the Quota tab, and then clicking New Quota Entry on the Quota menu. This allows you to choose the user account for which you want to establish a quota and configure appropriate quota limits for that user. This updates the Quota Entries dialog box to reflect the quota for that user account, as shown in Figure 7-19.

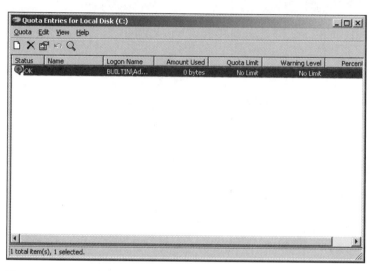

Figure 7-19   The Quota Entries window

It is important to keep in mind that the amount of disk space a user is currently occupying changes when ownership of files transfers from one user account to another. For example, imagine if Moira creates a database called Clients.mdb that occupies 1022 KB on a volume with disk quotas enabled. After Moira creates and saves the database, her available disk space is decreased by 1022 KB. If Moira later changes job roles within the company and John takes ownership of the database, Moira's available disk space would increase by 1022 KB, while John's would be decreased by the same amount.

TIP   At any time, you can click the Quota Entries button to view both the disk quota limit and warning level configured for any account, as well as the amount of disk space currently being used by an account.

In Activity 7-6 you configure a disk quota for a volume on your server as well as a quota entry for a specific user.

Activity 7-6: Configuring and Managing Disk Quotas

Time Required: 10 minutes

Objective: Enable and manage disk quotas settings.

Description: The IT manager at Dover Leasing is very concerned about the amount of disk space that users are allocated to store their personal files. In the past, users were told that they could use a maximum of 40 MB of disk space in their home folder, but a third-party quota-management system was never implemented. As such, many users simply ignored the directive, and available disk space is constantly an issue on Dover's servers. Understanding that Windows Server 2003 allows you to configure disk quotas for users on a partition-by-partition basis, the IT manager has asked you to test the implementation of quotas to determine whether or not they will meet Dover's needs.

1. Open My Computer.

2. Right-click drive **D:** and then click **Properties**.

3. Click the **Quota** tab. Notice that the status notice and icon both point out disk quotas are currently disabled for the partition.

4. Click the **Enable quota management** check box.

5. Click the **Limit disk space to** radio button, then type **100** in the text box and select **MB** in the drop-down box.

6. In the Set warning level to text boxes, type **80** and select **MB**.

7. Check the **Log event when a user exceeds their quota limit** check box.

8. Check the **Log event when a user exceeds their warning level** check box.

9. Review all of the choices selected. Notice that although quota information is tracked for this volume, the option to Deny disk space to users exceeding quota limit was not selected. As such, these quotas settings would be considered "soft" because they do not actually deny disk space to users and would instead be used for monitoring purposes. Click **OK**.

10. When the Disk Quota dialog box opens, read the message and then click **OK**. Allow a few minutes for the disk to be rescanned and quota information gathered if necessary.

11. Open the Properties of drive **D:** and click the **Quota** tab. Notice that the Disk quota system is now active and that the quota icon has changed.

12. Click the **Quota Entries** button.

13. In the Quota Entries dialog box, double-click the entry that appears for the Administrator user account to view its properties. Note the quota used and quota remaining information provided.

14. Change the quota entry for Administrator such that the quota limit and warning level are both set to **1 KB**. Click **OK**. Notice that the icon next to the quota entry changes to a warning because this user is now over their quota limit.

15. Close all open Windows.

Managing Disk Quotas from the Command Line

Windows Server 2003 also provides the ability to manage disk quotas from the command line with the FSUTIL utility. The FSUTIL QUOTA command provides six different sub-commands that allow an administrator to disable, enforce, modify, query, and track quota information, as well as report quota violations.

For example, to enable disk quotas on drive E using the FSUTIL QUOTA command, the correct syntax would be:

```
fsutil quota enforce e:
```

To display disk quota information for a particular partition or volume with quotas enabled, the command would be:

```
fsutil quota query e:
```

Example output from the FSUTIL QUOTA QUERY command is shown in Figure 7-20.

Figure 7-20   Using FSUTIL to query a volume or partition for quota information

The FSUTIL quota command can also be used to configure quota entries for individual users. For example, to create a new quota entry on drive E for the Mark Manore user account that limits disk space to 100 MB and issues a warning at 80 MB, the correct command syntax would be:

```
fsutil quota modify e: 80000 100000 mmanore
```

When a quota is created or modified using the FSUTIL QUOTA command, the warning threshold and limit values are specified in bytes.

As a method of helping to keep administrators informed of disk quota violations, Windows Server 2003 writes events to the System log (accessible via Event Viewer) periodically. Quota violations for users are written to the system log every hour by default. In some cases, administrators might want to change the interval associated with these events being written to the System log, especially if the log files are filling up too quickly or becoming unmanageable. The FSUTIL BEHAVIOR command can be used to change the interval associated with these events. For example, to change the default notify interval from the default of one hour (3600 seconds) to once every three hours (10800 seconds), the correct command syntax would be:

```
fsutil behavior set quotanotify 10800
```

For a complete list of the sub-commands and capabilities associated with both the FSUTIL QUOTA and FSUTIL BEHAVIOR commands, see the Fsutil : quota : Command-line reference and Fsutil : behavior : Command-line reference topics in Help and Support Center.

7

DISTRIBUTED FILE SYSTEM

The **Distributed File System** allows administrators to simplify access to multiple shared-file resources by making it appear as though multiple shared-file resources are stored in a single hierarchical structure. For example, if the network has eight Windows Server 2003 systems that provide a variety of shared folders to network users, DFS can be set up so that users do not have to know which specific server offers which shared folder. All of the folders can be set up to appear as though they are on one server and under a single folder structure. This eliminates the need for users to have to browse the network looking for shared resources. DFS also makes managing folder access easier for server administrators.

DFS is configured using the Distributed File System console in the Administrative Tools menu, as illustrated in Figure 7-21.

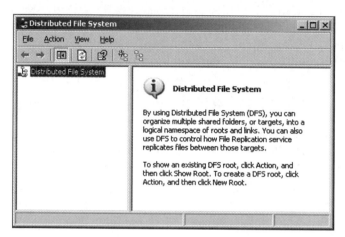

Figure 7-21   The Distributed File System console

A DFS share resembles a tree structure and consists of a root and DFS links. When configuring DFS, the root is configured first, then the DFS links. The DFS root is at the top of the tree structure and is the container for DFS links. The DFS links point to shared folders throughout the network, as illustrated in Figure 7-22.

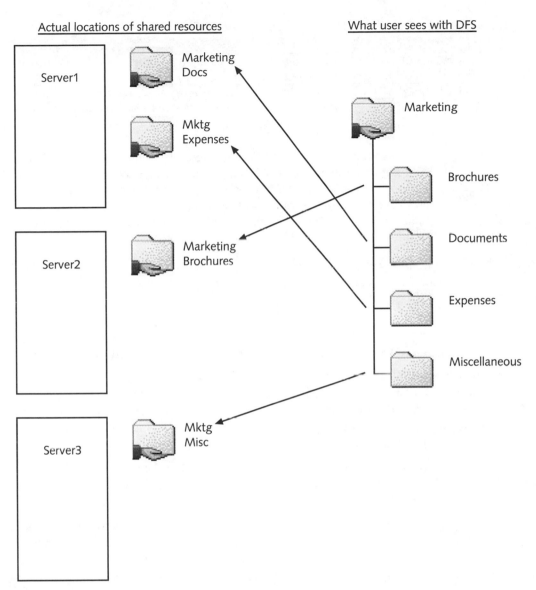

Figure 7-22   Shared folders organized using DFS

DFS Models

There are two models for implementing DFS: the **standalone DFS model** and the **domain-based DFS model**. The standalone DFS model offers limited capabilities compared to the domain-based model. Table 7-2 summarizes the two models.

Table 7-2   Standalone DFS and domain-based DFS

DFS Model	Description
Standalone DFS	DFS information is stored on the local server where DFS is configured. This model offers no fault tolerance.
Domain-based DFS	DFS information is stored within Active Directory. Links can be configured to point to multiple copies of a share for fault tolerance. DFS root must be on an NTFS partition.

NOTE   To access Windows Server 2003 DFS resources, clients must be running DFS client software. Although new Windows versions such as Windows 2000 and XP include this ability by default, older versions such as Windows 98 or NT 4.0 must have the Active Directory client extensions installed to access resources through DFS. You can download the Active Directory client extensions from the Microsoft Web site.

The hierarchical structure of DFS in the domain-based model is called the DFS topology or logical structure. There are three elements to the DFS topology:

- The DFS root
- The DFS links
- Servers on which the DFS shared folders are replicated as replica sets

A **DFS root** is a main container that holds links to shared folders that can be accessed from the root. The server that hosts the DFS root is called the host server. When a network client views the shared folders under the DFS root, all of the folders appear as though they are physically located in one main folder on the DFS root computer, even though the folders may actually reside on many different computers in the domain.

A **DFS link** is a pointer to the physical location of shared folders that are defined in the root. DFS links can also be made to another DFS root on a different computer or to an entire shared volume on a server.

A **replica set** is a set of shared folders that is replicated or copied to one or more servers in a domain. Configuring a replication set includes establishing links to each server that participates in the replication, as well as setting up synchronization so that replication takes place among all servers at a specified interval, such as every 15 minutes.

The first step in creating a DFS is to configure a DFS root of either the standalone or domain-based variety. Once the root is configured, you can create DFS links that point to the actual physical location of the shared files and folders. In Activity 7-7, you create a new domain-based DFS root along with multiple DFS links.

Activity 7-7: Implementing Domain-Based DFS and Creating Links

Time Required: 15 minutes

Objective: Create a new domain-based DFS root and add DFS links.

Description: The IT manager at Dover Leasing has recognized that based on the large number of servers that the company plans to implement, users may have difficulty finding the resources that they most commonly need access to. Because of this, he has asked you to investigate whether or not the distributed file system will help to make resource access easier for users. In this activity, you create a new domain-based DFS root and then add DFS links for shared folders on multiple servers.

1. Click **Start**, select **Administrative Tools**, and then click **Distributed File System**.

2. Right-click the **Distributed File System** icon and then click **New Root**. The Welcome to the New Root Wizard screen appears. Click **Next**.

3. At the Root Type screen, ensure that the **Domain root** radio button is selected and click **Next**.

4. At the Host Domain screen, ensure that your domain is selected on the Trusting domains list and then click **Next**.

5. At the Host Server screen, click the **Browse** button. In the Find Computers screen, select your server and then click **OK**. Click **Next** to continue.

6. At the Root Name screen, type **dfsroot** in the Root name text box and click **Next**.

7. At the Root Share screen, type **d:\dfsroot** in the Folder to share text box and click **Next**. When asked whether you want to create the folder, click **Yes**.

8. Click **Finish** to close the New Root Wizard.

9. Right-click your new DFS root and then click **New Link**.

10. In the New Link dialog box, type **Marketing Applications** in the Link name text box.

11. In the Path to target (shared folder) text box, type **\\serverXX\applications** (where *XX* is your student number), and then click **OK**. The new link appears under your DFS root, as shown in Figure 7-23.

7

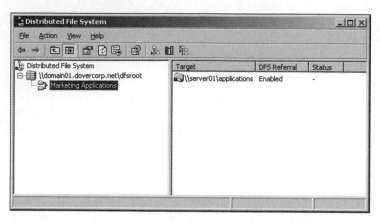

Figure 7-23   A DFS link named Marketing Applications

12. Open My Computer, and create a new shared folder on your D: drive called **partner**. Ensure that the shared folder permissions on this folder are set to allow the Everyone group the Read permission at a minimum.

13. In the Distributed File System window, add another DFS link named **Partner**, specifying the path to the partner folder on your partner's server in the Path to target (shared folder) text box.

14. To test whether the DFS root functions correctly, open the **Run** command, type **\\domain*XX*.dovercorp.net\dfsroot** (where *XX* is your assigned student number), and click **OK**. Ensure that both the Marketing Applications and Partner folders appear beneath as the contents of the dfsroot folder.

15. Right-click the **Partner** folder in the dfsroot window and click **Properties**. Notice the Location path specified on the General tab.

16. Click the **DFS** tab. Notice that the actual path to the shared folder on your partner's server is listed in the Referral list.

17. Close all open windows.

Managing DFS

After a new DFS root system is set up, there are several tasks involved in managing the root including:

- Deleting a DFS root
- Removing a DFS link
- Adding root and link replica sets
- Checking the status of a root or link

Each of these tasks is described in the following paragraphs.

After a DFS root is created, it is possible to delete it—when you want to configure it differently, for example. To delete a DFS root, open the Distributed File System console, and right-click the root you want to delete. You can then click Delete Root on the shortcut menu.

To remove a link from the DFS root, right-click the link in the details pane, and then click Delete Link on the shortcut menu.

One of the features of a domain-based DFS is that an entire DFS root or specific DFS links in a root can be replicated on servers other than the one that contains the master folder. The replication capability is what enables you to provide fault tolerance as well as load balancing of requests between servers. On a network in which there are multiple servers, replication can prove to be a vital service to provide uninterrupted access for users, in case the computer with the master folder is inaccessible. Load balancing also is vital as a way to provide users with faster service and better network performance by enabling users to access the nearest server containing the DFS shared folders. DFS takes advantage of Active Directory sites by ensuring that users are forwarded to a replica within their own site, if one exists. You can set up a DFS link for replication by right-clicking the link and selecting the Configure Replication option. This opens a wizard that walks you through the various DFS replication options and topologies available. In order to configure a new replica, at least one additional server in the same domain is required.

 You can configure replication to occur manually or automatically. If you choose to use automatic replication, ensure that the File Replication Service is started and set to start automatically because automatic DFS replication relies on this service. For more information on configuring DFS replication, see the Configuring Replication option in Help and Support Center.

The most common problem associated with DFS shared folders is that one or more DFS links are inaccessible because a particular server is disconnected from the network, shut down, or has failed. You can quickly check the status of a DFS root, link, or replica by right-clicking it in the right pane of the Distributed File System management tool, and then clicking Check Status. A DFS root, link, or replica that is working and fully connected has a green check mark in a white circle through its folder icon, as shown in Figure 7-24. One that is disconnected has a white "x" in a red circle through its folder icon.

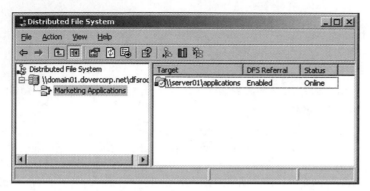

Figure 7-24   Viewing the status of a DFS link

CHAPTER SUMMARY

❑ The four standard file and folder attributes supported by Windows Server 2003 are archive, hidden, read-only, and system. Attributes can be configured using Windows Explorer and the ATTRIB command-line utility.

❑ Windows Server 2003 supports advanced attributes on NTFS partitions including archiving, indexing, compression, and encryption settings.

❑ NTFS includes built-in support for compression, allowing individual files or the contents of directories to be compressed to save disk space. Compression can be configured from the properties of a file or folder, or by using the COMPACT command-line utility.

❑ NTFS also includes support for the encrypting file system (EFS), a public key cryptography method for providing additional security for sensitive files. EFS can be configured from the properties of a file or folder, or by using the CIPHER command-line utility.

❑ Administrators can implement disk quotas to control the amount of disk space a user's files can consume on a particular NTFS partition or volume.

❑ The Distributed File System (DFS) provides a method to make shared folders on different servers appear to be part of a single logical hierarchy. Windows Server 2003 supports two models known as standalone and domain-based DFS.

KEY TERMS

archive attribute — A standard attribute used to determine the backup status of a file or folder.

compression — An advanced attribute of the NTFS file system used to reduce the amount of space that files and folders occupy on a partition or volume.

data decryption field (DDF) — The storage location for the file encryption key (FEK) is an EFS-encrypted file.

data recovery agent — A user account capable of gaining access to EFS-encrypted files encrypted by other users. In a domain environment, the domain Administrator account is the default data recovery agent.

data recovery field (DRF) — The storage location for the file encryption key (FEK) encrypted by the data recovery agent.

disk quotas — A Windows Server 2003 feature that is used as a means of monitoring and controlling the amount of disk space available to users.

Distributed File System (DFS) — A system that enables folders shared from multiple computers to appear as though they exist in one centralized hierarchy of folders instead of on many different computers.

domain-based DFS model — A DFS model that uses Active Directory and is available only to servers and workstations that are members of a particular domain. The domain-based model enables a deep root-based hierarchical arrangement of shared folders that is published in Active Directory. DFS shared folders in the domain-based model can be replicated for fault tolerance and load balancing.

Encrypting File System (EFS) — An advanced attribute of NTFS that enables a user to encrypt the contents of a folder or a file so that it can only be accessed via private key code by the user who encrypted it or a data recovery agent by default.

file encryption key (FEK) — The session key used to encrypt the contents of a file when EFS encryption is used.

hidden attribute — A standard attribute that controls the visibility of files and folders.

read-only attribute — A standard attribute, that when configured, does not allow the contents of a file or folder to be changed.

standalone DFS model — A DFS model in which there is no Active Directory implementation to help manage the shared folders. This model provides only a single or flat level share.

system attribute — A standard attribute typically associated with critical operating system files.

REVIEW QUESTIONS

1. Which of the following is not a standard attribute?
   a. Hidden
   b. System
   c. Compressed
   d. Read-only

2. Which of the following attributes can be configured from the properties of a folder residing on a FAT32 volume?

    a. Hidden

    b. System

    c. Read-only

    d. Archive

3. Which of the following attributes combined to make a file or folder "super hidden"? (Choose all that apply.)

    a. Hidden

    b. System

    c. Read-only

    d. Archive

4. When a folder's encryption attribute is configured, which of the following cannot be configured at the same time?

    a. Read-only

    b. System

    c. Hidden

    d. Compression

5. Which of the following is used to encrypt a file encryption key with EFS?

    a. A user's public key

    b. A user's private key

6. Which of the following users can access an EFS-encrypted file by default?

    a. The user who encrypted the file

    b. Any users in the same group as the user who encrypted the file

    c. The data recovery agent

    d. All users

7. Which of the following file systems support the ability to implement disk quotas?

    a. FAT

    b. FAT32

    c. NTFS

8. Which of the following tools can be used to encrypt files from the command line?

    a. COMPACT

    b. COMPRESS

    c. CIPHER

    d. ENCRYPT

9. Which of the following tools can be used to compress files from the command line?

    a. COMPACT

    b. COMPRESS

    c. CIPHER

    d. ENCRYPT

10. Which of the following tools can be used to review disk quota settings from the command line?

    a. QUOTAUTIL

    b. QUOTA

    c. FSUTIL

    d. COMPACT

11. What would be the result of issuing the command attrib –s –h file1.txt from the command line?

    a. File1.txt will have the system attribute added

    b. File1.txt will have the hidden attribute added

    c. File1.txt will have the system attribute removed

    d. File1.txt will have the hidden attribute removed

12. Which of the following are DFS models supported in Windows Server 2003? (Choose all that apply.)

    a. Domain-based DFS

    b. Standalone DFS

    c. Enterprise DFS

    d. Limited DFS

13. What term is used to describe alternative copies of a DFS link stored on other servers?

    a. Copy

    b. Replica

    c. Match

    d. Mount

14. A standalone DFS root is not fault tolerant.

    a. True

    b. False

15. Which of the following file systems are capable of natively supporting both encryption and compression? (Choose all that apply.)

   a. FAT

   b. FAT32

   c. NTFS

16. What is the result of copying a compressed file to another folder on the same NTFS volume?

   a. The file inherits the compression attribute of the target folder.

   b. The file retains its compression attribute.

17. What is the result of copying an EFS-encrypted file to a folder on a FAT32 partition?

   a. The copied file remains encrypted.

   b. The copied file is decrypted.

18. What happens when the COMPACT command is issued in a directory without any additional switches specified?

   a. All files in the directory are compressed.

   b. All files and subfolders in the directory are compressed.

   c. The compression attributes of files are listed.

19. The disk quota feature in Windows Server 2003 allows disk quotas to be configured on a server-wide basis.

   a. True

   b. False

20. Disk quotas can be configured according to group membership.

   a. True

   b. False

CASE PROJECTS

Case Project 7-1

Management has expressed a concern over disk usage because of the number of support calls indicating that server volumes are full. You have been sending memos asking users to delete any temporary or old files. Discuss how Dover Leasing can use disk quotas to limit usage and plan for future storage capacity requirements.

Case Project 7-2

Many of the executives at Dover Leasing have expressed concerns that even though NTFS permissions control user access to files, junior administrators could potentially grant themselves permissions to read sensitive documents. What solution could be implemented to help mitigate this risk?

Case Project 7-3

Users at Dover Leasing have been complaining that as additional servers are added to the network, shared file resources are becoming confusing. Some users consistently save files to the wrong folders because they forget to use the designated folder on a new server. Also, some users have been upset because certain folders have periodically not been accessible due to maintenance issues. What can be done to solve this issue?

7

CHAPTER

8

IMPLEMENTING AND MANAGING PRINTERS

> **After reading this chapter and completing the exercises, you will be able to:**
>
> ♦ Understand Windows Server 2003 printing terms and concepts
> ♦ Install and share printer resources
> ♦ Configure and manage installed printers
> ♦ Publish printers in Active Directory
> ♦ Troubleshoot printer problems

The concept of sharing resources among many different users is a primary reason why companies implement networks today. Networks have evolved from simple peer-to-peer arrangements where users would share files from their local workstations, to large and complex entities that may include hundreds, if not thousands, of interconnected and shared resources. This evolution means that an administrator is not only responsible for ensuring that shared resources are available to users but also that these resources are monitored and managed effectively.

Although sharing file resources is still the most common reason to implement a network, sharing access to print devices is probably a close second. Windows Server 2003 includes the ability to act as a print server, allowing both locally attached and network-interface print devices to be installed and shared amongst network users. In this chapter, you learn how to install and share print resources, and how to configure permissions to control printer access. Some of the more advanced configuration features of print devices in a Windows Server 2003 environment are also discussed.

Once you have created and shared file and print resources on your network, users may need a simple and effective way to search for these objects. Publishing resources into Active Directory allows any Active Directory-aware client to perform a simple search on the network. This chapter illustrates how to configure resource publishing and perform Active Directory searches.

The chapter closes with a look at some of the most common problems that may arise with respect to printers, and troubleshooting techniques that can be used to solve these problems.

WINDOWS SERVER 2003 PRINTING CONCEPTS

Managing a Windows Server 2003 network includes configuring and maintaining an efficient network of shared printers. You need to know how to install and configure these printers to ensure that users have an appropriate level of access when needed. One of the most common troubleshooting tasks for any network administrator is ensuring the continued availability of the shared network printers.

To successfully configure and troubleshoot Windows Server 2003 printing, you should be aware of very specific terms used to define the components of the printing system.

- Print device—The actual hardware device that produces the printed document. There are two main types of print devices: a **local print device** and a **network print device**. Local print devices are connected directly to a port on the print server or workstation. A network print device connects to a print server through its own network adapter and connection to the network.

- Printer—A configurable object in Windows Server 2003, the **printer** controls the connection to the print device.

- Print driver—Files that contain information Windows Server 2003 uses to convert raw print commands to a language that the printer understands; a specific **print driver** is needed for each print device model used and for each type of operating system in place.

- Print server—The computer in which the printers and print drivers are located; the **print server** is usually where you set up and configure the shared printing system.

- Print client—The computer from which a particular print job originates.

To set up an efficient printing environment, it is also important to make sure that your network meets the following hardware requirements:

- One or more computers to act as print servers—Although both Windows Server 2003 and Windows XP Professional can be used as print servers, Windows XP Professional only supports a maximum of 10 simultaneous client connections. This makes XP an inappropriate choice as a print server in all but the smallest network environments.

- Sufficient space on the hard drive for the print server—This is very important because Windows Server 2003 uses space on the hard drive to queue and buffer documents as they are being directed to the print device.

■ Sufficient RAM beyond that of the minimum Windows Server 2003 requirements—This is critical if you expect to have a large number of print jobs and still wish to maintain an acceptable performance level.

Understanding Network Printing

When a user sends a print job to a locally attached printer, the job is spooled on the local machine, and ultimately directed to a particular port, such as LPT1. When a user attempts to print a document to a network printer, however, the process is somewhat more involved. Both the **print client** and the print server run specific processes to deliver a print job to a network printer.

1. A print file is generated by the software application at the print client.

2. The application communicates with the Windows **graphics device interface (GDI)** as it creates the print file. The GDI integrates information about the print file—such as word-processing codes for fonts, colors, and embedded graphics objects—with information obtained from the printer driver installed at the client for the target printer, in a process that Microsoft calls rendering.

3. The print file is formatted with control codes to implement the special graphics, font, and color characteristics of the file. At the same time, the software application places the print file in the client's spooler by writing the file, called the spool file, to a subfolder used for spooling. In the Windows 95, 98, NT, 2000, XP, and 2003 operating systems, a **spooler** is a group of dynamic-link libraries, information files, and programs that processes print jobs for printing.

4. The remote print provider at the client makes a remote procedure call to the network print server to which the print file is targeted, such as a Windows Server 2003 print server. If the print server is responding and ready to accept the print file, the remote printer transmits that file from the client's spooler folder to the Server service on Windows Server 2003.

5. The network print server uses four processing elements to receive and process a print file; router, print provider, print processor, and print monitor. The router, print provider, and print processor are all pieces of the network print server's spooler.

6. The Server service calls its router, the Print Spooler service, once the remote print provider at the client contacts it. The router then directs the print file to the print provider, which stores it in a spool file until it can be sent to the printer.

7. The print provider works with the print processor to ensure that the file is formatted to use the right data type, such as **TEXT** or **RAW**, while the file is spooled.

8. The print monitor pulls it from the spooler's disk storage and sends it to the printer, when the spool file is fully formatted for transmission to the printer.

Ultimately, the final step in the printing process should result in the production of the intended file. In the following sections you learn more about the main administrative tasks associated with installing, configuring, and troubleshooting printing on Windows Server 2003 systems.

INSTALLING AND SHARING PRINTER RESOURCES

In order to allow users on a network to gain access to shared printer resources, printers must first be connected and installed, and then shared. In the following sections you learn more about installing a local printer, sharing it for access to network users, and then connecting to an existing network printer using different methods.

Adding a Printer as a Local Device

Smaller networks may have workstations or servers that share print devices connected directly to a local port on the computer. To add and share a local print device, you need to have administrator privileges on the computer that acts as the print server. Use the Add Printer Wizard to install and configure printers on systems running Windows Server 2003. Access this tool from the Printers and Faxes program (available on the Start menu), as illustrated in Figure 8-1.

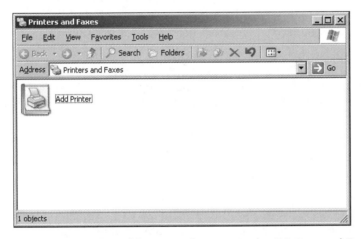

Figure 8-1   The Add Printer shortcut in the Printers and Faxes tool

The Add Printer Wizard provides access to all of the necessary configuration options to get a local printer up and running. As with Windows 2000, the Windows Server 2003 Add Printer Wizard lets you detect printers via Plug and Play. Conversely, the Wizard also allows you to manually configure printers by make and model, allowing you to add a manufacturer's driver from a supplied disk if necessary, as shown in Figure 8-2.

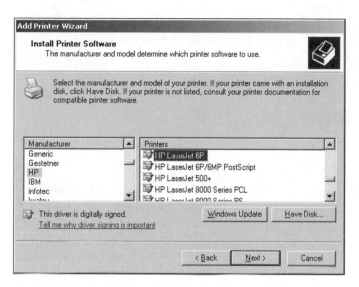

Figure 8-2   Manually configuring a printer

Additional configuration options specified during the local printer installation process include the port that the print device connects to, as illustrated in Figure 8-3.

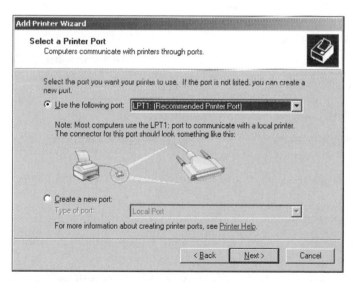

Figure 8-3   Configuring printer port settings

The Add Printer Wizard also allows you to specify if the device serves as the Windows default printer and whether the printer should be shared to provide network access. More advanced options, such as configuring printer permissions, priorities, and features such as print pooling, are handled once the printer is already installed by accessing its properties. Configuring additional printer settings is looked at later in this section.

In Activity 8-1 you install a local printer using the Add Printer Wizard accessible from the Printers and Faxes tool.

Activity 8-1: Installing a Local Printer

Time Required: 10 minutes

Objective: Use the Add Printer Wizard to install a local printer.

Description: The IT manager at Dover Leasing is interested in migrating all corporate printers from various platforms to Windows Server 2003-based print servers. He has asked you to begin the testing process by installing and configuring a locally connected print device that will eventually be shared for access by network users. In this activity, you install and configure a new local printer using the Add Printer Wizard from the Printers and Faxes tool.

1. If necessary, log on using your **AdminXX** account. Click **Start**, and then click **Printers and Faxes**.

2. In the Printers and Faxes window, double-click the **Add Printer** icon to start the Add Printer Wizard. At the Welcome screen click **Next**.

3. At the Local or Network Printer screen, ensure that the **Local printer attached to this computer** radio button is selected. Uncheck the **Automatically detect and install my Plug and Play printer** check box. Click **Next**.

4. At the Select a Printer Port screen, ensure that **LPT1: {Recommended Printer Port}** is selected in the Use the following port list box and click **Next**.

5. At the Install Printer Software screen, click **HP** in the Manufacturer list. In the Printers list, click **HP LaserJet 6P** and click **Next**.

6. At the Name Your Printer screen, type **HPLaserJet-ServerXX** in the Printer name text box (where *XX* is your assigned student number). Click **Next**.

7. At the Printer Sharing screen, select the **Do not share this printer** radio button and click **Next**.

8. At the Print Test Page screen, select the **No** radio button and click **Next**.

9. At the Completing the Add Printer Wizard screen, review the stated configuration information and then click **Finish**.

10. Verify that the new printer appears in the Printers and Faxes windows with a check mark icon specifying that it is the default printer. Close the **Printers and Faxes** window.

In order to allow other users on a network to access a printer, the printer must be shared in a manner similar to a folder. In Activity 8-2 you share the local printer created in Activity 8-1, making it accessible to network users.

ACTIVITY

Activity 8-2: Sharing a Local Printer for Network Access

Time Required: 5 minutes

Objective: Share an installed printer to allow network access.

Description: Having created a local printer in the previous activity, you now decide to share this printer to allow network clients to print to it. In this activity, you access the properties of the printer to configure sharing.

1. Click **Start**, and then click **Printers and Faxes**.

2. Right-click the **HPLaserJet–Server*XX*** icon and then click **Properties**.

3. On the General tab, type **Marketing Laser Printer** in the Comment text box.

4. Click the **Sharing** tab, and then click the **Share this printer** radio button. In the Share name text box, type **MarketingLaser** (as shown in Figure 8-4) and then click **OK**.

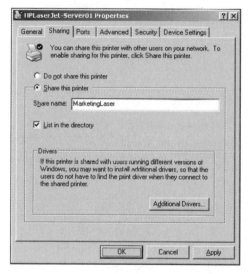

Figure 8-4   Sharing an existing printer

5. When the Printer Properties dialog box opens, read the message about access from MS-DOS workstations and then click **Yes**. Notice that a hand icon appears under the printer in the Printers and Faxes windows, designating it as a shared resource.

6. Click **Start**, and then click **Run**. In the Open text box, type **\\Server*XX*** (where *XX* is your assigned student number), and then click **OK**.

7. When the \\Server*XX* window opens, look for the MarketingLaser printer icon as shown in Figure 8-5. Notice that it also includes the description specified in Step 3.

8. Close all open windows.

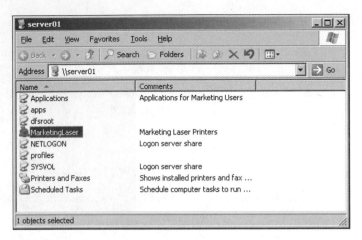

Figure 8-5   Viewing shared resources on Server01

In the same way that you can hide a shared folder by appending the $ symbol to the end of its share name, this method can also be used to stop printers from being displayed in lists of shared resources.

TIP

Adding a Printer as a Network Device

Many corporate print devices have integrated network interface cards that do not require a direct connection to the computer acting as the print server via a parallel port or USB connection. These network print devices use TCP/IP or other protocols to allow communication over the network.

You can also use the Add Printer Wizard to add network print devices to your network. The main difference is that instead of choosing to configure the device using a local port, you need to create a new TCP/IP port to facilitate communication directly over the network. To create this new TCP/IP port, click the Create a new port radio button on the Select a Printer Port screen, and then click the Standard TCP/IP Port option. Ultimately, doing this opens the Add Standard TCP/IP Printer Port Wizard, as illustrated in Figure 8-6. Once the configuration of the TCP/IP port is complete, the Add Printer Wizard continues as it does for any local printer.

In Activity 8-3 you install a network printer using two different methods.

Figure 8-6 The Add Standard TCP/IP Printer Port Wizard

Activity 8-3: Installing a Network Printer

Time Required: 10 minutes

Objective: Install a network printer using the Add Printer Wizard and by browsing the network.

Description: After successfully sharing a printer over the network, you decided to explore some of the methods used to install network printers. In this activity, you install a network printer connected to your partner's server using both the Add Printer Wizard and by browsing the network.

1. Click **Start**, and then click **Printers and Faxes**.

2. Double-click the **Add Printer** icon to open the Add Printer Wizard. At the Welcome screen, click **Next**.

3. At the Local or Network Printer screen, click the **A network printer**, **or a printer attached to another computer** radio button, and click **Next**.

4. At the Specify a Printer screen, click the **Connect to this printer** radio button and then type **\\serverXX\MarketingLaser** in the Name text box (where *XX* is your *partner's* student number). Click **Next**. Select the **No** radio button on the Default Printer screen, then click **Next**.

5. Click **Finish** to close the Add Printer Wizard.

6. Verify that the new network printer appears in the Printers and Faxes window. Notice that the icon used to represent a network printer is different from the one used to represent a local printer.

7. In the Printers and Faxes window, right-click your partner's network printer and click **Delete**. When the Printers dialog box opens, click **Yes**.

8. Click **Start**, and then click **Run**. In the Open text box type **\\ServerXX** (where *XX* is your *partner's* student number), and then click **OK**.

9. In the list of shared resources that appears, right-click the **MarketingLaser** icon and then click **Connect**, as shown in Figure 8-7. This installs the printer on your computer.

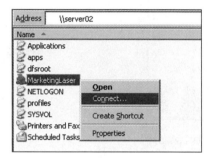

Figure 8-7   Connecting to an existing network printer

10. Verify that the MarketingLaser printer installed in the previous step appears in the Printers and Faxes window.

11. Close all open windows.

CONFIGURING AND MANAGING PRINTER RESOURCES

Although the basic settings encountered in the Add Printer Wizard can provide a suitable configuration to allow users to access shared printer resources, the properties of an installed printer provide access to many additional configuration settings. In the following sections you learn more about some of the settings and features involved with configuring and managing printers installed on a Windows Server 2003 system.

Configuring an Existing Printer

Once you have a printer installed, you may want to modify some of the configuration options such as sharing, permissions, and other advanced settings. To modify these options, right-click the printer icon and click Properties to access the properties of the printer. Figure 8-8 illustrates some of the configuration options and tabs available in the properties of a printer.

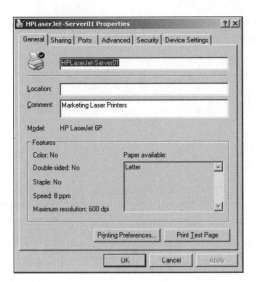

Figure 8-8 The properties of an existing printer

In Activity 8-4 you explore the properties of an existing local printer installed on your server.

Activity 8-4: Exploring Printer Properties

Time Required: 15 minutes

Objective: Explore the configurable properties for an installed printer.

Description: The IT manager at Dover Leasing has given you the responsibility of config-uring the properties of all printers to be installed on the network. You decide to explore the property settings associated with a printer to better prepare yourself. In this activity, you open and explore the properties of the printer originally installed in Activity 8-1.

1. Click **Start**, and then click **Printers and Faxes**.

2. Right-click the **HPLaserJet–ServerXX** icon (where *XX* is your assigned student number), and then click **Properties**.

3. On the General tab, click the **Printing Preferences** button. This opens the Print-ing Preferences dialog box for the printer, allowing you to configure settings such as paper layout and quality settings. Browse through the configurable settings and then click **OK**.

4. Click the **Sharing** tab, as originally seen in Figure 8-4. Notice that this tab is used to configure sharing settings, as well as to specify whether this printer should be listed in the directory. Click the **Additional Drivers** button, noting that this dialog box shows you which drivers are currently installed, while also allowing you to install additional drivers. Click **Cancel** to close the Additional Drivers dialog box.

5. Click the **Ports** tab. Notice that this tab is used to configure printer port settings, as well as enable settings like printer pooling.

6. Click the **Advanced** tab. Notice that this tab allows you to configure settings such as the availability of the printer as well as the printer spooling options. Click the **Separator Page** button, and then click the **Browse** button. This allows you to configure a separator page to be printed before a user's print job. Click **Cancel** twice to return to the printer properties dialog box.

7. Click the **Security** tab. Notice that this tab allows you to configure security settings for the printer.

8. Click the **Device Settings** tab. Notice that this tab allows you to configure properties specific to the printer model, such as the types of paper used in various trays and the amount of physical memory installed in the print device, as shown in Figure 8-9.

9. Click **Cancel** to close the printer properties dialog box, and then close the Printers and Faxes window.

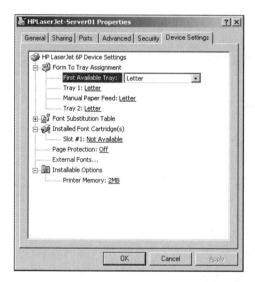

Figure 8-9   The Device Settings tab

Two of the most important configuration options for printers are the Sharing and Security tabs. The Sharing tab allows you to enable or disable printer sharing and Active Directory publishing, as well as install additional drivers for other operating systems that may need to use the printer. The Security tab allows you to control **printer permissions**, in much the same way that this tab is used to control NTFS permissions for files and folders. There are three main levels of print permissions, as well as the ability to configure more granular special permissions. Print permissions are outlined in Table 8-1.

Table 8-1   Printer permissions

Permission	Description
Print	Allows connection to a printer, printing of documents, and editing a user's own print jobs; the Everyone group has this permission by default
Manage Documents	Allows all of the Print permissions with the addition of controlling document print jobs for all users; the Creator Owner group has this permission by default
Manage Printers	Allows all of the Print and Manage Documents permissions and also allows sharing, modification, and deletion of printers and their properties; the Administrators, Print Operators, and Server Operators have this permission by default
Special Permissions	Much like NTFS special permissions these provide a more granular level of control over printer security including: controlling user ownership of a printer, viewing printer permissions, and changing printer permissions

Like NTFS and shared-folder permissions, printer permissions are cumulative.

NOTE

In Activity 8-5 you configure security permissions for an existing printer installed on your server.

Activity 8-5: Configuring Printer Permissions

ACTIVITY

Time Required: 15 minutes

Objective: Configure printer security permissions.

Description: Dover Leasing has a number of different printers scattered through a variety of departments and business units. Because each department is responsible for paying maintenance costs associated with their printers, the department heads want to ensure that only users within their own departments have the ability to print to these printers. The IT manager at Dover Leasing has asked you to ensure that all printers are properly secured according to this requirement. However, he also wants to ensure that members of the Help Desk group have the ability to manage documents, while all domain administrators are granted the Manage Printers permission. In this activity, you configure permissions on the Marketing Department's laser printer.

1. Click **Start**, and then click **Printers and Faxes**.

2. Right-click the **HPLaserJet-ServerXX** icon (where *XX* is your assigned student number), and click **Properties**.

3. Click the **Security** tab, as shown in Figure 8-10.

4. In the Group or user names list, click the **Everyone** group, and then click **Remove**.

8

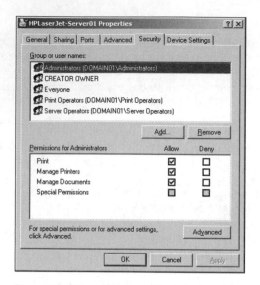

Figure 8-10   The Security tab for a printer

5. Click the **Add** button. In the Select Users, Computers, or Groups dialog box, type **Marketing Users** in the Enter the object names to select text box, and then click **OK**. Notice that once added, the Marketing Users group is granted the Allow Print permission by default.

6. Click the **Add** button. In the Select Users, Computers, or Groups dialog box, type **Help Desk Users** in the Enter the object names to select text box, and then click **OK**. In addition to the Allow Print permission, grant the Help Desk Users group the **Allow Manage Documents** permission.

7. Click the **Add** button. In the Select Users, Computers, or Groups dialog box, type **Domain Admins** in the Enter the object names to select text box, and then click **OK**. In addition to the Allow Print permission, grant the Domain Admins group the **Allow Manage Printers** permission.

8. Click **OK** to close the Properties dialog box.

9. Open the **Run** command and in the Open text box type **notepad.exe** and press **Enter**. This opens Notepad. In the Notepad window, type **testing**. Click **File** on the menu bar, and then click **Print**.

10. In the Print dialog box, ensure that the default printer is selected and then click **Print**. Close Notepad, click **No** when asked to save the changes.

11. In the Printers and Faxes window, double-click the **HPLaserJet–ServerXX** icon (where *XX* is your assigned student number). This displays the print queue for the HPLaserjet-Server*XX* printer, including the print job that you just sent. Close the HPLaserjet-Server*XX* and the Printers and Faxes windows.

12. Log off and then log back on as the user **cmedved** with the password **Password01**.

13. Open **Notepad**, type some text, and then attempt to print the document to the HPLaserJet-Server*XX* printer. Notice that it doesn't appear in the list of available printers because the Chris Medved user account is not a member of a group with sufficient permissions to print to the device.

14. Close all open windows and log off. Log on using your **AdminXX** account.

 Windows Server 2003 also lets you determine a user's effective printer permissions via the Effective Permissions tab in the Advanced Security Settings of a printer, as shown in Figure 8-11.

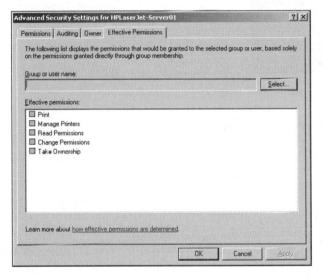

Figure 8-11   The Effective Permissions tab in the Advanced Security Settings of a printer

Printer Pools and Priorities

Some advanced features of Windows Server 2003 printing include setting up printer pools and configuring printer priorities.

A **printer pool** consists of a single printer that is connected to a number of print devices. The advantage of a printer pool is that it allows many physical print devices to function as a single logical printer, thus providing better document distribution in high-volume environments while reducing the time that users must wait for documents to print. One cautionary note is that all print devices configured to be part of the same printer pool must be capable of using the same print driver, or output problems will almost certainly occur. A printer pool is configured by clicking the Ports tab and then placing a check mark in the box next to the Enable printer pooling command, as shown in Figure 8-12.

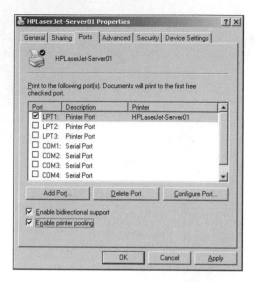

Figure 8-12   Enabling printer pooling

There may be times when you need to set **printer priorities** for different groups of users. For example, you may want to configure your print environment to give precedence to any printouts from the CEO of the company, even if there are other documents already ahead of it in the print queue.

Print priorities are especially useful in cases where you want different groups of users to have different levels of priority to a limited number of print devices. To configure printer priorities, install two printers on the print server and connect them both to the same print device. Configure the priority of each printer by clicking the Advanced tab and then adjusting the Priority to a number between 1 and 99, with 1 being the lowest priority and 99 being the highest priority, as shown in Figure 8-13. Again, higher priority printers print first.

Figure 8-13   Printer priority settings

The next step in configuring print priorities is to only allow specific users to print to a specific printer. For example, if you want the CEO to always have first priority at printing, only allow the CEO to print to the printer with the higher priority setting. All other users print to the printer with the lower priority setting. To do this, configure the printer security settings, as discussed earlier in this section.

In Activity 8-6 you configure a printer pool on your server.

Activity 8-6: Configuring Printer Pooling

Time Required: 10 minutes

Objective: Configure two printers to use the printer pooling feature in Windows Server 2003.

Description: The Marketing Department creates the largest volume of documents on a regular basis at Dover Leasing. Although the department is planning to upgrade all print devices later in the year, they currently have a number of spare HP LaserJet 6P units that they would like to better utilize. Because you are aware of the fact that Windows Server 2003 provides the printer pooling feature, you decide to configure printer pooling for two units in the Marketing Department. In this activity, you install an additional HP LaserJet 6P printer and then configure printer pooling with the original printer installed in Activity 8-1.

1. Click **Start**, and then click **Printers and Faxes**.

2. In the Printers and Faxes window, double-click the **Add Printer** icon to start the Add Printer Wizard. Click **Next** at the Welcome screen.

3. At the Local or Network Printer screen, ensure that the **Local printer attached to this computer** radio button is selected. Uncheck the **Automatically detect and install my Plug and Play printer** check box if necessary. Click **Next**.

4. At the Select a Printer Port screen, select **LPT2: {Printer Port}** in the Use the following port list box and click **Next**.

5. At the Install Printer Software screen, ensure that **HP** is selected in the Manufacturer list, and that **HPLaserJet 6P** is selected in the Printers list. Click **Next**.

6. At the Use Existing Driver screen, ensure that **Keep existing driver (recommended)** is selected, then click **Next**.

7. At the Name Your Printer screen, type **HPLaserJet2-ServerXX** in the Printer name text box (where *XX* is your assigned student number). In the Do you want to you use this printer as the default printer section, click the **Yes** radio button and click **Next**.

8. At the Printer Sharing screen, ensure that the **Do not share this printer** radio button is selected and click **Next**.

9. At the Print Test Page screen, ensure that the **No** radio button is selected and click **Next**.

10. At the Completing the Add Printer Wizard screen, review the stated configuration information and then click **Finish**.

11. Right-click the **HPLaserJet2-ServerXX** icon and then click **Properties**.

12. Click the **Ports** tab. Click the **Enable printer pooling** check box in the lower left of the window. If necessary, click the check box next to **LPT2** in the Port: column. Check the check box next to **LPT1**, then click **OK**. This allows documents sent to the HPLaserJet2-Server*XX* printer to print from both printers as availability dictates.

13. Close all open windows.

Setting Up and Updating Client Computers

Once the printer is added and configured, you must next set up the client computers to be able to print to the print server. If there is a mix of client operating systems throughout the network, a different version of the print driver is needed for each operating system that is connected to the print server.

Any client computers that run Windows 2000, Windows Server 2003, or Windows XP automatically download the print driver when they initially connect to the printer. Windows 95, Windows 98, Windows ME, and Windows NT 4.0 clients also automatically download the print driver, but only if there is a copy of the appropriate driver on the print server. Install additional print drivers by accessing the Additional Drivers dialog box from the Sharing tab, as shown in Figure 8-14.

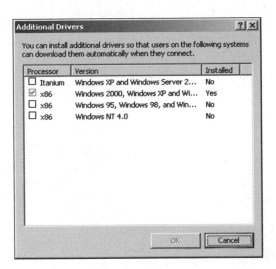

Figure 8-14   The Additional Drivers dialog box

If you have any older Windows clients on your network such as Windows 3.x, or non-Microsoft clients such as Macintosh or UNIX clients, you must manually install the necessary print driver. Non-Microsoft clients may also require additional print services such as Print Services for Macintosh or UNIX to be installed on the print server.

In Activity 8-7 you install additional print drivers for an existing printer.

Activity 8-7: Installing Additional Print Drivers

Time Required: 5 minutes

Objective: Install additional print drivers for the Windows 98 operating system.

Description: Although Dover Leasing has almost fully migrated all of their existing workstations to Windows XP, a number of Windows 98 clients continue to exist and will for the foreseeable future. The IT manager at Dover Leasing has asked you to ensure that the appropriate drivers for Windows 98 are installed on the server in addition to the default drivers. In this activity, you install additional drivers for Windows 98 in the properties of the HPLaserJet2-Server*XX* printer.

1. Click **Start**, and then click **Printers and Faxes**.

2. Right-click the **HPLaserJet2-Server*XX*** icon (where *XX* is your assigned student number), and then click **Properties**.

3. Click the **Sharing** tab, and then click the **Additional Drivers** button.

4. In the Additional Drivers dialog box, click the check box next to **x86** for **Windows 95**, **Windows 98**, **and Windows Millennium Edition** and then click **OK**.

5. When prompted for the location of the driver files, type the path **D:\Source\I386** in the Copy files from text box and then click **OK**.

6. Click **Close** to close to properties of the printer.

7. Close all open windows.

Managing Print Queues

Once users have sent print jobs to a printer from a particular application, these jobs are queued while waiting to be output. The most common way for a user to view the **print queue** for a particular printer is to simply double-click on that printer's icon in the Printers and Faxes tool. This displays the current contents of the print queue, as shown in Figure 8-15.

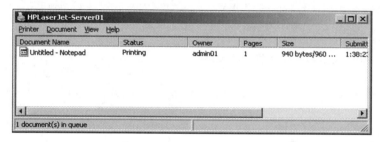

Figure 8-15   Viewing the contents of a print queue

Once a print job has been queued, a user with the Print permissions can pause, resume, restart, or cancel the printing of their own documents by clicking on the document in the queue and then selecting the appropriate option from the Document menu. Users cannot pause, resume, restart, or cancel print jobs belonging to other users unless they have the Manage Documents permission for that printer. In some cases, problems with the printer might be stopping the printer from physically printing the required documents. This might be a result of the physical printer being offline, the Print Spooler service stalling or hanging, or the printer having simply run out of paper. Troubleshooting printing issues is looked at in more detail later in this chapter.

Internet Printing Protocol

In addition to the standard method of configuring and gaining access to printers via the Printers and Faxes tool, Windows Server 2003 also supports the **Internet Printing Protocol (IPP)** specification, which allows printers to be managed via a Web browser, and print jobs to be submitted to a URL. Although IPP support is built into Windows Server 2003, Internet Information Services (IIS) must be installed on a print server to take advantage of it (IIS is not installed by default with Windows Server 2003). IIS is looked at in more detail in Chapter 13.

Once enabled, IPP allows an administrator to connect to and manage the printers on a Windows Server 2003 system using a Web browser like Internet Explorer. The URL to access the management interface is in the form http://*printservername*/printers. Connecting in this method provides a list of all of the configured printers on the server, their status, location, jobs, and model, as shown in Figure 8-16.

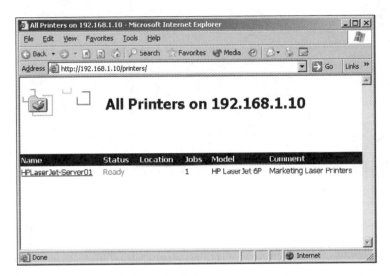

Figure 8-16 Web-based printer management

Clicking on the hyperlink for a particular printer allows an administrator to view and control print jobs currently queued, to pause and resume them, and to print documents, as well as install a printer if necessary, as shown in Figure 8-17. Normal users can also utilize this interface, although their configured permissions will limit the capabilities they have access to.

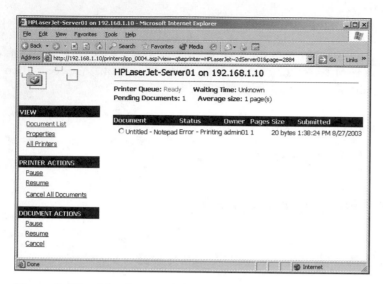

Figure 8-17   Viewing a print queue using Web-based printer management

Once IPP is installed and configured on the print server, clients running Windows 2000, Windows XP, and Windows Server 2003 can easily connect to existing printers using either the Web interface just discussed, or using the Add Printer Wizard. The URL used to connect to a printer using the Add Printer Wizard is *http://printservername/printers/printername/ .printer*, as shown in Figure 8–18.

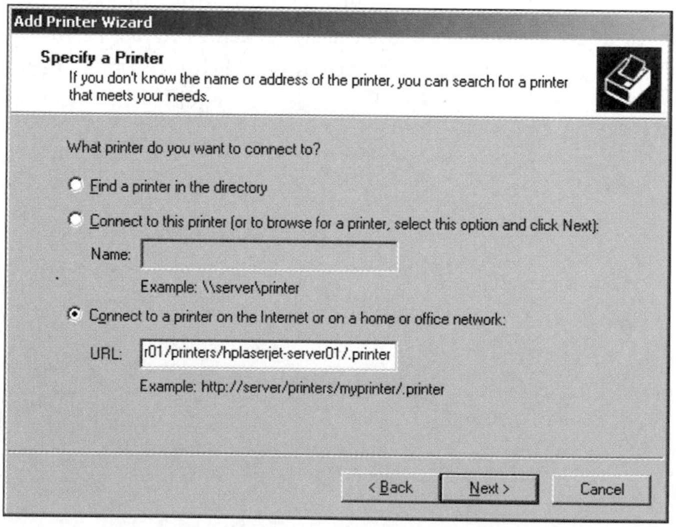

Figure 8-18   Specifying a URL in the Add Printer Wizard

One of the main benefits of using IPP is that it greatly simplifies the ability of an administrator to manage printers from any system on the network, without requiring those printers to be installed on the local client system. Another benefit is the fact that IPP can be used to print to other locations over the Internet, allowing users a method to easily gain access to remote printers using the standard HTTP protocol.

 The installation and basic configuration of IPP is looked at in more detail in Chapter 13.

Printer Command-Line Utilities

8

Along with the Printers and Faxes tool and Web-based printer management, Windows Server 2003 also provides a number of built-in VBScript files that allow printers and related properties to be managed from the command line. These commands include:

- Prncnfg.vbs—configures a printer or displays configuration information for a printer
- Prndrvr.vbs—adds, deletes, or lists printer drivers
- Prnjobs.vbs—views existing print jobs, as well as pauses, resumes, and cancels print jobs in a queue
- Prnmngr.vbs—adds, deletes, or lists printers and related connections, as well as sets and displays the default printer
- Prnport.vbs—creates, deletes, or lists standard TCP/IP printer ports, as well as displays or changes the configuration of an existing port
- Prnqctl.vbs—pauses or resumes a printer, cancels all jobs queued for a particular printer, and prints a test page

Because the files listed in the preceding bullet points are VBScripts rather than standard executables, they must be invoked from the command line using the **Windows Script Host (WSH)**. WSH serves as a controller for the ActiveX scripting engines, and is provided in both Windows-based and command-line versions. The Windows-based version is named Wscript.exe, and the command-line version is Cscript.exe. As such, when you wish to access a VBScript file from the command line, the correct syntax first issues the Cscript command (from the WINDOWS\system32 directory), followed by the name of the appropriate script, and any necessary switches. For example, the following command would display the current configuration of a printer named HPLaserJet-Server01 on the local system:

```
C:\WINDOWS\system32>cscript prncnfg.vbs -g -p hplaserjet-server01
```

The output from the preceding command is shown in Figure 8-19.

```
Command Prompt                                                              _ □ ×
C:\WINDOWS\system32>cscript prncnfg.vbs -g -p hplaserjet-server01
Microsoft (R) Windows Script Host Version 5.6
Copyright (C) Microsoft Corporation 1996-2001. All rights reserved.

Server name
Printer name hplaserjet-server01
Share name MarketingLaser
Driver name HP LaserJet 6P
Port name LPT1:
Comment Marketing Laser Printers
Location
Separator file
Print processor WinPrint
Data type RAW
Parameters
Priority 1
Default priority 0
Printer always available
Attributes local shared published enable_bidi do_complete_first

Printer status Other
Extended printer status Unknown
Detected error state Unknown
Extended detected error state Unknown

C:\WINDOWS\system32>_
```

Figure 8-19   Listing the configuration of a local printer using the `Prncnfg.vbs` command

 For more information on the capabilities of WSH, see the topic Windows Script Host overview in Help and Support Center. For a complete list of the switches and options supported with the various command-line printing utilities, search for the command by name in Help and Support Center.

Print Spooler

As users send print jobs to a printer, they are spooled on the hard disk of the print server by default. On a Windows Server 2003 system, spooling occurs in the WINDOWS\system32\spool\PRINTERS folder by default. Although the default location of the print spool folder is generally sufficient for low-volume printing, it is not optimal for higher-volume requirements, mainly a result of it being located in the same volume as the Windows operating system files. Ultimately, leaving the spool folder in the default location can lead to printing delays, especially on busy systems.

For best performance, Microsoft recommends moving the print spool folder to a different partition, preferably one located on a disk that has its own controller. For example, many companies will set up dedicated print server systems running Windows Server 2003, and dedicate an entire second hard disk to print spooling.

In Activity 8-8 you move the print spool folder from its current location to a dedicated folder on drive D on your server.

Activity 8-8: Changing the Location of the Spool Folder

Time Required: 5 minutes

Objective: Move the print spool folder to a different volume to improve printing performance.

Description: Having learned that placing the spool folder on a different volume can help to improve printing performance, the IT manager has asked you to test the process. In this activity you move the spool folder from its default location to a folder named Spool on drive D on your server by reconfiguring the print server's properties.

1. Click **Start**, and then click **Printers and Faxes**.

2. Click the **File** menu, and then click **Server Properties**.

3. Click the **Advanced** tab, as shown in Figure 8-20. In the Spool folder text box, type **D:\Spool**, and then press **OK**.

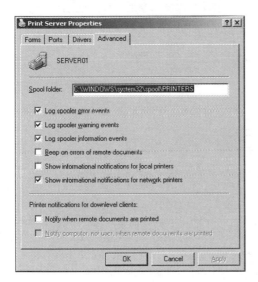

Figure 8-20   The Advanced tab of the Print Server Properties window

4. When the Print Server Properties dialog box appears, read the message that appears, and then click **Yes**.

5. Complete the process of moving the spool folder location by restarting your server, and then logging on using your AdminXX account. This step can also be substituted with restarting the Print Spooler service, which is looked at in Activity 8-10.

PUBLISHING PRINTERS IN ACTIVE DIRECTORY

Shared printers can be published into Active Directory to help users find network printer resources. In fact, any Windows Server 2003- or Windows 2000-compatible printer that is installed on a domain print server is automatically **published** into Active Directory during installation. By default, published printer objects are hidden in the Active Directory Users and Computers interface.

To view the published printers in Active Directory Users and Computers, click View on the menu bar, and click Users, Groups, and Computers as containers. This option modifies the view to show objects that are associated with a user, group, or computer object. Printer objects are associated with the computer object that acts as its print server. When the container in which the print server is located is expanded, computer objects can also be expanded to view the printer objects associated with them, as shown in Figure 8-21.

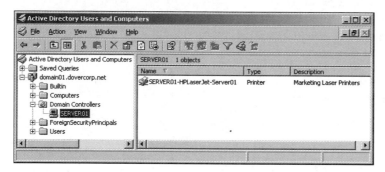

Figure 8-21 Viewing published printers in Active Directory Users and Computers

Printer shares that are created on pre-Windows 2000 print servers are not published into Active Directory by default. However, these printers can be added manually to the directory by creating new published printer objects in Active Directory Users and Computers. Like shared folder objects, these printers can be published in whichever container makes the most sense, based on environment and administrative goals. The New Object – Printer dialog box is illustrated in Figure 8-22.

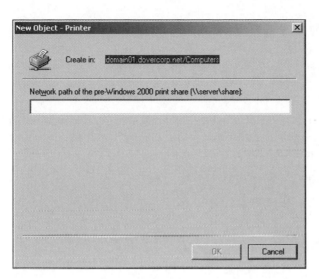

Figure 8-22   The New Object - Printer dialog box

In Activity 8-9, you will publish a printer to Active Directory.

Publishing printers into Active Directory manually can involve a great deal of administrative effort in large environments. To help ease this burden, a script called Pubprn.vbs in the WINDOWS\system32 directory can be used to help automate the process. View the header of the Pubprn.vbs script (right-click on the script file and choose the Edit option to open it in Notepad) for more information on its configuration.

Activity 8-9: Publishing Printers in Active Directory

Time Required: 10 minutes

Objective: Configure printer publishing settings and publish printers manually in Active Directory.

Description: Dover Leasing's network includes such a wide variety of printers connected to different operating systems, that the IT manager has asked you to explore how printers can be made easier to find in Active Directory. Although he wants most printers to be published in the directory, he is also concerned with users finding and attempting to access the printers belonging to the Marketing Department. In this activity, you browse existing published printers, manually publish a fictitious printer object in Active Directory, and then manually disable the publishing of printers belonging to the Marketing Department.

1. Click **Start**, select **Administrative Tools**, and then click **Active Directory Users and Computers**.

2. Click **View** on the menu bar, and then click **Users, Groups, and Computers as containers**.

3. Click the **plus signs (+)** next to the Domain*XX*.Dovercorp.net icon and the Domain Controllers OU to expand their contents.

4. Click the **Server*XX*** icon (where *XX* is your assigned student number) to view the new objects that are now visible. Notice that the shared printer created earlier in the chapter is now visible as a published object in Active Directory.

5. Right-click the **SERVER*XX*-HPLaserJet-Server*XX*** printer icon listed and click **Properties**. Notice that searchable features of the printer including its description and ability to print in color are configurable from this interface.

6. Click the **Color** check box and then click **OK**.

7. Click **Start**, and then click **Search**.

8. In the Search Companion pane, click **Other search options**, click **Printers, computers, or people** and then click **A printer on the network**.

9. In the Find Printers window, ensure that your domain is selected in the In list box. Click the **Features** tab, check the **Can print color** check box, and then click the **Find Now** button. The HPLaserJet-Server*XX* printer configured in Step 5 should appear in the Search results pane, as shown in Figure 8-23.

10. Right-click **HPLaserJet-Server*XX*** listed in the Search results pane to view the available options. Notice that a user can install a printer from this interface by choosing the Connect option.

11. Close the Find Printers window and the Search Results window.

12. Click **Start**, and then click **Printers and Faxes**.

13. Right-click the **HPLaserJet-Server*XX*** icon, and then click **Properties**.

14. Click the **Sharing** tab, uncheck the **List in the directory** check box, and then click **OK**.

15. Open the Search program from the Start menu and then attempt to search for a printer that is capable of printing in color again (see Steps 7-9 for explicit steps). Note that the HPLaserJet-Server*XX* printer is not found because it is no longer published in Active Directory.

16. Close all open windows.

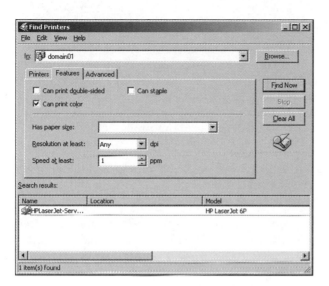

Figure 8-23   Searching for a printer based on its capabilities

8

TROUBLESHOOTING PRINTER PROBLEMS

Because printers installed on a Windows Server 2003 system include a wide variety of configurable options and settings, problems eventually can (and probably will) occur. The most common printing problems that you are likely to encounter and their appropriate solutions include:

- Print jobs will not print—Print jobs may not physically print from a particular print device for a variety of reasons. The most common causes include the print device being off-line, there not being enough hard disk space available to spool the job, or the print device simply being out of paper. To fix these problems, ensure that the print device is online, consider moving the spool folder to a different location (or free up disk space on the current volume), or add more paper to the device, respectively.

- Printer output appears garbled—Printed output may appear garbled or not print complete pages. The usual source of this problem is that an incorrect driver for the device is installed. Download the correct drivers from the manufacturer's Web site for the appropriate platforms, and then reinstall these drivers on the print server.

- Users receive an Access Denied message when attempting to print—An Access Denied message is received when attempting to send a job to a printer from a particular application. This message usually indicates incorrectly configured permissions. Review and correct permissions for the printer from the Security tab in the printer's properties to solve the problem.

- Users cannot find an existing printer when searching Active Directory—If a user cannot find an existing printer by searching Active Directory, begin by ensuring that the printer is still published. If it is not, publish the printer manually using Active Directory Users and Computers, or the PUBPRN.VBS script.

- Printer only works at certain times of the day—Windows Server 2003 allows schedules to be configured to control printer availability by the time of day. If a printer is not available during certain times, either change the availability from the Advanced tab of the printer's properties, or direct the user towards another configured printer that allows printing at those times.

- Windows 95/98/ME users cannot connect to a printer—When a printer is installed on a Windows Server 2003 system, drivers for Windows 95/98/ME are not installed by default. If users on these platforms require access to the printer, make the required drivers available from the Sharing tab of the printer's properties.

- Print jobs become stuck in the print queue—Some documents may appear in the print queue, but they do not print, and they cannot be deleted. To fix this problem, on the print server, open the Services console on the Administrative Tools menu, right-click the Print Spooler service, and then click Restart. Note that any print jobs that are in the queue are deleted.

- Print device failure—A print device may fail because of a paper jam, hardware failure, or a stuck print job. Any documents that are behind the current document in the queue can be redirected to a new print device. To redirect the print jobs, access the properties of the printer that is connected to the failed print device. Click the Ports tab, and then click the port to another printer assigned on the print server. If you need to redirect to another print server, click the Add Port button to add a local port that is directed to the IP address and share name of the other print server.

In Activity 8-10 you review the properties of the Print Spooler service, and use the Services console to restart the service.

Activity 8-10: Configuring the Spooler Service

Time Required: 10 minutes

Objective: View and configure properties of the spooler service.

Description: Dover Leasing's IT manager informs you that in the past printers have stopped printing due to the Print Spooler service hanging. Because of this, he has asked you to familiarize yourself with stopping and restarting the spooler service. In this activity, you use the Services node in the Computer Management console to view Print Spooler service settings and restart the service.

1. Click **Start**, right-click **My Computer**, and then click **Manage**.

2. In the Computer Management window, click the **plus sign (+)** next to the Services and Applications node to expand it.

3. Click the **Services** node to view it contents.

4. Scroll through the list of services until you find the Print Spooler service.

5. Double-click **Print Spooler** to view its properties. Notice that the service is configured to start automatically when Windows Server 2003 starts.

6. Click the **Log On** tab. Notice that the Print Spooler service is enabled as part of the only existing hardware profile.

7. Click the **Recovery** tab. Notice that when the service fails, it is configured to restart automatically.

8. Click the **Dependencies** tab. Notice the services upon which the Print Spooler service depends in order to function correctly. In this case, if the Remote Procedure Call is not running, the Print Spooler service cannot function.

9. Click **OK** to close the properties window of the Print Spooler service.

10. Right-click the Print Spooler service in the list of services and then click **Restart**. Notice the dialog box indicating that the service is restarting.

11. Close all open windows and log off.

CHAPTER SUMMARY

- Windows Server 2003 printing has its own unique terminology, and understanding this terminology is critical towards understanding how print devices function in a Windows environment.

- Printers are configurable objects that ultimately represent an interface to a print device. The primary tool used to install printers is the Add Printer Wizard, available from the Printers and Faxes tool.

- In order for a printer to be made available to network users, it must be shared in a manner similar to a shared folder.

- Printer permissions can be used to control user access to printers and the manner in which users can interact with a printer. Printer permissions follow the same general concepts as NTFS permissions.

- Printers on a Windows Server 2003 system can be configured with different priorities to control the order in which print jobs will be queued before being output to a particular print device.

- Printer pooling can be used to increase the speed and availability of a printer by making use of multiple physical print devices.

- Additional drivers can be installed from the properties of a printer in order to allow access to clients running different operating systems such as Windows 95/98/ME to gain access to a printer.

- The Internet Printing Protocol (IPP) allows printers to be managed via a Web browser, and allows users to print using the HTTP protocol.

8

- For best performance, the print spool folder should be located on its own dedicated partition, preferably on a separate disk than the Windows Server 2003 operating system files.

- Printer publishing allows users to query Active Directory for a list of available printers based on different criteria, such as a printer's ability to print in color.

- Common printer problems encountered on Windows Server 2003 systems include the print device being off-line, misconfigured printer permissions, the Print Spooler service hanging, or incorrect drivers being installed.

KEY TERMS

graphics device interface (GDI) — An interface on a Windows network print client that works with a local software application, such as Microsoft Word, and a local printer driver to format a file to be sent to a local printer or a network print server.

Internet Printing Protocol (IPP) — A specification supported by Windows Server 2003 that allows printers to be managed from a Web browser, and print jobs to be sent to a printer using the HTTP protocol.

local print device — A printer, such as a laser printer, physically attached to a port on the local computer.

network print device — A printing device, such as a laser printer, connected to a print server through a network.

print client — Client computer or application that generates a print job.

print driver — Files that contain information that Windows Server 2003 uses to convert raw print commands to a language that the printer understands.

print queue — A stack or lineup of all requested print jobs waiting to be sent from the spooler to the printer.

print server — The computer in which the printers and print drivers are located. This is usually where you set up and configure the shared printing system.

printer — A configuration object in Windows Server 2003 that controls the connection to the print device.

printer permissions — Security permissions that allow an administrator to control access to printer resources, in a manner similar to NTFS permissions.

printer pool — Consists of a single printer that is connected to a number of print devices.

printer priorities — Configuring multiple printers to print to the same print device. One printer is then configured to print before any of the other printers by adjusting the priority setting from 1 (lowest priority) to 99 (highest priority).

published — An Active Directory object that represents a link to or direct information on how to use or connect to the shared resource.

RAW — A data type often used for printing MS-DOS, Windows 3.x, and UNIX print files.

spooler — In the Windows 95, 98, Me, NT, 2000, XP, and 2003 environment, a group of DLLs, information files, and programs that process print jobs for printing.

TEXT — A data type used for printing text files formatted using the ANSI standard that employs values between 0 and 255 to represent characters, numbers, and symbols.

Windows Script Host (WSH) — A controller for the ActiveX scripting engines provided in both Windows-based and command-line versions.

REVIEW QUESTIONS

1. Which of the following is not a print permission in Windows Server 2003?
   a. Print
   b. Full Control
   c. Manage Documents
   d. Manage Printers

2. Which of the following permissions allows a user to pause not only their own print jobs, but also those of other users?
   a. Print
   b. Manage Documents
   c. Full Control
   d. Change

3. Printers installed on a Windows Server 2003 system are published to Active Directory by default.
   a. True
   b. False

4. Which of the following must be used to invoke the Prncnfg.vbs command from the command line?
   a. Cscript
   b. Wscript
   c. Script
   d. Vbscript

5. Which of the following is the highest printer priority on a Windows Server 2003 system?
   a. 100
   b. 99
   c. 1
   d. 0

6. Which of the following scripts can be used to publish printers in Active Directory?

   a. Pubprn.vbs

   b. Prncnfg.vbs

   c. Publish.vbs

   d. Pub.vbs

7. When a new printer is installed, drivers will be made available for which of the following operating systems by default?

   a. Windows 2000

   b. Windows Server 2003

   c. Windows 95

   d. Windows 98

8. What term is used to describe a printer that can send output to more than one print device?

   a. Printer pooling

   b. Multithreaded

   c. Multihomed

   d. Dual-port

9. The output from a configured printer is garbled. What is most likely the cause of the problem?

   a. The printer priority is incorrect

   b. The wrong driver is installed

   c. The print device is malfunctioning

   d. The wrong port is configured

10. When documents appear to be stuck in the print queue, which of the following services should be restarted?

    a. Print Spooler

    b. Server

    c. Workstation

    d. Plug and Play

11. What is the default printer permission assigned to the Administrators group on a Windows Server 2003 system?

    a. Print

    b. Manage Documents

    c. Manage Printers

    d. Full Control

12. A page that contains user information and prints before a user's print job is called what?

    a. Separator page

    b. Split page

    c. Document handle

    d. Outline document

13. In order to use the Internet Printing Protocol (IPP), which of the following services must be installed?

    a. Clustering

    b. Internet Information Services

    c. Network Load Balancing

    d. Routing Information Protocol

8

14. Which of the following represents the correct URL syntax to connect to a printer named Printer1 on Server01?

    a. http://server01/printers/printer1/.printer

    b. http://server01/.printer

    c. http://printer1/printers/server01/.printer

    d. http://server01/.printer/printer1

15. The printer spool folder is located on the same partition or volume as the WINDOWS folder by default.

    a. True

    b. False

16. In order for a printer to be made available to network users, it must be shared.

    a. True

    b. False

17. Only the drivers supplied with Windows Server 2003 can be used when installing a printer.

    a. True

    b. False

18. Which of the following script files is used to view the print jobs queued on a printer?

    a. Pubprn.vbs

    b. Prncnfg.vbs

    c. Prnmngr.vbs

    d. Prnjobs.vbs

19. Which of the following script files is used to set the default printer on a Windows Server 2003 system?

    a. Prnmngr.vbs

    b. Pubprn.vbs

    c. Prnjobs.vbs

    d. Prndrvr.vbs

20. Only one printer can be designated as the default printer at any point in time on a Windows Server 2003 system.

    a. True

    b. False

CASE PROJECTS

CASE
PROJECTS

Case Project 8-1

Dover Leasing is in the process of adding two new print devices to the network. One is for the Managers group and the other is for the Sales and Accountants groups. Both printers are identical and are connected to two separate servers. You have been asked to advise the Help Desk users about how to set up the printers.

1. How should the new print devices be configured to ensure that network users can connect to them?

2. What permissions should be assigned to those users responsible for managing the printers?

3. Explain how printer permissions are configured so the appropriate groups have access to the printers.

Case Project 8-2

To understand how printer permissions work, consider the information provided in the table below, and then answer the questions that follow.

Users / Printers	Group Memberships / Permissions
User1	Sales Users, Marketing Users, Managers, Domain Users
User2	Help Desk Users, Managers, Domain Users, Domain Admins
User3	Accounting Users, Domain Users, Project Planners
LaserJetA	Sales Users – Print Managers – Manage Documents Domain Users – Print Everyone – Print Domain Admins – Manage Printers
LaserJetB	Domain Users – Manage Documents Domain Admins – Manage Printers Help Desk Users – Print
LaserJetC	Accounting Users – Print Project Planners – Print Everyone – Deny Print Help Desk Users – Manage Documents

8

1. What permissions would User1 have to the LaserJetA printer?

2. What permissions would User2 have to the LaserJetC printer?

3. What permissions would User3 have to the LaserJetB printer?

4. What permissions would User1 have to the LaserJetB printer?

5. What permissions would User2 have to the LaserJetA printer?

6. What permissions would User3 have to the LaserJetC printer?

9

IMPLEMENTING AND USING GROUP POLICY

> ### After reading this chapter and completing the exercises, you will be able to:
>
> ♦ Create and manage Group Policy objects to control user desktop settings, security, scripts, and folder redirection
> ♦ Manage and troubleshoot Group Policy inheritance
> ♦ Deploy and manage software using Group Policy

An important part of your Windows Server 2003 management skills is the ability to effectively incorporate Group Policy into your Active Directory structure. Group Policy allows you to easily manage and control various configurations, such as user desktop settings, desktop and domain security, as well as deploy and manage software.

Another important aspect of Group Policy involves understanding how to control the inheritance and application of Group Policies throughout the Active Directory hierarchy. The following sections discuss these concepts as well as basic Group Policy troubleshooting techniques.

INTRODUCTION TO GROUP POLICY

Group Policy enables the centralized management of user and computer configuration settings throughout your network. A **Group Policy object (GPO)** is an Active Directory object that is used to configure and apply policy settings for user and computer objects. It performs a variety of administrative tasks, including:

- Configuring desktop settings using administrative templates
- Controlling security settings for users and computers
- Assigning scripts to run when a user logs on or off, or when a computer is started up or shut down
- Redirecting folders, such as the My Documents folder, out of a user's local profile to a different network location
- Automating software distribution and maintenance to computers throughout the network

To implement Group Policy, you must first create a GPO or modify one of the default GPOs to meet the company requirements.

There are two default GPOs created when Active Directory is installed. The first GPO is linked to the domain container and is called the **Default Domain Policy**. The second is linked to the domain controllers organizational unit (OU) and is called the **Default Domain Controllers Policy**.

Once a GPO is created, you can then link it to a site, domain, or OU. When you link a GPO to one of these container objects, its policy settings are applied to all users and computers in the container, including those within child OUs.

Group Policy can only be applied to computers running Windows Server 2003, Windows 2000, and Windows XP. If you still have down-level clients, such as those running Windows NT or Windows 9x, you must use system policies to control environment settings.

Creating a Group Policy Object

You can create a GPO in two different ways: use the Group Policy standalone Microsoft Management Console (MMC) snap-in, or use the Group Policy extension in Active Directory Users and Computers. In Activity 9-1 you create a new GPO by adding the Group Policy Object Editor snap-in to an empty MMC.

Activity 9-1: Creating a Group Policy Object Using the MMC

Time Required: 10 minutes

Objective: Use the Group Policy Object Editor MMC snap-in to create GPOs.

Description: The IT manager at Dover Leasing has decided that the company will use GPOs for the purpose of configuring a standard user desktop environment, as well as the deployment of software applications and updates. You have been asked to explore some of the different ways in which GPOs can be created from a Windows Server 2003 system. In this activity, you create a new GPO using the Group Policy Object Editor MMC snap-in.

1. Log on with your **AdminXX** account (where *XX* is your assigned student number).

2. Click **Start**, and then click **Run**. In the Open text box, type **mmc** and press **Enter**.

3. Click **File** on the menu bar, and click **Add/Remove Snap-in**.

4. Click **Add**. In the Add Standalone Snap-in dialog box, click **Group Policy Object Editor** as shown in Figure 9-1 and click **Add**.

Figure 9-1   Adding a standalone snap-in

5. In the Select Group Policy Object dialog box, click **Browse**.

6. In the Browse for a Group Policy Object dialog box, click the **All** tab to display a list of all GPOs that currently exist.

7. In the All Group Policy Objects stored in this domain section, right-click a blank area and click **New**.

8. Rename the new GPO using the name **Test Policy** and press the **Enter** key. Click **OK**, and then click **Finish**.

9. Click **Close** at the Add Standalone Snap-in window, and click **OK** at the Add/Remove Snap-in window.

10. Close the MMC window without saving your changes.

Group Policy objects can be applied to Active Directory sites, domains, and organizational units. In Activity 9-2 you create a number of new OU objects, and then move some existing user accounts into these OUs. Ultimately, these OUs will be used to test the application of Group Policy settings in activities later in the chapter.

Activity 9-2: Creating OUs and Moving User Accounts

Time Required: 10 minutes

Objective: Create new OUs and then move existing user accounts into those OUs.

Description: The IT manager at Dover Leasing would eventually like to take advantage of using OUs as a method of controlling the application of Group Policy settings. In this activity you create a number of new OUs, and then move some existing user accounts out of the Users container and into these new OUs.

1. Click **Start**, select **Administrative Tools**, and click **Active Directory Users and Computers**.

2. Right-click on the **DomainXX.Dovercorp.net** domain object, select **New**, and click **Organizational Unit**.

3. In the New Object – Organizational Unit window, type **Marketing** in the Name text box, and click **OK**. This creates a new OU named Marketing.

4. Right-click on the **DomainXX.Dovercorp.net** domain object, select **New**, and click **Organizational Unit**.

5. In the New Object – Organizational Unit window, type **Information Technology** in the Name text box, and click **OK**. This creates a new OU named Information Technology.

6. Right-click on the **DomainXX.Dovercorp.net** domain object, select **New**, and click **Organizational Unit**.

7. In the New Object – Organizational Unit window, type **Sales** in the Name text box, and click **OK**. This creates a new OU named Sales.

8. Click the **Users** container to view its contents. Right-click on the **Moira Cowan** user account, and click **Move**. In the Move window, click on the **Marketing** OU, and click **OK**. Click on the **Marketing** OU to confirm that the Moira Cowan user account has been moved.

9. Repeat Step 8 to move the John H. Smith user account to the Marketing OU, and the Mark Manore user account to the Information Technology OU.

10. Close Active Directory Users and Computers.

In Activity 9-3 you create a new Group Policy object and browse through various Group Policy settings.

Activity 9-3: Creating a Group Policy Object and Browsing Settings Using Active Directory Users and Computers

Time Required: 15 minutes

Objective: Use Active Directory Users and Computers to create a GPO.

Description: While the Group Policy Object Editor MMC snap-in provides one method used to create new or edit existing GPOs, you have learned that another alternative is to create and edit these objects from within the Active Directory Users and Computers tool. Because this tool is the primary administrative application in use at Dover Leasing, you have decided to explore its integrated GPO management features. In this activity, you create a new GPO and explore some of the settings that can be configured through the use of Group Policy.

1. Click **Start**, select **Administrative Tools**, and click **Active Directory Users and Computers**.

2. Click the **plus sign (+)** next to the **DomainXX.Dovercorp.net** domain object to view its contents, if necessary.

3. Right-click the **Marketing** OU and click **Properties**.

4. Click the **Group Policy** tab.

5. Click **Add**. The Add a Group Policy Object Link window opens. Click the **All** tab.

6. In the All Group Policy Objects stored in this domain section, click **Test Policy** and click **OK**. Notice that the GPO named Test Policy now appears in the list of Current Group Policy Object Links for Marketing.

7. Click the **New** button, type **Marketing Policy**, then press **Enter** to create a new GPO. This new GPO is now linked to the Marketing OU.

8. Ensure that **Marketing Policy** is selected and click **Edit**. The Group Policy Object Editor opens to allow the configuration settings of the Marketing Policy to be viewed and configured, as shown in Figure 9-2.

9. In the User Configuration section, click the **plus sign (+)** next to **Administrative Templates** to expand its contents, and then click the **Start Menu and Taskbar** icon.

10. Double-click **Remove My Documents icon from Start Menu**. Notice that the configuration settings include Not Configured, Enabled, and Disabled. Do not change any configuration settings at this point.

11. Click the **Explain** tab, and read the purpose and notes associated with this setting. Click **OK** to close the window.

12. As time permits, browse through additional Group Policy settings in both the User Configuration and Computer Configuration sections. Do not configure any settings during this exercise.

13. Close the Group Policy Object Editor window when you are finished, along with the properties of the Marketing OU. Leave Active Directory Users and Computers open.

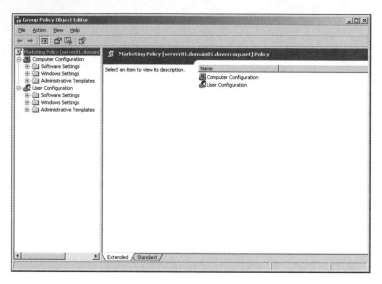

Figure 9-2   Viewing a Group Policy object

Editing a GPO

After a GPO has been created, it needs to be edited to control specific user or computer settings that should be applied. Table 9-1 lists the configuration categories available in both the Computer Configuration and User Configuration sections of a GPO.

Table 9-1   Configuration categories available for GPOs

Configuration Category	Explanation
Software Settings	Centralizes the management of software installation and maintenance; the installation, upgrading, and removal of applications can be controlled from one central location
Windows Settings	Manages the deployment and oversight of scripts, security settings, Internet Explorer settings, and features such as Remote Installation Services and folder redirection
Administrative Templates	Sets registry-based settings to configure application and user desktop settings; this includes access to the operating system components, access to Control Panel settings, and configuration of offline files

To enable a particular setting as you create or edit a GPO, choose the appropriate configuration category in the left console pane of the MMC snap-in and then, in the details pane, right-click the specific configuration setting, and click Properties.

Figure 9-3 shows the User Configuration\Administrative Templates\Control Panel category selected and the properties of the option to hide specified control panel applets. The Setting tab allows you to enable or disable the setting, as well as set any parameters that may be needed. The Explain tab provides information on what the effect of applying that setting is.

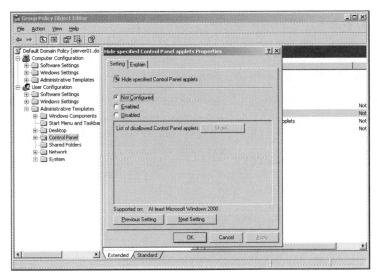

Figure 9-3   Configuring a Group Policy setting

When a GPO is created, the GPO content is stored in two different locations on the server:

- **Group Policy container (GPC)**—An Active Directory container that stores information about the GPO and includes a version number that is used by other domain controllers to ensure that they have the latest information. The version number is also used to make sure that the Group Policy template is synchronized. The GPC is located in Active Directory Users and Computers\System\Policies.

The Advanced Features view must be enabled in Active Directory Users and Computers to view the GPC.

NOTE

- **Group Policy template (GPT)**—The GPT contains the data that makes up the Group Policy. The template includes all the settings, administrative templates, security settings, software installation settings, scripts, and so forth. The registry changes are stored in a configuration file named Registry.pol. A configuration file is stored for both the user settings and computer settings. The GPT is stored in the %systemroot%\Sysvol\<Domain Name>\Policies folder.

The GPC and GPT are identified by a unique 128-bit number known as a **globally unique identifier (GUID)**, which is assigned to the object upon creation. GUIDs are guaranteed to be unique for the entire forest. When a computer accesses the GPO, it uses the GUID to distinguish between GPOs.

In Activity 9-4, you permanently delete an existing GPO.

Activity 9-4: Deleting Group Policy Objects

Time Required: 5 minutes

Objective: Use Active Directory Users and Computers to permanently delete a GPO.

Description: Having learned how to create new GPOs, you are interested in learning what happens if you attempt to delete one of these objects when it has been linked to one or more containers. In this activity, you attempt to delete a linked GPO to learn more about the options presented to you.

1. In Active Directory Users and Computers, right-click the **Marketing** OU and click **Properties**.

2. Click the **Group Policy** tab.

3. Ensure that the **Test Policy** GPO is selected and press the **Delete** button.

4. In the Delete dialog box, click the **Remove the link and delete the Group Policy Object permanently** radio button and click **OK**.

5. When the Delete Group Policy Object dialog box opens, click **Yes**. Notice that the Test Policy GPO is removed from the list.

6. Click **Add** and click the **All** tab to confirm that the Test Policy GPO has been deleted. Click **Cancel**.

7. Click the **Close** button to close the Marketing Properties window, leaving Active Directory Users and Computers open.

Application of Group Policy

GPOs can apply a variety of configuration options to the local computer, site, domain, and OU. There are two main categories to a Group Policy:

- Computer Configuration—Any configuration settings set within this category affect computers located in the container to which the GPO is linked.

- User Configuration—Any configuration settings set within this category apply to any user objects located in the container to which the GPO is linked.

When a computer is started and a user logs on, the following process takes place:

1. A Windows 2000, Windows XP, or Windows Server 2003 computer in a domain starts up. The client computer queries the domain controller for a list of GPOs that it needs to apply. The domain controller examines all of the GPOs to see

which policies apply to the computer. Policies that are executed on the computer include the computer settings and startup scripts.

2. The domain controller presents the client with the list of GPOs that apply to it in the order that the GPOs need to be processed. The computer contacts the domain controller and extracts the Group Policy templates from the Sysvol share, then applies the settings and runs the scripts.

3. When the user logs on, the same process happens again, except this time the user settings, logon scripts, and software policies are applied.

Controlling User Desktop Settings

Companies spend a lot of time and money designing standard computer installation configurations only to have users change settings, thus resulting in nonstandard configurations and increased calls to the help desk. Group Policy helps reduce administrative costs by allowing the enforcement of standard computer configurations, limiting user access to various areas of the operating system, and ensuring that users have their own personal desktop and application settings. Administrative templates consist of a number of administrative configurations, which can be used to apply these settings.

Administrative templates are basically registry settings that can be configured to manage computer and user desktop settings. There are seven main categories of configuration settings that can be applied to either the computer or user section of a GPO.

Table 9-2 explains each of the main categories of configuration settings for administrative templates and the section of the GPO to which each can be applied.

Table 9-2 Configuration categories of administrative templates

Configuration Category	Explanation	Configuration
Windows Components	Configures settings for applications such as Internet Explorer, NetMeeting, Task Scheduler, and the Microsoft Management Console	User and computer
System	Configures settings related to Group Policy, disk quotas, logons, and code signing	User and computer
Network	Configures settings for off-line files and network and dial-up connections	User and computer
Printers	Configures settings related to installing, publishing, and maintaining printers	Computer
Start menu and taskbar	Configures settings related to options available on the Start menu and taskbar	User
Desktop	Configures user desktop settings such as wallpaper, display of icons, and Active Desktop	User
Control Panel	Restricts various icons and applets within Windows Control Panel	User
Shared Folders	Configures shared folder and DFS root publishing settings	User

In Activity 9-5, you create a new GPO that assigns desktop settings to users in the Marketing OU.

Activity 9-5: Configuring Group Policy Object User Desktop Settings

Time Required: 15 minutes

Objective: Configure and test the application of Group Policy settings.

Description: The IT manager at Dover Leasing has asked you to test the use of GPO settings for the purpose of controlling the user desktop environment. In this activity, you attempt to remove the Recycle Bin icon, as well as restrict access to Control Panel for users whose accounts exist within the Marketing OU.

1. Using Active Directory Users and Computers, access the configuration settings of the **Marketing Policy** GPO. See Activity 9-3 for details, if necessary.

2. Under the User Configuration settings section, click the **plus sign (+)** next to **Administrative Templates** to view its contents.

3. Click the **Desktop** folder to view its contents. Double-click the **Remove Recycle Bin icon from Desktop** item to view its properties.

4. Click the **Enabled** radio button as shown in Figure 9-4, and click **OK**.

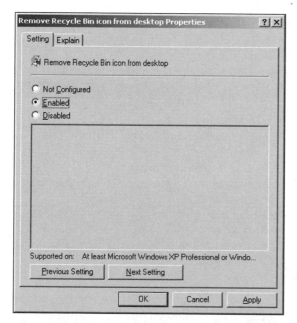

Figure 9-4 Configuring Recycle Bin settings

5. Click the **Start Menu and Taskbar** folder to view its contents. Double-click the **Remove Run menu from Start Menu** item to view its properties.

6. Click the **Enabled** radio button and click **OK**.

7. Click the **Control Panel** folder to view its contents. Double-click the **Prohibit access to the Control Panel** item to view its properties.

8. Click the **Enabled** radio button and click **OK**.

9. Close the Group Policy Object Editor window, close the properties window of the Marketing OU, and then close Active Directory Users and Computers.

10. Log off and then log on as the Marketing OU user **mcowan**, using the password **Password01**.

11. Confirm that the Recycle bin does not appear on the user desktop. Click **Start** to confirm that both the Run command and access to Control Panel are unavailable.

12. Log off and log back on using your **AdminXX** account.

Managing Security Settings with Group Policy

Windows Server 2003 allows an administrator to control a number of security settings using Group Policy. In Chapter 3, you learned that a variety of Group Policy settings could only be configured in GPOs assigned to domain objects, namely Password Policy, Account Policy, and Kerberos Policy settings.

The other nodes under the Security Settings category can be applied to both the domain and OU levels. Here is a summary of the functions of each node:

- Local Policies—Applies security settings to the local account database of the workstation or server; settings may be overwritten at the site, domain, or OU level but remain in effect if there are no other policies at those levels

  There are three subcategories of Local Policies that can be configured:

  - Audit Policy—Defines various successful or unsuccessful events that can be audited and recorded in the event logs

  - User Rights Assignment—Controls local computer rights that may be assigned to users or groups (e.g., the right to log on locally or shut down the computer)

  - Security Options—Defines a wide variety of configuration settings that adjust the registry (e.g., logon banner configurations, restricting floppy or CD-ROM access, and removing the last logged-on user name from the logon screen)

- Event Log—Defines configuration settings for event log size, retention period, and access restrictions

- Restricted Groups—Gives the administrator the ability to control who is a member of any security group; each time the policy is refreshed, any users that have been added to the group by any means other than the security template are removed automatically; can also control the other groups to which a particular security group belongs

- System Services—Allows an administrator control over service startup mode, disabling of a service, permissions to edit the service mode, and auditing of the service

- Registry—Defines security and auditing access control list (ACL) settings for Registry keys and subkeys; allows an administrator to control who has the ability to change or overwrite various registry settings

- File System—Defines and maintains NTFS security permissions and auditing permissions for any folder or file listed in the policy; files or folders must reside on an NTFS partition

- Wireless Network (IEEE 802.11) Policies—Defines security settings for wireless networks, including which wireless networks a client can connect to, whether access points should be used, and the data encryption settings

- Public Key Policies—Defines configuration settings for different public key-based applications like the Encrypting File System (EFS), certificate auto-enrollment settings, and Certificate Authority (CA) trusts

- Software Restriction Policies—Defines security settings for the deployment of software, such as the ability to manually define which file extensions are considered executable, control security settings of software-related Registry paths, and override software settings from other GPOs

- IP Security Policies on Active Directory—Defines different IP Security settings based on the role of a server or workstation; three default policies exist, but none are applied by default

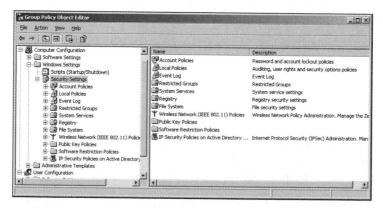

Figure 9-5   Viewing configuration areas under Security Settings

In Activity 9-6 you configure security settings for an existing GPO.

Activity 9-6: Configuring Group Policy Object Security Settings

Time Required: 10 minutes

Objective: Use Group Policy settings to configure a logon banner for domain users.

Description: Windows Server 2003 enables you to configure a variety of different security settings using GPOs. The IT manager at Dover Leasing is concerned about legal issues relating to the fact that the user authentication process does not include any type of warning message about which users are authorized to access Dover's computers. In this activity, you configure and test Group Policy settings to require that users accept the parameters of a warning message before logging on.

1. Using Active Directory Users and Computers, access the configuration settings of the **Default Domain Policy** GPO. (See Activity 9-3 for details, if necessary.)

2. In the Computer Configuration section, click the **plus signs (+)** next to **Windows Settings**, **Security Settings**, and **Local Policies** to expand them.

3. Click **Security Options** to view its settings.

4. Double-click **Interactive logon: Message text for users attempting to log on** to view its properties.

5. Click the **Define this policy setting in the template** check box. In the text box, type **Only authorized users of Dover Leasing are permitted to log on** as shown in Figure 9-6, and click **OK**.

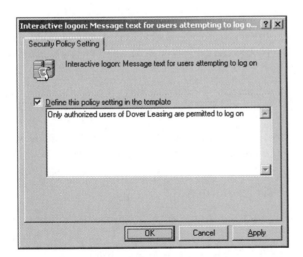

Figure 9-6   Configuring an interactive logon message

6. Double-click **Interactive logon: Message title for users attempting to log on** to view its properties.

7. Click the **Define this policy setting** check box. In the text box, type **Dover Corporate Security Policy** and click **OK**.

8. Close the Group Policy Object Editor window, as well as the properties of Domain*XX*.Dovercorp.net.

9. Close Active Directory Users and Computers and restart your server.

10. Press **Ctrl+Alt+Delete** to begin the logon process. The Dover Corporate Security Policy window opens. Click **OK**.

11. Log on using your **AdminXX** account.

In Activity 9-7 you configure file system security settings using Group Policy.

Activity 9-7: Configuring File System Security Using Group Policy Settings

Time Required: 15 minutes

Objective: Use Group Policy settings to configure security permissions on a file or folder.

Description: Users in the Marketing Department at Dover Leasing use a custom application requiring that a folder named Reports be present on their D: drive. The security requirements of this application dictate that only users in the Marketing Department should have access to the folder. The IT manager at Dover Leasing has asked you to attempt to find a way to use Group Policy settings to configure the necessary folder security, to avoid the need to manually configure each and every computer. In this activity, you test the ability to control file and folder permissions through the use of Group Policy file system settings.

1. Click **Start**, click **My Computer** and then double-click drive **D:** to view its contents.

2. Right-click in a blank area, select **New**, and click **Folder**.

3. Name the new folder **Reports**, and then close My Computer.

4. Open Active Directory Users and Computers and access the configuration settings of the **Marketing Policy** GPO. (See Activity 9-3 for details, if necessary.)

5. In the Computer Configuration section, click the **plus signs (+)** next to **Windows Settings** and then **Security Settings** to expand it.

6. Right-click **File System** and click **Add File**, as shown in Figure 9-7.

7. In the Add a file or folder dialog box, browse to the **Reports** folder on drive **D:** and click **OK**. The Database Security for D:\Reports window opens.

8. Click **Add**. In the Enter the object names to select text box, type **Moira** and click **OK**.

9. In the Permissions for Moira Cowan section, click the **Allow** check box next to the **Full Control** permission and click **OK**. When the Add Object dialog box opens, read the available options and then click **OK**.

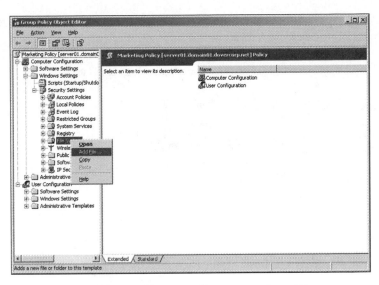

Figure 9-7   Adding a file to configure security settings

10. Close the Group Policy Object Editor window, as well as the properties of the Marketing OU.

11. Click **Start**, and then click **Run**. In the open text box, type **gpupdate.exe** and click **OK**. This will update Group Policy settings on your server.

12. Open My Computer and browse to the **D:\Reports** folder. Right-click the folder and click **Properties**. Click the **Security** tab, making note of the fact that no permissions for the Moira Cowan user account are explicitly defined. Close the Reports Properties window, then close My Computer.

13. Close Active Directory Users and Computers and restart your server.

14. Log on as the user **mcowan** using the password **Password01**.

15. Open My Computer and browse to the **D:\Reports** folder. Right-click the folder and click **Properties**. Click the **Security** tab, making note of the fact that permissions for the Moira Cowan user account are now explicitly defined, as per the GPO linked to the Marketing OU.

16. Log off and log back on using your **AdminXX** account.

Assigning Scripts

Most administrators are familiar with the application of various types of scripts or files that incorporate a number of commands used to automate routine operations. Logon scripts were most popular in the past and used to automate such tasks as drive mapping or application updates.

Windows Server 2003 can use scripts to perform tasks at various times during the logon or logoff process. Group Policy allows you to configure computer startup and shutdown scripts, which are configured in the computer section of a GPO, as shown in Figure 9-8. The user section of a GPO can be accessed to configure logon and logoff scripts.

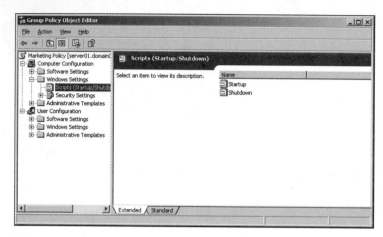

Figure 9-8   Viewing the startup and shutdown script configuration icons

If you assign multiple logon/logoff or startup/shutdown scripts to the configuration containers, each script is run synchronously in order from top to bottom. You can modify the order by selecting the script and clicking the Up or Down buttons in the Properties dialog box. In addition to modifying the order, other policy settings for groups allow you to specify script time-outs, change the running of the scripts to asynchronous, and specify whether scripts are hidden when they are executed.

In Activity 9-8 you assign a logon script to users using Group Policy.

Activity 9-8: Assigning Logon Scripts to Users Using Group Policy

Time Required: 15 minutes

Objective: Use GPOs to assign logon scripts to domain users.

Description: Dover Leasing has traditionally used logon scripts to easily define user environment settings, such as mapped network drives, printers, and so forth. Although the logon scripts in use at Dover currently meet all requirements, they have become very long and difficult to manage based on the specific requirements of users from different departments. Because of this, the IT manager at Dover Leasing has asked you to evaluate the ability to deploy logon scripts using GPO settings. In this activity, you deploy a logon script that maps a drive for Marketing users only through the use of a GPO.

1. Open My Computer, click **Tools** on the menu bar, and then click **Folder Options**.

2. Click the **View** tab. In the Advanced settings section, ensure that the **Hide extensions for known file types** check box is unchecked, and click **OK**.

3. Open drive D: and create a new folder called **Scripts**.

4. Open the Scripts folder. Right-click an area of free space, select **New**, and then click **Text Document**.

5. Double-click **New Text Document.txt** to open it.

6. In the first line of the file, type **net use x: \\instructor\shared**. Save the file and then close it.

7. Right-click **New Text Document.txt** and click **Rename**. Rename the file to **logon.bat** and press **Enter**. When prompted, click **Yes** to confirm the change.

8. Right-click the **logon.bat** file and click **Copy**. Close My Computer.

9. Open Active Directory Users and Computers and access the configuration settings of the **Marketing Policy** GPO.

10. Under User Configuration, click the **plus sign (+)** next to **Windows Settings** to expand it and then click **Scripts (Logon/Logoff)**.

11. Double-click **Logon** to access its properties. Click the **Show Files** button.

12. In the new window that opens, right-click an area of free space, click **Paste**, and then close the window.

13. In the Logon Properties window, click **Add**. In the Add a Script window, click **Browse** and then double-click **logon.bat**. Click **OK** to close the window, and then click **OK** again to close the Logon Properties window shown in Figure 9-9.

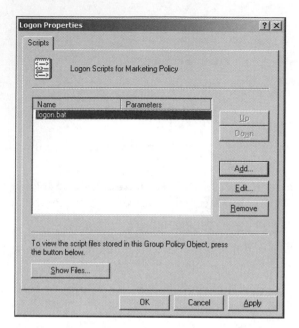

Figure 9-9   Assigning a startup script in group policy

14. Close the Group Policy Object Editor window, close the properties of the Marketing OU, and then close Active Directory Users and Computers.

15. Log off and then log back on as the user **mcowan** using the password **Password01**.

16. Open My Computer and verify that drive **X** has been mapped to the \\instructor\shared folder. Close My Computer.

17. Log off and then log back on using your **AdminXX** account. Open My Computer to verify that drive *X* has not been mapped because the Admin*XX* account does not fall under the scope of the Marketing Policy GPO.

18. Close My Computer.

Redirecting Folders

Folder redirection is a Group Policy feature that enables you to redirect the following contents of a user's profile to a network location:

- Application data
- Desktop
- My Documents
- Start menu

Some of the reasons why you would want to redirect the folders out of a user's profile include:

- Storing the folders on the network ensures that user information is backed up at all times, as opposed to being stored on the local workstation.
- User logon time is reduced because the contents of the folder do not have to be copied from the workstation to the server each time the user logs on or off.
- Folder redirection allows you to create a standard desktop for multiple users.

The Settings tab has a number of options that control the behavior of folder redirection. Table 9-3 describes each setting.

Table 9-3   Folder redirection settings

Configuration Setting	Description
Grant the user exclusive rights to <folder name>	This setting makes sure that only the individual user that owns the folder has access; this is enabled by default.
Move the contents of <folder name> to the new location	This setting moves the contents of the folder to the new location specified; if this check box is cleared, the contents of the folder before the redirection are not moved to the new location (this is enabled by default).
Policy removal	When a folder redirection policy is removed, by default the redirected folder remains in the redirected location; you can choose to redirect the folder back to the user's profile if the policy is removed.

9

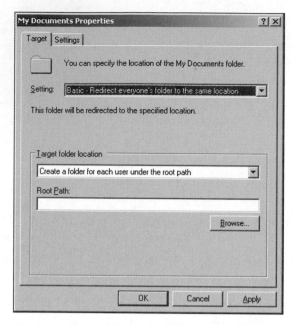

Figure 9-10   Configuring Folder Redirection settings

MANAGING GROUP POLICY INHERITANCE

As a Windows 2000, Windows XP, or Windows Server 2003 computer starts, GPOs are applied in the following order:

1. Local computer
2. Site
3. Domain
4. Parent OU
5. Child OU

All of the individual GPO settings are inherited by default. For example, a Group Policy setting on a parent container is also applied to child containers and, therefore, to all the users and computers in the child containers. One computer or user can process many policies during startup and logon.

At each level, more than one GPO can be applied. If there is more than one GPO per container, the policies are applied in the order that they appear on the Group Policy tab for the container, starting with the bottom GPO first.

Be careful about the number of GPOs that are applied. Computer startup and logon performance can be affected if a large number of GPOs need to be applied to the user or workstation.

Because of the multiple policies that can be applied to a user or computer, there is the chance of a conflict in the settings between policies. The computer uses the following steps to determine which policy to apply:

1. If there is no conflict, then both policies are applied. For example, if a policy at a domain level enables a certain setting and the policy at an OU level has that setting set as "Not Configured," then the domain policy is applied.

2. If there is a conflict, later settings overwrite earlier settings. If both a domain-level policy and an OU-level policy configure the same setting differently, then the OU-level policy is applied.

3. If computer and user policy settings directly conflict, computer policies usually override user policies.

After a user has logged on, the computer refreshes its policies every 90 minutes plus a random number of minutes (no more than 30) so that all the computers don't contact the DC to refresh at the same time. If a user does not shut down his computer, or a setting has changed in the Group Policy, then refreshing the policy ensures that the computer and user settings are up-to-date. Domain controllers refresh their policy settings for groups every five minutes.

You can refresh Group Policy settings manually by running GPUPDATE.EXE from the command prompt. The SECEDIT.EXE command used with Windows 2000 has been replaced with GPUPDATE.EXE in Windows Server 2003.

As mentioned previously, GPOs can be linked to site, domain, or OU containers in Active Directory. This allows the administrator maximum flexibility when applying Group Policies in the domain. There are a number of possibilities for how to apply Group Policy settings in a domain, as outlined in the following list:

- Certain policies that apply to everyone in a physical location can be applied at the site level. Other settings can be configured at a domain level. Some policy settings, such as account policy, can only be set at the domain level. If account policies are set at levels other than the domain level, they apply to local computer accounts and local user accounts on those systems only. Very specific policies can then be set based on OUs.

- Multiple Group Policies can be assigned to one container. Several GPOs can be created that define different settings and then link all of them to a specific container. For example, you might want to create a policy that defines security settings and another that defines user desktop settings, and then link both of them to the same container.

- The same Group Policy can be used to link it to multiple containers. A policy can then be created once and used for different containers. For example, you may create a policy for software distribution and then link that policy to the OUs where the policy should be applied.

In Activity 9-9 you link a Group Policy object to multiple containers.

Activity 9-9: Linking a Group Policy Object to Multiple Containers

Time Required: 10 minutes

Objective: Link a single GPO to multiple containers.

Description: As part of planning the deployment of GPOs for the *DomainXX.Dovercorp.net* domain, you have recognized that there are some cases where users in different departments (but not the entire domain) require the same configuration settings. Instead of configuring multiple GPOs that contain identical settings, you have decided that a smaller number of more generic policies linked to multiple containers might better meet your needs. In this activity, you create a new GPO that removes the Run command from user Start menus and then links that policy to multiple containers.

1. Open Active Directory Users and Computers, if it is not already opened.

2. Expand the **DomainXX.Dovercorp.net** domain if necessary, right-click on the **Information Technology** OU, and click **Properties**.

3. Click the **Group Policy** tab and then click **New**. Type **Remove Run Command**, then press **Enter** to name the new GPO.

4. Click **Edit** to access the properties of the Remove Run Command GPO.

5. Under User Configuration, click the **plus sign (+)** next to **Administrative Templates** to expand it, and then click **Start Menu and Taskbar** to view its settings.

6. Double-click the **Remove Run menu from Start Menu** icon to access its properties, as shown in Figure 9-11. Click the **Enabled** radio button, and then click **OK**.

7. Close the Group Policy Object Editor window and then close the properties of the Information Technology OU.

8. Right-click the **Sales** OU and then click **Properties**.

9. Click the **Group Policy** tab and then click **Add**.

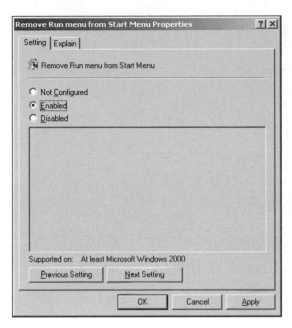

Figure 9-11   Viewing the Remove Run menu from Start Menu Properties

10. In the Add a Group Policy Object Link window, click the **All** tab. Click the **Remove Run Command** GPO and then click **OK**. The Remove Run Command GPO is now linked to both the Information Technology OU as well as the Sales OU.

11. Close the properties of the Sales OU, but leave Active Directory Users and Computers open.

Configuring Block Policy Inheritance, No Override, and Filtering

By default, all policy settings for groups are inherited from parent containers. However, there are several ways to change this default behavior, as outlined in the following sections.

Blocking Group Policy Inheritance

If you do not want any of the higher-level settings to be applied to a particular child container, then check the Block Policy inheritance check box on the Group Policy tab for the container properties. Figure 9-12 shows the interface.

Checking this option means that all higher-level policies for other containers are blocked. For example, if the properties of the Marketing OU were set to block Group Policy inheritance, then GPOs from the site or domain levels would not be applied. Blocking Group Policies can be very useful if you have one OU that has very different policy requirements than all of the other OUs, or if the OU must be separately managed.

9

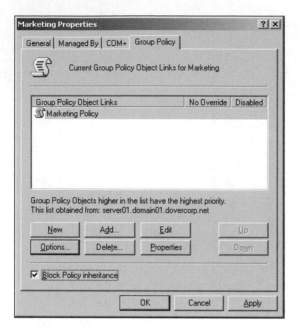

Figure 9-12 Blocking Group Policy inheritance

Configuring No Override

If you want a particular GPO's settings to always be enforced, you can configure the policy using the No Override option, as shown in Figure 9-13.

This results in the policy being enforced even if a lower-level policy that is processed later tries to change a setting. The No Override setting also enforces a policy on a container that has Block Policy inheritance set. Use this option if there is a particular group of settings that must be enforced in the entire network and then link this policy to the domain or site level so that it applies to all containers.

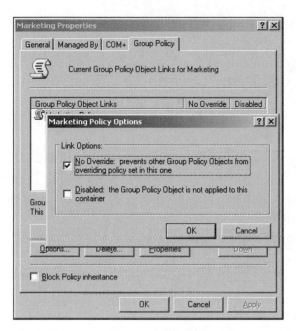

Figure 9-13   Configuring No Override on a Group Policy Object

Filtering Using Permissions

Another way of controlling the inheritance of Group Policies is to prevent policy settings from applying to a particular user, group, or computer within a container. For example, the Marketing OU may have a GPO linked to it, but you don't want the settings from the GPO to apply to the Marketing Vice President. To filter the Marketing Vice President so that she does not have the GPO applied, you could access the security settings associated with the GPO and deny the Read and Apply Group Policy permissions for the Marketing Vice President user account only. This would prevent the Group Policy from being applied to the Marketing Vice President, while the settings would still affect all other users within the OU.

In Activity 9-10 you configure Group Policy inheritance settings for existing GPOs.

Activity 9-10: Configuring Group Policy Object Inheritance Settings

Time Required: 20 minutes

Objective: Configure Group Policy inheritance settings.

Description: As part of his decision to deploy configuration settings using GPOs, the IT manager at Dover Leasing has identified a number of potential issues about how GPOs are processed in Active Directory environments. In particular, the IT manager is concerned that if administration is ultimately decentralized, administrators responsible for a particular OU might configure policy settings that override those configured at the domain level. You have been asked to configure and test Group Policy inheritance settings that ensure settings configured at the domain level can not be overwritten by OU-level configurations. In this activity, you configure and test the Group Policy No Override setting.

1. Open Active Directory Users and Computers (if necessary) and then access the configuration settings of the **Default Domain Policy** GPO.

2. Under the User Configuration settings section, click the **plus sign (+)** next to **Administrative Templates** to expand it, and then click **Start Menu and Taskbar** to view its settings.

3. Double-click **Remove Run menu from Start Menu**, click the **Enabled** radio button, and then click **OK**. This will disable the Run command for all domain users.

4. Close the Group Policy Object Editor window, and close the properties of the DomainXX.Dovercorp.net domain.

5. Access the configuration settings of the **Marketing Policy** GPO.

6. Under the User Configuration settings section, click the **plus sign (+)** next to **Administrative Templates** to expand it, and then click **Start Menu and Taskbar** to view its settings.

7. Double-click **Remove Run menu from Start Menu**, click the **Disabled** radio button, and then click **OK**. This will stop the removal of the Run command for all users in the Marketing OU.

8. Close all open windows and log off.

9. Log on using your **AdminXX** account, noting that the Run command is no longer available. Log off.

10. Log on using the **mcowan** account with the password **Password01**. Note that the Run command is now available because OU-level policies are applied after domain-level policies.

11. Log off and then log on using your **AdminXX** account.

12. Open Active Directory Users and Computers and then access the properties of the **DomainXX.Dovercorp.net** domain.

13. Click the **Group Policy** tab and ensure that the **Default Domain Policy** is selected. Click the **Options** button. Under Link Options, check the **No Override** check box and then click **OK**. Notice the check mark next to the Default Domain Policy in the No Override column. This will prevent settings in the Default Domain Policy from being overridden by policy settings applied at the OU level.

14. Close all open windows and log off.

15. Log on as user **mcowan** using the password **Password01**.

16. Click **Start** to verify that the Run command no longer appears.

17. Log off and then log back on using your **AdminXX** account. Remove the **No Override** setting from the **Default Domain Policy** GPO. Close all open windows.

In Activity 9-11 you use security permissions to filter the application of GPO settings.

ACTIVITY

Activity 9-11: Filtering Group Policy Objects Using Security Permissions

Time Required: 10 minutes

Objective: Use security permissions to filter and control the application of Group Policy settings.

Description: Although the OU structure in place in the *DomainXX.Dovercorp.net* domain was designed with network administration issues in mind, the IT manager is concerned about the fact that in some cases he does not want Group Policy settings to apply to all users. For example, in some departments he would rather not restrict the desktop settings of managers, many of whom find it intrusive. In this activity, you configure and test the ability to filter the application of Group Policy settings through the use of security permissions.

1. In Active Directory Users and Computers, access the properties of the **Marketing** OU.

2. Click the **Group Policy** tab, ensure that the **Marketing Policy** is selected, and then click **Properties**.

3. Click the **Security** tab, and review the permissions associated with the Authenticated Users group. Note that this group has both the Read and Apply Group Policy permissions set to allow.

4. Click **Add**. In the Enter the object names to select text box, type **Moira** and then click **OK**.

5. Ensure that the Moira Cowan user account is selected and then note the permissions associated with the account. Check the **Deny** check box for the **Apply Group Policy** permission. This will stop settings in the Marketing Policy GPO from applying to Moira Cowan. Click **OK**. Click **Yes** in the Security dialog box.

6. Close all open windows and log off.

7. Log on as the user **jhsmith** with the password **Password01**. Click the **Start** menu to confirm that the Run command is available for jhsmith as per the Marketing Policy GPO setting. Log off.

8. Log on as the user **mcowan** with the password **Password01**. Click the Start menu to confirm that the Run command is not available for mcowan because the Marketing Policy GPO does not apply due to permission filtering. As such, the policy settings applied by the Default Domain Policy are applied to the mcowan user account.

9. Log off and then log back on using your **AdminXX** user account.

9

Troubleshooting Group Policy Settings

There may be times when a GPO does not work as expected. For example, restrictions may not be enforced as configured, or may be too restrictive and thus interfere with user productivity.

A careful inspection of the Active Directory hierarchy could possibly uncover the reasons for a Group Policy not working correctly. Do not forget the order of Group Policy processing: local computer, site, domain, and OU. Be sure to inspect all containers above and below the OU that is causing the problem. In some cases, improper use of No Override or Block Policy inheritance settings can cause problems. Another area to be aware of is the Group Policy's Security tab. Make sure that the user or group has been assigned the Read and Apply Group Policy permissions.

Group Policy settings are refreshed every five minutes on domain controllers by default. User and computer Group Policy settings are refreshed every 90 minutes, with a 30-minute maximum offset. Group Policy settings can be refreshed immediately by issuing the GPUPDATE command.

Windows Server 2003 also includes two main utilities that allow you to view the effective Group Policy settings that have been applied to a particular user or computer in the form of the command-line **GPRESULT** tool and the graphical **Resultant Set of Policy (RSoP)** tool. These utilities are useful because they can be used to discover Group Policy-related problems and to illustrate which GPOs were applied to a user or computer. GPRESULT also lists all group memberships of the user or computer being analyzed, along with information about any GPOs that may have been filtered using security permissions.

If you are experiencing performance problems that relate to the processing of GPOs, you may want to disable the unused portion of the computer or user section of the policy. For example, if a particular GPO is only used to apply computer-related settings, then disabling the user configuration section of the policy would improve group policy processing performance. To disable processing of the computer or user configuration section of a policy, access the policy's properties and choose the appropriate setting, as shown in Figure 9-14.

Figure 9-15 shows the output of the GPRESULT command for a specified user.

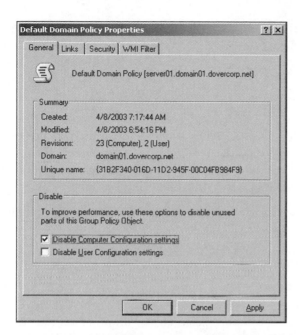

Figure 9-14   Disabling a section of a Group Policy Object

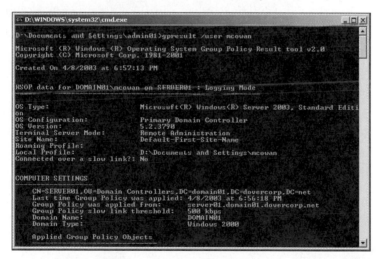

Figure 9-15   Using the GPRESULT tool

In Activity 9–12 you use the RSoP tool to view resultant Group Policy settings for a user on a particular computer.

Activity 9-12: Determining Group Policy Settings Using the Resultant Set of Policy Tool

Time Required: 10 minutes

Objective: Use RSoP to determine effective Group Policy settings.

Description: Although GPRESULT.EXE provides all of the information necessary to troubleshoot effective Group Policy settings, you have decided that the data it provides can be overwhelming from the command line. As an alternative, you have decided to try the graphical Resultant Set of Policy (RSoP) tool. In this activity, you again evaluate the effect of Group Policy settings for a domain user but this time using the RSoP tool.

1. Open Active Directory Users and Computers and then access the configuration settings of the **Default Domain Policy** GPO.

2. Under the User Configuration settings section, click the **plus sign (+)** next to **Administrative Templates** to expand it, and then click **Start Menu and Taskbar** to view its settings.

3. Double-click **Remove Run menu from Start Menu**, click the **Disabled** radio button, and then click **OK**. This will once again enable the Run command for all domain users.

4. Close the Group Policy Object Editor window, and close the properties of the Domain*XX*.Dovercorp.net domain. Close Active Directory Users and Computers.

5. Log off, and then log on again using your **Admin*XX*** account.

6. Open a new MMC and add the **Resultant Set of Policy** snap-in. (Refer to Activity 9-1 for details on opening an MMC console if necessary.)

7. Right-click the **Resultant Set of Policy** icon and click **Generate RSoP Data**, as shown in Figure 9-16.

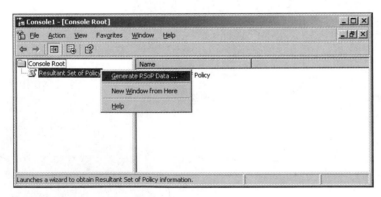

Figure 9-16 Generating RSoP data

8. At the Resultant Set of Policy Wizard welcome screen, click **Next**.

9. At the Mode Selection window, ensure that the **Logging mode** radio button is selected and click **Next**.

10. At the Computer Selection window, ensure that the **This computer** radio button is selected, and click **Next**.

11. At the User Selection window, click the **Select a specific user** radio button. Click the **DOMAINXX\mcowan** user account and then click **Next**.

12. At the Summary of Selections window, click **Next** to begin the analysis process.

13. Click **Finish** to complete the Resultant Set of Policy Wizard.

14. Click the **plus sign (+)** next to **mcowan on ServerXX – RSOP**. Under the Computer Configuration section, click the **plus signs (+)** next to **Windows Settings**, **Security Settings**, and **Local Policies** to expand them. Click **Security Options** to view its settings.

15. Scroll through the list to view the Security Options that are applied to the Moira Cowan user account as a result of Group Policy settings.

16. If time permits, browse through additional sections to view other policies that have been applied to the Moira Cowan user account via GPO settings.

17. Close the MMC without saving changes.

DEPLOYING SOFTWARE USING GROUP POLICY

In addition to managing user desktops, maintaining security, applying scripts, and redirecting folders, Group Policy can also help you deploy and maintain software installations throughout the domain. There are a variety of applications that can be deployed using Group Policy, including business applications such as Microsoft Office, utilities such as anti-virus software, and software updates such as service packs.

When a company rolls out a new software application, there are four main phases that are addressed:

- Software preparation
- Deployment
- Software maintenance
- Software removal

Software Preparation

The first phase of software deployment is to prepare the software for distribution. Windows Server 2003 Group Policy uses a special installation file called a **Microsoft Windows installer package (MSI)**. An MSI file contains all of the information needed to install an application in a variety of configurations. Many software vendors are starting to include preconfigured MSI packages with their applications to enable administrators to take advantage of the features provided by Windows Server 2003 Group Policy. For older applications, you can create your own MSI packages using third-party utilities, such as a program called WinINSTALL from Veritas.

After you obtain or create an MSI package file, place the file, along with any related software installation files, in a shared folder on the network. You configure Group Policy to access this shared folder so that a successful installation is ensured.

If an MSI package is not available for an application, and you cannot repackage the application using an application like WinINSTALL, you have the option to use another file type called a **ZAP file**. A ZAP file is a text file that can be used by Group Policy to deploy an application. However, applications deployed using the ZAP file:

- Can only be published and not assigned

- Are not resilient and do not repair themselves automatically

- Usually require user intervention and require the user to have the proper permissions to install applications on their local computer

 For more information on creating a ZAP file, consult KB article 231747 on the Microsoft Web site.

Deployment

Using Windows Server 2003 Group Policy, applications can be deployed in one of two ways:

- Assigning applications
- Publishing applications

Assigning Applications

When you create a policy to assign an application, any user to which the policy applies has a shortcut to the application advertised on the Start menu. The application is installed when a user clicks the shortcut for the first time or double-clicks a document that is associated with the application. If the user does not click the shortcut, the application is not installed, which saves space on the hard drive.

If the policy was configured in the computer section of the Group Policy, any computer to which the policy applies has the application automatically installed the next time that the computer is started.

One other advantage to assigned applications is that these applications are resilient, meaning that if files were to become corrupted, the application would automatically reinstall itself.

Publishing Applications

When a policy is created to publish an application, the application is not advertised on the Start menu. Users can install published applications by accessing the Add/Remove Programs applet in Control Panel or by double-clicking a document associated with the application. Applications can only be published to users and not to computers.

Configuring the Deployment

Configuring the deployment of the software package involves creating or editing a GPO and then specifying application deployment options. For example, an administrator might choose to assign a certain application to all computers at the domain level, which would automatically install the application the next time individual computers were started. Similarly, a different application might be published to members of the Marketing OU only, allowing users to whom this policy applies to install the application, if necessary, at their own discretion.

In Activity 9-13 you publish an application to users using Group Policy.

ACTIVITY

Activity 9-13: Publishing an Application to Users Using Group Policy

Time Required: 15 minutes

Objective: Publish an application using Group Policy settings.

Description: Dover Leasing has traditionally used Microsoft's System Management Server to deploy software packages and updates to domain users. Although the system is effective, the IT manager at Dover has found it both difficult and expensive to train system administrators in the use of this product. Understanding that Windows Server 2003 Group Policy includes features associated with software deployment, the IT manager has asked you to evaluate the ability to make software available for installation by users without administrative privileges. In this activity, you publish an application to users in the Information Technology OU.

1. Click **Start**, and then click **My Computer**. Double-click on drive **D:**, right-click an area of blank space, select **New**, and then click **Folder**. Name the new folder **shared**.

2. Right-click on the **shared** folder and click **Properties**. Click the **Sharing** tab. Click the **Share this folder** radio button, and then click **OK**.

3. Double-click the **D:\Source\SUPPORT\TOOLS** folder to open it. Copy the files named **suptools.msi** and **support.cab** to the **D:\shared** folder.

4. Open Active Directory Users and Computers and create a new GPO named **Support Tools Publishing** linked to the **Information Technology** OU.

5. Click **Edit** to access the configuration settings of the **Support Tools Publishing** Group Policy Object.

9

6. Under User Configuration, click the **plus sign (+)** next to **Software Settings** to expand it.

7. Right-click **Software installation**, click **New**, and then click **Package**, as shown in Figure 9-17.

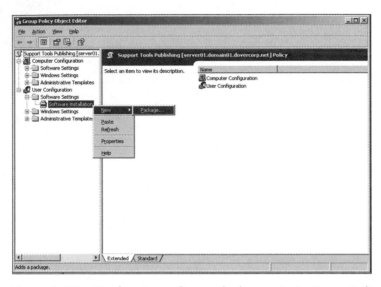

Figure 9-17   Configuring software deployment via Group Policy

8. In the Open dialog box, type **\\serverXX\shared\suptools.msi** (where *XX* is your assigned student number) in the File name text box and click **Open**.

9. In the Deploy Software dialog box, ensure that the **Published** radio button is selected and click **OK**. Click on the **Software installation** icon. Notice that the Windows Support Tools application, source folder, and deployment option information is now listed, as illustrated in Figure 9-18.

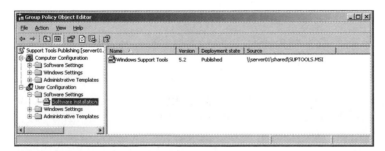

Figure 9-18   Viewing a published application

10. Close all open windows, log off, and then log back on as **mmanore** using the password **Password01**.

11. Click **Start**, click **Control Panel**, and then double-click **Add or Remove Programs**. Click the **Add New Programs** button. Notice that the Windows Support Tools are now available for installation by the mmanore user account.

12. Close all open windows, log off, and then log back on using your **AdminXX** account.

13. Open Active Directory Users and Computers and delete the **Support Tools Publishing** GPO (the entire GPO, not just the link) from the properties of the **Information Technology** OU. Close the properties of the Information Technology OU, but leave Active Directory Users and Computers open.

In Activity 9-14 you assign an application to users using Group Policy.

ACTIVITY

Activity 9-14: Assigning an Application to Users Using Group Policy

Time Required: 10 minutes

Objective: Assign an application using Group Policy settings.

Description: Having now seen the results of publishing applications to users, the IT manager at Dover Leasing has asked you to evaluate whether it is possible to ensure that the Windows Support Tools are always available for all users in the Information Technology OU without the need for them to manually install the application. In this activity, you configure and test a GPO designed to assign the Windows Support Tools to users in the Information Technology OU.

1. In Active Directory Users and Computers, create a new GPO named **Support Tools Assignment** linked to the **Information Technology** OU.

2. Click **Edit** to access the configuration settings of the **Support Tools Assignment** GPO.

3. Under User Configuration, click the **plus sign (+)** next to **Software Settings** to expand it.

4. Right-click **Software installation**, click **New**, and then click **Package**.

5. In the Open dialog box, type **\\serverXX\shared\suptools.msi** (where *XX* is your assigned student number) in the File name box and click **Open**.

6. In the Deploy Software dialog box, ensure that the **Assigned** radio button is selected and click **OK**. Click on the **Software installation** icon. Notice that the Windows Support Tools application, source folder, and deployment option information is now listed. Close all open windows.

7. Restart your server, and then log back on as **mmanore** using the password **Password01**.

8. Click **Start**, select **All Programs**, select **Windows Support Tools**, and then click **Command Prompt**. The Windows Support Tools install, and the Command Prompt opens.

9. Close all open windows, log off, and then log on using your **AdminXX** account.

Software Maintenance

After an application has been deployed, there are various types of maintenance tasks that usually need to be performed. Most vendors provide periodic updates and service patches to fix reported problems with their applications. You have the task of keeping the deployed software updated with the latest service releases. If vendors release new versions of the software, your users may want to transition slowly to the new version. You may want to allow the users to use both the old and new versions of the software.

When deploying application patches or upgrades, you have three choices for how the deployment is performed:

- A mandatory upgrade
- An optional upgrade
- Redeploying an application

A mandatory upgrade automatically replaces the old version of the software with the new version that is being deployed. Figure 9-19 shows the Upgrades tab found in the properties of a deployed application.

Figure 9-19 Configuring a mandatory upgrade

NOTE If the original package and the updated package are both native Windows installer files, the update automatically knows that it is to replace the original package; just the mandatory selection box needs to be configured.

To perform an optional upgrade, do not check the Required upgrade for existing packages option. If the user has installed the original application, all shortcuts still open the first version of the program. To install the upgrade, the user has to access Add or Remove Programs from Control Panel and choose to install the upgrade. If the original version was never installed, clicking the advertised icons invokes an installation of the updated version.

Redeployment of a package means to force an application to reinstall itself everywhere that it is already installed. You may have to do this if you need to deploy an application service pack or hot fix. The main requirement for redeployment is that the patch has to come with an MSI file. To configure redeployment, place the update in the same installation folder as the original application. Open the original GPO that deployed the package, right-click the application, and click All Tasks, Redeploy application.

Software Removal

The final phase of an application life cycle is the removal process. When you need to remove an application that you no longer want to deploy in the organization, Group Policy can save a great amount of time and money. The only caution is that the application must have been originally installed using a Windows installer package.

When removing an application, you are given two choices about how the removal process takes place:

- A forced removal
- An optional removal

A forced removal automatically uninstalls the application from all computers and prevents the software from being reinstalled. The removal takes place either the next time the computer restarts (for computer-based policies) or when the user logs on (for user-based policies).

An optional removal does not remove any of the installed copies of the software, but it does prevent any future installations from taking place. If users remove the application, they are not able to reinstall it.

CHAPTER SUMMARY

- Group Policy enables the centralized management of user and computer settings throughout the network. GPOs can be used to perform a variety of administrative tasks, including configuration of desktop settings, control of security settings for users and computers, assignment of scripts, the redirection of folders, and the automation of software distribution on computers throughout the network.

- Group Policy is applied in the following order: local computer, site, domain, OU, child OU.

- Group Policy is automatically inherited from parent containers to child containers. This can be modified by applying Block Policy inheritance, No Override, or by filtering the policy for specific users.

- When deploying software, Group Policy uses an MSI file to determine the installation options.

- Applications can either be assigned or published within a GPO. Assigned applications are advertised for users and automatically installed for computers. Published applications appear in the Add/Remove Programs applet for users. Computers cannot have applications published.

KEY TERMS

Default Domain Policy — The name of the GPO that is linked to the domain container in Active Directory; used primarily for configuration of domain-wide password policies.

Domain Controllers Policy — The name of the default GPO that is linked to the domain controllers OU. Used primarily for configuration of policy settings that are only to be applied to the domain controllers in the domain (i.e., auditing).

Folder redirection — A Group Policy feature that enables you to redirect the contents of the Application Data, Desktop, My Documents, My Pictures, and Start menu folders from a user's profile to a network location.

globally unique identifier (GUID) — A unique 128-bit number assigned to the object when it is created.

GPRESULT — This utility can be used to discover Group Policy-related problems and to illustrate which GPOs were applied to a user or computer. GPRESULT also lists all group memberships of the user or computer being analyzed.

Group Policy — Enables the centralized management of user desktop settings, desktop and domain security, and the deployment and management of software throughout your network.

Group Policy container (GPC) — An Active Directory container that stores information about the GPO and includes a version number that is used by other domain controllers to ensure that they have the latest information.

Group Policy object (GPO) — An Active Directory object that is configured to apply Group Policy and linked to either the site, domain, or OU level.

Group Policy template (GPT) — The GPT contains the data that makes up the Group Policy. The template includes all the settings, administrative templates, security settings, software installation settings, scripts, and so forth.

Microsoft Windows installer package (MSI) — A file that contains all of the information needed to install an application in a variety of configurations.

Resultant Set of Policy (RSoP) — A graphical utility included with Windows Server 2003 that enables you to review the aggregated Group Policy settings that apply to a domain user or computer.

ZAP file — A text file that can be used by Group Policy to deploy an application; it has a number of limitations compared to an MSI file.

REVIEW QUESTIONS

1. Which of the following MMC snap-ins is used to configure Group Policy settings?

   a. Group Policy Object Editor

   b. Disk Management

   c. Disk Defragmenter

   d. Active Directory Domains and Trusts

2. Which command-line tool can be used to view effective Group Policy settings?

   a. GPRESULT

   b. GPUPDATE

   c. SECEDIT

   d. SFC

3. Joe attempts to publish an application to a computer, but the publish setting is disabled. What is wrong?

   a. Applications can only be published to users

   b. The GPO is corrupted

   c. Applications can only be published to computers

   d. The user is not logged on

4. What is the order in which GPOs are applied?

   a. Local, Domain, Site, OU

   b. Local, Site, Domain, OU

   c. Local, OU, Site, Domain

   d. Domain, Site, OU, Local

9

5. Group policy settings cannot be applied to which of the following?

   a. Users

   b. Computers

   c. Security groups

   d. Distribution groups

6. Which of the following permissions should be applied to ensure that GPO settings apply to users?

   a. Apply Group Policy

   b. Read

   c. Write

   d. Modify

7. Two user accounts in a certain OU need to be configured without a GPO application, while the remaining users still need restrictions. How can this be accomplished?

   a. Allow the Apply Group Policy permission for these users

   b. Block inheritance for the policy

   c. Configure No Override for the policy

   d. Deny the Apply Group Policy permission for these users

8. Published applications are resilient in that they reinstall automatically if any files become corrupt.

   a. True

   b. False

9. Assigned applications are added to Add or Remove Programs, allowing them to be installed by a user if necessary.

   a. True

   b. False

10. When a GPO is created, its content is actually stored in which two locations on the server? (Choose two.)

    a. The Group Policy container within the Active Directory database

    b. The Group Policy container in the Sysvol folder

    c. The Group Policy template within the Active Directory database

    d. The Group Policy template in the Sysvol folder

11. You have created a GPO that removes the Run command and have linked it to the domain level. At the OU level, you have created a GPO to enable the Run command. Which GPO takes effect for a user in this OU?

    a. The GPO applied to the domain

    b. The GPO applied to the OU

    c. Both settings

    d. Neither setting

12. You have just made a change to the computer portion of a Windows Server 2003 GPO and want to manually refresh the policy settings. Which command accomplishes this?

    a. GPREFRESH

    b. SECEDIT

    c. GPUPDATE

    d. GPREF

13. A GPO can use a ZAP file to publish an application for which an MSI file is not available.

    a. True

    b. False

14. If an application has been assigned to a computer using Group Policy, when is the application installed?

    a. When a user logs on

    b. The next time the computer is restarted

    c. The next time the computer is shut down

    d. When a user logs off

15. A user has accidentally deleted a required file on his local machine for an application that you had previously assigned to the domain using an MSI file and Group Policy. What must you do to make sure that the application continues to function?

    a. Redeploy the application using the original GPO and MSI file.

    b. Do nothing; the application automatically fixes itself.

    c. Publish the application to the domain.

    d. Reinstall the application locally on the user's machine using a CD-ROM or the installation point.

16. Which removal option allows users to continue to work with an installed application but prevents any new installations?

    a. Forced removal

    b. Optional removal

    c. Installation removal

    d. None of the above

9

17. In which folder do scripts have to be stored to ensure proper functioning and replication to all domain controllers?

    a. The temp folder

    b. The sysvol folder

    c. The replication folder

    d. The system32 folder

18. For Group Policy settings to apply to a user, that user must be a member of a group with both the Read and Apply Group Policy permissions set to Allow.

    a. True

    b. False

19. You need to redirect the My Documents folder to a server location based upon security group memberships. Which setting do you choose?

    a. Basic

    b. Advanced

    c. None of the above

20. Both the GPRESULT and Resultant Set of Policy tools can be used to view the aggregated Group Policy settings that apply to a user.

    a. True

    b. False

CASE PROJECTS

Case Project 9-1

A fellow administrator is having problems with GPOs not being applied as expected. List five troubleshooting methods that you would use to diagnose problems with GPOs.

Case Project 9-2

Dover Leasing has decided to implement GPOs to configure different settings for all users within the Information Technology OU and its child OUs. All Information Technology users should have the Windows Server 2003 Administrative Tools installed regardless of the workstation that they log on to and have the Run command enabled. Users in the Network Support OU only should have the ability to install the Windows Support Tools if necessary. Finally, all users in the Help Desk OU should have access to the Microsoft Management Console in user mode only. Given these requirements, what OUs should be created and which settings should they contain to deploy Group Policy in the most efficient manner possible?

Case Project 9-3

Dover Leasing has decided to deploy GPOs for the purpose of controlling desktop settings for users in the Marketing OU of the *DomainXX.Dovercorp.net* domain. Although these settings should apply to almost all marketing staff, the IT manager has decided that the new settings should not apply to three marketing executives. Given these requirements, how should Group Policy settings be applied so that only the required marketing users are affected by the new settings?

9

CHAPTER

10

SERVER ADMINISTRATION

After reading this chapter and completing the exercises, you will be able to:

♦ Distinguish between the various methods, tools, and processes used to manage a Windows Server 2003 system

♦ Understand and configure Terminal Services and Remote Desktop for Administration

♦ Delegate administrative authority in Active Directory

♦ Install, configure, and manage Microsoft Software Update Services

Administering a network involves a wide variety of different tasks. On a network that includes Windows Server 2003 systems, an administrator's responsibilities will usually include the administration of more than one server, and as such, require the administrator to be familiar with some of the different tools and techniques that can be used to manage servers remotely.

This chapter begins with a look at Windows Server 2003 network administration procedures, and how tools like the MMC can be used in different ways to manage servers remotely. The concept of secondary logon is also introduced, outlining how an administrator can open tools or issue commands using alternate credentials when necessary.

In larger network environments, an administrator will not always have the luxury of being able to access the desktop environment of a server locally. For this reason, Windows Server 2003 provides access to the desktops of servers remotely via Remote Desktop. This feature can be accessed using a variety of different methods ranging from client software to a Web browser, and allows an administrator to interact with a server as though sitting in front of it. Remote Desktop is effectively a subset of the Terminal Services, a feature that allows users to access and interact with applications installed on a server, again as if sitting at the console of that server. The configuration of Terminal Services settings is also explored in this chapter.

One of the most important roles of any network administrator is to try and determine what level of access different users should be granted in an Active Directory environment. For example, which users should be able to reset passwords, create user accounts, and so forth. Active Directory permissions control the capabilities of different users or groups. In this chapter you learn how these permissions are configured, and how the delegation of administrative authority can be assigned through tools like the Delegation of Control Wizard.

Finally, an absolutely critical component of both server and desktop administration involves ensuring that all systems are up-to-date with the latest security fixes and patches as they are released. In this chapter you learn more about Microsoft Software Update Services, a server software package that can be installed on Windows Server 2003 systems to customize the deployment of critical security updates to client and server systems alike.

NETWORK ADMINISTRATION PROCEDURES

Managing a Windows Server 2003 network environment usually involves having administrative responsibility for more than one server. Because of this, it is important for administrators to be familiar with the primary server management tools and techniques at their disposal. In this section you learn more about using the Microsoft Management Console (MMC) to administer remote servers, how to use the Windows Server 2003 **secondary logon** feature, and some general steps for troubleshooting network issues that may arise.

Windows Server 2003 Management Tools

Windows Server 2003 provides a number of features and utilities to assist in daily server management tasks. Two of these key features are:

- The Microsoft Management Console (MMC)
- The secondary logon feature

Before undertaking any administrative tasks on Windows Server 2003, the network administrator is required to log on to the server. Although the logon process is very similar to previous Windows versions, the steps involved in shutting down or restarting a server have changed. Windows Server 2003 includes a feature known as the Shutdown Event Tracker that logs each time a server is shut down or restarted, allowing you to include comments on why the action took place. This information is logged as event 1074 in the Event Viewer system log. In Activity 10-1, you restart the server to generate a 1074 event, and in Activity 10-2, you view that event in the Event Viewer system log.

Activity 10-1: Restarting Windows Server 2003

Time Required: 10 minutes

Objective: Restart Windows Server 2003.

Description: A server running Windows Server 2003 will sometimes need to be restarted after installing new software or services, or to perform hardware upgrades and maintenance, or because of security issues. Because the Shutdown Event Tracker feature has been implemented in Windows Server 2003, the IT manager at Dover Leasing has decided to implement a new policy where all administrators must provide an appropriate comment explaining the reasons why a server was shut down or restarted. In this activity, you are asked to restart the server to gain a better understanding of this new process.

1. If necessary, log on to your server using your **AdminXX** account (where *XX* is your assigned student number). Click **Start** and then click **Shut Down**.

2. In the Shut Down Windows dialog box, click **Restart** in the What do you want the computer to do? drop-down box. The Shut Down Windows dialog box is illustrated in Figure 10-1.

Figure 10-1   The Shut Down Windows dialog box

3. In the Shutdown Event Tracker section, ensure that the **Planned** check box is checked.

4. On the Option drop-down list, ensure that **Other (Planned)** is selected.

5. In the Comment field, type **Server reboot for testing purposes**.

6. Click **OK** to restart the server.

ACTIVITY

Activity 10-2: Viewing Shutdown Events in the Event Viewer System Log

Time Required: 10 minutes

Objective: Use Event Viewer to view server shutdown events.

Description: All server shutdown events in Windows Server 2003 are recorded as event 1074 in the Event Viewer system log. The IT manager at Dover Leasing wants you to be familiar with the process of checking the system log on a daily basis to determine and document all of the reasons why a server was shut down or restarted. In this activity, you log on to your server and use Event Viewer to locate event **1074** in the system log.

1. Log on to your server using your **AdminXX** account.

2. Click **Start**, select **Administrative Tools**, and click **Event Viewer**.

3. Click **System** in the left-hand pane. The contents of the system log appear in the details pane of Event Viewer.

4. Use the Event column to find the most recent information event with Event ID number 1074. Clicking on the column sorts the contents of the log in ascending or descending order, making items easier to find. Double-click the **1074** event to view its details, as shown in Figure 10-2.

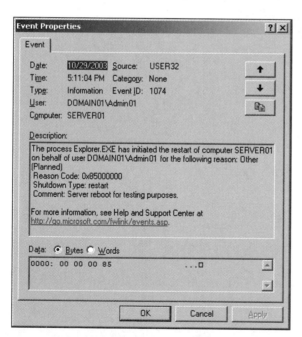

Figure 10-2   The details of event 1074

5. Read the event description data. Notice that both the shutdown type and comment from the last shutdown event are documented.

6. Close the Event Properties window.

7. With the most recent 1074 event still selected, click the **Event** column header to group all events with the same identification number together.

8. Double-click on a different 1074 event to view its contents.

9. Close the Event Properties window, and exit Event Viewer.

The Microsoft Management Console

The MMC is a customizable management framework that can host a number of management tools, thus providing a single, unified application for network administration. The management tools that are added to the interface are called snap-ins and can be obtained from Microsoft or a variety of third-party companies. For example, if you need to create a console to administer your DNS and DHCP servers, you might add the DNS and DHCP snap-ins to an MMC interface. This would provide you with a single administration console to manage both DNS and DHCP.

The advantage of using the MMC is that you can add or remove management tools as necessary and save custom tools for use by authorized administrators. The console is saved as a **Management Saved Console (MSC)** file with the .msc extension.

The supplied Windows Server 2003 Administration Tools, such as Computer Management or Active Directory Users and Computers, are actually prebuilt MMCs with various snap-ins added.

TIP

Perform a search for *.msc to view all of the prebuilt consoles available in Windows Server 2003.

One of the most useful features of the MMC is that it enables you to manage both local and remote computers. By default, most MMC snap-ins will be focused on the computer on which the console is running. However, the focus of many snap-ins can be changed to point to remote clients or servers. For example, an administrator in a domain environment could easily view the Event Viewer system logs on a remote Windows Server 2003 by changing the focus of the Event Viewer snap-in to point to that server. The remote administration capabilities supported by the MMC provide network administrators with a single point of management for common monitoring, configuration, and troubleshooting tasks. In Activity 10-3, you use remote management capabilities of the MMC to view information stored on a remote computer.

ACTIVITY

Activity 10-3: Using the MMC To View Information on a Remote Computer

Time Required: 10 minutes

Objective: Use the remote administration capabilities of the MMC.

Description: Because your domain at Dover Leasing includes many Windows Server 2003 servers, the IT manager wants you to be familiar with the procedure for switching the focus of MMC snap-ins to other computers. This will allow you to gather information and carry out administrative tasks on remote computers using a single management utility. In this activity, you use the remote management capabilities of the MMC to view Event Viewer system logs on another computer.

1. Right-click the **My Console.msc** file that you originally created in Activity 1-5 and click **Run as**. In the Run As dialog box, click the **The following user** radio button. In the User name text box type **DOVERCORP\Administrator** and then type **Password01** in the Password text box. Click **OK**.

2. Right-click the **Event Viewer** icon and click **Connect to another computer**.

3. In the Select Computer dialog box, ensure that the **Another computer** radio button is selected and type the name of your partner's computer in the Another computer text box. This should be in the format **SERVERXX**, where *XX* is your partner's student number. Click **OK** to continue.

4. With the focus of Event Viewer now changed to your partner's computer, expand **Event Viewer** by clicking the **plus sign (+)** to the left. Browse through the system and application logs on the remote computer.

5. Right-click the **Event Viewer** icon and click **Connect to another computer**. In the Select Computer dialog box, ensure that the **Local computer** radio button is selected, and click **OK**. Close the MMC console and save your changes when prompted.

Some of the MMC snap-in tools may be confusing to an inexperienced administrator. To better understand these tools, you can create a **taskpad** view of the console. Taskpad views simplify administrative procedures by providing you with a graphical representation of the tasks that can be performed in an MMC. In Activity 10-4, you create a taskpad that provides access to the Event Viewer system log.

ACTIVITY

Activity 10-4: Creating a Taskpad

Time Required: 15 minutes

Objective: Create a taskpad to simplify administrative tasks.

Description: Although the MMC provides access to all of the Windows Server 2003 administrative tools, situations may arise where users not familiar with the various snap-ins may be asked to carry out a task. Taskpads enable you to define a simplified environment from which shortcuts to common tasks can be created. The IT manager at Dover Leasing has asked you to begin creating a taskpad that will ultimately be used by the network help desk staff for the purpose of checking the Event Viewer system log. In this activity, you create a new MMC and define a taskpad that creates a shortcut to the system log on the local computer.

1. Click **Start**, click **Run**, and then type **mmc** in the Open text box. Click **OK**.

2. Click the **File** menu, and click **Add/Remove Snap-in**.

3. Click **Add** to view the list of available snap-ins. On the list, click **Event Viewer** and click **Add**. Ensure that the **Local computer** radio button is selected, and click **Finish**. Click **Close**, and then click **OK** to close the Add/Remove Snap-in dialog box and return to the console.

4. Right-click **Console Root** and click **New Taskpad View**. Click **Next** at the Welcome screen.

5. In the Taskpad Display dialog box, click **No list**, and click **Next**.

6. In the Taskpad Target dialog box, accept the default settings, and click **Next**.

7. In the Name text box, type **Network Helpdesk Taskpad**. In the description text box, type **Network Help Desk Management Utility**. Click **Next**.

8. At the Completing the New Taskpad View Wizard, click the **Start New Task wizard** check box if it is not already selected. Click **Finish**.

9. Click **Next** at the Welcome screen.

10. Verify that **Menu command** is selected, and then click **Next**.

11. At the Shortcut Menu Command screen, click **Tree item task** on the Command source drop-down menu.

12. In the lower left column, expand **Event Viewer**. Click **System**, and then click **Open** in the Available commands column. Click **Next**.

13. In the Task name text box, type **Shortcut to System log**, type an appropriate description, and click **Next**.

14. Choose an icon for the task, and click **Next**.

15. At Completing the New Task Wizard, click **Finish**.

16. From the Network Helpdesk Taskpad, click the **Shortcut to System log** icon to open the system log, as shown in Figure 10-3.

17. Click the **back arrow**, then right-click **Console Root** and click **Edit Taskpad View**.

18. In the Network Helpdesk Taskpad Properties dialog box, click the **Tasks** tab. Note that you can add additional tasks to this taskpad by clicking the New button.

19. Click **Cancel** to close the Network Helpdesk Taskpad Properties dialog box.

20. Save this new MMC to your desktop using the filename **Help Desk.msc**.

21. Close the console window.

10

Figure 10-3   The Network Helpdesk Taskpad

Secondary Logon

It is a recommended best practice for network administrators to have two logon accounts. One account is granted administrative rights and is only used for network management. A second account has normal user rights and is used for any non-administrative tasks. The problem with this recommendation is that you may have to log on and off many times throughout the day to gain the rights needed to complete your tasks.

To save the time required to log on and off, Windows Server 2003 provides the secondary logon feature. This feature allows you to log on with your regular user account and then open administrative tools as an administrator. In Activity 10-5, you use the secondary logon feature to open Event Viewer using the built-in administrator account.

You can disable this feature by stopping the Secondary Logon service found in the Services administrative console.

Activity 10-5: Using the Windows Server 2003 Secondary Logon Feature

Time Required: 5 minutes

Objective: Use the Run as command to open a program using alternate credentials.

Description: In most network environments, administrative staff members are provided with both a normal user account and one used to carry out administrative tasks. The Run as command provides a simplified way of allowing an administrator to carry out normal network functions as a regular user, while accessing administrative tools with appropriate credentials. The IT manager has decided that administrators at Dover Leasing should follow this model beginning next month. He has asked you to test the Run as command in Windows Server 2003 to see whether it will meet Dover's requirements. In this activity, you use the graphical version of the Run as command to open Event Viewer using the credentials of the domain administrator account.

1. Click **Start**, select **Administrative Tools**, and then right-click **Event Viewer**.

2. Click **Run as**. The Run As dialog box opens. Select the **The following user** radio button on the lower half of the screen, as shown in Figure 10-4. Type **Password01** in the Password text box, and then click **OK**.

Figure 10-4   The Run As dialog box

3. Close Event Viewer.

You can also use a command prompt to start applications under the administrator account. The command to do so is runas /user:<domain\username> cmd. The domain\username is the domain and user account in which you want to start the application, and cmd is the command used to start the application. In Activity 10-6, you use the secondary logon feature to open Event Viewer from the command line.

Activity 10-6: Using the Secondary Logon Feature from the Command Line

Time Required: 5 minutes

Objective: Log on using alternate credentials from the command line.

Description: Although the graphical version of the Run as command is useful for Windows Server 2003 administrators who primarily work from the graphical environment, a command-line version also exists in the form of the "runas" command. This command allows an administrator to open programs from the command line with alternate credentials. In this activity, you start Event Viewer from the command line, again using the credentials of the domain administrator account.

1. Click **Start**, and then click **Run**.

2. In the Open text box, type **cmd** and then press **Enter** to open a command prompt.

3. At the command prompt, type **runas /user:<domain>\administrator eventvwr** where <domain> is the name of your domain in the format DOMAIN*XX*. Press **Enter**.

4. Type **Password01** at the password prompt, and press **Enter**.

5. Event Viewer opens. Browse the various logs in Event Viewer.

6. Close all open windows.

Network Troubleshooting Processes

A major task for you, as a network administrator, is troubleshooting computer and network problems. A systematic approach to troubleshooting helps to define the exact problem and quickly solve it.

A successful troubleshooting process involves the following steps:

1. Define the problem

2. Gather detailed information about what has changed

3. Devise a plan to solve the problem

4. Implement the plan and observe the results

5. Document all changes and results

Define the Problem

Problems are often indicated by some cryptic error message or a general complaint from a user. The first step is to ask questions of the user having the problem. Be specific in your questioning; you want exact answers on what the problem is and how long it has been evident. If possible, you should also try to recreate the problem in a test lab so you can attempt various solutions.

Windows Server 2003 provides the net utility to assist you in identifying specific error messages. At a command prompt, type "NET HELPMSG *number*" (where *number* is the number associated with the error message) to retrieve additional information about a specific error message. In addition, Windows Server 2003 includes a new and improved Help & Support Center that you can access directly from the Start menu. You can also access the Microsoft Help and Support Web site at *support.microsoft.com* to learn the specifics on various error messages.

Gather Detailed Information About What Has Changed

Once the problem is identified, it is important to find out what has changed recently to cause the issue. Important factors to consider include whether any new components have been installed on the computer, who has access to the computer and might have changed previous settings, and whether any software or service patches that were installed recently might be causing conflicts. Knowing any changes that have occurred makes it easier for you to devise a plan to solve the problem, which is the next step in the troubleshooting process.

Devise a Plan To Solve the Problem

Before making any additional changes to the system, you should devise a plan to ensure that no additional problems are created. A rollback strategy should also be in place in case the proposed fix does not work.

When devising the plan to solve the problem, you should consider the following:

- Interruptions to the network or its components (e.g., restarting the server)
- Possible changes to the network security policy (e.g., permission or group membership changes, firewall adjustments, etc.)
- The need to document all changes and troubleshooting steps

Implement the Plan and Observe Results

Once you have devised a plan, be sure to notify all users on the network if availability will be interrupted. As you implement your plan, do not make too many configuration changes at one time. It can be difficult to roll back or test a specific step if too many changes have taken place.

Once you implement your plan, if the problem still occurs, you must document what was tested or adjusted up to this point and start the troubleshooting process all over again.

Document All Changes and Results

It is essential that you document all troubleshooting steps, results, and configuration changes to keep track of what has changed on the network. If the problem occurs again, the documentation helps explain the possible cause and provide the solution that was discovered during the previous troubleshooting phase.

10

CONFIGURING TERMINAL SERVICES AND REMOTE DESKTOP FOR ADMINISTRATION

Terminal Services provides remote access to a server desktop through "thin client" software, which serves as a terminal emulator. Terminal Services transmits only the user interface of the program to the client. The client then returns keyboard and mouse clicks back to be processed by the server. Traditionally, Terminal Services has been used for two main purposes: centralized access to applications for users, and remote administration of servers. In Windows Server 2003, the ability of users to connect to a server for the purpose of running applications is properly referred to as Terminal Services. However, the ability of an administrator to connect to a server for administration purposes is now known as **Remote Desktop for Administration**. Although Remote Desktop for Administration is installed as part of Windows Server 2003, the feature is disabled by default. Terminal Services is not installed unless explicitly added to a server by an administrator.

Terminal Services can be used to centralize control of applications, allowing organizations to maintain control over specific applications such as financial applications. With Remote Desktop for Administration, a server administrator can remotely access management tools, such as Active Directory Users and Computers, the Computer Management tool, the DNS tool, and others as if physically sitting in front of that server.

In the next section of this chapter, you learn how to install and manage both Terminal Services and Remote Desktop for Administration.

Enabling Remote Desktop for Administration

The ability to enable Remote Desktop for Administration is a rather simple process. Because it is installed by default, an administrator only needs to change a single setting in the Control Panel System program to allow connections to occur. By default, only members of the Administrators group can connect to a server using Remote Desktop for Administration. However, additional users can also be granted access via the System program. To connect to a server using Remote Desktop for Administration, users need to access the Remote Desktop Connection software from their client system. In Activity 10-7, you enable and then connect to your server using a Remote Desktop connection.

Activity 10-7: Enabling and Testing Remote Desktop for Administration

Time Required: 10 minutes

Objective: Enable and test Remote Desktop for Administration.

Description: To help reduce administrative costs, the IT manager at Dover Leasing is interested in using the Remote Desktop for Administration feature of Windows Server 2003 to facilitate administrator access to corporate servers. In this activity, you first enable

Remote Desktop for Administration on your server and then connect to the server using the Remote Desktop Connection tool.

1. Click **Start**, select **Control Panel**, and then click **System**.

2. Click the **Remote** tab.

3. Click the **Allow users to connect remotely to this computer** check box, as shown in Figure 10-5.

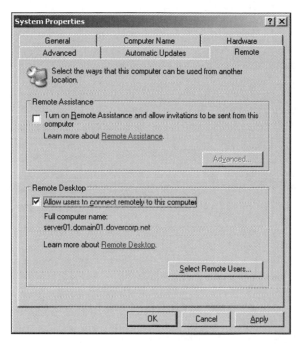

Figure 10-5   The Remote tab of the System program

4. When the Remote Sessions dialog box opens, click **OK**.

5. Click the **Select Remote Users** button. Read the dialog box that opens, and then click **OK**.

6. Click **OK** to close the System Properties dialog box.

7. Click **Start**, select **All Programs**, select **Accessories**, select **Communications**, and then click **Remote Desktop Connection**.

8. In the Remote Desktop Connection dialog box, type **192.168.1.XX** in the Computer text box, where *XX* is your assigned student number. Click the **Options** button.

9. On the General tab, type **AdminXX** in the User name text box if necessary, your password in the Password text box, and **DomainXX.Dovercorp.net** in the Domain text box, as illustrated in Figure 10-6. Click **Connect**.

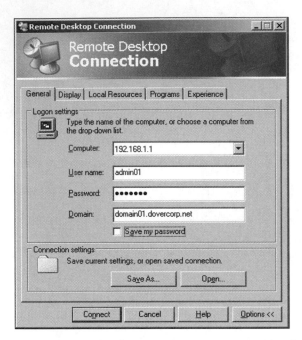

Figure 10-6   Configuring a username, password, and domain name for Remote Desktop
Connection

10. When the Remote Desktop window opens displaying your desktop, browse through
    the environment as time permits. Click the **Close** button on the connection bar
    found at the top of the screen.

11. When the Disconnect Windows session dialog box opens, read the message and then
    click **Cancel**. If this method is used to close a Remote Desktop session, the session
    remains active on the server.

12. In the Remote Desktop window, click **Start**, and then click **Log Off**. Click the **Log
    Off** button. This closes the Remote Desktop session.

Installing Terminal Services

Terminal Services is installed from the Add/Remove Windows Components section of the
Add or Remove Programs applet found in Control Panel. Also, if you plan to set up an
application server, then one Windows Server 2003 server on the network must also be
configured as a Terminal Services licensing server, which would necessitate installing this
option. In Activity 10-8, you install Terminal Services on your server.

Windows Server 2003 is capable of running without a license server for up to
120 days. After that period of time, clients will not be able to connect to a
Terminal Server unless a license server is present on the network.

Activity 10-8: Installing Terminal Services

Time Required: 10 minutes

Objective: Install Windows Server 2003 Terminal Services.

Description: Based on the number of client applications to which Dover Leasing employees need access, related administrative tasks are taking up a disproportionate amount of time for the company's IT staff. Because of this, the IT manager at Dover Leasing is seriously considering implementing Terminal Server to centralize the install, management, and access of a number of applications. In this activity, you install Terminal Services on your server.

1. Click **Start**, select **Control Panel**, and then click **Add or Remove Programs**.

2. Click the **Add/Remove Windows Components** button.

3. In the Windows Components Wizard window, click the check box next to **Terminal Server**. If a Configuration Warning dialog box appears, click **Yes**. Click **Next**.

4. At the Terminal Server setup screen, read the message that appears, and click **Next**.

5. At the Terminal Server Setup screen, read the options associated with both Full Security and Relaxed Security, as illustrated in Figure 10-7. Leave the Full Security radio button selected, and click **Next**.

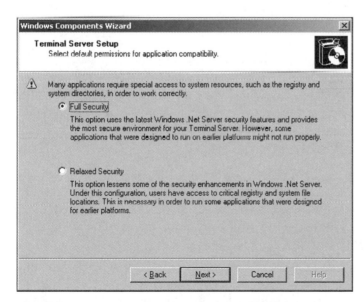

Figure 10-7   The Terminal Server Setup screen

6. Click **Finish** to complete the installation of Terminal Server. When prompted to restart your server, click **Yes**.

7. Log on with your **AdminXX** user account once the reboot is complete. Close the Terminal Server Help window that appears.

 By default, members of the Domain Users group are added to the Remote Desktop Users group when Terminal Server is installed. The Remote Desktop Users group has the ability to log on to a Terminal Server by default.

Managing Terminal Services

There are various tools available to administer a computer running Terminal Services once it is installed. The three primary tools used for Terminal Services administration include Terminal Services Manager, Terminal Services Configuration, and Terminal Services Licensing.

Table 10-1 describes the Terminal Services administration tools.

Table 10-1   Terminal Services administrative tools

Administrative Tool	Description
Terminal Services Manager	monitors and controls client access to one or more terminal servers
Terminal Services Configuration	configures terminal server settings and connections
Terminal Services Licensing	stores and tracks Terminal Services client access licenses

In the following sections, you learn how to configure remote connections and a Terminal Services client, how to install applications, and how to configure Terminal Services user properties. After you complete these sections, you have all the knowledge you need to create and configure a Terminal Server and provide client access to installed applications.

Configuring Remote Connection Settings

Before configuring client access to a Terminal Server, it is important that you configure the various security and connection-related settings that you require using the Terminal Services Configuration tool. This tool allows you to configure settings related to connection attempts, such as the level of encryption or authentication that is required, or the permissions assigned to various user or group accounts.

Connection settings for a Terminal Server are configured from the properties of a Terminal Server connection object. By default, one connection object exists, which allows multiple user connections to take place. Table 10-2 describes the various configuration areas found within the properties of a connection object.

Table 10-2   Property tabs for a terminal connection

Tab	Description
General	Configures authentication and encryption
Logon Settings	Configures how the user logs on, by supplying information or using pre-configured information
Sessions	Configures timeout settings
Environment	Configures a program to run automatically when a user connects
Remote Control	Enables remote control of a client
Client Settings	Configures client settings such as drive mappings and port mappings
Network Adapter	Configures the number of simultaneous connections
Permissions	Controls user access based on standard permissions, such as allow or deny access

Some of the settings outlined in Table 10-2 can also be configured on a user-by-user basis under the properties of a user account. Any settings configured for a connection override those configured on a user account.

One of the most important settings that you should check when configuring a Terminal Server connection is the implementation of encryption and authentication. Authentication can be set to use either no authentication or standard Windows authentication when the clients are Windows 95, 98, NT, or 2000. The encryption options available include:

- Client Compatible—All data is encrypted and sent from the client to the server using a key based on the maximum strength supported by the client

- High—Data sent from the client to the server and from the server to the client is encrypted at the server using the highest encryption level available. Clients that do not support this level will not be able to connect.

In Activity 10-9, you explore connection settings for your Terminal Server.

Activity 10-9: Exploring Terminal Services Settings

Time Required: 10 minutes

Objective: Explore Terminal Services settings.

Description: As part of considering the implementation of Terminal Servers at Dover Leasing, the IT manager is very concerned about retaining a high degree of control over the user environment and how users connect to the server. In this activity, you use the Terminal Services Configuration tool to configure settings related to a client connection.

1. Click **Start**, select **Administrative Tools**, and then click **Terminal Services Configuration**. The Terminal Services Configuration window opens, as illustrated in Figure 10-8.

2. Right-click the **RDP-Tcp** icon and click **Properties**.

3. On the General tab, click the **Use standard Windows authentication** check box.

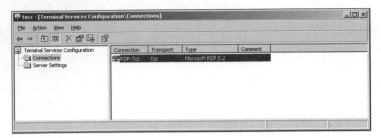

Figure 10-8   The Terminal Services Configuration window

4. Click the **Logon Settings** tab. Click the **Always prompt for password** check box.

5. Click the **Sessions** tab. Click the **Override user settings** check box. In the End a disconnected session list box, click **1 day**. In the Idle session limit list box, click **2 hours**, as illustrated in Figure 10-9.

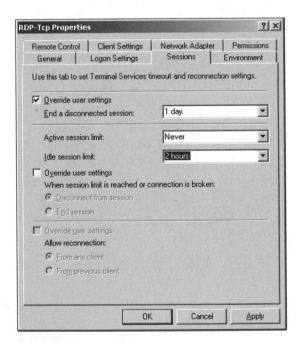

Figure 10-9   Configuring Session settings

6. Click the **Environment** tab and read through the purpose of the settings that appear.

7. Click the **Remote Control** tab and read through the purpose of the settings that appear.

8. Click the **Client Settings** tab and read through the purpose of the settings that appear, as illustrated in Figure 10-10.

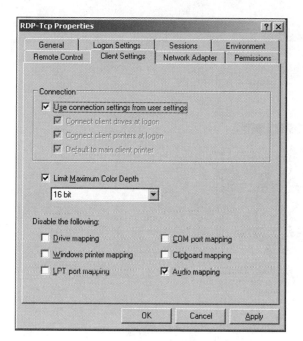

Figure 10-10   The Client Settings tab

 9. Click the **Network Adapter** tab and read through the purpose of the settings that appear.

10. Click the **Permissions** tab, and then click **Remote Desktop Users** in the Group or user names list box. Notice that this group has only the Allow User Access and Guest Access permissions by default, as illustrated in Figure 10-11.

11. Click **OK** to close the RDP-Tcp properties dialog box, and then close the Terminal Services Configuration window.

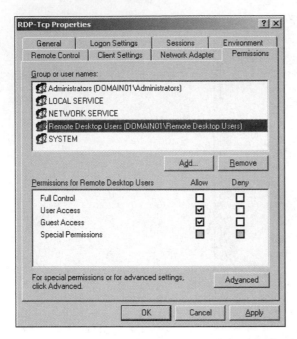

Figure 10-11   Permissions associated with the Remote Desktop Users group

Terminal Services Client Software

Once Terminal Server is installed, client software packages are automatically added to the %Systemroot%\system32\clients\tsclient\win32 folder on the Terminal Server. This folder contains the files necessary to install the **Remote Desktop Connection** software that is used by clients to connect to a Windows Server 2003 Terminal Server. The client software is provided as both an MSI file (msrdpcli.msi) and as a standard Win32 executable (setup. exe). The MSI file is particularly convenient because it can be deployed using Active Directory Group Policy settings. These files can be installed on a variety of operating systems including Window 95, 98, NT 4.0, and 2000. Installation of the client files is not necessary on Windows Server 2003 or Windows XP because the Remote Desktop Connection software is already installed on these operating systems by default.

The recommended method of installing the Remote Desktop Connection software is to share the %Systemroot%\system32\clients\tsclient\win32 folder and then initiate the installation process over the network either manually or through the use of Group Policy software deployment features.

 Windows Server 2003 is also capable of handling client connections via a Web browser if the Remote Desktop Web Connection is installed on the server. See Help and Support Center for more information.

NOTE

Installing Applications

When you install Windows Server 2003 Terminal Server, applications need to be installed in a compatible mode for multiple users to access them simultaneously. For this reason, you may need to reinstall some applications, as indicated by the Windows Components Wizard when you install Terminal Services. The proper method of installing applications involves using the Add or Remove Programs applet in Control Panel after Terminal Server is installed. Use the same applet to uninstall and reinstall programs that were installed before setting up the server for Terminal Server.

On a terminal server, software applications should be installed only in what is known as **install mode**, which is automatically invoked when Add or Remove Programs in Control Panel is used. You should avoid installing programs by using the Run option or by double-clicking the installation program from Windows Explorer or My Computer. However, it is possible to place a Windows Server 2003 system in install mode from the command line if you choose to circumvent the Add or Remove Programs method. To do this, first issue the command CHANGE USER /INSTALL. Then, after installing the application normally, issue the command CHANGE USER /EXECUTE to switch back to **user mode**. This will ensure that the program is installed in a multiuser mode compatible with Terminal Server.

Configuring Terminal Services User Properties

When Terminal Server is installed in Windows Server 2003, it adds extra configuration options to the properties of user accounts. There are four extra tabs available when Terminal Server is installed:

- Terminal Services Profile—This tab enables the user as a Terminal Services client, to configure a special profile used when users connect to a terminal server, and to configure a home directory.

- Remote control—This tab configures remote control properties for the user account. These settings can also be configured under the properties for the connection and any settings specified under the user account properties can then be overridden.

- Sessions—This tab configures a maximum session time and disconnect options. These properties can also be configured under the properties for the connection and any settings configured under the user account can then be overridden.

- Environment—This tab configures a program to automatically run when the user connects to the terminal server. For example, you can use this tab to configure a special logon script to be run when a user connects to the terminal server.

In Activity 10-10 you explore Terminal Services user account settings.

10

Activity 10-10: Exploring Terminal Services User Account Settings

Time Required: 10 minutes

Objective: Explore Terminal Services user account settings.

Description: Although you can configure general connection and environment settings on a global basis using the Terminal Services Configuration tool, the IT manager at Dover Leasing has asked you to explore the various settings that can be configured in the properties of a user account relating to the service. In this activity, you explore the various tabs added to the properties of a user account after Terminal Server is installed.

1. Click **Start**, select **Administrative Tools**, and click **Active Directory Users and Computers**. Click the **Users** folder to display its contents, if necessary.

2. Right-click the **AdminXX** account and then click **Properties**.

3. Click the **Terminal Services Profile** tab, as displayed in Figure 10-12. This tab allows you to configure specific user profile settings used when a user initiates a Terminal Server connection.

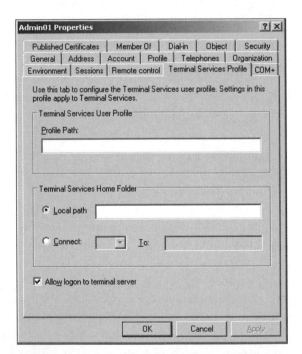

Figure 10-12   The Terminal Services Profile tab

4. Click the **Remote control** tab. This tab allows you to configure settings related to whether an administrator is allowed to connect to and control a user's Terminal Server session, as illustrated in Figure 10-13.

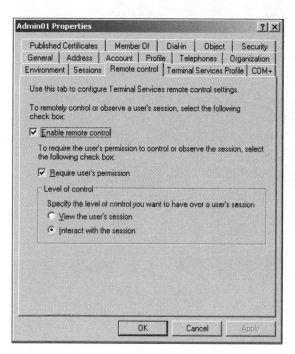

Figure 10-13   The Remote control tab

5. Click the **Sessions** tab. This tab allows you to configure session settings for this user only.

6. Click the **Environment** tab. This tab allows you to configure settings related to the user's Terminal Server environment, such as whether a program is run when the user logs on, as illustrated in Figure 10-14.

7. Close all open windows.

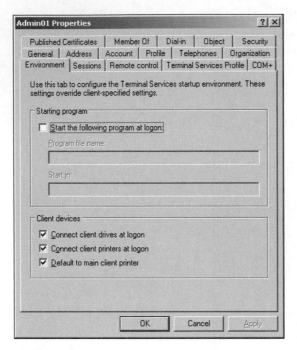

Figure 10-14   The Environment tab

DELEGATING ADMINISTRATIVE AUTHORITY

Active Directory is a database that must be protected like any other network resource. Active Directory uses permissions much like regular NTFS file permissions to protect the creation, deletion, or viewing of objects within the database. By default, administrators have full access to all objects within the domain. Users are given the initial permission to read most attributes of the objects stored in the database. You, as an administrator, can easily edit the object permissions within the database, although care must be taken not to assign permissions that might make an object inaccessible by everyone including yourself.

Active Directory Object Permissions

Active Directory objects can be assigned permissions at two levels:

- Object-level permissions—Define which types of objects a user or group can view, create, delete, or modify within Active Directory
- Attribute-level permissions—Define which attributes of a certain object a user or group can view or modify within Active Directory

Object-level permissions must be granted for a user to have the right to create or modify an object such as an OU, user, or group account. **Attribute-level permissions** are administered to control which attributes a user or group can view or modify. For example, if you want the address information of user accounts to be viewed only by the Human Resources Department, you would modify the attribute-level permissions to apply this restriction.

Object-level permissions can be applied according to a preconfigured set of standard permissions. Table 10-3 lists some common standard permissions available for most objects in Windows Server 2003.

Table 10-3 Common standard permissions available in Windows Server 2003 Active Directory

Permission	Description
Full Control	Performs all standard permissions plus change permissions and take ownership of an Active Directory
Read	Views Active Directory objects and their attributes
Create All Child Objects	Adds child objects to an OU
Delete All Child Objects	Removes child objects from an OU

10

For each permission listed in Table 10-3, you can allow, deny, or not specify the permission. If you do not explicitly select the Allow or Deny check boxes to specify a permission, you allow the object to inherit the permission settings from its parent container. In Activity 10-11 you explore Active Directory object permissions.

Activity 10-11: Exploring Active Directory Object Permissions

Time Required: 10 minutes

Objective: Use Active Directory Users and Computers to explore Active Directory object permission settings.

Description: The ability to administer resources in a granular fashion is one of the main reasons that Dover Leasing originally decided to implement Windows Server 2003 and Active Directory. The IT manager at Dover has asked you to evaluate the ability to configure permissions on both objects and their properties to see whether this is a reasonable way to attempt to control administration capabilities throughout the forest. In this activity, you explore the various permission settings for Active Directory objects.

1. Click **Start**, select **Administrative Tools**, and then click **Active Directory Users and Computers**.

2. Click **View** on the menu bar, and click **Advanced Features**. Notice a number of additional containers and objects appear in the Active Directory Users and Computers interface.

3. Right-click the **Sales** OU and click **Properties**.

4. Click the **Security** tab, as illustrated in Figure 10-15.

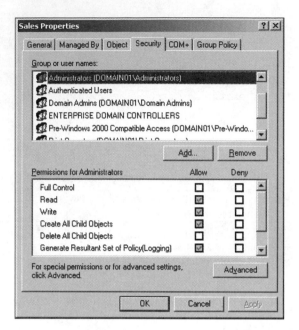

Figure 10-15   The Security tab of the Sales OU

5. Click some of the different group names found in the Group or user names list. As different groups are selected, the corresponding permissions found at the bottom of the screen are shown for that group. Note the difference in permissions available for the Domain Admins group versus the Account Operators group. Note also that some permissions are inherited, whereas others are configured directly on the object.

6. Click the **Advanced** button. On the Permissions tab, there is a list of all permissions assigned to the object, as shown in Figure 10-16. In the Permission entries section, double-click the first entry for the Account Operators group. This shows the details of the permission entry.

7. Use the scroll bar to view the individual object permissions included in this permission entry.

8. Click the **Properties** tab and use the scroll bar to view the permissions associated with individual account properties.

9. Click the **Apply onto** list arrow to view all of the different ways in which permissions can be applied to objects and their properties.

10. Click **Cancel** to close the Permission Entry for Sales dialog box, click **Cancel** to close the Advanced Security Settings for the Sales OU, and then click **Cancel** again to close the Sales OU properties.

11. Leave Active Directory Users and Computers open.

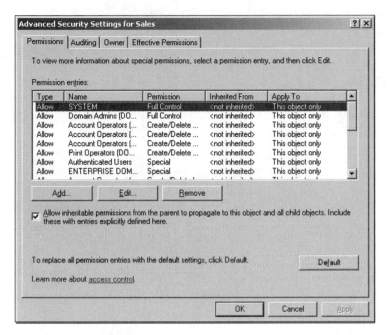

Figure 10-16   Viewing detailed permissions for the Account Operators group

NOTE   The Advanced Features mode must be turned on for you to view the Security tab on each object in Active Directory. To turn on the Advanced Features setting, click View on the menu bar in Active Directory Users and Computers and click Advanced Features.

Permission Inheritance

By default, all child objects inside a container object inherit permissions from parent objects. By using this inheritance and planning carefully, you can eliminate the need to assign permissions to every container object or to every object inside a container. The permissions are inherited from the parent container when the object is created. If the permissions to the parent container are changed after the child object has been created, the permissions can be forced to the child container by ensuring that all child objects inherit any change in permissions. You can do this by selecting "This object and all child objects" in permission entries for the Active Directory parent container.

You can modify the default inheritance of permissions by blocking the inheritance at a container or object level. For example, you may want to have all of the permissions that are set at an upper-level OU inherited by all child OUs except for one. You may want to give the Help Desk personnel the right to reset the passwords for all of the users at the corporate head office OU except for the executives. In this case, you could put all of the executives in an Executives OU, and then accept the default inheritance for all child OUs but block the inheritance for the Executives OU.

Delegating Authority Over Active Directory Objects

The delegation of administration allows you to distribute and decentralize the process of administering Active Directory. To accomplish this goal, the first step is to design the OU structure so that the administration work can be distributed. For example, you may want to assign the task of managing one small part of the network to a junior administrator or an administrator in a remote location. Creating an OU and then delegating the administrative control to that person is an ideal solution to accomplish this step.

The second step in delegating the administrative control is to configure the appropriate level of administrative permissions for each administrator. You may want to give another administrator full control of one particular OU, but you may not want that person to have any administrative permissions anywhere else. Again, assigning permissions to specific OUs allows you to achieve this goal.

Implementing Delegation

You can manage the permissions on every Active Directory object by directly viewing and modifying the Security tab on the object. However, this can be a very complicated task, especially if you are delegating a variety of tasks in a complex OU structure.

To make the delegation quicker and easier, Windows Server 2003 provides the **Delegation of Control Wizard**. This wizard guides you through the process of determining the permissions that you want to delegate and then configures the permissions for the object and child objects. In Activity 10–12 you explore settings related to the Delegation of Control Wizard.

Activity 10-12: Using the Delegation of Control Wizard

Time Required: 10 minutes

Objective: Use the Active Directory Users and Computers Delegation of Control Wizard to delegate control of an OU.

Description: After you walked the IT manager through the permission settings in the previous exercises, he decided that, although the level of granularity was useful, it would also be difficult to track any mistakes that might be made. Instead, he has asked you to evaluate the Delegation of Control Wizard to see whether it represents a feasible alternative. In this activity, you use the wizard to attempt to grant help desk staff the ability to reset passwords for users in the marketing OU.

1. In Active Directory Users and Computers, right-click the **Marketing** OU and click **Delegate Control**. The Delegation of Control Wizard starts.

2. Click **Next** at the Welcome screen.

3. At the Users or Groups screen, click **Add**. In the Enter the object names to select text box, type **Help Desk Users**, click **OK**, and click **Next**.

4. At the Tasks to Delegate screen illustrated in Figure 10-17, click the **Reset user passwords and force password change at next logon** check box under Delegate the following common tasks. Click **Next**.

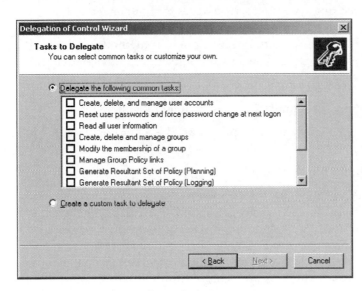

Figure 10-17   The Tasks to Delegate screen

5. Click **Finish** to complete the Delegation of Control Wizard.

6. Click the **Marketing** OU to display its contents, if necessary.

7. Right-click the **Moira Cowan** user account, then click **Properties**. Click the **Security** tab, and then click the **Advanced** button.

8. Scroll through the Permission Entries until you find the **Reset Password** entry for the Help Desk Users group. Double-click this entry to view it.

9. Scroll through the Permissions list on the Object tab until you find the Reset Password permission. Notice that this permission is allowed for the Help Desk Users group and has been inherited from the Marketing OU.

10. Close all open windows and exit Active Directory Users and Computers.

If you decide to change the permissions you have granted to a user, you can run the Delegation of Control Wizard again and assign new permissions to the user. The new permissions overwrite or add to all previous permissions.

SOFTWARE UPDATE SERVICES

One of the most critical day-to-day tasks of any network administrator is the management and maintenance of operating system security updates for both client and server computers. In the past, companies have relied upon a variety of methods to keep systems updated, and by extension, protected against security threats. Common methods used to update systems with current security patches (also referred to as hot fixes) and service packs have included:

- Manual download and installation

- Installation using scripting techniques, such as a logon script

- Automated deployment using applications like Microsoft Systems Management Server (SMS)

- Installation using Windows Update

While a variety of different methods can be used to deploy service packs and hot fixes to network computers, each presents challenges, especially with regards to the amount of administrative effort involved. As a solution to this issue, Microsoft has developed server-side software that allows administrators to deploy hot fixes and security updates to computers in a streamlined manner. Known as **Software Update Services (SUS)**, this tool allows an administrator to control how updates are deployed through an organization, providing a more granular level of control than any of the other techniques provides. Ultimately, SUS helps an administrator to ensure that systems are protected against any known or new flaws in a manner that requires much less administrative effort than has typically been associated with these tasks in the past.

While SUS can be used to deploy security updates and other critical packages made available by Microsoft, it cannot be used to deploy service packs or other third-party software.

SUS consists of two main elements—a client component and a server component. The server component of SUS can be installed on a server running Windows 2000 Server or Windows Server 2003. The client component, which is effectively an updated version of the Windows Automatic Updates tool, allows clients to contact the server running SUS to determine which updates are available for download, which server the client should obtain these updates from, and how they should be installed.

In the following sections you learn more about both the client and server components of SUS, including how both are installed and configured.

Installing Software Update Services

Microsoft makes both the client and server components of SUS available for download from their Web site. The current version of SUS (as of this writing) includes SUS Service Pack 1, and includes enhancements not available in the original version, such as the ability to install the SUS server component on a system configured as a domain controller.

 The Microsoft Software Updates Services Web site can be found at *http://go.microsoft.com/fwlink/?LinkId=6930.*

The recommended hardware requirements for installing the SUS server component are as follows:

- Pentium III 700 MHz or higher processor

- 512 MB of RAM

- 6 GB of free disk space for setup and storage of security packages

Although not explicitly required, Microsoft recommends dedicating a server to running SUS if possible. When the recommended hardware requirements are met, the SUS server should be capable of handling requests from up to 15,000 client systems.

The SUS server component can be installed on servers running the following operating systems:

- Windows 2000 Server (Service Pack 2 or higher)

- Windows Server 2003

- Microsoft Small Business Server 2000 (Service Pack 1 or higher)

Since the administration of the SUS server component is Web-based, the installation of Internet Information Services (IIS) version 5.0 or higher is a prerequisite before installing SUS. Administration of SUS also requires a system configured with Internet Explorer version 5.5 or higher.

In Activity 10-13 you first install IIS on your Windows Server 2003 system, and then install the server component of SUS.

Activity 10-13: Installing Software Update Services

Time Required: 20 minutes

Objective: Install the server component of Software Update Services.

Description: Based on a number of recent security flaws identified with Windows 2000 and Windows XP client computers, the IT manager at Dover Leasing is very interested in finding an effective method of deploying updates while at the same time reducing the amount of administrative effort involved in the process. You have been asked to evaluate SUS as a potential solution. In this activity you first prepare your server for SUS by installing IIS, and then install the SUS server component.

1. Click **Start**, select **Control Panel**, and then click **Add or Remove Programs**.

2. Click the **Add/Remove Windows Components** button.

3. At the Windows Components screen, double-click **Application Server**.

4. At the Application Server screen, check the **Internet Information Services (IIS)** check box. This ultimately installs IIS, upon which Software Update Services is dependent. Click **OK**.

5. At the Windows Components screen, click **Next**.

6. At the Completing the Windows Components Wizard screen, click **Finish**. Close the Add or Remove Programs window.

7. Click **Start**, and then click **Run**. In the Open text box, type **\\instructor\shared** and click **OK**.

8. Double-click the **SUS10SP1.exe** file to begin the installation of Software Update Services Service Pack 1.

9. At the Welcome to the Microsoft Software Update Services Setup Wizard screen, click **Next**.

10. At the End-User License Agreement screen, click the **I accept the terms in the License Agreement** radio button and click **Next**.

11. At the Choose setup type screen, press the button next to **Typical**.

12. At the Ready to install screen, click **Install**.

13. At the Completing the Microsoft Software Update Services Setup Wizard screen, click **Finish**. Close all open windows.

How Software Update Services Works

The basic purpose of SUS is to provide a centralized facility from which client systems can obtain security update packages made available by Microsoft in an automated fashion. When the **Windows Update** feature is used in non-SUS environments, a user with administrative privileges must run the tool, review the list of updates that are available based on a system scan, and then manually choose which updates to install. In a large environment, hundreds or even thousands of client computers might need to connect to Internet-based Windows Update download servers, a very inefficient use of limited Internet bandwidth. When SUS is installed, the SUS server can download these updates, and network clients can then connect to the SUS server to download and install those updates that have been approved (and hopefully tested) by an administrator.

SUS provides administrators with a great deal of flexibility as to how security updates are obtained by client systems and ultimately deployed. For example, by default an SUS server will download all updates available from Internet-based Windows Update download servers, and store those updates locally. However, if the administrator prefers, SUS can also be configured to only download an information catalog of the updates available from the

Windows Update download servers, and then have clients download packages from these Internet-based servers directly once they have been approved.

The SUS approval process is the most critical element of the entire SUS update process. When security updates are posted to the Windows Update download servers, they are not deployed automatically by default. Instead, an administrator must first approve the update before clients can connect to the SUS server and install it. This gives an administrator time to first install the security update on test systems to ensure that it functions as expected, rather than risk updating hundreds or thousands of systems and then determining that a problem has occurred. Prior to approving any security update, an administrator should always test it to ensure that test systems function correctly prior to deploying it to all client systems in the organization.

The process of approving an update is as simple as checking off a check box next to the update information and then clicking an Approve button. Once approved, client systems will connect to the SUS server to download and install the update according to their configured settings. In order to interact with an SUS server, an updated version of the Automatic Updates software must be installed on the client. This software is provided as an MSI file, meaning that it can be deployed via Group Policy settings in Active Directory environments. The configuration of the Automatic Updates software can also be configured via Group Policy, further easing its deployment. The installation and configuration of the updated Automatic Updates software will be looked at later in this section.

Configuring Software Update Services

Once the server component of SUS has been installed on a Windows 2000 Server or Windows Server 2003 system, it must be configured in order to allow clients to connect to the server and obtain updates. By default, an SUS server is ready to begin deploying updates immediately once the installation process is complete. However, an administrator must first approve the updates that clients should be allowed to download and install.

The following settings are configured on an SUS server by default when the Typical option is selected during installation:

- Updates are downloaded from Internet-based Windows Update download servers
- Proxy server settings used by SUS are set to Automatic
- All downloaded content is stored locally on the SUS server
- Available packages are downloaded in all supported languages
- Packages that are approved and then later updated by Microsoft are not automatically approved

TIP

In environments where client operating systems like Windows 2000 or XP are all configured with the same language settings, configure the SUS server to download updates in those languages only. This significantly reduces the size of the updates that need to be downloaded to the SUS server, helping to reduce Internet bandwidth requirements.

The administration of an SUS server is handled via a Web browser, specifically Internet Explorer 5.5 or later. The address to connect to the SUS administration Web site is *http://servername/susadmin*, where servername is the name of the server on which SUS is installed. Once accessed, the SUS administration Web site presents a dialog box requiring an administrator to log on with a valid username and password combination.

When the Microsoft Software Update Services Welcome screen appears, it provides links to both the SUS Overview Whitepaper and SUS Deployment Guide. The menu on the left side of the page provides links to the various configurable SUS settings, as outlined in Table 10-4. The See Also section provides access to additional online resources, such as the Microsoft Windows Update and Microsoft Security Web sites.

Table 10-4   Software Update Services main menu configuration areas

Menu item	Purpose
Welcome	Provides links to whitepapers such as the SUS deployment and overview guides
Synchronize server	Allows an administrator to manually force synchronization updates, or schedule them to happen in the future
Approve updates	Allows an administrator to approve individual updates, thus allowing them to be deployed to client systems
View synchronization log	Opens the SUS synchronization log, allowing an administrator to review any synchronization processes that have taken place
View approval log	Opens the SUS approval log, allowing an administrator to review any updates that have been approved
Set options	The main configuration screen for SUS server settings, allowing an administrator to control how updates will be made available to clients, which locales updates will be downloaded for, proxy server settings, and so forth
Monitor server	Lists information about available updates which have been loaded into memory cache, the number of updates available, and the date of the most recent update for each

In Activity 10-14 you configure SUS server settings on your Windows Server 2003 system.

ACTIVITY

Activity 10-14: Configuring Software Update Services Settings

Time Required: 15 minutes

Objective: Configure Software Update Service settings.

Description: After completing the installation of SUS, the IT manager has asked you to explore the software's available configuration settings. In this activity you log on to the SUS server administrative interface for the first time, reviewing and configuring various options.

1. Click **Start**, select **All Programs**, and then click **Internet Explorer**.

2. In the Address text box, type **http://serverXX/susadmin** (where XX is your assigned student number). Click the **Go** button.

3. When the Connect to serverXX.DomainXX.Dovercorp.net dialog box appears, type **AdminXX** in the User name field, and type your password in the Password field. Click **OK**. This opens the Microsoft Software Update Services Welcome screen, as shown in Figure 10-18.

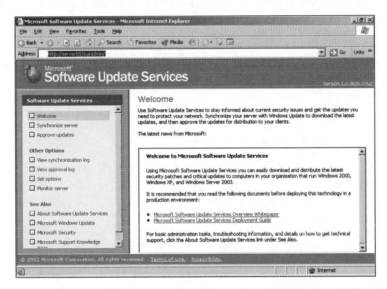

Figure 10-18   The Microsoft Software Update Services Welcome screen

4. In the Microsoft Software Update Services menu to the left, click the **Set options** link. Review the settings available on this page, noting that by default, the server synchronizes content from the Microsoft Windows Update servers, and that updates are stored to a local folder.

5. Scroll down to the Select where you want to store updates section. Click the **Maintain the updates on a Microsoft Windows Update server** option. In a real office environment an administrator might choose to download all updates locally. Configuring this setting eliminates the need for all available updates to be downloaded in the classroom environment.

6. Leave the Software Update Services Web page open.

In order for an SUS server to be aware of available security updates that can be applied to client systems, the server must be synchronized regularly. SUS provides the option to synchronize this information manually, but most administrators will appreciate the ability to schedule the synchronization process, allowing automatic synchronization to occur in the middle of the evening or other less busy times if necessary.

In Activity 10-15 you synchronize SUS content on your server manually.

Activity 10-15: Synchronizing Software Update Services Content

Time Required: 20 minutes

Objective: Synchronize Software Update Services content.

Description: Having configured various settings on your SUS server system, the IT manager has asked you to test the security update synchronization process for a single update. In this activity you configure SUS to download a single update, and then approve that update.

1. In the Microsoft Software Update Services menu of the Internet Explorer window to the left, click the **Synchronize server** link. Click **Yes** in the VBScript dialog box to apply the changes. This opens the Synchronize server screen, as shown in Figure 10-19.

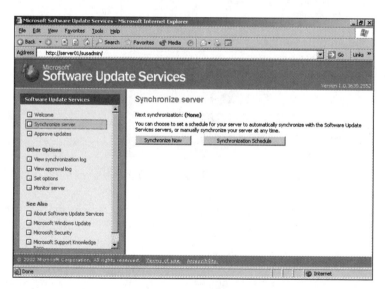

Figure 10-19   The Synchronize server screen

2. Click the **Synchronize Now** button. This initiates the process of downloading information about updates from the Microsoft Windows Update servers. Note that this process may take quite some time if you were to choose to download all updates locally, depending on how many updates are available.

3. When the VBScript dialog box appears, read the message stating that the server has been successfully synchronized, and then click **OK**.

4. At the Approve Updates screen, scroll through the list of Available Updates, as shown in Figure 10-20. Review the information about the available updates, including the download size, the basic details of the update, and which operating systems the update applies to.

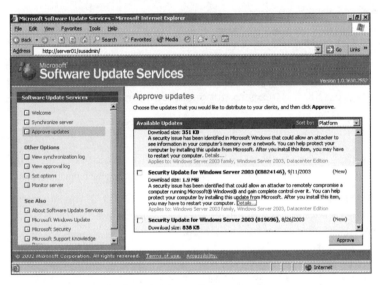

Figure 10-20   The Available updates screen

5. Click the **Sort by** drop down menu and click **Platform**. This lists updates according to the platform(s) they apply to.

6. Scroll down until you find Security Update for Windows Server 2003 (KB824146).

7. Click on the **Details** link found within the update information. This opens another window that lists the details of the update including available languages, as shown in Figure 10-21. Click the **Close** button.

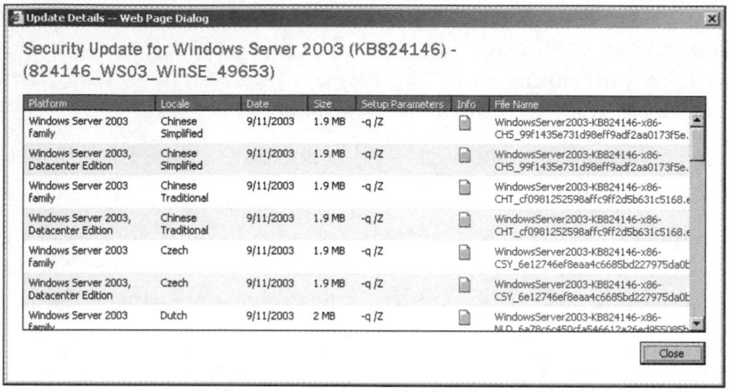

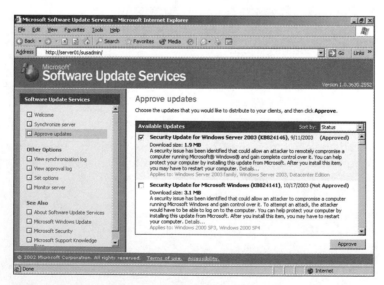

Figure 10-21   Details of an available update

8. Check the check box next to **Security Update for Windows Server 2003 (KB824146)**, and then click **Approve**. This approves the update, allowing config-ured Windows Server 2003 systems to download and/or install this update.

9. At the VBScript: Software Update Services dialog box, read the message and click **Yes**.

10. When the Software Update Services – Web Page Dialog window opens, click **Accept**.

11. At the VBScript: Software Update Services dialog box, read the message and click **OK**. This brings you back to the Approve updates screen, where the update is now listed as (Approved), as shown in Figure 10-22.

Figure 10-22   Viewing an approved update

12. In the left-hand Microsoft Software Update Services menu, click the **View synchronization log** link. This will open the Synchronization log screen, as shown in Figure 10-23.

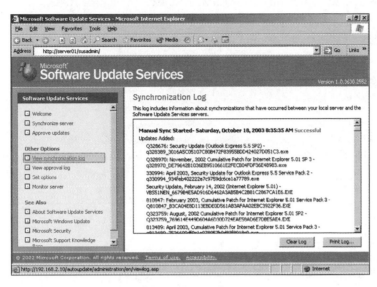

Figure 10-23   The Synchronization log screen

13. In the Microsoft Software Update Services menu to the left, click the **View approval log** link. This opens the Approval log screen, as shown in Figure 10-24. This screen lists information about which updates have and have not been approved.

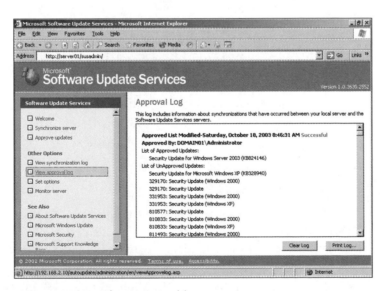

Figure 10-24   The Approval log screen

14. In the Microsoft Software Update Services menu to the left, click the **Monitor server** link. The Monitor server screen lists information about available updates which have been loaded into memory cache, the number of updates available, and the date of the most recent update for each, as shown in Figure 10-25.

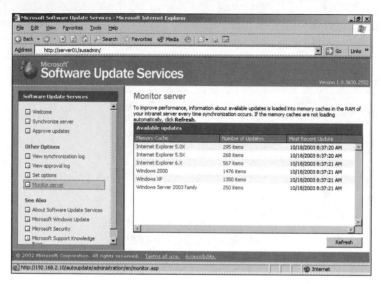

Figure 10-25   The Monitor server screen

15. Close the Internet Explorer window.

Automatic Updates

In order for client systems to obtain security updates from an SUS server, they must have the updated version of the **Automatic Updates client** installed. This updated client software is available for the SUS Web site in the form of an MSI file named WUAU22.MSI. The download and installation of this file is not always necessary, as it is already included with certain operating systems, or as part of a service pack installation. The following systems already have the updated Automatic Updates software installed:

- All Windows Server 2003 systems
- Windows XP systems with Service Pack 1 installed
- Windows 2000 systems with Service Pack 3 installed

For other systems, such as Windows 2000 or Windows XP without the necessary service pack installed, the updated Automatic Updates client can be installed manually by running the WUAU22.MSI file, or automatically by assigning the file to computers via Group Policy.

The basic settings associated with Automatic Updates are configured from the Automatic Updates tab of the System applet in Control Panel on Windows Server 2003 and Windows

XP systems. The Automatic Updates tab from a Windows XP Professional system is illustrated in Figure 10-26.

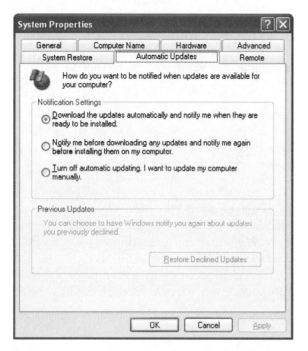

Figure 10-26   The Automatic Updates tab from a Windows XP client system

Automatic Updates can be manually enabled or disabled by checking or unchecking the Keep my computer up to date check box on the Automatic Updates tab. Once enabled, the available settings include:

- Notify me before downloading any updates and notify me again before installing them on my computer.

- Download the updates automatically and notify me when they are ready to be installed.

- Automatically download the updates, and install them on the schedule that I specify.

The configured settings on the Automatic Updates tab forces the client to attempt to connect to an Internet-based Windows Update download server by default. In order to configure clients to connect to an internal SUS server to obtain updates, an administrator must either manually configure the client system's Registry or configure Automatic Updates settings in Group Policy. In an Active Directory environment, Group Policy would be the preferred method, as it would avoid the need to manually configure all client systems. In non–domain environments, an administrator would need to configure Registry entries manually, via a scripted installation, or use the Group Policy Object Editor MMC to configure the necessary settings on individual systems.

 In order to configure Automatic Updates settings for use with an internal SUS server in a non-domain environment using the Group Policy Object Editor MMC, a template named WUAU.ADM must be added to the console beforehand. You manually add this administrative template to your server for practice purposes in Activity 10-17.

 For more information on configuring a non-domain client system to use an internal SUS server to obtain update information and downloads, see the Software Update Services Overview White Paper. A link to this document can be found on the Software Update Services administration Web site Welcome screen.

Automatic Update settings are typically configured via Group Policy in Active Directory environments. Settings are configured from the Computer Configuration > Administrative Templates > Windows Components > Windows Update section of a Group Policy object. Table 10-5 outlines the 4 configurable settings found in this section. Once Automatic Updates are enabled and configured via Group Policy, these settings cannot be configured manually on client systems, and will override any previous-configured local settings.

Table 10-5 Automatic Updates Group Policy settings

Setting	Purpose
Configure Automatic Updates	When enabled, an administrator must configure one of three options for how updates will occur. Choices include Notify for download and notify for install, Auto download and notify to install, and Auto download and schedule for install. If a notify option is chosen, a logged-on administrator will be notified of the availability of updates for download or installation.
Specify intranet Microsoft update service location	When enabled, this option allows an administrator to specify the location of the SUS server that the client should contact for information about updates, or to download the updates themselves. The format for this information is http://servername, where servername is the NetBIOS name or hostname for the SUS server.
Reschedule Automatic Updates scheduled installations	When enabled, this option controls when a rescheduled installation of updates will take place if the schedule is missed, for example if the client computer was turned off when the update was scheduled to occur.
No auto-restart for scheduled Automatic Updates installations	When enabled, this option prevents the client computer from restarting as part of applying an update if there is a user currently logged on to the client system.

In Activity 10-16 you configure Automatic Updates settings via the Default Domain Policy Group Policy object.

Activity 10-16: Reviewing Automatic Updates Group Policy Settings

Time Required: 15 minutes

Objective: Review Automatic Update Group Policy settings.

Description: In order to streamline the configuration of Automatic Updates client to contact and obtain updates from your SUS server, you decide to use Group Policy settings. In this activity you review and configure available Group Policy settings related to Automatic Updates.

1. Click **Start**, select **Administrative Tools**, and then click **Active Directory Users and Computers**.

2. Right-click on the **domainXX.dovercorp.net** icon (where *XX* is your assigned student number). Click **Properties**.

3. Click the **Group Policy** tab.

4. Ensure that **Default Domain Policy** is selected, and then click **Edit**.

5. Right-click on the **Administrative Templates** folder under Computer Configuration and click **Add/Remove Templates**.

6. In the Add/Remove Templates window click **wuau**, as shown in Figure 10-27. Click **Add**. The wuau template is already installed on this server. However, for the purpose of knowing the process associated with adding the template when necessary, you add it again here.

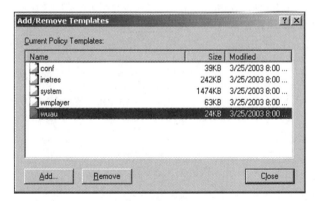

Figure 10-27   The Add/Remove Templates window

7. In the Policy Templates window, click **wuau.adm** and click **Open**. At the Confirm File Replace screen, click **Yes**. Click **Close** at the Add/Remove Templates window.

8. Click the **plus sign (+)** next to Administrative Templates in the Computer Configuration section to view its contents.

9. Click the **plus sign (+)** next to Windows Components to view its contents.

10. Click the **Windows Update** folder to view its contents, as shown in Figure 10-28.

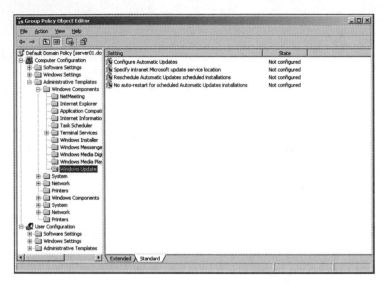

Figure 10-28   Windows Update Group Policy settings

11. Double-click on **Configure Automatic Updates** to view its properties. Click the **Enabled** radio button.

12. In the Configure automatic updating drop-down menu, click **4 – Auto download and schedule the install**. Click the **Next Setting** button.

13. At the Specify intranet Microsoft update service location Properties screen, click the **Enabled** radio button.

14. In the Set the intranet update service for detecting updates text box, type **http://serverXX** (where *XX* is your assigned student number). In the Set the intranet statistics server text box, again type **http://serverXX**, as shown in Figure 10-29. Click the **Next Setting** button.

15. At the Reschedule Automatic Updates scheduled installations Properties window, click the **Enabled** radio button. Click the **Next Setting** button.

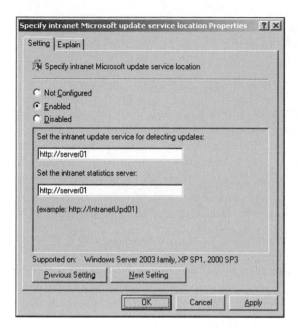

Figure 10-29   Configuring Specify intranet Microsoft update service location settings

16. At the No auto-restart for scheduled Automatic Updates installations Properties screen, click the **Explain** tab and read through the information about what this setting does. Once complete, click **OK**.

17. Close the Group Policy Object Editor window, click **OK** to close the domain*XX*.dovercorp.net Properties window, and then close Active Directory Users and Computers.

Planning a Software Update Services Infrastructure

One of the main advantages of implementing SUS within an organization is that many different deployment configurations are supported. The following sections outline some of the common methods that organizations can use to deploy and configure SUS, as well as the relative advantages and disadvantages of each method.

Small Networks

On a small business network, only a single server running SUS is usually required. As outlined earlier, a server that meets the minimum recommended hardware requirements for SUS has been tested to be capable of supporting up to 15,000 client systems. The main requirement for a small network with a single SUS server is that the SUS server requires some form of Internet connectivity to perform synchronization-related tasks.

Organizations with slightly more complex networks (such as those with multiple locations with individual Internet connections) might choose to deploy multiple SUS servers, perhaps one in each location. In this case, each SUS server would be managed independently, and client systems would be configured to connect to the SUS server in their particular location via Group Policy settings.

Enterprise Networks

In a large network environment with different locations and thousands of clients, an organization would typically deploy multiple SUS servers. Rather than have each SUS server connect to the Internet individually for synchronization purposes, an organization would probably decide to have only a single server synchronize from the Windows Update servers, and then have other internal SUS servers connect to that server to obtain updates. This model resembles a traditional hub-and-spoke, and can help to greatly reduce the bandwidth burden of multiple SUS servers connecting to the Internet to obtain the same required updates.

In a case where client systems are geographically dispersed over WAN links, having an SUS server in a remote office makes more sense than having all clients connect to an SUS server in a central office over WAN links. Instead, the remote SUS server can obtain updates from the central SUS server once, and then distribute those updates to clients in that particular location, minimizing WAN traffic.

An alternate method for deploying SUS in a large enterprise environment is to configure multiple SUS servers, and then use the Windows Server 2003 Network Load Balancing (NLB) feature to balance client requests amongst these servers. NLB supports load-balancing arrangements for between 2 and 32 server systems.

High Security Networks

On high security networks, the corporate intranet is typically disconnected from the public Internet, and client systems may not have direct Internet connectivity. In these arrangements, a company would typically choose to deploy multiple SUS servers, anywhere from two to many more, depending on the size of the organization. In this case, at least one SUS server requires Internet connectivity for synchronization purposes with the Windows Update servers. However, all other SUS servers (which would likely lack Internet connectivity) would be configured to obtain all updates from the SUS server with Internet connectivity, making that single server act as a distribution point for the network.

In Activity 10-17 you remove SUS from your server and uninstall Internet Information Services. This is necessary so as not to interfere with activities in Chapter 13.

Activity 10-17: Uninstalling Software Update Services and Internet Information Services

Time Required: 10 minutes

Objective: Uninstall Software Update Services and IIS.

Description: Having installed and configured SUS for testing purposes, the IT manager at Dover Leasing has asked you to remove it from the test server until a final decision for its deployment has been made. In this activity you remove both SUS and IIS from your server.

1. Click **Start**, select **Control Panel**, and then click **Add or Remove Programs**.

2. Ensure that **Microsoft Software Update Services** is selected, and then click the **Remove** button.

3. At the Add or Remove Programs dialog box, click **Yes**.

4. Once Microsoft Software Update Services has been removed, click the **Add/Remove Windows Components** button.

5. At the Windows Components screen, double-click **Application Server**.

6. At the Application Server screen, uncheck the **Internet Information Services (IIS)** check box. Click **OK**.

7. At the Windows Components screen, click **Next**.

8. At the Completing the Windows Components Wizard screen, click **Finish**.

9. Close the Add or Remove Programs window.

CHAPTER SUMMARY

- Windows Server 2003 includes the secondary logon feature as a way to allow users and administrators to open tools or issue commands using alternate credentials. For example, an administrator could use a regular user account and then use this feature when administrative tasks need to be performed.

- The Microsoft Management Console is the primary administrative environment for Windows Server 2003 systems. Snap-ins added to the MMC allow an administrator to manage different services such as Active Directory or DNS. The MMC also supports taskpad views, which can simplify the environment for less experienced users.

- Terminal Services is a Windows Server 2003 feature that allows users to connect to and run applications on a Windows Server 2003 system from their desktop as if sitting at the server console.

- Remote Desktop for Administration is a Windows Server 2003 feature that allows an administrator to connect to servers remotely for administrative purposes. When connected, the administrator interacts with the server desktop as if sitting at the server console.

- In much the same way that files and folders stored on NTFS volumes can be secured with permissions, Active Directory objects also have associated permissions. Object-level permissions apply to objects like users, while attribute-level permissions apply to the attributes associated with an object.

❑ The Delegation of Control Wizard simplifies the task of delegating administrative authority over a portion of Active Directory to specified users or groups. This wizard is the recommended method for delegating authority, and is more simple to manage than changing individual object and attribute permissions.

❑ Microsoft Software Update Services is a software application that can be installed on Windows Server 2003 systems, allowing an administrator to control and manage the deployment of security patches and hot fixes for network systems.

KEY TERMS

attribute-level permissions — Active Directory permissions that control whether users or groups can read or modify the attributes associated with Active Directory objects.

Automatic Updates client — The client software component of Software Update Services.

Delegation of Control Wizard — The wizard available in Active Directory Users and Computers to simplify the delegation of administrative authority.

Install mode — The mode used to install a program that will be used in a Terminal Services environment.

Management Saved Console (MSC) — The extension associated with a saved Microsoft Management Console (MMC) file.

object-level permissions — Active Directory permissions that control the level to which a user can modify an object such as a user account.

Remote Desktop Connection — The client software used to connect to a server running Terminal Services or Remote Desktop for Administration.

Remote Desktop for Administration — A feature that allows administrators to remotely connect to the desktop of a Windows Server 2003 system for administrative purposes.

Secondary logon — A feature that allows users to open certain administrative tools or issue commands using alternate credentials.

Software Update Services (SUS) — A server application designed to add control and flexibility over the deployment of security patches and hot fixes to client and server systems on a network.

Terminal Services — A Windows Server 2003 feature that allows users to connect to a Windows Server 2003 system and interact with applications as if sitting at the server console.

user mode — The normal running mode for a Terminal Services environment.

Windows Update — The Windows feature that allows operating systems to download service packs, patches, and hot fixes from Microsoft in an automated fashion rather than by manual download.

REVIEW QUESTIONS

1. Which of the following allows a user to run certain administrative tools or issue commands using alternate credentials?

   a. MMC

   b. Secondary logon

   c. Terminal Services

   d. Taskpad

2. Which of the following file extensions is associated with a saved MMC?

   a. MMC

   b. MSC

   c. MCS

   d. MOS

3. Which of the following tools simplifies the administration of administrative authority?

   a. Administration Wizard

   b. Delegation of Control Wizard

   c. Active Directory Permission Wizard

   d. Delegation MMC

4. What is the recommended minimum CPU requirement for a Windows Server 2003 system running SUS?

   a. P4 1 GHz

   b. P4 800 MHz

   c. PIII 700 MHz

   d. PII 500 MHz

5. What is the recommended minimum RAM requirement for a Windows Server 2003 system running SUS?

   a. 128 MB

   b. 256 MB

   c. 512 MB

   d. 1 GB

6. When configured according to the minimum requirements, what is the maximum number of clients that a single SUS server can support?

   a. 10000

   b. 15000

10

   c. 20000

   d. 30000

7. Which of the following should be done prior to installing software that will be accessed by multiple users on a Windows Server 2003 system running Terminal Services?

   a. Issue the change user /user command

   b. Issue the change user /install command

   c. Issue the change user /mode command

   d. Issue the change user /run command

8. Which of the following pieces of client software can potentially be used to connect to a Windows Server 2003 system running Terminal Services?

   a. Remote Desktop Connections

   b. Runas

   c. Command line

   d. Internet Explorer

9. Which of the following is not a Terminal Services administrative tool?

   a. Terminal Services Manager

   b. Terminal Services Configuration

   c. Terminal Services Applications

   d. Terminal Services Licensing

10. Which piece of software must be installed on a Windows 2000 Professional system to allow it to interact with an SUS server?

   a. Automatic Updates client

   b. SUS

   c. Remote Desktop Connections

   d. HyperTerminal

11. Which tab in the properties of a user account is used to configure a maximum session time and disconnect options for a Terminal Service session?

   a. Environment

   b. Sessions

   c. Remote Control

   d. Security

12. Which tab in the properties of a user account is used to configure a program to automatically run when the user connects to the terminal server?

    a. Environment

    b. Sessions

    c. Account

    d. Terminal Services

13. A Windows Server 2003 system cannot support both Terminal Services and Remote Desktop for Administration sessions concurrently.

    a. True

    b. False

14. The secondary logon feature is available to administrators only.

    a. True

    b. False

15. Which of the following commands is used to initiate secondary logon from the command line?

    a. Run

    b. Runas

    c. Runnow

    d. Runasuser

16. Which of the following services must be installed in order to install SUS on a Windows Server 2003 system?

    a. Terminal Services

    b. IIS

    c. DNS

    d. DHCP

17. Which of the following features enables you to define a simplified administrative environment from which shortcuts to common tasks can be created?

    a. Taskpad

    b. Secondary logon

    c. SUS

    d. Windows Update

18. Only an administrator can create user accounts in Active Directory, with no exceptions.

    a. True

    b. False

10

19. SUS cannot be installed on a domain controller.

   a. True

   b. False

20. Which of the following should be used to configure client Automatic Updates settings in an Active Directory environment?

   a. Group Policy

   b. The configuration of an SUS server

   c. Manual settings

   d. Terminal Services

CASE PROJECTS

Case Project 10-1

The IT manager at Dover Leasing has decided that using a custom taskpad is the best administrative strategy for network help desk staff until complete training on the various administrative tools can be provided later in the quarter. Using the Help Desk.msc taskpad originally developed in Activity 10-4, you have been asked to add additional shortcuts to tasks and tools that the help desk staff will be responsible for using. In particular, the IT manager has asked you edit the existing taskpad to include the following:

1. A shortcut to the application log

2. A shortcut to the command prompt

3. A shortcut to connect to another computer

4. Shortcuts to save both the application and system logs

Each of these tasks should include both a description and an appropriate icon. After you have added all of the new tasks, save the console file and have the instructor check your work.

Case Project 10-2

The IT manager has asked you to begin planning for the deployment of an SUS infrastructure at Dover Leasing. Some of the issues that he has expressed concern about include having more than one SUS server monopolize an already busy Internet connection, ways to limit the amount of SUS-related traffic that traverses WAN links, the installation of the Automatic Updates client, and the configuration of client settings.

1. If Dover Leasing currently has six locations, each with 1000 clients, which method of deploying SUS would be best, based on the IT manager's concerns?

2. What technique could be used to ensure that SUS-related traffic over Dover's WAN links is kept to a minimum? Be sure to consider Internet-based traffic as well.

3. What would be the most effective method to deploy the Automatic Updates client to computers on the network?

4. What would be the most effective method to configure Automatic Updates settings on client computers?

10

11

MONITORING SERVER PERFORMANCE

After reading this chapter and completing the exercises, you will be able to:

♦ Identify the importance of monitoring server performance

♦ Use Task Manager to monitor server performance and resource usage

♦ Use Event Viewer to identify and troubleshoot problems

♦ Use the Performance console to monitor server performance using both System Monitor and Performance Logs and Alerts

♦ Optimize server performance through the configuration of service settings

Many businesses today rely heavily on their servers for day-to-day operations. Expectations are set for network server availability and performance. When a server goes down or starts to perform poorly, many routine functions are affected and the complaints soon filter in. This means that as a network administrator, you need to ensure that a server is capable of meeting performance expectations and that server downtime is minimal.

Windows Server 2003 includes a variety of tools that can be used to monitor server performance, and potentially troubleshoot problems as they arise. For example, the Windows Task Manager utility provides administrators with a snapshot of current CPU and memory performance information, as well as data about the CPU utilization and memory usage of running processes. Although the information that Task Manager provides allows an administrator to obtain a real-time snapshot of system performance, it is rather limited, and is generally used as a starting point before gathering additional information using other tools and utilities. This chapter begins with a look at the Task Manager utility.

Event Viewer is another invaluable server monitoring tool; logging errors, caution messages, and general information about both operating system processes and applications. A proactive server management strategy involves checking the Event Viewer log files regularly as a method of trying to identify small issues and problems before they have a larger impact on server availability and performance. Both the Event Viewer system and application logs are looked at in this chapter.

One of the most robust tools that can be used to monitor server performance is the Performance console, which includes both the System Monitor and Performance Logs and Alerts tools. These tools are both capable of monitoring and logging data from countless different objects ranging from memory to processor utilization to the performance of various applications. This tool also provides a great deal of flexibility, allowing data to be represented both graphically or logged in files for export to other analysis applications. The Performance console is covered in detail in this chapter.

Windows Server 2003 performance is mainly impacted by the hardware resources installed in the server, and the various processes that are running at any given point in time. Examples of processes include not only applications, but also the various services that run in the background. This chapter closes with a look at how unnecessary services can be disabled to reduce resource usage, and how service settings can be configured such that different actions are taken when an error occurs.

INTRODUCTION TO MONITORING SERVER PERFORMANCE

Maintaining a server is similar to maintaining an automobile. When you purchase a new automobile, it must be serviced on a regular basis to ensure its performance over time. Many of the new cars and trucks today also come with tools that can alert you to problems when they occur. Server maintenance is similar. Often, administrators configure servers for network use, while not realizing that over time, server performance can deteriorate for a number of reasons.

One of the more important reasons for monitoring the health of your server is that it can help alert you to problems before they occur or become more serious. Over time, networks change; the demands placed on a server can vary or increase. Monitoring server performance can help you determine what normal behavior is for your server under the current demands and alert you to any performance issues that may be occurring if the normal behavior changes. This normal behavior is known as **baseline** performance.

Windows Server 2003 comes with several built-in tools that can be used to monitor server health and performance, including:

- Task Manager
- Event Viewer
- Performance console

The following sections introduce you to these tools, providing you with a description of how they can be used to monitor your server and how to use them.

TASK MANAGER

Although Windows Server 2003 provides a variety of tools that can be used to monitor and manage server performance, one of the fastest ways to obtain a snapshot of system performance is via the **Task Manager** tool. While the information provided by Task Manager is rather high-level in nature, it provides an effective method to quickly gauge server performance.

The Windows Task Manager interface can be accessed using a variety of different methods, such as by right-clicking on the Windows taskbar and clicking the Task Manager shortcut, or by pressing the Ctrl+Alt+Delete key combination and clicking the Task Manager button in the Windows Security dialog box. Once opened, Windows Task Manager consists of five main tabs, each of which provides different information and capabilities. These tabs are:

- Applications
- Processes
- Performance
- Networking
- Users

Each of the tabs found in the Windows Task Manager interface are looked at in more detail in the following sections.

Monitoring and Managing Applications

You can use Task Manager to view applications running on the server by pressing Ctrl+Alt+Del while logged on as Administrator or as a member of the Administrators group. Click the Task Manager button, which displays a dialog box with five tabs: Applications, Processes, Performance, Networking, and Users. An alternate way to start Task Manager is to right-click an area of open space on the Windows taskbar, and click the Task Manager shortcut item.

When you select the Applications tab, a list of all foreground software applications is displayed, as shown in Figure 11-1. To stop an application, select it from the list and click the End Task button. If an application is listed as Not Responding (no longer responding to user input), you can select that application and press End Task to stop the program, thus freeing up server resources such as memory and CPU cycles. The Switch To button brings the highlighted application to the foreground, and the New Task button enables you to start another application at the console, in a manner similar to the Run command.

11

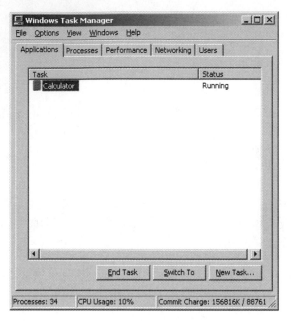

Figure 11-1   The Task Manager Applications tab

If you right-click a particular task, several active options appear in a shortcut menu, as follows:

- Switch To—Takes you into the highlighted program

- Bring To Front—Brings the highlighted program to the foreground, but leaves the focus on Task Manager

- Minimize—Causes the program to be minimized

- Maximize—Causes the program to be maximized, but leaves you in Task Manager

- End Task—Stops the highlighted program

- Go To Process—Takes you to the Processes tab and highlights the main process associated with the program

Monitoring and Managing Processes

The Task Manager Processes tab lists all of the processes in use by applications and services, including those running in the background, as shown in Figure 11-2. Besides allowing you to right-click on a process to end it, the Processes tab also displays important information about each running process, as summarized in Table 11-1.

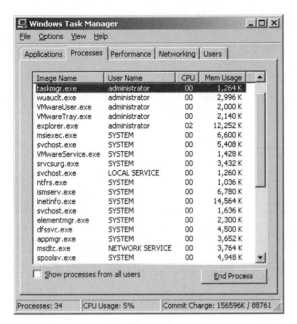

Figure 11-2   The Task Manager Processes tab

Table 11-1   Information provided by the Task Manager Processes tab

Process Information	Description
Image Name	The process name, such as winword.exe for Microsoft Word
User Name	The user account under which the process is running
CPU	The percentage of CPU resources currently used by the process
Mem Usage	The amount of memory currently used by the process

In Activity 11-1 you use Task Manager to manage applications on your Windows Server 2003 system.

Activity 11-1: Using Task Manager to Manage Applications and Processes

Time Required: 10 minutes

Objective: Use Task Manager to manage applications and processes.

Description: The IT manager at Dover Leasing wants all junior administrators to be able to identify tasks and processes running on all Windows Server 2003 systems with minimal effort. He has asked you to explore the settings available on the Task Manager Applications and Processes tab in order to train the junior staff. In this activity you use Task Manager to identify running tasks, determine the process associated with a task, and then end the task from the Task Manager interface.

1. If necessary, log on using your **AdminXX** account (where *XX* is your assigned student number).

2. Press **Ctrl+Alt+Delete**. At the Windows Security dialog box, click the **Task Manager** button.

3. If necessary, click the **Applications** tab. Assuming that you have no foreground applications running, this tab should not currently list any running tasks.

4. Click **Start**, and then click **Run**. In the Open text box, type **calc.exe** and click **OK**. This opens the Calculator program, which is now listed on the Applications tab with a status of Running.

5. Click on the **Calculator** icon on the Applications tab to select it, and then click the **Switch To** button. This minimizes Task Manager and brings the Calculator program to the foreground.

6. Click on **Windows Task Manager** on the taskbar to restore it.

7. Right-click on the **Calculator** icon on the Applications tab to view the items available on the shortcut menu that appears. Click **Go To Process**. Notice that this action switches focus to the Processes tab, with the process calc.exe highlighted. Review the User Name, CPU, and Mem Usage columns associated with the process.

8. Right-click on the **calc.exe** process to view the items available on the shortcut menu that appears. Click **End Process**.

9. At the Task Manager Warning dialog box, read the message that appears, and click **Yes**. Notice that the Calculator window closes, and that the calc.exe process no longer appears on the Processes tab.

10. Click the **Applications** tab and confirm that the Calculator task is no longer present.

11. Close the **Windows Task Manager** window.

Outside of providing an excellent snapshot of how resources like memory and CPU cycles are currently being consumed by running processes, the Processes tab also allows you to configure the priority associated with a process. By default, processes run under the Normal priority, meaning that all running processes are granted the same level of access to system CPU resources. In some cases, an administrator might want to grant certain processes a higher or lower level of access to these resources, based on their perceived importance or for performance-tuning purposes. For example, on a Windows Server 2003 system running a time-critical application, an administrator might choose to run the associated process at a higher priority to ensure it gains access to the processor immediately when necessary. To change the priority of a running process, right-click on a selected process in the Image Name column, select Set Priority, and then click the priority level required for the process.

Use the Realtime priority with caution. If assigned to a process, that process may completely monopolize the server's CPU resources, preventing necessary access by any other processes.

Monitoring Real-Time Performance

The Task Manager Performance tab shows vital CPU and memory performance information through bar charts, line graphs, and performance statistics, as shown in Figure 11-3. The CPU Usage and PF Usage bars show the current use of CPU and page file use. To the right of each bar is a graph showing the immediate history statistics. The bottom of the Performance tab shows more detailed statistics, which are described in Table 11-2. Typically, an administrator uses the Performance tab of Task Manager to gain a quick snapshot of the current performance of a Windows Server 2003 system, and then uses a more detailed tool like System Monitor (looked at later in this chapter) to gather more detailed information.

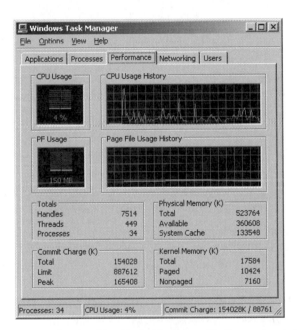

Figure 11-3   The Task Manager Performance tab

Table 11-2   Information provided by the Task Manager Performance tab

Performance Information	Description
CPU Usage/CPU Usage History	Shows the percentage of CPU being used and graphs both current and historical CPU usage
PF Usage/Page File Usage History	Shows the amount of page file usage and graphs historical page file usage
Totals	Displays the total number of handles, threads, and processes

Table 11-2   Information provided by the Task Manager Performance tab (continued)

Performance Information	Description
Physical Memory	Displays the total amount of memory, how much is available, and the amount of memory used for the system cache
Commit Charge	Displays the amount of memory that has been committed to all applications currently running
Kernel Memory	Displays the amount of memory that has been allocated to kernel functions, the amount of memory that could be paged to disk, and the amount of nonpaged memory

In Activity 11–2 you explore information on the Task Manager Performance tab.

Activity 11-2: Using Task Manager to Monitor Performance

Time Required: 5 minutes

Objective: Use Task Manager to monitor server performance.

Description: Some of the users at Dover Leasing have been complaining that server performance seems sluggish at different times during the day. As a first-level response, the IT manager would like junior administrators to quickly gauge server CPU and memory performance prior to passing this information off to network engineering staff. In this activity you review server performance using the Task Manager Performance tab.

1. Press **Ctrl+Alt+Delete**. At the Windows Security dialog box, click the **Task Manager** button.

2. Click the **Performance** tab. Review the information provided on this tab, such as CPU Usage, CPU Usage History, PF Usage, and Page File Usage History.

3. Leave the Windows Task Manager window open. Click **Start**, and then click **Run**. In the **Open** text box, type **wmplayer.exe** and click **OK**. Review the CPU Usage History graph on the Performance tab. A small spike should be visible at the point when Windows Media Player 9 Series was opened.

4. Click the **Applications** tab. In the Task list, click the **Windows Media Player 9 Series** icon, and then click **End Task**. This closes the Windows Media Player 9 Series program.

5. If time permits, open additional applications to view the impact on both CPU and Page File usage. As more applications are opened and active, these counters should increase, at least temporarily.

6. Close all open windows, and then close **Windows Task Manager**.

Monitoring Network Performance

The Task Manager Networking tab allows you to monitor network performance of all network cards installed on a Windows Server 2003 system. The graphical interface on this tab displays total network utilization information, which is roughly the percentage of the network bandwidth in use.

The lower portion of the Networking tab displays network performance data for each installed network card, as shown in Figure 11-4. It lists the name of the adapter (or connection), the network utilization detected by the adapter (from 0% to 100%), the speed of the network link, such as 10 Mbps, and the operational state of the adapter. This information can be valuable if you suspect there is a problem with a NIC in the server and you want an immediate determination if it is working. The information on the tab also can be an initial warning that something is causing prolonged high network utilization—80% to 100%, for instance.

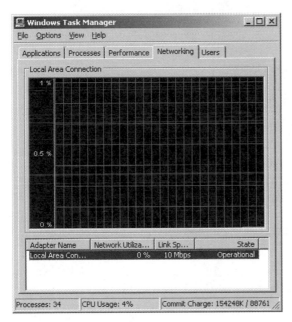

Figure 11-4   The Task Manager Networking tab

Monitoring Users

The Task Manager Users tab provides a listing of the users currently logged on to a system, including network clients with connections to the system. You can log off a user by selecting user and clicking the Logoff button (this ensures that any open files are closed before the user is logged off), or select the Disconnect option to disconnect a user's session (usually if that session is hung or cannot be logged off). Other options available from this tab include the ability to send a network message to a connected user, or connect to another user's session. The Users tab is shown in Figure 11-5.

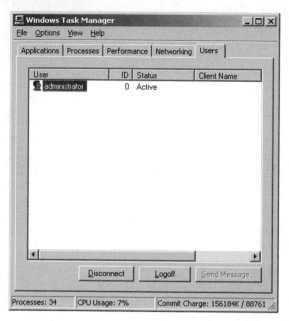

Figure 11-5   The Task Manager Users tab

EVENT VIEWER

Perhaps the most common and effective monitoring and troubleshooting tool in Windows Server 2003 is **Event Viewer**. You can use Event Viewer to gather information and troubleshoot software, hardware, and system problems. Figure 11-6 shows the Event Viewer console.

Events that occur on a system are tracked and recorded in different log files. You can use Event Viewer to view the contents of the log files. For example, you can use Event Viewer to view the contents of the **system log** to determine when, and possibly why, a specific service failed to start.

Whenever you are troubleshooting a problem with a server, one of the first places to look to gather information about the cause is Event Viewer. Entries in the log files can alert you to warnings and errors that are occurring, the component or application that is generating the message, and possibly why the problem is happening. Most entries also include an event ID that you can research on Microsoft's Support Web site (or the vendor's Web site in the case of third-party counters) to gather more detailed information on the problem and find a possible solution.

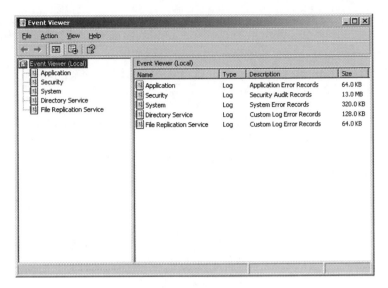

Figure 11-6   The Event Viewer console

Events are typically written to one of three log files:

- Application log — Information, warnings, and errors generated by programs installed on the system are written to the **Application log**.

- Security log — Events pertaining to the audit policy are written to the **Security log**. For example, if the audit policy is tracking failed logon attempts, an event is written to the security log each time a user is unsuccessful in logging on. By default, security logging is disabled until an audit policy is configured.

- System log — Information, warnings, and errors generated by Windows Server 2003 system components, such as drivers and services, are written to the System log.

A domain controller has two additional logs: the directory service log, which records events logged by Active Directory, and the file replication service log, which logs file replication events. A server installed with the DNS service also includes the DNS server log, which records events related to the DNS server service.

By default, any user can view the contents of the application and system log. Only administrators can view the security log, as well as those users who have been assigned the Manage Auditing and Security Log right.

The system and application logs display the following types of events:

- Information — When a component or application successfully performs an operation; information events are identified by an "I" icon.

- Warning — When an event occurs that may not be a problem at the current time, but may become a problem in the future; an exclamation point icon indicates warnings.

- Error — When a significant event has occurred, such as a service failing to start or a device driver failing to load, an "x" icon indicates errors.

There are two other types of events that are logged. These are successes and failures of actions that are performed on the network based on the configuration of an audit policy. Refer to Chapter 14 for more information about the configuration of security audit policies.

Interpreting Events

When you click a log file within Event Viewer, the details pane lists all the events that have occurred and provides general information about each one, such as:

- Type of event (information, warning, or error)

- The date and time that the event occurred, along with associated user information

- The source of the event (the component or application that logged the event)

- The category and event ID

- The computer on which the event occurred

An example of an event message is shown in Figure 11-7.

The header for an event provides the same information listed above. The event description provides an administrator with a description of what occurred and why the event is significant, which is usually the most useful information.

The data field of an event displays information that is generated by the program or component. It contains binary data that can be used by support technicians to troubleshoot the problem.

In Activity 11-3, you explore events in your server's system and application logs.

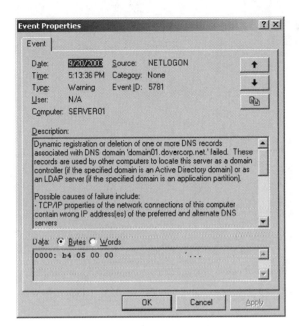

Figure 11-7 Viewing the details of a specific event

Activity 11-3: Viewing Event Viewer System and Application Log Events

Time Required: 10 minutes

Objective: View events in the Event Viewer system and application logs.

Description: The IT manager at Dover Leasing has decided that all IT staff needs to be familiar with using the Windows Server 2003 Event Viewer tool to monitor system and application events on corporate servers. In this activity, you explore events in both the Event Viewer system and application logs.

1. Click **Start**, select **Administrative Tools**, and then click **Event Viewer**.

2. Click the **Application** icon to view the contents of the application log.

3. Double-click the first **Information** event found in the list to view its properties. The Event Properties dialog box opens, similar to the one shown in Figure 11-8.

4. Read the information contained in the event header and Description fields, and then click the **down arrow** button. The next event in the application log is displayed.

5. Click the **Cancel** button.

6. Click the **System** icon to view the contents of the system log.

7. Double-click the first **Error** event found in the list to view its properties. Read through the details of the event header and Description fields.

11

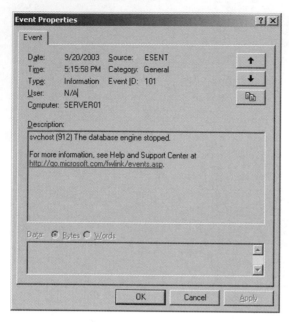

Figure 11-8   Viewing the properties of an Information event

8. Scroll to the bottom of the description field, if necessary, and then click the hyperlink at the bottom of the section to visit the Microsoft events Web site. Click **Yes** in the Event Viewer dialog box. The site opens in the Help and Support Center window automatically.

9. Close all open windows.

PERFORMANCE CONSOLE

Although Task Manager provides administrators with an easy way to quickly gauge server performance, Windows Server 2003 also includes an administrative tool known as the **Performance console** that allows more detailed information to be gathered using various methods. The Performance console consists of two different tools – System Monitor, and Performance Logs and Alerts. System Monitor allows an administrator to view data gathered from a wide variety of counter objects in real time, usually by viewing a graphical representation of collected data. Performance Logs and Alerts allows an administrator to gather similar information, but periodically log samples to a data file to be imported into other applications (such as Microsoft Excel or SQL Server), or to generate alerts when certain configured thresholds are met. The Performance console is displayed in Figure 11-9.

The following sections take a look at both the System Monitor and Performance Logs and Alerts components of the Performance console in more detail.

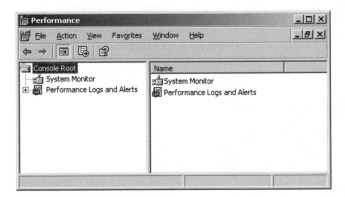

Figure 11-9   The Performance console

System Monitor

System Monitor is one of the most useful tools for collecting data on real-time server performance. As part of the Windows Server 2003 Performance MMC, this tool allows you to track how system resources are being used and how they are behaving under the current workload. System Monitor collects data that you can use for the following tasks:

- Server performance — If you use System Monitor on a regular basis, it can help you understand how the server performs under the current workload.

- Problem diagnosis — You can use the data that is collected to diagnose server components that may not be performing optimally, causing a bottleneck within the server.

- Capacity planning — You can use the information to see how server usage is changing over time and plan ahead for future upgrades.

- Testing — If configuration changes are made, you can use the data to observe the impact that the changes have on the server.

Using System Monitor, you can define the components you want to monitor and the type of data you want to collect. You choose the performance objects you want to monitor, such as memory, and the specific type of performance counters or data associated with the object for which you want to gather data. You can further customize the data you want to capture by specifying the source or computer you want to monitor. You can use System Monitor to gather data from the local computer or from a network computer for which you have appropriate permissions. Although the System Monitor tool includes a number of performance objects and associated counters to monitor by default, additional objects and counters are added when various services and applications are added to a server, such as DNS or Microsoft SQL Server.

Using System Monitor

When you first open the Performance tool, System Monitor automatically begins displaying performance data. By default, the tool displays data related to the memory, processor, and physical disk objects for the local computer, as displayed in Figure 11-10.

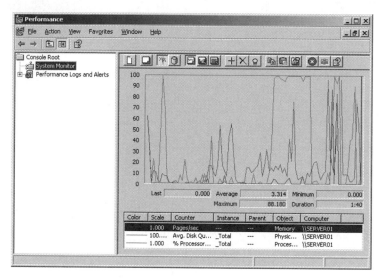

Figure 11-10   The default display of System Monitor

The information that System Monitor captures can be displayed in one of three views:

- Graph — Displays counter information as a continuous graph updated onscreen in real time

- Histogram — Displays counter information as a histogram, with information updated onscreen in real time

- Report — Displays a text-based report view of counters, with information updated onscreen in real time

The System Monitor interface provides a number of options for viewing performance data, including the ability to add additional performance counters as required, switch between display views, highlight a selected counter, copy and paste selected information, and freeze the display for analysis purposes. The System Monitor toolbar, found at the top of the details pane in System Monitor, allows you to easily control these functions. In Activity 11-4, you explore the various settings of the System Monitor tool.

Activity 11-4: Exploring System Monitor Settings

Time Required: 10 minutes

Objective: Explore Windows Server 2003 System Monitor settings.

Description: The IT manager at Dover Leasing has informed you that all corporate servers will eventually be monitored for performance purposes using the Windows Server 2003 System Monitor utility. He has asked you to become familiar with the tool and explore its various features because all networking-related staff will eventually need to be trained on this tool. In this activity, you explore the various features of System Monitor.

1. Click **Start**, select **Administrative Tools**, and click **Performance**. The Performance console opens and System Monitor begins running automatically using the three default counters.

2. Click the **View Histogram** button on the toolbar at the top of the System Monitor details pane, as shown in Figure 11-11. This illustrates the same counter information as a histogram.

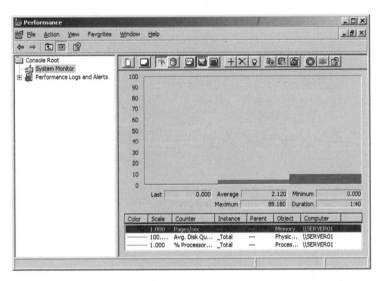

Figure 11-11   Viewing System Monitor data as a histogram

3. Click the **View Report** button on the System Monitor toolbar. This shows the same counter information using the report view.

4. Click the **View Graph** button to return to the original graph view.

5. Click the **% Processor Time** counter at the bottom in the details screen, and then click the **Highlight** button. Notice that the % Processor Time counter in the graph now appears as a thick white line to make it easier to distinguish from the other counters. Click the **Highlight** button again to remove highlighting from the counter.

6. Right-click on any area within the counter listing at the bottom of the details pane and click **Properties**.

7. In the System Monitor Properties dialog box, click **\Processor(_Total)\% Processor Time** if necessary, and then click on the largest line thickness in the **Width** list box, as shown in Figure 11-12. Click **OK**. The % Processor Time counter now appears as a thick red line on the graph.

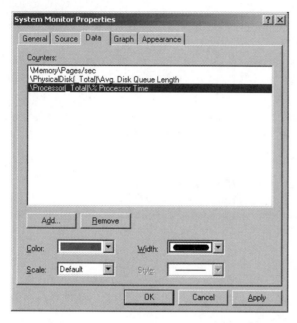

Figure 11-12   Configuring counter properties

8. Click the **Freeze Display** button on the System Monitor toolbar. This pauses the System Monitor view until the button is pressed again.

9. Click the **Update Data** button four or five times to allow the graph to move forward. This button allows you to update the onscreen data manually.

10. Click the **Freeze Display** button again to allow data to be gathered.

11. Click the **Clear Display** button on the System Monitor toolbar to clear and restart all onscreen counters.

12. Leave the Performance console window open.

Performance Objects and Counters

Monitoring performance on your server should be a regular maintenance task. The information you gather can help to establish a baseline of server performance and identify what is considered normal server performance under typical operating conditions. As you continue to monitor your server over time, you can compare the data against the baseline to identify how performance is changing as the network changes and workloads increase. Doing so allows you to pinpoint bottlenecks, such as components that may be hindering server performance, before they become a serious problem.

Any time you upgrade or add a component to a system, whether it is a hardware or software component, you should run System Monitor to determine the effect the change has on server performance.

When monitoring server performance, there are a few performance objects that should be included, as well as specific performance counters associated with each one.

- % Processor Time—This processor counter measures the percentage of time that the processor is executing a non-idle thread. If the value is consistently at or above 80%, a CPU upgrade may be required.

- % Interrupt Time—This processor counter measures hardware interrupts. If you experience a combination of Processor Time exceeding 90% and % Interrupt Time exceeding 15%, check for malfunctioning hardware or device drivers.

- Pages/Second—This memory counter measures the number of pages read in or out to disk to resolve hard page faults. If this number exceeds 20 page faults per second, add more RAM to the computer.

- Page Faults/Second—This memory counter measures the number of hard and soft page faults per second. A hard page fault refers to a request that requires hard disk access, whereas a soft page fault refers to a request found in another part of memory.

- % Disk Time—This physical and logical disk counter measures the percentage of elapsed time that the selected disk drive is busy. If this is above 90%, try moving the page file to another physical drive or upgrading the hard drive.

- Avg. Disk Queue Length—This physical and logical disk counter measures the average number of requests currently outstanding for a volume or partition. If averaging over two, then drive access may be a bottleneck. You may want to upgrade the drive or hard drive controller. Implementing a Stripe Set with multiple drives may also fix this problem.

In Windows NT, all disk counters were turned off by default. In Windows 2000, the physical disk object is turned on by default and the logical disk object is turned off by default. In Windows Server 2003, all disk counters are enabled by default. Disk counters can be turned on or off by using the DISKPERF –Y and DISKPERF –N commands, respectively.

In Activity 11-5 you add various counters to the System Monitor interface.

Activity 11-5: Adding Counters to System Monitor

Time Required: 10 minutes

Objective: Add object counters to the System Monitor tool.

Description: After exploring the various features of the System Monitor interface, you decide to add various counters to the tool to get a better sense of server performance and the purpose of the various counters. In this activity, you add counters to the System Monitor interface, explore the Explain feature for counter objects, and view the counter results using the graph, histogram, and report views.

1. In the Performance console, click the **New Counter Set** button on the System Monitor toolbar. Notice that all counters are removed from the System Monitor details pane.

2. Click the **Add** button on the System Monitor toolbar. The Add Counters dialog box opens, as shown in Figure 11-13.

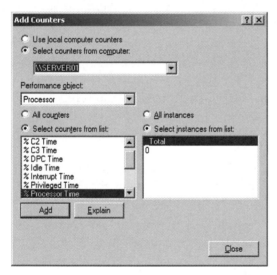

Figure 11-13   The Add Counters dialog box

3. In the Performance object list box, click **PhysicalDisk**.

4. In the Select counters from list list box, click **% Disk Read Time**. In the Select instances from list list box, click the first entry under **_Total**, and then click **Add**.

5. In the Performance object list box, click **Memory**.

6. In the Select counters from list list box, click **Available MBytes**. In the Select instances from list list box, click **_Total** if possible.

7. Click the **Explain** button. This opens a window that explains the purpose of the selected counter, as shown in Figure 11-14.

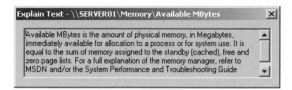

Figure 11-14   Using the Explain button to view the purpose of a selected counter

8. Close the **Explain Text** window.

9. Click the **Add** button to add the counter to System Monitor.

10. In the Performance object list box, click **Network Interface**.

11. Click the **All counters** radio button, and then click **Add**. This adds all of the performance counters for the Network Interface object to the graph.

12. Click **Close**.

13. Notice that the number of counters now available on the graph has increased dramatically. Click the **View Histogram** button to view the counter data using that method, and then click the **View Report** button.

14. Click the **New Counter Set** button to clear all counters from System Monitor.

15. Close the **Performance** console window.

Gathering data with a tool like System Monitor is the easy part. The more difficult part is interpreting the information to determine which component is affecting performance. The difficulty lies in the fact that the performance of some components can affect other components. It may appear from the data that one component is performing poorly when this can be the result of another component performing poorly, or even too well. For example, if you determine that your processor is running over 80%, your first instinct may tell you to upgrade the processor or install multiple processors if the motherboard supports it. Through further analysis by monitoring the Pages / Second Memory counter, however, you may find a lack of memory is the bottleneck causing excess paging. Thus, monitoring multiple components on a regular basis should give you an idea of how they perform together and make troubleshooting server performance that much easier.

The System Monitor tool provides a number of alternatives in terms of saving or viewing historical performance data. One particularly interesting feature is the ability to save System Monitor data to an HTML file. This allows an administrator to post performance data on a Web server, such that it could subsequently be easily viewed and retrieved. When System Monitor data is saved in this format, many of the control functions of the tool are still available through the Web interface. In other words, the data presented is not a simple graphics file, but rather an interactive interface.

The System Monitor tool is also capable of displaying older data that may have been saved to a log file or database using the **Performance Logs and Alerts** tool. This tool is looked at in more detail in the next section.

11

In Activity 11-6, you use the System Monitor tool to save and view a System Monitor graph.

Activity 11-6: Saving and Viewing System Monitor Data

Time Required: 10 minutes

Objective: Explore options for saving System Monitor data.

Description: Although the IT manager at Dover Leasing is aware of the fact that multiple servers can be monitored on a single System Monitor graph, he has asked you to explore the possibility of making counter data available via a Web browser for those users who will not have access to the MMC. In this activity, you save the output of various System Monitor counters to an HTML file and then access that HTML file using Internet Explorer to monitor your server.

1. Click **Start**, select **Administrative Tools**, and then click **Performance**.

2. Allow the System Monitor graph to gather information until the end right side of the window is almost reached, and then click the **Freeze Display** button.

3. Right-click on an area within the graph and click **Save As**.

4. In the Save As dialog box, click the **D:** drive in the Save in list box.

5. In the File name text box, type **sysmon**, and then click the **Save** button.

6. Click **Start**, and then click **My Computer**. Browse to the **D:** drive, and then double-click the file **sysmon.htm**.

7. The sysmon.htm file opens in Internet Explorer and displays the System Monitor details pane, as shown in Figure 11-15.

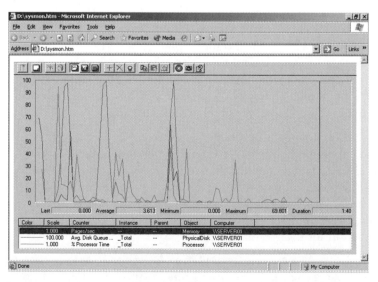

Figure 11-15 Viewing System Monitor data in a Web browser

8. In the Internet Explorer window, click the **Avg. Disk Queue Length** counter at the bottom of the window, and then click the **Highlight** button. Notice that even though the System Monitor information is displayed in a Web browser, some of its ordinary functions are still available.

9. Click the **View Histogram** button, and then click the **View Report** button. Notice that both of these functions are also supported from the Web browser interface. Click the **View Graph** button.

10. Click the **Freeze Display** button in the Internet Explorer window to deselect it. When the System Monitor Control dialog box opens, click **Yes**. Notice that the Web page automatically begins updating counter data again.

11. Close **Internet Explorer**.

12. In the Performance window, click the **New Counter Set** button to clear all counters from System Monitor.

13. Close the **Performance console** window, and close all open windows.

Performance Logs and Alerts

11

Another tool available within the Performance console is Performance Logs and Alerts. This tool allows you to automatically collect data on the local computer or from another computer on the network, and then view it using System Monitor or another program such as Microsoft Excel or a relational database such as Microsoft SQL Server.

Performance Logs and Alerts allows you to perform the following tasks:

- Collect data in a binary, comma-separated, tab-separated format, or SQL Server database format; the binary versions of the log files can be read with System Monitor, but comma- and tab-separated data can easily be imported into another program for analysis
- View data both while it is being collected and after it has been collected
- Configure parameters such as start and stop times for log generation, file names, and file size
- Configure and manage multiple logging sessions from a single console window
- Set up alerts so a message is sent, a program is run, or a log file is started when a specific counter exceeds or drops below a configured value

You can access Performance Logs and Alerts through the Performance console. There are three options available under Performance Logs and Alerts:

- Counter Logs
- Trace Logs
- Alerts

Counter logs take the information that you view using System Monitor and save it to a log file. One of the main advantages of using counter logs is that you can configure logging to start and stop at different intervals. **Trace logs** are similar to counter logs but are triggered to start when an event occurs. You can use **Alerts** to configure an event to occur when a counter meets a predefined value. For example, you might choose to run a specific program or utility automatically when a certain threshold is reached, or send a message to a network administrator.

Configuring Alerts

Logging does increase overhead on a server, so it is generally not something you want to have running all the time. It is essential that you set up a regular schedule for collecting data, and then review this data regularly as part of a proactive server monitoring strategy. Because logging should not be running constantly, alerts should be set up to notify you of a potential problem. For example, you can configure an alert to monitor processor usage, and notify you if it exceeds 80%.

Table 11-3 summarizes the available options on the Action tab, as illustrated in Figure 11-16.

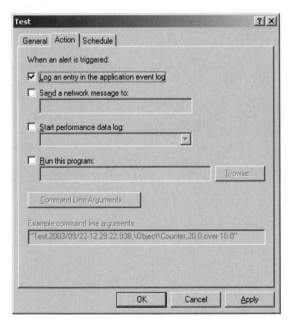

Figure 11-16   The Action tab of an alert

Table 11-3   Actions that can be taken when an alert is triggered

Action	Description
Log an entry in the application event log	An entry is added to the application log when the event is triggered
Send a network message to	Messenger service sends a message to the specified computer when the alert is triggered
Start performance data log	Counter log is run when the alert is triggered
Run this program	Specified program is run when the alert is triggered
Command Line Arguments	Specified command line arguments are copied when the Run this program option is used

In Activity 11-7, you configure Performance Logs and Alerts settings on your Windows Server 2003 computer.

ACTIVITY

Activity 11-7: Configuring Performance Logs and Alerts

Time Required: 15 minutes

Objective: Configure performance logging and alerts.

11

Description: Although the servers at Dover Leasing are monitored regularly during business hours, the company still does not have staff on hand outside of business hours to monitor system performance. Because of this, the IT manager has asked you to look into features of the Performance console that will allow data to be gathered after hours. Similarly, he would also like to have alerts configured such that an administrator would receive an onscreen message in the event that a critical server threshold is reached. In this activity, you will explore and configure various logging options as well as configure alerts using Performance Logs and Alerts.

1. Click **Start**, select **Administrative Tools**, and then click **Performance**.

2. Click the **plus sign (+)** next to **Performance Logs and Alerts** to expand its contents.

3. Click the **Counter Logs** icon to view its contents. Notice that a single sample log exists by default with the name System Overview.

4. Double-click the **System Overview** icon to view its properties. The System Overview Properties dialog box opens, as shown in Figure 11-17.

5. Notice the log file name associated with the log, the counters that the log includes, and the interval at which data is being gathered.

6. Click the **Log Files** tab.

7. Click the **Log file type** list arrow to view all of the different log type options available, as illustrated in Figure 11-18.

8. Click the **Schedule** tab. This tab allows you to schedule stop and start times for the log if necessary.

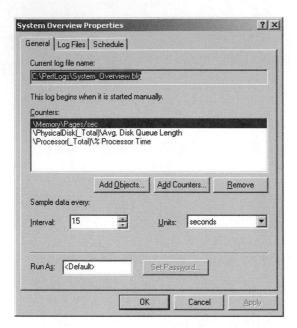

Figure 11-17   The System Overview Properties dialog box

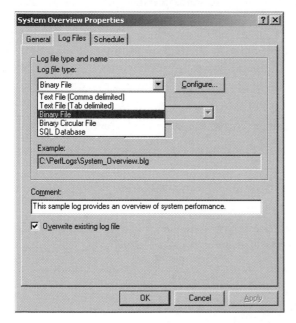

Figure 11-18   Configuring Log type options

9. Click **Cancel**.

10. Right-click the **System Overview** icon and click **Start**. Notice that the icon turns from red to green.

11. Wait approximately two minutes, and then right-click the **System Overview** icon and click **Stop**.

12. Click the **System Monitor** icon. On the System Monitor toolbar, click the **View Log Data** button.

13. When the System Monitor Properties dialog box opens, click the **Log files** radio button, and then click **Add**.

14. In the Select Log File dialog box, browse to **C:\PerfLogs**, click the **System_Overview.blg** file to select it, click **Open**, and then click **OK**. This loads the data stored in the System_Overview.blg log file into the System Monitor window.

15. Under Performance Logs and Alerts, click the **Alerts** icon to view its contents. There are no alerts configured by default.

16. Click **Start**, select **Administrative Tools**, and then click **Services**.

17. Right-click the **Alerter** service icon and click **Properties**.

18. In the Startup type list box, click **Automatic**. Click **OK**.

19. Right-click the **Alerter** service and click **Start**.

20. Right-click the **Messenger** service icon and click **Properties**.

21. In the Startup type list box, click **Automatic**. Click **OK**.

22. Right-click the **Messenger** service and click **Start**.

23. In the Performance window, right-click **Alerts** and click **New Alert Settings**.

24. In the New Alert Settings dialog box, type **CPU Utilization** in the Name text box and click **OK**.

25. On the General tab of the CPU Utilization dialog box, click the **Add** button.

26. In the Add Counters dialog box, click the **Add** button to add the % Processor Time counter, and then click **Close**.

27. Type **30** in the Limit text box to have the alert triggered when CPU utilization reaches a value over 30%, as illustrated in Figure 11-19.

28. In the **Interval** spin box, type **1**.

29. Click the **Action** tab. Click the check box next to **Send a network message to** and then type **Admin01** in the associated text box. Click **OK**.

30. Click **Start**, click **Run**, and type **wmplayer.exe** in the Open text box. Click **OK**. The Windows Media Player opens, which usually increases the CPU utilization for brief periods.

31. When the Messenger Service dialog box opens onscreen, as illustrated in Figure 11-20, read its contents and click **OK**.

32. Close all open windows.

11

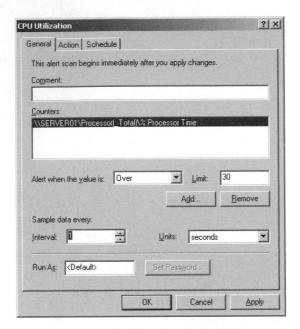

Figure 11-19   Configuring alert settings

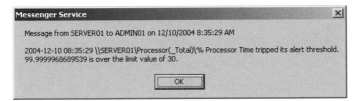

Figure 11-20   The Messenger Service dialog box, triggered by an alert

CONFIGURING AND MANAGING SERVICES

When it comes to optimizing and securing your server, one of the first things you can do is disable any unnecessary components, such as services. When a service is unnecessarily installed during setup or is no longer used, it should be disabled. Running unnecessary services consumes additional system resources such as memory and CPU, thus adding overhead to a system. For example, if you have installed Internet Information Services on a server for testing purposes and then no longer require it, the service should be uninstalled, or associated services should be disabled via the Services MMC. If not, it continues to run in the background and consumes resources, even though it may not be performing any valuable system function.

The services that you disable depend on the role the server plays on the network. For example, a Web server requires different services than a print server. Another consideration is service dependencies. Before you stop or disable a service, check to see if there are any other services running that depend on the service. Use the Dependencies tab of a service to view the other services it depends upon to function correctly. Use this tab in the properties of a service to view the other services that are dependent upon the one you are disabling. Figure 11-21 illustrates the Dependencies tab of the Messenger service.

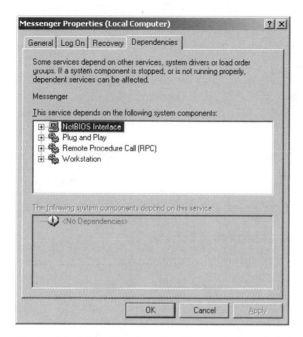

Figure 11-21   Viewing the Dependencies tab for the Messenger service

The Services MMC allows you to configure a variety of settings related to how services function and respond to potential problems on a Windows Server 2003 system. The properties of a service include four different configuration tabs, as follows:

- General — Displays a service's name, description, the path to the executable file, service startup parameters, and buttons allowing you to start, stop, pause, and resume a service

- Log On — Allows you to specify the user name that a service runs as, along with the hardware profiles for which the service is enabled

- Recovery — Allows you to configure the computer's response when a service fails, including different actions depending on the number of failures; also allows you to specify a program that should be run when a service failure occurs

- Dependencies — Specifies the services that a service depends upon to function correctly, as well as the services that depend on this service to function

In Activity 11-8, you configure the properties of various services on your server.

Activity 11-8: Configuring Windows Server 2003 Services

Time Required: 10 minutes

Objective: Configure the startup properties and settings of Windows Server 2003 services.

Description: The IT manager at Dover Leasing is very concerned about the levels of resource utilization of corporate servers, including the impact that this ultimately has on performance for users. He is also concerned about the security risks associated with having unnecessary services running on various servers throughout the organization. In this activity, you configure service startup settings, as well as other configuration options, such as how a service reacts to a failure.

1. Click **Start**, select **Administrative Tools**, and then click **Services**. The Services MMC opens, as illustrated in Figure 11-22.

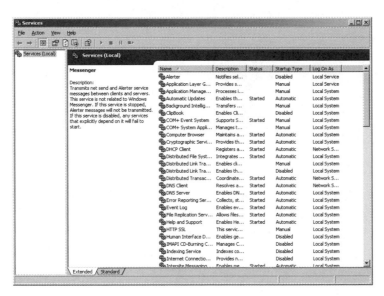

Figure 11-22   The Services MMC

2. Right-click the **Remote Desktop Help Session Manager** service icon, and then click **Properties**. The Remote Desktop Help Session Manager Properties dialog box opens, as shown in Figure 11-23.

3. In the Startup type list box, click **Automatic**. This sets the Remote Desktop Help Session Manager service to start automatically the next time the computer restarts.

4. Click the **Apply** button, and then click the **Start** button. This manually starts the Remote Desktop Help Session Manager service.

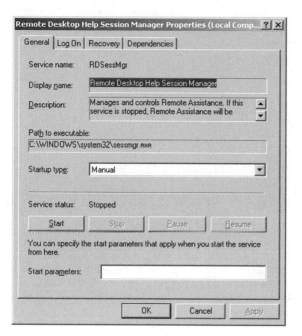

Figure 11-23   The General tab in the properties of a service

5. Click the **Log On** tab. This displays the properties of the account under which the Remote Desktop Help Session Manager service will run, as shown in Figure 11–24.

6. Click the **Recovery** tab.

7. In the First failure list box, click **Restart the Service**.

8. In the Second failure list box, click **Run a Program**, as shown in Figure 11–25.

9. In the Program text box, type **cmd.exe**. This causes the Command Prompt program to start in the event that the Remote Desktop Help Session Manager service fails for a second time.

10. Click the **Dependencies** tab. Review the list of services that the Remote Desktop Help Session Manager service depends upon. Click **OK**.

11. Right-click the **Messenger** icon and click **Properties**.

12. In the Startup type list box, click **Disabled**. This prevents the Messenger service from starting the next time the computer reboots. Click **OK**.

13. Close all open windows.

11

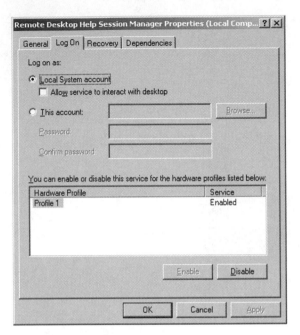

Figure 11-24   The Log On tab in the properties of a service

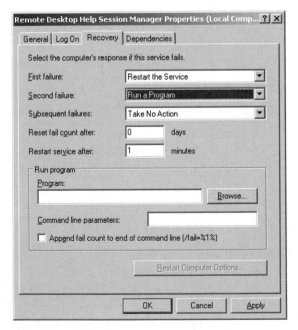

Figure 11-25   The Recovery tab in the properties of a service

CHAPTER SUMMARY

- The Windows Task Manager utility can be used to view and control running applications and processes, obtain basic performance information, view network utilization information, and view connected users.

- The Event Viewer tool is used to view information, warning, and error events relating to the operating system and installed applications. All Windows Server 2003 systems include system, security, and application logs. Additional logs may also be present based on the role of the server, such as in the case of a domain controller.

- The Performance console is the primary server monitoring utility provided with Windows Server 2003. It consists of two main tools: System Monitor and Performance Logs and Alerts.

- System Monitor is a Windows Server 2003 performance-monitoring utility that allows various server resources to be monitored graphically or in a report view. Monitoring can be configured for a combination of local and remote systems in a single graph, histogram, or report.

- Performance Logs and Alerts is another Windows Server 2003 performance-monitoring utility that allows data about server resources to be collected for additional analysis. Both counter and trace logs can be configured with this tool, and alerts can be configured to identify when performance moves outside of predefined parameters.

- A number of background services run on a Windows Server 2003 system by default, with the exact services dependent upon the applications and server services installed on the system. Disabling unnecessary services, or uninstalling unnecessary applications can help to optimize a server.

KEY TERMS

Alert — An alert performs a specified action once a counter meets the specified setting. Once an alert is triggered, a message can be sent, a program can be run, a counter log started, or an event can be written to the application log.

Application log — Where applications that are written to Microsoft standards record event information. The application developer determines the type of information an application writes to the log file.

baseline — A performance benchmark that is used to determine what is normal server performance under a specific workload.

counter logs — Performance data that is collected into a comma-separated or tab-separated format.

Event Viewer — A utility used to view the contents of the system, security, and application logs.

Performance console — A pre-defined MMC that includes both the System Monitor and Performance Logs and Alerts tools.

performance counters — Data items associated with a particular performance object used to measure a certain aspect of performance.

Performance Logs and Alerts — A tool included with Windows Server 2003 that enables you to create counter logs, trace logs, and configure alerts.

performance objects — System components that you can monitor using System Monitor.

Security log — The spot where events pertaining to the audit policy are written. By default, security logging is disabled until an audit policy is configured.

System log — The spot where system components such as services and device drivers record information, warnings, and errors.

System Monitor — A tool that allows you to gather and view real—time performance statistics of a local or network computer.

Task Manager — A tool used to view the processes and applications currently running on a system. Also provides basic resource usage statistics.

trace logs — Where data provider collects performance data when an event occurs.

REVIEW QUESTIONS

1. Which of the following Task Manager tabs allows the priority of a running process to be configured?

    a. Applications

    b. Processes

    c. Performance

    d. Users

2. Which of the following methods can be used to access the Task Manager utility?

    a. Press Ctrl+Alt+Delete, then click Task Manager

    b. Press Ctrl+T

    c. Right-click on the taskbar, click Task Manager

    d. Click Start, click Task Manager

3. Which of the following are logs found in Event Viewer on a Windows Server 2003 system?

    a. system log

    b. application log

    c. security log

    d. program log

4. Which of the following Task Manager tabs can be used to view the current status of a foreground program?

   a. Processes

   b. Applications

   c. Users

   d. Networking

5. Operating system events are always written to the application log in Event Viewer.

   a. True

   b. False

6. Which of the following tools is included in the Performance console?

   a. System Monitor

   b. Task Manager

   c. Performance Logs and Alerts

   d. Computer Management

7. Which of the following is not an action associated with an alert?

   a. Send a network message to

   b. Start performance data log

   c. Run this program

   d. Disable a service

8. Which of the following counters is displayed by default in the System Monitor display when the Performance console is opened?

   a. Pages/sec

   b. Avg. Disk Queue Length

   c. % Memory Time

   d. % Processor Time

9. What term is used to describe a service that must be running in order for another service to function?

   a. Dependency

   b. Dedicated

   c. Process

   d. Processor

10. Windows Server 2003 systems will only log information events in the system log in Event Viewer by default.

    a. True

    b. False

11

11. System Monitor can be used to monitor performance information on a remote computer.

    a. True

    b. False

12. Disk performance counters are enabled by default on a Windows Server 2003 system.

    a. True

    b. False

13. Which command is used to enable or disable disk counters on a Windows Server 2003 system?

    a. DISKPERF

    b. DISKPART

    c. DISKPARK

    d. DISKLOT

14. Which of the following is not a type of event stored in the system log in Event Viewer?

    a. information

    b. warning

    c. error

    d. success

15. The data displayed on the Task Manager Performance tab can be exported to a text file.

    a. True

    b. False

16. Which of the following is a valid Recovery action in the event of a service failure?

    a. Take No Action

    b. Restart the Service

    c. Run a Program

    d. Stop the Service

17. Which of the following are available views in the System Monitor tool? (Choose all that apply.)

    a. Report

    b. Histogram

    c. Graph

    d. Pie Chart

18. The CPU column on the Task Manager Processes tab displays point-in-time CPU usage information.

   a. True

   b. False

19. Which of the following are valid performance objects in System Monitor on a Windows Server 2003 system? (Choose all that apply.)

   a. Memory

   b. Processor

   c. Server

   d. System

20. It is not possible to monitor objects on more than one server at the same time using System Monitor.

   a. True

   b. False

11

CASE PROJECTS

CASE
PROJECTS

Case Project 11-1

You are responsible for the administration of three Dover Leasing servers. You have recently installed a new service on your server. The service is set to start automatically and run continuously to service user requests. Your manager is concerned about server performance after the service is installed, and you assure him that performance should not suffer. Answer the following questions based on the scenario.

1. After you install the service, what is one of the first things you should do?

2. During peak hours, your manager stops in to see how the server is performing under the added workload. What tool can you use to quickly show your manager the current processor usage on the server?

3. You have a slight concern that the service may indeed have an impact on the amount of time the processor is utilized. The % utilization was running at times near 50% before the service was installed. You would like to be notified if the processor utilization exceeds 60%. Explain how this can be done. What other actions can be configured if this occurs?

4. Because the server is working under an increased workload, you want to disable any unnecessary services to eliminate the overhead associated with running them. What should you consider before disabling any services on the server?

Case Project 11-2

The IT manager at Dover Leasing is looking for a quick way for junior administrators to monitor the performance of Windows Server 2003 systems on the network from any internal desktop system. Given that desktops are running a range of operating systems including Windows 98, Windows 2000, and Windows XP, what would be the best way to accomplish this?

Case Project 11-3

The development staff at Dover Leasing is in the process of developing an SQL Server-based application for the purpose of monitoring historical server performance and baseline data. Which Windows Server 2003 tool and specific data gathering option would be best suited to obtaining this information?

12

MANAGING AND IMPLEMENTING BACKUPS AND DISASTER RECOVERY

After reading this chapter and completing the exercises, you will be able to:

♦ Plan for disaster recovery of Windows Server 2003 systems

♦ Back up and restore data

♦ Implement shadow copy volumes

♦ Understand the purpose of the Automated System Recovery feature

♦ Understand Windows Server 2003 advanced startup options

♦ Install and use the Recovery Console

One of the most important roles of any network administrator is to ensure that systems and user data remain available, even under adverse circumstances. Part of ensuring server availability involves implementing and maintaining an effective backup and disaster recovery strategy such that when issues arise, they can be dealt with quickly and effectively.

Windows Server 2003 includes a number of different tools, utilities, and features that can be used as part of a backup and disaster recovery strategy. Throughout this chapter you not only learn about how to use the various tools and utilities effectively, but also how to plan and implement an effective disaster recovery strategy using both traditional methods and new features introduced in Windows Server 2003.

PLANNING FOR DISASTER RECOVERY

Although the accidental deletion of user data files is far more common than a full server failure, administrators still need to be prepared in case disaster strikes. When such issues do arise, an administrator should be prepared to get systems up and running again as quickly as possible, ensuring that all necessary data is also available. To make this easier, Windows Server 2003 includes a number of different features:

- The Backup utility—This backs up and restores operating system, application, and user data files. The Backup utility included with Windows Server 2003 allows backup jobs to be scheduled, critical System State information to be backed up and restored, and provides access to the Automated System Recovery feature.

- Shadow Copies of Shared Volumes—A new feature that allows users to access previous versions of files in shared folders when older versions need to be restored, when a file is accidentally deleted, or when they simply want to compare the current version of a file to an older version. Ultimately, this feature helps to reduce administrative burden by providing users with access to previous versions of files, without the need to contact an administrator to manually restore that file from backup.

- Automated System Recovery (ASR)—Another new feature that provides a mechanism for recovering a server from configuration information stored on floppy disks when used in conjunction with the Windows Server 2003 CD-ROM. Although this feature helps an administrator to restore the operating system and configuration settings quickly, applications need to be reinstalled and data needs to be restored from backup, since ASR handles neither process.

- Advanced startup options—These include familiar startup methods such as Safe Mode, Last Known Good Configuration, and others. These different modes allow an administrator to attempt to boot Windows Server 2003 when recent configuration settings make a normal boot unavailable.

- The Recovery Console—A command-line environment into which an administrator can boot a server in order to troubleshoot or make configuration changes when the operating system will not boot normally.

Each of the tools, utilities, and features listed here are looked at in more detail in subsequent sections.

BACKING UP AND RESTORING DATA

Windows Server 2003 includes a backup utility that allows you to restore an operating system or data in the event of a total hardware or storage media failure. The Windows Server 2003 Backup utility builds on the backup utility originally introduced in Windows 2000 and represents a significant improvement over backup utilities included with previous versions of Windows. Using the Windows Server 2003 Backup utility, you can perform a variety of tasks, including:

- Back up and restore files and folders
- Schedule a backup
- Back up Windows 2003 System State data
- Restore all or a portion of the Active Directory database
- Create an Automated System Recovery (ASR) backup

The Windows Server 2003 Backup utility also supports a wide variety of storage devices and media, such as tape drives, recordable CD-ROM drives, logical drives (such as local partitions and volumes), and removable disks.

12

Backup and Restore Concepts

The main reason for backing up both operating system and user data files is to ensure that both are available in the case of accidental deletion by users, or when some type of server failure occurs. A primary goal of any network administrator is to ensure that in the event of accidental deletion or failure, data can be restored (and made available to users) as quickly as possible. To meet this goal, data backup processes must be performed regularly, or the possibility exists that newer or updated files will not be available when a restoration process is necessary. Thankfully, the Backup utility included with Windows Server 2003 provides administrators with a great deal of flexibility when it comes to performing backups, allowing different types of backups to be performed according to the needs and requirements of an organization. Each of the backup types supported with this utility is looked at later in this section.

In many corporate environments, the amount of data that needs to be backed up regularly varies greatly. For example, a small organization may be able to simply back up user data files to a dedicated partition or volume on a server, since the total size of user files may be relatively small. In larger organizations, however, many servers may be present, and hundreds of gigabytes of backup storage space may be required. In these situations, companies typically invest in dedicated tape backup devices, ranging from simple single-tape hardware devices on individual servers to large centralized (and potentially automated) storage systems. The biggest single issue that determines the backup hardware and software implemented is usually the amount of user and application data present on network systems. However, operating system files are also typically backed up to ensure that these files can also be restored when necessary.

One key consideration that should be part of any backup strategy is determining which users should (or should not) have the ability to back up files and folders. In order to perform a backup, certain rights and permissions are required. By default, members of the following local groups can back up any files and folders on a member server running Windows Server 2003:

- Administrators
- Backup Operators
- Server Operators

In a domain environment, an administrator might instead choose to grant certain users the ability to back up any files and folders on all domain systems. Members of the Administrators, Backup Operators, or Server Operators domain local groups on a domain controller can back up any files or folders on any system within a domain.

Users who are not members of the Administrators or Backup Operators groups (on either their local system or a domain controller) are limited in terms of the files and folders that they can back up. In order for these users to back up files, they must either be listed as the owner of the file, or have one or more of the following NTFS permissions:

- Read
- Read and execute
- Modify
- Full Control

The primary purpose of limiting the files and folders that a normal user can back up is to ensure proper security. In cases where users need to be able to back up files and folders belonging to other users, they should be granted membership in the Backup Operators group, assigned at least the read permission for the files and folders in question, or granted the appropriate rights.

Two main rights are associated with the ability to back up and restore files and folders. These settings are configured via Group Policy, in the Computer Configuration > Windows Settings > Security Settings > Local Policies > User Rights Assignment section, as shown in Figure 12-1. The two main settings that impact the ability to back up and restore files are the Back up files and directories and Restore files and directories rights, respectively. If granted in a Group Policy object applied to the Domain Controllers OU, these rights apply to all domain systems. However, these settings can also be configured locally, or in a Group Policy object. When applied in a Group Policy object at the site, domain, or OU level, systems that fall under the scope of these policies have the settings applied. Figure 12-2 illustrates the Back up files and directories Properties dialog box as configured in the Default Domain Controllers Policy.

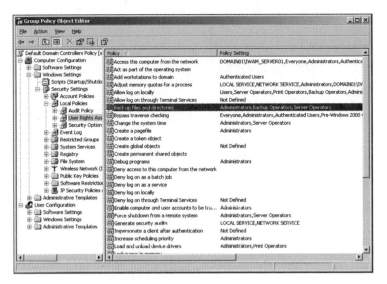

Figure 12-1   The Back up files and directories right in the Default Domain
Controllers Policy

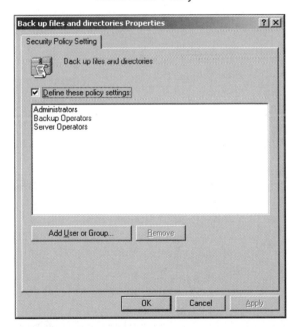

Figure 12-2   The Back up files and directories Properties window

The Windows Server 2003 Backup utility also provides additional security for any backup jobs created by selecting the Allow only the owner and the Administrator access to the backup data check box in the Backup Job Information dialog box, as shown in Figure 12-3. When selected, only the person who created the backup or an administrator has the ability to restore the backup, regardless of which users have the rights or permissions to restore files.

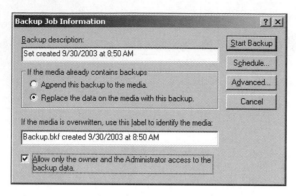

Figure 12-3   The Backup Job Information dialog box

Backup Types

Like most major backup programs, the Windows Server 2003 Backup Utility supports a variety of backup types, including:

- Normal backup
- Incremental backup
- Differential backup
- Daily backup
- Copy backup

Each of these backup methods and their impact on backup procedures are looked at in the following sections.

Normal Backup

The most common (and default) type of backup performed by the Backup utility is known as a **normal backup**. When chosen, this backup type backs up all selected files and folders, and clears the archive attribute on these files and folders. The purpose of clearing the archive attribute is to mark files as having been backed up, an important distinction when a normal backup is used in conjunction with some of the other backup methods outlined in this section.

Although the normal backup type backs up all selected files and folders, it is not always the best choice for backup jobs. For example, if an administrator were to specify a normal backup for Monday, and then complete another normal backup of the same files and folders for Tuesday, all files would be backed up again, regardless of whether any changes had taken place. This would result in larger-than-necessary backups, and duplicate copies of identical files being stored. While there is nothing explicitly wrong with this, it can be very inefficient. In most situations, administrators will begin the week with a normal backup of all necessary files, and then use either incremental or differential backups on subsequent days. Both incremental and differential backups, along with their impacts on backup processes, are looked at shortly.

Incremental Backup

The **incremental backup** type is significantly different from a normal backup. Instead of backing up all selected files and folders, it only backs up those files that have changed since the last normal or incremental backup took place. In a similar manner to a normal backup, an incremental backup also clears the archive attribute associated with any files and folders that it does back up.

The main purpose of an incremental backup is to reduce the overall size of backup jobs. For example, let's say that an administrator creates a normal backup of selected files and folders on Monday. If an incremental backup is then performed on these same files and folders on Tuesday, only those files that have changed since Monday will be backed up. Then, if another incremental backup is performed on Wednesday, only those files that have changed since Tuesday will be backed up, and so on. This method ensures that backups created after the initial normal backup take as little time as possible.

While an incremental backup strategy ensures that backups take the least time possible, they do result in a more involved restore process. For example, let's say that a folder containing user data is accidentally deleted on Thursday morning. In order to restore this data completely, an administrator needs to first restore the normal backup from Monday, and then the incremental backups from both Tuesday and Wednesday. This ensures that all files that have been backed up since Monday are again available.

12

Figure 12-4 illustrates the backup and restore processes for a folder named Data using a combination of normal and incremental backup types.

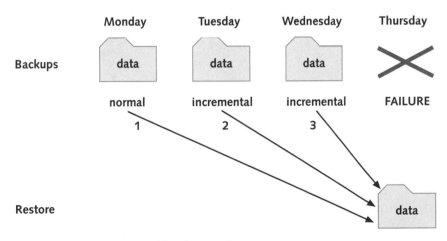

Figure 12-4   Incremental backup and restore operations

Differential Backup

The **differential backup** type is different from both a normal and incremental backup. Instead of backing up all selected files and folders, it only backs up those files that have changed since the last normal or incremental backup took place. In contrast to a normal or incremental backup, a differential backup does not clear the archive attribute associated with any files and folders that it backs up.

The main purpose of a differential backup is to reduce the overall size of backup jobs, although not to the same degree as an incremental backup. For example, let's say that an administrator creates a normal backup of selected files and folders on Monday. If a differential backup is then performed on these same files and folders on Tuesday, all files that have changed since Monday are backed up. Then, if another differential backup is performed on Wednesday, again all files that have changed since Monday are backed up, and so on.

While a differential backup strategy ensures that the restore process is less involved, they do result in a more involved backup process. For example, let's again say that a folder containing user data is accidentally deleted on Thursday morning. In order to completely restore this data, an administrator would need to first restore the normal backup from Monday, and then only the differential backup from Wednesday. Because the differential backup performed on Wednesday includes all changes to files since Monday, this ensures that all files that have been backed up since Monday are again available.

Figure 12-5 illustrates the backup and restore processes for a folder named Data using a combination of normal and differential backup types.

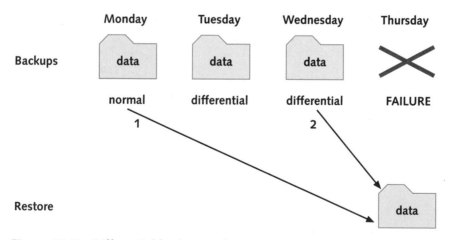

Figure 12-5   Differential backup and restore operations

Daily Backup

Unlike the other backup types explored already, the **daily backup** backs up selected files or folders that have been created or changed on the day that the backup takes place. When this method is used, the archive attribute is not changed, and, as such, it does not interfere with any existing backup procedures that may already be in place.

Copy Backup

In the same way that a normal backup backs up all selected files and folders, a **copy backup** does the same. However, a copy backup doesn't change the archive attribute associated with a backed up file or folder to mark it as having been backed up. The main purpose of a copy backup is to create the equivalent of a normal backup (perhaps for a backup tape to ultimately be stored offsite) without interrupting any other backup procedures in place.

Using the Backup Utility

The most common use of the Windows Server 2003 **Backup utility** is to back up critical data and operating system files to ensure that recovery is possible in the event that files are accidentally deleted or a disaster occurs. The Backup utility can be used in two different modes, known as Wizard mode and Advanced mode. As the name suggests, Wizard mode walks you step-by-step through the process of creating a backup or restoring files, while Advanced mode provides complete control over the file and folder selection process through a standard graphical interface. The Backup or Restore Wizard interface is show in Figure 12-6.

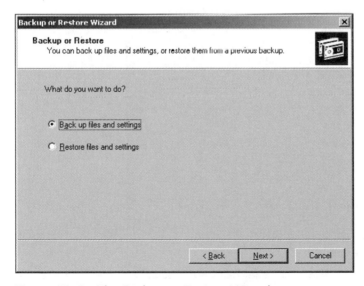

Figure 12-6   The Backup or Restore Wizard

As outlined earlier in this section, the Backup utility allows you to back up and restore files, schedule backups if necessary, back up critical operating system information known as System State data, restore Active Directory or related objects, and access the Automated System Restore (ASR) feature. In Activity 12-1 you use the Backup utility to back up the contents of a folder on your server using Advanced mode.

Activity 12-1: Backing Up Files and Folders Using the Backup Utility

Time Required: 15 minutes

Objective: Back up files and folders using the Windows Server 2003 Backup utility.

Description: The IT manager is currently in the process of trying to select a backup software solution for all Windows Server 2003 systems at Dover Leasing. You have been asked to test the capabilities of the Backup utility included with Windows Server 2003 as part of this process. In this activity you use the Backup utility to back up a folder and the files that it contains on your server.

1. Click **Start**, select **All Programs**, select **Accessories**, select **System Tools**, and then click **Backup**.

2. In the Backup or Restore Wizard dialog box that opens, click the **Advanced Mode** link to access the complete functionality of the Backup program. The Backup utility window appears, as shown in Figure 12-7.

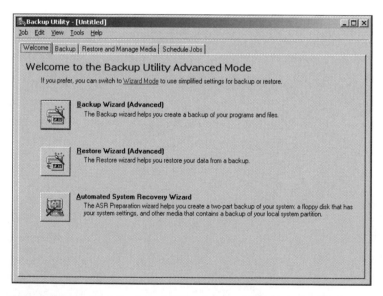

Figure 12-7   The Backup Utility Advanced Mode window

3. Click the **Backup** tab.

4. Click the **plus sign (+)** next to **Local Disk (C:)** to expand its contents.

5. Click the **plus sign (+)** next to **WINDOWS** to expand its contents.

6. Click the **plus sign (+)** next to **system32** to expand its contents.

7. Click the **config** folder to view its contents. Click the check box next to **config** to select the entire folder for backup, as illustrated in Figure 12-8.

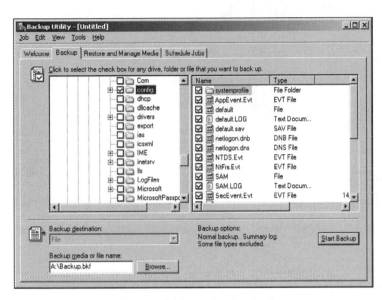

Figure 12-8   Selecting a folder to be backed up

8. In the Backup media or file name text box, type **d:\backup-config.bkf**, and then click the **Start Backup** button.

9. In the Backup Job Information dialog box, review the details provided, and then click the **Advanced** button.

10. In the Advanced Backup Options window, check the **Verify data after backup** check box, as shown in Figure 12-9. Click the **Backup Type** drop-down menu to view available backup options, but be sure that settings are left in the Normal configuration setting. Click **OK**.

11. Click the **Start Backup** button.

12. Once started, the Backup Progress window appears. Once the backup is complete, click the **Report** button, shown in Figure 12-10.

13. Close the **backup01.log** window (the number following the name of your log file may be different).

14. Close the Backup Progress window, and then close the Backup Utility window.

In Activity 12-2 you restore the files that you backed up in Activity 12-1.

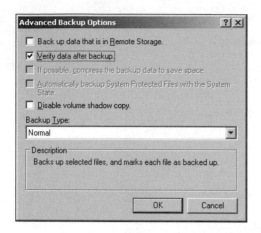

Figure 12-9   The Advanced Backup Options dialog box

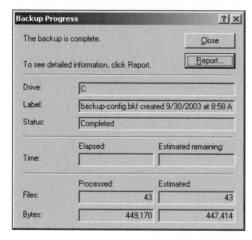

Figure 12-10   The Backup Progress dialog box

Activity 12-2: Restoring Files and Folders Using the Backup Utility

Time Required: 10 minutes

Objective: Restore files and folders using the Windows Server 2003 Backup utility.

Description: Having used the Backup utility to back up a folder and its contents in the previous activity, you decide to test the restore capabilities of this program. In this activity you restore a folder using the Backup utility Advanced Mode interface.

1. Click **Start**, and then click **Run**. In the Open text box type **ntbackup.exe** and click **OK**.

2. In the Backup or Restore Wizard dialog box that opens, click the **Advanced Mode** link to access the complete functionality of the Backup program.

3. Click the **Restore and Manage Media** tab. The backup job just created is listed, as shown in Figure 12-11.

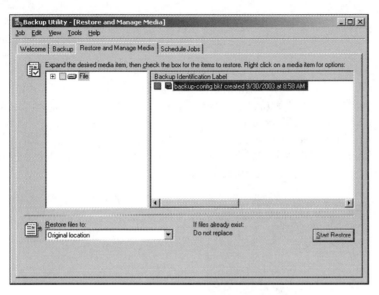

Figure 12-11   The Restore and Manage Media tab

4. Click the **plus sign (+)** next to the **File** icon to expand its contents.

5. Click the **plus sign (+)** next to **backup-config.bkf** to expand its contents.

6. Click the **plus sign (+)** next to **C:** to expand its contents.

7. Click the **plus sign (+)** next to **WINDOWS** to expand its contents.

8. Click the **plus sign (+)** next to **system32** to expand its contents.

9. Click the **config** folder to view the contents of the backup file. Check the check box next to the **config** folder.

10. In the Restore files to list box, click **Alternate location**.

11. In the Alternate location text box, type **D:\configbackup** and click the **Start Restore** button. Ultimately, this restores the contents of the backup-config.bkf file to the configbackup folder.

12. In the Confirm Restore dialog box, click **OK**.

13. After the Restore process is complete, click the **Close** button in the Restore Progress screen.

14. Close the Backup Utility window.

15. Click **Start**, and then click **My Computer**. Double-click drive **D:**, and then double-click the **configbackup** folder.

12

16. Double-click the **WINDOWS**, **system32**, and **config** folders to view their contents, confirming that the contents of the backup file were restored to an alternate location.

17. Close all open windows.

Scheduling Backups

In order to ensure that backups are completed without any interaction from an administrator, the Windows Server 2003 backup utility also supports the ability to schedule configured backups to take place according to the customer needs and requirements. For example, backups can be scheduled to take place daily, weekly, or monthly, at predefined times, or on predefined days. Figure 12-12 illustrates the Schedule Job dialog box from the Advanced settings of the Backup or Restore Wizard.

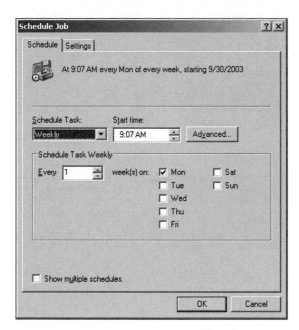

Figure 12-12   Scheduling backups

In Activity 12-3 you use the Backup or Restore Wizard to create and then schedule a backup operation on your server.

Activity 12-3: Scheduling Backup Operations Using the Backup Utility

Time Required: 10 minutes

Objective: Schedule a backup using the Windows Server 2003 Backup utility.

Description: Having manually created a backup of a folder and its files in Activity 12-1, you decide to test the ability to have this folder backed up automatically using the scheduling feature of the Windows Server 2003 backup utility. In this activity you use the Backup or Restore Wizard to define a new backup job, and then schedule this backup job to occur daily.

1. Click **Start**, and then click **Run**. In the Open text box type **ntbackup.exe** and click **OK**.

2. In the Backup or Restore Wizard dialog box that opens, click **Next**.

3. At the Backup or Restore screen, ensure that **Back up files and settings** is selected, and click **Next**.

4. At the What to Back Up screen, click the **Let me choose what to back up** radio button, and click **Next**.

5. At the Items to Back Up screen, click the **plus sign (+)** next to **My Computer** in the Items to back up section. Click the **plus signs (+)** next to **Local Disk (C:)**, **WINDOWS**, and **system32** to view their contents. Check the check box next to the **config** folder, and then click **Next**.

6. At the Backup Type, Destination, and Name screen, click the **Browse** button.

7. At the Save As dialog box, select drive **D:** in the Save in drop-down menu and click **Save**.

8. In the Type a name for this backup text box, type **ScheduledBackup** and click **Next**.

9. At the Completing the Backup or Restore Wizard screen, click the **Advanced** button.

10. At the Type of Backup screen, click **Next**.

11. At the How to Back Up screen, check the **Verify data after backup** check box, and click **Next**.

12. At the Backup Options screen, click the **Replace the existing backups radio** button, and then check the **Allow only the owner and the Administrator access to the backup data and any backups appended to this medium** check box. Click **Next**.

13. At the When to Back Up screen, click the **Later** radio button, as shown in Figure 12-13. Click the **Set Schedule** button.

14. In the Schedule Job window, select **Daily** in the Schedule Task drop-down menu, and select a Start time approximately 10 minutes after the current time. Click **OK**.

15. In the Set Account Information dialog box, type your **AdminXX password** in both the Password and Confirm password text boxes. Click **OK**.

12

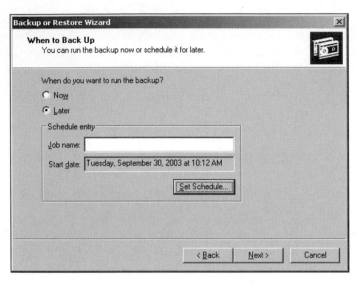

Figure 12-13   The When to Back Up screen of the Backup or Restore Wizard

16. At the When to Back Up screen, type **ScheduledBackup** in the Job name text box, and click **Next**. The Set Account Information dialog box opens again. Enter **your AdminXX password** in both the Password and Confirm password text boxes, then click **OK**.

17. At the Completing the Backup and Restore Wizard screen, click **Finish**.

18. Click **Start**, select **Control Panel**, and then double-click **Scheduled Tasks**. In the Scheduled Tasks window, confirm that a task named ScheduledBackup exists. Close the Scheduled Tasks window.

19. Once the 10 minutes since completing Step 14 has passed, click **Start**, and then click **My Computer**. Double-click on drive **D:** and confirm that a file named ScheduledBackup.bkf exists. This is the backup created automatically as part of the scheduled backup process.

20. Close all open windows.

Backing Up and Restoring System State Data

Besides the ability to back up normal data files and folders, the Windows Server 2003 Backup Utility also provides the ability to back up what is referred to as **System State** data. Backing up the System State data on a Windows Server 2003 system includes the following elements:

- Registry (always)
- COM+ Class Registration database (always)
- Boot files (always)

- Certificate Services database (if Certificate Services is installed)
- Active Directory (only on domain controllers)
- SYSVOL directory (only on domain controllers)
- Cluster service (if the server is part of a cluster)
- IIS Metadirectory (if IIS is installed)
- System files (always)

You should also back up these components regularly with your standard backup schedule. In the event of an Active Directory or system startup failure, the most common solution is to restore the System State data.

One limitation to the Windows Server 2003 Backup utility is that you cannot back up individual components of the System State data. Third-party backup applications, like Veritas Backup Exec, often allow individual component backups.

If you are restoring the System State because of a corrupt Active Directory database, you must restart the computer and choose the Directory Services Restore Mode advanced startup option. You can then use the backup utility to restore the latest System State data from backup. After you restart the computer and Windows Server 2003 starts normally, Active Directory is automatically reindexed and updates Active Directory and the file replication service.

In the event that you are attempting to restore a portion of the Active Directory tree, a few additional steps may be required. For example, if an OU was inadvertently deleted by an administrator, you can still use the Windows Server 2003 Backup Utility to restore the System State in an attempt to restore the deleted OU. One problem with this scenario is that when an Active Directory object is restored from backup, the other domain controllers still think that the object should be deleted. When replication takes place with the other domain controllers, the newly restored object is again deleted.

This problem can be overcome by performing an authoritative restore. An authoritative restore marks specific objects in the Active Directory as the master copy and forces the other domain controllers to receive the change.

To perform an authoritative restore, restart the computer in directory service restore mode, restore the most recent System State from backup, and then run the NTDSUTIL utility at a command prompt in authoritative restore mode.

For more information about the NTDSUTIL utility and its syntax, see the Windows Server 2003 Help and Support Center.

12

In Activity 12-4, you use the Windows Server 2003 Backup Utility to back up System State data on your server.

Activity 12-4: Backing Up System State Data

Time Required: 15 minutes

Objective: Back up the System State data on a Windows Server 2003 domain controller.

Description: Because your server is also a domain controller, the IT manager at Dover Leasing has asked you to explore the capabilities of the Backup Utility in terms of backing up System State data, including individual components. Ultimately, this will be an important consideration in whether the IT manager decides to rely on the Backup Utility or a third-party alternative. In this activity, you back up the System State data for your server.

1. Click **Start**, click **Run**, and in the Open text box type **ntbackup** and press **Enter**. Click the **Advanced Mode** link in the Backup or Restore Wizard screen.

2. In the Backup Utility window, click the **Backup** tab.

3. Click the **System State** icon to view its contents. Notice that the individual check boxes are grayed out because individual System State components cannot be backed up by this utility.

4. Click the check box next to the **System State** icon, as illustrated in Figure 12-14.

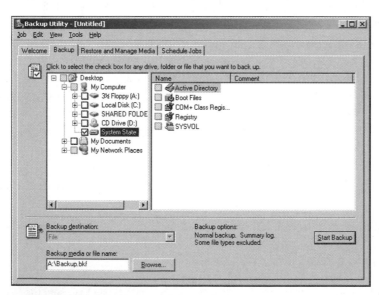

Figure 12-14   Backing up System State data

5. In the Backup media or file name text box, type **d:\systemstate.bkf** and click the **Start Backup** button.

6. In the Backup Job Information dialog box, click the **Start Backup** button.

7. After the Backup process is complete, click the **Close** button in the Backup Progress screen.

8. Click **Start**, and then click **My Computer**. Double-click on drive **D:** to view its contents.

9. Right-click on the file **systemstate.bkf** and click **Properties**. From the General tab, review the size of this file to get a better sense of how large a System State backup of your system is.

10. Close all open windows.

SHADOW COPIES OF SHARED FOLDERS

Windows Server 2003 introduces a new feature to help make the recovery of user data files stored in shared folders easier than ever before. Traditionally, if a user were to accidentally delete a file from a shared folder, an administrator would need to be contacted in order to restore the file from a previously created backup. Although this method is tried and tested, it does result in obvious inefficiencies. Firstly, the user needs to contact an administrator, which may result in delays, and lost user productivity. Secondly, the administrator has to take time from their schedule to find the backup media that contains a backed up version of the file, and restore it. The **Shadow Copies of Shared Folders** feature was designed to make recovering previous versions of files stored in shared folders simple for users, without the need for intervention from an administrator.

 The Shadow Copies of Shared Folders feature is not intended for use as a replacement for or alternative to creating regular backups. Regular backups should be performed normally in order to ensure that all data is available in the case of accidental deletion or some other disaster.

Implementing the Shadow Copies of Shared Folders feature on a Windows Server 2003 system allows users three main advantages:

- restoration of files that they accidentally delete

- recovery of previous versions of files when necessary

- comparison of the current version of a file to a previous version

The Shadow Copies of Shared folders feature is not enabled on a Windows Server 2003 system by default. When required, this feature is enabled on a volume-by-volume basis from the Shadow Copies tab of the properties of a drive, as shown in Figure 12-15.

Once enabled, the Shadow Copies of Shared Folders feature periodically creates shadow copies of all files stored in shared folders on that particular volume. It cannot be individually enabled or disabled for certain folders—the setting is volume-wide. By default, shadow copies of files are created according to a pre-defined scheduled, every Monday through

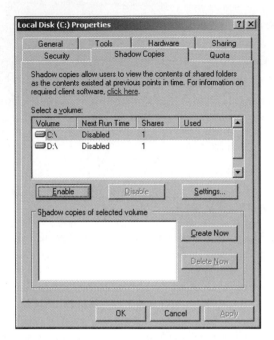

Figure 12-15   The Shadow Copies tab in the properties of a volume or partition

Friday at 7:00 a.m. and 12:00 p.m.. This schedule can be changed, but Microsoft recommends that shadow copies be created no more than once per hour at a maximum.

By default, the Shadow Copies of Shared Folders feature uses 10% of the available disk space on a volume for storing shadow copies, with a minimum of 100 MB allocated for this purpose. When space limits are reached, the older shadow copies are deleted, and a maximum of 64 shadow copies are stored per volume. As more shadow copies are created, the oldest ones are deleted to make way for newer versions.

In Activity 12-5, you enable and configure the Shadow Copies of Shared Folders feature for your server's D: drive.

ACTIVITY

Activity 12-5: Enabling and Configuring Shadow Copies of Shared Folder Settings

Time Required: 15 minutes

Objective: Enable and configure the Shadow Copies of Shared Folders feature for a selected volume.

Description: The IT manager at Dover Leasing is concerned about the amount of time lost and productivity wasted when users accidentally delete a file or need a previous version restored from backup. Because of this, he has asked you to test the Shadow Copies of Shared

Folders feature in Windows Server 2003. In this activity you enable and configure Shadow Copy settings for drive D: on your server.

1. Click **Start**, and then click **My Computer**.

2. Double-click on drive **D:** to view its contents. Right-click on an area of blank space, select **New**, and then click **Folder**. Name the new folder **shadow**.

3. Right-click on the **shadow** folder and click **Properties**. Click on the **Sharing** tab, and then click the **Share this folder radio** button. Click the Permissions button. Check the **Full Control** check box in the Allow column, and then click **OK**.

4. Click the **Security** tab. Click on the **Users** group, and then check the **Full Control** check box in the Allow column. Click **OK**.

5. Double-click on the **shadow** folder to open it. Right-click on an area of blank space, select **New**, and then click **Text Document**. Name the new text document **test.txt**.

6. Double-click on the **test.txt** document to open it in Notepad. Type **Testing shadow copies**, click **File**, and then click **Save**. Close Notepad.

7. Click **Start**, then click **My Computer**. Right-click on drive **D:** and then click **Properties**.

8. Click the **Shadow Copies** tab. In the Select a volume section, click on volume **D:**, and then click **Enable**.

9. When the Enable Shadow Copies dialog box appears, read the message and then click **Yes**. Note that enabling shadow copies for the volume may take a minute or more. Once complete, notice that a new shadow copy is listed in the Shadow copies of selected volume section.

10. Click the **Settings** button. This opens the Settings window, as shown in Figure 12-16. This screen allows you to change the volume where shadow copy files are stored, the amount of disk space allocated to shadow copy storage, and so forth.

11. Click the **Schedule** button. Click the drop-down menu at the top of the window to view the currently configured schedule for creating new shadow copies. By default, new shadow copies are created at 7:00 a.m. and 12:00 p.m., Monday through Friday.

12. Click **New** to add a third schedule to the list. Use the Start time spin box to set the schedule for this new task to **4:00 PM**. This adds one additional shadow copy creation task at 4:00 p.m. each day. Click **OK**.

13. Click **OK** to close the Settings window, and then click **OK** to close the properties windows of drive D:.

14. Double-click on drive **D:** to view its contents, and then double-click on the **shadow** folder to open it.

12

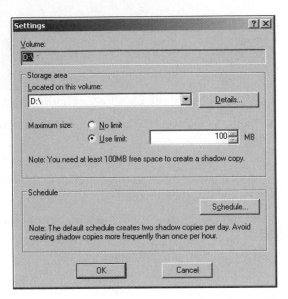

Figure 12-16   The Settings window for a volume with shadow copies enabled

15. Double-click on the **test.txt** file to open it in Notepad. Highlight the text in the document, press the **Backspace** key, and then type **Second shadow copy test**. Click **File**, and then click **Save**. Close the Notepad window.

16. Close all open windows.

Previous Versions

In order for network users to be able to access previous versions of files via the Shadow Copies of Shared Folders feature, additional software must be installed on their systems. The client software can be found on a Windows Server 2003 system in the %systemroot%\system32\clients\twclient\x86 folder for Intel-based systems. The client software is provided in MSI format, meaning that an administrator can install it manually, or deploy it using methods like Group Policy. Once installed, this software adds an additional tab to the Properties pages of files stored in shared folders called Previous Versions. This name was chosen to make it easier for users to understand the purpose of the tab, and the functions it allows them to carry out.

In Activity 12-6 you install the **Previous Versions Client** software on your server and explore settings on the Previous Versions tab in the properties of a file.

Activity 12-6: Installing and Using the Previous Versions Client

Time Required: 10 minutes

Objective: Install and use the Previous Versions Client and then view and restore a previous copy of a file.

Description: Having configured Shadow Copies on drive D:, you decide to install and test the Previous Versions Client as part of trying to determine how users will interact with the Shadow Copies of Shared Folders feature enabled in the previous activity. In this activity you first install the Previous Versions Client software, and then use the functionality that it provides to restore a previous version of the test.txt file created in the last activity.

1. Click **Start**, and then click **Run**. In the Open text box, type **%systemroot%\ system32\clients\twclient\x86** and click **OK**. This opens the x86 folder in Windows Explorer.

2. Double-click on the **twcli32.msi** file to launch the installer.

3. Once the installation is completed, click **Finish**.

4. At the Installer Information dialog box, click **Yes** to restart your server if necessary. Once the reboot is complete, log on with your **AdminXX** account.

5. Click **Start**, and then click **Run**. In the Open text box, type **\\serverXX** (where *XX* is your assigned student number) and click **OK**.

6. Double-click on the **shadow** folder to view its contents. Double-click on the **test.txt** file to open it, confirming that it contains the text Second shadow copy test. This is the most recent version of the file. Close Notepad without making or saving any changes.

7. Right-click on the **test.txt** file and click **Properties**. Notice that the properties of this file now includes a tab named Previous Versions.

8. Click the **Previous Versions** tab, as shown in Figure 12-17.

9. In the File versions list, review the Time information next to the test.txt file, and click **View**. This opens the previous version of the test.txt file. Close Notepad.

10. With the test.txt file still selected, click **Copy**. This allows you to save this copy of the file to an alternate location, if necessary. Click **Cancel**.

11. With the test.txt file still selected, click **Restore**. This restores the previous version of the test.txt file to the folder. When the Previous Versions dialog box appears, click **Yes**.

12. Close all open windows.

12

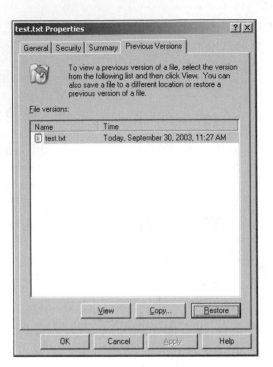

Figure 12-17   The Previous Versions tab in the properties of a shared file

AUTOMATED SYSTEM RECOVERY

Windows Server 2003 introduces a powerful new utility for the purpose of restoring system configuration information. The **Automated System Recovery (ASR)** feature allows you to restore system configuration settings in the event that a system cannot be repaired using the various safe-mode startup options or the last known good configuration feature.

ASR consists of two different elements on a Windows Server 2003 system. The first is the ASR backup, which you access from the Backup Utility. The second is a floppy disk that contains information about the backup, disk configuration information, and how the restore should be performed.

The main purpose of the ASR feature is to restore a Windows Server 2003 system to a functional state. However, ASR is only used to back up and restore system configuration information and not data files. You should back up any user data files separately before initiating ASR and then restore them once the ASR process is complete, using a tool such as the Windows Server 2003 Backup utility.

TIP

You should create a new ASR backup any time the system configuration of a server running Windows Server 2003 is changed.

If an ASR backup exists, you can restore system configuration settings by booting from the Windows Server 2003 CD and then selecting the Repair option. The information stored on the ASR floppy disk and in the ASR backup is then used to restore appropriate settings.

You create an ASR backup set using the Automated System Recovery Wizard, which you access from the Windows Server 2003 Backup Utility Advanced Mode Welcome tab. The Automated System Recovery Preparation Wizard Backup Destination screen is shown in Figure 12-18.

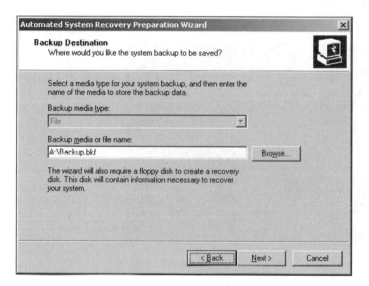

12

Figure 12-18   The Automated System Recovery Preparation Wizard Backup Destination screen

NOTE

Both Windows NT Server 4.0 and Windows 2000 included a system-restore feature known as an Emergency Repair Disk (ERD). ASR replaces the ERD feature on Windows Server 2003 systems.

For more information on using the Automated System Recovery feature, see the topic of the same name in the Windows Server 2003 Help and Support Center.

ADVANCED STARTUP OPTIONS

Several things can cause a system not to start, such as the installation of new software or device drivers, or changes made to the system's configuration. If your computer fails to start, you can try using one of the advanced startup options to troubleshoot the problem. For example, you can start the computer in **safe mode**, which only loads the default Windows Server 2003 settings and the device drivers necessary to start the operating system. If you have installed new software that you think is causing the problem, you can uninstall it once in safe mode.

You can access the Windows Advanced Startup Options screen during system startup by pressing F8 while viewing the Boot Loader Operating System Selection menu. The screen that appears (see Figure 12-19) presents you with a list of eight advanced startup options, summarized in Table 12-1.

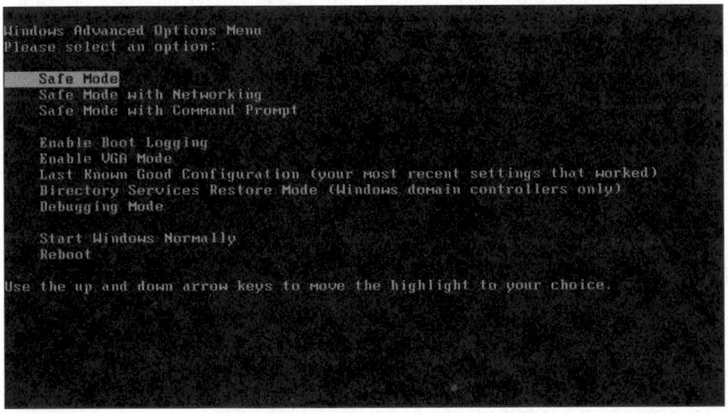

Figure 12-19   The Windows Advanced Startup Options screen

Table 12-1   Advanced startup options

Startup Option	Description
Safe Mode	Only the basic files and drivers required to start Windows Server 2003 are loaded. The default Windows Server 2003 settings are used. This option is useful when an application or component that is causing a problem needs to be uninstalled or disabled.
Safe Mode with Networking	This option starts the computer the same as in safe mode, but provides network connectivity. Use this option if you need access to the network to repair the problem.
Safe Mode with Command Prompt	This option starts the computer the same as in safe mode, but provides access to the Windows Server 2003 command line rather than the graphical user interface.

Table 12-1   Advanced startup options (continued)

Startup Option	Description
Enable Boot Logging	This option starts Windows Server 2003 while creating a log file that lists all the installed drivers and services that were loaded or not loaded. Use this option to determine the exact cause of startup problems. The file is called ntbtlog.txt and is stored in the %systemroot% folder.
Enable VGA Mode	This option starts Windows Server 2003 with the basic VGA driver for the video card. This is useful if you've installed a new video driver that is causing Windows Server 2003 not to start.
Last Known Good Configuration	This option starts Windows Server 2003 using registry information saved after the last successful logon. This option is useful if incorrect configuration changes have been made and you need to return to the computer's previous configuration.
Directory Services Restore Mode	This option enables you to restore the Sysvol and Active Directory Services on a domain controller. The system must be a domain controller to have this option available.
Debugging Mode	Debugging information is sent to another computer via a serial cable connection when Windows Server 2003 boots. Use this option to provide software developers with detailed debugging information about the problem.

12

In Activity 12-7 you explore some of the various advanced startup options on your Windows Server 2003 system.

Activity 12-7: Viewing and Testing Advanced Startup Options

Time Required: 20 minutes

Objective: View and Test Windows Server 2003 Advanced Startup Options.

Description: Based on his experiences in troubleshooting problems in Windows 2000, the IT manager at Dover Leasing has asked you to familiarize yourself with the advanced startup options that can be used to repair a Windows Server 2003 server if necessary. In this activity, you access the advanced startup options menu and then boot your server using the Safe Mode and Safe Mode with Command Prompt advanced options.

1. Click **Start**, and then click the **Shut Down** button. In the What do you want the computer to do? list box, click **Restart**. In the Comment text box, type **testing advanced startup options**, and click **OK**.

2. At the operating system selection screen, press the **F8** key to access the Windows Advanced Options Menu. If your system is not configured to dual boot, press **F8** prior to the Windows Server 2003 boot screen appearing.

3. Select **Safe Mode** on the list of available options, and press **Enter**.

4. If the operating system selection screen appears, select **Windows Server 2003, Enterprise** (or **Standard** if applicable) if necessary, and press **Enter**. If prompted to select a hardware profile, select **Profile1** and press **Enter**.

5. Log on using the **Administrator** user account with the password **Password01**.

6. When the Desktop dialog box opens, read the message it provides and click **OK**.

7. Click **Start**, click **Run**, and then type **cmd.exe** in the Open text box. Click **OK**.

8. At the command line, type **ping www.course.com** and press **Enter**. Notice that the ping fails because network functionality is disabled in Safe Mode.

9. Restart your server, and access the Windows Advanced Options Menu as outlined in Step 2.

10. Select **Safe Mode with Command Prompt** on the list of available options, and press **Enter**.

11. At the operating system selection screen, select **Windows Server 2003, Enterprise** (or **Standard** if applicable) if necessary, and press **Enter**. If prompted to select a hardware profile, select **Profile1** and press **Enter**.

12. Log on using the **Administrator** user account with the password **Password01**. Notice that the Command Prompt opens as the Windows shell environment.

13. At the command line, type **ping www.course.com**. Notice that this command also fails because Safe Mode with Command Prompt also provides no networking support.

14. Press **Ctrl+Alt+Delete** to access the Windows Security dialog box.

15. Click the **Shut Down** button, and then reboot your server normally, logging on with your **AdminXX** account.

Last Known Good Configuration

The **last known good configuration** allows you to recover your system from failed driver and registry changes. For example, installing a device driver that is incorrect for your hardware can cause a system to fail on startup. The last known good configuration information is stored in the registry and is updated each time the computer restarts and the user successfully logs on.

Normally when a computer is restarted, any configuration changes made before the reboot process was initiated are used. Each time you make configuration changes, these changes are copied to the default configuration that will be used the next time the computer is restarted. If these changes damage the default configuration, your computer may not be able to boot successfully. For example, the installation of new device drivers may cause the computer to stop responding and, ultimately, result in stop errors during the boot process, also known as the "Blue Screen of Death" (BSoD).

The last known good configuration can be thought of as a backup that can be used to restart the system in the event that the current configuration fails.

 Because the last known good configuration is updated each time you log on, make sure you do not log on to your server if problems are evident during the boot process. Once you do, the last known good configuration is updated with the incorrect configuration changes.

The last known good configuration is useful in situations where Windows Server 2003 configuration changes have been made that negatively impact the system. However, it cannot resolve problems such as missing or corrupt files, or if you restart and log on after the configuration changes have been made. Additional tools for system recovery are discussed later in this chapter.

In Activity 12-8, you test the use of the last known good configuration advanced startup option on your server.

Activity 12-8: Testing Last Known Good Configuration

Time Required: 15 minutes

Objective: Test the last known good configuration advanced startup option.

Description: Because any change to a server can severely impact user productivity if it results in system failure, the IT manager at Dover Leasing has asked you to familiarize yourself with the process for using the last known good configuration feature of Windows Server 2003. In this activity, you simulate errors by disabling both your network adapter card and DVD/CD-ROM drive, and then restore a previous server configuration by using the last known good configuration feature.

1. Click **Start**. Right-click the **My Computer** icon and click **Properties**.
2. In the System Properties dialog box, click the **Hardware** tab.
3. Click the **Device Manager** button.
4. In the Device Manager window, click the **plus sign (+)** next to the **Network adapters** icon to expand it.
5. Right-click your computer's network adapter, and click **Disable**. When prompted, click the **Yes** button.
6. In the Device Manager window, click the **plus sign (+)** next to the **DVD/CD-ROM drives** icon to expand it.
7. Right-click your computer's CD-ROM or DVD drive, and click **Disable**. When prompted, click the **Yes** button.
8. Click **Start**, and then click **Run**. In the Open text box, type **cmd** and press **Enter**.
9. At the command line, type **ping www.course.com** and press **Enter**. The ping fails because your network adapter has been disabled.

12

10. Click **Start**, and then click the **Shut Down** button. In the Shut Down Windows dialog box, choose **Restart**, type **Testing LKGC** in the Comment text box, and click **OK**.

11. At the operating system selection screen, press **F8**. If your system is not configured to dual boot, press **F8** prior to the Windows Server 2003 boot screen appearing.

12. On the Windows Advanced Options menu, select **Last Known Good Configuration** and press **Enter**.

13. At the operating system selection screen, select **Windows Server 2003, Enterprise** (or **Standard** if applicable) if necessary and press **Enter**. If prompted to select a hardware profile, select **Profile1** and press **Enter**.

14. When prompted, log on with your **AdminXX** account.

15. Click **Start**. Right-click the **My Computer** icon and click **Properties**.

16. In the System Properties dialog box, click the **Hardware** tab.

17. Click the **Device Manager** button.

18. Click the **plus signs (+)** next to both the **Network adapters** icon and the **DVD/CD-ROM drives** icon to expand them and verify that these devices are no longer disabled.

19. Close all open windows.

THE RECOVERY CONSOLE

Another Windows Server 2003 tool that can be used for system recovery is the **Recovery Console**. The Recovery Console is an advanced tool for experienced administrators, allowing them to gain access to a hard drive on computers running Windows Server 2003. It can be used to perform the following tasks:

- Start and stop services
- Format drives
- Read and write data on a local hard drive
- Copy files from a floppy or CD to a local hard drive
- Perform administrative tasks

Installing the Recovery Console

You can start the Recovery Console in one of two ways. The first option is to run it from the Windows Server 2003 CD once a serious error occurs by booting from the CD. The second option is to install it on your computer permanently before you need it to resolve a problem. Once you have installed the Recovery Console, it is listed as an option from the list of available operating systems during the initial boot process. You can then start the Recovery Console by selecting it on the boot loader menu, as shown in Figure 12-20.

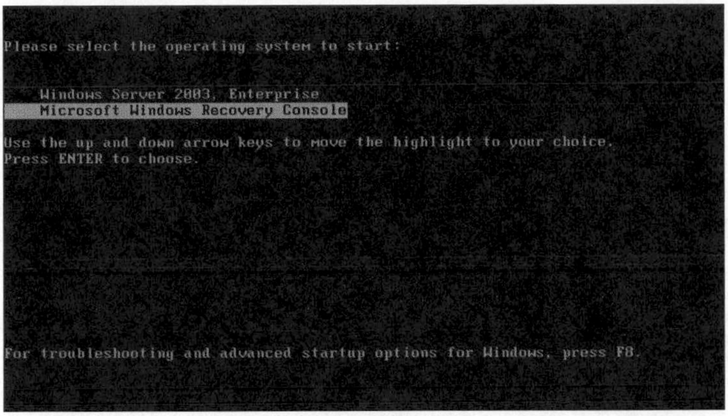

Figure 12-20   Accessing the Microsoft Windows Recovery Console

If you choose not to install the Recovery Console on your system, you can start by booting your system from the Windows Server 2003 CD. Instead of choosing to reinstall the operating system, you would initiate the recovery process by selecting the option to repair using the Recovery Console.

NOTE

You must be an administrator to run the Recovery Console, so accessing the console requires users to provide the correct local administrator's password for the system.

There are a variety of commands available through the Recovery Console. The following list includes some of the common commands that are used. For a complete list of commands that are available, use the Help command from within the console.

- Copy—Copies a file from removable media to the system folders
- Disable—Disables a system service or a device driver
- Enable—Enables or starts a system service or a device driver
- Exit—Closes the Recovery Console and restarts your computer
- Fixboot—Writes a new partition boot sector onto the system partition
- Fixmbr—Repairs the master boot record of the boot partition
- Listsvc—Lists all the services on the computer

In Activity 12-9, you first install and then use the Windows Server 2003 Recovery Console.

Activity 12-9: Installing and Using the Recovery Console

Time Required: 20 minutes

Objective: Install and use the Recovery Console.

ACTIVITY

Description: The IT manager has mandated that the Windows Server 2003 Recovery Console should be installed on all corporate servers to provide an alternate troubleshooting and repair environment in cases where the last known good configuration feature fails to fix an issue. In this activity, you first install and then test the Recovery Console to become familiar with the basic operation of its interface.

1. Click **Start**, and then click **Run**. In the Open text box, type **D:\SOURCE\ i386\winnt32.exe /cmdcons** and click **OK**.

2. In the Windows Setup dialog box, as illustrated in Figure 12-21, click **Yes**.

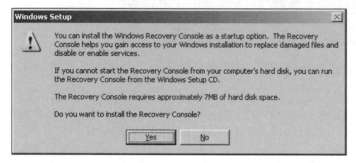

Figure 12-21   Installing the Recovery Console

3. Press **ESC** to cancel the dynamic update. Click **Yes**. Select the **Skip this step and continue installing Windows** radio button, then click **Next**.

4. In the Windows Server 2003, Enterprise Edition Setup dialog box, click **OK**.

5. Click **Start**, and then click the **Shut Down** button. In the Shut Down Windows dialog box, click **Restart**, and then type **Recovery Console Test** in the Comment text box. Click **OK**.

6. At the operating system selection screen, select the **Microsoft Windows Recovery Console** option, and press **Enter**.

7. When the Which Windows installation would you like to log onto prompt appears, type **1** and press **Enter**.

8. At the Type the administrator password prompt, type **Password01** and press **Enter**. This brings you to the C:\WINDOWS prompt.

9. Type **help** and press **Enter**. This displays a list of commands available via the Recovery Console. Press the **spacebar** to scroll though the remainder of the list and return to the command prompt.

10. Type **listsvc** and press **Enter**. This lists all of the services on the server, along with information about their status, as shown in Figure 12-22.

11. Press the **spacebar** until the RemoteAccess service is visible onscreen. Notice that its status is set to Disabled.

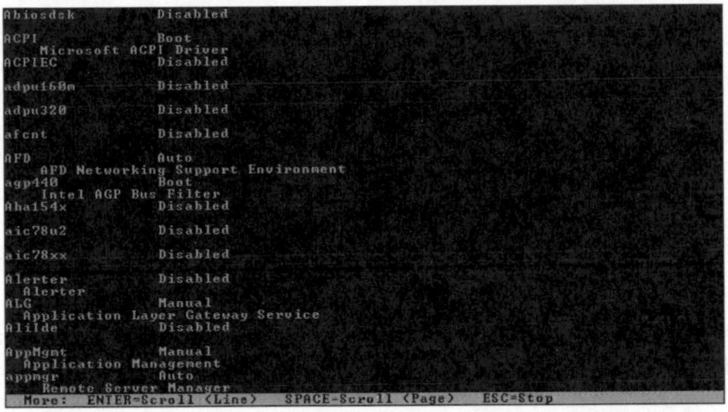

Figure 12-22 Viewing the results of the Recovery Console LISTSVC command

12. Press the **spacebar** until you return to the command prompt.

13. Type **enable RemoteAccess SERVICE_AUTO_START** and press **Enter**. This will configure the Remote Access service to start automatically once the server reboots.

14. Type **listsvc** and press **Enter**. Press the **spacebar** until the RemoteAccess service is visible. Notice that its status is now set to Auto.

15. Press the **ESC** key to return to the command line.

16. Type **exit** and press **Enter**. This exits the recovery console and initiates a reboot of the server.

17. Boot your server normally, and log on using your **AdminXX** account.

CHAPTER SUMMARY

❏ One of the most critical roles of any network administrator is to be able to restore a server and related data quickly in the event of failure or accidental deletion. Windows Server 2003 includes a variety of tools and utilities to restore a server to a previous configuration, undo problematic configuration changes, and back up and restore operating system, application, and user data files.

❏ In order to ensure that operating system, application, and user data files are not lost in the event of a server failure or accidental deletion, critical files and folders can be backed up and restored using the Windows Server 2003 Backup utility. This tool provides the option of using a wizard interface to perform these tasks along with what is known as Advanced mode.

❏ The Windows Server 2003 Backup utility supports five different types of backups including normal, incremental, differential, copy, and daily backups.

- As part of ensuring that critical operating system files are available in the event of a server failure or accidental deletion, the Windows Server 2003 Backup utility provides the ability to back up this information via a single element known as System State.

- Shadow Copies of Shared Folders is a new feature in Windows Server 2003 that allows an administrator to make previous versions of files available to users for the purpose of restoring a previous version, restoring a file that has been accidentally deleted, or to compare versions of files. This feature allows users to access these previous versions without the intervention of an administrator, or the need to restore data from backup.

- Automated System Recovery (ASR) is another new feature in Windows Server 2003 that allows an administrator to quickly recover from a server failure by storing server configuration information on floppy disks. These disks are used in conjunction with the Windows Server 2003 installation CD to restore a server to a previous configuration state, although it does not restore applications or user data files.

- Windows Server 2003 supports a variety of different advanced startup options that can be used to attempt to boot a server in the event that the normal boot process will not complete correctly. Examples of these options include Safe Mode and Last Known Good Configuration.

- The Windows Server 2003 Recovery Console provides administrators with an alternate environment into which a server can be booted to make various configuration changes if necessary. This tool is useful when a server will not boot due to errors or other incorrect configuration settings.

KEY TERMS

Automated System Recovery (ASR) — A new Windows Server 2003 feature that allows an administrator to restore server configuration settings in the event that a system cannot be repaired using other methods such as safe mode or last known good configuration. This technique involves creating floppy disks that include system configuration information, and then using these in conjunction with the Windows Server 2003 installation CD to restore a server to its previous configuration. ASR does not restore applications or user data files.

Backup utility — The tool included with Windows Server 2003 used to back up and restore files and System State information.

copy backup — A backup type that backs up all selected files and folders, but does not change the archive attribute setting. This allows a copy backup to be performed without interrupting any other backup processes currently in place.

daily backup — A backup type that backs up selected files or folders than have been created or changed on the day that the backup takes place.

differential backup — A backup type that only backs up those files that have changed since the last normal or incremental backup took place, but does not clear the archive attribute associated with those files.

incremental backup — A backup type that only backs up those files that have changed since the last normal or incremental backup took place and clears the archive attribute associated with those files.

last known good configuration — An advanced startup option that you can use to recover a system from failed Windows Server 2003 configuration changes.

normal backup — A backup type that backs up all selected files and folders, and clears the archive attribute on these files and folders.

Previous Versions Client — The client software component that allows users to access the Previous Versions tab to view or restore previous versions of files stored on a volume with Shadow Copies of Shared Folders enabled.

Recovery Console — A command-line interpreter that you can use to gain access to a local hard drive in the event that the system fails to boot.

safe mode — An advanced boot option that allows a Windows Server 2003 system to be booted with minimal services or drivers loaded, typically used for troubleshooting or diagnostic purposes.

Shadow Copies of Shared Folders — A new feature in Windows Server 2003 that can be enabled on a volume-by-volume basis to allow a user to view or recover previous versions of files stored in shared folders. In order to access this feature, user systems must have the Previous Versions Client software installed.

System State — A group of critical operating system files and components that can be backed up as a single group on a Windows Server 2003 system. System State data always includes the Registry, COM+ Registration database, boot files, and system files. On a domain controller, it also includes Active Directory and the SYSVOL directory. Other components that are included (assuming their associated services are installed) include the Certificate Services database, the Cluster Service, and the IIS Metadirectory.

12

REVIEW QUESTIONS

1. Which of the following backup types backs up all selected files and folders and changes their archive attribute?

    a. Normal

    b. Incremental

    c. Differential

    d. Daily

2. Which of the following backup types backs up all files that have changed since the last incremental or normal backup?

    a. Normal

    b. Incremental

    c. Differential

    d. Daily

3. Which of the following backup types backs up only the selected files and folders that have changed since the last differential or normal backup and does not change their archive attribute?

   a. Normal

   b. Daily

   c. Incremental

   d. Differential

4. Which of the following backup types backs up only the selected files and folders that have changed since the last incremental or normal backup and changes their archive attribute?

   a. Normal

   b. Copy

   c. Daily

   d. Incremental

5. Which of the following backup types only backs up the selected files and folders that have changed on the current day?

   a. Daily

   b. Normal

   c. Copy

   d. Incremental

6. Which of the following backup types backs up all selected files and folders and does not change their archive attribute so as not to interfere with any existing backup process?

   a. Daily

   b. Copy

   c. Differential

   d. Normal

7. Members of which of the following groups can back up any files and folders on a Windows Server 2003 domain controller?

   a. Administrators

   b. Backup Operators

   c. Server Operators

   d. Users

8. Which of the following permissions allows a user to back up files and folders that they do not own?

   a. Read

   b. Read and Execute

c. Full Control

d. Modify

9. Individual users can be granted rights that allow them to back up and restore files on a Windows Server 2003 system if necessary.

a. True

b. False

10. Having only the Read permission to a file is sufficient to allow a user to back up that file.

a. True

b. False

11. Which of the following advanced startup options allows a user to access the network on a Windows Server 2003 system?

a. Safe Mode

b. Safe Mode with Command Prompt

c. Safe Mode with Networking

d. Enable Boot Logging

12. What must be installed on a client workstation in order for a user to access previous versions of files in shared folders?

a. Shadow Copies Client

b. Previous Versions Client

c. Automated System Recovery

d. Windows Backup utility

13. Which of the following features allows an administrator to create floppy disks that can be used in conjunction with the Windows Server 2003 CD to restore a server?

a. Automated System Restore

b. Recovery Console

c. Last Known Good Configuration

d. Shadow Copies of Shared Folders

14. Which of the following advanced startup options boots Windows Server 2003 using a basic video driver?

a. Safe Mode

b. Safe Mode with Networking

c. Enable VGA Mode

d. Enable Boot Logging

15. The Backup utility included with Windows Server 2003 allows backup jobs to be scheduled.

    a. True

    b. False

16. How much disk space is required to enable the Shadow Copies of Shared Folders feature for a particular volume?

    a. 10 MB

    b. 100 MB

    c. 1 GB

    d. 10 GB

17. Which of the following options are available to a user from the Previous Versions tab in the properties of a file stored in a shared folder? (Choose all that apply.)

    a. View

    b. Copy

    c. Restore

    d. Delete

18. A normal user cannot restore a file from the Previous Versions tab without the intervention of an administrator.

    a. True

    b. False

19. Which of the following switches is used in conjunction with the WINNT32 command to install the Recovery Console?

    a. /recovery

    b. /console

    c. /cmdcons

    d. /conscmd

20. Any user can log on to a Windows Server 2003 installation using the Recovery Console.

    a. True

    b. False

CASE PROJECTS

Case Project 12-1

The IT manager at Dover Leasing has asked you to design a new backup strategy for Windows Server 2003 systems. Each server has a tape backup drive attached, and the IT manager wants backups performed each evening, Monday through Friday. Because of the large amount of user data to be stored on each server, a normal backup should be performed on Monday evenings, and then a less intensive option should be chosen for Tuesday through Friday. Assuming that the IT manager would like to be able to restore from backup as quickly as possible, what backup method would you suggest for these other days?

Case Project 12-2

A new administrator has been hired at Dover Leasing to work during evenings and weekends under your direction. One evening he decides to install a new device driver on one of the servers to enhance performance. Before checking with you or any other administrators on staff, he installs the device driver. You receive a call that upon restart the new administrator discovered that the server no longer boots successfully. The server needs to be available to users in the morning.

1. What options in Windows Server 2003 are available to recover from a failed reboot? What is each option used for?

2. What recovery tool would be appropriate for this situation?

3. You noticed after the server is recovered that the Recovery Console was not listed as an option during the operating system selection. It is company policy that this tool be installed on all servers. How can the tool be installed? If you needed to use the Recovery Console and it wasn't installed, how could you start it?

Case Project 12-3

After a serious server failure at Dover Leasing, you decide to attempt to restore the server using the Automated System Recovery (ASR) feature. Although the server now boots, users are calling to complain that their files are no longer accessible on the server. What is the cause of this, and what can you do to remedy the situation?

12

13

ADMINISTERING WEB RESOURCES

After reading this chapter and completing the exercises, you will be able to:

♦ Install and configure Internet Information Services (IIS)

♦ Create and configure Web-site virtual servers and virtual directories

♦ Configure Web-site authentication

♦ Configure and maintain FTP virtual servers

♦ Update and maintain security for an IIS server

♦ Create and modify Web folders

♦ Install and use the Remote Administration (HTML) tools

♦ Install and configure Web-based printing and printer management

♦ Troubleshoot Web client-browser connectivity

Windows Server 2003 includes a variety of Internet-related services that can assist a company in developing an effective online Internet or intranet presence. Companies are beginning to realize the potential and importance of Web-based services to provide employees and customers with efficient and alternative ways of interacting with the organization.

To help develop and host these services, Microsoft has included an application called Internet Information Services (IIS) within Windows Server 2003. IIS provides the foundation for the Web-related services that an organization needs to create an effective and secure Internet or intranet presence. In this chapter, you learn how to install, configure, maintain, and secure a Windows Server 2003 IIS server. You also learn how to configure each of the components that IIS has to offer an organization, such as Web and FTP services. The final section of this chapter discusses client connectivity troubleshooting issues that you may face as users attempt to access the Internet or your internal intranet.

INSTALLING AND CONFIGURING INTERNET INFORMATION SERVICES

Internet Information Services (IIS) 6.0 is a Windows Server 2003 application that provides Web-related services to an organization. IIS consists of four main components:

- World Wide Web (HTTP) services—Provides the capability of hosting multiple Web sites accessible from the Internet or an intranet

- File Transfer Protocol (FTP) services—Can be installed and configured to have the ability to copy files between the server and a remote location

- Network News Transfer Protocol (NNTP) services—Used to provide a means of maintaining a list of topics and threaded conversations between users, such as a corporate discussion newsgroup in which employees can post messages and read replies related to various company matters

- Simple Mail Transfer Protocol (SMTP) services—Included in IIS to provide e-mail capabilities to the other services, such as HTTP or NNTP; for example, you might create a Web form that requires the response to be e-mailed to another location

These services can be implemented to host a corporate intranet or Internet presence. An organization that hosts a corporate intranet can provide employees with the following:

- Interactive online company resources, such as employee handbook information, employee news, or department meeting minutes

- Team collaboration using various applications, such as Office XP

- Web-based applications to assist employees in filling out forms or other internal business processes

An Internet presence for an organization can provide customers with the following:

- Additional customer service, such as online manuals or frequently asked questions about products or services

- The ability to order products online and track shipping progress

- Dynamic company information and news bulletins

To make these services available to your employees and customers, it is important that you understand how to configure, maintain, and secure IIS. These concepts are discussed in the sections that follow.

Installing Internet Information Services

Unlike previous versions in Microsoft server platforms, IIS 6.0 is not installed by default during a standard installation of Windows Server 2003. Instead, you can manually install individual IIS components via the Add or Remove Programs applet in Control Panel.

Table 13-1 lists and explains each of the individual components you can install as part of IIS.

Table 13-1   Internet Information Services components

IIS Component	Purpose
Background Intelligent Transfer Service (BITS) extension	Allows clients to use spare bandwidth for data transfers and resume server transfers in the event that a session disconnects or a computer restarts
Common Files	The required IIS program files
File Transfer Protocol (FTP) Service	Used to install and create FTP sites, which allow you to upload and download files to and from the server
FrontPage 2002 Server Extensions	Enables creating, developing, and maintaining Web sites with Microsoft FrontPage and Visual InterDev
Internet Information Services Manager	Installs the Internet Information Services MMC snap-in to allow IIS server management
Internet Printing	Enables Web-based printer management and allows printing to a shared printer via the HTTP protocol
NNTP Service	Enables an IIS server to function as an NNTP server to distribute, receive, and post private news messages or Usenet articles
SMTP Service	Enables an IIS server to function as an SMTP Server, which gives the ability to provide support for e-mail on a network or the Internet
World Wide Web Service	Enables an IIS server to function as a Web server on an intranet or the Internet

13

In Activity 13-1, you install IIS components on your server.

ACTIVITY

Activity 13-1: Installing Internet Information Services

Time Required: 20 minutes

Objective: Install Internet Information Services components.

Description: Dover Leasing has hosted their Web site on an Apache-based Linux server for the past four years. Although this Web site has met their needs, the IT manager has decided that the entire site should be moved over to a Windows Server 2003 system running IIS to eventually take advantage of advanced features such as ASP.NET. In this activity, you install IIS 6.0 on your server for testing purposes.

1. Click **Start**, select **Control Panel**, and then click **Add or Remove Programs**.

2. In the Add or Remove Programs dialog box, click the **Add/Remove Windows Components** button to open the Windows Components Wizard.

3. On the Windows Components screen of the Windows Components Wizard, as shown in Figure 13-1, click **Application Server** in the Components list box and then click the **Details** button.

4. In the Application Server dialog box, click **Internet Information Services (IIS)** in the Subcomponents of Application Server list box and then click the **Details** button.

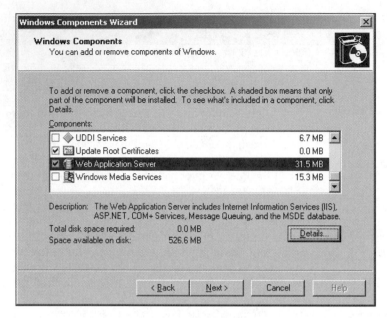

Figure 13-1   The Windows Components screen of the Windows Components Wizard

5. In the Internet Information Services (IIS) dialog box, shown in Figure 13-2, click on each individual component listed in the Subcomponents of Internet Information Services (IIS) list box to read its description.

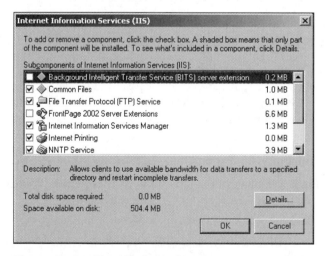

Figure 13-2   The IIS dialog box

6. Ensure that the check boxes next to the following services are checked: **Common Files**, **File Transfer Protocol (FTP) Service**, **Internet Information Services Manager**, **Internet Printing**, **NNTP Service**, **SMTP Service**, **World Wide Web Service**.

7. Once these boxes are checked, click **OK**.

8. On the Application Server screen, notice that the Internet Information Services check box is checked but slightly grayed out. This means that only some of the IIS subcomponents were selected. Click **OK**.

9. At the Windows Components screen, click **Next**.

10. If prompted with the Files Needed dialog box, type **D:\Source\i386** in the text box and click **OK**.

11. Once all components have installed, click the **Finish** button, and then close the Add or Remove Programs dialog box.

After a successful installation of IIS, you notice a number of changes on the server. Some of these changes include the addition of user objects in Active Directory, folders on the hard drive, and services installed within the operating system.

It is important to understand the location and purpose of the folders that are created by IIS during installation. By default, these folders contain the IIS system files and the physical files for your Default Web or FTP site. Table 13-2 explains these folders in greater detail.

13

Table 13-2 IIS folder structure

Folder	Contents
%systemroot%\system32\inetsrv	Contains all of the program files and dll files needed for IIS to function
C:\Inetpub	Contains various sub-folders, such as ftproot, wwwroot, nntpfile, and mailroot, which store all of the source content for the FTP, Web, NNTP, and SMTP services provided by the server
C:\Windows\help\iishelp	Contains the IIS documentation

Installing IIS also adds two new user accounts and one new group account to Active Directory Users and Computers. The first user object is IUSR_*servername,* which is an account that IIS uses to provide **Anonymous access** to the server. The second user object is IWAM_*servername,* which is an account used to allow IIS to start out-of-process applications. The IIS_WPG group is the IIS 6.0 worker process group that serves individual namespaces like *www.dovercorp.net* configured on the server. Individual user accounts should not be added to the IIS_WPG group.

Figure 13-3 highlights the new accounts created in Active Directory after IIS is successfully installed.

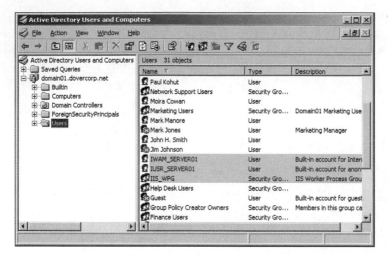

Figure 13-3   IIS-related user objects

Installing IIS also adds several operating-system services to Windows Server 2003, which you can view and control from the Services console on the Administrative Tools menu. The new services available after an IIS installation include:

- FTP Publishing Service—Provides an FTP Server service (daemon) that enables FTP clients to upload and download files to and from the FTP Server

- IIS Admin Service—Provides the programmatic interface for managing IIS and its components; it is also the parent process for all IIS services, which means that to stop this service, all other IIS services must be stopped

- Network News Transfer Protocol (NNTP)—Provides an NNTP Server that enables newsreader clients to post and read messages, and enables IIS to exchange NNTP messages with other NNTP servers in your organization and on the Internet

- Simple Mail Transfer Protocol (SMTP)—Provides an SMTP Server that enables the sending and receiving of SMTP e-mail messages

- World Wide Web Publishing Service—Provides a Web Server that can host one or more Web sites

Figure 13-4 shows the Services console open with the FTP Publishing Service highlighted.

Additionally, installing IIS allows you to use the Web sharing feature to make files and folders available to network clients via the HTTP protocol. We explore Web sharing in more detail later in this chapter. In Activity 13-2, you explore the system changes that occur as a result of installing IIS.

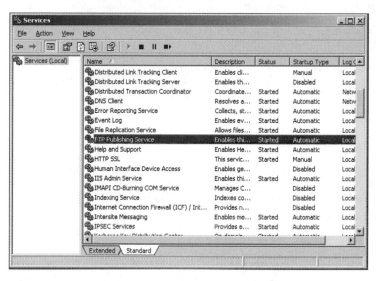

Figure 13-4   Viewing services after IIS is installed

Activity 13-2: Viewing System Changes after Installing IIS

Time Required: 10 minutes

Objective: View changes made to Windows Server 2003 after installing IIS.

Description: Because you will be responsible for the configuration and security of Dover Leasing's Web servers once implemented, you want to better understand the changes that IIS makes to a Windows Server 2003 system once installed. In this activity, you browse through user, group, directory, and service changes to obtain a picture of how an IIS installation will impact your servers.

1. Open Active Directory Users and Computers.

2. Click on your domain to expand it, if necessary, and then click the **Users** container to view its contents.

3. Browse for the IIS_WPG, IUSR_SERVER*XX* and IWAM_SERVER*XX* accounts (where *XX* is your assigned student number) to read the description associated with each. Open the properties of each to view the groups of which these objects are members.

4. Close Active Directory Users and Computers.

5. Open My Computer and browse to the **C:** drive.

6. Double-click the **Inetpub** folder to view its contents. This is where the various 'root' folders are located for different IIS services.

7. Open the wwwroot folder, and then double-click the file **iisstart.htm** to open it. The file opens in Internet Explorer and displays the "Under Construction" message.

13

8. In the Internet Explorer address bar, type **http://localhost** and press **Enter**. Notice that your Web server opens the page viewed in Step 7.

9. Close Internet Explorer.

10. In the My Computer window, browse to the **C:\WINDOWS\system32\inetsrv** folder to view the files and folders required by IIS to function.

11. Close My Computer.

12. Click **Start**, select **Administrative Tools**, and then click **Services**.

13. In the Services window, browse for the following services, making note of their current status and startup types: **FTP Publishing Service**, **IIS Admin Service**, **Network News Transfer Protocol (NNTP)**, **Simple Mail Transfer Protocol (SMTP)**, **World Wide Web Publishing Service**.

14. Double-click the **Network News Transfer Protocol (NNTP)** icon to view its properties.

15. On the General tab, click the **Stop** button to stop the service, click **Manual** in the Startup type list box, and then click **OK**. This prevents the NNTP service from starting automatically the next time your server reboots.

16. Close all open windows.

Architectural Changes in IIS 6.0

Although IIS version 6.0 is in many ways similar to the 5.0 version included with Windows 2000, a number of architectural changes have been introduced. Most of these changes relate to how processes are managed and maintained by IIS, although the central storage location for IIS configuration information, known as the **metabase**, has also changed. In previous IIS versions, the metabase was stored as a single binary file named Metabase.bin. Although this file served its function well, its binary nature made it difficult to read the file directly and make changes to it. In IIS 6.0, the metabase is now stored in two standard Extensible Markup Language (XML) files, known as MetaBase.xml and MBSchema.xml. The purpose of each file is outlined as follows:

- MetaBase.xml—This file contains the actual configuration settings for IIS 6.0

- MBSchema.xml —This file contains the XML schema that provides the default values of the various metabase properties

One advantage of the metabase configuration being stored in XML format is the ability to easily read and diagnose issues, because the files are stored in a human-readable format that can be viewed with any text editor. Secondly, the XML files provide better read performance than the old Metabase.bin file, resulting in faster service startup. Finally, the metabase being stored in XML format provides an industry-standard data representation method that can easily be programmed to.

Both the MetaBase.xml and MBSchema.xml files can be found in the %systemroot%\system32\inetsrv directory.

A number of process management and administration features have also been introduced with IIS 6.0. These features are designed to help ensure a more robust environment that provides better overall system stability, performance, and administrative capabilities. Table 13-3 outlines some of these new features and their intended purposes.

Table 13-3   IIS 6.0 process management and administration features

New Feature	Purpose
HTTP.SYS	A kernel-mode driver that now accepts and manages all incoming HTTP requests. All HTTP responses are cached in kernel mode, eliminating the need to switch to user mode and thus delivering better performance.
IIS 5.0 Isolation Mode	An application mode that ensures compatibility for applications designed to run on IIS 5.0.
Worker Process	An application mode that puts different applications into their own application pool. Each Isolation Mode pool has its own worker processes and remains independent of other pools, thus providing a higher level of system reliability, given that one pool will not crash another.
Remote Administration (HTML) tool	IIS 6.0 provides the Remote Administration (HTML) tool to allow administrators to manage an IIS server from any Web browser.

13

For more information on the new architectural and management features of IIS 6.0, see the Internet Information Services 6.0 Administrator Guide — %systemroot%\Help\iis.chm.

Configuring Web Server Properties

After installing the IIS components, the IIS MMC snap-in is the primary tool used for configuration purposes. This tool is available on the Administrative Tools menu, and is shown in Figure 13-5.

Windows Server 2003 also includes a number of Visual Basic scripts that allow you to configure individual sites and their elements from the command line. Many of these scripts are explored in activities later in this chapter.

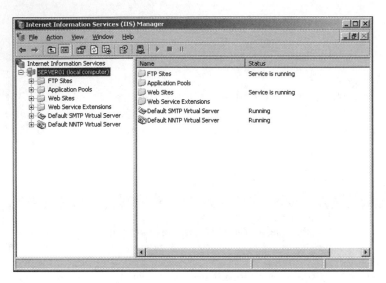

Figure 13-5   The Internet Information Services (IIS) Manager console

As illustrated in Figure 13-5, the IIS console displays the default sites and services that are initially installed. As more Web sites and FTP servers are added to the server, they appear as individual nodes in the interface that can be independently started, stopped, and configured. The default sites and services are described as follows:

- FTP Sites—This folder holds all configured FTP sites, including the Default FTP Site that responds to TCP port 21 on all of the server's configured IP addresses that are not assigned to another FTP site.

- Application Pools—This folder holds applications that are assigned to one or more Web sites, which isolates their processes from other Web sites.

- Web Sites—This folder holds all configured Web sites, including the Default Web Site that responds to TCP port 80 on all unassigned IP addresses of the server. This Web site is initially empty except for the "under construction" page placed in the wwwroot directory by default and may be used to create a custom Web site for your organization.

- Web Service Extensions—By default, IIS disables all request handlers designed to process dynamic content such as Active Server Pages or CGI extensions. This folder allows you to control the status of existing extensions and add new ones.

- Default SMTP Virtual Server—This e-mail component server responds to port 25 on all of the server's IP addresses that have not been assigned to another SMTP site.

- Default NNTP Virtual Server—This newsgroup server responds to port 119 on all of the server's configured IP addresses that have not been assigned to another NNTP site.

As you create new Web or FTP sites, each has its own icon listed in an appropriate folder in the details pane of the console. Creating new Web and FTP sites is discussed in greater detail later in the chapter. In Activity 13-3, you explore the interface of the IIS MMC snap-in.

Activity 13-3: Exploring the Internet Information Services MMC Snap-in

Time Required: 10 minutes

Objective: Explore the IIS MMC snap-in.

Description: Although it has been decided that you will ultimately be responsible for managing all IIS servers at Dover Leasing, a number of users in the Web groups will be responsible for the day-to-day administration of individual servers. The IT manager at Dover Leasing is worried that these users will not properly understand the impact of any changes that they make and has asked you to develop a short training class that will teach them how to use the IIS MMC console. In this activity, you explore the basic console layout and navigation.

1. Click **Start**, select **Administrative Tools**, and then click **Internet Information Services (IIS) Manager**.

2. If necessary, click the **plus sign (+)** next to your server to expand its contents. Click the **FTP Sites** node to view its contents. Notice that the Default FTP Site is listed, along with its status.

3. Click the **plus sign (+)** next to **Application Pools** to view its contents. By default, only a single Application Pool known as the DefaultAppPool exists.

4. Click the **plus sign (+)** next to **Web Sites** to view its contents. Notice that only the Default Web Site exists because no additional Web sites have been defined.

5. Click **Web Service Extensions** to view its contents. Notice the default statuses of the built-in extensions, as shown in Figure 13-6.

6. Click **Default SMTP Virtual Server** to view its contents.

7. Click **Default NNTP Virtual Server** to view its contents. Also notice that the icon associated with the service identifies it as being stopped, a result of stopping the service in the previous activity.

8. Leave the Internet Information Services window open.

To increase security, it is recommended to stop any IIS site or service that you are not using in your organization.

TIP

The first step in configuring IIS is to understand how configuration settings can be implemented on a server-wide basis. By accessing the properties of the Web Sites or FTP Sites folder in the Internet Information Services tool, **master properties** can be configured

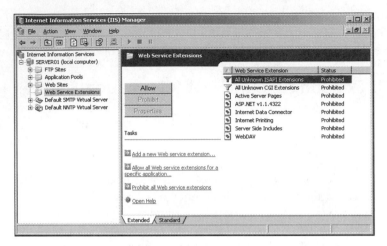

Figure 13-6   Viewing the statuses of Web Service Extensions

for all Web and FTP sites hosted on the server, as shown in Figure 13-7. Master properties are IIS parameters that are configured at the site-folder level and are inheritable by all Web or FTP sites hosted on the server. If your IIS server hosts a large number of sites, this feature is convenient because you can quickly set various common configurations, such as security and performance tuning, on all Web or FTP sites at once rather than configuring each setting on each site individually.

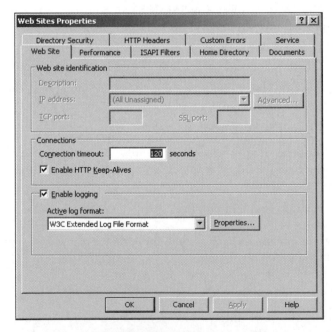

Figure 13-7   Viewing master property settings

Any property that is not specific to an individual site can be set at the site-folder level. For example, you cannot set the TCP port at the site-folder level because each Web site might be using different port numbers. However, if you want to limit all Web sites on your server to a specific number of connections, you are able to configure this as a site-folder property and have it be inherited by all sites on the server.

If an individual site has its own configuration settings and you decide to change the master properties, IIS gives you the option of whether or not to apply the changes to the preconfigured site. For example, if you configure the **Default Web Site** to only allow 500 connections and then set the master properties on the Web Sites folder to allow 700 connections, you will be prompted with the Inheritance Overrides dialog box asking which existing sites should inherit the new settings. This is illustrated in Figure 13-8.

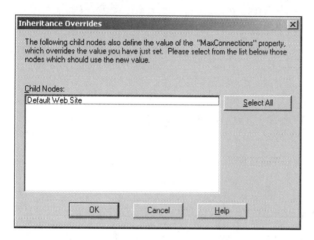

Figure 13-8　The Inheritance Overrides dialog box

Any configuration settings that are changed at the site, folder, or file level override the Master Properties and allow you to determine how inheritance takes place for any objects below the level that you are modifying. In Activity 13-4, you configure the master properties of the WWW service on your server.

Activity 13-4: Viewing and Configuring the Master Properties of the WWW Service

ACTIVITY

Time Required: 10 minutes

Objective: Configure the master properties of the WWW service.

Description: Although Dover Leasing currently has only one public Web site, the company is looking to move more of their internal processes to Web-based platforms in the future. Ultimately, this could lead to each Web server at Dover having 10 or more Web sites installed. Although changing the properties of these Web sites individually might be possible, you would rather avoid it based on your growing workload. In this activity, you explore and configure settings on the master property sheets of a Web server.

1. In the Internet Information Services (IIS) Manager window, right-click the **Web Sites** folder and click **Properties**.

2. On the Web Site tab, click the **Properties** button in the Enable logging section.

3. In the Logging Properties dialog box, click the **Weekly** radio button in the New log schedule section. Notice the location and naming convention for the log file as listed on the lower portion of the screen. Click **OK**.

4. Click the **Performance** tab. In the Web site connections section, click the **Connections limited to** radio button, and in the corresponding spin box type **700**.

5. Click **OK** to exit the Web Sites Properties dialog box.

6. To test whether the master properties configuration settings were inherited, click the **plus sign (+)** next to the **Web Sites** folder to expand it if necessary, right-click **Default Web Site**, and then click **Properties**.

7. Click the **Properties** button in the Enable logging section to verify that Weekly is specified in the New log schedule section. Click **OK** in the Logging Properties dialog box.

8. Click the **Performance** tab to verify that the Default Web Site now has a Connections limited to value of 700. Click **OK** to close the Default Web Site Properties dialog box.

9. Leave the Internet Information Services (IIS) Manager window open.

CREATING AND CONFIGURING WEB-SITE VIRTUAL SERVERS

IIS has the ability to host a large number of Web sites or **virtual servers** on a single server. A virtual server is simply a unique Web site that behaves as if it were on its own dedicated server. To make sure that no configuration conflicts take place between sites, you should consider the following details about each site before beginning the configuration process:

- Identify the IP address to which the Web site responds.

- Identify the TCP port to which the Web site responds.

- If you have multiple virtual servers responding to the same IP address, identify the host header name to which your new Web site responds.

Each Web site on your server must have a way of being uniquely identified. There are three ways that you can be sure each Web site is unique:

- Use a separate IP address to distinguish each Web site. This requires you to configure multiple IP addresses on the server's network interface(s).

- Use a single IP address with a specific port number for each Web site. For example, you might have a Web site at 192.168.1.100 with a host name of www.dovercorp.net that uses the default port 80, and another Web site using the same IP address, but with the host name www.sevenacres.com, which uses port 8000. The client connecting to www.sevenacres.com would then have to append a colon and the port number to the IP address or fully qualified domain name (FQDN) to access the second site, as in 192.168.1.100:8000 or www.sevenacres.com:8000.

■ Use a single IP address with multiple host headers representing each Web site. A **host header** is usually the fully qualified DNS name that clients type in to their browser for a Web site. For example, if you host two Web sites on your server, you may create www.dovercorp.net and www.sevenacres.com as host headers for the single IP address 192.168.1.100.

To enable the use of host names or FQDNs, you must configure proper DNS entries for each of the preceding points. DNS resolves host names and FQDNs to IP addresses. For example, you could type www.dovercorp.net instead of having to remember the IP address associated with the Web site.

In Activity 13-5, you configure a new Web site to accept requests on TCP port 8080.

Activity 13-5: Creating a New Web Site Using the Web Site Creation Wizard

Time Required: 20 minutes

Objective: Create a new Web site using the Web Site Creation Wizard.

Description: After you showed the IT manager your basic configuration of the Default Web Site, he asked you to create a new and dedicated site for the *Dovercorp.net* domain. This site will initially be used for testing purposes as the Web designers at Dover work on designing and testing the use of various dynamic-content programming features. Because your server only has one IP address currently assigned, you decide to change the port number of the existing site so that the designers can access the new site using the default HTTP port. In this activity, you first change and test the port number assigned to the Default Web Site and then create a new site to be used by the designers at *Dovercorp.net*.

1. In the Internet Information Services (IIS) Manager window, click the **plus sign (+)** next to the **Web Sites** folder to expand it, if necessary. Right-click the **Default Web Site** and click **Properties**.

2. On the Web Site tab, type **8080** in the TCP port text box, and then click **OK**.

3. Right-click the **Default Web Site** icon and click **Stop**. Click the **Web Sites** folder to view state information for the individual Web sites on your server. Once the site is listed as stopped in the State section of the details pane, right-click the **Default Web Site** again, and click **Start**.

4. To test whether the Default Web Site is still responding on TCP port 80, open Internet Explorer and type **http://localhost** in the address bar and press **Enter**. A message stating that the page cannot be displayed appears because the Default Web Site is now listening for requests on TCP port 8080.

13

5. In the Internet Explorer address bar, type **http://localhost:8080**, and press **Enter**. The "Under Construction" message should now appear.

6. Open My Computer, and create a new folder on your **D:** drive called **Dovercorpwebsite**. Close My Computer.

7. In the Internet Information Services window, right-click the **Web Sites** folder, select **New**, and then click **Web Site**.

8. At the Web Site Creation Wizard welcome screen, click **Next**.

9. At the Web Site Description screen, type **Dovercorp.net** in the Description text box and click **Next**.

10. At the IP Address and Port Settings screen, illustrated in Figure 13-9, accept the default values and click **Next**.

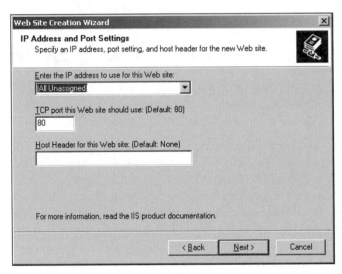

Figure 13-9   The IP Address and Port Settings screen

11. At the Web Site Home Directory screen, type **D:\dovercorpwebsite** in the Path text box and click **Next**.

12. At the Web Site Access Permissions screen, as illustrated in Figure 13-10, click the **Browse** check box and then click **Next**.

13. Click **Finish** to complete the Web Site Creation Wizard.

14. Verify that the new Dovercorp.net Web site appears under the Web Sites folder.

15. Leave the Internet Information Services (IIS) Manager window open.

16. Open My Computer and browse to the **D:\Dovercorpwebsite** folder.

17. Create a new text file in the folder called **index.txt**, and then open the file.

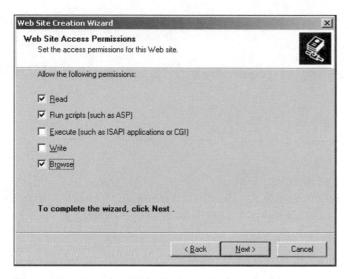

Figure 13-10   The Web Site Access Permissions screen

18. Type the following HTML code into the file:

    <html>

    <head>

    <title>Dovercorp.net Web Page</title>

    </head>

    <body>

    <h1>Dovercorp.net Web Site Test</h1>

    </body>

    </html>

19. Save and close the file, and then rename it **index.htm**. At the Rename warning message, click **Yes**.

20. In Internet Explorer, attempt to open the page **http://localhost**. The HTML page created in Step 18 appears.

21. Close all open windows.

The Web Site Creation Wizard provides a simple, step-by-step method of creating and initially configuring Web sites. However, administrators are often required to create many different Web sites on different servers throughout an organization. To help facilitate and automate this process, Microsoft provides a variety of VBScripts that an administrator can use to automate IIS configuration tasks. An example of such a script is IISWEB.VBS, which can

13

be used to create new Web sites from the Windows Server 2003 command line. In Activity 13-6, you create a new Web site from the command line using the IISWEB.VBS script.

Activity 13-6: Creating a New Web Site Using the IISWEB.VBS Script

Time Required: 10 minutes

Objective: Create a new Web site using a script instead of the Internet Information Services tool.

Description: While exploring the Windows Server 2003 Help and Support Center documentation, you learn that you can also create Web sites using VB scripts provided when IIS was installed. In this activity, you create a new Web site for testing purposes using the IISWEB.VBS script.

1. Click **Start**, click **Run**, and then type **cmd** in the Open text box. Click **OK**.

2. Type **mkdir d:\testsite** at the command prompt and press **Enter**. This directory will be used as the home directory for the new Web site. Type **cd c:\windows\ system32** and press **Enter**.

3. Type **cscript iisweb.vbs /create d:\testsite "New Web Site Test" /b 8100 /dontstart** at the command prompt and press **Enter**. This command creates a new Web site called New Web Site Test that uses TCP port 8100 for connections and is not started by default.

4. The results of the iisweb command are displayed, as shown in Figure 13-11.

```
C:\windows\system32\cmd.exe                                          _|□|x|

C:\WINDOWS\system32>cscript iisweb.vbs /create d:\testsite "New Test Web Site" /
b 8100 /dontstart
Microsoft (R) Windows Script Host Version 5.6
Copyright (C) Microsoft Corporation 1996-2001. All rights reserved.

Connecting to server ...Done.
Server       = SERVER01
Site Name    = New Test Web Site
Metabase Path = W3SVC/46802899
IP           = ALL UNASSIGNED
Host         = NOT SPECIFIED
Port         = 8100
Root         = d:\testsite
Status       = STOPPED

C:\WINDOWS\system32>
```

Figure 13-11   Using the IISWEB command to create a Web site

5. Close the command prompt, and then open the Internet Information Services (IIS) Manager tool.

6. If necessary, expand **ServerXX** (where *XX* is your assigned student number). Click the **plus sign (+)** next to the **Web Sites** folder to expand it, if necessary. The new Web site with the name New Web Site Test should appear, with its state set to Stopped, as shown in Figure 13-12.

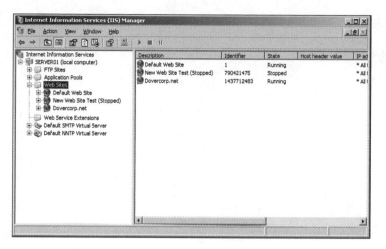

Figure 13-12 Viewing a new Web site using Internet Information Services (IIS) Manager

7. Right-click **New Web Site Test** and then click **Properties** to confirm that it is configured to use TCP port 8100 for connections.

8. Close all open windows.

 Windows Server 2003 includes a variety of VBScripts for the purpose of configuring and managing Internet Information Services. See the Help and Support Center for more information.

Modifying Web-Site Properties

Once the Web Site Creation Wizard or a script like iisweb.vbs has been used to create your Web site, you can then modify a number of properties to fine-tune some of the parameters of the site. Configuring the properties pages for a specific Web site affects only that site and no others. The Default Web Site Properties screen is shown in Figure 13-13.

You may have noticed that the Properties dialog box is very similar to the master properties dialog box discussed earlier in the chapter. It is important to remember that any parameters configured at the Web-site level override the master properties that may have been set at the server level.

Table 13-4 explains each of the tabs on the Properties dialog box.

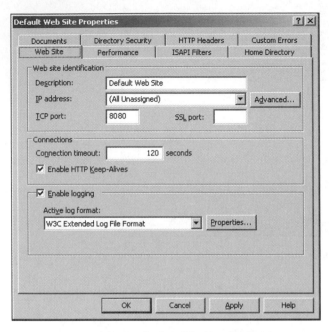

Figure 13-13   The Default Web Site Properties screen

Table 13-4   Web site properties tabs

Properties Tab	Purpose
Web Site	Configures the IP address, TCP port, number of connections, and logging
Performance	Modifies performance-based parameters such as **bandwidth throttling** and maximum Web-site connections
ISAPI Filters	Sets up Internet Server Application Programming Interface (ISAPI) filters that respond to events that occur on the server during the processing of an HTTP request
Home Directory	Controls where the Web site looks for Web content and sets security on that specific folder
Documents	Defines a default Web page search order for the Web site and enables a common footer to be placed at the bottom of each Web page
Directory Security	Configures security for the Web site, such as authentication control, IP address or domain name restrictions, and SSL certificate configurations
HTTP Headers	Configures expiration dates on Web-site content, custom HTTP headers, and content ratings; content expiration is effective when you want to control the amount of time that your Web-site material is to be cached in a client's Web browser cache folder
Custom Errors	Customizes common Web browser error messages that may be displayed to users who experience an error

In Activity 13–7, you configure the properties of the *Dovercorp.net* Web site.

Activity 13-7: Configuring Web Site Properties

Time Required: 15 minutes

Objective: Configure properties for an individual Web site.

Description: The IT manager at Dover Leasing is very interested in the ability to configure Web sites with different properties based on their individual requirements. Although many of Dover's Web sites will use common security settings, he wants you to become familiar with the individual property settings and how these can be used to control the way in which users will ultimately interact with the *Dovercorp.net* site to begin with. In this activity, you explore and configure individual property settings of the *Dovercorp.net* Web site.

1. Open the Internet Information Services (IIS) Manager tool.

2. If necessary, expand **ServerXX** (where *XX* is your assigned student number). Click the **plus sign (+)** next to the **Web Sites** folder to expand it, if necessary. Right-click the **Dovercorp.net** Web site and then click **Properties**.

3. Click the **Performance** tab. In the Web site connections section, type **500** in the Connections limited to spin box.

4. Click the **Documents** tab, and then click the **Add** button. In the Add Content Page dialog box, type **index.html** in the text box and then click **OK**.

5. Click the **Move Up** button until index.html appears at the top of the list content pages.

6. Click **OK** to save the properties configured thus far.

7. Open My Computer and create a new text file in the D:\Dovercorpwebsite folder. Open the new file in Notepad and type the following:

   <html>

   <body>

   <p>This is a test document footer</p>

   </body>

   </html>

8. Save the file and rename it **footer.html**. Click **Yes** in the Rename warning box.

9. In the Internet Information Services tool, right-click the **Dovercorp.net Web site**, click **Properties**, and then click the **Documents** tab.

10. Click the **Enable document footer** check box. Click the **Browse** button, then click **D:\Dovercorpwebsite\footer.html**, and click **Open**.

11. Click the **Directory Security** tab. Click the **Edit** button in the Authentication and access control section. Notice that the Web site is configured to use Integrated Windows authentication and that Anonymous access is enabled using the IUSR_ *servername* account. Click **OK**.

13

12. Click the **HTTP Headers** tab and click the **Enable content expiration** check box. This sets the content to expire after 1 day.

13. Click the **Edit Ratings** button in the Content rating section.

14. Click the **Enable ratings for this content** check box. Click each individual RSACi rating category to view its default configuration, and then click **OK**.

15. Click the **Custom Errors** tab. In the list of HTTP errors, click the entry for error **404**, as shown in Figure 13-14, and then click the **Edit** button. Note the File path listed. Click **Cancel**.

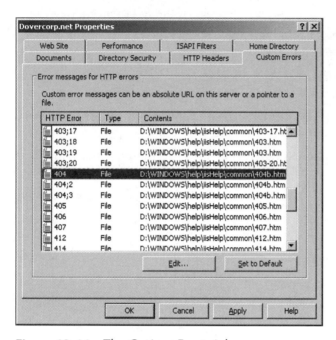

Figure 13-14   The Custom Errors tab

16. Click **OK** to close the Dovercorp.net Properties dialog box.

17. In the My Computer window, browse to the **C:\WINDOWS\Help\ iisHelp\common** folder. Right-click the file **404b.htm**, select **Open With**, and then click **Notepad**.

18. Edit the line <h1>The page cannot be found</h1> to read **<h1> The page cannot be found on the Dovercorp.net Web site</h1>**. Close the file, saving your changes.

19. Open Internet Explorer, type **http://localhost** in the address bar, and press **Enter**.

20. Notice that the Dovercorp.net Web page opens, but that this time it includes the footer configured in Step 10.

21. Type **http://localhost/unknown** in the Internet Explorer address bar and press **Enter**.

22. Notice that the custom 404 error message configured in Step 17 now appears when a page cannot be found.

23. Close all open windows.

CREATING VIRTUAL DIRECTORIES

You may have information that is stored on multiple servers throughout your organization. If you want any of this information to be included in your Web site, you can create a **virtual directory** that specifically points to the shared folder that stores the data. Clients would then access the information by appending the **alias** name of the virtual directory to the Web site host name. An alias can be used to hide the real directory name and to simplify the path that the server should use to access the information. For example, Dover Leasing may have a shared folder called Company Customers. For your intranet site, you might create a virtual directory that has an alias name of Customers. Employees would then type "www. dovercorp.net/customers" to access the virtual directory. The employees will not be able to tell that the information has come from a different server and folder. In Activity 13-8, you configure a virtual directory that points to a shared folder on your partner's server.

ACTIVITY

Activity 13-8: Creating and Configuring a Virtual Directory

Time Required: 15 minutes

Objective: Create and configure a virtual directory.

Description: The Legal and Marketing Departments at Dover Leasing create large volumes of documents over the course of a year. Although many of these documents are contracts stored in paper form, the staff often needs access to electronic versions for revision or review purposes. One issue that makes this difficult is the fact that these documents are often spread across different directories on different servers, which can make individual documents difficult to find. Eventually, the IT manager at Dover Leasing would like the network to be configured such that all Marketing and Legal users will have access to their required documents via a browser interface. In this activity, you create and configure a virtual directory on the *Dovercorp.net* Web site that points to a folder on a different server.

1. Open My Computer. Create a new folder called **D:\virtualdirectory**. Share the folder with the same name. Configure the folder such that the Everyone group also has the **Allow Read** shared folder and NTFS permissions.

2. Create a new text file in the D:\virtualdirectory folder. Open the file in Notepad and type the following:

   <html>

   <body>

13

<H1>This is a virtual directory on ServerXX</H1>

</body>

</html>

3. The *XX* in this code should be replaced with your server number. Save the file, and then rename it **index.htm**. Click **Yes** when prompted to confirm the change of the file's extension. Close My Computer.

4. Open the Internet Information Services (IIS) Manager tool. Click the **plus sign (+)** next to your server name and then click the **plus sign (+)** next to **Web Sites**.

5. Right-click the **Dovercorp.net** Web site, select **New**, and then click **Virtual Directory**. The Virtual Directory Creation Wizard opens. Click **Next**.

6. At the Virtual Directory Alias screen, type **customers** in the Alias text box, and then click **Next**.

7. At the Web Site Content Directory screen, type **\\serverXX\virtualdirectory** in the Path text box, where *XX* is your partner's student number. Click **Next**.

8. On the Security Credentials screen, ensure that the **Always use the authenticated user's credentials when validating access to the network directory** check box is selected, then click **Next**.

9. At the Virtual Directory Access Permissions screen, accept the default values by clicking **Next**.

10. Click **Finish** to complete creating the virtual directory.

11. Ensure that the customers virtual directory is visible, as illustrated in Figure 13-15.

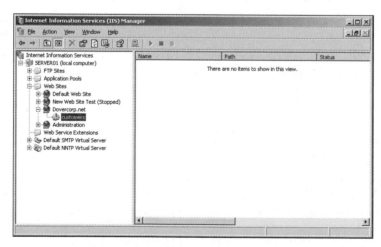

Figure 13-15　The customers virtual directory

12. Right-click the **customers** virtual directory and click **Properties**.

13. The customers Properties dialog box will open listing the network directory acting as the source for the virtual directory, as illustrated in Figure 13-16. Click **Cancel**.

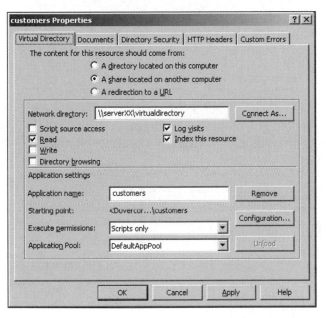

Figure 13-16   Viewing the properties of a virtual directory

14. Open Internet Explorer and type **http://localhost/customers** in the address bar. Press **Enter**. The Web page with the message This is a virtual directory on Server*XX* (where *XX* is your partner's student number) appears.

15. Close all open windows.

You can also create a virtual directory by using the Windows Server 2003 Web Sharing feature, which you explore later in this chapter.

CONFIGURING AUTHENTICATION FOR WEB SITES

All Windows Server 2003 servers require that any user who tries to access the server be authenticated to a valid user account. **Authentication** refers to determining whether or not a user has a valid user account with the proper permissions to access a resource, such as a shared folder or Web site. After a user account has been validated, it is given access to all resources to which it has the proper permissions. Windows Server 2003 Web servers are no exception to this rule. Proper authentication and permissions have to be in place before a client can access a Web site on the server.

IIS provides five levels of authentication that can be used to validate users that are trying to access a Web site stored on the server:

- Anonymous access

- Basic authentication

- Digest authentication

- Integrated Windows authentication

- .NET Passport authentication

Authentication settings are configured from within the properties of a Web site in the Authentication and access control section of the Directory Security tab. The Authentication Methods dialog box is shown in Figure 13-17.

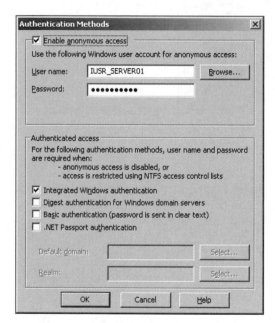

Figure 13-17 The Authentication Methods dialog box

Anonymous Access

Anonymous access allows users to access a Web site without having to provide a user name and password. When a user attempts to access your Web site, IIS uses the IUSR_*servername* user account to provide the required authentication credentials. This user account is a member of the Domain Users (on a domain controller) and Guests groups by default. Alternatively, you can change these credentials by specifying the user name and password of a different user account.

Basic Authentication

Basic authentication prompts users for a user name and password to be able to access the Web resource. The user needs to have a valid Windows Server 2003 user account to be able to gain access to the Web site. One problem with Basic authentication is that the user name and password are transmitted using Base64 encoding (not encryption) and can easily be captured and read by hackers.

Digest Authentication

This authentication method was originally introduced in Windows 2000 with IIS 5.0. **Digest authentication** works the same way as Basic authentication except that the user name and password are hashed using the MD5 algorithm to prevent hackers from obtaining the information. To use Digest authentication, users must be running Internet Explorer 5.0 or higher and have an account in Active Directory or a trusted domain. An IIS server using Digest authentication must also be part of an Active Directory domain and must be running HTTP 1.1 and WebDAV.

Integrated Windows Authentication

Integrated Windows authentication does not ask the user for a password but rather uses the client's currently logged-on credentials to supply a challenge/response to the Web server. This option is primarily used on internal intranets. Once this choice has been enabled, it can only be used if Anonymous access is disabled on the Web site and Windows file permissions have been set, requiring users to provide authentication to access the resources.

.NET Passport Authentication

IIS 6.0 supports a new authentication method not found in previous versions. **.NET Passport authentication** is a configurable option that allows a Web site to use the functionality of the .NET Passport service to authenticate user identities. Although this feature is a configurable option in the Authentication Methods dialog box, this is only for testing purposes. Ultimately, the ability to authenticate users with a .NET Passport will rely on a company carrying out a variety of preproduction tests with Microsoft, as well as a registration process.

Note that if multiple authentication methods are configured, the following rules apply:

- If Anonymous authentication and one other method are selected, the other method only applies if Anonymous authentication fails.
- FTP sites cannot use Digest, Integrated Windows, or .NET Passport authentication.
- Both Digest and Integrated Windows authentication take precedence over Basic authentication.

In Activity 13-9, you configure and test Web-site authentication options.

ACTIVITY

Activity 13-9: Configuring and Testing Web Site Authentication Options

Time Required: 10 minutes

Objective: Configure different Web-site authentication options.

Description: Although the *Dovercorp.net* Web site will ultimately allow access to anonymous public Internet users, the IT manager would like to have the ability to require authenticated access to various Dovercorp Leasing Web sites that may be created in the future. To better understand some of the different authentication options available, you decide to change the authentication settings of the *Dovercorp.net* Web site for testing purposes. In this activity, you configure and then test the impact of both Anonymous access and Basic authentication.

1. Open the Internet Information Services (IIS) Manager tool. Click the **plus sign (+)** next to your server name and then click the **plus sign (+)** next to **Web Sites**.

2. Right-click the **Dovercorp.net** Web site and click **Properties**.

3. Click the **Directory Security** tab.

4. In the Authentication and access control section, click the **Edit** button.

5. Note that both Anonymous and Integrated Windows authentication are currently configured for the Dovercorp.net Web site.

6. Open Internet Explorer, and in the address bar type **http://localhost**, and press **Enter**. Because Anonymous access is allowed, you are not required to authenticate to access the site. Close Internet Explorer.

7. Switch to the Dovercorp.net Properties dialog box. In the Authentication Methods window, uncheck the **Enable anonymous access** and **Integrated Windows authentication** check boxes.

8. Click the **Basic authentication** check box. When the IIS Manager dialog box opens, read the message it presents, as shown in Figure 13-18, and then click **Yes**. Click **OK** to close the Authentication Methods dialog box.

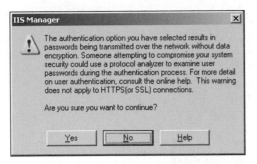

Figure 13-18   The IIS Manager dialog box

9. Click **OK** to close the Dovercorp.net Web site properties dialog box.

10. Open Internet Explorer. In the address bar, type **http://localhost**, and press **Enter**. When the Connect to localhost authentication dialog box opens, type **mcowan** in the User name text box and **Password01** in the Password text box. Click **OK**.

11. The Dovercorp.net Web site homepage opens once authentication is complete.

12. Configure the Dovercorp.net Web site back to its original authentication settings.

13. Close all open windows.

Configuring Server Certificates and Secure Sockets Layer

The Directory Security tab also allows you to configure secure Web communications by implementing **Secure Sockets Layer (SSL)** protocol. This protocol is used to encrypt Web traffic between a client and the Web server. Clients can access a secure server using SSL by using URLs that begin with https:// instead of the common http:// prefix. HTTPS communication is established by default over TCP port 443.

The first step in using SSL on a Web server is to obtain and install a server certificate from a certificate authority (CA) such as Verisign, Inc., or you can install certificate services on a server in your organization and create your own for internal purposes. Until a certificate is installed on the server, IIS is not capable of providing secure connections to clients using SSL. Certificates are installed and configured from the Directory Security tab of a Web site's Properties dialog box, as shown in Figure 13-19.

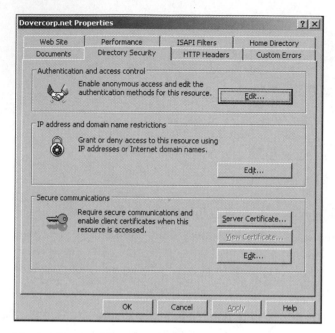

Figure 13-19   The Directory Security tab of a Web site's Properties dialog box

For Internet Web sites that will be made accessible to the general public, you should obtain a proper certificate from a recognized CA to ensure a path of trust. Once you obtain a certificate, you can install it using the IIS Certificate Wizard, as shown in Figure 13-20.

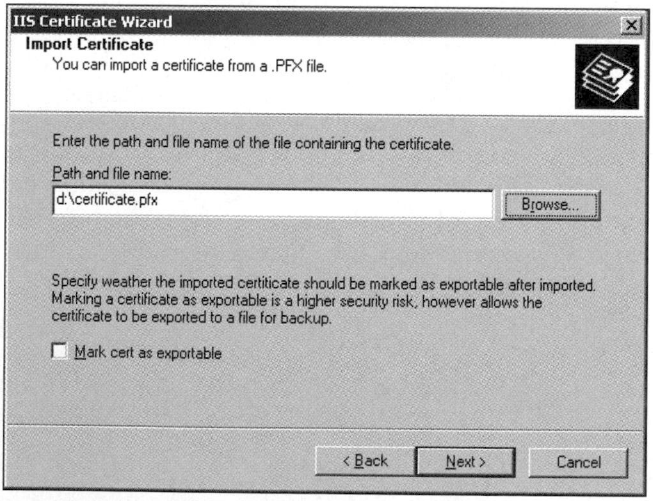

Figure 13-20   The IIS Certificate Wizard

Once you install a certificate, you must enable a Web site for SSL as shown in Figure 13-21. TCP port 443 is the default HTTPS port and must be used unless users explicitly state the port number when they connect.

Figure 13-21   Enabling a Web site for SSL

13

CONFIGURING FTP VIRTUAL SERVERS

File Transfer Protocol (FTP) is used to transfer files between two computers that are both running TCP/IP. The FTP service included with IIS 6.0 enables users to transfer files to and from it using FTP client software such as the command-line ftp utility or a Web browser. The following section looks at some of the basic concepts behind FTP, how to configure the FTP properties, as well as how to create and manage an FTP site.

File Transfer Protocol

FTP is an industry-standard method of transferring files between two hosts running TCP/IP. Although HTTP has replaced FTP for many download functions, it is still a useful protocol for file transfers and is still widely used on both private networks and the Internet today. Unlike HTTP, which only uses a single port for connections during a single session, FTP uses two ports, TCP ports 20 and 21. TCP port 21 is usually used to initiate the connection and for diagnostic functions, while data is usually ultimately passed over TCP port 20.

FTP uses the **Transmission Control Protocol (TCP)** for file transfers. TCP is a connection-based protocol, which means a session is established between the two hosts before any data is transferred.

Some of the important features of TCP include the following:

- The sending computer sends a number of packets to a recipient at once but then waits for an acknowledgment that data was received before sending any more packets. If the sending computer does not receive an acknowledgement, it retransmits the original data.

- All packets at the sending computer are assigned a sequence number so the receiving computer can reassemble the data.

- Each packet also contains a checksum for ensuring the integrity of the data.

To use FTP to transfer files between two computers, one machine must be running FTP client software and the other FTP server software. For example, the server might be running FTP server software such as IIS 6.0, while the client could be using the FTP command-line utility included with Windows Server 2003.

There are a number of easy-to-use, graphical FTP utilities that you can download from the Internet as shareware and freeware. Perform a search for FTP using your favorite search engine to find a list of available downloads.

Configuring FTP Properties

Like the WWW service, you can configure multiple FTP sites running on a single IIS 6.0 server. Each site behaves and operates independently, and it appears to a client as though they are running on separate FTP servers. Each site has its own set of property sheets allowing you to customize settings on a site-by-site basis. There are five tabs available from the site properties, as shown in Figure 13-22 and summarized in Table 13-5.

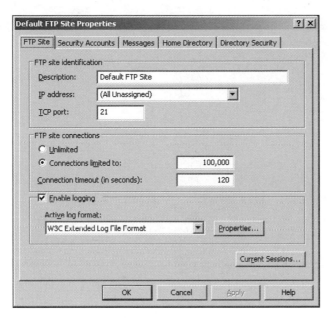

Figure 13-22   The properties of an FTP site

Table 13-5   FTP site property tabs

Properties Tab	Purpose
FTP Site	Configures site identification and connection limits, and enables FTP logging
Security Accounts	Configures which account is used for Anonymous access to the FTP site; also disables Anonymous access, requiring all users to have a user account and password to access the site
Messages	Configures both the welcome and exit messages that are displayed to users that connect to and disconnect from the FTP site
Home Directory	Where the files published through your FTP site are stored; changes the default home directory location to another directory on the server or to a directory located on another server; sets the type of access allowed to the folder (read and/or write); the directory style listing selects the folder style listing that is displayed to FTP users
Directory Security	Grants or denies access to the FTP site based on IP addresses, as shown in Figure 13-23; grants access to all computers except those listed in the exception box, or denies access to all computers except the ones listed; configures access based on individual IP addresses, network addresses, or fully qualified domain names

13

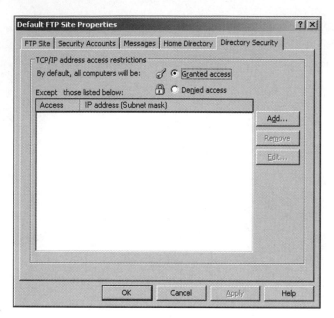

Figure 13-23   FTP site security settings

In Activity 13-10, you configure the properties of the **Default FTP site** and connect to it for testing purposes.

Activity 13-10: Configuring and Testing the Default FTP Site

Time Required: 15 minutes

Objective: Configure and test the Default FTP site.

Description: Dover Leasing has always provided customers with access to various sample contracts via a fax-back service. Although the company plans to place many sample contracts on their new Web site in the future, the IT manager has asked you to explore the possibility of providing access to contracts via FTP as well. In this activity, you configure the properties of the Default FTP site and then test it to ensure that anonymous users can connect without issue.

1. Open the Internet Information Services (IIS) Manager tool.

2. Click the **plus sign (+)** next to your server name and then click the **plus sign (+)** next to the **FTP Sites** folder to expand it.

3. Right-click the **Default FTP Site** and click **Properties**.

4. On the FTP Site tab, browse the information provided, noting that the port number is set to the default value of 21. Click the **Current Sessions** button.

5. Because no users are currently connected via FTP, there should be no users listed in the FTP User Sessions window. Click **Close**.

6. Click the **Security Accounts** tab. Notice that the FTP service allows Anonymous access by default. If this option is de-selected, basic authentication is required.

7. Click the **Messages** tab.

8. In the Banner text box, type **Dovercorp.net FTP server**.

9. In the Welcome text box, type **Thank you for logging on to the Dovercorp.net FTP Server**.

10. In the Exit text box, type **Thanks for stopping by – goodbye!**.

11. Click the **Home Directory** tab. In the FTP site directory section, click the **Write** check box. This allows users to upload files to this FTP server.

12. Click **OK** to close the Default FTP Site Properties dialog box.

13. Click **Start**, click **Run**, and in the Open text box type **cmd** and press **OK**. At the command prompt, type **ftp localhost** and press **Enter**. Notice the banner message that appears.

14. At the User prompt, type **anonymous** and press **Enter**.

15. At the Password prompt, type the e-mail address **user@dovercorp.net**. This is required when logging on using the anonymous user account. Press **Enter**. Notice the Welcome message that appears, as shown in Figure 13-24.

Figure 13-24 Viewing the welcome message after logging on to an FTP site

16. In the Internet Information Services (IIS) Manager window, right-click the **Default FTP Site**, click **Properties**, and then click the **Current Sessions** button. The currently logged-on user appears in the list.

17. At the command prompt, type **bye** and press **Enter** to close the FTP session. Notice the Exit message that appears.

18. Close all open windows.

Now that you are familiar with the different configuration settings associated with an FTP site, let's look at how to create a new FTP virtual server using the Internet Services Manager.

Creating an FTP Site Virtual Server

Much like virtual Web servers, you can create new FTP sites using either the Internet Information Services tool or by scripting. These FTP sites also follow the same principles as Web sites in that they allow you to create virtual directories that can be both local and remote to the IIS server. In Activity 13-11, you create a new FTP site as well as an FTP virtual directory.

ACTIVITY

Activity 13-11: Creating and Testing a New FTP Site and Configuring a Virtual Directory

Time Required: 20 minutes

Objective: Create a new FTP site and virtual directory.

Description: After viewing the FTP server that you configured in Activity 13-10, the IT manager at Dover Leasing has asked you to configure an additional FTP site for the purpose of testing multiple sites, as well as FTP virtual directories. Ultimately, the IT manager thinks it may be possible to enable various customer service representatives working from home to gain quick and easy access to various documents on different servers, using FTP. In this activity, you create and test a new FTP site that includes a virtual directory located on a different server.

1. Open My Computer and create two new folders on your D: drive named **ftpsite** and **ftpvirdir**, respectively. Grant the Everyone group the **Allow Full Control** NTFS permissions to both folders. Share the **ftpvirdir** folder and grant the Everyone group the **Allow Full Control** shared folder permission.

2. Create a new text file in the D:\ftpvirdir folder called **customers.txt**. Open this file, type **Customer readme file from ServerXX** (where *XX* is your assigned student number) and then save and close the file.

3. Close My Computer.

4. Click **Start**, select **Control Panel**, select **Network Connections**, and then click **Local Area Connection**. Click the **Properties** button.

5. Click **Internet Protocol (TCP/IP)** and then click **Properties**.

6. On the General tab, click the **Advanced** button.

7. In the IP addresses section, click the **Add** button. In the TCP/IP Address dialog box, type **192.168.100.XX** in the IP address text box (where *XX* is your assigned student number) and **255.255.255.0** in the Subnet mask text box. Click **Add**.

8. Click **OK** twice, and then click **Close**. Close the Local Area Connection Status dialog box.

9. Open the Internet Information Services (IIS) Manager tool.

10. Click the **plus sign (+)** next to your server name, and then right-click the **FTP Sites** folder, select **New**, and click **FTP Site**. The FTP Site Creation Wizard opens. Click **Next**.

11. At the FTP Site Description screen, type **FTP site for clients** in the Description text box and click **Next**.

12. At the IP Address and Port Settings screen, click the IP address configured in Step 7 in the Enter the IP address to use for this FTP site list box. Click **Next**.

13. At the FTP User Isolation screen, click **Next**.

14. At the FTP Site Home Directory screen, type **D:\ftpsite** in the text box, and click **Next**.

15. At the FTP Site Access Permissions screen, click the **Write** check box, as shown in Figure 13-25, and click **Next**.

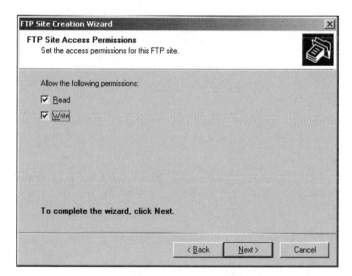

Figure 13-25   The FTP Site Access Permissions screen

16. Click **Finish** to create the new FTP site.

17. Test the new FTP site by opening a command prompt and typing **ftp 192.168.100.XX** (where *XX* is your assigned student number) and pressing **Enter**. When prompted for a user name and password, use the user name **anonymous** and the password **user@dovercorp.net**. Once connected, type **bye** to close the connection.

18. In the Internet Information Services window, right-click **FTP site for clients**, select **New**, and then click **Virtual Directory**.

19. At the Virtual Directory Creation Wizard welcome screen, click **Next**.

20. At the Virtual Directory Alias screen, type **customers** in the Alias text box and click **Next**.

21. At the FTP Site Content Directory screen, type **\\ServerXX\ftpvirdir** (where *XX* is your partner's student number in the text box), and click **Next**.

22. At the Security Credentials screen, ensure that the **Always use the authenticated user's credentials when validating access to the network directory** check box is checked and click **Next**.

23. At the Virtual Directory Access Permissions screen, click **Next**, and then click **Finish**.

24. At the command prompt, type the command **d:** and then press **Enter** to change the focus of the command prompt to the root of your D: drive. At the command prompt, type **ftp 192.168.100.XX** (where *XX* is your partner's student number) and press **Enter**.

25. Log on with a user name of **anonymous** and a password of **user@dovercorp.net**.

26. At the ftp> prompt, type **cd customers** and press **Enter**. This moves you into the customers virtual directory.

27. At the prompt, type **ls** and press **Enter** to view a listing of all files. Note that a file named customers.txt appears in the list.

28. At the command prompt, type **get customers.txt** and press **Enter**. This transfers the customers.txt file to your server. Type **bye** at the command prompt and press **Enter**.

29. Open My Computer and verify that the file **customers.txt** exists in the root of your D: drive. Open the file to verify that it came from your partner's server.

30. Close all open windows.

UPDATING AND MAINTAINING SECURITY FOR AN IIS SERVER

Whenever information is published to users on the Internet, the topic of security arises. You want to be able to provide users access to certain information on your Web servers while restricting access to all other information and the rest of the network. There are several ways an administrator can secure access to information on a Web server. These alternatives are discussed in the following section.

As with any other type of server, once it is installed and configured, an IIS server still needs to be maintained and updated. This usually includes performing regular backups, stopping and starting IIS-related services, and applying updates. These topics are discussed in the next few sections.

Resource Permissions

One of the first ways to control access to information is to set permissions specifying the types of access users are granted. When securing Web content, there are two types of permissions that you can apply to secure resources: NTFS permissions and IIS permissions. To provide the most security for your Web content, you should take advantage of both Windows Server 2003 NTFS security as well as IIS security.

NTFS Permissions

You can control access to Web-server resources stored on an NTFS volume by using NTFS permissions. You should apply NTFS permissions to any Web pages and virtual directories published to your Web server to obtain the highest degree of security possible.

 One of the differences between NTFS permissions and IIS permissions is that different NTFS permissions can be assigned to users and groups, whereas IIS permissions are global.

NOTE

IIS Permissions

Combining NTFS permissions and IIS permissions provides the most security for your Web content. IIS permissions can be configured for any of the following:

- Web sites and FTP virtual servers
- Virtual directories
- Physical directories
- Files

When restricting access to virtual directories, physical directories, and files, there are two primary types of permissions that can be set: the Read permission and/or Write permission. The Read permission allows users to view the contents and the Write permission allows users to add content to virtual directories and folders, as well as change the contents of a file.

If a Web site or virtual directory contains any scripts or executables, you can also configure the Execute permission by choosing None, Scripts only, or Scripts and Executables from the Home Directory or Virtual Directory tab.

 When combining NTFS permissions and IIS permissions, the most restrictive permission is the effective permission.

NOTE

In Activity 13-12, you restrict access to a Web site using both IIS and NTFS permissions.

13

Activity 13-12: Configuring IIS and NTFS Permissions

Time Required: 10 minutes

Objective: Protect Web site resources using both IIS and NTFS permissions.

Description: As part of your role at Dover Leasing, you are responsible for the overall security of network resources. Because the *Dovercorp.net* Web site will be accessible by the general public once completed, you are worried about resources being properly secured. Having read that the highest degree of security in IIS is provided when both IIS and NTFS permissions are applied, you decide to test their impact to be sure that they work correctly. In this activity, you test denying the Read permission to the *Dovercorp.net* customers virtual directory using both IIS and NTFS permissions.

1. Open the Internet Information Services (IIS) Manager tool.

2. Click the **plus sign (+)** next to your server name to expand it. Click the **plus signs (+)** next to the **Web Sites** folder and then the **Dovercorp.net** Web site to expand them. Right-click the **customers** virtual directory and then click **Properties**.

3. On the Virtual Directory tab, click the **Read** check box to uncheck it and then click **OK**.

4. Open Internet Explorer. In the address bar, type **http://localhost** and press **Enter**. The Dovercorp.net Web site opens.

5. In the address bar, type **http://localhost/customers** and press **Enter**. The page is not displayed because IIS Read access was disabled. Note that the HTTP error code listed on the page is 403.2, which means that Read access is denied. Close Internet Explorer.

6. In the Internet Information Services (IIS) Manager tool, access the properties of the customers virtual directory and click the **Read** check box to re-enable the permission. Click **OK** to close the customers Properties dialog box.

7. Open My Computer, and access the properties of your D:\virtualdirectory folder. This is the folder that your partner's server connects to as the customers virtual directory.

8. Click the **Security** tab and set the **Deny Read** permission for all listed groups. Click **OK** to close the virtual directory Properties dialog box. Click **Yes** in the Security dialog box. Ensure that your partner has completed this step before moving on to Step 9.

9. Open Internet Explorer, type **http://localhost/customers** in the address bar, and press **Enter**. Notice that the Connect to server*XX*.Domain*XX*.Dovercorp.net authentication dialog box opens. This is because all users have been explicitly denied the NTFS Read permission to the folder.

10. Close all open windows.

IP Address and Domain Name Security

You can secure Web content by granting or denying access to users based on their IP address or domain name. You can grant or deny access to an individual IP address or to a particular address range.

An example of how an administrator might use IP address and domain name security is when your company provides Web content to another business such as a business partner or a client. The administrator could deny access to all IP addresses except those on the business partner's or client's network. In Activity 13-13, you restrict access to the *Dovercorp.net* Web site using IP address restrictions.

Activity 13-13: Testing IP Address Restrictions

Time Required: 10 minutes

Objective: Test the ability to control Web site access by IP address.

Description: The current Dover Leasing Web server has been the target of attacks by three different hackers. Although you were not able to determine the identities of these users by viewing the security logs, you were able to determine their IP addresses. Based on these previous experiences, you decide to test the ability to block access to Web sites based on a user's configured IP address. In this activity, you block access to the *Dovercorp.net* Web site from your server's configured IP address for testing purposes.

1. Open the Internet Information Services (IIS) Manager tool.

2. Click the **plus sign (+)** next to your server name to expand it. Click the **plus sign (+)** next to the **Web Sites** folder to expand it, and then right-click the **Dovercorp.net** Web site and click **Properties**.

3. Click the **Directory Security** tab. In the IP address and domain name restrictions section, click the **Edit** button.

4. In the IP Address and Domain Name Restrictions dialog box, click the **Add** button.

5. In the Deny Access dialog box, as shown in Figure 13-26, type **127.0.0.1** in the IP address text box to deny access to this Web site for your computer. Click **OK** twice. Click **OK** to close the Dovercorp.net Properties dialog box.

6. Open Internet Explorer, type **http://localhost** in the address bar, and press **Enter**. The page does not display because your IP address has been rejected. Notice that the error code listed on the page is a 403.6 forbidden error.

7. In the Internet Information Services window, right-click the **Dovercorp.net Web site** and click **Properties**.

8. Click the **Directory Security** tab. In the IP address and domain name restrictions section, click the **Edit** button.

9. In the IP Address and Domain Name Restrictions dialog box, click the entry for **127.0.0.1** and click the **Remove** button. Click **OK**.

13

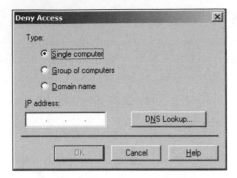

Figure 13-26   The Deny Access dialog box

10. Click **OK** to close the Dovercorp.net Properties window.

11. Close all open windows.

Starting and Stopping Services

At some point, for administrative purposes, you may need to stop and restart services related to IIS. IIS 6.0 makes it simple to stop and restart services by allowing services, along with individual sites, to be stopped and restarted through the Internet Information Services console.

Backing Up the IIS Configuration

It is generally a good idea to periodically back up the configuration settings of your IIS Server. IIS 6.0 stores its configuration settings in a database referred to as the IIS metabase that can be backed up separately. This is useful in the event that you have to restore your IIS Server settings.

The default location for backups is the %systemroot%\system32\inetsrv\Metaback directory. The metabase can be backed up using one of five methods:

- Back up the database with the backup utility in the IIS console
- Copy the contents of the backup directory to another folder to provide redundancy after an initial backup has been performed
- Export the contents of the database to a text file using the metabase editor tool
- Use the IISBACK.VBS script
- Back up System State data with the Windows Server 2003 Backup utility or a third party utility

The easiest way to back up the metabase is to use the Internet Information Services tool. In Activity 13-14, you back up and restore the IIS configuration of your server.

Activity 13-14: Backing Up the IIS Configuration

Time Required: 10 minutes

Objective: Back up and restore the configuration of an IIS server.

Description: The IT manager at Dover Leasing is concerned about all server data being backed up on a regular basis. He is also worried, based on past experience, about the *Dovercorp.net* Web site being down for extended periods due to lost data or server problems. To help ensure a quick response in the future, he has asked you to test the backup and restore features found within the Internet Information Services console. In this activity, you use the backup and restore facilities of IIS to back up, verify, and then restore your server's configuration.

1. Open the Internet Information Services (IIS) Manager tool.

2. Right-click the **ServerXX (local computer)** icon, select **All Tasks**, and then click **Backup/Restore Configuration**.

3. In the Configuration Backup/Restore dialog box, click the **Create Backup** button, as shown in Figure 13-27.

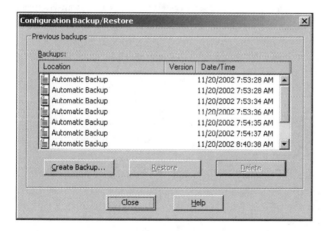

Figure 13-27   The Configuration Backup/Restore dialog box

4. In the Configuration Backup dialog box, type **test IIS backup** in the Configuration backup name text box and click **OK**.

5. Notice that your new backup appears in the Configuration Backup/Restore dialog box. Click the **Close** button.

6. Open My Computer and browse to the **C:\WINDOWS\system32\inetsrv\ Metaback** folder. Confirm that two files that begin with the name "test IIS backup" are stored in this folder.

7. Close My Computer.

8. In the Internet Information Services window, right-click your server, select **All Tasks**, and then click **Backup/Restore Configuration**.

9. In the Configuration Backup/Restore dialog box, click **test IIS backup**, and then click **Restore**.

10. Read the message that appears in the IIS Manager dialog box, and then click **Yes**.

11. When the IIS Manager dialog box opens specifying that the operation completed successfully, click **OK**.

12. Close all open windows.

You can also export the IIS 6.0 metabase configuration using the iiscnfg.vbs script. Exporting the configuration of the metabase is useful in cases where you want to import your configuration to another computer running Windows Server 2003. For more information on importing or exporting the IIS metabase, see the Internet Information Services 6.0 Administrator Guide or the Help and Support Center.

IIS 6.0 also introduces a new history feature that tracks changes to the MetaBase.xml and MBSchema.xml files. Whenever changes are made to these files via system configuration tasks (or by directly editing them), copies of the changed files are written to the %system-root% \system32\inetsrv\History folder on the server. You can subsequently use these files if the metabase ever needs to be rolled back to a previous configuration.

Updating IIS 6.0

As with most software that you install on your server, updates are regularly released to fix any known bugs and security issues that are reported. The two common types of updates that you apply to your IIS Server are service packs and hot fixes. Hot fixes are usually released between service packs and to fix a certain component. They are small software fixes designed to solve a known security issue. Service packs are usually an accumulation of software patches and fixes that fix bugs that have been discovered. Service packs are more significant upgrades than hot fixes.

Before you apply any patch, hot fix, or service pack, make sure you perform a full backup of your server.

Security is one of the most important aspects of running a Web server. Often, hot fixes and patches are released to fix a known security issue. Therefore, it's crucial that network administrators know which hot fixes have been applied to a Web server and, more importantly, which hot fixes have not been applied. One of the tools you can use to determine what hot fixes and service packs need to be installed on a server is the Microsoft Baseline Security Analyzer, originally discussed in Chapter 2. You can use this tool to determine which IIS hot fixes are currently installed on your Web server.

Microsoft provided a utility known as the IIS Lockdown Tool to secure previous versions of IIS. In Windows Server 2003, the ability to further secure Web services is provided via the Web Service Extensions node in the IIS console.

CREATING AND MODIFYING WEB FOLDERS

Once you have IIS installed on servers, your organization may have data that they want shared via HTTP or FTP access by clients. For example, your company may want its yearly financial reports to be publicly available on the Internet.

Windows Server 2003 also includes a feature that allows you to create and share files on a Web server using a **Web folder**. A Web folder is designed to be accessed from the Internet or an intranet using the HTTP or FTP protocols. Once IIS is properly installed and Web folders are configured, many common applications such as Office XP are capable of opening and saving files to the Web folder just like any standard Windows shared folder.

Configuring a folder to be shared over the Web is similar to regular folder sharing except you use the Web Sharing tab to configure folder properties. If the IIS Web server is configured properly, you can choose the specific Web site from which you want this folder to be available. Figure 13-28 shows the Web Sharing tab for a folder named apps.

13

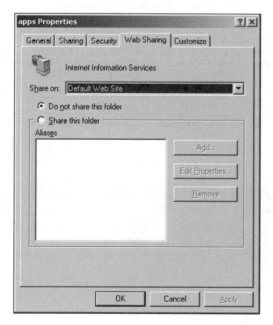

Figure 13-28   The Web Sharing tab of a folder

Shared Web folders do not have to use the actual folder name to be referenced. Web folders can instead use an alias name to which you want your Web clients to refer when accessing the shared resource. Figure 13-29 illustrates the Edit Alias dialog box.

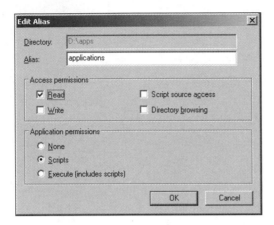

Figure 13-29   The Edit Alias dialog box

In the Edit Alias dialog box, you should also configure the access permissions and application permissions that you would like Web clients to have for the data within the shared resource. Tables 13-6 and 13-7 explain the various Web folder access permissions.

Table 13-6   Web folder access permissions

Access Permission	Description
Read	Allows users to read and display Web-based information
Write	Allows users to modify the contents of the shared Web folder
Script source access	Allows users to view the contents of Web-based scripts
Directory browsing	Allows users to browse the actual folder structure of the shared resource

Table 13-7   Application permissions

Application Permission	Description
None	Provides no permissions to execute script or application commands
Scripts	Allows the user to run scripts to perform Web-based functions
Execute (includes scripts)	Allows users to run scripts or applications over the Web-based connection

Network clients can open a Web-based file share using one of three main methods:

- Internet Explorer—To open a Web folder using Internet Explorer, click the File menu, and then click Open. Type the URL of the folder share (http://web server/share) in the Open text box, and then click the check box next to Open as Web Folder.

- My Network Places—Open My Network Places, and double-click the Add Network Place Wizard. You can then type the URL of the Web folder in the form of http://webserver/share.

- Microsoft Office XP—In a Microsoft Office application, click File, click Open, and then type the URL of the Web folder in the File name text box.

In Activity 13-15, you configure and access a folder using Web Sharing.

ACTIVITY

Activity 13-15: Configuring Web Folders and Exploring Access Methods

Time Required: 10 minutes

Objective: Configure and access a Web shared folder.

Description: Although users at Dover Leasing still use mapped network drives as their primary method of accessing file server resources, the IT manager has asked you to explore the possibility of also providing browser-based access to files and folders. In this activity, you use the Web Sharing feature of Windows Server 2003 to create and test access to a new virtual directory.

1. Open My Computer.

2. Create a new folder on your D: drive called **websharing**. Create a new text document in the folder called **test.txt**. Open the file, type **Web sharing test**, then save and close the file.

3. Right-click the new **websharing** folder and click **Properties**.

4. Click the **Web Sharing** tab.

5. In the Share on list box, click the **Dovercorp.net** Web site.

6. Click the **Share this folder** radio button.

7. When the Edit Alias dialog box opens, accept all default values and click **OK.** Click **OK** again to close the websharing folder properties dialog box.

8. Open the Internet Information Services (IIS) Manager tool. Verify that a new virtual directory called "websharing" now appears under the Dovercorp.net Web site.

9. Open Internet Explorer, type **http://localhost/websharing**, and press **Enter**.

10. Notice that a directory listing appears for this folder because directory browsing is enabled for Web Sharing folders by default and because a default document page was not found in the folder.

13

11. Click the **test.txt** file to view its contents. It appears within the browser window because text files can be viewed in Internet Explorer.

12. Close all open windows.

INSTALLING AND USING REMOTE ADMINISTRATION (HTML) TOOLS

As discussed earlier in this chapter, IIS 6.0 provides the ability to manage IIS servers remotely via the Remote Administration (HTML) tools. Once installed, use these tools to manage not only IIS 6.0 servers, but also a variety of system elements including network settings, disk quotas, and more via a standard Web browser. This allows an administrator to easily configure system settings from any computer on the network.

The Remote Administration (HTML) tools are not installed on Windows Server 2003 by default, and must be added manually via the Add/Remove Windows Components feature of Add or Remove Programs in Control Panel. In Activity 13-16, you first install and then explore the Remote Administration (HTML) tools using Internet Explorer.

Activity 13-16: Install and Explore the Remote Administration (HTML) Tools

Time Required: 15 minutes

Objective: Install and then explore the Remote Administration (HTML) tools to manage your server.

Description: Although the IT manager intends to have administrative staff use the Internet Information Services MMC to manage IIS servers normally, he has asked you to install the Remote Administration (HTML) tools for evaluation purposes. In this activity, you will first install these tools and then explore various settings from Internet Explorer.

1. Click **Start**, select **Control Panel**, and then click **Add or Remove Programs**.

2. Click **Add/Remove Windows Components**.

3. In the Components text box, click **Application Server** and then click the **Details** button.

4. In the Application Server window, click **Internet Information Services (IIS)** and then click the **Details** button.

5. In the Internet Information Services (IIS) window, click **World Wide Web Service** and then click the **Details** button.

6. In the World Wide Web Service window, click the check box next to **Remote Administration (HTML)** as shown in Figure 13-30. Click **OK**.

7. Click **OK** to close the Internet Information Services (IIS) window, click **OK** to close the Application Server window, and then click **Next**.

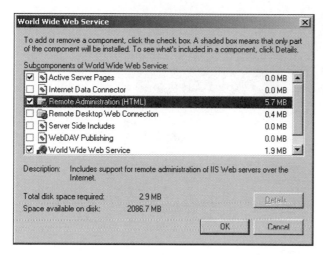

Figure 13-30   Installing Remote Administration (HTML) tools for IIS

8. Click **Finish**.

9. Click the **Close** button to close the Add or Remove Programs window.

10. Click **Start**, select **All Programs**, and then click **Internet Explorer**. To add a site to the Trusted Sites list, click **Tools**, and then click **Internet Options**. Click the **Security** tab, and select **Trusted sites** in the zones list. Click the **Sites** button. In the Trusted sites dialog box, type **127.0.0.1**. Click **Add**, and then click **Close**. Click **OK** to close the Internet Options dialog box.

11. In the Internet Explorer address bar, type **https://127.0.0.1:8098** and press **Enter**. This connects you to the Remote Administration Web site using a secure connection.

12. When the first Security Alert window appears, click **OK**. When the second Security Alert window appears, click **Yes**.

13. In the User name text box, type **AdminXX** (where *XX* is your assigned student number). Type your password in the Password text box, and then click **OK**. The Server Administration Web site opens, as shown in Figure 13-31.

14. Click on the **Sites** link in the blue menu bar. This opens the Web Site Configuration page, which allows site properties to be changed or new sites to be created.

15. Click on the **Web Server** link in the blue menu bar. This opens the Web Server administration page, allowing you to change different server settings.

16. Click on the **Web Master Settings** link. In the Maximum connections section, type **1000** in the Limited to text box and click **OK**.

17. Click on the **Network** link in the blue menu bar, and then click on the **Interfaces** link. This page allows you to change the configuration settings of the server's network adapters.

13

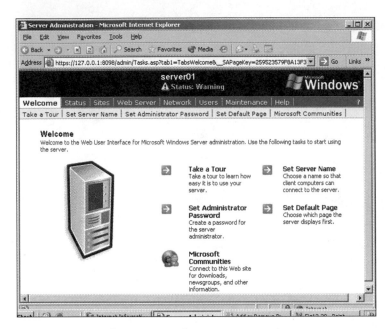

Figure 13-31   The Server Administration Web site

18. Click on the **Maintenance** link in the blue menu bar. Browse through available settings as time permits.

19. Close Internet Explorer.

INSTALLING AND CONFIGURING INTERNET PRINTING

In Chapter 8 you learned about the installation and configuration of printers in Windows Server 2003. This included a brief look at the Internet Printing Protocol (IPP), the facility that allows printers to be managed via a Web browser, and clients to send print jobs to printers using the HTTP protocol. In order for Internet printing to be used on a Windows Server 2003 system, IIS must be installed, as must the Internet Printing component, which was originally installed in Activity 13-1.

Once installed, Internet Printing is still not necessarily enabled. To enable this feature, an administrator must ensure that the Internet Printing Web Service Extension is set to Allow, along with Active Server Pages, as shown in Figure 13-32.

Once these two extensions are allowed, it is possible to manage and install printers via a Web browser like Internet Explorer, as well as configure client systems to print via the HTTP protocol. In Activity 13-17 you verify the correct configuration to allow Internet Printing on your server, manage printers using Internet Explorer, and install a printer to use Internet Printing via the Add Printer Wizard.

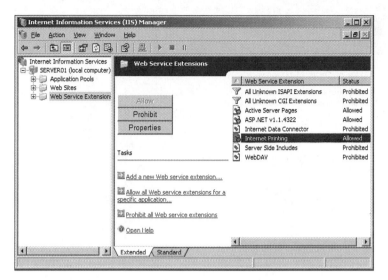

Figure 13-32   Allowing the Internet Printing Web Service Extension

Activity 13-17: Configuring and Managing Internet Printing

Time Required: 15 minutes

Objective: Configure and manage Internet Printing on a Windows Server 2003 system.

Description: In order to consolidate the manner in which printers are configured and managed at Dover Leasing, the IT manager has asked you to explore Internet Printing settings in Windows Server 2003. In this activity you verify the correct configuration to allow Internet Printing on your server, manage printers using Internet Explorer, and install a printer to use Internet Printing via the Add Printer Wizard.

1. Open the Internet Information Services (IIS) Manager tool.

2. Click the **plus sign (+)** next to your server to expand its contents if necessary. Click the **Web Service Extensions** folder to view its contents.

3. Ensure that both the Internet Printing and Active Server Pages extensions have their status set to Allowed. If they are not set to allow, click on each, and then click the **Allow** button. Close the Internet Information Services (IIS) Manager window.

4. Open Internet Explorer. Type **http://localhost:8080/printers** and press **Enter**.

5. At the All Printers on localhost screen, click the **HPLaserJet–ServerXX** link.

6. Under the View menu on the left side of the screen, click **Properties**. This displays the various property settings for the printer, as shown in Figure 13-33. Close Internet Explorer.

7. Click **Start**, and then click **Printers and Faxes**.

8. Double-click on the **Add Printer** icon. At the Welcome screen, click **Next**.

13

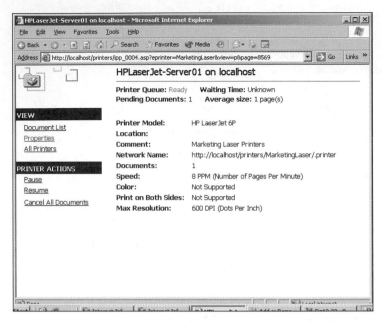

Figure 13-33   Viewing the properties of a printer using Internet Explorer

9. At the Local or Network Printer screen, ensure that **A network printer, or a printer attached to another computer** is selected, and click **Next**.

10. At the Specify a Printer screen, click the **Connect to a printer on the Internet or on a home or office network** radio button. In the URL text box, type **http://192.168.1.XX/printers/HPLaserJet-ServerXX/.printer** (where *XX* is your partner's student number). Click **Next**.

11. At the Default Printer screen, click **No**, and then click **Next**.

12. Click **Finish**.

13. Right-click on the **HPLaserjet-ServerXX on http://serverXX** icon in the Printers and Faxes window, and click **Properties**.

14. Click on the **Ports** tab. Notice that the configured port points to the URL of the printer, as shown in Figure 13-34.

15. Close all open windows.

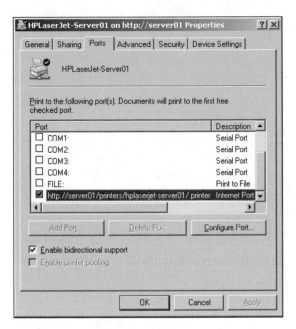

Figure 13-34   Viewing the Ports tab in the properties of an HTTP printer

TROUBLESHOOTING WEB CLIENT CONNECTIVITY PROBLEMS

A major part of any administrator's job is troubleshooting network problems. One of the most common problems that may occur when running an IIS server is clients are not able to access one of the sites. The following section looks at some of the common client connectivity problems that can occur and how you can troubleshoot the various problems.

Client Access Problems

If users are unable to gain access to an IIS Server, there are several configuration settings that you can verify to troubleshoot the problem.

- Verify the TCP/IP configuration settings that have been configured on the client. Use the IPCONFIG command on Windows NT, 2000, or XP machines to verify that the correct IP settings have been assigned. You can use WINIPCFG to verify IP settings on Windows 9x machines. Use the PING command to verify connectivity with remote computers.

- Check the proxy settings that have been configured through the client's Web browser. To be able to access intranet Web sites, be sure to click Bypass proxy server for local addresses in the proxy server configuration settings of your Web browser.

- Check for obvious problems such as whether the proxy server is available and online and whether the client is connected to the network.

- Enable or disable the Show friendly HTTP error messages option in the properties of Internet Explorer. If enabled, full details of connection errors are shown.

- Use a protocol analyzer to capture packets moving between the client and the Web server to determine where communications errors may be taking place.

If users complain that they are unable to gain access to a Web site or FTP site configured on an IIS server, check any one of the following:

- Check the permissions assigned to the site. Make sure that the Users group has been assigned the NTFS Read permission to the directory. Make sure the IIS Read permission has been assigned to the site's home directory.

- Check to see which authentication method has been configured for the site.

- Check to see what IP address and domain name restrictions have been applied to the site.

- If there is a connection limit set for the site, make sure this limit has not been exceeded.

- If the service has been configured to use a port other than the default, make sure the client is specifying the correct port number.

- If you have not enabled Anonymous access, make sure the client has a valid user account.

- Client computers may contain invalid cached DNS information about a specific Internet location. From the command prompt, type IPCONFIG / FLUSHDNS to clear the DNS cache.

Chapter Summary

- Internet Information Services (IIS) includes four main components: the World Wide Web (HTTP) services, File Transfer Protocol (FTP) services, Network News Transfer Protocol (NNTP) services, and Simple Mail Transfer Protocol (SMTP) services.

- The first step to configuring IIS is to understand how the master properties affect the overall Web server. The master properties are IIS parameters that can be configured on the server and are inheritable by all Web and FTP sites hosted on the server. If an individual site has its own configuration settings and you decide to change the Master Properties, IIS gives you the option of whether or not to apply the changes to the preconfigured site.

- Multiple Web sites can be distinguished on a single Web server by either configuring individual IP addresses for each site, configuring individual port numbers for each site, or by configuring a host header for each site.

- A virtual directory can be used to include information that may be stored on a server different from the one on which the Web site home directory is located.

- By default, Anonymous access is used to allow public access to a Web site.

❑ Five main authentication methods used in IIS are Anonymous, Basic, Digest, .NET Passport, and Integrated Windows authentication.

❑ Regular IIS maintenance tasks include backing up the IIS configuration, starting or stopping services, and installing hot fixes and service packs.

❑ Windows Server 2003 supports the Internet Printing Protocol (IPP), which allows printer configuration, management, and connections via the HTTP protocol.

KEY TERMS

.NET Passport authentication — An IIS authentication method that utilizes .NET Password user names and passwords.

Alias — The name of a virtual directory, or the name used to hide the real name of a directory and to simplify the directory name that would be used to access the information.

Anonymous access — Allows users to access a Web site without having to provide a user name and password.

Authentication — Refers to determining whether a user has a valid user account with the proper permissions to access a resource such as a shared folder or Web site.

bandwidth throttling — Allows you to limit the network bandwidth that is available for Web and FTP connections to the server.

Basic authentication — Prompts users for a user name and password to be able to access the Web resource. The user name and password are then transmitted using Base64 encoding.

Default FTP site — An FTP server that responds to TCP/IP port 21 on all configured IP addresses of the server that are not assigned to another site.

Default Web Site — A configured Web site that responds to TCP/IP port 80 on all unassigned IP addresses of the server. This Web site is initially empty and may be used to create a custom Web site for your organization.

Digest authentication — Prompts users for a user name and password to be able to access the Web resource. The user name and password are hashed to prevent hackers from obtaining the information.

File Transfer Protocol (FTP) — Used to transfer files between two computers that are both running TCP/IP.

host header — The fully qualified DNS name that is used to access a Web site on an IIS Server.

Integrated Windows authentication — Does not ask the user for a password but rather uses the client's currently logged-on credentials to supply a challenge/response to the Web server.

Internet Information Services (IIS) — A Windows Server 2003 component that provides Web-related services to an organization.

master properties — IIS parameters that are configured on the server and are inheritable by all Web and FTP sites hosted on the server.

metabase — IIS 6.0 stores its configuration settings in a database referred to as the IIS metabase.

13

Secure Sockets Layer (SSL) — This protocol is used to encrypt Web traffic between a client and the Web server.

Transmission Control Protocol (TCP) — A connection-based protocol, which means a session is established between the two hosts before any data is transferred.

virtual directory — A mapping to a physical directory containing content to be included on a Web site.

virtual servers — A unique Web or FTP site that behaves as if it were on its own dedicated server.

Web folder — A folder designed to be accessed from the Internet or an intranet using the HTTP or FTP protocols.

REVIEW QUESTIONS

1. You are planning to install a Web-enabled e-mail package in your organization. Which IIS service is used to enable the sending of e-mail messages?

   a. NNTP

   b. SMTP

   c. HTTP

   d. FTP

2. IIS is automatically installed during a standard installation of Windows Server 2003.

   a. True

   b. False

3. Which of the following are the two user accounts automatically created during an installation of IIS? (Choose two.)

   a. IWAM_*servername*

   b. Anonymous_user

   c. WEBUser_*servername*

   d. IUSR_*servername*

4. Master properties can be configured to set the IP address and TCP port for all sites located on the server.

   a. True

   b. False

5. Individual site properties override master properties by default.

   a. True

   b. False

6. You are a network administrator responsible for maintaining your company's Web servers. There have recently been several hot fixes released for IIS 6.0. What tool can you use to determine the hot fixes currently installed on your Web servers?

   a. Add or Remove Windows Components

   b. Device Manager

   c. MBSA

   d. System Information

7. A client is reporting that he is unable to connect to your server running IIS. Which of the following could be causing the problem?

   a. permissions assigned to the Web and FTP sites

   b. TCP/IP parameters assigned to the client

   c. any IP address and domain name restrictions applied

   d. whether or not Anonymous access has been disabled

8. Which of the following IIS permissions can be assigned to a virtual directory?

   a. Full Control

   b. Read

   c. Write

   d. Delete

9. You have configured a new FTP site on your Web server. The site has been configured to only allow Read access. You have also enabled Anonymous access using the IUSR_Server1 account. In addition, you also notice that the following NTFS permissions are in place: *Users: Full Control*; *IUSR_Server01: Modify*; and *Guests: Modify*. What type of permission do users have to your new FTP site?

   a. Full Control

   b. Change

   c. Read

   d. No Access

10. You are the administrator of your company's Web server. You changed the FTP port from 21 to 1223. Clients report that they are not able to access the FTP server. What is most likely causing the problem?

    a. You have configured clients with incorrect permissions.

    b. There are IP address restrictions in place.

    c. Clients are connecting to the default port.

    d. There are domain name restrictions in place.

11. Directory security can be configured using which of the following?
    a. IP address
    b. Network address
    c. Username
    d. Domain name

12. You are configuring directory security for your FTP site. You select the granted access option and add the IP network group address 129.10.0.0. You also add the single computer IP address 135.15.121.10. Which of the following statements are true? (Choose all that apply.)
    a. All computers on the 129.10.0.0 network are granted access to your FTP site.
    b. The IP address 135.15.121.10 is not granted access to your FTP site.
    c. All computers on the 129.10.0.0 network are not granted access to your FTP site.
    d. The IP address 135.15.121.10 is granted access to your FTP site.

13. Which protocol does FTP use to establish a session?
    a. TCP
    b. HTTP
    c. UDP
    d. POP3

14. When you are creating a virtual directory, which of the following are possible options for the location of the directory? (Choose all that apply.)
    a. a directory other than the home directory
    b. a URL
    c. a directory in a remote computer
    d. none of the above

15. Which of the following options can be used to back up the configuration settings of your IIS Server?
    a. Use the backup program included with Windows.
    b. The IISBACK.VBSscript
    c. Use the backup program within the IIS console.
    d. Use third-party backup software.

16. Which TCP port number does HTTP use by default?
    a. 21
    b. 80
    c. 443
    d. 119

17. What TCP port number does HTTPS use by default?

    a. 400

    b. 433

    c. 443

    d. 8080

18. You are configuring authentication for your IIS server. You want all users to provide their Windows Server 2003 user name and password before gaining access to the Web resources. You also do not want the user names and passwords sent in clear text. Which authentication method should you configure?

    a. Anonymous authentication

    b. Basic authentication

    c. Digest authentication

    d. Integrated Windows authentication

19. You want to configure a maximum connection limit for all sites configured on your Web server. At what level should you make the configuration change?

    a. master

    b. site

    c. folder

20. Which of the following are valid IIS authentication methods? (Choose all that apply.)

    a. Anonymous access

    b. Basic authentication

    c. Digest authentication

    d. Integrated Windows authentication

13

CASE PROJECTS

CASE
PROJECTS

Case Project 13-1

Dover Leasing is planning to install a Web server on their corporate network. In a planning session, managers and representatives from each department raise several concerns. You have been asked to address these concerns in the next planning session.

1. Managers are unsure of the different authentication methods available. List the various methods of authentication and the differences between them.

2. Each department will have their own Web site and wants to control whether users from other departments will be able to access their site. List the various ways in which access to these sites could be controlled.

3. If the Web server will host multiple sites, what methods can be used to uniquely identify each one?

Case Project 13-2

You are configuring a new FTP site for Dover Leasing's Web server. The managers would prefer the information to be physically stored on another server. The site will be used to provide access to some of your company's Web content to network users and an external customer. Your managers are concerned about security because no other external clients or business partners should be allowed to access this content. You have been asked to create a document addressing some of the issues and concerns.

1. Outline each of the steps in creating and configuring the new FTP site.

2. Security is a major issue and has been emphasized by your managers. Include in your document the various options you will use to secure the new FTP site so that only the appropriate users have access.

3. Include in your document how NTFS and IIS permissions can be used together to provide the most security.

4. Your managers are also concerned with the security of IIS 6.0 and want to make sure that the latest service packs and hot fixes are always applied. How will you track what hot fixes and patches need to be installed on your server?

Case Project 13-3

A friend who owns an ISP has come to you for advice about offering services based on the Windows Server 2003 version of Internet Information Services. Mainly he is concerned about the large number of Web sites that he will need to create and the amount of time this will take. Secondly, he has security concerns about implementing services he doesn't require such as NNTP and FTP. What can you suggest that would help to alleviate his concerns?

14

WINDOWS SERVER 2003 SECURITY FEATURES

After reading this chapter and completing the exercises, you will be able to:

♦ Identify the various elements and techniques that can be used to secure a Windows Server 2003 system

♦ Use Security Configuration and Analysis tools to configure and review security settings

♦ Audit access to resources and review Security log settings

One of the most important roles of any network administrator is to ensure that servers and the data they hold are properly secured. In practice, implementing proper security is a far-reaching endeavor that varies from organization to organization. Considerations not only include the various security features and capabilities of an operating system like Windows Server 2003, but also the various policies and procedures of an organization. Although securing a server to the greatest possible extent might seem like the most logical choice in the eyes of an administrator, in practice the ability for users to access systems in a timely and straightforward manner also needs to be considered. Implementing security always involves finding the right balance between both business and technical factors. In other words, there is more to implementing sound security practices than often meets the eye, especially for inexperienced administrators.

Windows Server 2003 includes a number of different security features and capabilities, many of which have been looked at in previous chapters. This chapter begins with a basic review of the key security features of Windows Server 2003, and then takes a closer look at two additional capabilities not yet explored, namely Security Configuration and Analysis tools, as well as the auditing capabilities that allow administrators to review various security-related events.

SECURING YOUR WINDOWS 2003 SYSTEM

Windows Server 2003 includes a number of different security-related features and tools that help an administrator to properly secure both server and desktop systems. Although a wide variety of tools and features exist, they can generally be categorized into one of the following areas:

- Authentication
- Access control
- Encryption
- Security policies
- Service packs and hot fixes

The following sections provide an overview of each security category, and how various features and tools relate to these categories.

Authentication

Authentication is a concept at the heart of any network security strategy. At the most basic level, Windows Server 2003 authentication processes require a user to submit a valid user name and password combination to gain access to desktop systems (such as those running Windows NT, Windows 2000, and Windows XP) or domain environments.

In a domain environment, a Windows Server 2003 system configured as a domain controller handles authentication functions in a centralized manner. In a workgroup environment, users are authenticated by the local Security Accounts Manager (SAM) database on the computer they are logging on to. In both cases, the end result is the same—the user's identity is confirmed, and this confirmation later serves to dictate which resources a user can and cannot access on either their local computer or the network. This identification process is a critical element of security in any network environment.

In the same way that users can be authenticated to their local computer or a domain controller in their home domain, trust relationships extend this process to other domains, and possibly other forests. Ultimately, this means that users in domain environments can authenticate themselves a single time, and then potentially access resources across many domains and forests without the need to authenticate again.

Other Windows Server 2003 services support additional authentication methods. One example is Internet Information Services (IIS), which provides a variety of authentication methods for users accessing resources stored on a Web server (for more information on IIS authentication options, revisit Chapter 13). These authentication methods make it possible to not only authenticate internal network users, but also users from the Internet when necessary.

For the highest degree of security possible, all network users should be required to authenticate themselves. While it is possible to allow users access to a network without authentication, this is inherently insecure and should be avoided whenever possible.

Windows Server 2003 user authentication methods were originally explored in Chapter 3, while IIS authentication settings were outlined in Chapter 13.

Access Control

In order to secure resources like files, folders, and printers, Windows Server 2003 also supports another key security capability known as access control. As the name suggests, access control literally controls which users, groups, and computers can access resources, along with the level of access granted. For example, NTFS permissions are used to provide access control to resources stored on NTFS partitions and volumes such as the ability to read, write, or modify a file. Shared folder permissions allow an administrator to control who can access the files and subfolders or a shared folder, and to what extent. Similarly, printer permissions extend the concept of access control to printers and associated print devices.

As a general rule, users should only be granted the lowest level of access to resources that they require to carry out necessary functions. For example, if a user only needs to be able to read a file and not make changes, they should be granted no more than the Read permission to that file. This concept is known as the "principal of least privilege". Although the concept is fundamentally sound, implementing it is often easier said than done, since the effective permissions of a user are impacted by the permissions directly applied to them, as well as any groups they are members of. For this reason, Windows Server 2003 includes features like the Effective Permissions tab in the properties of resources, allowing an administrator to quickly determine the impact of these combined permissions for an individual user, group, or computer.

Shared folder and NTFS access control permissions were explored in detail in Chapter 5. Printer access control permissions were explored in Chapter 8.

In the same way that access control is used to control access to traditional network resources like files, folders, and printers, permissions can also be used to control access to Active Directory objects. For example, using techniques like the Delegation of Control Wizard or by explicitly configuring permissions on the Security tab of objects like a user account, an administrator can control what level of access users have to that particular object. In a manner similar to file, folder, and printer permissions, the principle of least privilege should be followed when applying access control settings to Active Directory objects.

Active Directory object access permissions were outlined in Chapter 10.

Encryption

In order to further protect data on a server beyond what access control settings provide, Windows Server 2003 also supports the ability to encrypt confidential files. This capability is provided via the Encrypting File System (EFS), which uses a combination of private and public keys to encrypt and decrypt the symmetric files encryption key that was used to actually encrypt the contents of a file. EFS is only available for use with files stored on NTFS partitions and volumes, and only encrypts files locally. In other words, EFS does nothing to encrypt files or folders as they traverse a network. In a Windows Server 2003 environment, the encryption of network data is handled by a protocol known as IPSec.

The Encrypting File System (EFS) was looked at in detail in Chapter 7.

IPSec is an open-standard security protocol used to encrypt the contents of packets sent across a TCP/IP network. When implemented between network clients and servers, IPSec is running in what is known as transport mode, and can fully secure communications sessions across a network based on rules defined by an administrator. For example, an administrator might choose to encrypt the contents of all communications between the desktops of all executives and their local file servers, while maintaining unsecured communications for all other users. IPSec can also be used in a second mode known as tunnel mode, where data is secured between two pre-defined endpoints only. Such a configuration is common when a company wants to connect two LANs over an intermediate public network, such as the Internet.

IPSec should be implemented on networks that require a high degree of security for the transmission of sensitive data. This technique makes it extraordinarily difficult for hackers or other rogue users to capture network data packets and view their contents using network monitoring or packet capturing tools like Sniffer or Network Monitor.

IPSec is beyond the scope of Microsoft exam 70-290. For more detailed information on Windows Server 2003 IPSec functions and features see the Help and Support Center.

Security Policies

Security policies allow an administrator to control a wide range of security settings on Windows Server 2003, Windows 2000, and Windows XP standalone and domain systems. The tools that can be used to configure these settings include the Local Security Policy and the Group Policy Object Editor MMC snap-ins. In domain environments, these security settings are most easily applied via Group Policy, where settings can be configured once in a centralized manner, and then be applied to different domain systems.

Beyond the tools used to configure security policy settings, Windows Server 2003 also includes tools that allow an administrator to analyze policy settings to those stored in a number of pre-configured security templates. The two main tools for this purpose are the Security Configuration and Analysis MMC snap-in and the command-line SECEDIT utility. Later in this chapter you learn more about using the various Security Configuration and Analysis tools provided with Windows Server 2003.

Group Policy objects and related settings were looked at in detail in Chapter 9.

Service Packs and Hot Fixes

14

Although not explicitly considered a security feature, an important part of any security strategy involves ensuring that all network systems have critical updates and security patches applied as they are released. In the Microsoft world, updates are released as "hot fixes" when a security flaw or other issue is identified and corrected, effectively acting as a "patch" when applied. Over time, **hot fixes** and other updates are combined and released in a single **service pack**. A service pack includes all previous updates, and is always cumulative. In other words, applying Service Pack 2 to a Windows Server 2003 would also include all of the updates originally included in Service Pack 1, and any hot fixes released since Service Pack 1. Applying service packs and hot fixes helps to ensure that a Windows Server 2003 system is not susceptible to any security vulnerabilities that may have been identified.

Service packs and hot fixes can be downloaded and installed via Windows Updates and by downloading the individual executables from the Microsoft Web site. Microsoft never sends updates to customers as e-mail attachments. As such, any attachments in messages that appear to be from Microsoft should never be installed—more than likely, these attachments contain a virus or other malicious code.

In environments that include many internal systems running operating systems like Windows Server 2003, Windows 2000, and Windows XP, an update solution like Microsoft Software Update Services can help an administrator to automate and better control the process of distributing updates.

Software Update Services was explored in detail in Chapter 10.

Using Security Configuration Manager Tools

In the past, as network systems increased in size and complexity, administering security across the enterprise also became increasingly complex. Windows NT did not provide adequate tools or utilities to implement and manage an effective network security policy. For example, if administrators wanted to implement security auditing on a particular group of workstations, either they would have to visit each machine individually or try to find adequate third-party tools to assist in the configuration.

Another common problem with managing security policies in Windows NT involves maintaining the configuration. If a company or department has more than one administrator in charge of applying and maintaining the security settings, it can be difficult to keep track of configuration changes to the policy. Without proper documentation and good communication between the administrators, a great deal of time may be spent figuring out which auditing and security settings each administrator has changed.

Windows Server 2003 makes significant changes to how security configurations can be maintained. Tools included for this purpose are collectively referred to as the **Security Configuration Manager tools**. This tool set, together with Windows Server 2003 Group Policies, allows an administrator to configure a specific group of security settings to form a **Security Policy template**. This template can then be administered centrally and applied throughout Active Directory.

To assist with security policy changes, the Security Configuration Manager tools can also be used to analyze and implement security settings on a computer system. In the analysis, a comparison can be made between a computer system's security settings and a previously defined security template file. Differences between the computer system and the policy template can then be viewed and reported, and action can then be taken to change the settings on the computer to the desired settings.

For example, your security plan may provide detailed information on the security settings for the company's computers. Creating the design is only the first step, however. You also need to implement the design, which could mean making changes to every computer on the network. The Security Configuration Manager tools are designed to make the implementation of the security policy much easier. When the security policy has been designed and approved, the settings can then be defined in a security template. This template can then be compared to the current settings on the network by using the Security Configuration and Analysis tool. This shows which current settings match the security policy and which do not. You can then apply and implement the new settings with a simple command.

The Security Configuration Manager tools are also useful in maintaining security settings. In addition, it is easy to check the security settings for the network on a regular basis and reapply any settings that may have been changed.

The Security Configuration Manager tools consist of the following core components:

- Security templates
- Security settings in Group Policy objects
- Security Configuration and Analysis tool
- SECEDIT command-line tool

Security Templates

An administrator uses a security template to define, edit, and save baseline security settings to be applied to computers with common security requirements to meet organizational security standards. Templates help ensure that a consistent setting can be applied to multiple machines and be easily maintained.

The templates are text-based files that can be read but should not be changed or edited using any text editor. Be sure to use the Security Templates snap-in to create and edit the templates. The Security Templates snap-in is illustrated in Figure 14-1.

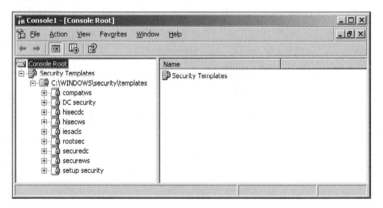

Figure 14-1   The Security Templates MMC snap-in

In Activity 14-1 you browse some of the default security templates provided with Windows Server 2003.

Activity 14-1: Browsing Security Templates

Time Required: 10 minutes

Objective: Exploring settings associated with built-in security templates.

Description: Windows Server 2003 includes a number of pre-defined templates that can be used to configure security settings on domain workstations and servers. The IT manager at Dover Leasing is interested in evaluating the potential impact of using these settings but wants to be sure that increasing the overall level of security will not render certain systems unable to communicate. In this activity, you browse through some of the default security templates included with Windows Server 2003 to evaluate their configuration settings.

1. If necessary, log on using your **AdminXX** account, where *XX* is your assigned student number.

2. Click **Start**, and then click **Run**. In the Open text box type **mmc** and then click **OK**.

3. Click **File** on the menu bar, click **Add/Remove Snap-in**, and then click **Add**.

4. In the Add Standalone Snap-in window, click **Security Templates** and click **Add**.

5. Click **Close** to close the window, and then click **OK**.

6. Click the **plus sign (+)** next to **Security Templates** to expand it, and then click the **plus sign (+)** next to **C:\WINDOWS\security\templates** to view the available templates.

7. Click the **plus sign (+)** next to **hisecdc** to view its contents.

8. Click the **plus sign (+)** next to **Account Policies**, and then click **Password Policy**. Browse through the password settings associated with the hisecdc security template.

9. Click **Account Lockout Policy** to view the template's associated settings. Click the **plus sign (+)** next to **hisecdc** to hide its contents.

10. Click the **plus sign (+)** next to the **securedc** template to expand it, and then click the **plus sign (+)** next to **Account Policies**.

11. Click **Account Lockout Policy** to view its settings, as shown in Figure 14-2. Compare the account lockout settings configured in the hisecdc template to those found in the securedc template.

12. As time permits, browse through some additional security templates to compare differences between settings configured in the various security templates.

13. Leave the MMC open.

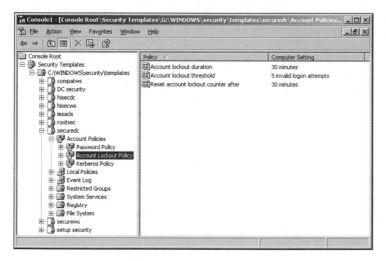

Figure 14-2   Account Lockout Policy settings in the securedc template

Analyzing the Pre-configured Security Templates

The first step in configuring and implementing security templates is to sort the network computers into three main categories: workstations, servers, and domain controllers. These three categories relate to the default security templates included with Windows Server 2003, although an administrator can also design custom templates. Keep in mind that only computers running Windows Server 2003, Windows XP, and Windows 2000 can take advantage of security template configurations and deployments.

The Default Template

When Windows Server 2003 is installed, the default security settings applied to the computer are stored in a template called **Setup Security.inf**. The contents of this template will be different depending upon the original configuration of the computer, such as whether the operating system was freshly installed or upgraded from a previous version of Windows. The purpose of this template is to provide a single file in which all of the original computer security settings are stored. If the security settings of a computer are ever changed and an administrator wishes to easily return the system to its original settings, the Setup Security.inf template could simply be reapplied.

NOTE

The Setup Security.inf template should never be applied using Group Policy because it contains a large number of settings that can seriously degrade Group Policy processing performance.

Incremental Templates

If the basic security settings do not meet your security needs, you can apply various additional security configurations using **incremental templates**. These templates modify security settings incrementally. However, these templates should only be applied to machines already running the default security settings because they do not include any of the initial configurations that the template created during the initial installation.

- Compatws.inf—This template can be applied to workstations or servers. Windows Server 2003 has increased the default security considerably over previous versions like Windows NT. In some cases, this increased security brings application compatibility problems, especially for non-certified applications that require user access to the registry. One way to run these applications is to make the user a member of the Power Users group, which has a higher level of rights and permissions than a normal user. Another option is for the administrator to increase the security permissions for the Users group. The Compatws.inf template provides a third alternative by weakening the default security to allow legacy applications to run under Windows Server 2003.

- Securews.inf and Securedc.inf—These templates provide increased security for areas such as account policy, auditing, and registry permissions. The securews template is for any workstation or server, whereas the securedc template should only be applied to domain controllers.

- Hisecws.inf and Hisecdc.inf—These templates can be incrementally applied after the secure templates have been applied. Security is increased in the areas that affect network communication protocols through the use of such features as packet signing. These templates should only be applied to client computers running Windows 2000 or higher, and all domain controllers must be running Windows 2000 or Windows Server 2003. If used, these templates should be applied to all computers on the network to ensure proper connectivity. The hisecws template is for workstations or servers, whereas the hisecdc template should only be applied to domain controllers.

- Iesacls.inf—This template contains settings to lock down Internet Explorer security settings.

- DC Security.inf—This template is applied automatically whenever a Windows 2000 or Windows Server 2003 member server is promoted to a domain controller. This is available to give the administrator the option to reapply the initial domain controller security settings if the need arises.

- Rootsec.inf—This template specifies the original permissions assigned to the root of the system drive. The main purpose of this template is for use in reapplying security permissions to resources on the system drive that have been changed, whether intentionally or accidentally.

The security templates included in Windows Server 2003 provide the administrator with acceptable security configurations for a variety of situations. If there is a unique situation where a pre-configured template is not suitable, you also have the ability to create a custom template to meet your needs.

> You can also use a pre-configured template as a baseline and save any changes to a new template. To do this, right-click a pre-configured template, and then choose Save As.

Applying Security Templates

Security templates can be applied to either the local machine or the domain via GPOs. To apply a security template to a local machine, open the Local Security Settings MMC snap-in by running SECPOL.MSC. Right-click Security Settings in the console pane, and choose Import Policy. You can then select the template file to be imported, as shown in Figure 14-3.

Figure 14-3   Importing settings from a security template

Security settings that are applied using Group Policy will always override local settings. Group Policy security settings are refreshed any time the machine is rebooted, at 90-minute intervals (with a maximum 30-minute offset) for servers and workstations, and every five minutes on domain controllers. Even if there have been no changes, the security settings are refreshed every 16 hours.

In Activity 14-2 you use the Security Templates MMC snap-in to create a custom security template.

ACTIVITY

Activity 14-2: Creating a Security Template

Time Required: 10 minutes

Objective: Define a new security template to meet custom requirements.

Description: Although the default security templates include a variety of different settings that can be used to increase the security level of Dover Leasing's servers and workstations, the IT manager has decided to explore the possibility of defining a custom template containing settings specific to Dover's requirements. Ultimately, a custom template will be defined that can be distributed to other Dover business units to standardize the security process if necessary. In this activity, you explore the process of defining a custom security template based on some of Dover's specific requirements.

1. In the MMC with the Security Templates snap-in added, right-click **C:\WINDOWS\security\templates** and click **New Template**.

2. In the Template name text box, type **dovercorptest**. In the Description text box, type **Test security template for the DomainXX.Dovercorp.net domain**. Click **OK**.

3. Browse through the configuration settings of the new dovercorptest security template. Notice that because the template is new, no settings have yet been configured.

4. Click the **plus sign (+)** next to the **dovercorptest** template to expand it, click the **plus sign (+)** next to **Account Policies** to expand it, click **Password Policy**, and configure the following settings:

   - Enforce password history – 5 passwords remembered
   - Maximum password age – 20 days
   - Minimum password age – 19 days
   - Minimum password length – 6 characters
   - Password must meet complexity requirements – Enabled

5. Click on **Account Lockout Policy** and then configure the following settings:

   - Account lockout duration – 30 minutes
   - Account lockout threshold – 3 invalid logon attempts
   - Reset account lockout counter after – 30 minutes

6. Right-click the **dovercorptest** security template and click **Save**. Close the MMC. Click **No** in the Microsoft Management Console dialog box.

7. Open My Computer and browse to **C:\WINDOWS\security\templates**. Double-click the **dovercorptest.inf** file to open it in a text editor, as shown in Figure 14-4. Notice that the settings originally configured in the Security Templates tool now appear in the text file.

8. Close the dovercorptest.inf file, and then close My Computer.

```
dovercorptest.inf - Notepad
File Edit Format View Help
[Unicode]
Unicode=yes
[Version]
signature="$CHICAGO$"
Revision=1
[Profile Description]
Description=Test security template for the Domain01.Dovercorp.net domain
[System Access]
MinimumPasswordAge = 19
MaximumPasswordAge = 20
MinimumPasswordLength = 6
PasswordComplexity = 1
PasswordHistorySize = 5
LockoutBadCount = 3
ResetLockoutCount = 30
LockoutDuration = 30
[Registry Values]
```

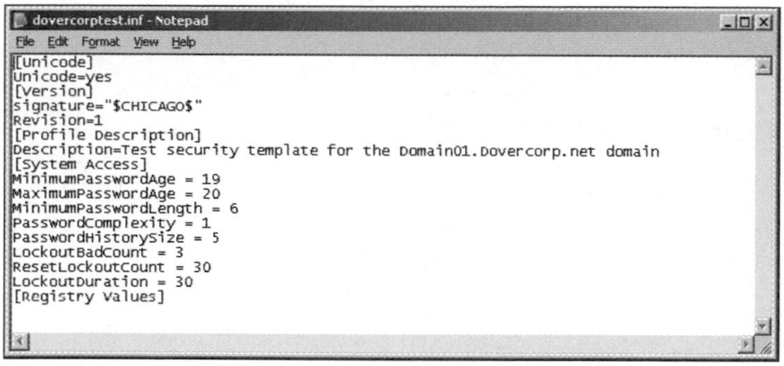

Figure 14-4 Viewing template settings using Notepad

In Activity 14-3 you apply the custom security template created in Activity 14-2 to the Default Domain Policy on your server.

ACTIVITY

Activity 14-3: Applying Security Template Settings to Group Policy Objects

Time Required: 10 minutes

Objective: Deploy security template settings using Group Policy.

Description: Although security templates allow you to configure security settings directly on a local computer, their settings can also be imported into GPOs to facilitate easier deployment. The IT manager at Dover Leasing has asked you to explore the possibility of using Group Policy to deploy settings configured in the template defined as part of the previous activity. In this activity, you import the security settings of a security template into an existing GPO.

1. Click **Start**, select **Administrative Tools**, and then click **Active Directory Users and Computers**.
2. Right-click the **Domain*XX*.Dovercorp.net** icon (where *XX* is your assigned student number) and click **Properties**.
3. Click the **Group Policy** tab, ensure that **Default Domain Policy** is selected, and then click **Edit** to view its settings.
4. In the Computer Configuration section, click the **plus sign (+)** next to **Windows Settings** to expand it.
5. Right-click **Security Settings** and click **Import Policy**.
6. In the Import Policy From window, click **dovercorptest.inf** and click **Open**.
7. After importing the security template settings to the Default Domain Policy, browse through the Password Policy and Account Lockout Policy sections. Verify that the settings from the dovercorptest security template have been imported into the GPO.

8. Close the Group Policy Object Editor window, as well as the properties of the Domain*XX*.Dovercorp.net domain. Close Active Directory Users and Computers.

Security Configuration and Analysis

The **Security Configuration and Analysis** snap-in illustrated in Figure 14-5 allows administrators to compare current system settings to a previously configured security template. The comparison identifies any changes to the original security configurations and any possible security weaknesses that may be evident when compared to a stronger security baseline template.

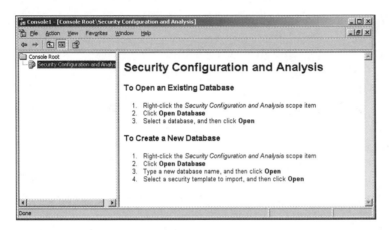

Figure 14-5   The Security Configuration and Analysis snap-in

The Security Configuration and Analysis tool uses a container, also referred to as a database, to store imported templates to be compared to the current system. The administrator imports a template into the database and then compares the template settings to the actual computer settings. If desired, the administrator can import more than one template to compare the effects of combining templates on the current settings. Once a combined template has been created, it can be saved and exported for future analysis, or it can be used to configure working computer systems.

After the analysis process is complete, the security categories appear. As each node is expanded, you can see the comparison between the database (imported templates) and the computer's current configuration. A green check mark indicates that the two settings match; a red "x" indicates a mismatch. You can make changes by double-clicking any configuration entry and selecting the desired configuration.

In Activity 14-4 you compare the current configuration of your domain controller with the settings found in the built-in hisecdc.inf security template.

Activity 14-4: Analyzing Security Settings Using Security Configuration and Analysis

Time Required: 15 minutes

Objective: Use the Security Configuration and Analysis tool to compare Group Policy and security template settings.

Description: As part of a new security initiative, the IT manager at Dover Leasing has decided that a mechanism must exist to allow systems to be periodically evaluated to ensure that they meet Dover's defined security-setting requirements. You have been asked to evaluate the Security Configuration and Analysis tool to determine whether or not this application will meet the stated requirements. In this activity, you compare the current configuration of your domain controller with the settings found in the built-in hisecdc.inf security template.

1. Open a new MMC and add the **Security Configuration and Analysis** snap-in. Follow the instructions in Activity 14-1 if necessary.

2. Right-click the **Security Configuration and Analysis** icon and click **Open Database**.

3. In the Open database window, type **SecurityTest** in the File name text box, as illustrated in Figure 14-6, and then click **Open**.

Figure 14-6   Opening a new database

4. In the Import Template window, click **hisecdc.inf** and click **Open**.

5. Right-click the **Security Configuration and Analysis** icon and click **Analyze Computer Now**.

6. In the Perform Analysis dialog box, click **OK** to accept the default log file location. The Analyzing System Security dialog box opens, as shown in Figure 14-7.

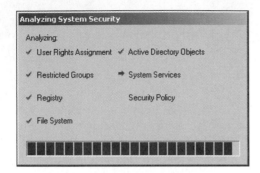

Figure 14-7   The Analyzing System Security dialog box

7. Click the **plus sign (+)** next to **Security Configuration and Analysis** and **Account Policies** to expand them, and then click **Password Policy**. An example of this screen is shown in Figure 14-8.

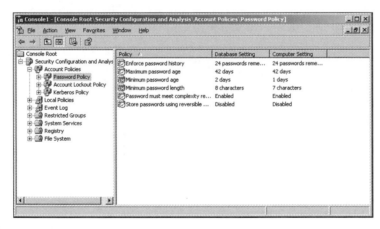

Figure 14-8   Reviewing Password Policy settings

8. Review both the Database Setting column and the Computer Setting column. The first column outlines the settings found in the database that relate to the template, whereas the second column outlines the settings currently configured on your server. Note that the icons displayed as part of each setting outline whether or not your server's current configuration meets or exceeds the settings outlined in the security database.

9. As time permits, browse through additional settings such as those found in the Account Lockout Policy, User Rights Assignment, and Security Options sections.

10. Close the MMC without saving any changes.

SECEDIT Command-Line Tool

SECEDIT.EXE is a command-line tool used to create and apply security templates, as well as analyze security settings. This tool can be used in situations where Group Policy cannot be applied, such as in workgroup configurations. SECEDIT, along with the Task Scheduler, can ensure that every computer in the workgroup maintains consistent security-policy settings. The SECEDIT command uses six main switches, as shown in Figure 14-9:

- /analyze—Analyzes database settings and compares them to a computer configuration
- /configure—Configures a system with database and template settings
- /export—Exports database information to a template file
- /import—Imports template information into a database file for analysis purposes
- /validate—Verifies the syntax of a template
- /GenerateRollback—Generates a template that saves the current security settings of a system; this template can be used to return to previous security settings in the event that settings are changed

Figure 14-9   The SECEDIT command

NOTE   The Windows Server 2003 version of SECEDIT.EXE no longer includes the /refreshpolicy switch that was used to manually refresh computer and user Group Policy settings in Windows 2000. Refreshing Group Policy settings is now accomplished using the command-line tool GPUPDATE.EXE.

AUDITING ACCESS TO RESOURCES AND ANALYZING SECURITY LOGS

Monitoring network events is an increasingly critical and important facet of any network security strategy. Monitoring helps detect potential threats, increases user accountability, and provides evidence of security breaches if or when they occur. Monitoring can also be used for resource planning. Auditing specific resources, such as printer and file shares, can tell you how often users are accessing them. For example, if you determine through auditing that a specific share is heavily used by users on the network, you may need to create another instance of the share on another server, or physically move it to a system that is more capable of handling the required workload.

Auditing in Windows Server 2003 is used to monitor and track activities on a network. You can specify which events to monitor based on your security or resource planning requirements. When an audited event does occur, a record of it is written to the **security log**. The audit entry in the security log provides you with information such as the user who performed the action, the specific action that was performed (for example, a logon attempt), and whether it was a success or failure. **Event Viewer** is used to view the audit entries stored in the security log.

Before you can begin auditing security events or the access of network resources, you must first set up an audit policy. An **audit policy** defines the events on a network that Windows Server 2003 records in the security log as they occur. For example, if you choose to monitor failed logon attempts, when a user attempts to log on with an invalid user name and/or password, an event is written to the security log. Keep in mind that an event is not written to the security log on the local computer; rather, the event is written to the security log on the domain controller that attempted to validate the user. In other words, events are stored in the security log of the computer on which the event transpires.

When implementing an audit policy, you need to determine those events you wish to track, along with whether you want to track the successes and/or failures. The audit policy settings available in Windows Server 2003 are illustrated in Figure 14-10. You explore these settings in Activity 14-5.

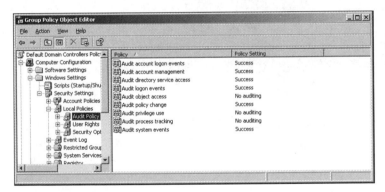

Figure 14-10   Windows Server 2003 Audit Policy settings

Activity 14-5: Exploring Default Auditing Settings

Time Required: 10 minutes

Objective: Explore the default audit settings configured on a Windows Server 2003 domain controller.

Description: Having read about Windows NT 4.0 in the past, you understand that by default, no auditing settings were configured on these servers. To verify whether this is still the case with Windows Server 2003, you decide to explore the default auditing settings configured on your domain controller. In this activity, you explore the properties of the default domain controller Group Policy object to view its default settings.

1. Click **Start**, select **Administrative Tools**, and then click **Active Directory Users and Computers**.

2. Right-click the **Domain Controllers** OU and click **Properties**.

3. Click the **Group Policy** tab. Ensure that **Default Domain Controllers Policy** is selected on the Group Policy Object Links list, and then click the **Edit** button.

4. In the Computer Configuration section, click the **plus signs (+)** next to **Windows Settings**, **Security Settings**, and **Local Policies** to expand them.

5. Click the **Audit Policy** node to view its contents. Notice the nine policy settings and their configured default values in the Policy Setting column.

6. Double-click the **Audit account logon events** icon to view its configured settings. Notice that the policy setting is enabled but that only success events are being audited by default, as shown in Figure 14-11.

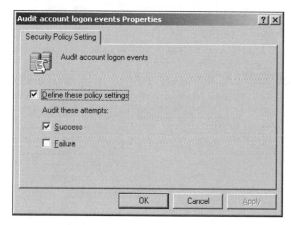

Figure 14-11   The Audit account logon events window

7. Browse through additional policy settings as time permits, but make no changes.

8. Close all open windows.

Table 14-1 outlines the different types of events that can be monitored in a Windows Server 2003 environment.

Table 14-1 Auditing events that can be monitored

Event	Explanation of Event
Audit account logon events	Activated when a user logs onto a computer; account logon events are generated where the user account is located (such as on the local computer or a domain controller), whereas logon events (outlined later in this table) are generated where the logon event occurs.
Audit account management	Activated whenever a user or group is created, deleted, or modified; this category also tracks successful or unsuccessful password changes.
Audit directory service access	Activated when an Active Directory object is accessed; the specific Active Directory object that is to be audited must also have auditing enabled.
Audit logon events	Activated when a user logs on or off a local computer or Active Directory; audits logon failures to find out if password hacking is taking place.
Audit object access	Activated when an object such as a folder or printer is accessed; the administrator must also configure the specific object for audit successes and failures.
Audit policy change	Activated when a policy that affects security, user rights, or auditing is changed.
Audit privilege use	Activated whenever a user uses an assigned right, such as changing the system time, or taking ownership of a file.
Audit process tracking	Activated any time an application process takes place; can assist developers in discovering which files or registry settings an application accesses when executing a command.
Audit system events	Activated when a system event takes place, such as the computer restarting.

Configuring Auditing

Once you have determined the events that need to be audited based on the security requirements of your network, you are ready to configure an audit policy. The following section outlines the requirements of which you should be aware, the steps in configuring an audit policy, and some general guidelines.

NOTE How you configure an audit policy is determined by the role of the computer on the network. If the computer is a member server or workstation in a domain, an audit policy can be implemented using Group Policy objects assigned to the domain or different OUs. For domain controllers, audit policy settings are implemented via the Default Domain Controllers Policy applied to the Domain Controllers OU. For non-domain standalone workstations and servers, audit settings can be defined by using the Local Security Policy tool on a system-by-system basis.

Requirements

The following requirements must be met to configure an audit policy:

- You must be a member of the Administrators group or be assigned the Manage auditing and security log user right.
- If you are auditing files and folders (via the audit object access setting), these files and folders must reside on an NTFS volume (auditing is not available on FAT volumes).

Configuring an Audit Policy

To set up an audit policy, you must first choose the events you wish to monitor and then decide whether to monitor the successes and/or failures of these events, as illustrated in Figure 14-12. However, if you are auditing access to files, folders, printers, and Active Directory objects, you also need to configure auditing settings on the specific resources for which you want to monitor access. Configuring object access auditing settings is looked at later in this section.

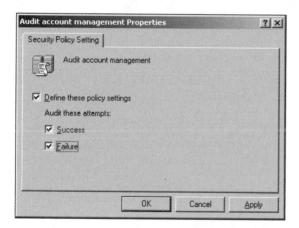

Figure 14-12   Configuring audit policy settings

In Activity 14-6 you configure and test new audit policy settings on your Windows Server 2003 system.

Activity 14-6: Configuring and Testing New Audit Policy Settings

Time Required: 10 minutes

Objective: Configure and test new audit policy settings.

Description: The IT manager at Dover Leasing has informed you that he wants to implement a new corporate security policy that will not only log all failed domain logon attempts, but that will also provide the capability to log different types of object access events. In this activity, you make changes to the default auditing policy such that all unsuccessful logon attempts are audited and the ability to audit object access is enabled.

1. Use Active Directory Users and Computers to open and view the settings of the Default Domain Controllers Policy GPO auditing settings, as described in Activity 14-5.

2. Double-click the **Audit account logon events** icon to view its properties.

3. In the Audit these attempts section, click the **Failure** check box and click **OK**.

4. Double-click the **Audit object access** icon to view its properties.

5. In the Audit these attempts section, click both the **Success** and **Failure** check boxes and click **OK**.

6. Close the Group Policy Object Editor window, the Domain Controllers Properties dialog box, as well as Active Directory Users and Computers.

7. Click **Start**, and then click **Run**. Type **gpupdate.exe**, then press **Enter**.

8. Log off.

9. Attempt to log on as the user **AdminXX** with the password **pass**. This logon attempt fails.

10. Log on as the user **AdminXX** with your correct password.

11. Click **Start**, select **Administrative Tools**, and click **Computer Management**. Click the **plus sign (+)** next to **Event Viewer** to view its contents.

12. Click the **Security** icon to view the contents of the security log.

13. Search through the security log for a Failure event in category Account Logon that uses the event ID number 675. Double-click this Failure event to open it and view its details, as shown in Figure 14-13.

14. Read through the information provided by the event and then close all open windows.

Windows Server 2003 will automatically refresh audit policy settings every 90 minutes (with a maximum 30-minute offset) on a workstation or server and every five minutes on a domain controller as per normal Group Policy processing. If no changes occur, these settings are also refreshed every 16 hours by default. If you want to apply the changes immediately, you can do one of the following:

- Restart the computer
- At the command prompt, issue the GPUPDATE.EXE command

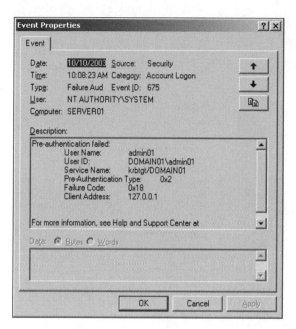

Figure 14-13 Viewing a failed logon event

Remember that Group Policy settings are applied in the order Local, Site, Domain, and Organizational Unit. As such, auditing settings configured at one level may be overridden by settings configured at another. Refer back to Chapter 9 for an overview of Group Policy processing settings.

Auditing Object Access

If your files and folders reside on an NTFS volume, you can set up auditing to monitor user access. For example, some information such as employee records or financial data may be confidential. To maintain a high level of security for this information, you need to enable auditing to detect any attempted or successful security breaches. This is especially useful if you want to track which users are attempting to access files or folders that contain sensitive data.

Auditing object access can result in a very large number of events being logged to the Security log. This can have a detrimental impact on system performance, and should be used sparingly.

To configure auditing settings for specific files or folders, access the Advanced Security Settings on the particular resource. Figure 14-14 illustrates the Auditing Entry dialog box for a folder called Accounting. Notice that the interface allows you to configure different types of access attempts, including whether these attempts were successful or failed.

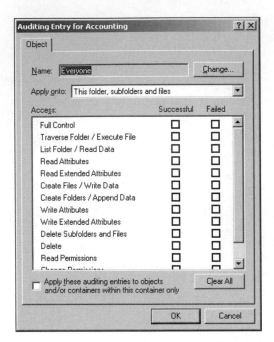

Figure 14-14   The Auditing Entry window

TIP

When configuring auditing of object access, you should generally audit access by the Everyone group to ensure that all access attempts, including those by unauthenticated users, are recorded.

Auditing can also be configured for objects that are stored within Active Directory. The process is very similar in that the audit policy is first configured, then auditing is enabled for individual objects within Active Directory such as computers, users, groups, and OUs.

In Activity 14-7 you configure auditing settings for a folder located on an NTFS volume on your server.

ACTIVITY

Activity 14-7: Configuring Auditing on an NTFS Folder

Time Required: 10 minutes

Objective: Audit failed and successful access to an NTFS folder.

Description: Although Dover Leasing has decided to implement NTFS security on all files and folders stored on corporate servers, the IT manager is still very interested in gathering information about which users are attempting to access restricted resources. In this activity, you configure object access auditing settings to track attempted access to a secured folder.

1. Click **Start**, and then click **My Computer**.

2. Double-click on drive **D:**, click **File** on the menu bar, select **New**, and then click **Folder**. Name this new folder **Accounting**. Secure this folder with NTFS permissions such that only the **Domain Admins** account has **Full Control** of the folder for the time being. Leave the properties dialog box of the folder open once complete.

3. On the Security tab, click the **Advanced** button, and then click the **Auditing** tab.

4. Click the **Add** button. In the Select User, Computer, or Group dialog box, type **Everyone** in the Enter the object name to select text box and click **OK**.

5. In the Auditing Entry for Accounting dialog box, click the **Failed** check box next to **List Folder / Read Data** along with the **Failed** check box next to **Delete** and then click **OK**.

6. Click **OK** to exit the Advanced Security Settings for Accounting dialog box, and then click **OK** again to close the properties dialog box of the Accounting folder.

7. Log off and then log back on using the **mcowan** user account with the password **Password01**.

8. Open My Computer, browse to drive **D:**, and then attempt to open the Accounting folder. Access should be denied according to the NTFS permissions you configured in Step 1.

9. Right-click the **Accounting** folder and click **Delete**. When asked if you're sure you want to delete the folder, click **Yes**.

10. When the Error Deleting File or Folder message appears, click **OK**.

11. Log off and then log back on using your **AdminXX** account.

12. Click **Start**, select **Administrative Tools**, and then click **Computer Management**. Click the **plus sign (+)** next to **Event Viewer** if necessary to expand it, and then click on the **Security** log icon to view its contents. Search for Failure events that use the event ID 560.

13. Double-click any event using ID **560** to view its contents, as shown in Figure 14-15. View additional 560 events as time permits.

14. Close all open windows.

14

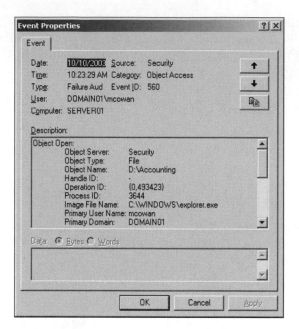

Figure 14-15 Viewing the properties of a failure event

Best Practices

To implement an audit policy that effectively meets your security requirements, it is a good idea to take some time to properly plan the implementation. Planning includes determining the computers for which auditing should be configured, what objects need to be audited, the type of events to audit, and whether to audit the successes, failures, or both. An audit policy can quickly become unmanageable and provide you with information that is of no use. By the same token, excessive auditing can seriously degrade the performance of network servers and workstations. Only choose to audit those events that are going to provide you with valuable information about your network. Here are some general guidelines that you should follow when you are planning your audit policy:

- Only enable auditing for those events that can provide you with useful information. Auditing unnecessary events increases overhead and fills up the security log with information that is not useful.

- Review the audit entries in the security log on a regular basis so you are aware of any security issues.

- Enable auditing for sensitive and confidential information.

- Audit the Everyone group instead of the Users group because the Everyone group includes unauthenticated users.

- Audit the use of user rights assignment so that administrative users are more accountable for their actions.

■ Always audit the Administrators group so you can track changes made by users who are members of this group.

Analyzing Security Logs

Once an audit policy has been created, an entry is written to the security log each time an event occurs that is defined within the policy. For example, if you enable auditing for object access and then audit all successful and failed read attempts on a folder called Accounting Docs, when a user opens the folder or attempts to open it, an entry would be written to the security log. You can then use Event Viewer to examine the contents of the log. All information written to the log is a result of the audit policy that you configure.

 For security purposes, only administrators and those users assigned the Manage Auditing and Security Log user right can view the contents of the security log.

TIP

To open Event Viewer and view the contents of the security log, access Event Viewer from the Administrative Tools menu, or from the Computer Management MMC. The contents of the security log are displayed in the details pane, providing a summary of each audit entry, including the date and time that the event occurred and the user who performed the action, as shown in Figure 14-16. A key icon represents a successful event, and unsuccessful events (failures to perform a specific action) are represented by lock icons. Double-click an event to provide detailed information about the specific event, as illustrated in Figure 14-17.

14

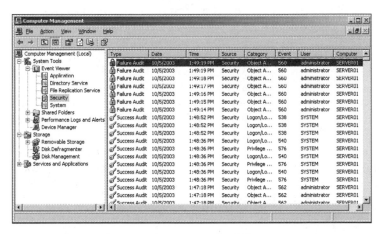

Figure 14-16 Viewing the contents of the Security log in Event Viewer

 By default, the security log shows events that occurred on the local computer. You can also use Event Viewer to view the security log on a remote computer by right-clicking Event Viewer (Local), and then clicking Connect to another computer.

TIP

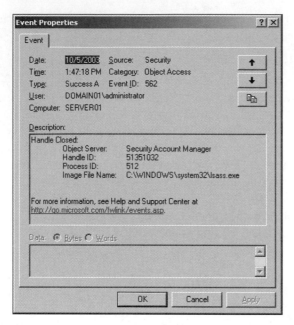

Figure 14-17 Viewing the properties of a success event

Depending on the number and type of events you choose to audit, the security log can quickly grow in size, making it difficult to pick out certain events. Fortunately, Event Viewer has a Find option that allows you to search through the security log to locate specific events. You can search for specific event types such as successful events or unsuccessful events, but you can also do a more detailed search by providing an event ID, category of event, or even a user logon name. To use the Find option, click the Security Log within the Event Viewer console, click View on the menu bar, and click the Find option. The Find in local Security dialog box opens, as shown in Figure 14-18.

Events in the security log can also be filtered so only those events matching your criteria are displayed in the details pane. This is useful if you have a large number of audit entries in the log and want to view entries based on event type or entries that occurred during a specific date and time. Similar to the Find option, you can also filter events based on event ID, category, user logon name, and computer name. To use the filter command, click the security log within the Event Viewer console, and click the Filter option located on the View menu. The Filter tab is shown in Figure 14-19.

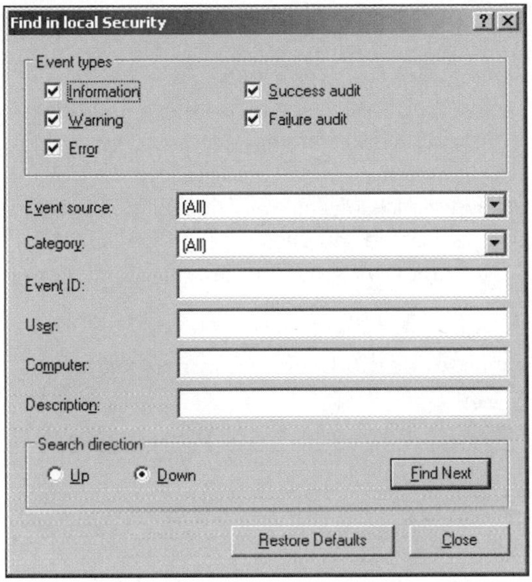

Figure 14-18   The Find in local Security dialog box

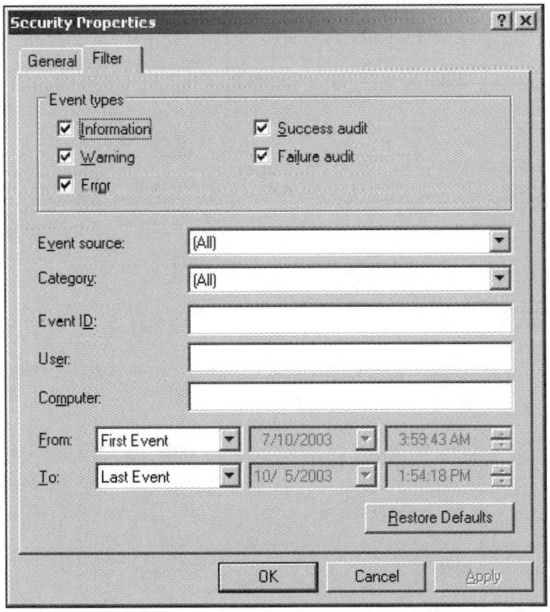

Figure 14-19   Use the Filter tab to filter events by various criteria

You may have noticed a number of other logs available within Event Viewer. The application and system logs are found on all computers running on Windows Server 2003. The application log contains information such as warnings and error messages generated by any programs coded to write events to this log. The system log contains information such as warnings and error messages that are generated by the operating system. Other logs, such as directory service, DNS server, and file replication service logs are only displayed in Event Viewer if the server is running their associated services. For example, all DNS servers include the DNS server log to track DNS-specific error and information messages.

In Activity 14-8 you configure the properties of the Event Viewer Security log.

Activity 14-8: Configuring Event Viewer Log Properties

Time Required: 10 minutes

Objective: Configure properties for log files in Event Viewer.

Description: After viewing the extremely large number of events that are found in the security log with only a very basic audit policy applied, you decide to look into alternative methods to quickly search for and find events. In this activity, you use both the find and filter features in Event Viewer to sort through log file entries.

1. Click **Start**, select **Administrative Tools**, and then click **Computer Management**.

2. Click the **plus sign (+)** next to **Event Viewer** to expand its contents if necessary, and then click the **Security** log to view all events. Click the first event in the list to highlight it.

3. Right-click the **Security** log, select **View**, and then click **Find**.

4. In the Event source list box, click **Security**.

5. In the Category list box, click **Logon/Logoff**. Uncheck both the **Information** and **Success audit** check boxes.

6. In the User text box, type **AdminXX**, and then click the **Find Next** button a number of times. Notice that the event highlighted in the background continues to change as the Find command moves through the list of events in the log that meet the criteria specified.

7. Click the **Close** button.

8. Right-click the **Security** log icon, select **View**, and then click **Filter**. The properties dialog box of the Security log opens to the Filter tab.

9. Repeat Steps 4 to 6 above to provide the information that should be used to filter the log. Click **OK** once complete.

10. Notice that the security log is now filtered to display only those events that have met the specified criteria.

11. Double-click any of the events listed to view its properties. Notice that the source, category, and user sections meet the criteria that you specified in Step 9. Click **OK** to close the Event Properties dialog box.

12. Right-click the **Security** log, select **View**, and then click **All Records**. Notice that all events now appear in the security log once again.

13. Close all open windows.

Configuring Event Viewer

In the past, one of the problems with auditing a large number of events was that the security log becomes full very quickly. By default, the security log of a Windows 2000 server was set to a maximum default size of 512 KB and once it reached this size, logging stopped. This has been changed in Windows Server 2003, where the default initial security log size is 16 MB. However, this should not be used as an excuse to prolong checking the security log on a regular basis because events may be overwritten once the maximum log file size is reached depending on configured settings. One way to avoid this problem, as previously mentioned, is to audit only those events that are essential. Another way is to change the default settings or properties of the security log. Ideally, making a point to review and archive the security log files on a regular basis is the best administrative strategy.

To configure the properties of the security log, in Event Viewer, right-click the Security log and click Properties. The Security Properties dialog box opens, as illustrated in Figure 14-20. Table 14-2 summarizes the configuration options available.

14

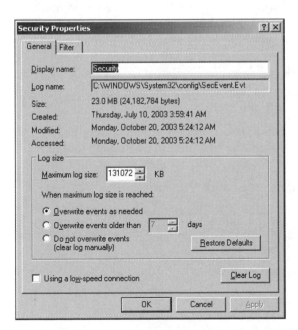

Figure 14-20   Configuring the properties of the Security log

Table 14-2   Security log configuration options

Option	Description
Log name	Changes the name and location of the log
Maximum log size	Specifies the size of the log file; the default is 128 MB
Overwrite events as needed	All new events overwrite the oldest events when the log file becomes full; if you plan to use this option, check the log file at regular intervals
Overwrite events older than X days	Sets the number of days before a log is overwritten (between 1 and 365)
Do not overwrite events (clear log manually)	Events in the log are not overwritten and when the log becomes full new events are discarded until the log is manually cleared
Using a low-speed connection	Specifies whether the log is located on another computer and whether you are connected using a low-speed device (such as a modem)

In Activity 14–9 you edit Security log settings and learn how to save the contents of an Event Viewer log file.

ACTIVITY

Activity 14-9: Editing Security Log Settings and Saving Events

Time Required: 10 minutes

Objective: Edit security log settings and save events for archiving purposes.

Description: The IT manager at Dover Leasing has asked you to implement a process to ensure that security log settings are never overwritten. Based on the large number of servers that will ultimately need to be managed at Dover, he has asked you to configure the security log settings to a maximum size of approximately 200 MB. Because log files must be emptied manually to ensure that events are not overwritten, he has also asked you to save the security log files using a date-related format. In this activity, you configure the properties of the security log to meet the requirements outlined by the IT manager.

1. Click **Start**, select **Administrative Tools**, and then click **Computer Management**. Click the **plus sign (+)** next to **Event Viewer** to expand it, if necessary.

2. Right-click the **Security** log and then click **Properties**.

3. In the Log size section, type **250000** in the Maximum log size text box.

4. In the When maximum log size is reached section, click the **Do not overwrite events (clear log manually)** radio button and then click **OK**.

5. A message appears telling you that the log file size must be an increment of 64K. Click **OK** to continue.

6. Click the **Security** log. Click **Action** on the menu bar, and then click **Save Log File As**.

7. In the File name text box, type **seclog-MM-DD-YY** using today's date for the file-name variables.

8. Click the **Save as type** list arrow to view the different formats in which a log file can be saved. On this list, click **Event Log (*.evt)**, and then click the **Save** button.

9. Note that the security log events are not cleared as part of a save operation. It's worth noting that you are prompted to save events when you attempt to clear an event log, however.

10. Right-click the **Security** node and click **Clear all Events**. When prompted with whether you want to save the security log, click **No**. This empties the security log with the exception of any new events.

11. Right-click the **Security** node and click **Open Log File**. Click the log file saved in Step 7 and then click **Security** in the Log Type list box. Click **Open**. Notice that the contents of the saved log now appear in the security log.

12. Close all open windows.

CHAPTER SUMMARY

- Windows Server 2003 includes a number of security-related features that can be used to ensure a high level of system security. The general areas that these features fall into include authentication, access control, encryption, security policies, and service packs and hot fixes.

- Security policies provide administrators with a way to configure a variety of security-related settings on Windows Server 2003, Windows 2000, and Windows XP systems.

- The primary tools used to configure security policy settings include the Local Security Policy and Group Policy Object Editor MMC snap-ins. Security settings can also be imported from pre-defined or custom security templates.

- Security Configuration and Analysis tools allow an administrator to compare the current security policy settings of a server to those stored in security templates. Both the Security Configuration and Analysis MMC snap-in and the SECEDIT command-line utility allow an administrator to compare, analyze, import, export, and configure security policy settings.

- Auditing is a Windows Server 2003 feature that allows an administrator to track a wide range of security-related events. Examples include the use of user rights, logon events, object access, system events, and more.

- The Event Viewer Security log is used to view the events relating to audit settings. A success event is depicted with a key icon in the log, while a lock icon represents a failure event.

14

KEY TERMS

audit policy — Defines the events on the network that Windows Server 2003 records in the security log as they occur.

Auditing — The process that tracks the activities of users by recording selected types of events in the security log of a server or a workstation.

Event Viewer — A component you can use to view and manage event logs, gather information about hardware and software problems, and monitor security events. Event Viewer maintains logs about program, security, and system events.

hot fixes — Interim updates to Windows Server 2003 that are released between major service pack releases. These are used to fix operating system bugs and security issues.

incremental templates — A set of text-based security template files that you can use to apply uniform security settings on computers within an enterprise. The templates modify security settings incrementally and do not include the default security settings.

IPSec — An open-standard security protocol used to encrypt the contents of packets sent across a TCP/IP network.

SECEDIT.EXE — A command-line tool used to create and apply security templates, as well as analyze security settings.

Security Configuration and Analysis — An MMC snap-in that allows an administrator to compare the configuration of a Windows Server 2003 system to settings stored in a security template and to apply template settings if necessary.

Security Configuration Manager tools — A security toolset consisting of security templates and utilities that can be used to analyze and apply security configurations.

security log — A Windows Server 2003 event log used to record security events such as auditing information.

Security Policy template — A template used to apply various security settings to an Active Directory container or object.

service pack — Periodic updates to the Windows Server 2003 operating system to fix reported bugs and security issues.

Setup Security.inf — The security template applied to Windows Server 2003 systems during the installation process.

REVIEW QUESTIONS

1. Which of the following Event Viewer log files are success and failure events written to?
   a. DNS
   b. Security
   c. System
   d. Application

2. What is the default size of the Security log on a Windows Server 2003 system?

   a. 512 KB

   b. 8 MB

   c. 16 MB

   d. 32 MB

3. Which of the following is not a default security template included with Windows Server 2003?

   a. Hisecdc.inf

   b. Securedc.inf

   c. Rootsec.inf

   d. Secureserver.inf

4. Which of the following audit settings should be configured to audit access to files and folders?

   a. Audit account logon events

   b. Audit policy change

   c. Audit object access

   d. Audit system events

5. Which of the following audit settings should be configured to audit server reboots?

   a. Audit system events

   b. Audit policy change

   c. Audit logon events

   d. Audit object access

6. Which of the following audit settings should be configured to audit the creation of group objects?

   a. Audit system events

   b. Audit account management

   c. Audit policy change

   d. Audit logon events

7. Which of the following audit settings should be configured to audit successful password changes?

   a. Audit account management

   b. Audit object access

   c. Audit policy change

   d. Audit logon events

14

8. No auditing settings are configured for domain controllers by default on Windows Server 2003 systems.

   a. True

   b. False

9. Which of the following security features is used to encrypt data as it is transmitted over a TCP/IP network?

   a. IPSec

   b. EFS

   c. Access Control

   d. Software Update Services

10. Which of the following security features is used to encrypt files and folders stored on an NTFS volume?

    a. IPSec

    b. EFS

    c. Access control

    d. Service packs

11. Which of the following security features is used to validate the identity of a user on a Windows Server 2003 network?

    a. IPSec

    b. Authentication

    c. EFS

    d. Hot fixes

12. Which of the following security features is used to secure files and folders on an NTFS partition?

    a. Access control

    b. IPSec

    c. Service packs

    d. Software Update Services

13. Which of the following security templates contains the default security settings applied to a Windows Server 2003 system by default?

    a. Setup Security.inf

    b. Secure.inf

    c. Setup.inf

    d. Hisecdc.inf

14. Security template settings can be applied via Group Policy.

    a. True

    b. False

15. Which of the following command-line tools can be used to create and apply security templates?

    a. GPUPDATE

    b. SECEDIT

    c. SECCONFIG

    d. GPREFRESH

16. Which of the following is not a supported switch with the SECEDIT command in Windows Server 2003?

    a. /configure

    b. /analyze

    c. /export

    d. /refresh

17. Where are security templates stored by default on a Windows Server 2003 system?

    a. C:\Windows

    b. C:\Windows\Security

    c. C:\Windows\security\templates

    d. C:\Templates

18. Which of the following MMC snap-ins can be used to compare current server security settings to those stored in a security template?

    a. Security Configuration and Analysis

    b. SECEDIT

    c. Active Directory Users and Computers

    d. Active Directory Sites and Services

19. Which security template is automatically applied to a Windows Server 2003 system when it is promoted to the role of domain controller?

    a. DC Security.inf

    b. Secdc.inf

    c. Securedc.inf

    d. Dcsec.inf

20. It is possible to configure access control settings on Active Directory objects such as user accounts.

    a. True

    b. False

14

CASE PROJECTS

Case Project 14-1

The IT manager at Dover Leasing is looking for a way to ensure that Windows Server 2003 systems have consistent security settings configured according to the role of the server. For example, he would like all file servers throughout the enterprise to have consistent security settings. Having analyzed all of the default built-in security templates provided with Windows Server 2003, he has decided that custom settings need to be applied. Based on these needs, which tool can first be used to create a new template? Once the template is defined, what would be the most efficient way of distributing these security settings to network servers?

Case Project 14-2

Dover Leasing is in the process of reviewing their current structure and practices. Management would like to know if there is a way to track user access so that if a security breach does occur, there is a record of it. Once the appropriate permissions have been established, you want to be able to track user access to various folders. Explain how you can use auditing and the general steps that you need to complete to implement an audit policy.

APPENDIX

A

Exam Objectives Tracking for MCSE Certification Exam #70-290 Managing and Maintaining a Microsoft Windows Server 2003 Environment

EXAM #70-290: MANAGING AND MAINTAINING A MICROSOFT WINDOWS SERVER 2003 ENVIRONMENT

Managing and Maintaining Physical and Logical Devices

Objective	Chapter: Section	Activities
Manage basic disks and dynamic disks.	Chapter 6: Managing Disks and Data Storage	Activity 6-1 Activity 6-2 Activity 6-3 Activity 6-4 Activity 6-5 Activity 6-6 Activity 6-7 Activity 6-8
Monitor server hardware. Tools might include Device Manager, the Hardware Troubleshooting Wizard, and appropriate Control Panel items.	Chapter 2: Managing Hardware Devices	Activity 2-1 Activity 2-3
Optimize server disk performance. • Implement a RAID solution. • Defragment volumes and partitions	Chapter 6: Managing Disks and Data Storage	Activity 6-9
Install and configure server hardware devices. • Configure driver signing options. • Configure resource settings for a device. • Configure device properties and settings	Chapter 2: Managing Hardware Devices	Activity 2-2 Activity 2-3 Activity 2-4 Activity 2-5 Activity 2-6

Managing Users, Computers, and Groups

Objective	Chapter: Section	Hands-on Activity(s)
Managing local, roaming, and mandatory user profiles.	Chapter 3: Creating and Managing User Accounts	Activity 3-2 Activity 3-3 Activity 3-4
Create and manage computer accounts in an Active Directory environment.	Chapter 3: Creating and Managing User Accounts	Activity 4-8
Create and manage groups. • Identify and modify the scope of a group. • Find domain groups in which user is a member • Manage group membership • Create and modify groups by using the Active Directory Users and Computers Microsoft Management Console (MMC) snap-in. • Create and modify groups using automation.	Chapter 4: Implementing and Managing Group and Computer Accounts	Activity 4-1 Activity 4-2 Activity 4-3 Activity 4-4 Activity 4-5 Activity 4-6 Activity 4-7

A

Objective	Chapter: Section	Hands-on Activity(s)
Create and manage user accounts. • Create and modify user accounts by using the Active Directory Users and Computers MMC snap-in. • Create and modify user accounts by using automation • Import user accounts	Chapter 3: Creating and Managing User Accounts	Activity 3-1 Activity 3-5 Activity 3-6 Activity 3-7 Activity 3-8 Activity 3-9
Troubleshoot computer accounts • Diagnose and resolve issues related to computer accounts by using the Active Directory Users and Computers MMC snap-in • Reset computer accounts	Chapter 4: Implementing and Managing Group and Computer Accounts	Discussed in Chapter 4
Troubleshoot user accounts • Diagnose and resolve account lockouts • Diagnose and resolve issues related to user account properties	Chapter 3: Creating and Managing User Accounts	Discussed in Chapter 3
Troubleshoot user authentication issues	Chapter 3: Creating and Managing User Accounts	Discussed in Chapter 3

Managing and Maintaining Access to Resources

Objective	Chapter: Section	Hands-on Activity
Configure access to shared folders • Manage shared folder permissions	Chapter 5: Managing File Access Chapter 7: Advanced File System Management	Activity 5-1 Activity 5-2 Activity 5-3 Activity 7-7
Troubleshoot Terminal Services • Diagnose and resolve issues relating to Terminal Services security • Diagnose and resolve issues related to client access to Terminal Services.	Chapter 10: Server Administration	Activity 10-8 Activity 10-9 Activity 10-10
Configure file system permissions • Verify effective permissions when granting permissions. • Change ownership of files and folders	Chapter 5: Managing File Access	Activity 5-4 Activity 5-5 Activity 5-6 Activity 5-7
Troubleshoot access to files and shared folders.	Chapter 5: Managing File Access Chapter 7: Advanced File System Management	Discussed in Chapter 5 Activity 7-4

Managing and Maintaining a Server Environment

Objective	Chapter: Section	Hands-on Activity
Monitor and analyze events. Tools might include Event Viewer and System Monitor.	Chapter 14: Windows Server 2003 Security Features	Activity 14-5 Activity 14-6 Activity 14-7 Activity 14-8 Activity 14-9
Manage software update infrastructure	Chapter 10: Server	Activity 10-13 Activity 10-14 Activity 10-15 Activity 10-16
Manage software site licensing	Chapter 10: Server Administration	Discussed in Chapter 10
Manage servers remotely • Manage a server using Remote Assistance • Manage a server using Terminal Services remote administration mode • Manage a server using available support tools	Chapter 10: Server Administration	Activity 10-3 Activity 10-4 Activity 10-5 Activity 10-6 Activity 10-7
Troubleshoot print queues	Chapter 8: Implementing and Managing Printers	Activity 8-1 Activity 8-2 Activity 8-3 Activity 8-4 Activity 8-5 Activity 8-6 Activity 8-7 Activity 8-8 Activity 8-9 Activity 8-10
Monitor system performance	Chapter 11: Monitoring Server Performance	Discussed in Chapter 11
Monitor file and print servers. Tools might include Task Manager, Event Viewer, and System Monitor • Monitor disk quotas • Monitor print queues • Monitor server hardware for bottlenecks	Chapter 7: Advanced File System Management Chapter 11: Monitoring Server Performance	Activity 7-6 Activity 11-1 Activity 11-2 Activity 11-3 Activity 11-4 Activity 11-6
Monitor and optimize a server environment for application performance. • Monitor memory performance objects • Monitor network performance objects • Monitor process performance objects • Monitor disk performance objects	Chapter 11: Monitoring Server Performance	Activity 11-5 Activity 11-7

A

Objective	Chapter: Section	Hands-on Activity
Manage a Web server • Manage Internet Information Services • Manage security for IIS	Chapter 13: Administering Web Resources	Activity 13-1 Activity 13-2 Activity 13-3 Activity 13-4 Activity 13-5 Activity 13-6 Activity 13-7 Activity 13-8 Activity 13-9 Activity 13-10 Activity 13-11 Activity 13-12 Activity 13-13 Activity 13-14 Activity 13-15 Activity 13-16 Activity 13-17

Managing and Implementing Disaster Recovery

Objective	Chapter: Section	Hands-on Activity
Perform system recovery for a server • Implement Automated System Recovery (ASR) • Restore data from shadow copy volumes • Back up files and System State data to media • Configure security for backup operations	Chapter 12: Managing and Implementing Backups and Disaster Recovery	Activity 12-4 Activity 12-5 Activity 12-6 Activity 12-10
Manage backup procedures • Verify the successful completion of backup jobs • Manage backup storage media	Chapter 12: Managing and Implementing Backups and Disaster Recovery	Activity 12-1
Recover from server hardware failure	Chapter 12: Managing and Implementing Backups and Disaster Recovery	Discussed in Chapter 12
Restore backup data	Chapter 12: Managing and Implementing Backups and Disaster Recovery	Activity 12-2

Objective	Chapter: Section	Hands-on Activity
Schedule backup jobs	Chapter 12: Managing and Implementing Backups and Disaster Recovery	Activity 12-3

B

DETAILED LAB SETUP GUIDE

HARDWARE

Classroom PCs should be configured as follows:

- Pentium 233–MHz processor or faster
- At least 128 MB of RAM
- At least 1.5 GB of available hard disk space
- CD-RW or DVD-RW drive
- Keyboard and mouse or some other compatible pointing device
- Video adapter and monitor with Super VGA (800 × 600) or higher resolution
- Sound card for the Instructor PC
- Self powered/amplified speakers for the Instructor PC
- Internal or external fax/modem
- Ethernet network interface controller
- 3.5-inch disk drive
- An Ethernet hub or switch with at least as many ports as there are PCs in the classroom
- One twisted-pair, Category 5 straight-through cable per PC

Other equipment that may be needed:

- An additional Instructor PC to act as an additional domain controller
- A generic printer

Consumable items that students should bring to class:

- Five blank CD-R disks
- Five blank 3.5-inch disks

SOFTWARE

The following software is needed:

- Microsoft Windows Server 2003 Enterprise Edition operating system (one CD media per student)
- Adobe Acrobat Reader (version 4 or later)
- Latest version of Software Update Services (SUS) (*www.microsoft.com/windows serversystem/sus*)
- Microsoft Virtual PC (*www.microsoft.com/windows/virtualpc*) (optional)

SETUP INSTRUCTIONS

B

To work on the material in this book, students need to have administrative privileges over their respective PCs. In a classroom setting, students should have the freedom to make administrative-level configuration errors. Normally such errors can render a PC unbootable or otherwise unusable for participation in the classroom. However, a student's mistakes should never impede completion of lab assignments. In this light, the lab should have a data recovery system and working backups that are both easy to use and reliable.

The most straightforward method of data recovery is the reinstallation of the operating system from the Microsoft factory CDs. However, having to reinstall the operating system from the factory CD every time a student corrupts his or her system can be time consuming and frustrating. There are no activities in the book that go over a Windows Server 2003 install. This leaves some flexibility for the instructor to decide how the students should install Windows Server 2003. Therefore, to ensure rapid and reliable data recovery, consider the following guidelines when setting up the lab:

- Microsoft's Virtual PC provides quick access to an operating system from a previous state. The ability to use undoable disks gives students the opportunity to restore their computers to the state before the lab. Students must Save State in Virtual PC after each successful lab. Virtual PC is very resource intensive and the student computers should exceed the hardware requirements if used.

- If using an imaging product, such as Norton Ghost, a single image file that contains all of the data stored on the reference installation is created. This image file even contains the partition table of the hard disk drive along with the master boot record. Restoring data from such an image brings the machine back to its original state at the time the backup was created.

- When creating a reference image file, it is important to remember that the image file will be an exact copy of the reference PC's hard disk drive. This means that data such as NetBIOS computer names and SIDs (security identifiers) are preserved as they were on the reference PC. This also means that unless further steps are taken, all PCs that are imaged from this reference image will have the *same* NetBIOS computer name, SIDs, and perhaps even IP address (if the IP addresses are set up statically). However, you do *not* want a classroom where all the PCs have the same NetBIOS name or IP address because such duplication can cause conflicts throughout the class. You may be able to get away with all the SIDs being the same for a while, but this should not be a permanent state. You especially do not want identical SIDs in an environment that employs Active Directory domains.

- To make a classroom of uniquely identifiable PCs, utilities such as Microsoft sysprep, Norton Ghost Walker, or REMBO Toolkit (the NTChangeName command) may be executed on each PC. The easiest to use is Ghost Walker; it is an MS-DOS program that not only changes the NetBIOS computer name but also creates a randomly generated SID in one easy step. If you don't feel the need to change the SID, you can manually change the NetBIOS name by simply right-clicking the My Computer icon, clicking Properties, clicking the Computer

Name tab, clicking the Change button, and typing the desired NetBIOS computer name in the Computer name field. Click OK when finished.

Keep the following in mind if imaging or Virtual PC is not available:

- The instructor needs to decide on the following key points and make them available to all students during their installs:

  - Computer naming convention

  - IP addressing (default gateways, DNS, and WINS, if necessary)

  - Workgroup/domain names

- Students should install Windows Server 2003 Enterprise Edition from the CD.

C

EXPANDED CHAPTER SUMMARIES

CHAPTER 1 SUMMARY

Windows Server 2003 has four editions that are targeted for different roles. They are the Web, Standard, Enterprise, and Datacenter Editions.

Web Edition is optimized to run Web applications and for hosting multiple Web sites on Internet Information Services 6.0. It is a more cost-effective solution than all other editions of the Windows Server 2003 family. A major feature that is missing from Web Edition is that you cannot configure it as a domain controller.

Standard Edition is the next step up from Web Edition. It includes all of the features that you get from Web Edition with the addition of Active Directory and other critical services that can be installed. Microsoft has targeted small to midsized businesses to use Standard Edition for File and Print services and even as Active Directory domain controllers. It is critical that you know what type of hardware you can put into a server running Standard Edition. Standard Edition can have a total of four physical processors and up to 4 GB of RAM.

Enterprise Edition is geared for midsized to large companies looking for servers that require additional hardware and better reliability. It includes all of the features from Standard Edition and adds the capability of 8-node clustering. That feature alone makes this operating system a more reliable one. Enterprise Edition supports up to eight physical processors and a maximum of 32 GB of RAM. The minimum system requirements for Enterprise Edition are exactly the same as Standard Edition.

The Web, Standard, and Enterprise Editions all have the same system requirements. Here are the minimum system requirements for the main system components:

- *Processor*—133 MHz
- *RAM*—128 MB
- *Disk space*—1.5 GB

The Datacenter Edition is designed for mission-critical applications and large databases. It includes the features from the previous editions. Datacenter Edition can support up to 32 processors and an amazing 64 GB of RAM. Here are the minimum system requirements for the main system components:

- *Processor*—400 MHz
- *RAM*—512 MB
- *Disk space*—1.5 GB

Windows Server 2003 was built to work within a network and to be able to communicate with other computers. There are two choices for how your server interacts with networks: workgroups or domains. Workgroups are great if you have a small number of computers that need to share resources. The one big problem in a workgroup is that each computer stores its own Security Accounts Manager (SAM). Accounts are stored in the SAM database, which means if you want to have an account for all the computers in your workgroup, you have to create one on each local computer. The other option is to join your computer to a domain or create your own Active Directory domain. This way, all of the accounts are stored in a centralized database called Active Directory that runs on your Windows Server 2003 server. Having the accounts stored in this manner allows for centralized management.

Windows Server 2003 can be configured as either a member server or a domain controller. Member servers are part of a domain and provide key services such as file, print, application, RRAS, and DNS. Domain controllers provide authentication for clients within a domain. It is very common to have domain controllers function in other roles that a member server would take. Web Edition is the only server that cannot become a domain controller. To promote a server to a domain controller, run the Active Directory Wizard.

A big part of a network administrator job is to manage and maintain the server hardware, as in adding new expansion cards to configuring fault tolerance through a Redundant Array of Independent Disks (RAID). Another common task would be to manage user and group accounts. Tasks such as creating new users, modifying existing users, and resetting passwords are not uncommon. By managing groups, an administrator can add users to groups to assign them permissions to resources and to grant them system rights.

An administrator can make resources, such as folders and printers, available over the network by sharing them. To properly secure shared resources, an administrator needs to assign permissions locally and remotely. Terminal Services allows users to connect to remote servers to access applications.

When a server needs monitoring, there are several tools available. One of those tools, System Monitor, allows an administrator to compare results against a baseline. Event Viewer, which is another tool, is the primary logging feature in Windows Server 2003. By applying patches and security updates, you can help secure your servers. The Software Update Service allows for centralized management of updates. The Backup utility allows an administrator to create new backups and restore old ones.

Active Directory domains contain objects such as users, computers, and printers. As an Active Directory administrator, you will be creating many of the objects within your domain.

Every object that is created in Active Directory has additional attributes that are associated with it. For example, a User object has attributes such as First Name, Middle Initial, Last Name, Address, Home Phone, and Manager. These objects and attributes are defined in what is known as the Active Directory schema.

Active Directory gives you the ability to logically organize your objects in what are known as organizational units (OUs). You place objects such as user accounts in these OUs. You can create your OU structure based on location, departments, or any other combination. These objects may initially seem like folders to you, but as your knowledge expands, you will see that they also have a crucial role in the management of your users and computers within Group Policy.

A powerful feature that senior-level Active Directory administrators will enforce is delegation. They delegate control of certain tasks, such as resetting passwords, to OU admins. That way, those OU admins can reset passwords for the users within the OU over which they have been granted control.

Trees and forests are also part of the logical structure of Active Directory. A tree is one or more domains with a contiguous namespace. A forest is one or more domains that have a noncontiguous namespace. The first domain you create in Active Directory is known as your forest root domain.

When users of a domain want to search for attributes in Active Directory, they search a domain controller with a special role known as the global catalog. Using the global catalog is much like dialing 411 to look for a phone number. If you want to look for users with last names that started with "McC," you would put that text into your search. The global catalog would perform the query.

Your network infrastructure is something that you must plan accordingly. You will be configuring Active Directory sites to conform to your current networks. Try to remember these two facts about sites: a site is one or more well-connected IP networks, and a site can have more than one network, but a network can be a member of only one Active Directory site.

Chapter 2 Summary

Before bringing a server into a production environment, an administrator reviews settings on hardware and drivers and checks whether there are any resource conflicts. If a new device is added, it may be easy to install because of Windows Server 2003 support for Plug and Play (PnP). Of course, a little more hands-on involvement may be needed for legacy devices.

Device drivers are written specifically for particular hardware and are usually tied to a specific operating system. Microsoft does have generic drivers for most hardware, but you should go to the hardware vendor's Web site to look for new drivers. You may also find updates to drivers on the Windows Update Web site.

A great tool to see what hardware is already installed on your machine is known as Device Manager. Device Manager not only shows you the hardware installed on your server, but also lets you control the drivers and configuration of those devices. For the most part you do not have to worry about this because most hardware is now PnP. PnP devices need only be plugged in to the system to have the appropriate driver installed and begin functioning.

For devices that are not PnP or for devices that connect to your server using the ISA slot on the motherboard, you have to check the documentation for directions on how to configure resources. For legacy devices, you can use the Add New Hardware Wizard in Control Panel. You can also use the disks and documentation that came with the hardware.

C

All devices that are installed on a server have specific resources assigned to them. These resources are:

- Direct Memory Access (DMA) channels
- Input/Output (I/O) ranges
- Memory address ranges
- Interrupt Requests (IRQ) lines

When conflicts arise between hardware settings, you may use the System Information tool to troubleshoot these conflicts. You can access this tool by typing msinfo32.exe from the Run dialog box. This tool reports invaluable information about settings and configurations on hardware devices. The area of importance when dealing with hardware is the Hardware Resources section. Another useful place to look is the Components section, which gives you I/O, IRQ, and driver settings.

Windows Server 2003 operating system files have all been digitally signed to ensure compatibility, quality, and authenticity. By default, a driver that is not signed still installs on your servers; however, you are warned that the driver may decrease system stability.

You have three options when it comes to driver signing:

- *Ignore*—This option ignores driver signing.
- *Warn*—If the driver is not signed, this option warns the user.
- *Block*—If the driver is not signed, this option does not permit the install.

If you inherit a server and are unsure as to which drivers are signed, you can run a utility called File Signature Verification from the Run dialog box which verifies all digital signatures for hardware devices. This utility identifies unsigned drivers, but does not tell you where to go to get new ones.

If you experience problems after the driver update, you have a couple of options. One choice would be to use a new feature that can roll back drivers. This feature is in the properties of the driver with which you are working. It can uninstall the current driver and reinstall the previous one, all with a click of a button. Depending on the type of device driver, you may have to restart the server, so make sure to notify users before restarting the server or make sure that you do the restart during off-peak hours.

In System Properties, you can set processor scheduling and memory usage. The processor schedule gives you the choice between giving the priority of your processor to user applications or the default background services. Your memory usage area lets you configure whether you want memory usage to be allocated for user programs or the default of system cache.

You can set options to control the location and size of the paging file. It has always been a best practice to move your paging file to a disk that does not contain your operating system. This increases system performance because your operating system and paging file will not be fighting to read and write on the same disk.

Your server can run with different hardware profiles. Hardware profiles tell the operating system which drivers to load when booting. After you configure the hardware profile and every time you start the server, you are asked which hardware profile you want to start.

Windows Server 2003 power management is set by default to be Always On. This mode shuts the monitor off after 20 minutes and never turns off the hard drive. You can configure the power options to best suit your needs by accessing the Power Schemes applet in Control Panel.

CHAPTER 3 SUMMARY

Each user account has dozens of attributes (also known as properties) that you can configure. Some of the common properties you may configure are group membership, profile settings, account settings, and address information.

The main tool you use to manage users accounts is called Active Directory Users and Computers. Every user account has properties that can be configured, and certain applications can add additional properties. These tabs can include a lot of additional information about the user, such as office location, telephone number, address, group membership, and terminal services settings—to name just a few.

Authentication is needed to grant users access to resources in an Active Directory environment. A user must log on with a valid user account and password. In a domain environment, this user account and password exists in Active Directory; however, in a workgroup, it is stored in the Security Accounts Manager (SAM) database. When a user logs on to a computer using the Log On to Windows dialog box, the logon is considered interactive authentication. If a user decides to connect to a network resource, the user uses network authentication.

Users who log on to an Active Directory domain use an authentication protocol called Kerberos v5. Kerberos v5 is a protocol that provides authentication services for computers in an Active Directory domain. Only computers running Windows 2000, Windows XP, and Windows 2003 can use Kerberos. This authentication protocol is an improvement in security from what NT domains used, which was either NTLM or NTLM v2. The NTLM authentication protocol is used by down-level clients running Windows NT 4.0 and Windows 9x.

The first time a user logs on to a computer, he or she creates a new user profile based on the Default User profile. A user profile stores settings specific to that user and includes the following:

- Application data
- Desktop settings
- Favorites
- Cookies

- Desktop
- Start menu

When the user logs off, those changes the user has made are saved to his or her unique profile, which is stored in the C:\Documents and Settings folder. This profile is known as a local profile and is stored only on that machine.

Users of domain accounts can have their profiles follow them from computer to computer. These profiles are called roaming profiles and are set up within the Domain Account properties. This allows for centralized backups of user profiles. The first time a user logs on to a computer with a roaming profile, the profile is copied to the local machine. Any changes that are made are then copied back to the server when the user logs off.

Administrators can force all the domain accounts to fit a specific profile by forcing the use of a mandatory profile. Administrators can create one by modifying an existing roaming profile. To create a mandatory profile, you need to change the name of the ntuser.dat file to ntuser.man. When you do this, users who get this profile can make changes, but the next time they log on, those changes revert to whatever was set up by the administrator.

Active Directory Users and Computers is available on the Administrative Tools menu, or you can add it to a custom MMC. The version that comes with Server 2003 is slightly different than the version that came with Windows 2000. This version gives you the ability to drag and drop, and it gives you a node called Saved Queries. This node allows administrators to quickly search for objects based on specific settings.

If you have been tasked with creating user accounts that have many of the same account properties, you should consider using a template account. A template account is a user account that you can create and configure with common attributes. With the templates feature, if you had 10 accounts that needed to be created for new sales employees, you would first create a sales template. In that template, you would define all the groups in which these new users would exist. As a best practice, you should start the name of this account with a symbol such as an underscore. When you do this, the template account is always going to be listed first in Active Directory Users and Computers and be easy to find. Now all you have to do is right-click your template account and select Copy. This requests a new user name and password and then copies most of the settings from the template account.

Windows Server 2003 has added command-line tools so that you can easily script accounts through the command line. The new command-line tools are:

- *DSADD*—Adds objects
- *DSMOD*—Modifies objects
- *DSQUERY*—Queries for objects
- *DSMOVE*—Moves objects
- *DSRM*—Deletes objects

You can also take advantage of bulk importing and exporting of accounts. The two supported formats are LDIFDE and CSVDE.

All accounts that you create follow certain guidelines set up in the domain account policy. Account policies include settings on user account passwords, such as the length, age, and complexity. Account Policies also define settings that lock out users from logging on to an account after a specified number of invalid logon attempts. Finally, your account policy helps with the configuration of your Kerberos settings. All of these account policies are defined in the default domain group policy and must be configured at the domain level for domain accounts. You can also set up auditing to check for the success or failure of an event such as account logons. The results of auditing are stored in the security log in Event Viewer.

CHAPTER 4 SUMMARY

A group is an object that you use to organize other objects, such as users, computers, contacts, or other groups. Groups sometimes seem like the same thing as OUs, but they are very different from each other. With groups, you can assign permissions to resources; you cannot do that with OUs. With OUs, you can link group policies, but you cannot link a group policy to a group.

There are two types of groups that you can create in an Active Directory domain: security groups and distribution groups. These two types have very different uses and should be used appropriately. Security groups are the most popular types of groups because they give you the ability to have a Security Identifier (SID) that can be assigned to resources. Thus, when you have a group that needs to be granted access to a folder, you create that group as a security group. In addition, a security group can be used as an e-mail entity. This means you could send an e-mail to that group, and it would be delivered to all of the members. Distribution groups can be used only as e-mail entities.

Once you decide the type of group you want to create, you then need to decide what type of scope this group will have. There are three group scopes from which to choose:

- Global
- Domain local
- Universal

Global groups are created for organizing users, computers, and other groups. Thus, when you have users that belong to the same department, you should create a global group and place those users into that global group. The membership of a global group is limited to user accounts only from its domain. If your Active Directory is in native mode, then you can also nest global groups into other global groups from the domain.

Domain local groups are primarily used for assigning permissions to resources such as files, folders, or printers. As their name states, they are local to their domain and can be assigned permissions only for resources in their domain. A domain local group can have users, computers, and global groups as members while in mixed mode. If you increase your domain mode from mixed mode to anything higher, such as native mode, you could have other domain local groups and universal groups as members.

Universal groups are primarily used in a multiple domain forest in which administrators want to aggregate users or other groups. You can use universal groups only while your domain is in native or Windows Server 2003 functional level. Universal groups can be members of domain local and other universal groups from any domain that is trusted. In addition, universal groups can have global, domain local, and universal groups—as well as users and computers—as members. Universal groups should be used with caution because certain membership changes with them increase your global catalog replication traffic. To cut down on this, make sure to place groups—and not individual user accounts—inside your universal group.

The primary tool used to create groups is called Active Directory Users and Computers. Using Active Directory Users and Computer, you can also manage group memberships and alter properties. If a group is accidentally created as the wrong group scope, it can be easily converted to another, as follows:

- Global to universal
- Domain local to universal
- Universal to global
- Universal to domain local

As with user accounts, you can also use the DSADD command utility to create new group objects. You can also manage groups by using these additional command-line utilities:

- *DSMOD*—Modifies objects
- *DSQUERY*—Queries for objects
- *DSMOVE*—Moves objects
- *DSRM*—Removes objects

Microsoft has included a number of groups that you can use for specific rights and tasks. These are known as built-in groups and you can find them in the Builtin container or the Users container. You can add users to these groups instead of creating a new group that does the same task if there is a task you want them to be able to accomplish.

Of course, there may be times where you have to create a new group and give it specific permissions because there is no default group. As an example of creating a custom group, consider that Backup Operators is a default group that gives members the right not only to back up files and folders but also the right to restore files. If you need a group that does only backups and another that does only restores, you would do better to create two new groups, assign those rights to the groups, and then add members to those groups.

Computers running Windows NT, 2000, XP, and 2003 all need valid computer accounts in your Active Directory domain. You can create these computer accounts much the same way you have created users and groups—with Active Directory Users and Computers or DSADD.

CHAPTER 5 SUMMARY

One of an administrator's most important jobs is to manage access to resources. For the most part, the management of those resources concerns access to files and folders over the network. Your primary task will be to ensure that users, groups, or computers have been granted the appropriate permissions to resources they access.

The FAT file system was developed long ago to support DOS. FAT was included in Windows Server 2003 only for backward compatibility and has some very serious limitations, such as no folder- or file-level security. It also supports volumes only up to 4 GB.

FAT32 is an enhancement that was released with Windows 95 OSR2 that overcame the 4 GB limitation and bumped this limitation up to 2 TB in Windows Server 2003. There is still no file- or folder-level security with FAT32.

NTFS was released with Windows NT 4.0 and has evolved to the version that is included with Windows Server 2003. This version supports volumes up to 16 EB, file- and folder-level security, quotas, and compression.

When you want to make a folder accessible over a network, you need to share an existing folder. This allows others to see that folder when they access your computer over the network.

You can create shared folders by using multiple methods, but the two most common methods are through Windows Explorer or the Computer Management console. With either method, the share name does not have to match the name of the folder; however, you will want to keep a couple of best practices in mind when you create a share:

- Older clients may have a difficult time connecting to names that are longer than 8.3 characters.

- You should make the name intuitive for users to connect.

- If you have a share that you want to keep hidden from users, you must append a $ to the share name. This makes it hidden to all users, including administrators, so you need to make sure that you remember the share name. Even though it is hidden, you still need to assign the appropriate permissions.

When you create a shared folder, users must connect to that share through a Universal Naming Convention (UNC) path. A UNC is a string of text that you type into the Run dialog box. UNC paths allow you to connect to a computer that has shares. You could also just connect with the computer name. Connecting in this manner would show you a list of all the shares on that computer. Remember that you must have the appropriate permissions to access those resources.

Shared folders have a simple set of permissions, as follows:

- Read
- Change
- Full Control

Share permissions apply only to shared folders and take effect only over the network. If you want to secure local files and folders and lock down access to resources over the network even more, you have to use NTFS permissions. NTFS has standard and special permissions. The standard permissions are as follows:

- Full Control
- Modify
- Read & Execute
- List Folder Contents (only on folders)
- Read
- Write
- Special Permissions

As an administrator, you have the ability to grant users, groups, or even computers access to specific files and folders stored on that computer. The special NTFS permissions are just subsets of the standard permissions. For example, Read is more than just read. There are special NTFS permissions that combine to make the Read permission. The special NTFS permissions that make up the Read permission are read attributes and read extended attributes.

Determining effective permissions to a resource is critical to resource administration. If you are a user in multiple groups who has been granted shared folder permission, then your effective permission is those cumulative shared permissions. The same goes for NTFS. If you are a member of multiple groups that have each been granted different access, then you just add up the permissions for the groups of which your account is a member. There is one exception to this rule: deny overwrites all other permissions.

On each file or folder that is created on an NTFS volume, you can use the Effective Permission tab. On this tab, you enter a user or group for whom you would like to see the effective permission. Note that this shows only the effective *NTFS* permission. When you have a shared folder that has both NTFS and shared folder permissions, it gets a little bit more difficult to find out the effective permission. The effective permission to that resource is going to be the permission that is common between the NTFS and shared folder permissions. For example, if you have Full Control as a shared permission and Read as an NTFS permission, then your effective permission is Read. You get this result because Read is also part of Full Control, and the permission that is common between the two types of permissions is Read.

Chapter 6 Summary

Traditionally, operating systems use basic disks for storage. With basic disks, you can create partitions. There are two types of partitions: primary or extended. A primary partition can be marked active, which means that you can boot an operating system from it. You are limited to four primary partitions per system. If you need to have more than four partitions, then you have to create extended partitions. Extended partitions cannot be marked as active, and you must create logical drives inside extended partitions.

By default, when you install Windows Server 2003, it installs into a single partition, which is the C: drive. During the setup, you have the option to change where Windows Server 2003 is going to be installed. The default directory is C:\Windows. This directory is called the boot partition, and it contains system files. The root of the C:\ drive is known as the system partition, and it contains boot files.

Windows Server 2003 also has support for what are known as dynamic disks. These are the same type of disks as basic disks, except Windows Server 2003 views them differently. For a disk to become a dynamic disk, you must convert the entire disk through the Disk Management tool.

With dynamic disks, you are able to create three types of volumes. The tools that you use to manage these volumes are either the Disk Management MMC or the command-line utility DISKPART. The Windows Server 2003 supported volumes are as follows:

- Simple
- Spanned
- Striped

A simple volume is a single area of space that is formatted on a dynamic disk. This truly is the simplest and easiest type of volume to create. If the volume is formatted with NTFS, then you can extend it in the future if you need additional space. However, you cannot extend a simple volume that is either the boot or system partition.

Spanned volumes contain between two and thirty-two dynamic disks that are treated as a single volume. Collectively, they are used to create a larger volume than the actual size of any single dynamic disk. The spanned volume fills up disk space one disk at a time. Just as with simple volumes, you can extend spanned volumes on NTFS partitions only. If one of your spanned volumes fails, then there is no fault tolerance feature that allows users to still connect and access data on the spanned volume. For that reason, do not place mission-critical data on spanned volumes.

Striped volumes are also known as RAID level 0. Unlike every other type of RAID volume, this one provides no fault tolerance. A striped volume contains between two and thirty-two physical hard disks. The striped volume appears as one volume; however, unlike spanned volumes, a striped volume stripes data across all disks evenly. Because of the striping, your disk performance increases for both reads and writes. Be aware that stripe sets provide no fault tolerance, so do not place mission-critical data on them.

The most common tool used for disk management is the Disk Management tool that resides inside the Computer Management console. Disk Management allows you to perform these management tasks:

- Manage disk properties
- Create new partitions and volumes
- Extend NTFS volumes
- Mount drives

Windows Server 2003 has the ability to support fault-tolerant drives. This is done through what is known as Redundant Array of Independent Disks (RAID). Windows Server 2003 can use software- or hardware-based RAID solutions. Windows Server 2003 supports only RAID 0, 1, and 5 for software-based solutions.

Striped volumes are known as RAID level 0 and provide no fault tolerance. They can be used to reduce the amount of wear on disks and increase disk performance. A minimum of two disks is needed.

A mirrored volume is a combination of two dynamic disks. One of the disks is the primary disk that is used by the system and users, and the other is used as a backup. Every time you write something to the primary disk, it mirrors that information on the other disk. Mirrored volumes are known as RAID level 1 and *do* provide fault tolerance. Mirrored volumes are a great place to install the system and boot partitions for a Windows Server 2003 server.

Stripe sets with parity are known as RAID level 5. They contain anywhere from three to thirty-two dynamic disks. They function much like stripe sets in that they stripe data across drives evenly. The big difference is that they also stripe parity information that can be used to rebuild data if one of the drives fails.

Disk management includes checking the health of disks. Status messages appear in the Disk Management tool to help show if there are any problems with disks. Common status messages you may encounter for volumes are as follows:

- Failed
- Failed Redundancy
- Formatting
- Healthy
- Regenerating
- Resyncing
- Unknown

Besides the Disk Management tool, there are several other command-line tools that allow you to perform disk management tasks. For instance, Check Disk allows you to scan a disk for bad sectors. The Convert command-line tool converts FAT16 or FAT32 partitions or volumes to NTFS. Disk Cleanup removes temporary and unnecessary files. Over time, as data is written to a disk, it eventually becomes fragmented. Windows Server 2003 includes a built-in disk defragmenter that can organize data that is stored on the disk. DISKPART allows administrators to create and extend volumes and partitions, import disks, and much more. You also can use the FORMAT command to format disks. FSUTIL is a command-line utility that gathers information about disks. MOUNTVOL is a tool that allows an administrator to use the command line to create mount points.

CHAPTER 7 SUMMARY

Each file and folder stored on a disk has attributes that can be configured. One of those attributes is the read-only attribute. As the name of this attribute implies, it makes all the files or folders with that attribute read-only. On a FAT volume, this can easily be unchecked because there is no local security for the FAT file system.

The archive attribute allows administrators to mark a file or folder as changed. When certain backups run, the backup program checks to see if a file has changed by looking at its archived attribute.

The system attribute is commonly used with the hidden attribute. The hidden attribute marks files or folders as hidden. With this attribute checked, normal users cannot see the files or folders and so are unable to harm them. When both of these attributes are checked, they can be an effective way to hide files and folders. Even if you select that you want to view hidden files in the Folder Options dialog box, they remain hidden. You must also choose to view system files be able to view the hidden files. So, in effect, using both the hidden and system attribute is like a doubly hidden attribute.

Windows Server 2003 supports advanced attributes. If an administrator wants to configure the archive attribute for a file or folder, it can be done within the advanced attributes. The advanced attributes is also where an administrator can go to index a file to help with searches. Windows Server 2003 also has the ability to compress files and folders. By using compression, you can save some space on your servers. This option is available only on volumes formatted with NTFS. Once you compress a file or folder, the text used for the name is displayed as blue instead of the default black.

There are two rules to remember when moving and copying files and folders:

- Moving a file or folder in the same volume retains the file or folder's attributes.
- Every other operation inherits the permission of its new parent folder.

These two rules work not only with the compression attribute, but also with NTFS permissions and EFS.

You can secure file and folder resources by using NTFS permissions, but there are times when an additional layer of security is needed. Consider this situation: You travel frequently with a laptop and you store sensitive documents on it. Laptops can easily be misplaced or stolen, and there are third-party tools that can be used to bypass NTFS security if someone were to gain physical access to the disk. Fortunately, Encrypting File System (EFS) can be used to add the additional layer of security needed. EFS encrypts the file or folder with a special session key known as a file encryption key (FEK). Once the encryption is done, the FEK is copied to a secured area on the file header called the data decryption field (DDF). That DDF is also encrypted by the user's public key. The entire encryption/decryption process is transparent to the user except when a user initially configures a file or folder for EFS.

When a user wants to decrypt the encrypted file or folder, he or she opens up the folder normally. However, it is a completely different story behind the scenes. Windows Server 2003 uses his or her private key to unlock the data recovery field (DRF). Depending on how the administrator sets up the DRF policy, that policy may automatically include the domain administrator account for recovery purposes. With the administrator added to the DRF, an administrator can always recover data that has been encrypted by any user.

Windows Server 2003 includes the option for users to add other users' private keys into the DDF. This is a common method for sharing access to an encrypted file or folder. In this way, only the users who were included can decrypt the file or folder. EFS and NTFS compression are mutually exclusive of each other, so you cannot encrypt *and* compress a file.

NTFS also allows you to limit how much space users can utilize on your file servers. This feature is called disk quotas and can be a lifesaver on file servers. You can assign disk quotas only to user accounts and not to groups. This can make it a little more difficult to set up for a large domain. You set this up per volume and not per disk. You can also set it up to warn users when they are getting close to their limits.

Another valuable feature of Windows Server 2003 for file servers is the distributed file system (DFS). DFS allows administrators to have multiple shared folders from multiple servers appear as if they are all under the same share hierarchy. There are two DFS models that you can configure. Standalone DFS provides no fault tolerance, and everything is stored on one server. Domain-based DFS stores information in Active Directory and can be configured to point to multiple copies of the shared folder to provided fault tolerance. This makes it extremely easy to perform maintenance on a file server because users are redirected to another server that has the same resources available.

CHAPTER 8 SUMMARY

Printing is an extremely important part of an administrator's responsibilities in almost every organization. There are few aspects of the job as widespread as printing. The first step in understanding printing in Windows is to understand Microsoft's perspective on terminology. The following are some of the most common terms encountered and their meanings:

- *Print device*—A print device is the actual hardware used for printing documents. There are two general types of print devices: a local print device, which is directly connected to a port on the print server or workstation, and a network print device, which connects to a print server through its network adapter.

- *Printer*—This is the software interface between the hardware print device and the user. It is configurable and controls the connection to the print device.

- *Print driver*—These are files that are used by Windows Server 2003 to send a raw print job to the print device in a language it understands. These are hardware specific, designed for a specific print device based on its model.

- *Print server*—This is a computer with one or more print devices connected to it, and which acts as a central server where end users can send print jobs.

- *Print client*—This is the computer that sends a job to the print device.

It is important to have an efficient printing environment. Such an environment would have the following:

- *One or more computers designated as print servers*—Both Windows Server 2003 and Windows XP Professional can act as a print server; however, Windows XP Professional has a limitation of 10 simultaneous client connections. This makes Windows XP a poor choice as a print server in most network environments.

- *Sufficient space on the hard drive for the print server*—Setting up print jobs for printing can be disk-space intensive; therefore, plenty of hard drive space is needed, preferably on a drive where the operating system files are not located. The space is used to queue and buffer documents in preparation to be sent to the print device.

- *Sufficient RAM beyond that of the minimum Windows Server 2003 requirements*—This allows a server to handle large jobs with greater ease; otherwise, several large print jobs may negatively impact the server's performance.

From a user's perspective, the printing process is fairly straightforward and can be initiated by a single press of a button. However, the actual process behind the scenes is much more complicated:

1. A print file is created by a software application on the print client.

2. The software communicates with the Windows graphics device interface (GDI) during creation of the print file. The GDI integrates characteristics of the print job—colors, fonts, and embedded graphics—with information provided by the print driver installed on the client for the target printer. This process is referred to as rendering.

3. The file is formatted with control codes that allow special graphics, fonts, and color information to be printed. The application places the print file in the client's spooler, which is a subfolder used for spooling.

4. The client's remote print provider uses a remote procedure call to the network print server where the file is being delivered. If the print server responds and is ready to accept the file, the remote printer sends the file to the Server service on the server.

5. The network print server has four different processing elements that receive and process a print file. These are the router, print provider, print processor, and print monitor. They are all pieces of the network print server's spooler.

6. The Server service calls its router, the Print Spooler service, once the remote print provider at the client contacts it. The router then directs the print file to the print provider, which stores it in a spool file until it can be sent to the printer.

7. The print provider works with the print processor to ensure that the file is formatted to use the right data type, such as TEXT or RAW, while the file is spooled.

8. When the spool file is fully formatted for transmission to the printer, the print monitor pulls it from the spooler's disk storage and sends it to the printer.

A printer can be added as a local device. This may require administrative privileges, depending on your network. This is most easily accomplished using the Add Printer Wizard.

Printers can also be network devices. When they are network devices, printers can use TCP/IP, and network print devices can include their own network card. To add network devices, you can use the Add Printer Wizard. When adding a printer, you define the Standard TCP/IP Port option with the TCP/IP address of the network device. Print jobs can then be sent directly to the print device.

The following printer permissions can be set to manage a user's control over specific printers:

- *Print*—This permission permits connection to a printer, the printing of documents, and the editing of a user's own print jobs. The Everyone group has this permission by default.

- *Manage Documents*—This permission grants all capabilities of the Print permission, plus it allows the controlling of document print jobs for all users. The Creator Owner group has this permission by default.

- *Manage Printers*—This permission grants all the capabilities of Print and Manage Documents. In addition, it allows sharing, modification, and deletion of printers and their properties. The Administrators, Print Operators, and Server Operators groups have this permission by default.

- *Special Permissions*—This permission is similar to NTFS special permissions. Special permissions allows a granular level of control over printer security, including controlling user ownership of a printer, viewing printer permissions, and changing printer permissions.

A printer pool consists of a single printer that is connected to a number of print devices. The advantage of a printer pool is that it allows many physical print devices to function as a single logical printer, thus providing better document distribution in high-volume environments while reducing the time that users must wait for documents to print.

Printer priorities allow you to grant some groups of users a higher priority to a print device than other users. For example, you may want to configure your print environment to give precedence to any printouts from the CEO of the company, even if there are other documents already ahead of the CEO's documents in the print queue.

If you need to manage your environment through scripts, the following are provided for you:

- *Prncnfg.vbs*—This file either configures a printer or displays configuration information about a printer.

- *Prndrvr.vbs*—This script can add, delete, or list printer drivers.

- *Prnjobs.vbs*—This script allows you to view existing print jobs. It can also pause, resume, and cancel jobs that are in the queue.

- *Prnmngr.vbs*—This script is used to add, delete, or list printers and related connections. It also can set a printer as default.

- *Prnport.vbs*—This script allows standard TCP/IP ports to be shown. In addition, you can create or delete ports, or change their current configurations.

- *Prnqctl.vbs*—This script allows you to pause or resume a printer, cancel all of the jobs currently queued for a printer, or print a test page.

The print spooler stores the spooled print jobs on the hard drive. By default, this location is in the WINDOWS\system32\spool\PRINTERS folder. You may need to change this location if the print server handles several print jobs. Ideally, it should be moved away from the Windows operating system files.

To make printers easy to locate in Active Directory, they can be published. This process adds information regarding the printer into Active Directory so that users can find it by searching.

Windows Server 2003 simplifies managing printers and enables you to effectively manage your printing environment. Through permissions, printer pools, priorities, and command-line utilities, there are a variety of ways for you to effectively manage and deploy print servers in your Windows environment.

CHAPTER 9 SUMMARY

Windows Server 2003 supports Group Policy Objects. GPOs are an Active Directory feature, so they are available only in a domain environment. When used effectively, group policies enhance an administrator's ability to manage the network and its policies. Group policies can be thought of as groups of policies, or rules, that can be applied to user accounts. User accounts with similar management needs can be grouped together in an organizational unit, or OU. Then, a GPO can be applied to the OU, defining sets of rules for objects, such as user or computer accounts, contained in the OU.

C

A Group Policy Object (GPO) is used to configure and apply policy settings for user and computer objects. It performs a variety of administrative tasks, including:

- Configuring a user's desktop settings using predefined templates
- Controlling desktop and domain security settings for users and workstations
- Creating and assigning scripts that run for particular users and computers during logging, starting up, or shutting down
- Redirecting folders, such as the My Documents folder, to a network location
- Automating the distribution of software and its maintenance to computers throughout the network

Group policies can also contain multiple categories. The policies controllable by a GPO can be broken into the following three categories:

- *Software settings*—These centralize software installation maintenance and management, including the installation, upgrading, and uninstallation of applications.
- *Windows settings*—These settings are for the management of scripts, security settings, Internet Explorer settings, and other features such as Remote Installation Services and folder redirection.
- *Administrative templates*—These enable defining registry-based settings to configure application and user desktop settings. Additional settings include those granting access to operating system components, Control Panel settings, and offline file configuration.

When a GPO is created, it can be located in two main locations. The first location is a Group Policy container (GPC). This is an Active Directory container located in the Active Directory Users and Computers console. The second is the Group Policy template (GPT). The template contains all the settings, administrative templates, security settings, software installation settings, and scripts. Note that the configuration file Registry.pol stores the registry changes. A configuration file defines settings for both users and computers. The template is stored in the Sysvol folder, which is located under the %systemroot%\Sysvol\ <Domain Name>\Policies folder.

GPOs can define a variety of settings. Administrators can assign a group policy to multiple locations, such as the local computer, site, domain, and OUs. Group policies have two main categories: computer configuration and user configuration.

Active Directory applies group policies as the computer starts up. The process of applying Group Policy is as follows:

1. A Windows 2000, Windows XP, or Windows Server 2003 computer in a domain boots and queries the domain controller for a list of GPOs that apply to it. The domain controller checks the GPOs to find policies that apply to the computer. Policies that are executed on the computer include the computer settings and startup scripts.

2. The domain controller gives clients the list of GPOs that apply to the client in the order that the GPOs must be processed. The client contacts the domain controller and pulls down the Group Policy templates from the Sysvol share. Next, it applies the settings and runs the scripts.

3. At user logon, the process is repeated, except that this time user settings are processed and user policy settings, such as scripts and software policies, are applied.

When editing GPOs, the manageable settings are broken down into nodes. These nodes are applicable to policies set at the domain and OU levels. The node functions are as follows:

- *Local Policies*—These apply settings to the local account database of the workstation or server.

- *Event Log*—These settings set configuration settings for event log size, retention period, and access restrictions.

- *Restricted Groups*—These settings grant the administrator the ability to control who is a member of any security group.

- *System Services*—These allow an administrator control over service startup mode, disabling of a service, permissions to edit the service mode, and auditing of the service.

- *Registry*—This group of settings sets security and auditing access control list (ACL) settings for registry keys and subkeys.

- *File System*—These manage and maintain NTFS permissions and auditing permissions for any folder or file listed in the policy. To be effective, the files or folders must reside on an NTFS partition.

- *Wireless Network (IEEE 802.11) Policies*—These policies define settings that govern wireless networks, including to which wireless networks a client can connect, whether access points should be used, and the data encryption settings used.

- *Public Key Policies*—These options govern configuration settings for different public key-based applications. These include the encrypting file system (EFS), as well as certificate autoenrollment settings and certificate authority (CA) trusts.

- *Software Restriction Policies*—These settings control software deployment. They include the ability to manually define which file extensions are considered executable, control security settings of software-related registry paths, and override software settings from other GPOs.

- *IP Security Policies on Active Directory*—These define different IP security settings based on the role of a server or workstation; three default policies exist, but none are applied by default.

Other options include the capability to force storage of user documents to a server. This option enables an administrator to ensure that documents are properly backed up. This policy is known as folder redirection. It is a Group Policy feature that enables you to redirect the following contents of a user's profile to a network location:

- Application data
- Desktop
- My Documents
- Start menu

Because Group Policy can be applied at multiple levels, it is important to understand the processing order of group policies. In a Windows 2000, Windows XP, or Windows Server 2003 computer, GPOs are applied in the following order:

1. Local computer
2. Site
3. Domain
4. Parent OU
5. Child OU

Note the following:

- If you do not want any of the higher-level settings to be applied to a particular child container, then check the Block Policy inheritance check box on the Group Policy tab for the container properties.
- If a conflict exists between policies at different levels, the last policy implemented applies. However, this behavior can be modified by blocking the inheritance of policies and by using the No Override option.
- If you want a particular GPO's settings to always be enforced, you can configure the policy using the No Override option.

Group Policy also includes the ability to install software across the network. This is done using a Microsoft Windows installer package (MSI). If an MSI package is not available, a ZAP file, created with a tool such as WinINSTALL, can be used.

Deployment can be accomplished using either of two methods: assigning applications or publishing applications. Assigning applications to a user advertises the program in the Start menu. The program is installed when a user clicks the shortcut or opens an associated file. If it is assigned to a computer, the next time the computer starts, the software is installed.

Publishing applications is an alternate method of deploying them. Published applications can be installed via the Add/Remove Programs applet in Control Panel.

You can also maintain and manage deployed applications. During maintenance, you can force upgrades for software, make them optional, and even redeploy an application.

CHAPTER 10 SUMMARY

Microsoft has provided several tools to help the administrator effectively manage his or her Windows Server 2003 environment. Some of these tools, such as the Microsoft Management Console, are customizable to meet the various needs of administrators. Other tools, such as the secondary logon feature, are designed to assist administrators in maintaining a secure environment while maintaining functionality and ease of use. Together these tools enhance an administrator's capabilities to manage the network.

The MMC is a management device that allows for extensive customization through snap-ins. Snap-ins are dedicated plug-ins for the MMC that allow management of a particular aspect of Windows Server 2003. For instance, snap-ins are available to manage the DNS and DHCP services. Another snap-in is Event Viewer. Multiple snap-ins can be added to a single MMC console. This allows an administrator to select the snap-ins most regularly used and add them to a single management console.

As a security best practice, administrators should have a nonadministrative account that they use for tasks such as checking their e-mail. Their administrative tasks should be completed with their second account, which is granted administrator privileges. This enhances network security.

To make it simpler to switch between accounts, Windows Server 2003 supports secondary login. This is a security feature that allows an administrator to start a program, such as a management tool or an installer, under the privileges of a second account. This keeps an administrator from being required to log on and off to execute programs with administrative privileges.

In addition to management tools, troubleshooting skills are important for an administrator. Resolving issues quickly saves time and money. To accomplish this, it is important to have a well-defined approach when attempting to resolve problems. A successful troubleshooting process involves the following steps:

1. Define the problem.
2. Gather detailed information about what has changed.
3. Devise a plan to solve the problem.
4. Implement the plan and observe the results.
5. Document all changes and results.

Another tool in the administrator's toolbox is Remote Desktop for Administration. This tool allows full access to a server from a remote location. Only members of the Administrators group can connect to the server, by default. Other users can be granted access using Control Panel's System applet.

C

Management for connections and for the services is taken care of through a variety of tools:

- *Terminal Services Manager*—Allows monitoring and controlling client access to terminal servers
- *Terminal Services Configuration*—Allows the configuration of terminal server settings and connections
- *Terminal Services Licensing*—Keeps track of Terminal Services client access licenses

When using the Terminal Services configuration tool, the connection object properties can be configured. Opening the properties displays eight tabs that allow a variety of configuration controls, as follows:

- *General*—This tab allows configuration of authentication and encryption.
- *Logon Settings*—This tab allows configuration of how the user logs on, by supplying information or using preconfigured information.
- *Sessions*—This tab allows configuration of timeout settings.
- *Environment*—This tab allows configuration for a program to run automatically when a user connects.
- *Remote Control*—This tab enables remote control of a client.
- *Client Settings*—This tab allows configuration of client settings such as drive mappings and port mappings.
- *Network Adapter*—This tab allows configuration of the number of simultaneous connections.
- *Permissions*—This tab controls user access based on standard permissions.

Terminal Services client software packages are installed under the %Systemroot%\system32\clients\tsclient\win32 folder on the terminal server. The files to install Remote Desktop Connection are located here. The MSI package is msrdpcli.msi.

When a terminal server is installed, additional tabs are added to the user account's properties. These tabs allow for user-specific configurations granting a granular control over the user's interactions with the terminal server. These tabs are as follows:

- *Terminal Services Profile*—Enables the user to configure a special profile to be used when connecting to a terminal server.
- *Remote control*—Configures remote control properties for the account, which can also be configured in the Properties dialog box for the connection. User account properties can then be overridden.
- *Sessions*—Configures the maximum session time and disconnect options, which can also be configured in the Properties dialog box for the connection. This overrides settings made to the user account.

- *Environment*—Configures a program to automatically run when the user makes a terminal services connection. It can be used to configure a special logon script to be run when a user connects to the terminal server.

Administrators can set permissions related to Active Directory as well. This allows an administrator to control access to different Active Directory objects. The common permissions are as follows:

- *Full Control*—This permission grants all standard permissions plus the ability to change permissions and take ownership of an Active Directory.

- *Read*—This permission allows viewing of Active Directory objects and their attributes.

- *Create All Child Objects*—This permission grants the ability to add child objects to an OU.

- *Delete All Child Objects*—This permission grants the ability to remove child objects from an OU.

One tool to allow an administrator to delegate authority of objects in Active Directory to others is the Delegation of Control Wizard. This can be used, for instance, to allow a manager to reset passwords for employees in his or her department.

Other responsibilities for an administrator include keeping systems up to date. Security patches and hot fixes distributed by Microsoft can be critical in maintaining a system's integrity. To deploy patches, these options are available:

- Manual download and installation

- Installation using scripting techniques, such as a logon script

- Automated deployment using applications such as Microsoft Systems Management Server (SMS)

- Installation using Windows Update

In addition to these options, Microsoft has developed a tool, Software Update Services (SUS), which can be used to deploy hot fixes and security updates. The recommended hardware requirements for installing the SUS server component are as follows:

- Pentium III 700 MHz or higher processor

- 512 MB of RAM

- 6 GB of free disk space for setup and storage of security packages

The SUS server component can be installed on servers running the following operating systems:

- Windows 2000 Server (Service Pack 2 or higher)

- Windows Server 2003

- Microsoft Small Business Server 2000 (Service Pack 1 or higher)

SUS is designed as a central location to update your network computers. It gives administrators a management tool to handle packages normally downloaded through Windows Update. Configuring Software Update Services includes the Typical option. This downloads updates from the Internet. SUS Proxy server settings are configured automatically. All downloaded content is stored locally and packages are downloaded in all supported languages.

The updated version of the Automatic Updates client can be downloaded from the SUS site, and it is included by default with Windows Server 2003, XP SP1, and Windows 2000 SP3. By knowing and using the variety of tools available to you, your effectiveness as an administrator increases. By exploring and using the tools available to you, your ability to administer the servers in your domain is improved and your efficiency increases.

CHAPTER 11 SUMMARY

A benchmark of a good administrator includes the ability to troubleshoot and maintain systems to perform optimally. If a system is performing poorly, several problems can result. Productivity can decrease when a system is not performing well, and users cannot accomplish their jobs. Windows Server 2003 includes several tools that make resolving performance issues, identifying bottlenecks, and tuning performance an easier task.

The first step in performance tuning is establishing a baseline. A baseline is a standard against which you can measure the system's performance. A baseline includes recorded observations regarding a computer system's behavior. Having a baseline allows you to identify bottlenecks, or areas of the system that slow the overall performance of the operating system.

Windows Server 2003 comes with several built-in tools that can be used to monitor server health and performance, including:

- Task Manager
- Event Viewer
- Performance console

Task Manager is a versatile and underutilized utility in troubleshooting a variety of performance-related issues. Task Manager includes several tabs to assist an administrator:

- The Applications tab displays information regarding currently running programs and allows you to start applications as well as end applications. It also informs you if a program appears to be unresponsive to the operating system.

- The Processes tab gives a detailed view of the processes running in the background on your system. Information includes the Process ID number, CPU usage, CPU time, and Memory Usage. Additional information can be added along with these default options. In addition, processor affinity can be set here. Processor affinity allows the user to assign a process to a single CPU, or multiple CPUs on a multiprocessor system.

- The Performance tab gives a graphical view of CPU and memory utilization. It includes graphical displays and real-time measurements of system performance and resource usage. The information includes:

  - *CPU Usage/CPU Usage History*—This shows the usage level of the CPU.

  - *PF Usage/Page File Usage History*—This shows the usage level of the page file and historical graphs.

  - *Totals*—This displays the count of all the handles, threads, and processes.

  - *Physical Memory*—This shows the entire amount of memory, the amount available, and the amount used by the system cache.

  - *Commit Charge*—This is the amount of memory committed to all running applications.

  - *Kernel Memory*—This is the amount of memory set aside for kernel functions.

- The Network tab displays information regarding the network adapter's utilization, showing the information in a real-time graph.

- The User's tab provides information regarding the currently logged-in users.

Events affecting performance may be recorded in Event Viewer, in one of three standard logs. Additional logs may be present depending on the services installed. The three logs are as follows:

- *Application log*—This log records information, warnings, and errors created by applications installed on the system.

- *Security log*—Security-related events are recorded in the security log. These are created in accordance with the audit policy.

- *System log*—This log contains information, warnings, and errors that have been logged by Windows Server 2003 system components, including drivers and services.

When viewing a log, different types of information may be recorded. In the system and application event logs, the following entries may be included:

- *Information*—These events are recorded when a component or application successfully performs an action.

- *Warning*—Warnings are recorded when an event may not require immediate attention; however, the event may eventually become a problem.

- *Error*—This event type indicates a significant problem. A service may not have started in a timely fashion, or a device driver may not have loaded.

In addition, the security log entries include success and failure entries. These are successes and failures of actions that are performed on the network based on the configuration of an audit policy.

For in-depth performance monitoring, System Monitor is the tool of choice. It is the standard on Windows Server 2003 for collecting data on real-time server performance. System Monitor facilitates the information gathering performed by administrators. It allows you to monitor how the system is performing under the current workload. You are also able to diagnose performance problems such as bottlenecks. You can use the information you gather to plan for growth, and you can also test changes on the server and observe their impact on the server's performance.

Performance Logs and Alerts, an additional performance monitoring tool in Windows Server 2003, provides useful analyses of your systems and includes the ability to alert you based on a system's performance compared to threshold values. Performance Logs and Alerts provides the ability to capture data in a variety of formats, such as binary, comma-separated, tab-separated, and a format compatible with SQL Server databases. Data can be viewed while it is being monitored, or administrators can view all of the collected data. Parameters can be set that govern the data collection, including start and stop times for logs, filenames, and file sizes. Multiple logging sessions can be managed from a single management console. Alerts that are sent when thresholds have been exceeded can also be created, and thresholds can be defined by the administrator.

The cumulative tools provided by Windows Server 2003 for performance tuning allow an administrator to maximize a company's hardware investment. By optimizing and tuning servers, the administrator can ensure maximum system performance. In addition, the administrator can troubleshoot bottlenecks and identify other performance issues, and he or she can wisely recommend upgrades and resolutions to performance-related problems.

CHAPTER 12 SUMMARY

Even in the best-managed networks, things go wrong. From power outages to equipment failure to natural disasters, administrators are tasked with insulating the corporate network infrastructure from a variety of calamities. An effective administrator plans for these events and has a contingency plan to mitigate negative effects. Windows includes a variety of tools to assist an administrator in these endeavors:

- *The Backup utility*—This utility allows an administrator to back up and restore the operating system, software applications, and user data files. Backup jobs can be scheduled.

- *Shadow Copies of Shared Volumes*—This new feature keeps previous versions of files in shared folders so that if a user needs to restore an older version, it is accessible. This gives end users a simple method to restore their own data, reducing an administrator's workload.

- *Automated System Recovery (ASR)*—This new feature allows the recovery of a server from configuration information stored on disks. It allows for a quick reinstall; however, applications still need to be reinstalled and data must be restored from backups.

- *Advanced startup options*—These options allow an administrator to control how the system boots, giving access to different methods of starting up that allow trouble-shooting and diagnostic steps. Modes available include Safe Mode, Last Known Good Configuration, and others.

- *Recovery Console*—This is a command-line environment to which an administrator can boot on a server. It allows the administrator to troubleshoot and make configuration changes when the system will not boot as expected.

One of the most important parts of your plan is the backup plan. By default, members of the following local groups can back up any files and folders on a member server running Windows Server 2003:

- Administrators
- Backup Operators
- Server Operators

If users are not members of the local groups in the preceding list, they cannot by default back up files. Instead, for users to back up files, the users must either be listed as the owner of the file or have one or more of the following NTFS permissions:

- Read
- Read and Execute
- Modify
- Full Control

The most common type of backup is the Backup utility's normal backup. This backup method backs up all files selected and clears the archive attribute on the selected files and folders. By clearing the archive attribute, any subsequent file changes are marked for backup during a subsequent backup.

The incremental backup type is another backup method. This method backs up all files that have changed since the last normal or incremental backup, and it clears the archive attribute.

Another backup type is the differential backup type. Unlike the first two backup types, the differential backup type does not reset the archive attribute. It backs up all files that have changed since the last normal backup, regardless if a differential has been performed since the last normal backup ran.

The preceding three types of backups are the most common. However, there are two additional backup types with which you should be familiar: daily backups and copy backups. Daily backups back up files that have changed on the day the backup is scheduled. The archive attribute is not modified, so other backup types remain unaffected.

A copy backup backs up all files and folders that are selected, and, as with the daily backup, the archive attribute is not modified. The copy backup is similar to a normal backup, except the archive attribute is not modified, so other backup types aren't interfered with.

In defining what to back up, you can select files and folders. In addition, you have an option to back up the System State data. Backing up the System State data on a Windows Server 2003 system includes the following choices:

- Registry (always)
- COM+ Class Registration database (always)
- Boot files (always)
- Certificate Services database (if Certificate Services is installed)
- Active Directory (only on domain controllers)
- Sysvol directory (only on domain controllers)
- Cluster service (if the server is part of a cluster)
- IIS Metadirectory (if IIS is installed)
- System files (always)

Another feature is Shadow Copies of Shared Folders. This feature allows for:

- Restoration of files that users accidentally delete
- Recovery of previous versions of files when necessary
- Comparison of the current version of a file to a previous version

The Automated System Recovery feature in Windows Server 2003 is another administrative tool that can assist you when a system cannot be repaired. This powerful new utility can restore system configuration information. The Automated System Recovery (ASR) feature is used to restore an operating system's configuration settings during a reinstallation, if a system cannot be repaired or otherwise restored to a normal running state.

The advanced startup options allow a number of ways to start the system in an attempt to diagnose or troubleshoot problems. Last Known Good Configuration boots the system with the registry information from the last successful logon. This allows registry changes to be undone so that the system can be restored to an operable state.

Recovery Console is an option that allows an administrator to boot into a command-line environment. In this environment, an administrator is able to manage files and services and make modifications to the operating system from a command prompt. Recovery Console can be used to fix more serious errors where one of the other advanced startup methods fails.

Chapter 13 Summary

Windows Server 2003 includes the latest version of Internet Information Services, IIS 6.0. IIS includes the following components:

- *World Wide Web (HTTP) service*—These services allow the hosting of one or more Web sites.

- *File Transfer Protocol (FTP) service*—This service allows the transfer of files between the server and a remote client.

- *Network News Transfer Protocol (NNTP) service*—This service is used to create topic-centered discussions.

- *Simple Mail Transfer Protocol (SMTP) service*—This service allows e-mail to be sent, enabling other IIS services to have a form e-mailed, for instance.

An organization can implement these services in a variety of ways:

- Through an internal company Web site containing company forms, manuals, and policies

- Through collaborative work using applications such as Office XP

- Through Web-based applications for internal business processes such as completing forms or entering data

In addition, if the services are accessible over the Internet, there are even more possibilities:

- Additional customer service information for end users including software, updates, manuals and support, or frequently asked questions about products or services

- Online ordering and shipment-tracking capabilities

- Press releases, news bulletins, and short articles

There are multiple components of the IIS suite of services. They include the following:

- *Background Intelligent Transfer Service (BITS) extension*—Spare bandwidth is used for data transfers, with the capability to resume the transfer in case it is interrupted.

- *Common Files*—These are the required IIS program files.

- *File Transfer Protocol (FTP) service*—This allows the creation of FTP sites to upload and download files.

- *FrontPage 2002 Server extensions*—This enhances Web site design and creation by creating compatibility with Microsoft FrontPage and Visual InterDev for Web site design.

- *Internet Information Services Manager*—This installs the Internet Information Services MMC snap-in, giving administrators a single tool to manage IIS services.

- *Internet Printing*—This allows Web-based printer management and printing.

- *NNTP service*—This enables the NNTP service for news articles and threaded discussion.

- *SMTP service*—This enables the IIS server to act as an SMTP Server, providing the capability to send e-mail.

- *World Wide Web service*—This enables an IIS server to host Web sites and Web pages, acting as a Web server on an intranet or the Internet.

IIS maintains several important folders in different locations. For content, help information, and critical system files, the following locations are notable:

- *%systemroot%\system32\inetsrv*—This location contains program files and .dll files needed for IIS.

- *C:\Inetpub*—This is the root repository of IIS, containing such subfolders as ftproot, wwwroot, nntpfile, and mailroot, which store all of the content for the FTP, Web, NNTP, and SMTP services.

- *C:\WINDOWS\Help\iishelp*—This contains the IIS documentation.

New changes in IIS 6.0 include the HTTP.SYS kernel mode driver. It accepts and manages all incoming HTTP requests. IIS 5.0 Isolation mode ensures compatibility with legacy IIS 5.0 applications to ensure that they can run on IIS 6.0. The worker process puts different applications into their own application pool. This provides a higher level of stability for the server. The Remote Administration (HTML) tool is a Web browser tool that is used to administer the IIS 6.0 installation.

IIS also supports virtual servers. While the server is installed on a single machine, it is capable of hosting multiple Web sites for different domains. For this to work, each Web site on your server must have a way of being uniquely identified. There are three ways that you can be sure that each Web site is uniquely identified:

- Use a separate IP address to distinguish each Web site.

- Use a single IP address with a specific port number for each Web site.

- Use a single IP address with multiple host headers, which are fully qualified domain names that belong to a specific site.

Web sites can be configured via multiple properties tabs, as follows:

- The Web Site tab is used to configure basic settings such as IP address, TCP port, and the number of allowed connections.

- The Performance tab allows the Web site to be tuned based on the server load and number of expected users.

- ISAPI filters can be set up on the ISAPI Filters tab.

- The Home Directory tab controls where the Web site holds its source data files.

- The Documents tab allows default documents to be specified and allows Web sites to have a common footer.

- The Directory Security tab allows you to configure security for the Web site.

- The HTTP Headers tab allows you to configure expiration dates for the content.

- The Custom Errors tab allows you to create custom Web site error messages, which are loaded instead of the default generic error pages.

For authentication, there are five methods supported by IIS natively, as follows:

- Anonymous access

- Basic authentication

- Digest authentication

- Integrated Windows authentication

- .NET Passport authentication

Anonymous access is the most common access method. It allows users to access a Web site without having to provide a user name and password. By default, users accessing a Web site use the IUSR_*servername* account, which is the user account associated with their anonymous access to the Web site. Basic authentication can be set up for Windows Server 2003. The security risk associated with basic authentication includes the transmission of the user name and password in an easily decodable format, Base64, which does not encrypt the data.

Digest authentication was introduced with Windows 2000 and IIS 5.0. It adds security over basic authentication because passwords are hashed using the MD5 algorithm to prevent them from being easily decoded Another authentication option is Integrated Windows authentication. This option uses the user's logon credentials to the operating system as the user name and password. This is typically an option for internal Web sites and intranets. A new authentication option, .NET Passport authentication, uses the .NET Passport service to authenticate users.

If you have configured more than one authentication method, it is important to know how the methods are handled. If there are multiple authentication methods, the following rules are used to determine which method is applicable:

- If Anonymous authentication and another method are the two options, the second method is used only if Anonymous authentication fails.

- FTP sites are limited and are unable to use Digest, Integrated Windows, or .NET Passport authentication.

- Digest and Integrated Windows authentication are used before Basic authentication.

SSL, a standard for encrypting Web communications, can be used to secure traffic between clients and the server. Web sites secured with SSL can be recognized by their URLs, which uses https:// instead of http://. SSL traffic is sent to port 443 on the server. To implement SSL, the Web server must use a server certificate from a certificate authority.

The File Transfer Protocol service can be used to transfer files between a client and a server. It uses multiple server ports for traffic, but TCP ports 20 and 21 by default. Port 21 is used to initiate the connection, and data is transferred over port 20.

There are several methods to secure your Web server. Data can be secured using resource permissions. Standard NTFS permissions can be used to secure data only to permissible users. IIS permissions are also effective and can be used for Web sites, FTP servers, virtual and physical directories, and files.

The default location used for backups is %systemroot%\system32\inetsrv\Metaback. You can back up the metabase using one of five methods:

- Use the backup utility to back up the database in the IIS console.
- Copy the contents of the backup directory to another folder on the same or another drive, thus providing fault tolerance once the initial backup has been performed.
- Use the metabase editor tool to export the contents of the database to a text file.
- Use the IISBACK.VBS script.
- Use the built-in Windows Backup utility to back up System State data or use a third-party utility.

IIS, just like the operating system, may require patches. Before patching, always perform a full backup of the server. Utilities such as the Microsoft Baseline Security Analyzer as well as the IIS Lockdown tool can be used to check the configuration of a server to ensure it has patches and is configured securely.

The Remote Administration (HTML) tools can be used to manage Web servers and other server functions through a Web browser. The tools can be added through the Add/Remove Windows applet in Control Panel. They are not installed by default.

Internet Printing, another feature in Windows Server 2003, is also not installed by default. It allows printers to be managed through a Web browser and allows clients to send print jobs to the printer using HTTP.

CHAPTER 14 SUMMARY

Various security features are built into Windows Server 2003. The available features can be broken down into these categories:

- *Authentication*—Ensures authorized access by requesting credentials before granting access to the system.
- *Access control*—Controls access to resources by allowing administrators to define levels of access.
- *Encryption*—Grants confidentiality by encrypting sensitive information so that it cannot be viewed by unauthorized users.

- *Security policies*—Allows granular definition and implementation of a company's desired security goals.

- *Service packs and hot fixes*—These are rollups of bug fixes and security flaws issued by Microsoft to ensure the stable and secure functioning of the operating system.

The Security Configuration Manager tools with Windows Server 2003 include these core components:

- Security templates

- Security settings in Group Policy objects

- Security Configuration and Analysis tool

- Secedit command-line tool

Security templates are primary tools for an administrator. They grant the ability to define, edit, and save baseline security settings to be applied to computers with common security requirements to meet organizational security standards. Several templates are included with Windows Server 2003, and it is important to be familiar with them.

The first template is the default template. This template is created when Windows Server 2003 is initially installed. The default security settings that are applied are stored in a template known as Setup Security.inf. These templates vary by installation, as the original configuration of the computer can alter them, especially when the initial installation is a fresh install or an upgrade. This file provides a single template that allows an administrator to restore the original computer security settings.

The next template category contains the incremental templates. Each incremental template has a specific level of security. To achieve the desired level of security within Windows, all templates up to the desired level of security must be applied. That is, each template builds on the templates that have lower security. You should apply these templates only to those machines already running the default security settings because they do not include any of the initial configurations created during the initial installation.

The incremental templates are as follows:

- *Compatws.inf*—This template is intended for either workstations or servers. Windows Server 2003 is more secure by default than earlier Windows versions because the default security is set to a higher level. However, this may cause problems with older applications, but this template might lower the security to enable the older applications to run successfully.

- *Securews.inf and Securedc.inf*—These templates increase the level of security for account policies, auditing, and registry permissions. The latter template is for domain controllers only; the former can be used for either a server or workstation.

- *Hisecws.inf and Hisecdc.inf*—These templates are intended to greatly increase security, especially in the area of network communications.

C

- *Iesacls.inf*—This template has settings designed to increase the security of Internet Explorer.

- *DC Security.inf*—This template is applied to Windows 2000 or Windows Server 2003 servers that are promoted to domain controllers. It allows an administrator to redeploy the initial security settings.

- *Rootsec.inf*—This template defines the original permissions assigned to the root of the system drive and can be used to reapply the settings if necessary.

Security templates can be applied to the local machine, or they can be applied across computers in the domain through a Group Policy Object (GPO).

The Security Configuration and Analysis snap-in enables administrators to compare configured, effective computer settings to a predefined template. This allows an administrator to compare the current policy to the desired policy. Differences between the actual policy and the desired policy are designated in the console tool so that the administrator can make appropriate corrections. In addition, the administrator can configure the computer with the desired settings.

Secedit.exe is a command-line tool used to create and apply security templates, as well as analyze security settings. This tool can be used in workgroups in which GPOs are not applied. The following switches can be used with this tool to define its behavior:

- */analyze*—Analyzes and compares security settings between the database and computer configuration

- */configure*—Implements the settings in the desired template

- */export*—Exports the current database information to a template file

- */import*—Imports a template file's information into a database file that can be used for analysis purposes

- */validate*—Verifies that a template has the correct syntax

- */GenerateRollback*—Creates a template with the current security settings of a system, which can be used to restore the settings in case the results of a change are undesirable

Auditing is a tool administrators can use to monitor and track activities on the network. Auditing should follow a defined security plan and meet specific needs. Auditing can be resource intensive, so it should be carried out with a definite plan. Audit information is logged in Event Viewer's security log and can include who performed an action, what the action was, and the result of the action.

Auditing can record these types of events:

- *Audit account logon events*—Indicate when a user logs onto a computer.

- *Audit account management*—Indicates when a user or group account is created, deleted, or modified. In addition, it also records successful or unsuccessful password changes.

- *Audit directory service access*—Indicates the access of an Active Directory object.
- *Audit logon events*—Indicate when a user logs on or off either a local computer or Active Directory.
- *Audit object access*—Indicates when objects, such as a file, folder, or printer, have been accessed.
- *Audit policy change*—Indicates when a policy that affects security, user rights, or auditing is modified.
- *Audit privilege use*—Indicates when a user invokes a right or privilege. Rights and privileges are actions, such as changing the system time or taking ownership of a file.
- *Audit process tracking*—Indicates that an application process has taken place.
- *Audit system events*—Indicates that a system event, such as a computer restart, has occurred.

To configure an audit policy, the following conditions must be met:

- Your user account must be a member of the Administrators group, or it must be granted the right to manage auditing and the security log.
- If auditing includes monitoring file and folder access, then the files and folders must be on an NTFS-formatted partition.

Setting up an audit policy includes two steps. You must first choose the events you wish to monitor and then decide whether to monitor the successes and/or failures of these events as the first step. If you are auditing access to files, folders, printers, and Active Directory objects, a second step is required. You need to configure auditing settings on the specific resources for which you want to monitor access.

If policies have been modified, you can apply changes immediately if necessary. To do so, either restart the computer, or, at a command prompt, issue the Gpupdate.exe command.

When configuring auditing, carefully consider what will actually be monitored. Auditing unnecessary items creates additional overhead and creates more log entries to filter. You should monitor log entries on a regular basis. It is typically a good idea to monitor sensitive and confidential information. Monitoring the Everyone group as opposed to Users includes unauthenticated users.

Event Viewer in Windows 2000 Server had a maximum default of 512 KB allotted for logging, and once it reached this limit, logging stopped. Windows Server 2003 has increased the log size to 16 MB. Depending on configuration, events may be overwritten when the maximum size has been reached, so it is important to only audit critical events and to monitor the log regularly.

Practice Exam

70-290 Managing and Maintaining a Microsoft Windows Server 2003 Environment

Name:_____

Date:_____

1. Which of the following statements regarding extended partitions is correct? (Choose all that apply.)
    a. Extended partitions can be divided into logical drives.
    b. Extended partitions can be created on basic or dynamic disks.
    c. A hard drive can contain up to four extended partitions.
    d. You do not format extended partitions.

2. Which of the following requires a computer restart when it is converted to NTFS? (Choose all that apply.)
    a. the system partition
    b. the boot partition
    c. all primary partitions
    d. all extended partitions

3. What is the maximum partition size that can be created with FAT32?
    a. 4 GB
    b. 8 GB
    c. 32 GB
    d. 2 TB
    e. unlimited

4. Which of the following volumes does *not* provide fault tolerance? (Choose all that apply.)
    a. spanned volume
    b. striped volume
    c. mirrored volume
    d. RAID-5 volume
    e. extended volume

5. What is the term for a fault tolerance solution that employs a separate hard disk controller to write all data to a second hard drive?
    a. RAID 5
    b. disk mirroring
    c. disk duplexing
    d. striped volume

6. You are configuring a RAID-5 volume to store important data files on a server. You have a 4-GB hard drive with 2 GB of free space. You have added three additional 4-GB hard drives. What is the largest RAID-5 volume you can create?
    a. 16 GB
    b. 12 GB
    c. 8 GB
    d. 4 GB

7. **You want to install a new network card in a Windows Server 2003 server. The network card is listed on the HCL, but the driver is not included in Windows. What must you do to locate the proper driver?**
    a. Download the driver from the Microsoft Web site.
    b. Download the driver from the manufacturer's Web site.
    c. Install the latest service pack.
    d. Install the network card driver in compatibility mode.

8. **You are having problems with a Windows Server 2003 application server that has many unsigned files installed. You want to use System File Checker to automatically replace all unsigned files with the correct system files from Microsoft. Which command do you use?**
    a. sfc /purgecache
    b. sfc /enable
    c. sfc /scannow
    d. sfc /quiet

9. **Which type of device driver *cannot* be rolled back? (Choose all that apply.)**
    a. video
    b. network card
    c. modem
    d. printer
    e. USB

10. **Which of the following statements regarding rolling back device drivers is incorrect?**
    a. You can restore only the previous version of the driver.
    b. Only the administrator can roll back device drivers.
    c. You can roll back device drivers in safe mode.
    d. The drivers for multifunction devices cannot be rolled back.

11. **What is the maximum number of characters that can be used in a user name?**
    a. 8
    b. 12
    c. 20
    d. 255
    e. 256

12. **Which of the following is an example of a User Principal Name (UPN)?**
    a. JDOE
    b. John.Doe
    c. John@ABC.COM
    d. John.Doe.ABC.COM

13. You need to create a new user. You want to copy an existing user's account as a template for the new user. Which field on the Organization tab is *not* copied to the new user account?

    a. Title

    b. Department

    c. Company

    d. Manager

    e. all of the above

14. An employee has taken a six-month leave of absence. What should be done to his user account?

    a. Delete the user account.

    b. Rename the user account.

    c. Disable the user account.

    d. Change the user account's password.

15. Which group does *not* have permission to disable a domain user account?

    a. Account Operators

    b. Server Operators

    c. Enterprise Admins

    d. Domain Admins

16. In native functional level, what can global groups contain? (Choose all that apply.)

    a. user accounts from any trusted domain

    b. user accounts from the same domain as the global group

    c. local groups

    d. universal groups

    e. global groups from the same domain as the global group

17. In native functional level, what can universal groups contain? (Choose all that apply.)

    a. users from any trusted domain

    b. global groups from any trusted domain

    c. computer accounts from any domain in the forest

    d. universal groups from any trusted domain

18. Local groups *cannot* be created on what type of Windows Server 2003 computers?

    a. domain controllers

    b. application servers

    c. DNS servers

    d. member servers

    e. none of the above

19. Which command can be used to display the groups of which a particular user is a member?

    a. DSLIST

    b. DSGROUP

    c. DSGET

    d. DSUSER

20. **What type of group is used for assigning permissions to a domain resource? (Choose all that apply.)**
    a. global
    b. universal
    c. domain local
    d. local

21. **You have shared a network folder. What is the default permission to the shared folder?**
    a. Everyone group Full Control
    b. Everyone group Read
    c. Authenticated Users Read
    d. Authenticated Users Full Control

22. **Which of the following is *not* an administrative share in Windows Server 2003?**
    a. C$
    b. Admin$
    c. Print$
    d. FAX$
    e. none of the above
    f. all of the above

23. **Which group has permission to share folders on a Windows Server 2003 domain controller? (Choose all that apply.)**
    a. Account Operators
    b. Server Operators
    c. Backup Operators
    d. Administrators

24. **Which NTFS permission overrides all other permissions on a folder?**
    a. Full Control
    b. Deny
    c. Take Ownership
    d. Change Permissions

25. **Audrey is a member of three groups: Users, Accounting, and Managers. The Users group has been assigned Read permission to the DATA share. The Accounting group has been assigned Modify permission to the DATA share, and the Managers group has been assigned Full Control to the DATA share. What is Audrey's effective permission to the DATA share?**
    a. Read
    b. Modify
    c. Full Control
    d. Write

26. You have shared a folder named Documents and assigned the default share permissions. You have also assigned Rebecca the NTFS permission Write, and assigned the group WORDPRO the Full Control NTFS permission. If Rebecca is also a member of the WORDPRO group, what are her permissions to the Documents share?

    a. Read

    b. Write

    c. Full Control

    d. None

27. What is the maximum number of concurrent connections allowed by Remote Desktop for administration in Windows Server 2003?

    a. 1

    b. 2

    c. 10

    d. unlimited

28. You want to connect to a Windows Server 2003 domain controller using Remote Desktop. You need to connect to the console session to view system messages, but another administrator is currently connected to it. What will happen if you log onto the console session?

    a. You cannot connect to the console session if another user is connected.

    b. You will lock the other administrator out of the console session.

    c. You will create a second console session.

    d. You cannot connect to the console session using Remote Desktop.

29. Using Remote Desktop for Administration, what protocol is used to transfer screen updates, keyboard inputs, and mouse clicks between the remote server and the client?

    a. RDP

    b. SAP

    c. ICA

    d. SNMP

30. You have connected to a remote server using Terminal Services to monitor the server's available memory. You have configured Performance Monitor to track the level of available memory. You want to be able to connect to the server tomorrow to view the information on the screen. How should you end the session?

    a. disconnect

    b. log off

    c. shut down

    d. any of the above

31. You notice a Windows Server 2003 application server is running sluggishly. After further examination, you discover the amount of available memory has steadily decreased over the past week. What could be causing the problem?

    a. excessive paging

    b. insufficient RAM

    c. processor bottleneck

    d. memory leak in an application

32. **Which of the following counters can be used to determine if the server has enough RAM?**
    a. Page Faults/sec
    b. Pool Nonpaged Bytes
    c. Committed Bytes
    d. Available Bytes

33. **Which of the following can cause processor bottlenecks? (Choose all that apply.)**
    a. low available network bandwidth
    b. slow hard drives
    c. multiple applications running on the same server
    d. older 8-bit network cards

34. **Which of the following does *not* improve disk performance on a Windows Server 2003 server?**
    a. defragmenting the hard disk
    b. adding additional hard drives to a RAID -5 volume
    c. upgrading on-board caching on the disk controller
    d. placing the page file on the same partition as the boot partition

35. **You have determined the network subsystem is a bottleneck. Which of the following actions would improve network performance? (Choose all that apply.)**
    a. subnetting the network
    b. adding additional servers to the network
    c. unbinding unused protocols from the adapter
    d. upgrading hubs to switches

36. **Which of the following statements regarding disk quotas is false?**
    a. Disk quotas are available only on NTFS volumes.
    b. Disk quotas cannot be applied to removable drives.
    c. Disk quotas can be enabled on local and network volumes.
    d. none of the above

37. **Which component is included in the System State only on domain controllers?**
    a. Registry
    b. Certificate Services database
    c. IIS metabase
    d. SYSVOL folder
    e. Cluster service information

38. **Which of the following backup types does *not* reset the archive bit? (Choose all that apply.)**
    a. Normal
    b. Copy
    c. Incremental
    d. Differential
    e. Daily

39. Which of the following is *not* stored on the ASR floppy disk? (Choose all that apply.)
    a. System State data
    b. boot files
    c. disk configuration information
    d. restore procedure

40. You need to restore Windows Server 2003 using the ASR disks. What key do you press when prompted in the Windows setup sequence to begin the ASR restore?
    a. F1
    b. F2
    c. F7
    d. F10
    e. none of the above

41. You want to configure Shadow Copies for critical accounting folders, but you are concerned that the shadow copies will consume too much disk space. What is the minimum amount of disk space you can assign for shadow copies?
    a. 50 MB
    b. 100 MB
    c. 200 MB
    d. 250 MB
    e. There is no minimum size.

42. You have enabled shadow copies on a server volume. By default, when will the shadow copies be created? (Choose all that apply.)
    a. 7:00 a.m. Monday to Friday
    b. 8:00 a.m. Monday to Friday
    c. 10:00 a.m. Monday to Friday
    d. 12:00 noon Monday to Friday
    e. 4:00 p.m. Monday to Friday

43. When is the LastKnownGood information updated?
    a. when the server is started
    b. when the server is shut down
    c. when a user logs on successfully
    d. when the System State is backed up

44. You need to repair Windows Server 2003 using the Recovery Console. Which user account has permission to access the Windows Server 2003 installation?
    a. All users
    b. Local Administrator
    c. Server Operators
    d. Domain Admins

45. Which of the following files is *not* required in a Windows Server 2003 boot disk? (Choose all that apply.)
    a. BOOT.INI
    b. NTLDR
    c. NTOSKRNL.EXE
    d. PAGEFILE.SYS
    e. NTDETECT.COM

46. You need to move the print spool location to another hard drive because of free space limitations. You have specified a new location in the print server's Advanced properties. What else must you do to change the print spooler location?
    a. nothing
    b. Restart the computer.
    c. Restart the print spooler service.
    d. Restore the Server service.

47. What is the minimum number of hard disks required to create a RAID-5 volume?
    a. 1
    b. 2
    c. 3
    d. 4

48. Which of the following group scope changes is *not* allowed?
    a. global to universal
    b. domain local to universal
    c. universal to global
    d. universal to domain local
    e. global to domain local

49. You need to move a hard disk from one Windows 2003 Server computer to another Windows Server 2003 computer. What must you do to view the new hard disk?
    a. Import the new hard disk.
    b. Rescan the disks.
    c. Reformat the new hard disk.
    d. Refresh the screen.

50. Which operating system does *not* require a computer account to join the domain? (Choose all that apply.)
    a. Windows 95
    b. Windows 98
    c. Windows NT
    d. Windows 2000
    e. Windows XP Professional

Glossary

.NET Passport authentication — An IIS authentication method that utilizes .NET Password user names and passwords.

access control entry (ACE) — An entry in an object's discretionary access control list (DACL) that grants permissions to a user or group. An ACE is also an entry in an object's system access control list (SACL) that specifies the security events to be audited for a user or group.

Active Directory (AD) — The directory service included with Windows Server 2003 that provides a single point of administration, authentication, and storage for user, group, and computer objects.

Active Directory schema — Contains the definition of all object classes and attributes used in the Active Directory database.

Active Directory Users and Computers — An Active Directory MMC tool that allows you to create various objects such as OUs, user accounts, groups, computers, and contacts.

active partition — The partition from which an operating system begins the boot process. Typically drive C: is configured as the active partition on a Windows Server 2003 system.

administrative shares — Hidden shared folders created for the purpose of allowing administrators to access the root of partitions and other system folders remotely.

Alert — An alert performs a specified action once a counter meets the specified setting. Once an alert is triggered, a message can be sent, a program can be run, a counter log started, or an event can be written to the application log.

Alias — The name of a virtual directory, or the name used to hide the real name of a directory and to simplify the directory name that would be used to access the information.

Anonymous access — Allows users to access a Web site without having to provide a user name and password.

application log — Where applications that are written to Microsoft standards record event information. The application developer determines the type of information an application writes to the log file.

archive attribute — A standard attribute used to determine the backup status of a file or folder.

attribute-level permissions — Active Directory permissions that control whether users or groups can read or modify the attributes associated with Active Directory objects.

attributes — Used to define the characteristics of an object class within Active Directory.

audit policy — Defines the events on the network that Windows Server 2003 records in the security log as they occur.

Auditing — The process that tracks the activities of users by recording selected types of events in the security log of a server or a workstation.

Authentication — Refers to determining whether a user has a valid user account with the proper permissions to access a resource such as a shared folder or Web site.

authentication — The process by which a user's identity is validated, which is subsequently used to grant or deny access to network resources.

Automated System Recovery (ASR) — A new Windows Server 2003 feature that allows an administrator to restore server configuration settings in the event that a system cannot be repaired using other methods such as safe mode or last known good configuration. This technique involves creating floppy disks that include system configuration information, and then using these in conjunction with the Windows Server 2003 installation CD to restore a server to its previous configuration. ASR does not restore applications or user data files.

Automatic Updates client — The client software component of Software Update Services.

Backup utility — The tool included with Windows Server 2003 used to back up and restore files and System State information.

bandwidth throttling — Allows you to limit the network bandwidth that is available for Web and FTP connections to the server.

baseline — A performance benchmark that is used to determine what is normal server performance under a specific workload.

Basic authentication — Prompts users for a user name and password to be able to access the Web resource. The user name and password are then transmitted using Base64 encoding.

basic disk — In Windows Server 2003, a partitioned disk that can have up to four partitions and that uses logical drive designations. This type of disk is compatible with MS-DOS, Windows 3.x, Windows 95, Windows 98, Windows NT, Windows 2000, Windows XP, and Windows Server 2003.

Basic Input/Output System (BIOS) — A program stored on a flash memory chip attached to the motherboard that establishes the initial communication between the components of the computer, such as the hard drive, CD-ROM, floppy disk, video, and memory.

clustering — The ability to increase access to server resources and provide fail-safe services by linking two or more computer systems so they appear to function as though they are one. Clustering is only supported in Windows Server 2003 Enterprise and Datacenter editions.

compression — An advanced attribute of the NTFS file system used to reduce the amount of space that files and folders occupy on a partition or volume.

Computer Management console — A predefined Microsoft Management Console (MMC) application that allows administration of a variety of computer-related tasks on the local computer or a remote computer.

copy backup — A backup type that backs up all selected files and folders, but does not change the archive attribute setting. This allows a copy backup to be performed without interrupting any other backup processes currently in place.

counter logs — Performance data that is collected into a comma-separated or tab-separated format.

CSVDE — A command-line utility that can be used to import and export data to and from Active Directory in a comma-separated file format.

daily backup — A backup type that backs up selected files or folders that have been created or changed on the day that the backup takes place.

data decryption field (DDF) — The storage location for the file encryption key (FEK) is an EFS-encrypted file.

data recovery agent — A user account capable of gaining access to EFS-encrypted files encrypted by other users. In a domain environment, the domain Administrator account is the default data recovery agent.

data recovery field (DRF) — The storage location for the file encryption key (FEK) encrypted by the data recovery agent.

Default Domain Policy — The name of the GPO that is linked to the domain container in Active Directory; used primarily for configuration of domain-wide password policies.

Default FTP site — An FTP server that responds to TCP/IP port 21 on all configured IP addresses of the server that are not assigned to another site.

Default Web Site — A configured Web site that responds to TCP/IP port 80 on all unassigned IP addresses of the server. This Web site is initially empty

and may be used to create a custom Web site for your organization.

defragmenting — A process by which fragmented files are rearranged into contiguous areas of disk space, improving file access performance.

Delegation of Control Wizard — The wizard available in Active Directory Users and Computers to simplify the delegation of administrative authority.

device driver — Software that includes the instructions necessary in order for an operating system to communicate with a hardware device.

differential backup — A backup type that only backs up those files that have changed since the last normal or incremental backup took place, but does not clear the archive attribute associated with those files.

Digest authentication — Prompts users for a user name and password to be able to access the Web resource. The user name and password are hashed to prevent hackers from obtaining the information.

Direct Memory Access (DMA) channels — A resource that allows hardware to access RAM directly without the intervention of the system CPU.

discretionary access control list (DACL) — A part of the security descriptor of an object that contains a list of user or group references that have been allowed or denied permissions to the resource.

Disk Management — The Windows Server 2003 utility used to manage disk partitions and volumes.

disk quotas — A Windows Server 2003 feature that is used as a means of monitoring and controlling the amount of disk space available to users.

distinguished name (DN) — An LDAP component used to uniquely identify an object throughout the entire LDAP hierarchy by referring to the relative distinguished name, domain name, and the container holding the object.

Distributed File System (DFS) — A system that enables folders shared from multiple computers to appear as though they exist in one centralized hierarchy of folders instead of on many different computers.

distribution group — A group that is only used for an e-mail distribution list.

domain — A logically structured organization of objects, such as users, computers, groups, and printers, that are part of a network and share a common directory database. Domains are defined by an administrator and administered as a unit with common rules and procedures.

domain controller — A Windows Server 2003 system explicitly configured to store a copy of the Active Directory database, and service user authentication requests or queries about domain objects.

Domain Controllers Policy — The name of the default GPO that is linked to the domain controllers OU. Used primarily for configuration of policy settings that are only to be applied to the domain controllers in the domain (i.e., auditing).

domain functional level — The level at which a Windows Server 2003 domain is configured, such as Windows 2000 mixed mode, Windows 2000 native mode, or Windows Server 2003.

domain local group — A group that can only be assigned permissions to a resource available in the domain in which it is created. However, group membership can come from any domain within the forest. Created on domain controllers within the domain.

domain-based DFS model — A DFS model that uses Active Directory and is available only to servers and workstations that are members of a particular domain. The domain-based model enables a deep root-based hierarchical arrangement of shared folders that is published in Active Directory. DFS shared folders in the domain-based model can be replicated for fault tolerance and load balancing.

down-level operating system — An operating system running Windows NT 4.0 or earlier.

driver signing — A digital signature that Microsoft incorporates into driver and system files as a way to verify the files and to ensure that they are not inappropriately overwritten.

DSADD — A command-line utility used to add objects to Active Directory.

DSMOD — A command-line utility used to modify Active Directory objects.

DSMOVE — A command-line utility used to move or rename Active Directory objects.

DSQUERY — A command-line utility used to query for Active Directory objects.

DSRM — A command-line utility used to delete Active Directory objects.

dynamic disk — A disk in Windows Server 2003 that does not use traditional partitioning, meaning there are no restrictions on the number of volumes that can be set up on one disk or the ability to extend volumes onto additional physical disks. Dynamic disks are only compatible with Windows Server 2003, Windows 2000, and Windows XP Professional systems.

effective permissions — The permissions that actually apply to a user or group based on the different permissions of the user or groups they are members of on a particular resource.

Encrypting File System (EFS) — An advanced attribute of NTFS that enables a user to encrypt the contents of a folder or a file so that it can only be accessed via private key code by the user who encrypted it or a data recovery agent by default.

Event Viewer — A component you can use to view and manage event logs, gather information about hardware and software problems, and monitor security events. Event Viewer maintains logs about program, security, and system events.

Event Viewer — A utility used to view the contents of the system, security, and application logs.

extended partition — A partition on a basic disk that is created from unpartitioned free disk space, and is not formatted with a file system. Space in an extended partition is allocated to logical drives.

FAT — A file system supported in Windows Server 2003 but traditionally associated with the MS-DOS operating system. FAT can be used on partitions or volumes up to 4 GB in size.

FAT32 — A derivative of the FAT file system that supports partition sizes up to 2 TB, but provides none of the security features of NTFS.

fault tolerance — Techniques that employ hardware and software to provide assurance against equipment failures, computer service interruptions, and data loss.

file encryption key (FEK) — The session key used to encrypt the contents of a file when EFS encryption is used.

File Signature Verification — A utility used to identify unsigned system and driver files that provides information such as the filename, location, modification date, and version number.

File Transfer Protocol (FTP) — Used to transfer files between two computers that are both running TCP/IP.

Folder redirection — A Group Policy feature that enables you to redirect the contents of the Application Data, Desktop, My Documents, My Pictures, and Start menu folders from a user's profile to a network location.

forest — A collection of Active Directory trees that do not necessarily share a contiguous DNS naming convention but do share a common global catalog and schema.

forest root domain — The first domain created within the Active Directory structure.

fragmented — A normal and gradual process in which files become divided into different areas of disk space in a volume, resulting in slower file access.

global catalog — An index of the objects and attributes used throughout the Active Directory structure. It contains a partial replica of every Windows Server 2003 domain within Active Directory, enabling users to find any object in the directory.

global group — A group that is mainly used for organizing other objects into administrative units. A global group can be assigned permissions to any resource in any domain within the forest. The main limitation of a global group is that it can only contain members of the same domain in which it is created.

globally unique identifier (GUID) — A unique 128-bit number assigned to the object when it is created.

GPRESULT — This utility can be used to discover Group Policy-related problems and to illustrate which GPOs were applied to a user or computer. GPRESULT also lists all group memberships of the user or computer being analyzed.

graphics device interface (GDI) — An interface on a Windows network print client that works with a local software application, such as Microsoft Word, and a local printer driver to format a file to be sent to a local printer or a network print server.

group — A container object that is used to organize a collection of users, computers, contacts, or other groups into a single object reference.

Group Policy — Enables the centralized management of user desktop settings, desktop and domain security, and the deployment and management of software throughout your network.

Group Policy container (GPC) — An Active Directory container that stores information about the GPO and includes a version number that is used by other domain controllers to ensure that they have the latest information.

Group Policy object (GPO) — An Active Directory object that is configured to apply Group Policy and linked to either the site, domain, or OU level.

Group Policy template (GPT) — The GPT contains the data that makes up the Group Policy. The template includes all the settings, administrative templates, security settings, software installation settings, scripts, and so forth.

hardware profile — A set of instructions telling the operating system which devices to start and drivers to load when a computer starts.

hidden attribute — A standard attribute that controls the visibility of files and folders.

host header — The fully qualified DNS name that is used to access a Web site on an IIS Server.

hot fixes — Interim updates to Windows Server 2003 that are released between major service pack releases. These are used to fix operating system bugs and security issues.

incremental backup — A backup type that only backs up those files that have changed since the last normal or incremental backup took place and clears the archive attribute associated with those files.

incremental templates — A set of text-based security template files that you can use to apply uniform security settings on computers within an enterprise. The templates modify security settings incrementally and do not include the default security settings.

Industry Standard Architecture (ISA) — A legacy 16-bit bus architecture that does not support the Plug and Play standard.

Input/Output (I/O) ranges — Dedicated memory areas that are allocated for the purpose of transferring information between a computer and a hardware device.

Install mode — The mode used to install a program that will be used in a Terminal Services environment.

Integrated Windows authentication — Does not ask the user for a password but rather uses the client's currently logged-on credentials to supply a challenge/response to the Web server.

interactive authentication — The process by which a user provides their user name and password to be authenticated from the Log On to Windows dialog box.

Internet Information Services (IIS) — A Windows Server 2003 component that provides Web-related services to an organization.

Internet Printing Protocol (IPP) — A specification supported by Windows Server 2003 that allows printers to be managed from a Web browser, and print jobs to be sent to a printer using the HTTP protocol.

interrupt request (IRQ) lines — Resource used by hardware devices to gain the attention of the system processor.

IPSec — An open-standard security protocol used to encrypt the contents of packets sent across a TCP/IP network

Kerberos version 5 (Kerberos v5) — The primary authentication protocol used in Active Directory domain environments.

Key Distribution Center (KDC) — An Active Directory domain controller that stores the directory database containing all users and passwords.

last known good configuration — An advanced startup option that you can use to recover a system from failed Windows Server 2003 configuration changes.

LDIFDE — A command-line utility that can be used to import and export data to and from Active Directory using the LDAP Interchange Format file format.

legacy devices — Devices that do not follow the Plug and Play standard, such as older Industry Standard Architecture (ISA) expansion cards.

Lightweight Directory Access Protocol (LDAP) — An access protocol that defines how users can access or update directory service objects.

local print device — A printer, such as a laser printer, physically attached to a port on the local computer.

local profile — A user profile stored on a particular computer that doesn't follow a user across the network.

logical drives — Dedicated and formatted portions of disk space created within an extended partition on a basic disk.

Management Saved Console (MSC) — The extension associated with a saved Microsoft Management Console (MMC) file.

mandatory profile — A user profile with settings that are not changed when a user logs off.

master properties — IIS parameters that are configured on the server and are inheritable by all Web and FTP sites hosted on the server.

member server — A Windows Server 2003 system that has a computer account in a domain, but is not configured as a domain controller.

Memory Address range — Memory ranges allocated for the purpose of communication between a hardware device and the operating system.

metabase — IIS 6.0 stores its configuration settings in a database referred to as the IIS metabase.

Microsoft Management Console (MMC) — A customizable management interface that can contain a number of management tools to provide a single, unified application for network administration.

Microsoft Windows installer package (MSI) — A file that contains all of the information needed to install an application in a variety of configurations.

mirrored volume — A fault-tolerant disk strategy in which a volume on one dynamic disk has its contents mirrored to a second dynamic disk.

mounted drive — A partition or volume accessible via an empty folder on an existing NTFS partition. Often implemented to circumvent the need to assign the volume or partition of a drive letter.

multimaster replication — A replication model in which any domain controller accepts and replicates directory changes to any other domain controller. This differs from other replication models in which one computer stores the single modifiable copy of the directory and other computers store back-up copies.

network authentication — The process by which a network resource or service confirms the identity of a user.

network print device — A printing device, such as a laser printer, connected to a print server through a network.

normal backup — A backup type that backs up all selected files and folders, and clears the archive attribute on these files and folders.

NT LAN Manager (NTLM) — The challenge-response protocol that is used for authentication purposes with operating systems running Windows NT 4.0 or earlier.

NTFS — The native file system of Windows Server 2003, provides better scalability and performance than FAT and FAT32, while also providing the ability to configure local security permissions, compression, encryption, and more.

object — A collection of attributes that represent items within Active Directory, such as users, groups, computers, and printers.

object classes — Define which types of objects can be created within Active Directory, such as users, groups, and printers.

object-level permissions — Active Directory permissions that control the level to which a user can modify an object such as a user account.

Organizational unit (OU) — An Active Directory logical container used to organize objects within a single domain. Objects such as users, groups, computers, and other OUs can be stored in an OU container.

paging file — Disk space, in the form of a file (pagefile.sys), for use when memory requirements exceed the available RAM.

Performance console — A pre-defined MMC that includes both the System Monitor and Performance Logs and Alerts tools.

performance counters — Data items associated with a particular performance object used to measure a certain aspect of performance.

Performance Logs and Alerts — A tool included with Windows Server 2003 that enables you to create counter logs, trace logs, and configure alerts.

performance objects — System components that you can monitor using System Monitor.

Plug and Play — A set of specifications originally developed by Intel that enables a system to automatically detect hardware and configure driver and resource settings.

Previous Versions Client — The client software component that allows users to access the Previous Versions tab to view or restore previous versions of files stored on a volume with Shadow Copies of Shared Folders enabled.

primary partition — A dedicated portion of a basic disk that is potentially bootable, and formatted with a file system. A basic disk can support a maximum of four primary partitions.

print client — Client computer or application that generates a print job.

print driver — Files that contain information that Windows Server 2003 uses to convert raw print commands to a language that the printer understands.

print queue — A stack or lineup of all requested print jobs waiting to be sent from the spooler to the printer.

print server — The computer in which the printers and print drivers are located. This is usually where you set up and configure the shared printing system.

printer — A configuration object in Windows Server 2003 that controls the connection to the print device.

printer permissions — Security permissions that allow an administrator to control access to printer resources, in a manner similar to NTFS permissions.

printer pool — Consists of a single printer that is connected to a number of print devices.

printer priorities — Configuring multiple printers to print to the same print device. One printer is then configured to print before any of the other printers by adjusting the priority setting from 1 (lowest priority) to 99 (highest priority).

published — An Active Directory object that represents a link to or direct information on how to use or connect to the shared resource.

RAID-5 volume — A fault-tolerant disk strategy that consists of creating a single volume across anywhere between three and 32 dynamic disks. RAID-5 volumes use disk striping with parity to allow the volume to remain accessible in the event that a single disk with the volume should fail.

RAW — A data type often used for printing MSDOS, Windows 3.x, and UNIX print files.

read-only attribute — A standard attribute, that when configured, does not allow the contents of a file or folder to be changed.

Recovery Console — A command-line interpreter that you can use to gain access to a local hard drive in the event that the system fails to boot.

Redundant Array of Independent Disks (RAID) — A collection of hard disks that act as a single unit for the purpose of providing fault tolerance or increasing performance.

relative distinguished name (RDN) — An LDAP component used to identify an object within the object's container.

Remote Desktop Connection — The client software used to connect to a server running Terminal Services or Remote Desktop for Administration.

Remote Desktop for Administration — A feature that allows administrators to remotely connect to the desktop of a Windows Server 2003 system for administrative purposes.

Resultant Set of Policy (RSoP) — A graphical utility included with Windows Server 2003 that enables you to review the aggregated Group Policy settings that apply to a domain user or computer.

roaming profile — A user profile stored on a centralized server that follows a user across a network.

safe mode — An advanced boot option that allows a Windows Server 2003 system to be booted with minimal services or drivers loaded, typically used for troubleshooting or diagnostic purposes.

SECEDIT.EXE — A command-line tool used to create and apply security templates, as well as analyze security settings.

Secondary logon — A feature that allows users to open certain administrative tools or issue commands using alternate credentials.

Secure Sockets Layer (SSL) — This protocol is used to encrypt Web traffic between a client and the Web server.

Security Accounts Manager (SAM) database — The local security and account database on a Windows Server 2003 standalone or member server.

Security Configuration and Analysis — An MMC snap-in that allows an administrator to compare the configuration of a Windows Server 2003 system to settings stored in a security template and to apply template settings if necessary.

Security Configuration Manager tools — A security toolset consisting of security templates and utilities that can be used to analyze and apply security configurations.

security group — A group that can be used to define permissions on a resource object.

security log — A Windows Server 2003 event log used to record security events such as auditing information.

Security Policy template — A template used to apply various security settings to an Active Directory container or object.

service pack — Periodic updates to the Windows Server 2003 operating system to fix reported bugs and security issues.

service ticket — A Kerberos ticket granted by a KDC allowing a client to gain access to a network resource or service.

Setup Security.inf — The security template applied to Windows Server 2003 systems during the installation process.

Shadow Copies of Shared Folders — A new feature in Windows Server 2003 that can be enabled on a volume-by-volume basis to allow a user to view or recover previous versions of files stored in shared folders. In order to access this feature, user systems must have the Previous Versions Client software installed.

shared folder — A data resource container that has been made available over the network to authorized network clients.

simple volume — A dedicated and formatted portion of disk space on a dynamic disk.

site — A combination of one or more Internet Protocol (IP) subnets connected by a high-speed connection.

site link — A low-bandwidth or unreliable/occasional connection between sites. Site links can be adjusted for replication availability, bandwidth costs, and replication frequency. They enable control over replication and logon traffic.

Software Update Services (SUS) — Microsoft software that allows security patches and updates to be deployed from a centralized server.

spanned volume — Dedicated and formatted space on between two and 32 dynamic disks that is treated as a single logical volume.

special NTFS permissions — A more granular set of NTFS permissions that allows an administrator a higher degree of control over the abilities assigned to users or groups for a particular resource.

spooler — In the Windows 95, 98, Me, NT, 2000, XP, and 2003 environment, a group of DLLs, information files, and programs that process print jobs for printing.

standalone DFS model — A DFS model in which there is no Active Directory implementation to help manage the shared folders. This model provides only a single or flat level share.

standard NTFS permissions — The permissions available on the Security tab of an NTFS file or folder.

striped volume — Dedicated and formatted space on between two and 32 dynamic disks that is treated as a single logical volume, with data striped across the disks in the volume in 64 KB blocks.

system attribute — A standard attribute typically associated with critical operating system files.

system log — The spot where system components such as services and device drivers record information, warnings, and errors.

System Monitor — A tool that allows you to gather and view real-time performance statistics of a local or network computer.

System State — A group of critical operating system files and components that can be backed up as a single group on a Windows Server 2003 system. System State data always includes the Registry, COM+ Registration database, boot files, and system files. On a domain controller, it also includes Active Directory and the SYSVOL directory. Other components that are included (assuming their associated services are installed) are the Certificate Services database, the Cluster Service, and the IIS Metadirectory.

Task Manager — A tool used to view the processes and applications currently running on a system. Also provides basic resource usage statistics.

Terminal Services — A Windows Server 2003 service that allows a user to connect to and run applications on a server as if sitting at the server console.

TEXT — A data type used for printing text files formatted using the ANSI standard that employs values between 0 and 255 to represent characters, numbers, and symbols.

ticket-granting ticket (TGT) — A ticket passed to a client system by the KDC once successful authentication occurs.

trace logs — Where a data provider collects performance data when an event occurs.

transitive trust — The ability for domains or forests to trust one another, even though they do not have a direct explicit trust between them.

Transmission Control Protocol (TCP) — A connection-based protocol, which means a session is established between the two hosts before any data is transferred.

uninterruptible power supply (UPS) — A device built into electrical equipment or a separate device that provides immediate battery power to equipment during a power failure or brownout.

universal group — A group that can be assigned permissions to any resource in any domain within the forest. Universal groups can consist of any user or group object except for local groups.

user account — An object that is stored in Active Directory that represents all of the information that defines a physical user who has access permissions to the network.

user account template — A special user account configured with settings that can be copied in order to simplify the creation of user accounts with common settings.

user mode — The normal running mode for a Terminal Services environment.

User Principal Name (UPN) — A user-account naming convention that includes both the user name and domain name in the format user@domain.com.

user profile — The desktop and environment settings associated with a particular user account.

virtual directory — A mapping to a physical directory containing content to be included on a Web site.

virtual memory — Disk storage used to extend the capacity of the physical RAM installed in the computer.

virtual servers — A unique Web or FTP site that behaves as if it were on its own dedicated server.

Web folder — A folder designed to be accessed from the Internet or an intranet using the HTTP or FTP protocols.

Windows 2000 mixed — The default domain functional level for a Windows Server 2003 Active Directory domain. Supports Windows NT Server 4.0, Windows 2000 Server, and Windows Server 2003 domain controllers.

Windows 2000 native — A domain functional level that supports both Windows 2000 Server and Windows Server 2003 domain controllers.

Windows Script Host (WSH) — A controller for the ActiveX scripting engines provided in both Windows-based and command-line versions.

Windows Server 2003 — A domain functional level that supports Windows Server 2003 domain controllers only.

Windows Server Catalog — The main listing of hardware devices that have been certified to function with Windows Server 2003, and officially carry the "Designed for Windows Server 2003" logo.

Windows Update — The Windows feature that allows operating systems to download service packs, patches, and hot fixes from Microsoft in an automated fashion rather than by manual download.

workgroup — A logical group of computers characterized by a decentralized security and administration model.

ZAP file — A text file that can be used by Group Policy to deploy an application; it has a number of limitations compared to an MSI file.

Index

asterisk (*), 123–124, 166

A

access control. *See also*
  authentication; passwords;
  permissions
    Access Denied message and, 325
    account lockout and, 132,
      135, 582
    entry (ACE), 193
    to files, managing, 181–216
    overview, 573–574, 651–652
account(s). *See also* passwords; users
    authentication and, 93–94
    bulk import/export and,
      126–128
    command-line utilities and,
      118–119
    creating, 85–142
    described, 86
    disabled, 135
    Group Policy and, 338
    introduction to, 86–93
    managing, 85–142
    moving, 338
    policies, 129–133
    properties, 87–89
    resetting, 175
    templates, 115–118
    troubleshooting, 129–136
    user profiles and, 98–110
Account is disabled option, 117
account lockout
    counters, 582
    duration, 132, 582
    policies, 132, 578
    settings, 132
    threshold, 132, 582
    troubleshooting, 135
Account Lockout Policy, 132, 578

Account Operators group, 170,
  404–405
Account tab, 90, 91, 114
ACE (access control entry), 193
ACPI (Advanced Configuration and
  Power Interface), 57
Action tab, 456
Active Directory (Microsoft). *See
  also* Active Directory Users and
  Computers (Microsoft)
    backups and, 487
    bulk import/export and,
      126–128
    communications standards, 32–33
    components, 28–33
    computer accounts and, 14,
      172–174
    delegation of administration and,
      402–407
    described, 25–28
    domains and, 10, 11–12
    file management and, 286, 290
    group accounts and, 144,
      170–172
    Group Policy and, 336,
      339–340, 346
    IIS and, 515–518
    Installation Wizard, 12–13
    logical structure, 28–33
    MMCs and, 383
    multimaster replication and, 25
    objects, described, 26–27
    permissions and, 402–405
    physical structure, 33–34
    printing and, 322–326
    properties, 27
    server administration and, 383,
      402–407
    sites, 34

support requirements, 3–6
user accounts and, 88–89, 94
Active Directory Users and Computers (Microsoft), 336, 338,
  339–340
    accessing, 14
    administering Web resources and,
      517–518
    computer accounts and, 172–174
    group accounts and, 151–154
    new features of, 16–17
    printing and, 322–324
    resetting passwords with, 17–18
    templates and, 116–118
    user accounts and, 87–93,
      104–105, 110–115
    user profiles and, 102–104
    viewing/configuring computer
      account settings in, 14–15
adapter cards, 56, 395, 559
Add a Group Policy Object Link
  window, 339
Add button, 152, 154, 275
Add Hardware Wizard, 52–54
Add or Remove Programs, 409–410
Add Printer icon, 302
Add Printer Wizard, 300–302,
  304–306, 313–314, 318, 560–561
Add Standalone Snap-in dialog box,
  22–23, 337
Add to a group option, 152
Additional Drivers dialog box, 307,
  314–316
Address tab, 90, 114
Add or Remove Programs applet,
  369, 392, 393, 399, 425, 512–517
Add/Remove Snap-in dialog box,
  21–23

Microsoft® Windows® Server 2003
Enterprise Edition 180-Day Evaluation

The software included in this kit is intended for evaluation and deployment planning purposes only. If you plan to install the software on your primary machine, it is recommended that you back up your existing data prior to installation.

System requirements

To use Microsoft Windows Server 2003 Enterprise Edition, you need:

- Computer with 550 MHz or higher processor clock speed recommended; 133 MHz minimum required; Intel Pentium/Celeron family, or AMD K6/Athlon/Duron family, or compatible processor (Windows Server 2003 Enterprise Edition supports up to eight CPUs on one server)
- 256 MB of RAM or higher recommended; 128 MB minimum required (maximum 32 GB of RAM)
- 1.25 to 2 GB of available hard-disk space*
- CD-ROM or DVD-ROM drive
- Super VGA (800 × 600) or higher-resolution monitor recommended; VGA or hardware that supports console redirection required
- Keyboard and Microsoft Mouse or compatible pointing device, or hardware that supports console redirection

Additional items or services required to use certain Windows Server 2003 Enterprise Edition features:

- For Internet access:
  - Some Internet functionality may require Internet access, a Microsoft Passport account, and payment of a separate fee to a service provider; local and/or long-distance telephone toll charges may apply
  - High-speed modem or broadband Internet connection
- For networking:
  - Network adapter appropriate for the type of local-area, wide-area, wireless, or home network to which you wish to connect, and access to an appropriate network infrastructure; access to third-party networks may require additional charges

Note: To ensure that your applications and hardware are Windows Server 2003–ready, be sure to visit **www.microsoft.com/windowsserver2003**.

* Actual requirements will vary based on your system configuration and the applications and features you choose to install. Additional available hard-disk space may be required if you are installing over a network. For more information, please see **www.microsoft.com/windowsserver2003**.

Uninstall instructions

This time-limited release of Microsoft Windows Server 2003 Enterprise Edition will expire 180 days after installation. If you decide to discontinue the use of this software, you will need to reinstall your original operating system. You may need to reformat your drive.